Advance Praise for *Twitter Marketing: An Hour A Day*

If you've been struggling—as I have—to figure out what exactly Twitter is for and how it can be used to build a business, this terrific book by Hollis Thomases is a godsend. It's filled with practical advice and hands-on exercises that will help companies of all sizes tap into Twitter's marketing potential. Best of all, it's a really good read and sheds much-needed light on what the excitement is all about.

—Bo Burlingham, editor-at-large, *Inc.* magazine, and author, *Small Giants: Companies That Choose To Be Great Instead of Big*

At last: A friendly Twitter handbook specifically for the unique needs of marketing professionals in the corporate and non-profit worlds! It's practical, pragmatic, and, best of all, packed with case studies and real-life illustrations. I've already been inspired to try a few new ideas from it."

—Anne Holland, founder, Marketing Sherpa; publisher, WhichTestWon.com; one of the 'Top 25 Businesswomen on Twitter' in 2009

Are you listening to your customers? On Twitter?

If you're not participating yet in social listening, welcome to your new textbook. Hollis Thomases lays down the plan for you to follow in the Hour-A-Day "eat-an-elephant" style, so you can be facile in minutes, effective in hours, and an expert in days. Whether Twitter is king in two years makes no matter; the technology is rewriting the future of customer interaction. You need to know this right now and for your future.

—Susan Bratton, CEO, Personal Life Media, Inc.; host, DishyMix show; author, *Masterful Interviews*

Think Twitter's more hype than substance? Think again.

Hollis Thomases, who's guided online marketing campaigns during boom and bust years alike, lays out a compelling case for businesses to tap this social network. Hollis, a ClickZ columnist for five years, embodies the best that Twitter has to offer; she's tuned into this online community. And in this book, she shares practical advice for marketers, public relations practitioners, and others to consider before plunging into this channel.

—Anna Maria Virzi, executive editor, ClickZ

Hollis Thomases has created an extremely practical guide to Twitter for neophytes and serious marketers alike. She clearly and completely demystifies the service. Chapters build from very basic topics, such as setting up an account, to more advanced areas, such as branding, direct response marketing, and PR crisis management. And Thomases "walks the walk;" her insights and advice are drawn from daily experience on Twitter as well as close study of successful (and unsuccessful) Twitter campaigns.

There are an increasing number of books on Twitter, but this one is an indispensable B2B guide for large or small businesses seeking to build effective social media marketing campaigns on this rapidly growing platform.

—Greg Sterling, principle, Sterling Market Intelligence

What is the Twitter phenomenon, and how can you capitalize on it for business, marketing, employee relations, crisis management, and sales? How have companies such as Dell used Twitter to account for more than $3 million in sales? This book walks you through Twitter processes and strategies step by step: from setting up an account to setting actionable business goals. Whether you're a Twitter newbie or a seasoned power user, there's something in here that will help you use Twitter more effectively—and more profitably.

—Rebecca Lieb, VP, Econsultancy, and author, *The Truth About Search Engine Optimization*

Twitter® Marketing

Twitter® Marketing

An Hour a Day

Hollis Thomases

Wiley Publishing, Inc.

Senior Acquisitions Editor: Willem Knibbe
Development Editor: Gary Schwartz
Technical Editor: Carlos Hernandez
Production Editor: Liz Britten
Copy Editor: Kathy Grider-Carlyle
Editorial Manager: Pete Gaughan
Production Manager: Tim Tate
Vice President and Executive Group Publisher: Richard Swadley
Vice President and Publisher: Neil Edde
Book Designer: Franz Baumhackl
Compositor: Maureen Forys, Happenstance Type-O-Rama
Proofreader: Candace English
Indexer: Ted Laux
Project Coordinator, Cover: Lynsey Stanford
Cover Designer: Ryan Sneed

Published simultaneously in Canada

ISBN: 978-0-470-56226-0

Library of Congress Cataloging-in-Publication Data:

Thomases, Hollis, 1965–
Twitter marketing : an hour a day / Hollis Thomases. — 1st ed.
p. cm.
ISBN 978-0-470-56226-0 (pbk.)
1. Twitter. 2. Internet marketing. 3. Business communication. 4. Online social networks. I. Title.
HF5415.1265.T53 2010
658.8'72—dc22

2009043718

10 9 8 7 6 5 4 3 2 1

Dear Reader,

Thank you for choosing *Twitter Marketing: An Hour a Day*. This book is part of a family of premium-quality Sybex books, all of which are written by outstanding authors who combine practical experience with a gift for teaching.

Sybex was founded in 1976. More than 30 years later, we're still committed to producing consistently exceptional books. With each of our titles, we're working hard to set a new standard for the industry. From the paper we print on, to the authors we work with, our goal is to bring you the best books available.

I hope you see all that reflected in these pages. I'd be very interested to hear your comments and get your feedback on how we're doing. Feel free to let me know what you think about this or any other Sybex book by sending me an email at `nedde@wiley.com`. If you think you've found a technical error in this book, please visit `http://sybex.custhelp.com`. Customer feedback is critical to our efforts at Sybex.

Best regards,

Neil Edde
Vice President and Publisher
Sybex, an imprint of Wiley

To my grandparents, who unfailingly believed me capable of all I've achieved, and to my husband, for bearing with me on this Homerian journey and for us coming out the other side better for the wear.

Acknowledgments

I am a humble and passionate student of my field. Longer than most, I have evangelized the Internet as a marketing medium, and Twitter has given me another means to spread the word. Having been warmly embraced by the Twitter community, I have learned, interpreted, and tried to share my education with others. Little did I know that all of this interaction would lead me to write this book. With this, my finished work, I feel I first ought to thank the Twitterverse at large for helping me make this possible. I have so enjoyed the support and conversations of which I've been the benefactor. Writing a book is a lonely business, and many times a simple "atta girl," helpful retweet, or validation of an idea carried me through many hours. I also need to acknowledge all the individuals and companies who provided feedback, case studies, and helpful anecdotes, all of which went into the contents of this book.

Writing this book has been an epic journey for me. I feel as though I have passed a series of Odysseus-like tests and have arrived back in Ithaca tired, yet unscathed. This wouldn't have been possible were it not for everyone who works for me at my agency, Web Ad.vantage, who suffered through months of my absentee ownership, and yet who managed not only to hold down the fort, but to thrive during this period. It's a testament to the potency of our team, and I'm so proud of you all. I'd especially like to acknowledge Jaime Hood, Katie Clay, and Virginia Bush for their direct assistance on this project, and David Cease for manning the fort in my stead.

I also need to thank those who voluntarily contributed to this book in no small measure, providing me with research, notes, tweets, and direct content: Carlos Hernandez (@CarlosHernandez, who did double duty as this book's technical editor and who is a huge supporter), Gini Dietrich (@ginidietrich), Tom Rowe (@thefrontrowe), Marivic Valencia (@techpr), Nancy Cawley Jean (@NancyCawleyJean), and Mike D. Merrill (@mikedmerrill). These people gave up their personal time to help me with this project, and I cannot thank them enough for doing so. My thanks too to Rachel Levy, who also aided me with content development.

In the spirit of Twitter, as I endeavored to produce this book, I also strove to collaborate with the at-large community. I sent out a request for help for Twitter assistants whom I asked to be "on call" to aid me, whether it was to answer single questions, to retweet requests, or to try to recruit other contributors to various parts of the book. I called this group of committed volunteers the "Hollis Twitter Army," and we used the hashtag #HTArmy to trumpet each new mission. Members of the Hollis Twitter Army grew to develop relationships of their own, and to this day they use the hashtag to share information about Twitter marketing they think would be valuable for us all to read. For this unity and spirit of sharing, I am so proud. I would like to acknowledge some particular members of the Hollis Twitter Army who really led the charge: my "lieutenant," Lauren Litwinka; my "captain," Juli Barcelona; and special members Sima Dahl, Chris Maddox, Mayra Ruiz, and Ericka Alston, as well as those I mentioned in the previous paragraph.

Special thanks to all-around fabulous person and author of *Social Media Marketing: An Hour a Day*, Dave Evans, who recommended me for this project and who has acted as a mentor and cheerleader throughout. And to the great crew at Sybex—Willem Knibbe, Gary Schwartz, Liz Britten, and Pete Gaughan—who patiently endured the onslaught of questions and communications from this type-A, first-time author.

For coaxing the writer out of me early on, I really need to thank Greg Sterling and Rebecca Lieb, both former editors at different online publications who have since moved on to other careers but who both gave me a voice and a reason to pursue greater knowledge.

And finally, I want to thank my friends who patiently tolerated my near-complete absence of a social life; my family, who instilled in me the work ethic to complete this undertaking; my beautiful babies, who loved having Mommy home day and night to stroke and nuzzle with; and to my husband, Tony, for allowing me always to pursue my dreams.

About the Author

Hollis Thomases, a self-confessed Twitter addict, is an award-winning online marketer who has spent much of her career educating and inspiring business professionals to tap into the marketing power of the Web. Hollis founded Web Ad.vantage (`http://www.webadvantage.net`), a boutique agency providing a broad range of strategic online marketing and advertising solutions, in 1998 when social networking meant participating in Usenet groups, email discussion lists, webrings, forums, and message boards. Hollis has seen a lot of digital marketing ideas come and go, but believes that Twitter has staying power.

Under Hollis's leadership and strategic planning, Hollis and Web Ad.vantage have provided consulting and tactical execution services, including social media marketing, to entities such as Nokia USA, Endo Pharmaceuticals, K'NEX, Johns Hopkins University, Visit Baltimore, Checkpoint Software, Starlight Children's Foundation, and Connections Academy.

A long-time popular speaker, Hollis has appeared at Internet and industry conferences for such varied organizations and events as the American Marketing Association, the Public Relations Society of America, Search Engine Strategies, the Newsletter and Electronic Publishers Association, The Kelsey Group, and the Vocus Worldwide User Forum. Since 2005, Hollis has authored the online biweekly ClickZ column, "*Planning the Buy.*"

Hollis was the 2007 U.S. SBA "Small Business Person of the Year" representing the state of Maryland and, in 2009, she was honored by the University of Baltimore's Merrick School of Business as Baltimore's "Distinguished Business Innovation Entrepreneur of the Year." Hollis holds a Bachelor of Arts in social relations from Cornell University. She has many interests, but her passions run to people, wining and dining, and any kind of activity that gets the heart rate going...probably in that order.

Hollis welcomes you to tweet her at `@hollisthomases`!

Contents

Foreword

When I first met Hollis in New York, we were both writing for ClickZ (`http://www.clickz.com`), an online publication for digital marketing professionals. We were getting ready for the ClickZ session at the Search Engine Strategies conference and talking about how social media had become a factor in search optimization programs. Hollis was presenting a set of case studies on the use of Twitter in the context of search and practical, applied business marketing. It was at this session that I saw in Hollis a source, a real insight into how to use Twitter effectively. Mostly what impressed me was the way in which she was able to simply and clearly convey what she knew, to show the people in the audience how to do what she had done. Those are the keys to mastering the "Hour a Day" writing approach.

Since that time, Hollis has continued to press her knowledge into further uses of Twitter as the service has literally exploded. This book brings her knowledge to you, in the characteristically practical, hands-on way for which the "Hour a Day" series is known.

I know what some of you may be thinking (although you're at least far enough down the purchase funnel to be reading this foreword!): "Twitter is a fad." You may have heard that a lot of the "accounts" are abandoned. Suppose that's true. Suppose that only 25% of the current installed base—something approaching 100 million—are active. That's 25 million people who are talking among themselves. Think "I'm standing in line at Starbucks…" is idle banter? Ask Howard Schultz, founder and returned CEO of the best-known coffee chain in the world. He literally "stopped the line," to borrow a term from Toyota, when he closed Starbucks for three hours partly out of concern for exactly what it was that was being talked about as people waited in those lines at Starbucks.

The bottom line is this: As a marketer, I don't really care if something is a fad or not; what I care about are sales, this quarter. If a powerful fad lasts two or more quarters and I can tap into it and build my business, I'm going to do it. For those keeping track, as of this writing, Twitter is in its 15th quarter, and millions of people are using it daily. That's what gets my attention, as a marketer, and that is what Hollis has captured and written about in *Twitter Marketing: An Hour a Day*. Minimum, it's worth understanding how Twitter can contribute to your marketing program. Maximum? That's up to you.

What Twitter brings to a marketing program, in my mind, was summed up nicely by blogger Jeff Jarvis when he stressed the importance of a "natural voice." Look at India's Kingfisher Airlines, or any of the Dell Twitter accounts. You'll find ordinary people, like "StefanieAtDell" that are ... *simply talking to customers.* Customers are talking back, and a conversation is forming. Airline tickets and computers are being sold as a direct result. Hollis shows you, step-by-step, how to do what these brands and dozens of others have now discovered: Twitter, used smartly, can contribute to your success.

Dive into this book. Do the exercises. Put what you learn to work in your business. Then test it, measure it, refine it, and grow it. Most of all, enjoy it. And thank you for choosing to explore Twitter from a business and marketing perspective.

—Dave Evans
Author, Social Media Marketing: An Hour a Day, *and founder of Digital Voodoo*

Introduction

Hello, my name is Hollis Thomases (`@hollisthomases`*), and I'm a Twitter addict. There, I said it. Like most Twitter addicts, however, there was a time when I was instead a Twitter skeptic. I'd been practicing online marketing for 11 years and couldn't for the life of me understand why I would want to answer the question "What are you doing?" for the world to read. Better yet, why would they care? I viewed Twitter as a place for the trivial and the mundane—a place that attracted people with time on their hands or those who had nothing better to do.*

Today, nothing could be further from my perception. I have seen the proverbial light and I evangelize Twitter whenever and wherever I can. These days, the most common question I'm answering for others is not "What am I doing?" but "Why should I Twitter? I don't get this thing or how it can help my company." The turning point came for me in early 2008 when a colleague pointed me to a brief about how the tax-preparation firm H&R Block was using Twitter to help answer tax-return-preparation questions as a means to woo new customers. Reading this brief made me realize the potential of Twitter as a marketing tool. As an online marketing practitioner, the dots were connected, and I haven't looked back since.

Each day I'm reminded how valuable Twitter is as a marketing tool. It's a place for research, for customer service, for product promotion, to distribute news, to build customer loyalty, and to get ideas. In fact, the use of Twitter for marketing is constantly evolving, where almost weekly one can read about a unique strategy or application of Twitter for marketing. Yet, at the same time, as a user representing either yourself or your brand, the daily use of Twitter can be overwhelming and mind-numbing. How are we supposed to process all this information, read everything people write, and just where and how are we supposed to allocate our time and resources, and for what end?

What I hope to accomplish by writing this book is to show you the marketing power of Twitter so you will truly believe the end justifies learning about the means. In college I majored in a funny little interdisciplinary field combining the study of psychology, sociology, and anthropology called social relations. In a class of 4,000 students, only two other people majored in social relations and, at the time, I put up with much ribbing: "What kind of major is that? Are you majoring in partying?!?" In hindsight, I now think I was quite prescient in my decision, but the reality was that I loved (and still do) to understand what motivated people. I wanted to understand both the internal forces and external ones, and social relations isn't a study so much of data as it is of what forces form and influences people. I believe that Twitter is one of these forces.

You see, Twitter helps foster one of social media's most powerful examples of *collectivism.* Collectivism, as defined by Wikipedia, is

> *...any moral, political, or social outlook that emphasizes the interdependence of every human in some collective group and the priority of group goals over individual goals. The philosophical underpinnings of collectivism are for some related to holism—the view that the whole is greater than the sum of its parts/pieces. Specifically, a society as a whole can be seen as having more meaning or value than the separate individuals that make up that society.*

Now, in no way am I claiming that everyone using Twitter is only out for the collective good, but there *is* a soul to Twitter that speaks to, nurtures, and prides itself on this kind of interdependence. The creators of Twitter unwittingly tapped into something much larger than a mere means to provide instant status updates of people. They tapped into the soul of this modern collective and gave everyone a means to communicate within it.

I have often joked that I am a "twanthropologist," my own Twitterese for someone who studies humans on Twitter. Part of the reason I chose to write this book was to further this observation, but moreover I wanted to use my abilities to write, educate, and train people on how to use Twitter by speaking in a way with which they'd feel comfortable (also known as *plain English*). It would have been clever to have written this book in 140-character bits, the limitation imposed by Twitter, but the reality is that such writing would be disjointed and hard to follow—even if the end result were not a printed book. Instead, I've used old-fashioned prose to walk you through logical processes, with my goal being that you come away feeling more fully informed than if you had tried to absorb all of this information in tiny-sized nuggets.

This book was written not as a simple primer; there are other great books that have taken this approach. Instead, *Twitter Marketing: An Hour a Day* is for the serious marketing and business professional seeking more in-depth and detailed information. Beyond teaching the basics, I hope that this book provokes thought and new creative ideas for using Twitter. If you execute these ideas, please don't hesitate to let me know through Twitter!

How to Use This Book

For cover-to-cover readers, Part I of this book will provide the background of Twitter, statistical information to offer perspective, common uses of Twitter, and information about how Twitter is being used by so many varying types of people and entities. In Part II, I want you to become familiar with Twitter, first as an individual user, before you start using it to help you market your company. In Part II, I introduce you to the hour-a-day format found in this popular series of online marketing books. You'll have daily exercises to guide your progress. Think of Part II as your warm-up. If you're already a fluent Twitter user, you may want to skim or altogether skip Part II and head straight to Part III. By Part III, you'll have your business marketing hat on, and we'll cover the kinds of details and concerns that commonly arise among marketers. Finally, in Part IV, we review some particular circumstances for using Twitter in a business context. Throughout the book, I'll also drop reminders because, although very versatile, the daily use of Twitter is somewhat routine.

You will also see #TMHAD along the book's outer border where you'll find the chapter title and page number. This #TMHAD is called a "hashtag," which you'll soon learn all about. We're including this particular #TMHAD hashtag because we're hoping when you discuss this book on Twitter you'll also use our hashtag in your tweet. That way, you, all the other book readers, Twitter users, and I can easily locate and join the conversation. Please give it a try!

Twitter is a real-time medium and one that's still experiencing rapid growth. Some of the material in this book may change completely by the time it is published, and I apologize in advance for any outdated content. None of us in this dynamic social media space, however, would expect otherwise, so I hope neither do you. The most important take-away, however, is that you learn and actually have fun. Yes, fun and business marketing—it is possible to combine the two!

Twitter® Marketing

Get to Know Twitter

I

Here's your mission: Read and use this book to help your company engage in Twitter marketing. This is not a CliffsNotes-Your-Way to-Twitter Marketing; it is packed with information and exercises, and it will require your attention and rigor. When you are through, you'll have the tools and knowledge needed to help you make wise decisions and succeed at Twitter marketing.

Part I of this book is designed to give you the historical background and statistical information you need to determine if Twitter marketing is right for your organization. It also gives you plenty of examples of how other companies have been using Twitter to help support their brands and generate action.

You're probably eager to start reading, learning, and using Twitter for marketing, so without further ado, let the class begin!

Understand Twitter

In so many ways, many people still don't get *Twitter. Bring up Twitter at any casual or business gathering, and you're bound to start a lively conversation. Most of the time, nonusers flat out and emphatically proclaim, "I just don't get Twitter!" Others, who just view Twitter as a crude tool to broadcast your every action, curl their upper lips with the challenge, "Why should I waste my time with Twitter?" The more timid or truly curious befuddledly ask, "Just what the heck* is *Twitter?"*

If you're among the curious, the first chapter of this book should satisfy your curiosity and then some. If you fall into the cynical, doubting Thomases (pun intended) or perplexed categories, be prepared to read beyond this first chapter to learn about and understand the true business value of Twitter.

1

Chapter Contents

Twitter History and Definitions

In early 2006, a young software engineer named Jack Dorsey approached the media syndication company Odeo with the idea of finding a simple way to share what his friends were doing—that is, their status at any given moment. Drawing on his previous work programming web-based emergency dispatch software and finding inspiration in instant-messaging applications, Dorsey was interested in developing a real-time status-communication platform with a social spin. Entrepreneur and Odeo founder Biz Stone, liked the idea. Stone and Dorsey collectively decided that short message service, or SMS (the technology used by mobile phones to send and receive text messages), would be ideally suited to this concept. They decided on a maximum message size of 140 characters, because it was fewer than the maximum 160 characters permitted by SMS text messaging, which would leave room for a user name and a colon.

In only two weeks' time, the first prototype of what would become Twitter was born. The service quickly grew popular with Odeo employees and other insiders, and attracted the attention of ex-Googler Evan Williams, who initially funded the project. Twitter was launched to the public in August 2006, and by May 2007, Dorsey, Stone, and Williams officially cofounded Twitter, Inc.

Twitter Defined

So what the heck is Twitter, anyway?

The common definitions of Twitter are mired in industry jargon such as "social networking" and "micro-blogging," so if you don't understand those terms, we need to take a step back for a minute. I find myself explaining Twitter to newbies as something akin to instant messaging or chat—that is, Twitter is a platform that allows you to share, in real time, thoughts, information, links, and so forth with the Web at-large and to be able to communicate directly, privately or publicly, with other Twitter users. The main difference, however, is that each Twitter communication cannot exceed 140 total characters.

I am also frequently asked questions about who can see these messages and if someone has to join Twitter to communicate. I stress that most Twitter posts, known as *tweets,* can theoretically be viewed by anyone with an Internet connection at any time. No one needs to have a Twitter account to view someone else's tweets. The public accessibility of Twitter makes it somewhat unique among social networking websites, where normally you can't see people's information without them first accepting your invitation. If you do want to communicate privately with other individuals on Twitter, though, you *will* need to join and create an account. (I'll tell you more about how you can send private messages through Twitter a little later.)

Twitter is based on the simple question "What are you doing?" and encourages users to answer exactly that. But if you use Twitter only to broadcast your commonplace activities, you're missing out on its real potential. After all, if all you ever write is "Going to the grocery store now," or "Just fixed the office copier," you're not really opening up the door for much conversation, are you?

Conversations of many kinds and the ease with which Twitter facilitates them compose the hidden power of Twitter, particularly as a branding and business marketing tool (Figure 1.1). Twitter has given the public unprecedented direct access to companies, celebrities, and power figures in a way that hasn't previously been seen. Conversely, Twitter enables unfettered and immediate direct access to the masses. For a brand, Twitter can rapidly reduce the timeline and costs of research, product launches, pilot tests, incentives, and promotions; plus Twitter offers a number of other possibilities that we will explore in depth later in this book.

Home
hollisthomases Did Twitter just add SSL or did I miss something?
less than 5 seconds ago from web
nancypub RT @HappyTown09: The storm ... @whitmoregroup #followfriday
1 minute ago from TweetDeck
Larkin appreciating how much I've been tweeting over the past few; wondering if I should unhinge twitter and facebook
1 minute ago from TwitterFox
chrisabraham Pit-stopping en route to a meeting in Pittsburgh at 13:30 then on to Columbus, OH - Photo: http://bkite.com/08FCO
1 minute ago from Brightkite
hollisthomases Online Web Brands ranked by Video Streams for May 2009; 49% growth in time per viewer, year over year: http://tr.im/p40c
2 minutes ago from TwitterFox
chrisabraham I'm at Bedford - http://bkite.com/08FCN
2 minutes ago from Brightkite
obilon IBM To Spend $100 Million On Mobile Research http://bit.ly/2lUpfl via @addthis
2 minutes ago from Seesmic Desktop
chrisabraham http://ping.fm/p/qZ8ul - Pit-stopping en route to a meeting in Pittsburgh at 13:30 then on to Columbus, OH
2 minutes ago from Ping.fm
mollyblock More Wright stuff: Frank Lloyd Wright's long-endangered, historic Ennis House for sale at $15M: http://bit.ly/16MMF2
2 minutes ago from TweetDeck
chrisbrogan RT @Radian6 join us w host @chrisbrogan for Rockstars of SocialCRM 6/24. Jam out live or on the web! http://bit.ly/SocialCRM
2 minutes ago from Tweetie
hotdogsladies An "aviatrix" sounds like a sexy bird lady who's into spanking, and I'd give practically anything for that not to seem kind of hot.
2 minutes ago from web
justinthesouth Hello @theredrecruiter I am now following you at the suggestion of @leaddawg #FollowFriday
2 minutes ago from TweetDeck

Figure 1.1 Twitter is a real-time looking glass into what people are doing, saying, observing, and thinking.

Why Should I Use Twitter?

Twitter humbly asks, "What are you doing?" Perhaps the more appropriate question for Twitter to ask would be, "What interests you?" Try thinking in this context as you begin marketing yourself or your business through Twitter. Remember that tweeting is like having a conversation. Imagine yourself at a conference or a business-networking event. If a perfect stranger came up to you and blurted out, "I'm eating the empanada hors d'oeuvres right now," you would probably look oddly at this person, give them an awkward smile, and move swiftly on your way. On the other hand, if a different person came up and said, "I found the information provided by the last speaker very valuable for my business. How about you?" you'd probably be more interested in what this person had to say, and more inclined to respond yes or no. That's how you should treat every Twitter interaction. The most successful people and brands using Twitter are the ones who treat Twitter as an ongoing, open, and thought-provoking conversation rather than just a broadcast medium. These users are knowledgeable about their business, responsive to feedback, and respectful of the community.

Some Important Twitter Vernacular

Before we go any further, it's important to familiarize yourself with the most common Twitter terminology as it will be used throughout this book to describe the process of Twitter marketing.

Twitter Terminology

Handle. A user's Twitter name (e.g., hollisthomases).

Tweet. The message, consisting of 140 or fewer characters, sent by a Twitter user. On Twitter, these tweets are tracked in your user profile as Tweets.

Tweeting or **Twittering.** The act of composing and sending a message.

Retweet (RT). When someone forwards your tweet, or retweets, they put RT in front of it to give you proper credit.

@ **reply.** The @ symbol directly in front of someone's name (`@hollisthomases`) indicates you're sending them a public message or responding to a message they sent you. It's a publicly visible type of Twitter messaging between two users or more.

Direct message (DM). A DM sends a private message to another Twitter user. In order for them to receive this private message, they need to be following you. In order for you to receive a DM back, you need to be following them. To send a DM, use "D," plus a space, plus the recipient's Twitter handle. Do not use the @ symbol when you send a DM.

Twitter Terminology *(Continued)*

Tweep. A nickname used to describe a Twitter user. (Tweep is shorter name than Twitterer and originates from the terms "Twitter" and "people," or "peeps.") Tweeps describes more than one tweep.

Follower. Someone who has opted in to receive your tweets in their Twitter Steam.

Following. Those who you have opted in to receive tweets from.

Friend. When a mutual Follower/Following relationship exists between two users.

Twitterverse. Describes the Twitter community at large—i.e., the Twitter universe.

Hashtag. The hashtag is a way of identifying a tweet related to a particular subject. The hashtag protocol is the hash or pound sign (#) directly followed by the word, words, or characters someone has assigned to that subject—the fewer characters, the better. For example, the hashtag for this book will be #TMHAD, an abbreviation for "Twitter Marketing: An Hour a Day."

Twitter by the Numbers

Twitter does not currently release the number of active accounts using the service. Independent market research companies, however, continually analyze Twitter's traffic and growth, which has been substantial. If understanding the definition of Twitter is any indication, Twitter most certainly has a lot of people's attention. Sites that monitor Wikipedia traffic show that the Twitter definition page, or article, jumped from being the 70th most accessed page in February 2009 to being in the Top 25 of all accessed pages on Wikipedia for March and April 2009, the latest statistics available at the time of this writing. Another source estimates that over a million people viewed the Wikipedia article for Twitter in May 2009. This is substantial when you consider that there are over three million articles on Wikipedia. The Twitter article on Wikipedia was created March 11, 2007 and has been repeatedly edited—2,183 times as of this writing. Nielsen statistics indicate that Twitter experienced an unprecedented 1,382 percent growth rate between February 2008 and February 2009, leaping from 475,000 to 7 million unique monthly visitors in the span of one year. This makes Twitter the fastest-growing social network for that time period (Figure 1.2). As of May 2009, Compete.com estimated Twitter to have 19.7 million unique monthly visitors, which ranks Twitter as the third-largest social network, behind Facebook and MySpace.

Demographically, Twitter is split closely between male and female audiences. As of May 2009, Quantcast reported that 55 percent of Twitter users were female (Figure 1.3). In June 2009, Sysomos, a social media analytics company, measured the gender breakdown of Twitter at 53 percent female and 47 percent male. For that

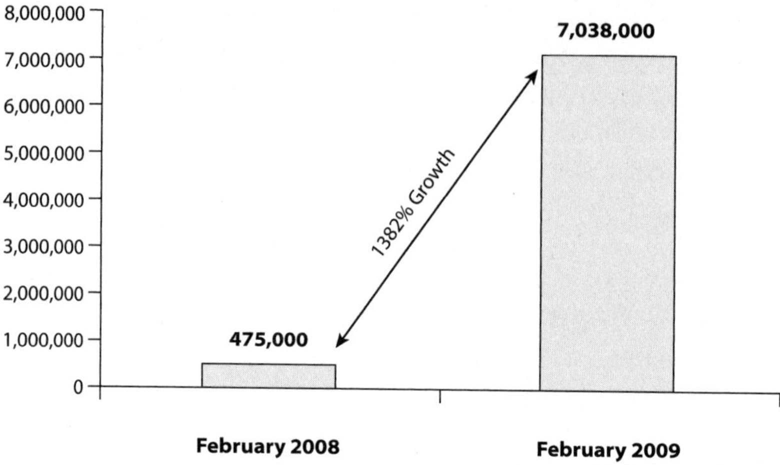

Figure 1.2 Twitter's year-over-year growth

same time period, Hitwise, a service that tracks data passing through Internet Service Providers (ISPs) and measures Twitter.com traffic, came up with similar numbers, citing the gender breakdown of Twitter as 51.5 percent female and 48.5 percent male. But a Harvard Business School study released around this same time argued that Twitter is very "male-centric," despite the larger number of female users. The study found that both sexes are more likely to follow more men than they are to follow women on Twitter, and that men are almost twice as likely to follow other men than women. Men have 15 percent more followers than women, and men are more likely to have reciprocal Twitter relationships (Male A follows Male B, who in turn follows back Male A). Study authors find these results so atypical that they describe them as "stunning … on a typical online social network, most of the activity is focused around women—men follow content produced by women they do and do not know, and women follow content produced by women they know."

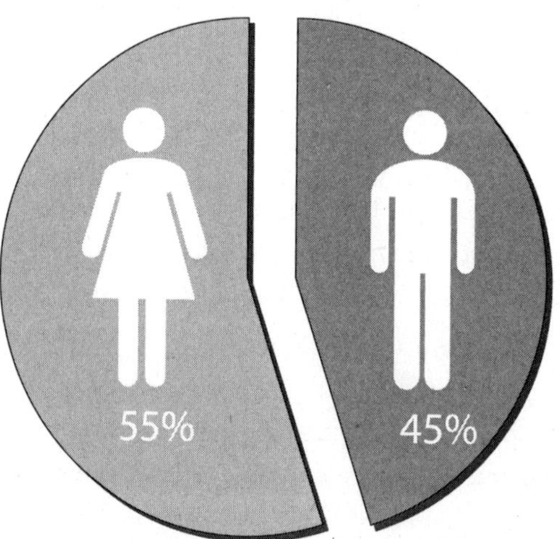

Figure 1.3 Twitter's narrow gender divide

Personally, I question whether the Harvard findings will stand up over time, and I would also like to see a study that analyzes gender and "tweep affinity." Men may have more followers, but I think that's because they view these relationships in either a casual or business way, whereas women take their Twitter relationships more seriously, and more loyally and frequently tweet among themselves. There's a whole community of interconnected moms on Twitter. I believe the strength of these tweep affinities is going to matter more over time than sheer numbers indicate.

When it comes to age, there's some disparity in the statistics. Some say that Twitter, like other social networks, is rooted firmly in the 18-to-34 demographic, claiming this bracket accounts for approximately 47 percent of all its users. Other sources say that Twitter users predominantly fall into the 35- to 49-year-old age bracket, which accounts for 35 percent. In the meantime, a surprisingly large number of seniors tweet, accounting for 21 percent of the Twitter population. Almost all researchers agree, however, that Twitter is not for the youth set, with only 1 percent of Twitter users falling under the age of 17.

What Twitter Is Not

Sometimes explaining Twitter in the context of what it's *not* helps to clarify things.

Twitter isn't accessible only on the Web. Twitter users can communicate via cell phone, mobile devices, or desktop applications.

Twitter isn't the "new" email or cell phone. Twitter's 140-character limitation is just that—limiting. For rapid-fire, short communications, Twitter is useful. However, email and telephones can still do a lot more than Twitter can. Twitter is just another tool in the digital communicator's toolkit.

Twitter isn't a form of instant messenger. Although it's true that Twitter shares many of the same characteristics as instant messaging or chat applications, the two operate using different technology, offer different functionality, and serve different purposes.

Twitter isn't a micro version of your blog. Although many users exploit Twitter to tease and link to every new blog post, using Twitter only in this manner is considered poor practice. Your tweets should be varied, with original content. Otherwise, why would anyone else want to read them?

Twitter isn't private by any means. Unless you lock them down, be prepared for your tweets to be read, responded to, and possibly forwarded (retweeted) by perfect strangers. It's almost pointless to be on Twitter and lock down your tweets unless you never want to be engaged by the greater community—the *Twitterverse*. This piece of advice, however, does not apply to direct messages, which *are* private.

Twitter isn't a replacement for Facebook, MySpace, or other social networks. Rather, Twitter can be a complement to social networks, as well as a different, albeit powerful, standalone tool.

Twitter isn't a competition. Having more followers does not equal having more authority, influence, or expertise. As you'll learn soon, many different types of people with different agendas are using Twitter to seek different types of personal gain. Don't get sucked into making Twitter a popularity contest.

Table 1.1 provides a quick look at how Twitter is similar to and different from other communication platforms.

▶ **Table 1.1** Twitter Compared to Other Popular Platforms

Characteristics	Twitter	Email	Instant Messaging	Facebook
Free	✓	✓	✓	✓
Easy to use	✓	✓	✓	
Unlimited message size		✓	✓	✓
Send unlimited messages	✓	✓	✓	✓
Status updates	✓		✓	✓
Mobile-smart phones	✓	✓	✓	✓
Privacy protections	✓		✓	✓
One-to-many conversations	✓	✓		✓
One-to-one conversations	✓	✓	✓	✓
Private conversations		✓	✓	
Sense of community	✓			✓
Reciprocal friends		✓		✓

Twitter's Technology

Twitter uses a proprietary message-routing system that processes text-based messages from the Web, SMS, mobile Web, and instant messages. It also allows outside entities, known collectively as third-party applications, to access its servers via its open-source application program interface (API) to pass data (messages and user information) back and forth. Twitter's flexible, extensible platform has given it wide reach as developers create new applications, tools, directories, functions, and the like. All of these Twitter solutions attract attention, trial and use, and subsequent mention by the Twitter community at large, which then helps to further broaden interest in Twitter. Many users prefer such third-party *apps* as their primary means of using Twitter, which often replaces entirely the need to go to the Twitter website.

On a simpler level, Twitter's technology can be divided into two key components: the Web and its mobile counterpart.

Twittering on the Web

The Twitter website itself is programmed using the Ruby on Rails web application framework, which is popular with Twitter's developers due to its facility for rapid development and ease of maintenance. Twitter users who tweet from the Web at `http://www.twitter.com` need only a basic web browser to use the service and access all of its features.

Twittering on the Go

Tweeting from a mobile phone while on the go is a slightly more complicated process. Twitter provides a special web-based interface at `http://m.Twitter.com`. It is a pared-down, faster-loading version of the original that works particularly well with browser-enabled mobile devices. If your device does not have a browser, mobile tweeting will require learning a few special keypad commands. It's important to note that using Twitter while on the go is possible from *any* mobile device with SMS capability. Just remember this: although using Twitter is free, text messaging (receiving *and* sending) is not. If you plan to use Twitter via text messaging, you might want to monitor your cell phone bills and upgrade to an unlimited text-messaging plan if your tweets really start to add up.

Follow the Leader

Twitter's unique subscription system allows you to *follow* (or *unfollow*) other users' tweets, similar to subscribing to or unsubscribing from a blog or email list. Among the statistics that Twitter displays prominently on every user's profile page (Figure 1.4) are a *followers count* (the number of people following someone) as well as a *following count* (the number of people someone follows).

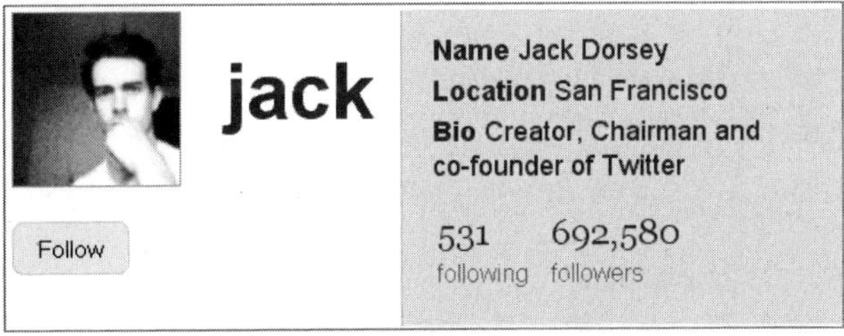

Figure 1.4 Not surprisingly, Jack Dorsey (Twitter cofounder and chairman) is a very popular guy on Twitter.

Twitter's very public statistics promote something of a popularity-contest atmosphere within Twitter. People may pass instant judgments about the caliber of a user based on their followers/following counts, and not necessarily on the quality of their tweets. There are some who have gone so far as to propose that Twitter do away with these followers/following statistics for this very reason.

Almost unilaterally, however, Twitter users aim to avoid losing followers. The best way for users to retain followers is by maintaining an active, engaging tweet stream that remains relevant and beneficial to their audience (Figure 1.5).

Figure 1.5 Sephora's tweet stream demonstrates active, engaging, and varied tweets.

The authentic side of the Twitterverse is an ecosystem that respects and rewards quality over quantity—both with tweets and tweeps—and reduces the *signal-to-noise ratio* when it comes to producing quality tweets. Most respectable tweeps frown on spammers, annoying tweeps, those who tweet too much, and those who take "What are you doing?" too literally. The objectives for brands utilizing Twitter should be the same: produce great content, be engaged with your community, seek out those with like-minded interests, and the followers will come. Ultimately, this kind of interaction-attraction will help support your brand.

Twitter's Open Source API

From the start, Twitter facilitated its rise in popularity by opening itself up to integration with other tools and applications built by web developers. Twitter's open-source API, the means by which these developers access Twitter's server to pass information back and forth, has led to the continuous development or upgrading of solutions that improve how people use Twitter or extend its functionality. Many such applications are simple. They are designed to do just one thing and do it well. It's, therefore, typical of tweeps to use a wide variety of specialized applications that suit their needs to improve the overall Twitter experience.

There are hundreds of Twitter applications, and new ones are constantly being developed. There are some common ones, however, that will be mentioned throughout this book, so they're worth listing here:

- TweetDeck is a popular downloadable desktop application with higher functionality to receive, read, respond, manage, group, and search tweets.
- Twirl is another early front-runner in downloadable desktop applications.
- Seesmic is a desktop application giving TweetDeck a run. It has now come out with a web-based version of its app.
- TwitterFox is a Firefox browser add-in application.
- Tweetie is a popular iPhone Twitter application.
- Twitterfon is another popular iPhone Twitter client.
- Tweetlater is a web-based application that lets you schedule tweets for future posting.
- Hootsuite is similar to Tweetlater. It combines with URL shortening and tracking metrics.
- CoTweet is an application that manages multiple users responding to single or multiple accounts with multiple users.

Obviously, there are many reasons why Twitter has grown so popular so quickly. The industry now questions if it can sustain this growth and, if so, what Twitter plans on doing to monetize it. In the meantime, we'll focus this book on ways in which you can monetize Twitter for business marketing gain.

Twittering on the Go

Tweeting from a mobile phone while on the go is a slightly more complicated process. Twitter provides a special Web-based interface at `http://m.Twitter.com`, a pared-down, faster-loading version of the original that works particularly well with browser-enabled mobile devices. If your device does not have a browser, mobile tweeting requires a few special keypad commands due to the lack of a Web-based interface (see Table 1.2). It's important to note that using Twitter while on the go is possible from *any* mobile device with SMS capability.

► **Table 1.2** Twitter Mobile-Only Commands

Command	Syntax	Purpose
Turn On	ON	Turns all mobile-device notifications on.
Turn Off	OFF	Turns all mobile-device notifications off.
Turn On User	ON *username*	Turns all notifications/tweets from a specific user on.
Turn Off User	OFF *username*	Turns all notifications/tweets from a specific user off.
Stop (same as QUIT)	STOP	Stops all Twitter messages from being sent to your phone.
Quit (same as STOP)	QUIT	Stops all Twitter messages from being sent to your phone.
Follow	FOLLOW *username*	Follow a user and begin receiving their notifications/tweets.
Leave	LEAVE *username*	Stop receiving notifications/tweets from a specific user.

Twitter's Rapid Ascent

Despite the enthusiasm among early adopters when Twitter was first launched, most of the public struggled to understand Twitter's appeal. At first, many users wondered, "Do people really want to know every little thing I do?"

Part of the initial hurdle in attracting users to Twitter was that people *were* just tweeting about the mundane. In its first few months before today's tools, applications, and enhancements arrived, it was hard to recognize Twitter's real value. As Twitter began to catch on, however, clever users started to use Twitter to share links and news and to integrate Twitter feeds into their blogs via RSS. Twitter's technology allowed developers to access its servers, and then they released new tools that made Twitter more manageable and interesting to more people.

As is common with unanticipated growth spurts in web technology, Twitter's increased use led to problems. By midyear 2007, Twitter began experiencing server-capacity problems related to its growing number of users, prompting the creation of the now infamous Fail Whale, which was both a humorous graphic and quick-to-catch-on description of the recurring circumstance (Figure 1.6).

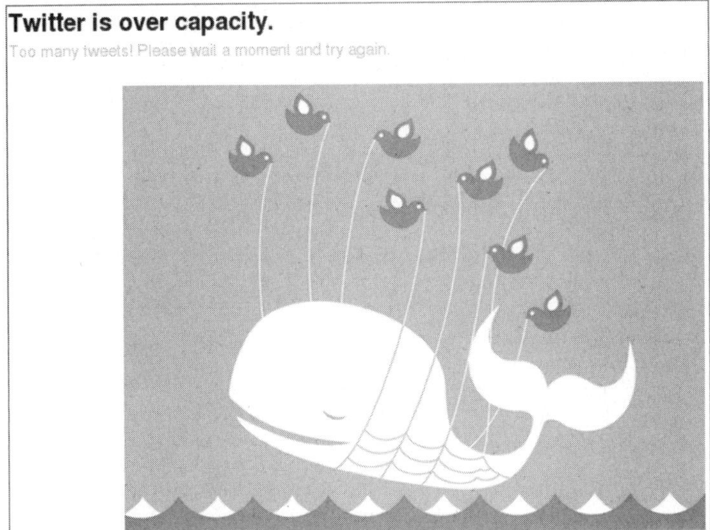

Twitter is over capacity.
Too many tweets! Please wait a moment and try again.

Figure 1.6 Twitter's infamous Fail Whale

Despite its technical problems, Twitter cultivated a bold and fiercely loyal user base, while developing its own sense of culture, etiquette, and even vocabulary. Twitter is one of the most unique social networks in this respect, as many of its social mores developed out of its requirement for brevity. Twitter users tend to be very matter-of-fact when it comes to tweeting, and very vocal about other users' *faux pas*. Because of this, new users, particularly big brands who by their very nature are targets and tend to be called out faster by the Twitter community, should be well aware and respectful of Twitter's unique culture so as to avoid engaging recklessly. That said, Twitter is also known to be one of the most honest, helpful, and welcoming online communities, and its reputation is perhaps one of the main reasons behind its surge in popularity over the course of 2007.

In 2008, Twitter attracted the media's attention when some American presidential candidates began using it on the campaign trail, most notably Barack Obama. According to Hitwise, on election day 2008, traffic on Twitter.com alone rose 43 percent. Later that year, Twitter users in India live-tweeted the horrific events of the 2008 Mumbai attacks as the tragedy unfolded. It was a significant turning point in Twitter's history, as people began to rely on this simple but effective service as a source for breaking news. In the summer 2009, Twitter again influenced history during the aftermath of the Iranian elections, which resulted in national tumult, culminating with the Iranian government's ousting of the traditional news media. During that time, the only breaking news came from tweets from the Iranian opposition.

Because Twitter is mobile, tweeps who are first on the scene of breaking news are able to get the word out quickly and efficiently. Smart phones not only let people tweet; they can also take and upload photos, enriching the value of a tweet. These days, news often breaks first on Twitter, and the media follows suit. Not to be usurped, many media outlets now deliver their news feeds via Twitter, as well as directly engaging with readers.

By the start of 2009, Twitter's popularity reached critical mass. Once thought of as a trivial fad, Twitter was now making headlines and becoming a household word. More brands began integrating Twitter into their social media strategies. Realizing its importance, entities from large corporations to small businesses were also racing to claim their Twitter handles, hoping to avoid the domain-squatting issues of the late 1990s.

Twitter has also become wildly popular in the mainstream media as more celebrities have joined the fray, reaching a pinnacle in April 2009 when Oprah (`@oprah`) signed up for Twitter live on her show with the already popular actor and producer Ashton Kutcher (`@aplusk`) in the role of guide, and drawing 76,000 followers to her account within less than 15 minutes of her first tweet! Popular tech blog TechCrunch estimated that Oprah's show alone may have brought more than one million new users to Twitter. Not long after, Kutcher laid down a challenge to acquire more than one million users before CNN's Breaking News (`@cnnbrk`). (See Figure 1.7.) Since then, Kutcher has completely surpassed Breaking News and is currently the Number One "most popular" Twitterer, as measured by the number of followers.

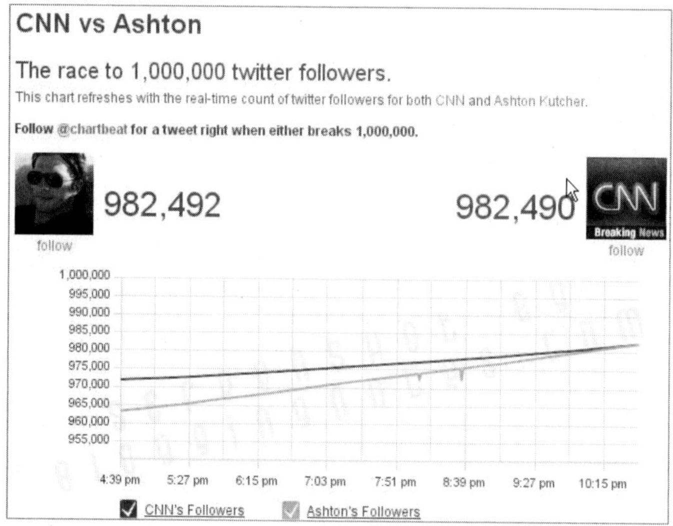

Figure 1.7 Ashton Kutcher's progress against CNN's Breaking News

Twitter's Financial Future

Twitter's popularity has also attracted potential mega-buyers. In November 2008, there were multiple unconfirmed reports that Facebook offered to acquire Twitter for $500 million of its stock, which included a cash component. The offer was roundly rejected. In April 2009, rumors furiously swirled that Google was also going to make an offer to acquire Twitter. Google squarely denied the rumor. In May 2009, Apple too, it was rumored, was interested in acquiring Twitter. To date, Twitter has rejected all offers to be acquired, stating on its blog that it intends to go it on its own:

`http://blog.twitter.com/2009/04/sometimes-we-talk.html`

All of these rumors have many of us wondering, "What *is* the future of Twitter?" Twitter seems to be investing in its future by courting investors, hiring experienced players, and keeping the media grasping at every publicly announced nuance or teased piece of information. For example, in March 2008 the *Wall Street Journal* reported that Twitter cofounder Biz Stone alluded to companies paying for more features in the future because Twitter had hired a product manager to develop these yet-to-be-defined features. In June 2009, a general partner of a firm that invested in Twitter hinted to *The New York Times* that Twitter's monetization lay in ecommerce, namely "links to products and turnkey payment mechanisms" and "filters and feeds to sort tweets by whom they are from and what they are about." That same month, Bloomberg.com reported that Biz Stone said that Twitter could make money by verifying corporate accounts. In August 2009, Biz Stone taped a television interview on the PBS show *Tavis Smiley* and alluded to the company's plans to monetize itself by selling more robust data-analysis features to brand companies. In September 2009, *The Wall Street Journal* reported that Twitter was close to raising as much as $100 million from multiple investors who valuated Twitter at $1 billion!

However Twitter plans to make money in the long run, one thing's for certain: plenty of people in Twitterdom will have an opinion about their decision.

What Makes Tweeps Tick?

Twitter creates value because it can be used in many clever and innovative ways to serve many different purposes (Figure 1.8).

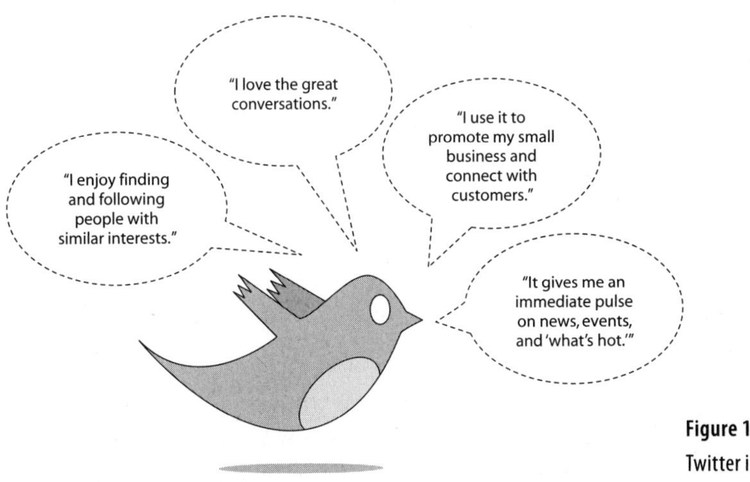

Figure 1.8 How and why Twitter is being used

For a marketer, it's just as important to understand the motivations behind why people use Twitter as it is to understand how Twitter serves as a marketing tool. What makes people want to follow and be followed? Why have so many people reluctantly joined Twitter, only soon to become Twitter addicts (`#twitteraddict`)? In short, what makes Twitter users tick? Let's take a closer look at some of the reasons why Twitterers use Twitter; understanding this will in turn help explain why Twitter continues to gain such widespread popularity.

Keeping in Touch Twitter is great for socializing. You can socialize with friends, clients, customers, prospects, the media, and anyone else with whom you might regularly be in touch. A single tweet is broadcast to all of your followers at once, making it easy to let everyone know where you are and what you're up to.

Making New Friends Some people want to use Twitter strictly to find new friends and contacts with whom to cyber-socialize. Twitter's low barriers to connecting make this especially easy.

Connecting with Like-Minded People The majority of Twitter users are people looking to connect with others who have similar interests and discuss the latest news and trends in their circles. Enthusiasts of all types are connected through Twitter.

> *Example*: There are tons of online gamers on Twitter who tweet about all things video games, love to "talk smack," and find new opponents.

Voyeurism Twitter's open system allows *anyone*—even non–Twitter users—to view whatever you tweet. Someone might want to keep an eye on another tweep's goings-on without the other knowing it. Twitter makes this possible.

Event Planning Twitter can be an easy way to organize an offline gathering of like-minded people. In fact, a *TweetUp* is Twitterese for "meet up" in which a group of tweeps interested in meeting face-to-face plan to congregate at a determined time and place, usually associated with an existing event or subject matter and usually in an informal setting.

> *Example*: I initiated the idea of a TweetUp at the 2009 Search Engine Strategies conference in New York and passed my idea on to the conference organizers, who then suggested the time and place and tweeted about it to all their followers. A healthy-sized group of people turned up and stayed several hours—networking, talking about the conference, and "stimulating the economy" of a local watering hole.

Activism On Twitter, it's easy to find and/or recruit people willing to support or work your cause, whether charitable, medical, environmental, or political.

> *Example*: Barack Obama's campaign managers used the `@barackobama` Twitter account as an essential tool for finding and organizing support for their candidate. They were obviously very successful. Twitter has also been used to help

severely ill people find donors or get medical assistance they might otherwise not be able to afford.

Entertainment There's no shortage of entertainment on Twitter, whether it's celebrities who tweet; bands updating their fans; comedians telling 140-character jokes; links to YouTube videos; sports scores; or otherwise fun, funny, or interesting people and entities using Twitter to amuse or be amused.

Example: Shaq O'Neal (`@THE_REAL_SHAQ`), Britney Spears (`@britneyspears`), and Ellen DeGeneres (`@TheEllenShow`) all use Twitter to both inform and goose their fans.

It is noteworthy that there are so many Twitter imposters posing as celebrities that Twitter had to create a verified accounts system that consists of a seal on a user's profile page once Twitter confirms that the user is who he/she/it claims to be. Currently, Twitter's Verified Accounts are offered only to high-profile individuals likely to have "impersonation problems or identity confusion," and not businesses. The only information Twitter currently offers about its verified accounts can be found here: `http://twitter.com/help/verified`. Twitter has hinted at selling Verified Accounts to businesses down the road, however, as a revenue stream.

Getting a Company's Latest Tweets Brands often use Twitter as a trumpet for news, developments, and promotions—even before press releases or official blog posts. Many consumers like to follow the companies that matter to them and connect with brands on a more personal level.

Example: Tony Hsieh (`@zappos`), CEO of Zappos.com, one of the Web's largest footwear and accessories stores, tweets regularly about new products, company news, and special promotions. He also shares tidbits from his exciting, always-on-the-go personal life.

Marketing and Business Development Twitter is an invaluable tool for businesses of all sizes. In fact, Twitter's level playing field gives small businesses and entrepreneurs an edge they can't necessarily get otherwise. Customers and prospects get to know the face behind the company, which can be helpful in building a brand. Through Twitter, entrepreneurs don't have to spend thousands to launch a new product or service, promote a marketing campaign, or drive traffic to their websites.

Example: `@smbusinesses` is a user who follows only small businesses on Twitter, serving as a portal to connect and network with similar users.

Monitoring Brands and Reputations Most tweeps aren't shy about speaking their minds, especially when it comes to things they like or dislike. Twitter makes it possible to monitor and measure what they're saying about you or your brand in real time.

Example: Comcast Cablevision, the company behind the Twitter handle `@ComcastCares`, often responds promptly to tweets about service interruptions and other complaints.

Keeping Up with the Latest News News breaks often on Twitter, especially tech-related news originating from tweets by people within the industry. Some traditional media have begun using Twitter as an additional broadcast medium.

Example: `@CNNbrk` is CNN's official Twitter account for breaking news. It continually tweets the news network's latest headlines to over 1.5 million followers.

Example: When a US Airways plane crash-landed in the Hudson River, the first photo was submitted by a Twitter user who posted it to the Web (see `http://twitpic.com/135xa`) and tweeted, "There's a plane in the Hudson. I'm on the ferry to pick up the people. Crazy."

Simplicity

Twitter's genesis sprung from the idea of serving as a status update tool, and at its most basic level, that's what it still is (Figure 1.9). Although its usage has evolved well beyond the "What are you doing?" premise, Twitter's simplicity makes answering the status question a common first activity for newcomers.

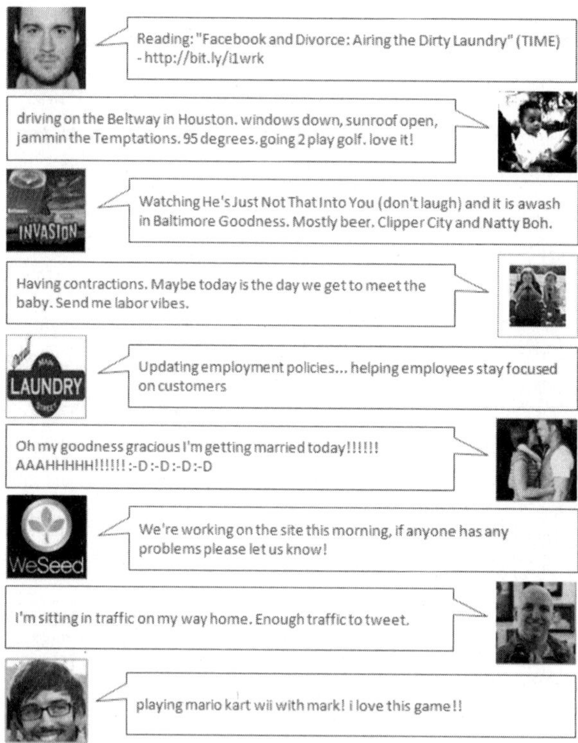

Reading: "Facebook and Divorce: Airing the Dirty Laundry" (TIME) - http://bit.ly/i1wrk
driving on the Beltway in Houston. windows down, sunroof open, jammin the Temptations. 95 degrees. going 2 play golf. love it!
INVASION
Watching He's Just Not That Into You (don't laugh) and it is awash in Baltimore Goodness. Mostly beer. Clipper City and Natty Boh.
Having contractions. Maybe today is the day we get to meet the baby. Send me labor vibes.
LAUNDRY
Updating employment policies... helping employees stay focused on customers
Oh my goodness gracious I'm getting married today!!!!!! AAAHHHHH!!!!!! :-D :-D :-D :-D
WeSeed
We're working on the site this morning, if anyone has any problems please let us know!
I'm sitting in traffic on my way home. Enough traffic to tweet.
playing mario kart wii with mark! i love this game!!

Figure 1.9 A few examples of simple status update tweets

Short and Sweet

Although Twitter limits messages to a meager 140 characters (Figure 1.10), many would argue that this seemingly strict limitation is one of Twitter's greatest strengths. Limited length means that every word counts. In an Internet age of information overload, most Twitter users relish in the brevity.

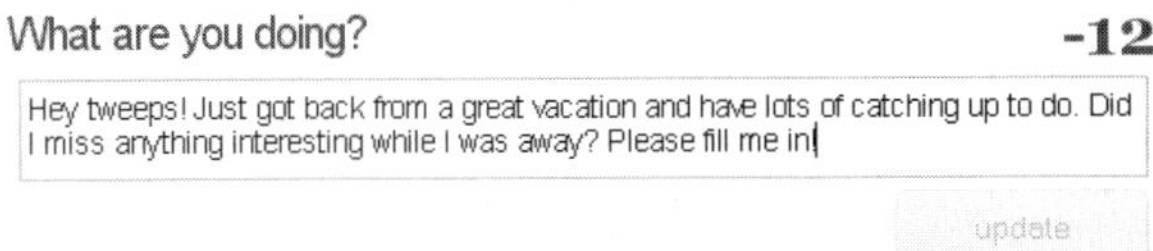

Figure 1.10 As you compose your tweet, once you get down to 20 characters remaining, Twitter's character "countdown" will turn red to warn you. If you exceed your character limitation, you will receive Twitter's warning.

Writing pithy yet informative tweets that convey the full value of your meaning is a skill. I think of it almost as the art of great copywriting or in a similar way to how I view writing a killer email subject line or news headline. If I don't get all the key information up front and with as few grammatical articles as possible, I might miss the opportunity to convince my reader to go any further.

Later in this book, we'll be going over the art of composing great tweets. Now, for fun, let me share a term first introduced to me by a colleague (`@dwplanit`): *twoosh*, which refers to a perfect and still sensible 140-character tweet. (It's cheating if you shorten or abbreviate words in your twoosh.) Intentionally trying to write a twoosh is almost as challenging as writing haiku, although twooshes do frequently occur on their own! (See Figure 1.11.)

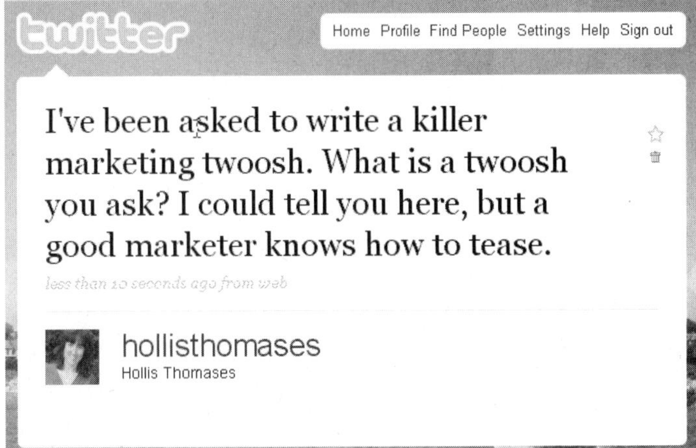

Figure 1.11 A twoosh is a perfect 140-character tweet.

Low Barriers to Entry

Twitter makes it easy to join: It's free! Using the web-based version of Twitter is still 100 percent free, although users accessing Twitter via mobile SMS might incur standard text messaging rates and users who elect to use third-party Twitter management solutions might also have to pay for those.

Twitter knows very few divides. Anyone of any nationality, race, or gender, anywhere in the world, is welcome to create a Twitter account (or more than one). (See Figure 1.12.) For the low price of your name and a valid email address, admission to the Twitterverse is granted. Email addresses are not validated, but using a false one prevents the user from being notified by Twitter about things such as new followers or direct messages.

Figure 1.12 Twitter users come from all over the world.

Account Creation

Talk about simplicity; Twitter's three-step account-creation process couldn't be easier (Figure 1.13):

1. Create a username and password.
2. Enter your email address to find contacts.
3. Start following people.

(You can even skip steps 2 and 3.)

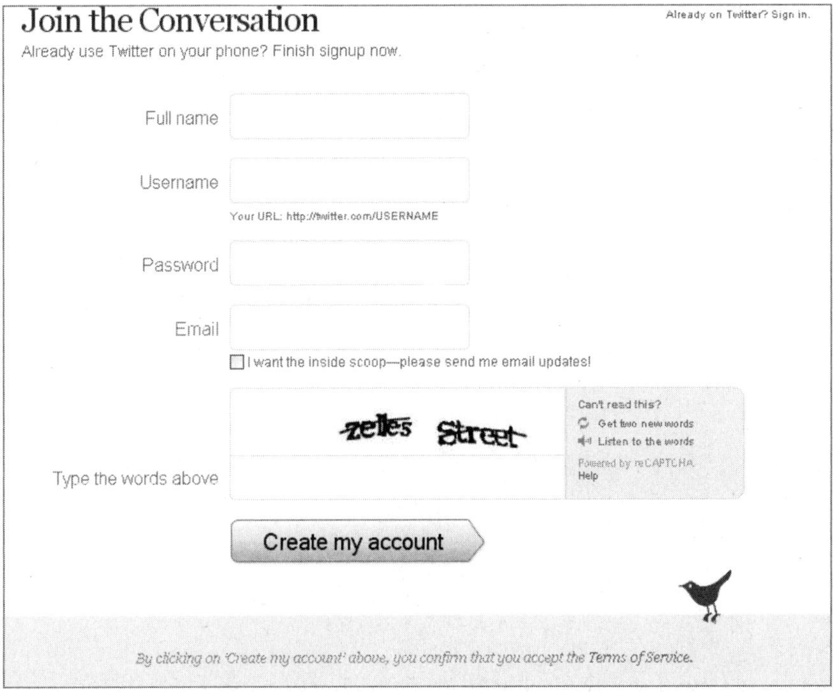

Figure 1.13 Creating a new Twitter account

Users are encouraged to share their real names, but doing so is not required. Twitter user profiles can be completed and customized, but they do not have to be to allow someone to use Twitter. Currently, there's no user agreement to read and sign or email confirmation link to click. (Although there is no user agreement, Twitter does have Terms of Service, which you can find at `http://twitter.com/tos`.)

Just Start Typing

Once your account is created, you're ready to start tweeting. You may simply tweet your status, or you may create a welcome tweet introducing yourself to the Twitterverse by telling a little about yourself and your reason(s) for joining Twitter. This is good practice for the art of pithy writing! You can also hang back and *lurk* a while. The term *lurking* has been around since the early days of the Internet, and it merely means to hang back, become familiar with the process and culture of the Internet channel you're about to get involved with, and look a little before leaping. On Twitter, lurking is reading other people's tweets before venturing out to post your own. The eager new user may seek the help of a willing friend who's already on Twitter to act as an accomplice, introducing you to their tweeps. Most Twitter users are warm and welcoming of new users who acknowledge their "newbiness," although these same experienced users might be less tolerant of newcomers who don't take time to learn or who intentionally ignore better twetiquette, and some might even make a point of calling the offender out. A very funny YouTube video showcases actor Kevin Spacey's appearance on the *Late Show with David Letterman*, in which he shows Dave how to use Twitter: `http://www.youtube.com/watch?v=2Z1aZ7Gs46A`.

Find Friends

Twitter has several tools to help you find friends and start building your Twitterverse. We'll cover this topic more in-depth in Chapter 4, "Week 1: Get on Twitter;" for now you just need to know that Twitter's friending functionality is both simple and without boundaries. If you find someone you want to follow, you do not need to send this person an invitation or even get their permission to start following them. Simply click the Follow button, and you will officially befriend this person (Figure 1.14).

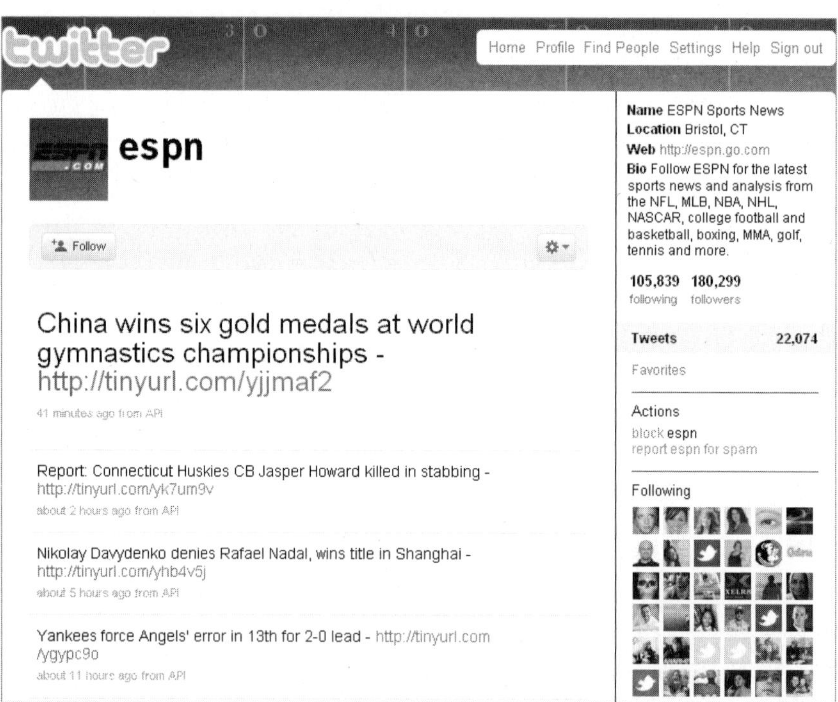

Figure 1.14 Twitter makes following as simple as one click.

When someone chooses to follow you on Twitter, Twitter sends you an email notification with the new follower's name, handle, and their followers/following/update stats. This not only alerts you to the fact that you have a new follower, but you can also click on the link in the email to view this new user's Twitter page (Figure 1.15).

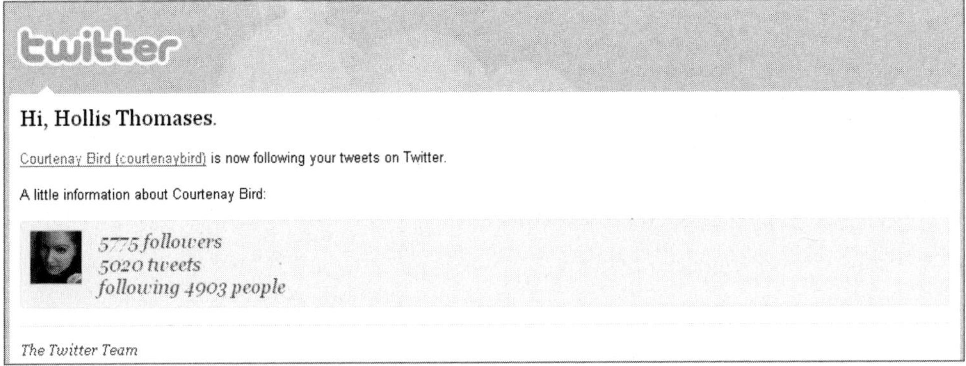

twitter
Hi, Hollis Thomases.
Courtenay Bird (courtenaybird) is now following your tweets on Twitter.
A little information about Courtenay Bird:
5775 followers
5020 tweets
following 4903 people
The Twitter Team

Figure 1.15 Twitter alerts you by email when you have a new follower.

Unlike other social communities, however, friending on Twitter is not a two-way arrangement. Following someone does not ensure that they are going to follow you, nor should you expect them to do so. Because Twitter has basically no barriers to friending, you will find yourself being followed by total strangers—and because you don't know these people, you may be reluctant to follow them. Some people have no problem with follower reciprocity and they might even use automated software to instantaneously follow you back; on the other hand, others are far more discriminatory about this practice. These latter types of Twitter users will usually visit your Twitter profile page to learn more about you and make their follow-back decision based on how follow-worthy they feel you are. Regardless, following someone back is just as easy: all anyone has to do is click the Follow button, and they'll become a new follower.

Ease of Use

Twitter's simplicity doesn't stop once you've gotten started. Twitter's clean interface and easy-to-understand activities make it incredibly accessible to anyone. Because, in theory, there are very few technical things you can do directly on Twitter, it has left little room for functional error.

Straightforward Design

Twitter's web interface is clean, attractive, and user-friendly, with little to detract from its purpose (Figure 1.16). You can really do only a handful of things on Twitter.com, and even listing them makes it all sound more complicated than it really is.

- Read tweets from your followers (your *tweet stream*).
- Mark a tweet as a Favorite.

- Send a message or reply to your followers.
- Read your direct messages.
- Send a direct message.
- View your followers.
- View who you're following.
- View your tweets (you also have the option to delete your own tweets individually).
- View your favorites.
- Conduct a search (you can also save a search as an option).
- View your saved searches.
- View Trending Topics.
- Subscribe to your feed by RSS.
- Modify your profile.
- Change your settings.
- Find friends.

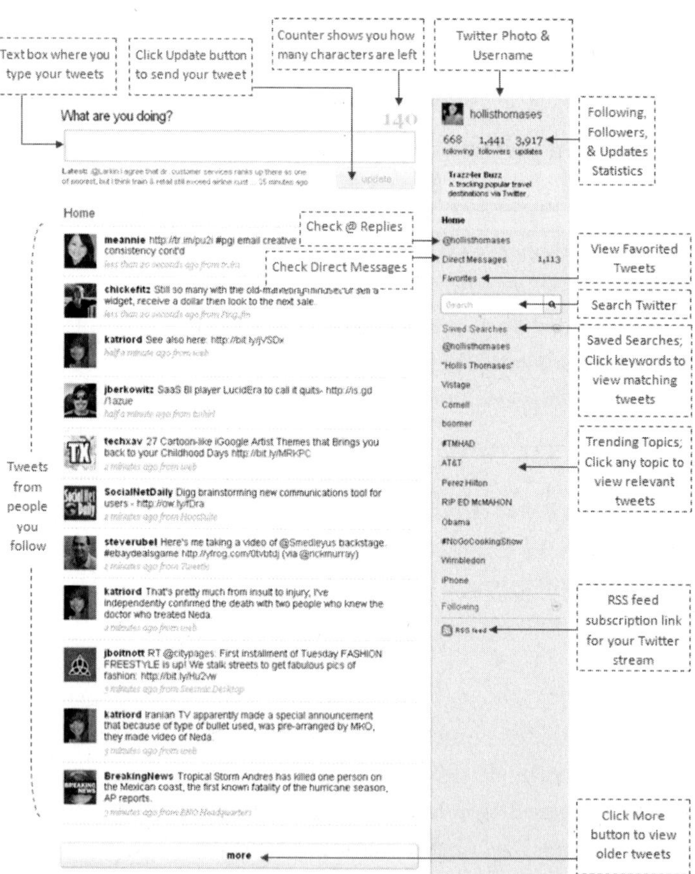

Figure 1.16 Twitter's finite activities

Simple Controls

Having such limited activity options reduces the room for confusion or error. For example, all of the View functions just require that someone click on the desired link. Twitter makes most of its links very easy to see—they're just ordinary underlined blue links. Twitter is so easy, in fact, that newbies first trying to get oriented through third-party tools commit more errors than those just using the simple Twitter interface, particularly when it involves responding. For example, if you receive a direct message via your cell phone's text messaging and just press Reply, a message you intended to send to a single person will be broadcast to the world. Oops! (See Figure 1.17.) It's tempting to reply via email to a direct message, but that just doesn't work. If you're trying to use some kind of third-party application that has built-in retweeting functionality, a new user might retweet everything instead of writing a simple @ reply, which really adds unintentional meaning to the tweet. Because of all these *faux pas*, I usually recommend that people get their feet wet by using Twitter.com before they venture into other platforms.

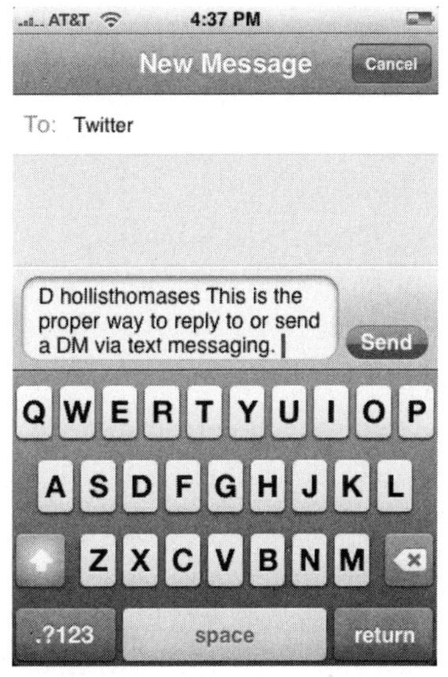

Figure 1.17 If you want a reply to be a direct message, you have to change the @ to a D.

Low Level of Commitment

People use Twitter for all kinds of reasons. In Twitter's "Getting Started" Help section (`http://help.twitter.com/forums/10711/entries`), there isn't any stipulation about how often you have to use Twitter or for what purpose. As a result, Twitter meets people's needs differently and, at its core, Twitter requires nothing of its users—not even active use. This low level of commitment has led to some criticism of Twitter. In April 2009 Nielsen Online claimed that 60 percent of Twitter users quit after their first month's use, so Twitter's rising user counts might be misleading (Figure 1.18).

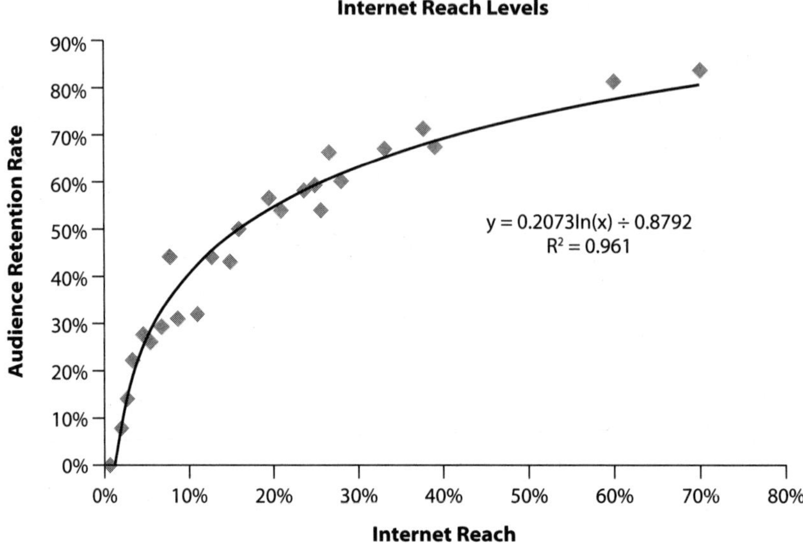

Figure 1.18 Nielsen's analysis of Twitter user retention

Does this matter to the marketer? Is this a trend that will continue or just a hiccup as people rushed to register for Twitter but then didn't find value in it? Let's remember how Twitter is being used.

Casual Conversations Because of its casual atmosphere, Twitter has become the water cooler of the Web, a popular hangout where users pause to shoot the breeze, catch up on things they may have missed, and gossip with friends.

Easy Come, Easy Go On Twitter, users can follow and unfollow people at will, with no real consequences. See someone tweet something interesting? Start following them and see what other cool things they might share. Don't like what someone has to say? Make a clean break and unfollow them. Most users don't take it personally.

Blogging, But Not Twitter is an easy way to jump-start blogging without a whole lot of effort. Blogging takes a lot of work: bloggers not only have to come up with content ideas, but they have to find time to flesh out and write these ideas into actual blog entries. Twitter users, on the other hand, can share news, opinions, links, music, and more—all without even knowing how to start a blog, let alone having to write a lengthy blog post.

Although I don't really question Nielsen's research, I somewhat disagree with its conclusions about why people might be abandoning Twitter. To begin with, accounts are created for many reasons: for preservation's sake ("I don't want someone else registering my name even if I don't plan on tweeting"); for creativity's sake ("I love this name as a Twitter handle, and there's no cost to creating a Twitter account, so why not just create the account just in case I ever want to use it?"); for marketing's sake ("We are eventually going to have a Twitter strategy where all our employees tweet, so let's have all our employees register a Twitter account [company name + their first name] now to get that out of the way.").

After ruling out possibilities like this, I'm still left thinking that success with Twitter, as with all other social networks, is directly related to engagement. Does anyone remember what it was like to have a pen pal, someone who committed to write you whenever you wrote them? You looked forward to having a letter in your mailbox from your pen pal every so often, and receiving that letter was possibly the highlight of your day. You may never have met this pen pal who might have resided in a foreign country, but through the relationship of writing, you and your pen pal grew very close and remained close through the years. Twitter reminds me of having pen pal, but with Twitter I'm lucky enough to have many pen pals (Figure 1.19). Still, in my earliest days on Twitter, I could count on a few reliable tweeps who always responded to my posts. Thanks to them, I am writing this book today. So if you're using Twitter for marketing, remember to create a pen pal–like relationship with your customer base. That relationship is the equivalent of brand loyalty, and every brand strives for this kind of customer loyalty.

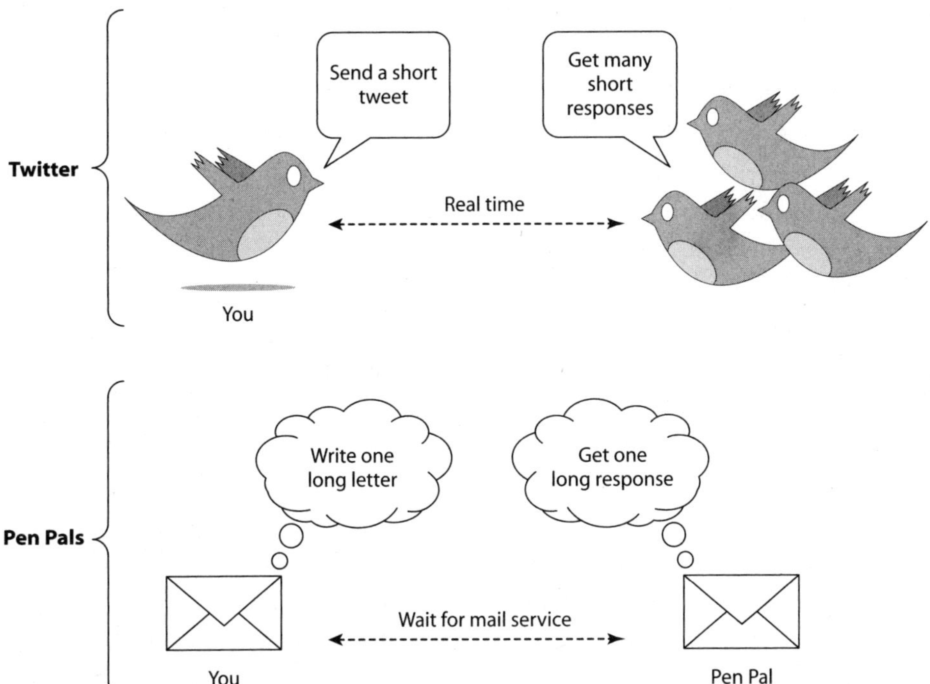

Figure 1.19 Twitter relationships can be like pen pal relationships...but better!

High Level of Control

For the small amount of commitment that Twitter requires, it offers a remarkably high level of individual user control. This is another feature that has led to its rise in popularity.

You Own Your Message

You are what you tweet. Other social networks generally summarize who you are with a one-shot profile and give you tools and features to embellish that profile with pictures, graphics, links, and so on. Twitter, however, has few distracting add-ons; it's pretty much stripped down to a singular focus: your tweets. Twitter and the Twitter community of users place a high value on what you have to say; by primarily using only words, a user can increase the authority and influence he or she has within the community. Tweet interesting things, and gain followers. Tweet uninteresting things, and lose them. Don't tweet much at all; don't expect much in return. Twitter not only gives users total control over their messages, but also gives them the opportunity to wield clout in the community.

Interact with Who You Want, When You Want

Twitter puts you in the driver's seat of who you interact with; whether that's the act of following, replying, @ or direct messaging, or retweeting, Twitter allows you to do so at a pace that's individually controlled. Certainly, the norms of twetiquette encourage reasonable response times; however, nothing dictates or even forces a user to respond in any particular timeframe.

This control is both very powerful and empowering. It also gives the user the ability to build a personalized network of people; that is, people selected by the user for the user's own reasons. Advanced third-party tools and a soon-to-be launched feature on Twitter called Lists, further help the individual user by organizing this network of users in customized, meaningful ways (Figure 1.20).

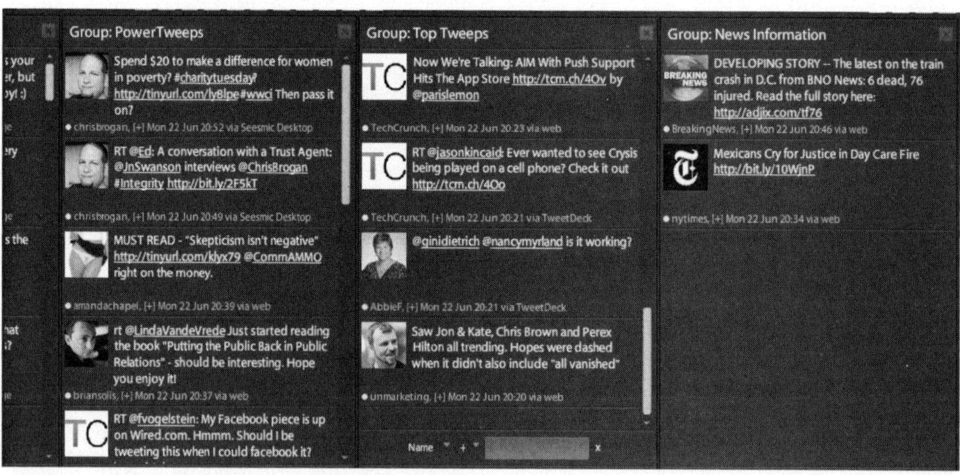

Figure 1.20 Third-party applications like TweetDeck can be used to organize groups.

Block Unwanted Users

If you really don't care for another Twitter user or suspect they're a spammer, Twitter's built-in block function enables you to silence them. They will be unable to send you tweets and blocked followers will not appear in your follower list. Additionally, blocked users will be unable to read your tweets in their Twitter stream. Blocking makes it appear as if you do not exist to each other.

Like everything else with Twitter, blocking someone is easy.

1. Identify the undesirable follower, and click the Block button (Figure 1.21).
2. Confirm the block (Figure 1.22).

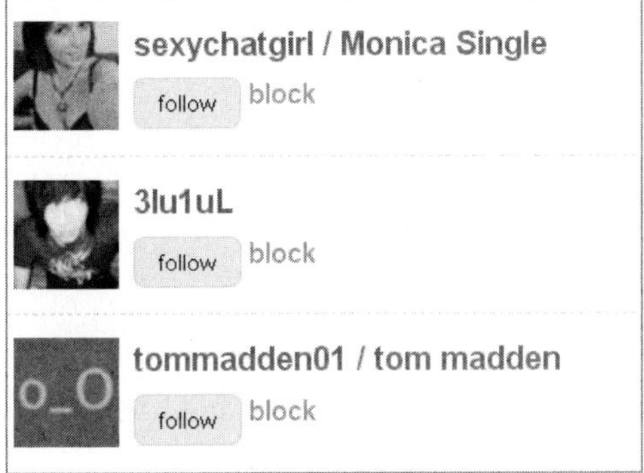

Figure 1.21 Identify the undesirable follower.

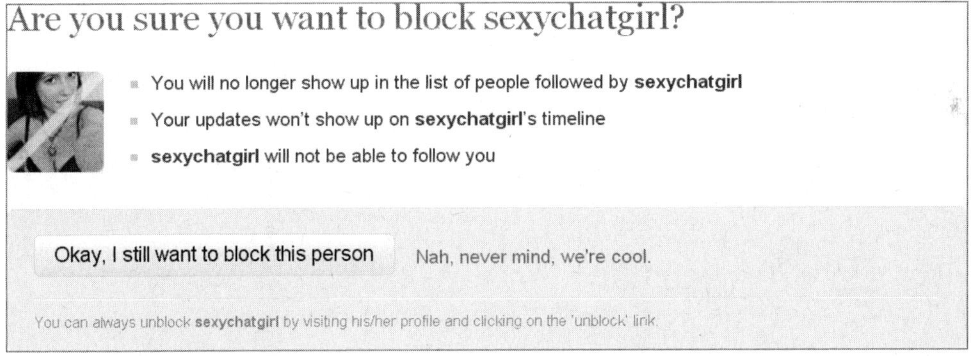

Figure 1.22 Confirm the block.

Privacy Protections

Twitter has several built-in privacy protections that let users control who sees their tweets. By default, these protections are disabled. It's easy to enable them, however, with Twitter's simple Protect My Tweets checkbox in the Settings console. (See Figure 1.23.)

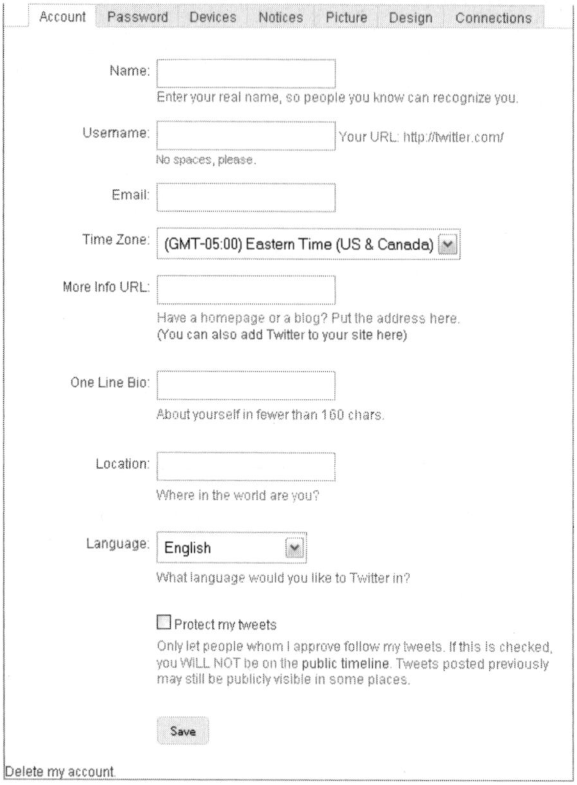

Account | Password | Devices | Notices | Picture | Design | Connections

Name:
Enter your real name, so people you know can recognize you.

Username: Your URL: http://twitter.com/
No spaces, please.

Email:

Time Zone: (GMT-05:00) Eastern Time (US & Canada)

More Info URL:
Have a homepage or a blog? Put the address here.
(You can also add Twitter to your site here)

One Line Bio:
About yourself in fewer than 160 chars.

Location:
Where in the world are you?

Language: English
What language would you like to Twitter in?

☐ Protect my tweets
Only let people whom I approve follow my tweets. If this is checked, you WILL NOT be on the public timeline. Tweets posted previously may still be publicly visible in some places.

Save

Delete my account

Figure 1.23 Twitter's privacy settings

Protected tweets mean that none of that user's tweets appear on Twitter's public timeline. Only users who are approved by the account owner can see the owner's tweets (Figure 1.24).

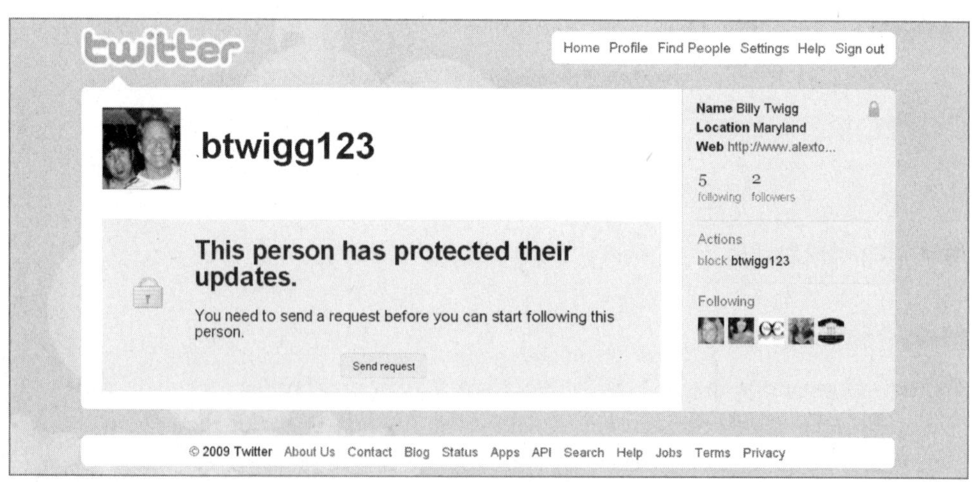

Figure 1.24 A profile with protected tweets

Twitter also has a Delete My Account option (a rarity for most social networks) that will completely erase all traces of your Twitter profile and every tweet associated with it. This feature is not something most account holders know about or choose to use, but it's comforting to know that it exists if needed. Remember, however, that even if you wipe out your Twitter identity and all your tweets, your tweets may have promulgated elsewhere in Twitter's search engine or Google (both of which index tweets) or on other people's websites or blogs. Watch those late-night drunken rants about your ex. Your tweets may live in infamy long after your Twitter account is gone. Always be mindful of what you're saying!

Twitter's Culture

As Twitter has grown in popularity, it has developed a culture of its own and, as with any culture, it has its own mores, expectations, and intricacies that users become aware of through self-education, regular use, and guidance by the Twitter community at large.

Sense of Community

Twitter has developed a strong reputation for being an open, accepting community of users who embrace new ideas and are willing to provide help to those who seek it. Twitter users often benefit from *crowdsourced* help—that is, users turn to the Twitter community as well as their followers to solicit input or to get help to make an informed decision.

Crowdsourcing: A Definition

According to Wikipedia, "Crowdsourcing is a [new word] for the act of taking a task traditionally performed by an employee or contractor, and outsourcing it to an undefined, generally large group of people or community in the form of an open call."

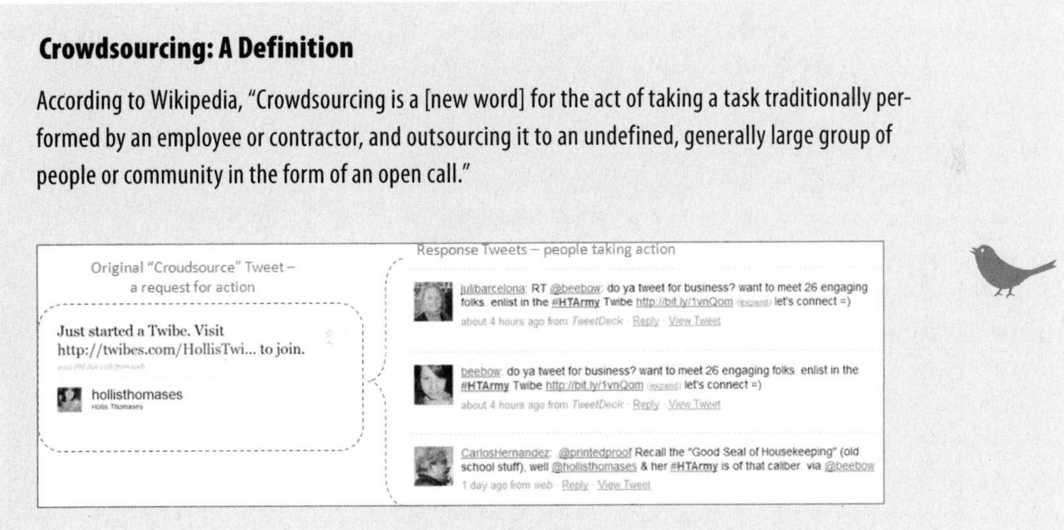

Rhetorical Nature

Twitter is a one-to-many communication platform. When you tweet, your message is not only broadcast to everyone who follows you, but your tweet is placed out in Twitter's public domain for anyone to find and read. Responses are welcome, but not demanded. Nobody really expects all of their followers to reply to everything they say. Just because a tweet does not receive a desired level of response, however, does not mean that it was not interesting, valuable, or useful to followers. In fact, if a user were to reply to every single tweet you made, you'd feel that they were odd—almost like a stalker.

Brutal Honesty

If you're a newcomer to Twitter, be prepared to have thick skin. Want an honest opinion? Twitter is one of your best bets. Twitter users aren't afraid to speak their minds, and most will happily tell you how they *really* feel about something. Because of this, Twitter is one of the best tools available for taking the public's collective temperature: what's hot, what's not, and everything in between. When Twitter users are enthusiastic about something, they tweet about it; when they are less than enthusiastic about something, they tweet about that too. One of the best things about Twitter is that you can tap into the whole community's crowd wisdom, regardless of who you follow.

Twitter is a real-time gauge of public opinion. Twitter's Trending Topics (Figure 1.25) aggregates and lists the most popularly tweeted topics at any given time. This shows you what's on people's minds. Sometimes it's nonsense, while at other times it's a major global event. Oftentimes, topics are hashtagged, abbreviated or coded by the Twitter community's vernacular. At a glance, Twitter's Trending Topics can help you stay in the know.

Trending Topics
#remember
#ranelection
go team carlisle
True Blood
Alan Carr
Mark Martin
Mousavi
#CNNfail
Twitter Blasts CNN
Tehran

Figure 1.25 What's hot? To find out, see Twitter's Trending Topics list.

Twitter's Advanced Search also helps inform Trending Topics and the court of public opinion. Chapter 4 will discuss Advanced Search in more detail.

Twetiquette

The Twitter culture has developed its own etiquette, or *twetiquette*. Although certain behavior, such as brutal honesty, can be expected from users, the way in which people deliver their tweets and act/react is still influenced by a degree of mutual respect. Twitter users who recognize and operate within the boundaries of good twetiquette will attract more followers, have more appeal to new ones, won't annoy the Twitter community, and will garner solid responses to their tweets. Those who don't follow common twetiquette may get called out by other users, ignored, unfollowed, blocked, or worse: reported by the Twitter community as spammers. Twitter *does* take action against confirmed spammers, removing them from Twitter altogether.

Common Twetiquette Standards

Some of the most common conventions of twetiquette include the following:

- **Complete your Twitter profile.** It's the Twitter equivalent of introducing yourself. Don't expect people to engage you unless they can find out a little bit about you first.
- **Upload a picture.** Profile pictures are sometimes referred to as *avatars*. (Only newbies keep the Twitter default avatar, mainly because they don't know how to change it.) Don't hide behind some strange graphic. Most people want to see the real person with whom they're tweeting.
- **Basic manners also apply on Twitter.** The time-honored Golden Rule line of thinking applies to your Twitter use. (Yes, people have already been sued for libel as a result of Twitter rants.)

- **Keep it clean!** Keep profanity and questionable language to a minimum. If you wouldn't say something out loud in public, it's probably not a good idea to say it on Twitter.
- **Don't just talk about yourself.** Self-promotion gets old really quickly.
- **Respond to @ or direct messages.** If someone sends you an @ message or direct message, it's courteous to respond. Provide context for your tweets. When publicly replying to a tweep, try to give some context to your tweet so others reading it can understand your message without having to backtrack on the whole conversation. Context in the form of a several-word reference should suffice.

Vocabulary and Acronyms

Over the years, Twitter users have developed their own vocabulary that cleverly plays on the word "Twitter" itself, appending the letters "T" and "W" to the beginning of the word, or featuring it somewhere in between. (As a friend put it to me, "We all sound like Elmer Fudd!") Words that rhyme with "Twitter" or contain the root "twit" are also favored. Twitter users often create new words on the fly, which are tweeted to other users and are quickly adopted and integrated into the Twitter vernacular. Many third-party websites and applications developed for Twitter—such as Twitterholic, Twollow, and Twhirl—perpetuate this trend. There are too many to list here, so they are included in the glossary at the end of this book.

Observe Tweets for Context

Clever tweeps do a great job of working context into their replies. When reading your Twitter stream, check out how and if different tweeps' replies convey the greater meaning of the whole dialog they're having with others and how you find this valuable.

- When retweeting, give credit where it's due. In other words, use the originator's Twitter handle to show who sent the tweet originally.
- Be mindful of what you say about others. You never know who is reading your tweets, and it could be the very people about whom you're making negative comments. (This is especially important for companies empowering employees to tweet on the company's behalf.)
- Keep self-promotion to a minimum, especially for new followers warming up to you. Nobody wants to follow you and suddenly receive numerous tweets and direct messages about whatever it is you're selling.
- When you ask a question and receive answers, thank the people who were kind enough to respond.

- It's courteous to follow people when they follow you, at least at first, to get a sense of who they are and what they're all about. (You can always unfollow them later.)
- If the number of tweeps you're following doesn't balance, to a fair degree, with the number of people following you, and you have very few tweets, you'll probably be considered to be someone with an ulterior motive (i.e., a spammer, an affiliate sales propagator, or a multilevel marketer).
- Don't constantly ask your followers to retweet, Digg, Stumble, and so on to get out your message. It's annoying, and your followers will most likely ignore your requests, or worse, unfollow you.
- Repeatedly reporting the number of followers you have comes across as arrogant. If people are curious, they know where to look for this information. The same goes for constantly touting your rankings on the various Twitter stat/vanity sites (Twitterholic, TwitterGrader, and so forth).
- Don't take unfollowing personally, and don't publicly reprimand people for doing so.
- Never violate Twitter's Rules, which you can find at `http://help.twitter.com/forums/26257/entries/18311`.

The Main Points

- Twitter is a simple, real-time, people-status updating platform turned social community with connections that are built on the concept of *followers*—that is, people who find you and what you have to say interesting.
- Tweeting is like having (or starting) a conversation and should be treated as such.
- People use Twitter for many different reasons and in many different ways, which has opened the door for different types of marketing opportunities.
- In its short history, the flourishing Twitter community has developed its own unique culture, complete with social conventions (twetiquette) and language.
- Twitter is continuing to grow in popularity and evolve as both a social network and marketing tool.

Who's Using Twitter for What?

Who, exactly, is using Twitter these days? A gadget-addicted tech geek? A twenty-something born-to-be-wired? Someone who has nothing better to do all day than post mind-numbing tweets?

Of course not! These days Twitter crosses a wide swath of people from all walks of life. This book teaches you how to reach these people and deliver your marketing message appropriately. Let's walk through some Twitter demographics relating to the kinds of individuals using Twitter. Then let's break out the various types of individuals and entities you're likely to come across on Twitter.

2

Chapter Contents

Demographics

As mentioned in Chapter 1, "Understanding Twitter," Twitter guards its user information and usage statistics closely, so no official demographic data is available from Twitter. To complicate matters, Twitter users who use third-party applications, such as TweetDeck and Twhirl (as opposed to posting straight to Twitter.com's web interface), are not taken into account by the established data-analysis companies. For Twitter demographics data, therefore, we can rely solely on studies done by firms such as Quantcast, comScore, Hitwise, and Sysomos.

The Data

Quantcast, whose measurement methodology couples machine learning with directly measured data and a variety of sample-based reference points, claims that Twitter is a Top 50 site (ranked at number 26) and that its estimated reach in the United States was over 26 million people in May 2009. Quantcast describes Twitter's audience as "young adult, slightly more female than male" and likely to visit pop culture websites.

In May 2009, comScore, one of the Web's largest measurement analysis companies, estimated that 37.3 million people visited Twitter.com, which is up 16 percent from April 2009. This, however, is a slowdown compared to the 68 percent growth in the previous month. Still, Twitter's web page views have exploded since the beginning of 2009, going from less than 50 million page views in May 2008 to 900 million page views globally in May 2009. (See Figure 2.1.)

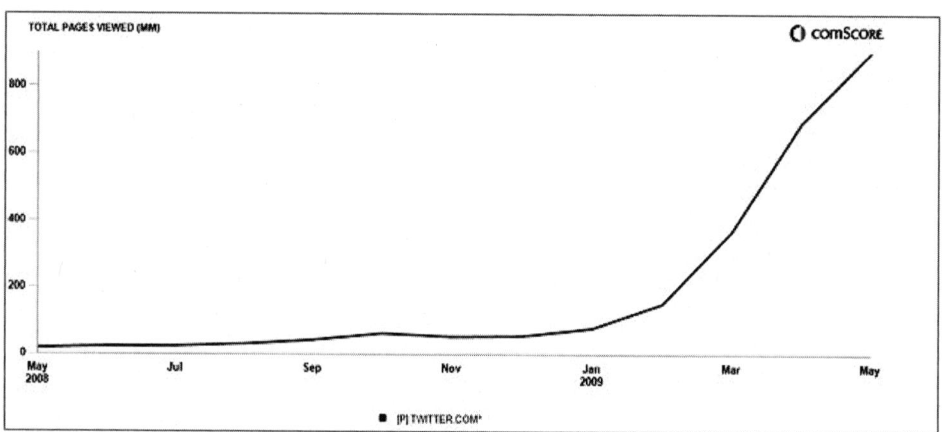

Figure 2.1 comScore shows Twitter's explosive growth in page views for 2009.

Erick Schonfeld, writing for popular resource site TechCrunch, reminds us that comScore is analyzing *all* visitors to Twitter.com, which combines users with accounts and the casual browser reading tweets or finding people. comScore does *not* measure users of Twitter who do not use the Twitter.com web interface to read, post, or reply. Some estimates place this kind of use of third-party desktop or mobile applications by active Twitter users at up to half of Twitter's volume.

Who are these users, numerically speaking?

Hitwise estimated the age breakdown of Twitter users as 39 percent 18- to 24-year-olds, 20 percent 25- to 34-year-olds, 16.5 percent 35- to 44-year-olds, nearly 15 percent 45- to 54-year-olds, and about 9.5 percent 55+ (Figure 2.2). As compared to the year prior, the largest gains being seen in the age brackets for 25- to 34-year-olds and 35- to 44-year-olds, with the 55+ bracket losing the most ground (see Figure 2.3).

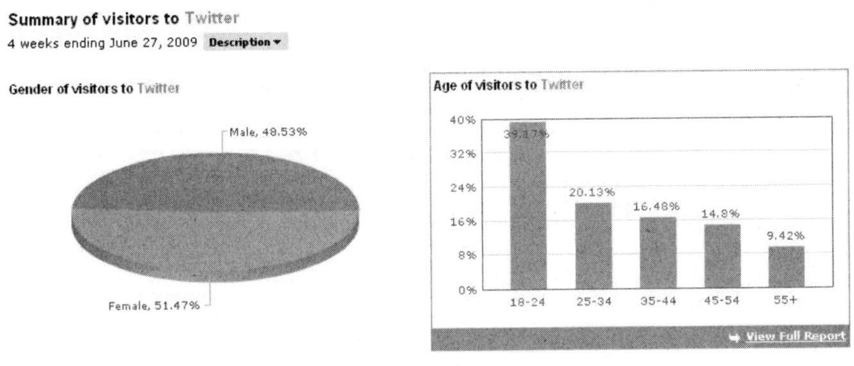

Figure 2.2 Hitwise 2009 Twitter gender and age data

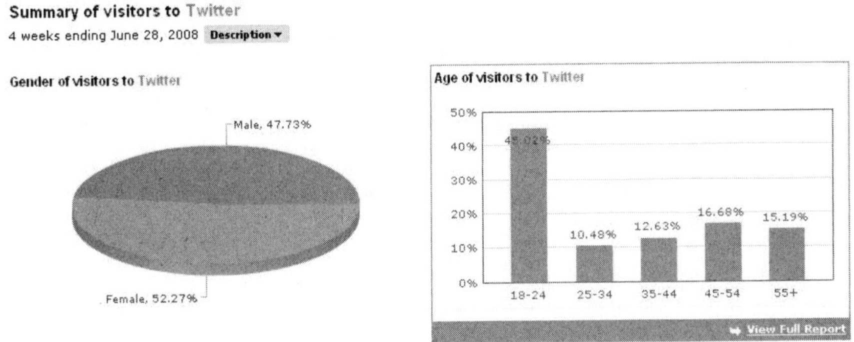

Figure 2.3 Hitwise 2008 Twitter gender and age data

Where are these tweeters? The Sysomos study found that New York has the most Twitters users, followed by Los Angeles, Toronto, San Francisco, and Boston. Detroit was the fastest-growing city over the first five months of 2009 (Figure 2.4).

Twitter Users by State

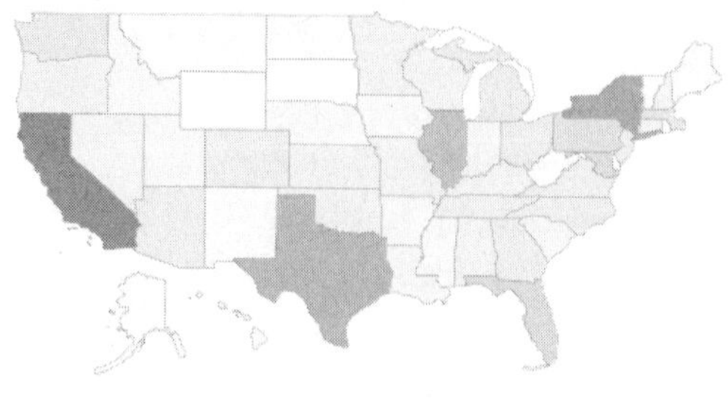

Heat Map of Twitter User Counts by State

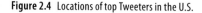

sysomos

Figure 2.4 Locations of top Tweeters in the U.S.

What does Twitter use tell us about someone? According to a July 2009 study by Anderson Analytics co-analyzed by *Ad Age*, if Twitter is your favorite site, you're more likely to be interested in sex than the average Facebook, MySpace, or LinkedIn user. Twitter users also skew particularly high in interest for all news categories, restaurants, sports, politics, personal finance, and religion. They especially like pop culture, music, movies, TV, and reading. They're more likely to buy books, movies, shoes, and cosmetics online than the other groups. Twitterers are also entrepreneurial multitaskers. They are more likely than others to use Twitter to promote their blogs or businesses, more likely to be employed part time (16 percent versus 11 percent average), and have an average income of $58,000. Survey respondents were noncommittal about Twitter, with 43 percent saying they could live without the service.

The Social Media Framework

Another way to look at Twitter demographics is to reference the important social media book *Groundswell* (Harvard Business School Press, 2008), by former Forrester Research analyst Charlene Li and her colleague Josh Bernoff. The authors examined social media users within a framework they named "Social Technographics," which defines the online population by an individual's role in a Web 2.0 world. It is from this global view that one can learn how an individual will likely react to the micro-blogging tool called Twitter.

Social Technographics classifies and ladders consumers into six overlapping levels of participation: Creators, Critics, Collectors, Joiners, Spectators, and Inactives (Figure 2.5).

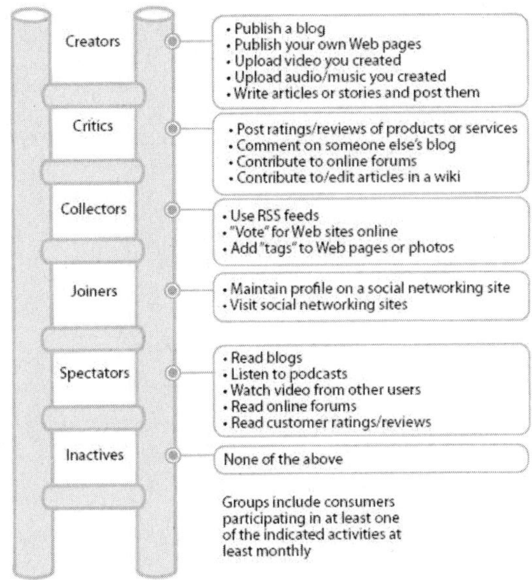

Figure 2.5 The Technographic Ladder

Creators Creators produce content such as web pages, blogs, photos and video, audio, and articles.

Critics Critics review, rate, comment upon, and contribute to the content produced by Creators.

Collectors Collectors tend to aggregate information. They're likely to subscribe to RSS feeds, vote for articles and websites, and bookmark or *tag* web content.

Joiners Joiners sign up for and visit social networking sites, but tend not to fully engage.

Spectators Spectators take in Web 2.0 content (read, listen, watch) but don't often participate.

Inactives Inactives just plain don't participate at all.

What do all these statistics and categorizations really mean in the context of Twitter? Though Twitter might be measured in terms of number of accounts, an account does not necessarily equate to a single person. The Twitterverse consists of many buckets of user types, and it's important to understand these user types as you prepare to develop your Twitter marketing strategy.

Individual Users

Twitter started out because Jack Dorsey wanted a way to keep up-to-date with other individuals. If only Jack had used Twitter, however, it would have been a pretty useless idea because it would never have served its purpose. Who flocked to Twitter in the early days? It's probably worth taking a look at the types of early adopters and their motivations for using Twitter in order to understand how the Twitter marketing channel might continue to evolve.

Twitter's Early Adopters

While the rest of us might have been ignoring this silly little texting/chat-like application known as Twitter, some in the cyberworld took a liking to it and soon grasped its potency.

The Geeks

Those techie types who have affectionately come to be labeled "geeks" embraced Twitter early on. They *got it*. The potency of Twitter was that it was a kind of unchained instant messenger to communicate your whereabouts and happenings with your buddies. Moreover, you didn't need to be limited to computer access or tied to a cell phone. One platform could serve all purposes.

The Evangelists

Twitter had a natural, built-in viral component: in order to have a dialog with your buddies via Twitter, they had to use it too. So it's likely that the first wave of people to tout Twitter did it for selfish reasons. Given its ease of use and portability, however, Twitter was easy for passionate users to evangelize. Not even a formal company yet, Twitter turned a corner at the March 2007 South by Southwest (SXSW) Conference, where the word about Twitter spread like wildfire. Those in the know used Twitter to find out about the best parties—although in those days, most tweeting occurred via SMS because everyone had their cell phones at hand. By November 2007, at BlogWorld Expo, Twitter was again on everyone's lips.

A BlogWorld Expo 2007 Attendee's Blog Entry about Twitter

"Twitter [has] tipped the tuna. By that I mean it started peaking. Adoption amongst the people I know seemed to double immediately, an apparent tipping point. It hasn't jumped the shark, and probably won't until Steven Colbert covers this messaging of the mundane. As Twitter turns 1 on March 13th, not only is there a quickening of users, but messages per user." (Ross Mayfield of SocialText: `http://ross.typepad.com/blog/2007/03/twitter_tips_th.html`)

The Curious

If you were among the people attending these kinds of conferences and events and hearing about Twitter, chances were great that you were going to at least check it out. If you wanted to be part of the cool, informed crowd, you'd better sign up if you hadn't already. As bloggers began writing about Twitter, word spread even further, and curiosity struck others beyond technology conference-goers (Figure 2.6). Once bloggers figured out that they could use Twitter to push blog post links and attract more traffic, they became evangelists—anyone with an active blog had to know about Twitter. As a consequence, Twitter gained more traction.

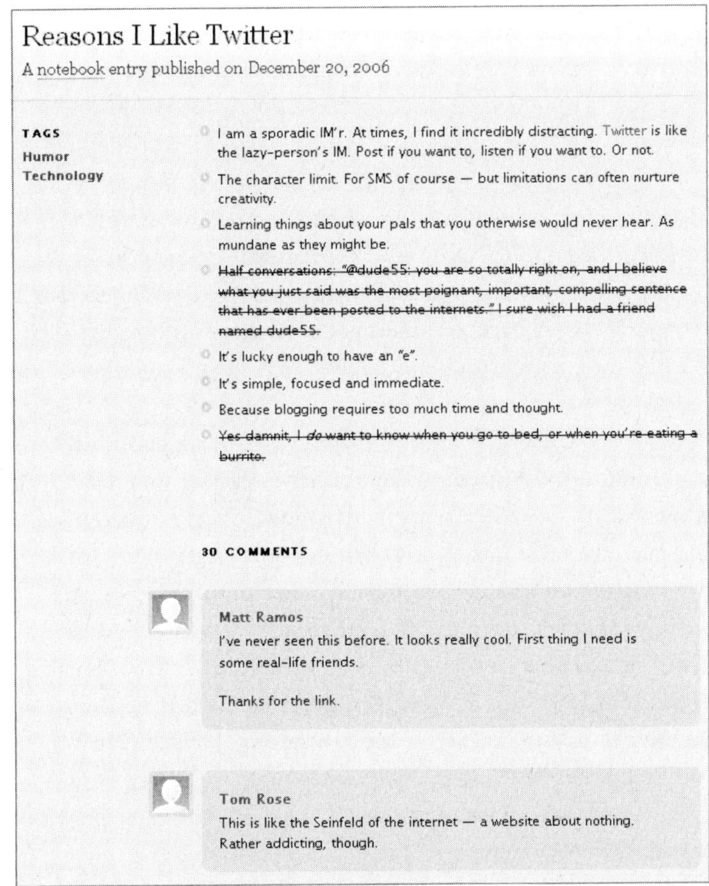

Reasons I Like Twitter
A notebook entry published on December 20, 2006
TAGS
Humor
Technology
I am a sporadic IM'r. At times, I find it incredibly distracting. Twitter is like the lazy-person's IM. Post if you want to, listen if you want to. Or not.
The character limit. For SMS of course — but limitations can often nurture creativity.
Learning things about your pals that you otherwise would never hear. As mundane as they might be.
~~Half conversations: "@dude55: you are so totally right on, and I believe what you just said was the most poignant, important, compelling sentence that has ever been posted to the internets." I sure wish I had a friend named dude55.~~
It's lucky enough to have an "e".
It's simple, focused and immediate.
Because blogging requires too much time and thought.
~~Yes damnit, I *do* want to know when you go to bed, or when you're eating a burrito.~~
30 COMMENTS
Matt Ramos
I've never seen this before. It looks really cool. First thing I need is some real-life friends.
Thanks for the link.
Tom Rose
This is like the Seinfeld of the internet — a website about nothing. Rather addicting, though.

Figure 2.6 An early blog post from the Twitter curious

The Reinventors

Reinventors early on saw the value in Twitter to do more or to do something different. Some reinventors came from a world of entrepreneurship—those who constantly strive to find the next big thing to commercialize. Those who made their living in communications saw the potential for Twitter as a new communication tool, and those in the media saw Twitter as another broadcast channel. Still others came from the corporate world and were just looking for new tools to get things done. Twitter, as it turned out, could help realize multiple realities.

Eventually, enough people flocked to Twitter that it started to take on a life of its own. Twitter became a kind of living organism, evolving from a variety of people using it for a variety of purposes. The diversity of Twitter users can be broken down further by individual profile types.

Twitter Profiles Types

Ignoring for a moment that Twitter isn't simply used by individuals (we'll get to other kinds of Twitter users in a little while), marketers need to understand the various Twitter profile types.

Newbies and Inactives

A *newbie,* quite simply, is a newcomer. A newbie might have joined Twitter out of curiosity or because he or she was encouraged to do so. One of the best things about being a genuine newbie on Twitter is that most Twitter users will gladly help you get acquainted.

Merely signing up for an account, however, does not a Twitter enthusiast make! For that matter, many who sign up for Twitter do not actively use their accounts. Various sources report a good portion of Twitter account holders are inactive. A *Harvard Business Review* report revealed that most Twitter users are passive, with 10 percent of all users accounting for 90 percent of the overall number of tweets. Hubspot, another web-data-tracking company, reported that more than 50 percent of Twitter accounts did not do even the most basic activities.

Accounts can remain inactive for a variety of reasons, including a user's fear of getting started, not really caring to introduce "yet another thing" into an already busy life, and having signed on for inconsequential reasons. For example, after Oprah's "big join," Twitter watchers learned that this kind of newly minted user came, saw, and left the building. There are even those who merely want to celebrity-gawk. Accounts are also created without any initial usage in mind, such as accounts created to hold or protect a name, accounts created for automated software (*bots*), and multiple identities created by a single person with different purposes for each account in mind.

As previously stated, younger users have been deemed a large user pool by some data analysts. Although these users may have Twitter accounts, they really seem to fall into the Inactives category, at least according to a May 2009 study conducted by the Participatory Marketing Network (PMN). This study found that only 22 percent of 18- to 24-year-olds use Twitter. My casual interactions with this age bracket (from speaking on panels aimed at high school and college students, as well as by interacting with them on Twitter) seem to confirm this study. Many young account holders enjoy Twitter mainly as a way to track their favorite celebrities.

Casual/Social Users

Casual or social users of Twitter primarily tweet as an alternative to instant messaging or text messaging. Twitter is open and easy to use, and social tweets are simple, often short, and don't pay heed to context (e.g., "Hey!" or "Thx!"). Casual tweeters don't necessarily pay attention to the Twitter world around them. They tweet either sporadically or just to socialize. Although these users might be in business, they tend not to use or rely on Twitter for business. Twitter is their way to journalize their thoughts and meet new people in a no-holds-barred way of connecting. The casual user may in time, however, evolve into another kind of user, depending on whom they connect with and what resonates with them.

Multilevel Marketers, Get-Rich-Quick Schemers, and Quickie Salesmen

Many legitimate marketers in the online community didn't like this category of marketer before Twitter—and like them even less now! These schemes may have redeeming value to someone, but it's hard to find a compelling argument for them—other than to make money without regard for social mores or standards. Although they might be marketing legitimate products, most Twitter users find members of this category difficult to differentiate from spammers. How do you know if you're dealing with a get-rich-quicker? Visit their profile page and view things such as their Following-to-Followers statistics. If they're following a disproportionate number of people to the number of followers they're actually attracting, this could be a red flag. Next, look at their Tweet stats: if they have very few tweets in comparison to the number of followers they have, they have probably acquired their followers by artificial means, which is another red flag. (These individuals pay to acquire a list of followers and use software that automatically follows and unfollows users, hoping to take advantage of the automated following to build their own follower base.) You'll probably also notice other common clues such as profile bios that literally say this individual just wants to get rich quick and Tweets that only promote get-rich-quick messages. If you do happen to follow this type, it's likely you'll get an automatic DM back with a link to more ways to make money. It doesn't take long before you can quickly discern this type.

Unfortunately, Twitter's easy-access platform has attracted multilevel marketers (MLMrs) in droves, and some out there believe that they will overrun Twitter with so much garbage and spam that it will lead to the downfall of Twitter. Because MLMrs never define themselves as such, tweeting negatively about them can even bring down a rain of new, useless MLM followers or *twitbots* (more on that later) to the defiant user. Thankfully, the Block button comes in handy to cut off these unwelcome followers and, of course, you can always opt not to follow them back.

Quickie sales may also fall into to another gray area, but Twitter was never created to be used solely as a sales pitch channel. Twitter's etiquette about sales messages is akin to that of social networking sites: one ought to be fostering relationships and contributing to the community as a whole. It's deemed bad practice to tweet only about what you're selling. If all you want to do is sell, go on eBay. That being said, Twitter can, of course, be used as a channel to help nurture sales in a way that's not off-putting to the community. That's what this book will help show you.

The Antagonist

Every so often, you might encounter one of these sorts on Twitter. You know the type: the person who just wants to give you a hard time and call into question everything that you do. The antagonist is typically different than an unhappy customer, who just wants their problem resolved to their satisfaction. The antagonist likes to stir the pot for controversy's sake and to gain attention. The larger the brand, the more vulnerable you are to harassment by this kind of unwelcome tweep. You could block them, but then you run the risk of them spreading their malcontent throughout Twitter. Addressing their concerns with factual responses and then mostly ignoring them is the best way to manage these types.

Company Guy/Gal

A company guy or gal uses Twitter for business on their company's behalf. When this occurs, whose voice do we hear? Do we hear that person's voice resonating the company brand and image, or do we hear a person speaking for themselves? Must the answer be one or the other?

In Chapter 5, "Week 2: Find and Attract Followers," we're going to go over best practices and answer these questions. For now, suffice it to say that certainly there are some people—and perhaps many people—currently tweeting on their company's behalf. On Twitter a company spokesman does not appear as a faceless brand from an anonymous source, but rather as an individual representing the company (Figure 2.7).

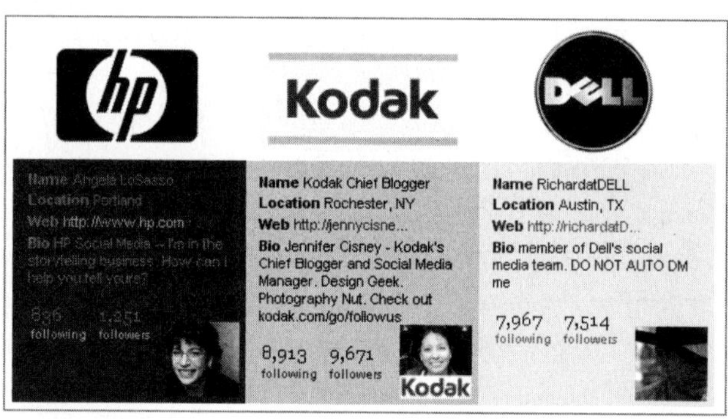

Figure 2.7 Individuals representing their companies on Twitter

Power Users

Let's start by defining what a Twitter *power user* is not. A power user is *not* someone who simply has tens of thousands of followers, as some might want you to believe. Power users come in a few different flavors; however, they all share some common attributes:

- They tweet...a lot!
- They tend to produce a lot of original content.
- The original content they tweet would be described as high quality.

- They tend to be retweeted a lot.
- They have a lot of followers because of their high-quality original content and because they're retweeted so often.
- Others describe them as thought leaders, and as authentic, real, or genuine (that is, it's clear that they're not just talking heads).
- They are responsive to their community of followers, which feeds all of the above.
- They seem to be supremely committed to and passionate about Twitter. (I often wonder how some power users have lives outside of Twitter or accomplish anything during their day jobs.)

Power users might be deemed the elite of Twitter. They've certainly attained a kind of "Twitter rock star" status. Most power users have earned their stripes (reputation) authentically—that is to say, without using follower-building tools and other chicanery.

Folks like Pete Cashmore (`@mashable`), Robert Scoble (`@scobleizer`), Tara Hunt (`@missrogue`), Chris Brogan (`@chrisbrogan`), Sarah Evans (`@PRSarahEvans`), Mari Smith (`@marismith`), and Scott Stratten (`@unmarketing`) are often cited as power users (Figure 2.8.) For more examples of power users, visit Twitalyzer's Top 100 (`http://www.twitalyzer.com/twitalyzer/list.asp`). Twitalyzer is a resource that uses its own proprietary methodology to track and measure Twitter's Top 100 users at any given time.

Figure 2.8 Some of Twitter's well-known power users

Moms as Power Users

Wired moms make up a huge segment of power users. A 2008 study by ad network BlogHer found that 36.2 million women actively participate in the blogosphere every week, with 15.1 million publishing and 21.1 million reading and commenting on blogs. These wired moms may have started out as *mommy bloggers* or they came to Twitter based on the recommendation of a friend or family member, got hooked, and stayed. It is easier to get started on Twitter than a blog, and unlike blogging, a mom doesn't have to be a content producer in order to take advantage of Twitter.

The mommy community on Twitter is huge, and their influence via the social media sphere continues to grow. Big brands salivate at the idea of successfully tapping into this community. Christine Young (`@YoungMommy`) touts herself as "one of Walmart's 11Moms & Nielsen's Power Moms." Jessica Smith (`@JessicaKnows`) has also been tapped: "Nielsen Media named me one of the Power Pack in their Power Mom 50." There's even an entire website devoted to TwitterMoms: The Influential Moms Network (`http://www.twittermoms.com`) is run by Megan Calhoun, another power mom (`@twittermom`). (See Figure 2.9.) Clearly, these moms are proud of and continue to cultivate their influence and standing in the mommy community. Anyone trying to market products or services to moms better pay close attention to this community and their tweets.

Figure 2.9 TwitterMoms

Experts

Wait a minute. Aren't power users experts? Shouldn't these categories be combined? As my algebra teacher would say, this relationship does not exhibit the "necessary and sufficient conditions" to say that experts are power users. Although it's likely that a power user is a Twitter expert, the converse is not necessarily true. Why? As in every other community, Twitter is full of windbags and frauds. Anyone on Twitter can hang up a shingle (their profile bio) and claim to be an expert at this or that—particularly when it comes to social media. Most true Twitter or social media experts don't come out and literally use the word "expert" to describe themselves. Real experts have more sense than that and let their tweets and Twitter statistics do the talking for them.

On Twitter, the community can and does function as a teacher. By following a user, the community and its response affirms and endorses a user's degree of expertise. The Twitter community, and not the individual, decides who's an expert and who's not. One of the highest forms of flattery a true user can receive are the tweets citing gratitude to those who have helped, inspired, motivated, or simply have listened to them. The other users are the ones who can rightfully call someone an "expert."

Pretenders will ultimately be ignored by all except their own ilk, and they tend to be false followers. For experts, the axiom should read, "He (or she) who claims to be an expert in social media is likely not to be one."

The transforming power of Twitter allows all players to be equals. A mere individual can carry more clout on Twitter than a brand. On Twitter, numbers can be misleading. One person may tweet more than another, but that other person may have something more important to say to the community. Therefore, the volume of tweets isn't wholly an indication of clout, nor is the number of followers, particularly if the user being followed doesn't have any real relationship with the follower base. Phonies and big brands who are accustomed to manipulating images, beware. Twitter is another Web 2.0 player demonstrating how the game has changed and how people can harness and wield their community power if they choose to do so.

Content Producers

Earlier I mentioned the evangelists, those who espoused Twitter during its infancy, somewhat for their own gain. These evangelists were primarily bloggers who today still actively exploit Twitter for their own gain. You can identify this type pretty easily: their tweets are mainly composed of links to their own blog posts. Although their means may be selfish, Twitter users like this still generate legitimate content (as opposed to MLMrs who mainly tweet links to things they think will make them money). A blogger can also opt to tweet their post as a way to inspire dialog. Chris Brogan does this effectively (see Figure 2.10).

Original tweet/teaser:

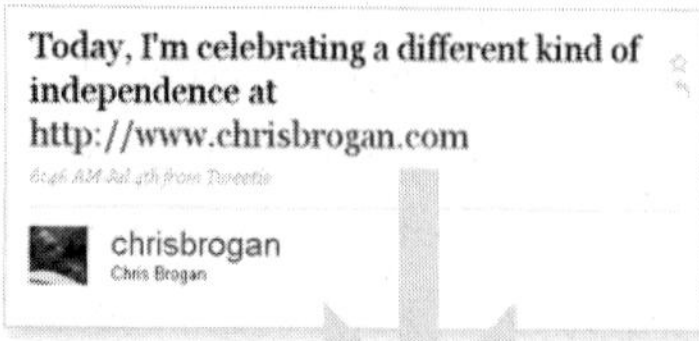

Blog post:

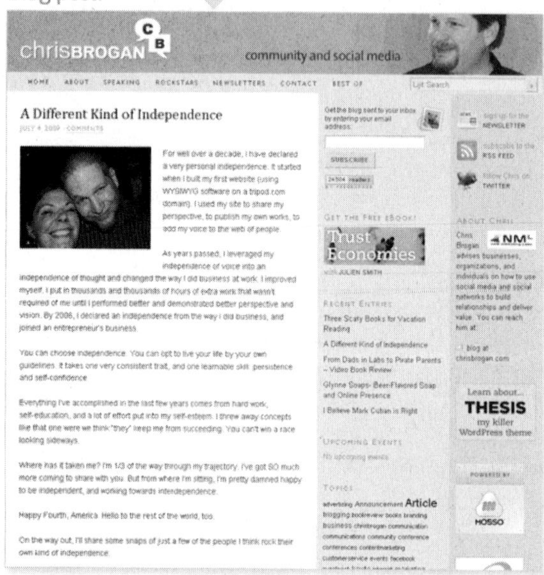

Figure 2.10 Chris Brogan's tweet tease tactic and a related blog post

URL-shortening systems such as TinyURL have been around for years; however, Twitter's 140-character limitation promulgated newer and even shorter URL-shortening solutions. The new solutions came with additional bells and whistles such as tracking statistics, aggregated referral source statistics, and on-page/in-frame data. Content producers in particular are apt to exploit these new tools to the greatest end.

Bloggers don't solely occupy the content producer mantle, however. Some people just enjoy the game of 140-character composition; others, like comedians, use Twitter to test material and build an offline audience; still others use Twitter as a platform to philosophize. In general, you can tell a content producer by their Tweet volume: it's typically as high as or higher than their follower count. When their follower count begins to exceed their tweets, they're probably moving into the territory of a power user.

Celebrities

Celebrities have had a huge impact on the growing Twitter phenomenon. In 2009, celebrities flocked to Twitter, seeing it as a way to connect directly with their fans (or, in some cases, revive a stagnating career). Chapter 1 discussed the Oprah Effect. Much of 2009's Twitter user account growth has been attributed to the fact that so many people want to read about their favorite celebrity's every last move (Figure 2.11). Entertainers, like *The Tonight Show*'s Conan O'Brien and *The Daily Show*'s Jon Stewart, have used Twitter for their show fodder; news celebrities tweet their audience; sports figures have tweeted from the sidelines; and musicians take their tweeps along for road shows.

Figure 2.11 Top celebrity tweeters (based on Follower counts)

Websites like TweeterWall, FollowFamous, and VIPTweets have cropped up to serve the devoted. NBC has launched an entire microsite, Twitter-Tracker.com, complete with advertisements, and a companion Twitter account (`@TW1TTERTRACKER`) that aggregates the tweets that *The Tonight Show* staffers post on Twitter (Figure 2.12).

Celebrities like Oprah have even gotten in on the marketing game. Chris Bulger of Compete.com described one 2009 campaign for KFC and its impact on his blog (`http://blog.compete.com/2009/06/09/kfc-oprah-wtitter-free-chicken`).

Figure 2.12 NBC's Twitter-Tracker.com

The big question is whether this free promotion had a lasting effect for KFC throughout the month of May. According to the graph in Figure 2.13, the answer to that question is no. Traffic to kfc.com and unthinkfc.com peaked during the week of the promotion. Unique Visitors were 2.85 million and 8.75 million, respectively. However, following that promotion week, traffic quickly dropped off. Unique visitors to kfc.com decreased 73 percent (week-over-week), and unique visitors to unthinkfc.com had a decrease of 98 percent.

The Oprah Effect is also clearly visible in Figure 2.14, as you can see in the third bar of each cluster. In the week of the free offer, 7.95 million unique visitors went to the Grilled Chicken Coupon landing page on Oprah.com. Many of these visitors were seeking further information following the mention on her show and others were following her Twitter feed.

Twitter Delivers the Chicken

"I first learned about the free Grilled Chicken meal offer from Oprah when I saw both 'KFC' and 'Oprah' were top trends on Twitter. Upon further investigation, I learned that a page on Oprah's website was redirecting traffic to KFC's new microsite for their new Grilled Chicken product, [`http://www.unthinkfc.com`]. Customers were able to receive their free Grilled Chicken meal via a coupon on [the microsite]. Lending a hand in guiding online attention to the free Grilled Chicken meal [`http://www.coupons.com`] also played a crucial role in referral traffic to the microsite. In May, Coupons.com accounted for 34.1 percent of unthinkfc.com referral traffic; Oprah.com accounted for slightly less with 30.2 percent.

In less than 24 hours, the promotion had received a tremendous amount of attention. Figure 2.13 shows the Daily Reach for the website unthinkfc.com from May 3 through May 9, 2009, the week in which the free offer was made available. Daily Reach is a metric that shows how many people visit a website as a percentage of all U.S. Internet users online. So, on May 6th, an astounding 3.73 percent of the U.S. Internet population visited unthinkfc.com."

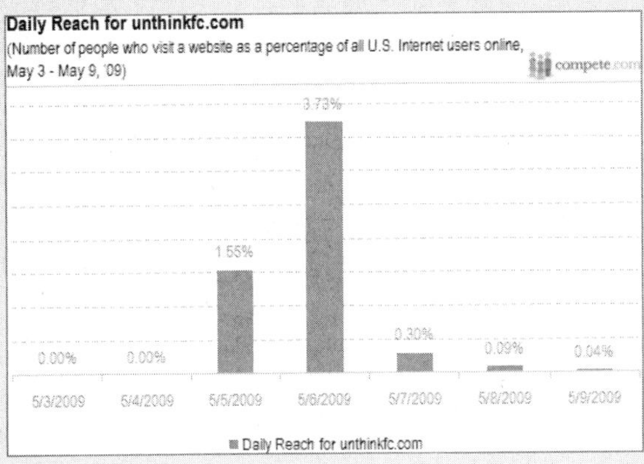

Figure 2.13 unthinkfc.com Daily Reach during coupon promotion

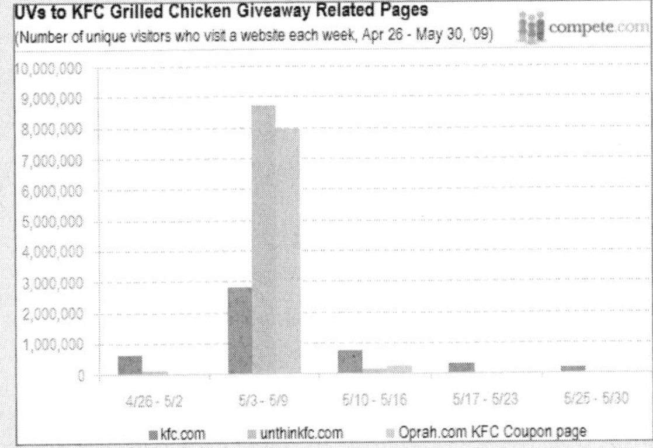

Figure 2.14 Traffic and the Oprah Effect on unthinkfc.com

KFC was not really prepared for the Oprah Effect, however. Apparently, stores could not handle the volume of requests, which obviously left consumers frustrated. Sales for KFC's grilled chicken did increase, though, which was the point of the promotion, so KFC could deem this campaign a success.

Bots, Games, and Memes

Individual users aren't the only entities you might come across on Twitter. The Bots, Games, and Memes category doesn't even include people. The contents of these user accounts are automated via software programs, so don't expect members of this category to be engaging in any way.

Let's define the members of this category and then move on to some examples. *Bots* have been on the Web for a long time. Search engines use bots to crawl through the contents of web pages so that they can index them. According to the definition in Wikipedia, "Typically, bots perform tasks that are both simple and structurally repetitive, at a much higher rate than would be possible for a human alone." Because it relies on them to perform certain operations, Wikipedia even has a Bot Policy: "...bots must be harmless and useful, have approval, use separate user accounts, and be operated responsibly."

Twitter games also run off software programs. Game developers must be creative because their programs need to play off the use of tweets somehow.

Memes, which rhymes with "dreams," refers to an idea, concept, phrase, or other unit of information that spreads quickly. On Twitter, memes might be a viral concept (not automated) or the aggregation of highly popular tweets by a software program.

Twitter Bots

Twitter bots fall into two primary categories: harmless and unwelcome. Harmless bots can be set up to generate frivolous results like trivia or funny phrases (`@xbetween`) or useful results like new bots (`@googlenews`). Typically created by spammers, unwelcome bots might try to mimic humans in an effort to generate followers when they are actually an annoyance at a minimum and a scourge at worst. It's a Bot (`http://www.itsabot.com`), although no longer in existence, was an interesting site that ran Twitter accounts through its software and tried to detect whether the account is a bot or real person (Figure 2.15).

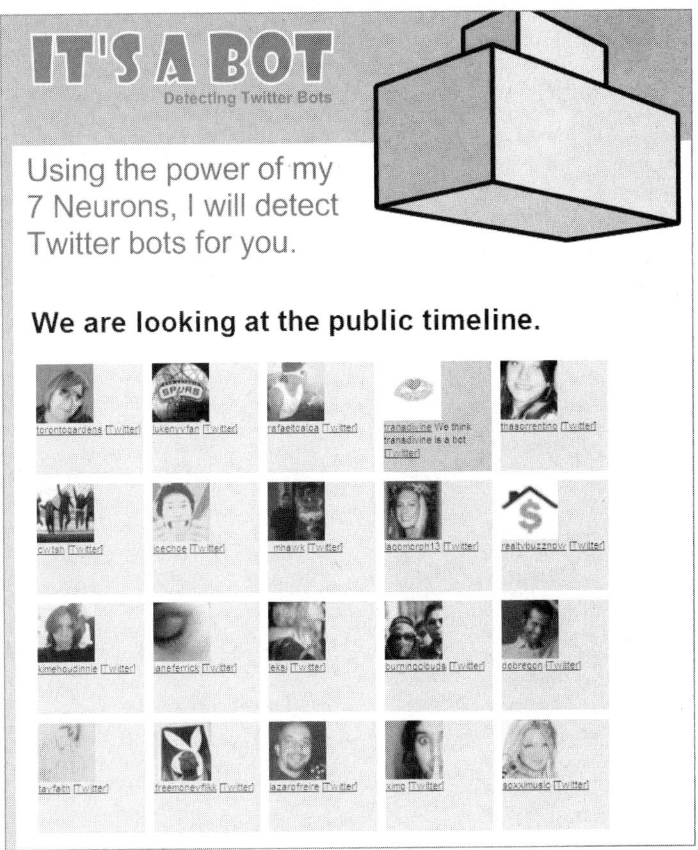

Figure 2.15 It's a Bot analyzed users to detect bots.

Games

People generally find Twitter games not only harmless but fun; however, as with any other kind of game, people can end up wasting valuable time playing them. Because the user has to follow the game in order to play, games can be considered opt-in choices (Figure 2.16). Twitter games seem to be in the early stages of development; however, there are some who believe that with advanced development and creativity, Twitter could become another major casual-gaming hub.

Twitter gaming often spreads by word of mouth, with a participating user pulling in their tweeps either by the nature of the game's operation (some games push tweets from that user out to all their followers) or literally by someone telling their friends about the game. At the moment, no single directory lists all the Twitter games out there, although many of them can be found on `http://twitdom.com/tag/games`.

Figure 2.16 Some games on Twitter

Memes

An example of a viral meme occurred during the 2009 Iranian presidential elections. When the election results led to charges of corruption by opposition voters and protestors took to the streets, the government intermittently shut down the Internet and forced out most of the external news media. Twitter became a major vehicle for the dissemination of news, both within Iran among the protestors and for the rest of the world observing the turmoil. Throughout the Twitterverse, users started adopting green avatars to show their support of the Iranian protestors (Figure 2.17).

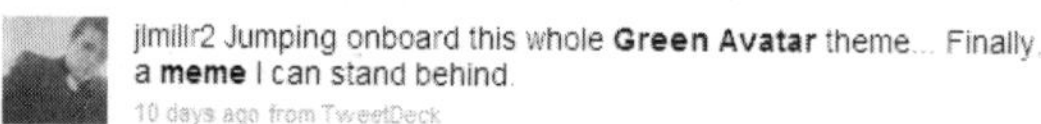

jlmillr2 Jumping onboard this whole Green Avatar theme... Finally, a meme I can stand behind.
10 days ago from TweetDeck

Figure 2.17 Green avatar memes were adopted to show support for fair Iranian elections.

Many viral memes wind up as Trending Topics on Twitter because they get so much attention and get people to tweet about them. Sometimes memes are also associated with hashtags, but just because a word has a hashtag doesn't mean it becomes a meme.

Automated memes capitalize on topics the software algorithm deems as current or popular. The most popular meme tool is TweetMeme (Figure 2.18), which aggregates and categorizes the most popular links on Twitter.

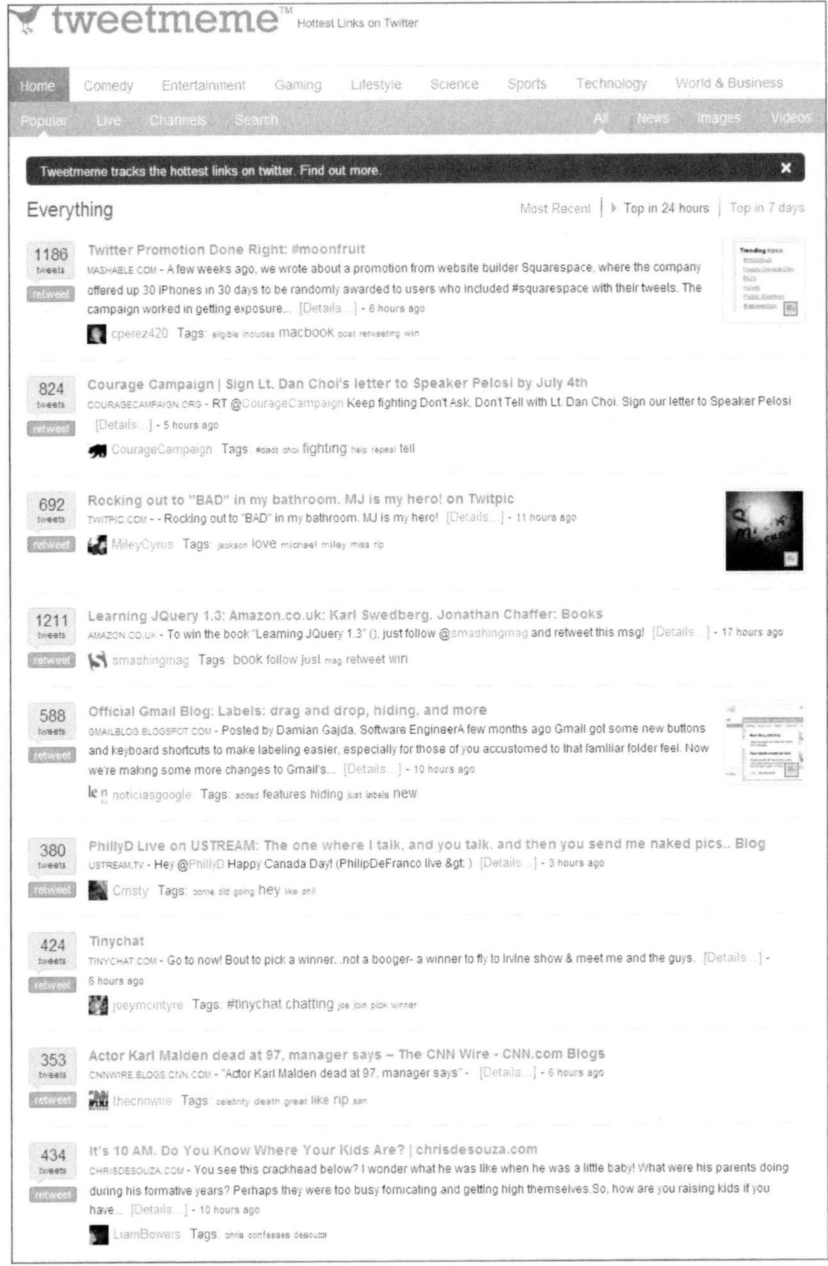

Figure 2.18 TweetMeme tracks popular tweets.

Small and Home-Based Businesses

For the small or home-based business, Twitter is probably the most important marketing leveler since email. Twitter gives everyone the chance to have an equal voice. Granted, big brands can pay to market their Twitter handles in all kinds of ways—in ad and marketing campaigns, on product packaging, through public relations, and so on. None of this external promotion, however, prevents the small business from reaching the same Twitter status as a top-selling brand. What's more important, the fact that Twitter is free completely eliminates a common marketing barrier to entry for small and home-based businesses.

Besides the "free factor" Twitter offers, there are several other compelling reasons for small and home-based businesses to embrace Twitter. For many small businesses, marketing doesn't come easy and business development proves to be even more challenging. Small business owners may not have the time, resources, or know-how to market their business, or they may not be comfortable with the notion of "small talk" that business networking involves. Social community platforms like Twitter change the dynamics of small business marketing in that the business owner can still network to the degree he or she feels comfortable without necessarily feeling vulnerable or exposed.

Perhaps that's why social media has attracted a growing number of small and home-based businesses. According to the April 2009 index of Discover Small Business Watch, 38 percent of small and home-based business owners were members of an online social networking community, up from 22 percent in October 2007. Sage North America, a small business software supplier, found that "65 percent of small businesses that used social networking sites said that they felt more comfortable doing so this year than they did last year, and 51 percent said that they had acquired and retained customers because of it." Sage estimates that more than 260,000 North American businesses currently use social networking to promote their businesses. MarketingProfs, a popular marketing resource site, conducted an informal survey in May 2009 that revealed that 84 percent of primarily small business Twitter users expected their company's use of Twitter to increase over the next six months, and 46 percent expect this increase to be significant. Forty-one percent of these same users say that Twitter delivers more value for business than LinkedIn or Facebook, topped only by company blogs (Figure 2.19)

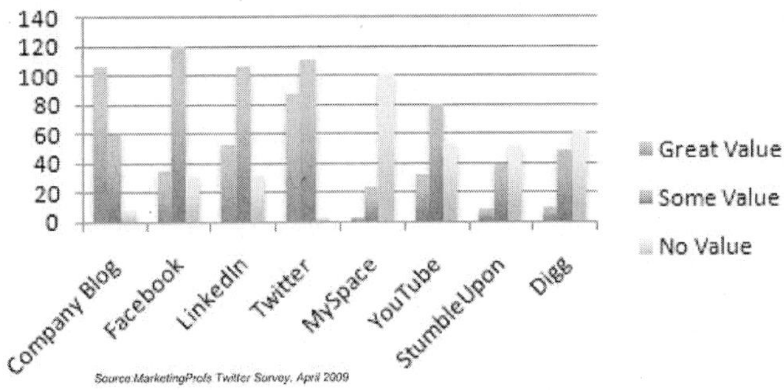

Figure 2.19 Twitter provides more value for business.

Small Business Twitter Stories

Throughout the Twitterverse, you'll find numerous small businesses represented, sometimes by their company moniker, sometimes by their leader, and sometimes by both. My company, Web Ad.vantage, is a great example of this. I use my Twitter account (@hollisthomases) to build brand awareness, publicize my company, tout job openings, and conduct networking. We also have an agency Twitter account (@webadvantage), which we all use to tweet about industry and company news, pose questions, answer questions, and network with peers and colleagues.

There are those on Twitter whose primary mission is to help or sell to small businesses (or a little of both). Twitter users like John Jantsch (@ducttape) and Matthew Ringer (@smallbizbee) tweet helpful links and respond to questions. Taking the community spirit a step even further, Anita Campbell (@smallbiztrends) has created a Who's Who on Twitter list of small business tweeps and resources (http://smallbiztrends.com/2009/01/the-ultimate-small-business-twitter-list.html). If your business is both small and local, you might find @LocalBizNews helpful to follow.

Some companies *became* companies because of social media and tools like Twitter. Wendy Piersall's company, Sparkplugging (http://www.sparkplugging.com; Figure 2.20) owes its roots to eMoms at Home, a blog she began as a hobby in 2006. During the time since the blog was founded, Twitter was also born and Piersall soon capitalized on it, joining in March 2007 and building a Twitter community in conjunction with what she was doing on her website, which was teaching others how to run home-based businesses. Her community grew, she found success and attracted others (not just moms) looking to do the same, and two years later she renamed her company and has been rolling ever since.

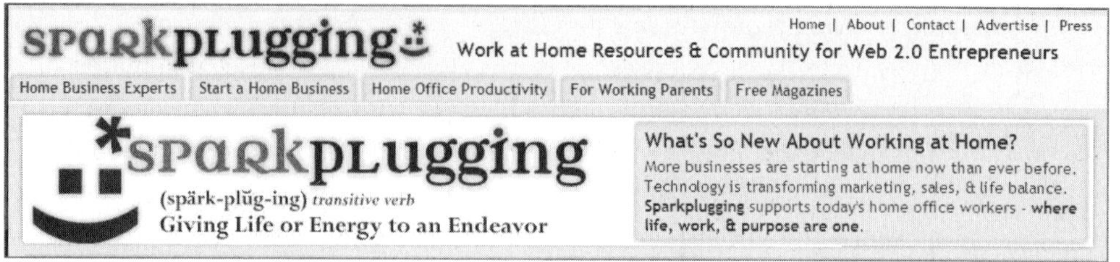

Figure 2.20 Sparkplugging website

Local Business Using Twitter

Unquestionably, the local small business sector has benefited from Twitter. Real estate agents, eateries, and even street peddlers have found ways to capitalize on Twitter. Enabled by tools such as Twitter Search, TwitterLocal, and LocalTweeps that help users find other users in their area, and keywords tied to their businesses (which might also be the names of competitors), these businesses can almost pinpoint, with near laser precision, Twitter users to whom they can market. Local businesses can work to build a following, and before they know it: voilà! They have a sale!

In fact, local business may be the darling of Twitter success stories. Much has already been written about the Twitter exploits of local businesses, and in Chapter 3, "Twitter: The Multipurpose Platform," we'll explore some of these case studies in greater detail.

Not-for-Profits: Charities, Causes, the Arts, Houses of Worship, and Associations

Because Twitter is free and easily accessed, not-for-profits are eager to understand and take advantage of the power of the Twitter community. Twitter, by its very nature, breeds coagulation of advocacy and affinity. Twitter gives nonprofits voices they may never have had. On Twitter, it's okay to express passion and the kind of devotion that's often found only within their inner circles. Twitter has been described by nonprofits as their "top listening tool" and key to "mending relationships." Nonprofits also feel that social media platforms like Twitter give them access to younger audiences at a key time to wield influence and break out of the mold of appearing stodgy, uninteresting, and inaccessible.

Some nonprofits have already successfully embraced Twitter, while others are in the early stages of learning. Some have been very clever in their use of Twitter, running contests to give away event tickets, live tweeting from conferences, teasing new studies and information reports, and creating completely new means for people to rally around a cause. One commonly cited example of this kind of Twitter success was the effort undertaken for the nonprofit group charity: water (`http://www.charitywater.org`), whose mission is to bring clean and safe drinking water to people in developing nations. To raise awareness and solicit donations for its cause, in February 2009, in a matter of two weeks, organizers created and promoted a 202-city simultaneous event, Twestival, exclusively through Twitter (Figure 2.21). The events gave local Twitter users an opportunity to meet and network for the greater good, but more importantly, charity: water raised over a quarter million dollars, mainly from people who had never heard of them before. Thanks to this success, subsequent Twestival events for September 2009 and February 2010 have been scheduled.

Figure 2.21 Twestival

Popular social media blog Mashable (`http://mashable.com/2009/03/19/twitter-nonprofits`) has a good list of nonprofits and charities on Twitter where you can learn how other nonprofits are using Twitter. Twitter, however, does pose challenges to the nonprofit sector. Twitter's need for care and feeding presents a challenge to understaffed and overtaxed employees who can't imagine adding just one more thing to their plate, and some in the sector wonder if their tiny organizations can benefit enough to merit allocating these scarce resources. I advise these organizations to recruit volunteer evangelists or student interns who believe in the organization's purpose and can tweet on its behalf. With some concerted effort, perhaps they can raise enough money in donations or new membership fees to fund a paid staffer.

Academia and Higher Education

The Academia/Higher Education sector is one that should be at the forefront of Twitter use and innovation, but which instead has been slow to adopt this technology. Of those institutions that have been actively using Twitter, it has primarily been seen as just another broadcasting tool. Rather than dwell on the reasons why this sector has underutilized Twitter to date, let's focus on the positive—that is, the ways in which some institutions uniquely can use or already are successfully using Twitter.

Here is list of ideas, some items of which are the work of Twitter user @lexrigby:

- **Student recruitment.** By actively engaging with the community at-large, the institution naturally makes itself more appealing to prospective candidates. @UBTowsonMBA provides a good example of this use of Twitter.
- **Courting alumni.** Alumni need to feel loved too, and merely asking them for donations and blasting them with news doesn't do much for the warm and fuzzies. Twitter can be used to reminisce by class, link to photos, tout events, and maintain school pride long after an alum has graduated.
- **Classroom communities.** Students using Twitter as a way to collaborate on homework may lead to more productive discussions in class.
- **Class communication.** Teachers/lecturers can be encouraged to use Twitter as a way to communicate with students about homework, room changes, time changes, class preparation, further reading, and so on.
- **Conference news.** Attendess can live tweet during conferences using hashtags so that nonattendees can keep up with the information being released.
- **Question and answer sessions.** Students and educators pose and answer questions, all via Twitter.
- **Feedback.** Rather than waiting until the end of a class or event to fill in a feedback form, Twitter can be used as a means to generate immediate feedback. It can be used to encourage particular teaching methods and offer advice about how to do things differently.
- **Distance learners.** Using Twitter to communicate with distance learners has the potential to offer students greater learning support and encouragement throughout their education.
- **Academic research.** Academia loves to take the pulse of society and tenured staff are under constant pressure to "publish or perish." Tapping into the Twitter community could serve as a launching pad for some new research report or larger, more scientific study.
- **Keeping current.** Both professors and students can keep up-to-date on the latest developments in their respective fields.
- **Student service.** Wayne State University in Michigan (@waynestate) uses Twitter as a customer service tool to listen, address, and reply to any problems raised by students.

Government

As part of his revolutionary Internet-based presidential campaign, candidate Barack Obama's team tapped Twitter as a means to keep the public informed of the candidate's whereabouts, website updates, and campaign points. Since then, many in government have joined Twitter, some to scandalous fault, tweeting inappropriate remarks about supposedly secret trips to war zones. Probably hoping to curtail more of the same, the Social Media Subcouncil, "a group of government web managers at the federal, state, and local levels bringing together social media best practices and other resources for the benefit of government agencies," has even put together a Twitter Best Practices page on its wiki site (`http://govsocmed.pbworks.com/TwitterBestPractices`). The movement of government into social media can be tracked on Twitter using the `#gov20` hashtag.

Another wiki, Twitter Fan Wiki USGovernment (`http://twitter.pbworks.com/USGovernment`) serves a different purpose—one more in the spirit of our democracy—that is, to connect the public with its tweeting government representatives. The wiki is regularly updated and chock-full of more Twitter accounts than you'd imagine possible. Don't expect too much recent activity from a lot of these accounts, though. Some are woefully undermaintained.

The government as an entity, however, must still conduct its daily business and, as with other kinds of business, Twitter has been changing how this business gets done. Government purchasing officers seeking vendors for unusual bids can reach out to their Twitter network for referrals (e.g., `@govloop` and `http://www.govloop.com`). Government agencies can use Twitter as another way to keep the public informed about important alerts and advisories. Of course, politicians can use Twitter to keep their constituency "in the know." TweetCongress, a grassroots effort to get Congress tweeting (`@tweetcongress` and `http://blog.tweetcongress.org`), has created Top Tweet Thursday, a selection of the top congressional tweets chosen by the TweetCongress staff.

Marketing, Advertising, Public Relations, and Communications Professionals

Perhaps, next to MLMrs, one of the fastest-growing industry segments on Twitter right now is the marketing, advertising, public relations, and communications professionals sector. (I count myself a member of this trade.) The June 2009 study by Sysomos found that, of the people who identify themselves as marketers, 15 percent follow more than 2,000 people; in the rest of the Twitter population, of which only 0.29 percent follow more than 2,000 people. *Marcomm* professionals are so prevalent on Twitter that one of my colleagues recently remarked to me, "Soon, all of Twitter is going to be just us talking to ourselves." Although I don't necessarily agree with this perspective, I can't deny that every day I see more and more professionals in this industry sector joining Twitter. And why not? The question really ought to be, "What took you so long?" I think traditional practitioners and firms within this sector have had a harder time embracing all things Web, as if it's altogether another discipline. Although there are certainly aspects of digital marketing that require different skills, we all need to remember that, among other things, the Internet facilitates communication. To any kind of marketer, the sheer importance of this fact cannot be ignored. Twitter, among other things, is a premier communications vehicle and, therefore, all marketers should become students of Twitter.

For all the ways and reasons Twitter is being used, this alone justifies why marketing and public relations (PR) people should be on Twitter and how they should be using it. Twitter should be part of the marketer's toolkit. Enumerating the ways in which this group uses Twitter might be restating the obvious; however, I will state them anyway:

- As a listening tool
- As an education tool
- As an engagement tool with existing and new audiences
- As a business networking tool
- As a soft-sell sales tool
- As a media relations builder
- As a media pitching tool
- As a brand monitoring tool
- As a reputation management tool
- As a CEO coaching tool
- As a research forum
- As an information sharing tool
- As a website traffic builder
- As an event marketing and creation tool (host Twitter-based live *events*)
- To reach the local community
- As a news distribution channel
- To build opt-in email lists
- To gain professional credibility

This last point is an important one. Twitter has at least reached a tipping point for marketing professionals to the extent that, if you are *not* on Twitter, it's likely to appear to your peers, prospects, and clients that you are "not with it," which certainly won't help your reputation. From my marketer's perspective, the exciting part about being on Twitter now is that it's in its infancy, and we all have so much to learn as it and the Twitterverse continue to evolve. If you're really smart, good, or lucky, you might actually influence its evolution!

Media Outlets

The media is all over the place when it comes to Twitter. Some, like CNN, have taken full advantage of Twitter, integrating it into many of their broadcasts, updating current news via its @CNNbrk account, and encouraging its journalists to have and post to their own Twitter accounts. Others, like the world of print publishing, have been slower to sign up for Twitter, let alone use Twitter for anything other than another means to broadcast the same content. Perhaps that's because most media outlets operate as *push mechanisms*: they distribute news and information; they don't necessarily dialog about it with their audience, let alone in a live, real-time way unless it's at a live event. A few print publishers, such as the *Palm Beach Post* (@Palm_Beach_Post) and the *Baltimore Business Journal* (@bbjonline) have gotten the hang of Twitter and use it as both a one-way and a two-way channel. The *Chicago Tribune* has gotten creative about its use of Twitter. In addition to having its regular editorial staff on Twitter, the *Tribune* hosts ColonelTribune (@ColonelTribune), a "gentleman-about-town" handling news and all things Chicago with whom you can converse. The colonel is quite popular. With close to 160,000 followers at this point, he's more popular than his own paper (@ChicagoTribune), which only has about 15,000 followers.

On Twitter, traditional media outlets are represented in two primary ways: by the media entity itself (e.g., @nytimes, @nprnews, @wsj) and by the journalists who write for these outlets. Journalists may actually have a leg up on their clunky old-school employers because they *can* more easily dialog and use Twitter as its use evolves. In fact, in certain ways, Twitter is a *perfect* medium for journalists who can now receive tips and scoops from Joe Everyman as well as their trusted contacts. Of course, with this kind of direct access, journalists need to be more cautious than ever and thoroughly vet their sources when they're not tried and true.

Want to reach a journalist? Try resources such as JournalistTweets (http://journalisttweets.com) and MediaOnTwitter (http://www.mediaontwitter.com). The latter is a joint endeavor between some of Twitter's PR powerhouses: Sarah Evans (@PRSarahEvans), Peter Shankman (@skydiver), and Brian Solis (@briansolis). These users, and others like them, have formed a kind of new category, the *Conduit*, a role that used to be played by only subscription services like PR Newswire's ProfNet. The Conduit helps the journalists gather information for their stories by tweeting to their follower base at the journalist's request. Shankman even coined the alert phrase HARO, which stands for Help A Reporter Out, to tweet out the requests. Urgent requests are tweeted from @helpareporter with the code URGHARO (Figure 2.22), and are then posted to the complementary Facebook page (http://www.facebook.com/helpareporter).

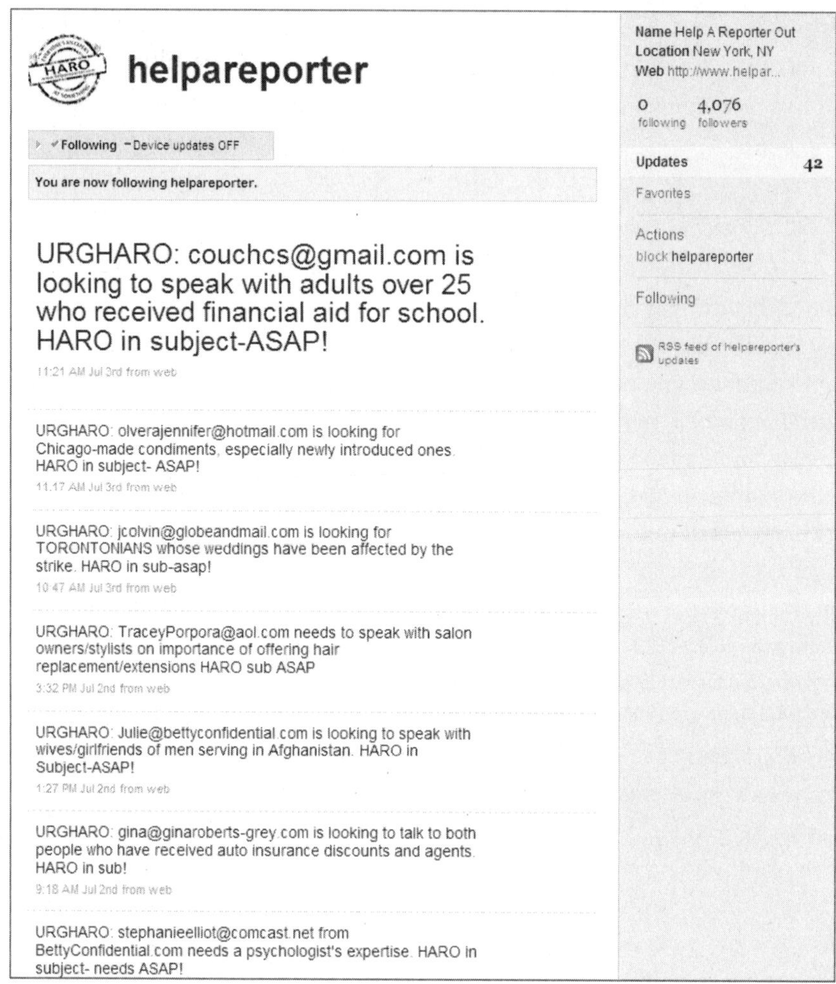

Figure 2.22 Help A Reporter Out urgent requests

The barring of journalists from Iran during its 2009 election protests also revealed Twitter's role for, in, and as part of the media. In *The New York Times,* Noam Cohen wrote about the six lessons learned about Twitter during this episode:

1. **Twitter is a tool and thus difficult to censor.** You do not have to visit the home site to send [or read] a message.
2. **Tweets are generally banal, but watch out.** Each update may not be important. Collectively, however, the tweets can create a personality or environment that reflects the emotions of the moment and help drive opinion.
3. **Buyer beware.** Nothing on Twitter has been verified. While users can learn from experience to trust a certain Twitter account, it is still a matter of trust.
4. **Watch your back.** Not only is it hard to be sure that what appears on Twitter is accurate, but some Twitterers may even be trying to trick you.

5. **Twitter is self-correcting but a misleading gauge.** Twitter is a certain kind of community—technology-loving, generally affluent, and Western-tilting.
6. **Twitter can be a potent tool for media criticism.** Just as Twitter can rally protesters against governments, its broadcast ability can rally them quickly and efficiently against news outlets—for example, `#CNNfail`, which called out CNN's failure to have comprehensive coverage of the Iranian protests. This criticism was quickly converted to an email-writing campaign, and CNN was forced to defend its coverage in print and online.

The topic of Twitter's role as a news medium took center stage at the all-Twitter June 2009 140-Characters Conference (`#140conf`) in New York. The schedule included sessions on the effect of Twitter on newspapers and television, and as a news-gathering tool. The latter session's panel featured some heavy hitters of the broadcast news world: Ann Curry (`@AnnCurry`), NBC's Today Show news anchor and host of Dateline NBC; Rick Sanchez (`@ricksanchezcnn`) of CNN Newsroom; Ryan Osborn (`@todayshow`), producer of NBC's *Today* show; and Clayton Morris (`@claytonmorris`) a Fox News anchor. Writing on the popular blog TechCrunch, Brian Solis did an excellent job of summarizing the panel discussion with his article, "Is Twitter the CNN of the New Media Generation?" (`http://www.techcrunch.com/2009/06/17/is-twitter-the-cnn-of-the-new-media-generation`). I point to this because it helps illustrate the news media's perspective as well as their issues and biases, but Solis also references an earlier article in which he wrote a very powerful opinion:

> *"What eludes publishers is the very thing that can save them: the new model for not only surviving the evolution, but also thriving in the future ecosystem of publishing and connecting content with audiences where they congregate online. The new media economy will embrace a shift in content creation and revenue generation from a top-down model to a bottom-up groundswell."*

I have to say, I first recognized Twitter's potential as a news medium during the 2008 presidential election debates. For the elections, Twitter coordinated a stream of all posts using a microsite version of Twitter, `http://election.twitter.com`, which is no longer active (Figure 2.23). Anyone posting within the microsite would have their tweet streamed live to everyone else within the microsite. During the debates, tweets flew madly as the stream refreshed constantly. Users commented on everything from the candidates' outfits to the substance of their arguments. Remarks varied from the profound to the hysterical, and I found myself sometimes more interested in what my fellow tweeters had to say than the candidates themselves. Never before during an election had I felt so interested, so engaged. My voice *could* actually be heard. I found the experience extremely powerful and realized Twitter was on to something huge.

Figure 2.23 Twitter's Election 2008 site

During the elections, Twitter also partnered with Current (`http://current.com`), which produced *Hack the Debate.* Current aired live debates online and integrated a Twitter overlay that simultaneously broadcast tweets from Election.Twitter.com. Since then, other networks such as CNN, MTV, and E! Entertainment have gotten in on the act; but seeing this innovation for the first time knocked my socks off.

Sports and Entertainment

Perhaps because of, or maybe just in conjunction with, the flood of celebrities to Twitter, the sports and entertainment industry has also gotten on the bandwagon. It's been postulated that Twitter might be able to curb the downward spiral of the music industry. According to a June 2009 report by The NPD Group, a market research company, "Twitter users are much more likely than average web users to be engaged in online music activities—one-third listened to music on a social networking site, 41 percent listened to online radio (compared to 22 percent among all web users), and 39 percent watched a music video online (versus 25 percent among all web users). Twitter users were also twice as likely as average web users to visit MySpace Music and Pandora." Critically, Twitter users also buy more: "33 percent of Twitter users reported buying a CD in the prior three months, and 34 percent claimed to have purchased a digital download, which compares positively to overall web users (at 23 percent and 16 percent, respectively). When Twitter users purchased music, they also spent more money than did their non-Twitter counterparts. In fact, people on Twitter purchased 77 percent more digital downloads, on average, than those who were not using Twitter."

When a fan-favorite TV show debuts its season premier or airs an episode with a crucial turn of events, the Twitterverse is abuzz with comments both good and bad. At this pace, the Tweet-o-Meter could practically replace Nielsen panels and, at the same time, provide far richer feedback to the producers. Not unaware of its potential, in May 2009, Twitter signed an agreement with entertainment production company Reveille and Brillstein to produce a show about Twitter. The agreement caused great controversy in celebritydom, as reports led people to believe the show would be a reality-based competition using celebrity stalking through Twitter. Twitter founder Biz Stone had to take to the Twitter blog to stop the rumor mill: the agreement was real; the show concept was not confirmed. It's not hard to imagine Twitter as another entertainment platform, however; by its nature, people already find the whole ecosystem entertaining. Where else can you get your dose of news and simultaneously find out what your friends and other interesting people are up to first thing in the morning?

The film industry sees Twitter as another way to promote movies virally. As of May 2009, four of the six major American motion picture studios had Twitter accounts. Going beyond film teaser links, Sony Pictures International generated a lot of buzz with its "Terminator Salvation Twitter Game" (`@TStheGame`), Universal Studios has integrated live tweets into its online ads, and Lions Gate Films promoted exclusive movie content for their followers. On the Entertainment Agent Blog, agent blogger Kenneth Tate II writes, "Entertainment agents take notice: If your client is not on Twitter, and if you are not consistently promoting their presence on Twitter, then you are not providing comprehensive representation. With that in mind, it might be best to start thinking of Twitter as an essential for publicity and promotion for clients. And if you don't have any clients, think of Twitter as a tool to use to passively follow the industry as you strategize your own business."

The sports industry, on the other hand, always seeking ways to tap into the power of the fan, has quickly warmed to Twitter. In a June 2009 article, "Twitter Craze Is Rapidly Changing the Face of Sports," *Sports Illustrated* stated, "The entire sports world is obsessed with the microblogging tool." College coaches tweet to showcase their programs to recruits. Niche leagues use Twitter to build audiences. Women's Professional Soccer "started a weekly series in which players answer real-time questions from fans on Twitter. Here, a cash-conscious league can engage its fans without paying a penny." Pro teams tweet scores, schedules, and highlight clips and try to engage with fans to bring them just a little closer to their sports heroes. The Phoenix Suns director of digital media and research, Amy Martin, had the luxury of probably the most popular sports figure on Twitter, Shaquille O'Neal (`@The_Real_Shaq`) to leverage. For his birthday, Martin thought up "Shaq Day," a contest of Twitter user-made videos. Martin also hosted virtual pep rallies and a tweet-up event where Twitter fans who bought tickets to that day's game got to meet the sports legend. For the 2009

Stanley Cup playoffs, the NHL organized a nationwide (24-city) tweet-up that made headlines (Figure 2.24).

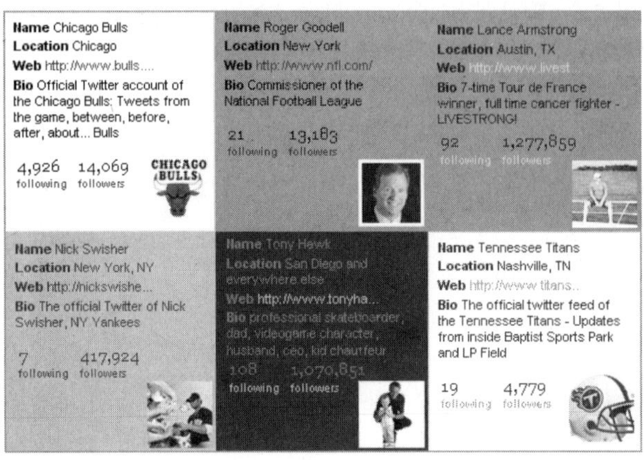

Figure 2.24 Sports figures on Twitter

Are you seeking to find sports figures on Twitter? Sportsin140.com (`http://www.sportsin140.com/`) has created a Twitter directory with what it claims to be "over 500 confirmed and validated Twitter accounts for pro athletes, coaches, members of the sports media, colleges and universities, companies and more."

Corporations and Brands

Yes, corporations and brands are on Twitter, but not nearly enough, and not very many of them have quite figured out how to use Twitter. They express concern about resources, value, and return on investment (ROI), control of their corporate image, and so on. These are the same brands that struggle with the notion of social media, but who don't have a good comeback when asked, "What are you doing about the consumers who are already talking about you when you're not even there with them?" Sit with them and do a Twitter search; they'll practically be stupefied by the results.

That being said, Twitter's gotten enough media attention to capture the interest of big corporations and brands and, to their credit, most are now pretty eager to listen and learn. Those that have already dived in have been (like the rest of us) figuring out Twitter as they go. As a marketing tool, Twitter demands flexibility, and sometimes that's hard for big companies to swallow. But brands should look at Twitter this way: with a fast-moving real-time medium of only 140 characters, if you do make a mistake, it's probably going to be a lot less costly than a traditional marketing and advertising failure. If you handle your mistakes promptly and appropriately, you can rebound a lot faster.

Brands on Twitter

In case you're wondering what brands have gotten in on the Twitter act, let's list some active ones here. In Chapter 3, we'll go into detail about what corporations and brands can accomplish by using Twitter. For now, let's just use this list and Figures 2.25 through 2.37 as a way for you to feel comfortable that you're not alone in your Twitter marketing pursuits.

Consumer Retail Products and Services

American Apparel (`@americanapparel`)

Best Buy (`multiple handles`)

Build-A-Bear Workshop (`@buildabear`)

Career Builder (`@CareerBuilder`)

Comcast (`@ComcastCares`)

Dick's Sporting Goods (`@dickssportingss`)

DKNY (`@DKNY`)

e.l.f. Cosmetics (`@askelf`)

Express (`@ExpressLisaG`)

Graco (`@gracobaby`)

Figure 2.25 Graco

Hanes (`@HanesComfort`)

Hewlett-Packard (`@HPCheer`)

Home Depot (`@homedepot`)

H&R Block (`@hrblock`)

Kodak (@kodakCB & @kodakidigprint)

Leap Frog (@LeapFrog)

Louis Vuitton (@LouisVuitton_US)

Nordstrom (@nordstrom)

Figure 2.26 Nordstrom

Pet Smart (@PetSmartTLC)

Petco (@NatalieatPETCO)

Rubbermaid (@rubbermaid & @RubbermaidTwo)

Sephora (@sephorablog)

Sharpie (@SharpieSusan)

Snapfish (@snapfishbyhp)

Target (@TargetINC)

Toys“R”Us (@toysrus)

Turbo Tax (@turbotax)

Uniball (@UniBall_USA)

Wachovia (@Wachovia)

ValuPack (@Valpakcoupons)

Vera Bradley (@verabradley)

Zappos (@zappos and http://twitter.zappos.com/employees)

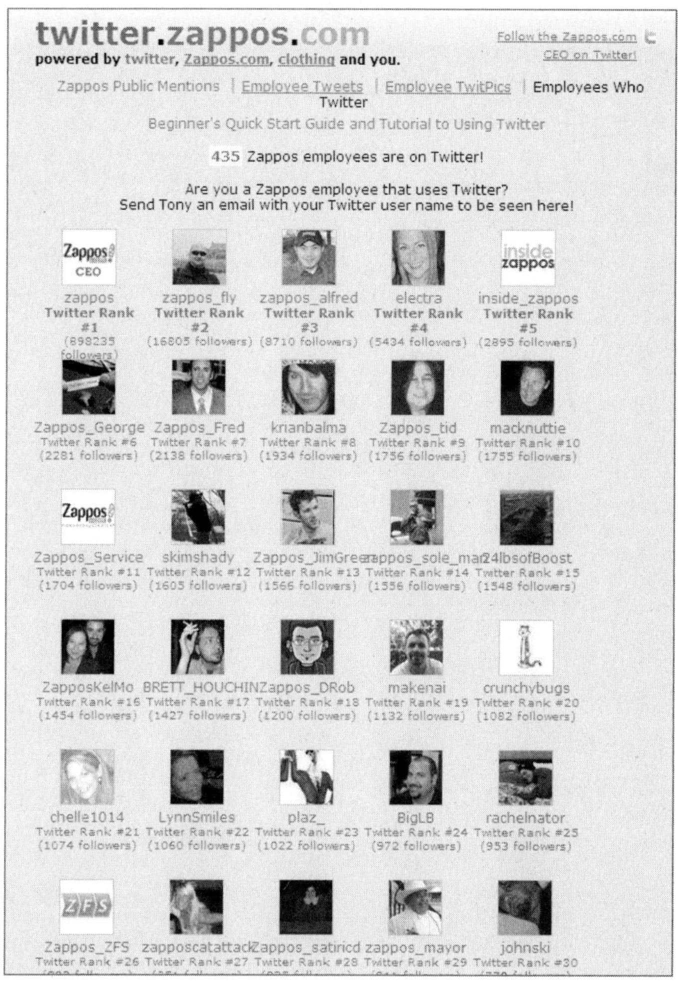

Figure 2.27 Zappos employees on Twitter

Packaged Goods, Food, and Beverage

Baskin Robbins (`@BaskinRobbins`)

Ben & Jerry's (`@cherrygarcia`)

Betty Crocker (`@BettyCrocker`)

Bigelow Tea (`@bigelowtea`)

BiLo Supermarket (`@BILOSuperSaver`)

Bob Evans (`@BobEvansFarms`)

Blue Bunny (`@Blue_Bunny`)

Coke (`@CocaColaCo`)

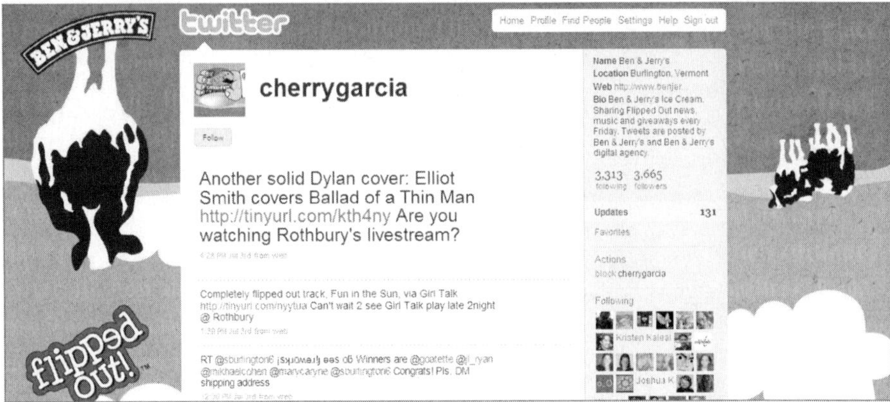

Figure 2.28 Ben & Jerry's

Community Market (@CommunityMarket)

DiGiorno Pizza (@DigiornoPizza)

Dunkin' Donuts (@DunkinDonuts)

Eggland's Best (@EgglandsBest)

Expo Markers (@ExpoMarkers)

Fast Fixin' (@FastFixin)

Flying Dog Brewery (@flyingdog)

Friendly's (@EatAtFriendlys)

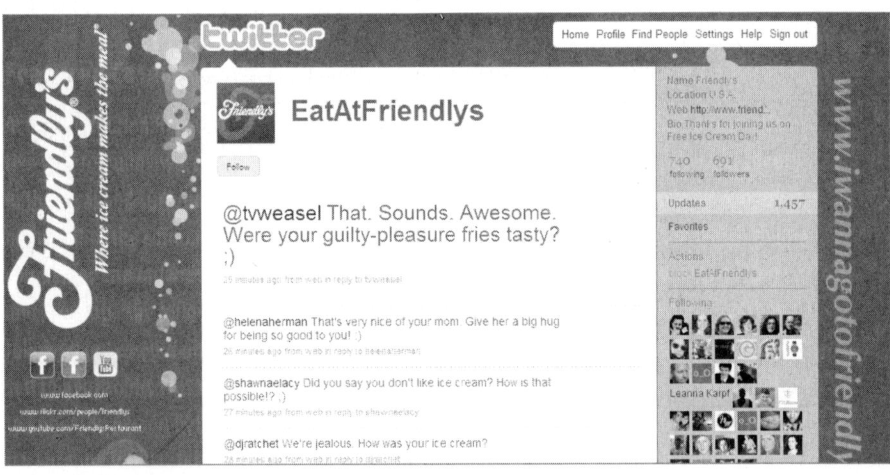

Figure 2.29 Friendly's

Hostess Snacks (@Hostess_Snacks)

Huggies (@huggiesmom)

KFC (@kfc_colonel & @thebklounge)

Little Debbie (@LittleDebbie)

Mambo Sprouts (@MamboSprouts)

Meijer (@Meijer)

method (@methodtweet)

Pepsi (@pepsi)

Plum Organics (@PlumOrganics)

Philadelphia Cream Cheese (@LoveMyPhilly)

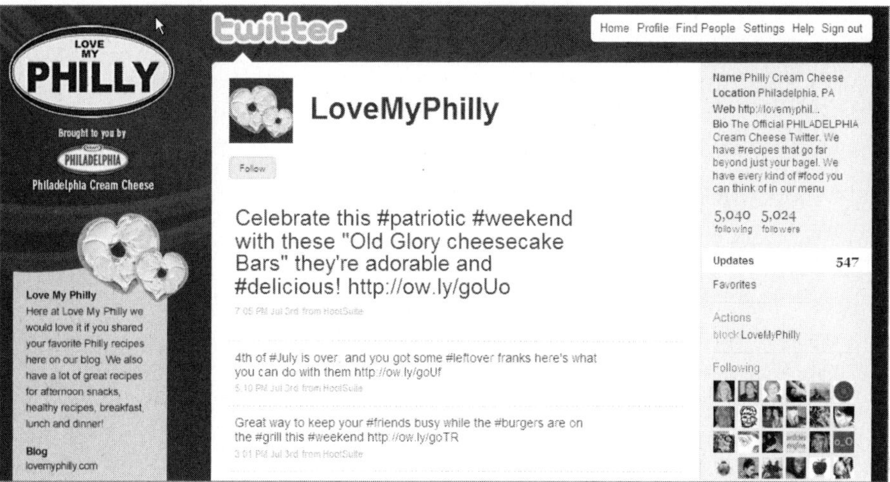

Figure 2.30 Philadelphia Cream Cheese

Popeye's Chicken (@PopeyesChicken)

Purex (@Purex)

Quaker (@QuakerTalk)

Revolution Foods (@RevolutionFoods)

Rita's Italian Ice (@ritasitalianice)

Scott (@ScottTips)

Seventh Generation (@SeventhGen)

SoftSoap (@LatherUp)

Starbucks (@Starbucks)

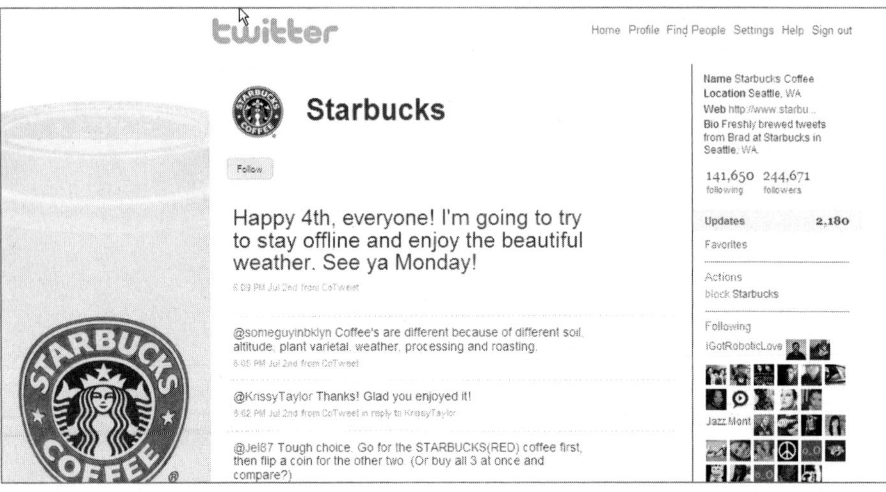

Figure 2.31 Starbucks

Success Rice (@Success_Rice)

Sun and Earth (@SunandEarth)

Sun Chips (FritoLay) (@SunChips)

tasti D-lite (@tastidlite)

Trader Joe's (@traderjoes)

Tyson Foods (@TysonFoods)

Whole Foods (@wholefoods)

Automotive

Chevrolet (@AdamDenison)

Ford Motors (@scottmonty & @fordcustservice)

General Motors (@gmblogs)

Harley Davidson (@harleydavidson)

Honda (@Alicia_at_Honda)

Figure 2.32 General Motors

Travel and Leisure

Carnival Cruise Line (`@CarnivalCruise`)

The Citizen Hotel (`@thecitizenhotel`)

Fairmont Hotels (`@fairmonthotels`)

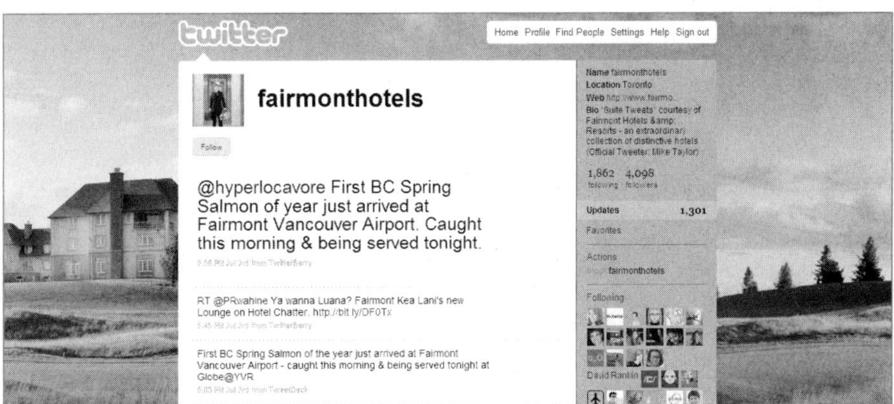

Figure 2.33 Fairmont Hotels

Four Seasons Resorts (`@Four_Seasons`)

Hertz (`@connectbyhertz`)

Hotel Casa del Mar (`@casadelmar`)

JetBlue (@jetblue)

Luxor Hotel & Casino (@LuxorLV)

Marriott International (@MarriottIntl)

MGM Grand Hotel (@mgmgrand)

Planet Hollywood Casino & Resort (@phvegas, @phresort)

The Ritz-Carlton (@simonfcooper, @ritzcarltonpr & @brucehimelstein)

Southwest Airlines (@southwestair)

Travel Channel (@travelchannel)

Figure 2.34 Southwest Airlines

Figure 2.35 Travel Channel

Technology

Delicious (`@Delicious`)

Dell (`@richardatdell` & `http://www.dell.com/twitter`)

EMC (`@emccorp`)

Google (`@google`...and many others)

HP (Store) (`@buyhp`)

HP Direct (`@HPCheer`)

HTC (`@htc`)

Intuit (`@intuit`, `@QuickBooks`, `@IntuitPayroll`, `@IntuitCommunity`, `@IntuitDeals` & `@1practicalgal`)

LinkedIn (`@LinkedIn`)

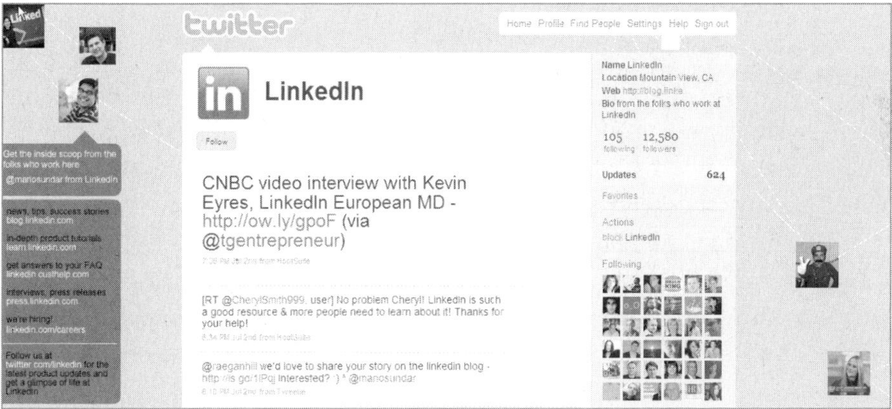

Figure 2.36 LinkedIn

Motorola (`@motodeals`)

Oracle (`http://wiki.oracle.com/page/Oracle+Tweeters?t=anon`)

Palm (`@palm_inc`)

The Sims 3 (`@thesims3`)

Sun Microsystems (`@sunmicrosystems`)

Yahoo! (`@yahoo`...and many others)

Figure 2.37 The Sims 3

The Role of the Community Manager

For large brands with many corporate layers, products, divisions, and even global units, one way to deal with the "social media fear factor" has been to promote or hire someone to oversee social media initiatives. This individual, most commonly referred to as the *community manager*, has a fairly daunting responsibility. Not only are community managers responsible for managing how the brand is portrayed and perceived with the online public, but they are also responsible for developing and overseeing the execution of strategies that are in constant flux due to the environment in which they're being executed. Community managers need to be individuals with 360-degree vision, *and* they need to be able to think on their feet.

What's been written thus far about community managers has primarily come from those within the industry who either study the phenomenon or participate in it. Jeremiah Owyang (`@jowyang`), an analyst with the Altimeter Group researching the social computing industry, distilled the role into four key tenants, here excerpted from `http://www.web-strategist.com/blog/2007/11/25/the-four-tenets-of-the-community-manager`.

- **Advocate.** The primary role of the community manager is to represent the customer. This includes listening, monitoring, and interpreting what corporate customers and consumers are saying, as well as engaging with these customers by responding to their requests and needs both in private and in public.
- **Evangelist.** In this capacity, the community manager acts as corporate promoter of events, products, and upgrades to customers by using, among other tactics, conversational discussions.

- **Communicator.** In this role, the community manager is fluent with all forms of jargon within social media communication: from forums, to blogs, to podcasts, and to Twitter. This individual is also responsible for mediating disputes within the community, turning to consumer advocates for assistance, and trying to work through challenges presented by detractors. In an editorial strategy and planning capacity, the community manager will work with multiple internal stakeholders to conceive, plan for, produce, and publish the necessary content to keep the brand's public community fresh and current.
- **Futurist.** The futurist collects, organizes, and presents to internal stakeholders input from the community about what it would like to see from the brand going forward.

Owyang has also compiled an extremely comprehensive list of "Social Computing Strategists and Community Managers for Enterprise Corporations" (which he makes no promises to maintain, but which is still useful): `http://www.web-strategist.com/blog/2008/06/20/list-of-social-computing-strategists-and-community-managers-for-large-corporations-2008`.

Connie Bensen (`@cbensen`), a very well-respected community strategist, hosts an informative blog by that same name (`http://www.communitystrategist.net`). On it, she has posted and maintains a description of the community manager responsibilities and goals, which can be summarized as follows:

Online Marketing, Outreach Strategies, and Building Brand Visibility

- Contribute to the development of the company's online marketing and outreach strategies.
- Foster a sense of community around the brand at both the brand properties and on the Web at large by building relationships.
- Monitor key online conversations and events to make sure the company is participating effectively and is being represented.
- Participate in social networking sites.
- Manage, maintain, and ensure the success of the company blog.

[Online] Public Relations

- Identify industry influencers with whom to establish relationships, partner, and collaborate.
- Engage, motivate, and recognize the Company's most active online advocates.
- Respond to crises.
- Coordinate, oversee, train, and recognize those involved in the execution of community projects.

Customer and Technical Support

- Learn the products inside and out.
- Listen to customers and gather their feedback; thank them for their input.
- Route customer needs to the appropriate department.
- Be responsible for the administration of the Company's online brand property(s).

Product Development and Quality Assurance

- Communicate customer suggestions and provide ideas for product improvement.
- Participate in discussions on product use.
- Report product defects.

Sales and Business Partnerships

- Identify and route potential sales opportunities to the appropriate teams.
- Be proactively strategic in building business-partner relationships.

Internal Web 2.0 Ambassador

- Encourage internal communication and provide leadership for cross-functional efforts.
- Increase awareness of and training for Web 2.0 tools across the company.
- Advocate for the culture shift that's required to be a customer-centric company.
- Develop company guidelines on outreach consistent with company brand positioning.

Reporting

- Participate in creating the online community plan, including a budget.
- Track and report the following on a regular basis:
  - Quantitative measures as outlined by business goals
  - Amount of activity at community site(s)
  - Qualitative report of consumer responses
  - Suggestions and feedback for management and executive levels
- Identify and offer solutions for breaking down barriers between customers and corporate.

Goal Setting and Professional Development

- Stay up-to-date on new social media tools, best practices, and how other organizations and companies are using them.
- Participate in professional networking by interacting with peers and thought leaders in online arenas and attend events.

Clearly, the job of the community manager should be filled by an experienced, multitalented multitasker. This isn't a position to take lightly or to foist onto a recent college grad just because they know more about Facebook, MySpace, and Twitter than their boss. The good community manager *facilitates the brand* in the social media space. This is a tremendous responsibility for anyone—don't take it lightly.

The Main Points

- Twitter's demographics are shifting. Don't assume the audience is static and predictable.
- Many different types of individuals and entities use Twitter and may have different agendas for doing so.
- The rules and tenants for Twitter are still being written and rewritten.
- The individual tasked with representing a company on Twitter has an important role as the face of the company to the public.

Twitter, the Multipurpose Platform

Describing Twitter, a platform limited to 140 characters, as "versatile" almost seems impossible—but truly that's what it's become. Twitter's full versatility has not even been tapped out yet. It seems like every few weeks, another innovative use of Twitter comes to light. The value of these diverse uses varies, but you can't evaluate them for your organization unless you first know they exist—and that's what we hope to accomplish in this chapter.

3

Chapter Contents

What Twitter Can Accomplish

At the start, Jack Dorsey and the rest of Twitter's creators didn't completely realize the far-reaching potential uses for the tool they had developed. Read the Twitter Blog (`http://blog.twitter.com`), and you'll find various references to Twitter being "very open." Twitter is open to developers, it's open to evolution, and it's open to new ideas. In other words, Twitter is allowing the community to shape it more than it's shaping itself. Twitter is a free-market system at its finest, driven like every other free market by supply and demand. Twitter's evolution happens so dynamically, in fact, that even before I complete writing this book, the ways in which people and organizations use Twitter will not only change; they might change substantially. As Steve Johnson (`@stevenbjohnson`) put it in his *Time* magazine article, "How Twitter Will Change the Way We Live," "...the most fascinating thing about Twitter is not what it's doing to us. It's what we're doing to it."

In Chapter 2, we gave you a nice starter list of brands on Twitter, and throughout this chapter, we've provided examples of the ways in which companies have used Twitter to accomplish different goals. To gain perspective, it's always helpful to read about what early adopters in a space have done (and what they have learned). Now that Twitter's been around a while, we have more information to go on. Regularly, you can find Twitter success stories in the news media, on blogs, and at conferences. Because Twitter success stories grab headlines quickly these days, some of the same companies are held up as standards and their stories are told over and over again.

Rather than recycle the same material you can find in countless other resources—and some of which I used earlier in this book—I've gathered new or lesser-known case studies and anecdotal information for you from an assortment of organizations, large and small, representing different applications of Twitter.

I sort of see Twitter this way: Twitter generates energy. Like any other energy source, Twitter fuels, ignites, and powers. Twitter fuels conversations, Twitter ignites controversy, and Twitter powers innovation. This innovation occurs all over the place: in the Web development community, in the media, in fundraising, in activism, and in business marketing. If this energy is harnessed correctly, it's got a bright future. If it's not, this energy could wind up wasted or, worse yet, depleted and we'll choose or be forced to move onto another platform.

One trait associated with the human form of energy is passion, and Twitter users have plenty of it. In fact, Twitter may embolden people outside of their ordinary zone. After all, how difficult is it to compose a 140-character tweet? Moreover, look how easy Twitter makes it to complain or rant, perhaps sometimes when we ought not. The question for any brand wishing to market through Twitter becomes, "How can I tap into that passion without offending users?" The larger your brand, the greater the chances are that passion for your most-popular products and services already exists on Twitter. For smaller business lacking a brand marquee, the great thing about Twitter is that it can be used to *create* your brand. All companies have the same opportunity to reach both existing customers and potential customers through Twitter, and the thing to remember is that, if you're thinking about marketing through Twitter, so too might be your competition.

Twitter moves fast. Faster than anything we've seen on the Internet before. Twitter breaks news faster than almost any media outlet today. In the summer of 2008, I first realized its potential for breaking news when I read a tweet from a colleague: "On conference call with California. They just had an earthquake!" Whoa! I didn't even need to turn on anything or navigate anywhere to get that news: it just appeared in my updated Twitter stream. In the normal course of the day, active tweeters, like the 24-hour news channels, fill the empty cyberspace with content. What kind of content? Sure, there are the random tweets about thoughts and activities, but there are also links to useful information and comments about positive (and negative) experiences they have had with the goods and services used in their daily lives. With the growth of Twitter, those comments and recommendations are also growing at an increased rate.

Featured Case: Planet Hollywood/Customer Service

Planet Hollywood Resort & Casino (`@phVegas`) joined the Twitterverse in April 2009, when Brandie Feuer, their director of interactive marketing, came over from the Luxor Casino, where she had been responsible for getting them onto Twitter. Feuer got both hotel/casinos onto Twitter for similar reasons: "Twitter is a great, easy entry into the social media space. It allows Planet Hollywood to listen to what others are saying, engage with past, present, and future guests, and better understand how we can provide increased value to them." At Planet Hollywood, customer service is the driving force behind anything they do, and Twitter allows the resort to provide one-on-one customer-service experiences to "facilitate positive engagements and proactively deflect incorrect or negative sentiments about Planet Hollywood." Planet Hollywood also strives to provide value to the community and, because the hotel empowered Feuer to put a personal voice behind the brand, it has provided them with "phenomenal feedback and a better understanding of what interests our guests." Through Twitter, Feuer can respond immediately to customers' requests for recommendations on places to eat or things to do.

By using Twitter Search, Feuer also proactively responds to general Twitterverse questions about Las Vegas to help travelers solve their problems. Feuer believes that, rather than worry about exposing themselves to negative sentiment by entering Twitter, brands should realize that people usually just want to know that their voice matters, that someone is listening, and that Twitter can be a tool to counterbalance disgruntled complaints that commonly result from misinformation. "When we provide correct or updated information in a timely manner, we typically receive an influx of positive responses. The best part about Twitter is that online conversations become offline realities. Previously, new ideas, new products, and new ways of doing things took years to attain and implement. Today, with the help of [forms of] social media [tools like Twitter], these things are garnered faster and, as an added, but invaluable bonus, new friendships are obtained as well."

How do you locate, track, and monitor these kinds of comments and recommendations? You'll have to get to Part II, "Master Twitter Fundamentals," to get the lowdown on all the tools and solutions at your brand's disposal. Right now, what you need to know is that by paying attention to what is being said about your brand within the Twitter community, you can develop new concepts, and possibly even new brand perceptions, with potentially no cost outlays other than someone's time. I caution you to enter Twitter with reasonable expectations, however. Chatter on Twitter *can* positively impact brands, but a May 2009 study by Knowledge Networks of social media users found that "while 83 percent of the Internet population ages 13 to 54 participates in social media, less than 5 percent regularly turn to these sites for guidance on purchase decisions in any of nine product/service categories." Measurably and anecdotally, though, numerous companies, large and small, express that Twitter has had an effect on their customers. Also, let's not forget that customer retention is just as important if not more important than acquiring new ones for many, many businesses.

What Brands Can Gain through Twitter

There are two primary and very different reasons why companies should be on Twitter. The first reason has less to do with brands and more to do with niche, small, or obscure companies—the kinds of companies that need to do more to bootstrap their marketing in general. With Twitter, they can help their search engine rankings and website traffic. When I speak to companies like this, they have a hard time connecting the dots. They think that no one in their potential marketplace could possibly be on Twitter, so why should they bother? In response, I say—and I'm going to utter blasphemy here—so what?!! Search engines love fresh content, just the kind of material Twitter and other social media platforms regularly provide. Search engine spiders specifically latch onto this fresh content for their indexes, which in turn help with search visibility. What company would turn down free, organic search engine rankings if it could achieve them? This doesn't even take into account that Twitter Search itself continues to play a more vital role in people finding up-to-the-moment information, what's being referred to as "real time search."

The second reason has nothing to do with bootstrap marketing; it has to do with resistance to Twitter from people working for bigger brands who, without even diving in as individuals, bellyache: "What's so great about Twitter, and why should we bother with it?" These are the same companies who feel they must only do something when their audience, or competition, is already there—the same companies who fear taking a leadership role. To them I urge, why not get in early when you can make mistakes and learn *before* your audience gets so entrenched and so educated that your late-entry naiveté makes you look bad? I'm not talking about companies that have done their due diligence and have elected not to participate on Twitter due to legal or other concerns. It's true that not every brand is right for Twitter. I do think, however, that there are many positives to be gained by participating on Twitter and that it's time to get serious enough to stop treating Twitter like some fly-by-night fad. Let me tell you why:

Branding and Awareness Building Trying to let your market know that you exist and what you're about? Trying to convey information? Trying to reinforce the market's perception of you that you've built through other marketing efforts? Sun & Earth (`@sunandearth`), a manufacturer of environmentally safe cleaning products, got on Twitter to do just that. Combating challenges such as lack of brand awareness in certain markets and looking to "increase awareness in current markets, identify commercial opportunities, interact more readily with consumers, and increase plant tour frequency," Sun & Earth says their Twitter efforts thus far have been good. "Awareness has been increasing," reported official Sun & Earth corporate tweeter J. Rotondo.

Direct-to-Consumer Opt-In Marketing Pretty much considered the holy grail of brand marketing, the direct-to-consumer (DTC) relationship can play a huge role in the lifecycle of a consumer. When the Web came about and brands could build websites and tools that allowed consumers to come directly to them, and register for this or join an email list about that, it expedited the development of the DTC relationship. The buzz phrase back then was, "building a one-to-one relationship." Although the notion of such a relationship is still a good one, in many cases it has yet to realize its full potential. Twitter, on the other hand, really *can* be a one-to-one relationship between the consumer and the brand. It can be active (consumer tweets brand; brand @ replies back) or passive (consumer follows brand and has the potential to be exposed to everything the brand pushes out via Twitter). This is opt-in marketing at its finest.

Provide Direct Customer Service When a consumer had a problem with your product in the past, they had to call during certain daytime hours, send an email via a website contact form or anonymous address, or snail mail your company about their concern or question. In today's fast-paced, two-income-household world, this method is inconvenient and unnecessarily time-consuming. With Twitter, if the consumer can distill their concern down to 140 characters and get a quick, satisfying, and equally brief solution back (or a way to transition the issue to another channel where it's already been elevated as a problem), this is a win-win. Not to mention that delivering customer service through Twitter costs a lot less than doing so through a call center! Ask a tweeter about a brand that does a good job of customer service through Twitter, and you'll often hear about JetBlue Airways (`@jetblue`). Read the JetBlue Twitter stream at any given time and you'll see all kinds of tweets; many replying directly back to users who have tweeted them…not an easy chore when you have close to one million followers!

Build Customer Loyalty and Retention Certainly, Twitter aids customer loyalty and retention through the customer service a brand can deliver via Twitter. This kind of loyalty, while fine, is passive. Twitter can also be a channel to cultivate loyalty and retention more actively. You can merely fuel devoted fans, as many urban food-truck vendors do when they send out a daily tweet about what corner they'll be parked on that day. Or you can go deeper, developing Twitter-only customer promotions or creating Twitter-centric events, such as a brand-lovers TweetUp. Starbucks (`@starbucks`) does a good job working in tweets about its rewards and discount cards to remind followers that such programs exist (see Figure 3.1).

Promote One of the most obvious ways to use Twitter for business is as another vehicle to broadcast promotions. Brands tweet about everything from coupons to deals to in-store offers. `@Amazon Deals` and `@DellOutlet` offer great examples of brands offering Twitter-only deals to their followers (see Figure 3.2).

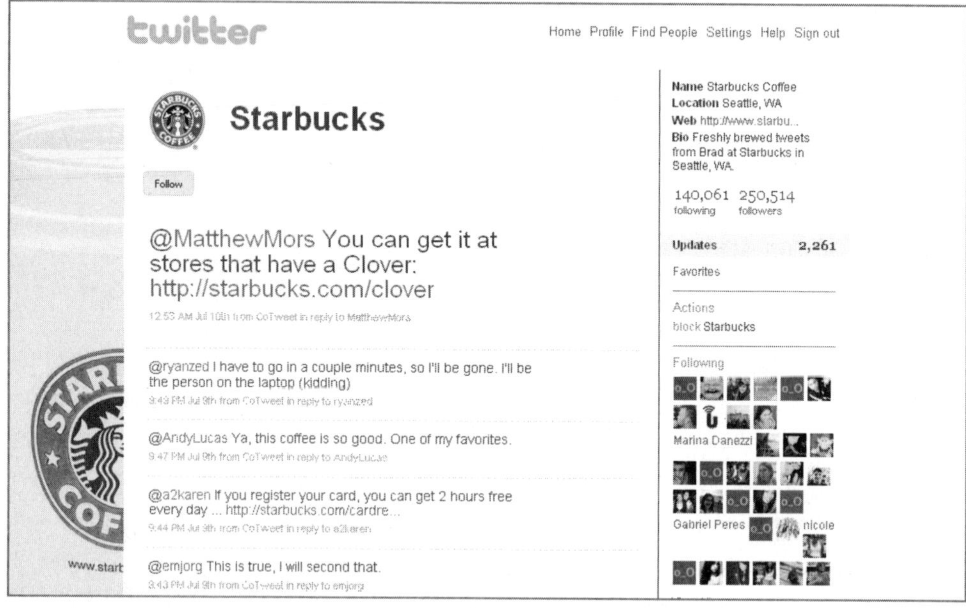

Figure 3.1 Starbucks promotes its card programs.

Figure 3.2 Dell's Twitter-only promotions

Lead Generation and Sales Lead generation or sales as a result of being on Twitter could be every business' ideal goal, and yet so many doubt Twitter's ability to impact sales directly. A little later in this chapter, we're going to go into more detail about leads and sales generated with Twitter's help. To help put this into perspective now, check out Best Buy's version of a Twitter sales force, its *Twelpforce* (`@TWELPFORCE`). A relatively new but ingenious, aggressive strategy in action, the Twelpforce leverages the potency of Twitter's real-time public search to identify consumers looking for items that Best Buy sells so that members of the Twelpforce can make contact and tickle them that Best Buy does sell these items. The Twelpforce also makes itself available to answer technical questions (see Figure 3.3).

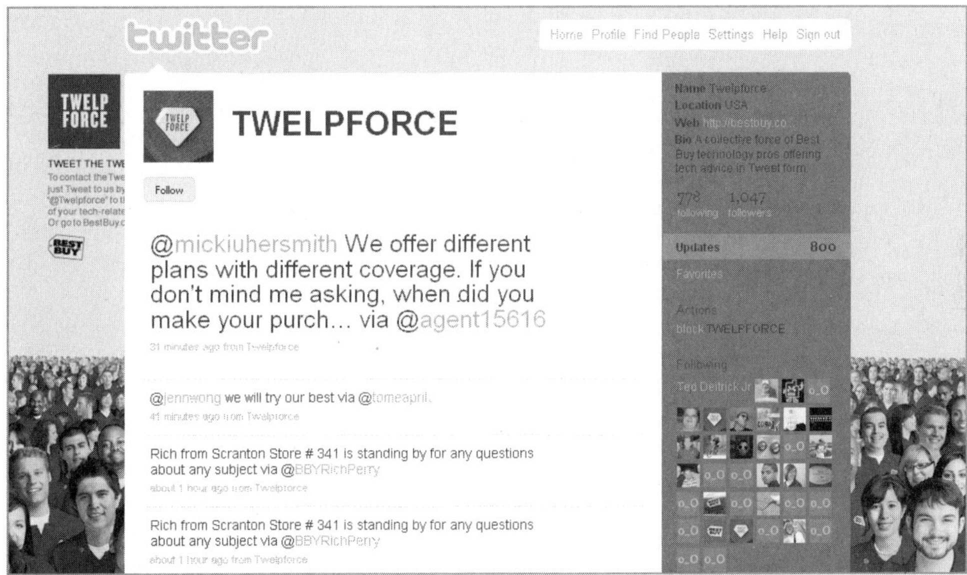

Figure 3.3 Best Buy's Twelpforce in action

Provide Instant Updates and Alerts Have a time-sensitive product or service? Twitter makes communicating updates and alerts easy and faster than by phone call. Two examples of brands using Twitter this way are Southwest Airlines (`@SouthwestAir`), which provides instant updates on flights (see Figure 3.4), and one-day, one-deal site woot (`@woot`), which pushes out its daily deal via Twitter (see Figure 3.5).

Get Instant Feedback Through Twitter, a brand can very quickly gauge the pulse of its audience, the value of which can be to help evaluate corporate moves or just play a part in a larger research effort. Brands can test new logo creative concepts and tag lines, advertising and promotional campaign ideas, or even the state-of-the-brand consumer check-in ("How are we doing?"). (See Figure 3.6.)

Figure 3.4 Southwest Airlines' timely updates

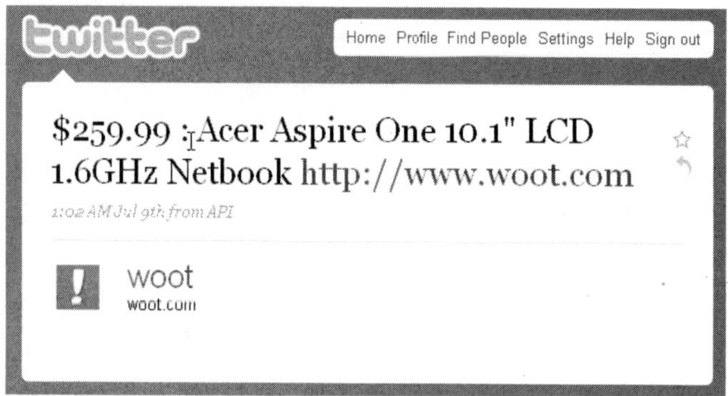

Figure 3.5 woot's daily deal

Figure 3.6 Network Solutions solicits feedback on its new brand and website.

Event Marketing Twitter is also a practical tool to use when you're trying to promote an event that's out on the timeline. One of the earliest event venues to adopt Twitter as this kind of communications channel was the South by Southwest festival and conference (`@sxsw`); but nowadays, if you're hosting a major event (like the LPGA) and you're not tweeting, you're behind the eight ball (see Figure 3.7).

Localized Information Are you a franchise? A business trying to sell exclusively into a local community? By using Search and other geo-specific Twitter tools, you can easily find users in your specific geographical vicinity, reach out to them by following and/or tweeting them, and then push out your localized information. You can also set up, save, and regularly review geo-specific searches to identify new users or track competitors.

Figure 3.7 LPGA using Twitter to promote upcoming tournaments

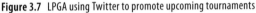

Featured Case: 1st Mariner Bank

As a local community bank, 1st Mariner Bank (`http://www.1stmarinerbank.com`) wanted to connect with consumers in their area and saw Twitter as an opportunity to emphasize the bank's local roots, promote local events, highlight activities in the community, and connect with customers and prospects on banking needs. They opened a Twitter account (`@1stMarinerBank`) in January 2009 and slowly began to get their feet wet. They started by following other local businesses and connecting with them. By July 2009, the bank described itself as "actively participating" on Twitter. Besides the positive connections to the community, the bank could directly tie at least two new banking relationships to their Twitter account and numerous issue resolutions. One placated customer even blogged about his satisfaction with the bank, calling 1st Mariner "A New Shining Star in Social Media PR" (see Figure 3.8). For their early and successful adoption of Twitter, the bank has been recognized by industry groups, including Net Banker and the Online Banking Report. Kevin Lynch, senior vice president at eCommerce/Contact Center, says, "[We are] very pleased with the results." The bank plans to remain active on Twitter for the foreseeable

Featured Case: 1st Mariner Bank *(Continued)*

future and, in fact, is now experimenting with more Twitter accounts to handle specific needs, such as `@FMBCustServ`, managed by the bank's Contact Center manager, and `@FirstAccess`, which is tied to a specific product aimed at the college-age audience.

TECHNOSAILOR emmense AaronBrazell.com

technosailor business, technology, government, communications

First Mariner Bank: A New Shining Star in Social Media PR

by AARON BRAZELL on JULY 10, 2008 5 COMMENTS

For all the fuss that has been made about Dell, Zappos, Comcast, JetBlue and a whole host of other big names utilizing Twitter and other forms of social media for their messaging and client support, there is one that stands out to me as the most impressive. I say this because of my own personal experience in the past few days. These encounters with my bank, 1st Mariner Bank, are fresh in my mind and, to me, demonstrate a truly productive means of "doing the job" with social media tools.

As an independent, self employed consultant, times can sometimes be tough. In fact, in many way, it's a feast or famine game. You go through spells where clients don't pay, they pay late, or you just can't get the business going enough to generate the income needed to run the business, and sadly, sometimes to pay the bills. So bank runs are important. They are pivotal moments where you might go from pennies in the account to plenty of money to fill the reserves. Those bank runs are always personally fulfilling because it's a statement that, hey, I don't have to go find a "real" job now... I can continue to press forward pursuing the dreams I've tried to find on my own for these past years. That deposit of some check is a rewarding thing that, honestly, sometimes makes the difference between having the will to go on or just quitting outright.

On Wednesday, I finally received one of these very important checks that was long overdue from a client. With a diminishing bank account, I jumped in the car late in the day and trucked the 45 minutes through rush hour traffic just to get to the bank and find they were closed. When I called their customer service toll free number, I was informed (inaccurately, as I later discovered) that the drive through was still open. Since there was a problem with my Visa debit card, I couldn't simply make the deposit at the ATM machine so I thanked the representative and tried the drive thru. As I said, I discovered it was closed as well.

Irritated, I jumped on Twitter and went ballistic, venting about how I was going to close my account and find a bank that was closer. I was livid and was letting the world know. These bank runs are not small things for me. They take gas and money and time away from my book. I have kept this account because I always valued the 1st Mariner Bank Customer Service, though, but even that wasn't going to be enough to keep me banking 45 mins away from home.

About Aaron Brazell

Aaron Brazell is the Lead Editor of Technosailor.com, a frequent public speaker, photographer, entrepreneur, and the author of the upcoming WordPress Bible from Wiley Publishing.

Email Aaron at aaron@technosailor.com

Figure 3.8 Call this a satisfied 1st Mariner customer!

Job/Member Recruitment Companies now have another online channel to turn to for their personnel recruitment efforts (as do associations and groups trying to recruit new members): Twitter. In addition to tweeting about their job openings and linking to their job descriptions, companies have used Twitter's two-way medium to adapt to individual recruitment situations. For example, in July 2009, Best Buy (@BestBuyCMO; @BestBuyRemix) posted a job description for "Emerging Media Manager." The job, as posted, required a graduate degree and 250 followers on Twitter. Almost immediately, Best Buy received feedback from the Twitter community, some of whom felt the job requirements inappropriate given the job itself. As a result of the outcry, Best Buy decided to pull the job posting and instead have Twitter followers crowdsource the development of the new job description (Figure 3.9). The experiment was not without bumps, as Best Buy CMO Barry Judge wrote on his blog:

> *"Thank you for participating, commenting, re-tweeting, blogging about, and contributing your thoughts to the discussion regarding the Emerging Media job description crowdsourcing effort so far. We're only a couple of days into it and the response has been phenomenal.... Although we're asking for ideas related to our job description, we're discovering that the issue of how to identify talent in this space may be a sore point for other companies as well. Hopefully, at the end of the day, the discussion resulting from this will also contribute to the larger discussion beyond our Emerging Media role."*

Thought Leadership Brands that want to be perceived as leaders in their fields should find Twitter an excellent vehicle to help reinforce this perception. Thought leaders conduct and release research findings, pose evocative questions, and take stances on issues. ING Direct (@INGDIRECT) exhibits this kind of leadership. Take a look at its stream and you'll see tweets that question controversial news articles, encourage support for our troops "who defend our freedom," and ask, "If you had to ask your significant other to give up one thing in order to save money, what would it be?"

Change Attitudes Brands that got into Twitter early benefited from Twitter's new-and-cool caché, even if they had been perceived previously as old and stodgy. Tie that into using the platform as a real way to deliver change, and you have a winning formula. Probably the best-known example of this is what one man did for cable enterprise Comcast. Frank Eliason, the visionary behind @ComcastCares and its director of digital care, saw Twitter as a way to combat the intense negative reputation the company had, particularly about its customer service. Through Frank's efforts and those of a team of Comcasters on Twitter, the company has been able to address customer concerns more quickly and satisfactorily than telephone customer service ever has. As a result, Comcast now has a reputation of "earnestly trying" rather than completely failing at customer service as it once had (Figure 3.10).

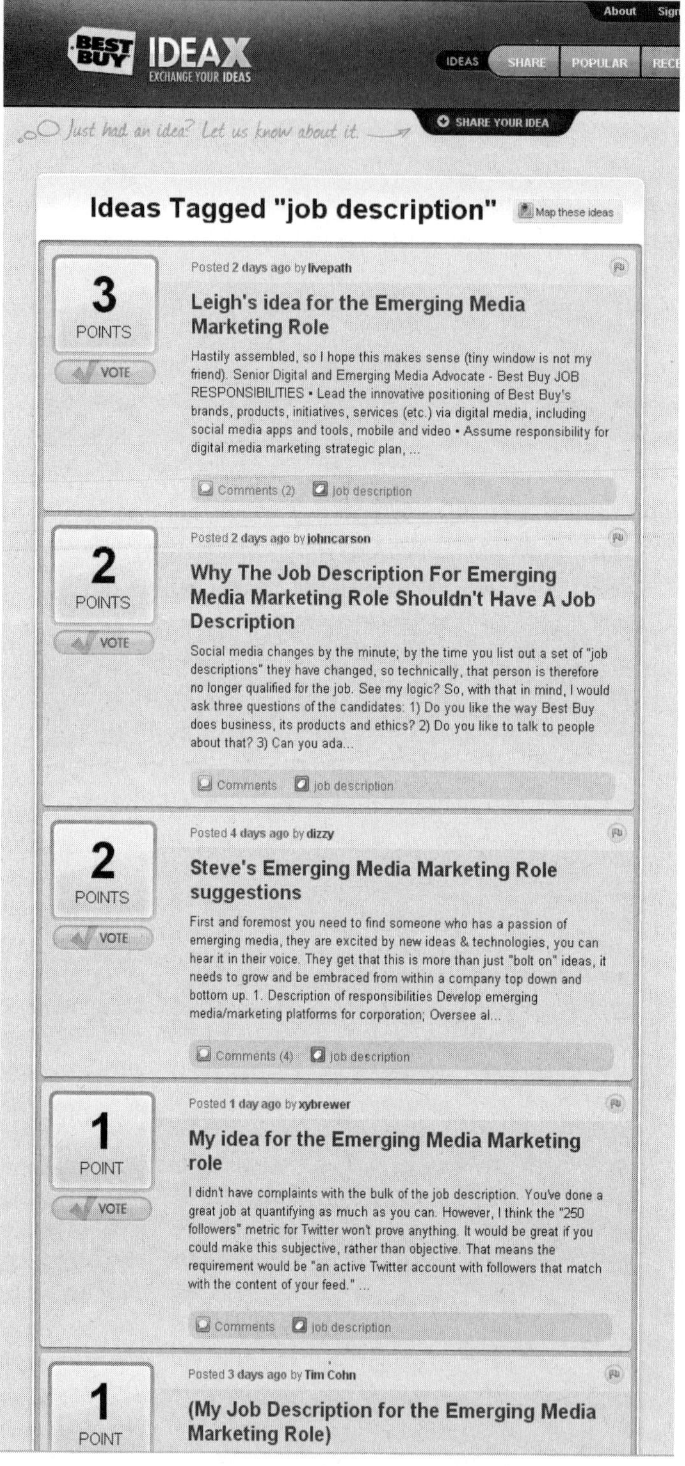

Figure 3.9 Best Buy's experiment in crowdsourcing a job description

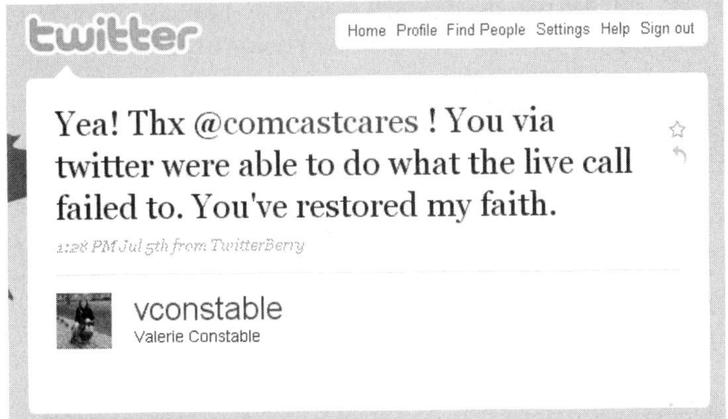

twitter
Home Profile Find People Settings Help Sign out
Yea! Thx @comcastcares ! You via twitter were able to do what the live call failed to. You've restored my faith.
1:28 PM Jul 5th from TwitterBerry
vconstable
Valerie Constable

Figure 3.10 A satisfied Comcast customer

Competitive Advantage The most obvious competitive advantages are gained when your competition is not active on Twitter and you are. What can you do to "out-Twitter" your competition when you are both on Twitter? Some classic rivals stack up fairly well on Twitter: Coke and Pepsi, Ford (`@scottmonty`) and GM, Google and Yahoo!, Domino's and Papa John's, while others, such as Microsoft versus Apple (the latter strangely missing in action as far as we can tell) and Burger King versus McDonald's (again, the latter hard to find due to poor account setup and unintuitive user handles like `@McCafeYourDay`), don't fare so well.

Manage Crises More often than not, brands let slip the opportunity to manage crises via Twitter. Disgruntled or slighted customers, empowered by social media, can at best lodge a legitimate complaint and at worse launch full-out (and often much deserved) brand warfare when their grievances go unaddressed. A musician whose $3,500 guitar was broken by United Airlines baggage handlers took his story to the blogosphere when United refused to handle the situation: `http://www.davecarrollmusic.com/story/united-breaks-guitars`.

On the other hand, a few have figured out how to make Twitter work for them in moments of crisis with positive results. As reported in *PRWeek*, London mayor Boris Johnson, inundated with tweets from disgruntled citizens after it emerged that many buses had their heaters turned up in the middle of the heat wave, looked into the issue, contacted his transport advisor, and soon had the issue resolved. Had the mayor not had a Twitter account or had he not monitored it closely, he might not have known of the problem or might not have handled it so swiftly. Instead, thanks to his active use of Twitter, his followers expressed their gratitude, publicly praising him. Crisis averted.

Authorize.Net, a popular credit card and electronic check payment processor had a major outage due to a hardware failure. Some of its merchants were affected. Informed of the outage, Authorize.Net's Twitter account (`@AuthorizeNet`) worked overtime, diligently responding to tweets and keeping its followers informed. Again, followers reacted favorably to how the company handled the crisis (see Figure 3.11).

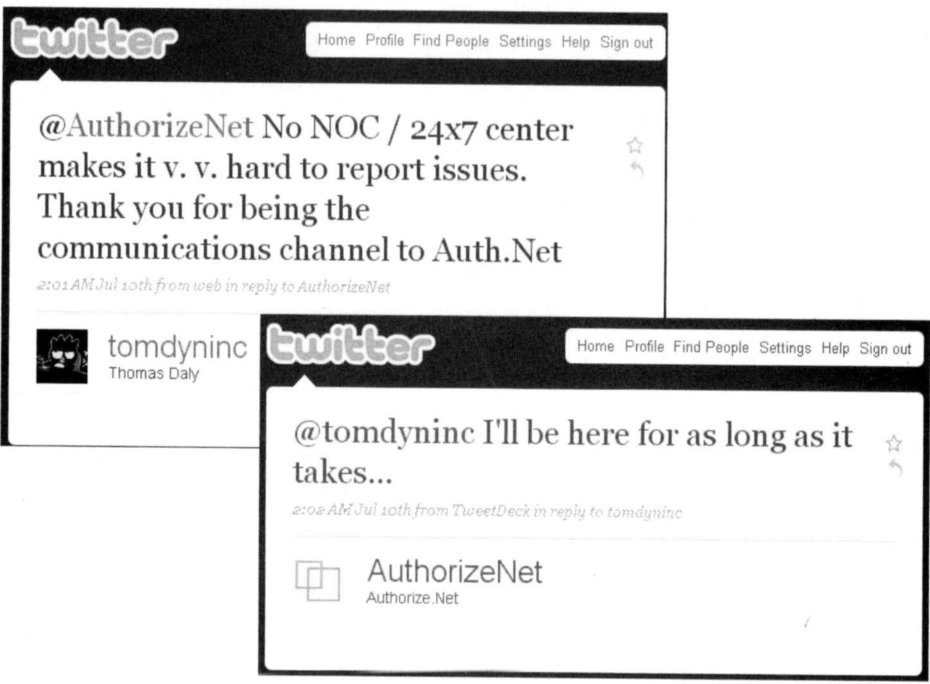

Figure 3.11 Authorize.Net successfully managed its crisis and used Twitter as an important communications channel throughout.

The examples show that brands have to learn to use Twitter to be on top of a crisis, to acknowledge the problem, and then to respond and do what they can to improve upon the situation. In these days of instant communications fueling a need for immediate gratification, ignoring problems and hoping they go away is no longer an option.

Create Spokespeople...for Free! The best part about arriving positively on the other side of a crisis is that the well-treated customer might not only be a retained one, but one you'll have for life. Used creatively, Twitter can grow spokespeople—the treasured "brand evangelist"—as easily as a Chia Pets! One local start-up establishment, a tavern in Baltimore called Bad Decisions (`@bad_decisions`), attributes its entire success to Twitter. With no marketing budget to speak of, Bad Decisions owner John Reusing decided to "throw himself out there" into the Twitterverse, and soon found himself the darling of the Baltimore Twitterati (Figure 3.12). Customers latching on and wanting to help him succeed devised special events to be held at the bar. In addition to frequently hosting tweet-ups at Bad Decisions, promotions like the bi-monthly "Bacon and Beer Happy Hours" and viewings of classic television shows like *The Muppets* tied into trivia contests with prizes sponsored by other local businesses have helped attract even more customers, as the Twitter curious have followed along to the "group tweeting" arising out of Bad Decisions' efforts.

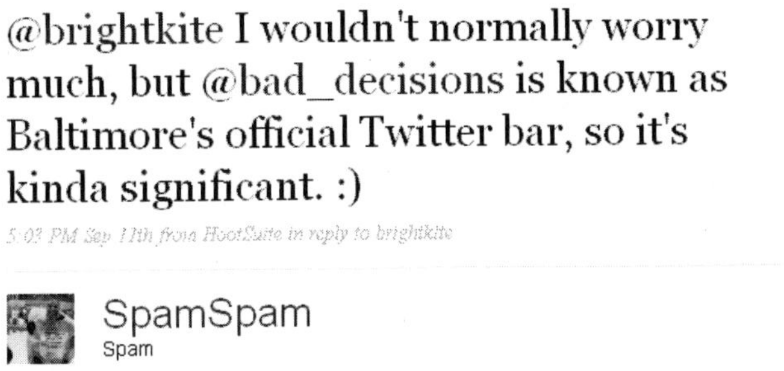

@brightkite I wouldn't normally worry much, but @bad_decisions is known as Baltimore's official Twitter bar, so it's kinda significant. :)

5:03 PM Sep 11th from HootSuite in reply to brightkite

Figure 3.12 Bad Decisions is now considered "the" Baltimore Twitter bar

Entertain Entertaining tweets, particularly those that link to entertaining content like funny videos or bizarre photos, have a fantastic viral effect on Twitter. Entertainment-oriented tweets are some of the most popularly retweeted and receive some of the highest click volume of anything tweeted. Think of it this way: anything that might have made the rounds as a humorous, forwarded email probably has viral value on Twitter. Content from popular humor sites such as The Onion, Funny or Die, and CollegeHumor often makes the rounds, but these days anyone with a camera, cell phone, or smart phone can produce funny content that goes viral. Twitter is a platform for *Candid Camera* on steroids!

Search Visibility Earlier, I mentioned the benefits of Twitter and search visibility. The facts are pretty straightforward: Google and other search engines index Twitter. If you tweet relevant content, you increase your odds of being found (see Figure 3.13).

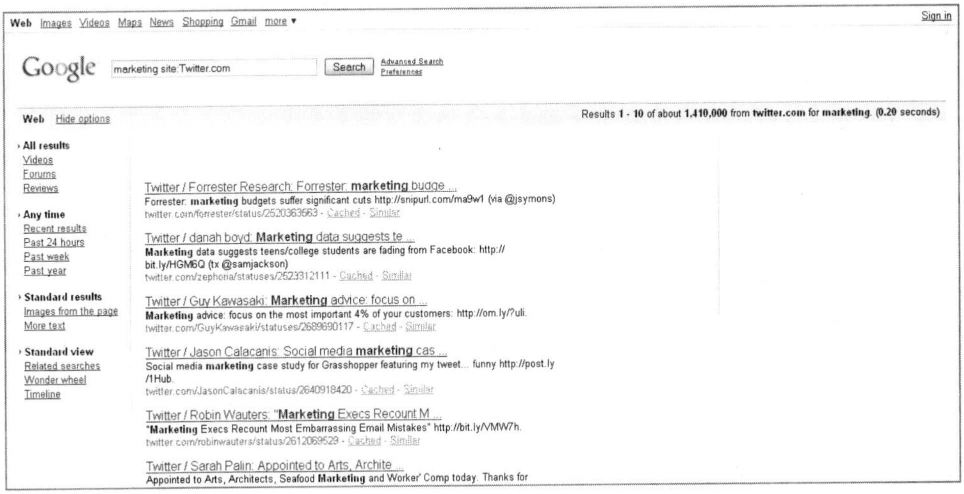

Figure 3.13 Google's indexed Twitter pages for *marketing* (1.4+ million results)

Shake Things Up Are you a brave brand? If so, push your own boundaries on Twitter. Get out of your comfort zone, try new things, and maybe have a little fun in the process. This suits Dogfish Head Craft Brewery of Delaware just fine. The company, which already describes itself as "an unconventional company" and "a little nuts," has embraced Twitter the same way it has embraced its zany persona.

Meet New People and Socialize Your Brand

Not that long ago, a client of mine described Twitter as "the best bar ever." At this point you might be thinking, "Why would I want my organization associated with a bar?" Nevertheless, let's take this analogy further. At a bar, you can walk in, sidle up to the bar, and eavesdrop on every conversation without repercussion or worrying about violating social etiquette. With Twitter, you can follow people based on location, job, area of interest, or just whether you find their tweets interesting. You can find out where the best beer special is, and you can learn about breaking news events such as when a plane crash landed in the Hudson River. You have this stream of commentary about a wide variety of topics that you can mine for information—or you can be as social as you want to be with the people at the "Tweetbar" and engage them in conversation. Before you know it, you'll have a whole new group of people you've connected with on some level. This connection could be fleeting or lasting, depending on how you pursue it and how deep the connection really runs (Figure 3.14).

Figure 3.14 All the (Twitter) world's a bar.

Brands might have a hard time with the concept of *meeting people*. Brands are used to promotions they push out to the masses or direct-marketing efforts they deliver under cover of some channel that doesn't even provide access to the actual people they're targeting. Even customer-service centers that deal with consumer questions and complaints don't really *meet* these customers, and they're certainly not forming any kind of direct relationship. Twitter, on the other hand, breaks down all these barriers. Brands, as scary or exciting as it may seem, really get to meet their customers in a very intimate sort of way. If someone makes contact with the brand, the brand can check out the customer's profile, their picture, their bio, and their tweets, which in turn reveal their thoughts, attitudes, passions, and dislikes. At the Tweetbar, brands cannot be the ones who refrain from interacting because they're shy. In fact, brands that take on the role of bartender might benefit even more; after all, who doesn't disclose all kinds of confidences to their favorite bartender?

Dogfish Head Craft Brewery

Mariah Calagione, Dogfish's vice president, wanted to get the word out about their off-centered beers, fun events, and "general craziness happening in our world each and every day." Calagione knew that *beer-geeks*, her affectionate term for hard-core, beer-loving folks, are active online because "thousands are posting blogs about the beer they drink, the beer they love, the beer they can't get their hands on, and the beer they hate." Over the past 15 years, Dogfish spent a lot of their marketing resources on their website and online presence, particularly in building a voice and a community, so engaging on Twitter just made sense for them. Twitter allows Dogfish to let people know when they put new beers on tap at their pub, when they're brewing something fun and new, or when they start shipping a just-released seasonal beer. Twitter also lets Dogfish find and engage with people who are out there talking about (or talking up!) their beers. "We just tell people what we are up to and how we're enjoying our beers, and our audience does the same." Calagione also tracks and retweets when people post links to their beer blogs about Dogfish, for which she gets "lots of great feedback." Calgione's attitude about Twitter is that she's going to tweet what she feels is appropriate for the brand—and if people don't like it, they can just unfollow.

Meet Your Customers on Twitter

Brands should be doing more than just idling at the Tweetbar, however. On Twitter, that's the equivalent of waiting for followers to find and follow you. Instead, be more active. There are various ways that, with a little bit of research, you as a brand manager can find people who are, could, or should be your customers. In Chapter 4, "Month 1: Master Twitter Fundamentals," we're going to go into deeper detail about the tools at your disposal to locate your consumers and build followers. Know, however, that there is a divergent school of thought about building followers. Some feel that a follower count is some kind of gauge of validity, popularity, or interest. Therefore, inflating this number quickly—even if it means artificially, for example, by purchasing them (yes, this is possible)—is an important step in their Twitter strategy. Others, I among them, see an artificially created follower count as less valuable and inauthentic. Such followers will never engage with your brand, never evangelize for your brand, and can't be mobilized to do anything regarding your brand. Twitter is not TV where ratings points matter; on Twitter, authenticity and transparency matter.

Featured Case: Potomac Valley Brick/Promotions

Potomac Valley Brick (@PVBrick) initially launched its for-fee competition Brick-Stainable, an international sustainability design competition, exclusively through Twitter. PVBrick used its tweets not only to steer following architects and architectural students to the competition website to enter, but also to solicit and secure sponsorships from related industry corporations. A regular stream of tweets on the competition attracted new, relevant followers, and all press releases encouraged new followers with a "Follow Us on Twitter" call to action.

What was the result? They got paid registrants, sponsorship dollars to sustain the competition, plus international trade media attention for PVBrick's innovative approach. Twitter helped position the company as an industry leader for its use of social media, and according to president Alan Richardson, "that's saying a lot for a brick manufacturer."

Zappos (@zappos), an online shoe retailer that has been acquired by Amazon thanks to its success, is one of the marquee brands on Twitter. It is represented first and foremost by its CEO, Tony Hsieh. Tony/Zappos has close to one million followers—and you can bet he didn't buy them. Tony has used Twitter to engage at a personal level, and in doing so, he has infused and enhanced his brand with a personality—that is, he's humanized his brand. The success of `@Zappos` isn't because one million people really like shoes; it's because Tony is a person talking about his life—and because so much of his life is consumed by his work hours, he can't help but sew his brand message into the fiber of his Tweets.

Hsieh believes in this power of Twitter so much that he wrote on his blog about four ways Twitter can make you a better and happier person (Figure 3.15):

1. *Transparency & Values: Twitter constantly reminds me of who I want to be, and what I want Zappos to stand for.*
2. *Reframing Reality: Twitter encourages me to search for ways to view reality in a funnier and/or more positive way.*
3. *Helping Others: Twitter makes me think about how to make a positive impact on other people's lives.*
4. *Gratitude: Twitter helps me notice and appreciate the little things in life.*

Whether you are into shoes or not, you have to admire someone so steadfast in his beliefs. If you're a student of Twitter, Hsieh is certainly someone to follow.

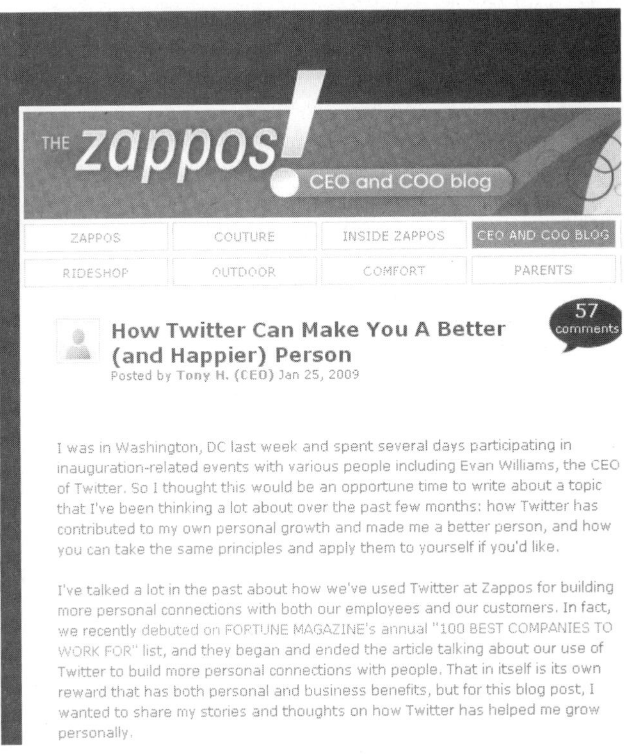

How Twitter Can Make You A Better (and Happier) Person

Posted by Tony H. (CEO) Jan 25, 2009

I was in Washington, DC last week and spent several days participating in inauguration-related events with various people including Evan Williams, the CEO of Twitter. So I thought this would be an opportune time to write about a topic that I've been thinking a lot about over the past few months: how Twitter has contributed to my own personal growth and made me a better person, and how you can take the same principles and apply them to yourself if you'd like.

I've talked a lot in the past about how we've used Twitter at Zappos for building more personal connections with both our employees and our customers. In fact, we recently debuted on FORTUNE MAGAZINE's annual "100 BEST COMPANIES TO WORK FOR" list, and they began and ended the article talking about our use of Twitter to build more personal connections with people. That in itself is its own reward that has both personal and business benefits, but for this blog post, I wanted to share my stories and thoughts on how Twitter has helped me grow personally.

Figure 3.15 Tony Hsieh believes Twitter can make you a happier, better person.

Meet Your Twitter Customers Offline

One of the really cool things about Twitter is that it has not only allowed people to connect through technology; it has also brought people together in person. Chapter 1, "Understand Twitter," introduced the concept of a tweet-up, when a face-to-face group gathering is organized and promoted through Twitter. Chapter 2, "Who's Using Twitter for What?" talked about how the Phoenix Suns organized a tweet-up (Shaq Day) for its fans. Brands on Twitter can foster relationships that they can develop further offline. Also, brands can seek out and invite local individuals in the nearby community to come out and engage with the brand offline.

Twitter Tools for Local Search

There are a number of ways organizations can initiate geographically targeted tweeps. Although we'll cover this further in Part II, let's review a few of these methods now so you can get the gist:

Twellow (`http://www.twellow.com`) Twellow is a kind of phone book for Twitter; you can search the site for geography either by drilling into their Twellowhood map or by performing a search. (See Figure 3.16.)

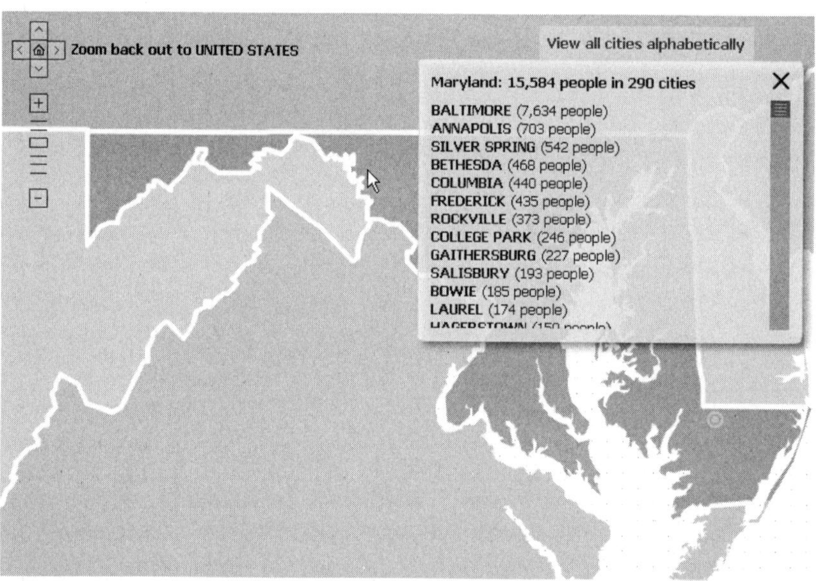

Figure 3.16 Twellowhood lets you drill down through its interactive map to find Twitter users in your area.

Tweetmondo (`http://www.tweetmondo.com`) Whereas the Twellowhood feature of Twellow is limited to the United States and Canada, Tweetmondo covers the entire world. It identifies someone based on their location and also displays a tweetcloud of geographic locations receiving a lot of buzz.

monitter (`http://www.monitter.com`) With monitter, you can combine a search phrase with a 10-plus-mile radius limitation to find tweets within a particular geographical location.

LocalTweeps (`http://localtweeps.com`) With Localtweeps, you use the Search tab to type in zip codes and find tweeps in your target area(s).

ChirpCity (`http://www.chirpcity.com`) This identifies and aggregates tweets by, from, and about cities.

Twibes (`http://www.twibes.com`) Twibes, short for "Twitter Tribes," allows you to create groups focused on subjects such as geography, personal or business interests, or anything else you like. If you're looking for people in a region with whom you want to connect, do a search on Twibes and see if any groups match your criteria. (See Figure 3.17.)

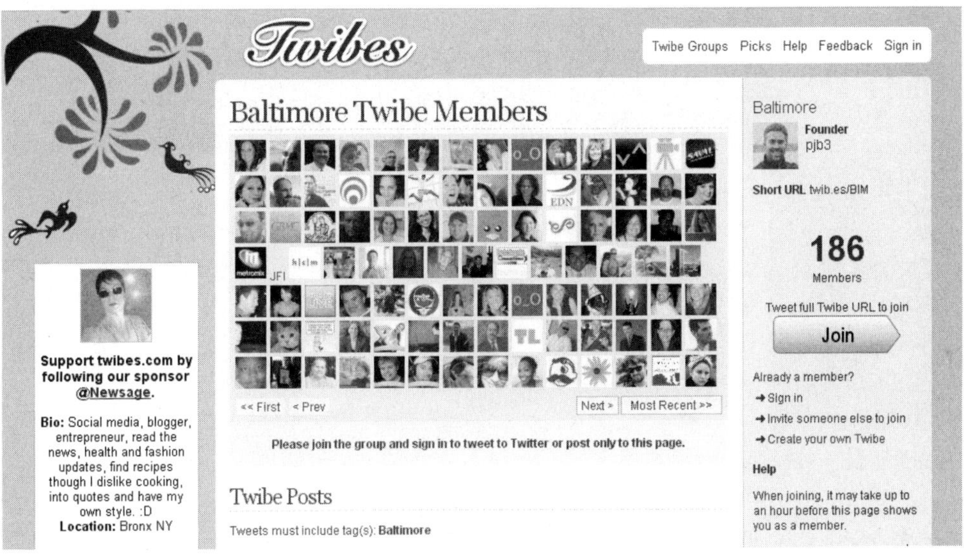

Figure 3.17 Baltimore Twibe

TwitterLocal (`http://www.twitterlocal.net`) TwitterLocal is a downloadable desktop application running on Adobe Air and it filters tweets by location. You can set a radius point to see all the tweets within a designated area (for example, 10-mile radius from Portland, Oregon).

Monitor and Attend Twitter Events in Your Area

The saying goes that birds of a feather flock together. People actively engaged in social media tools like Twitter have most definitely taken to establishing their own events and groups. Oftentimes, these events are open to the public and, if you're serious about engaging your brand in the community, representatives of your company should try to get out to these kinds of local events. Not only will your brand get connected more quickly with willing tweeps, but the community will be impressed by your presence and your desire to connect with them.

For example, in my metropolitan community of Baltimore, events such as Ignite Baltimore (`http://www.ignitebaltimore.com`; `@ignitebaltimore`; Figure 3.18); Barcamp Baltimore (`@BarCampBmore`), TEDxMidAtlantic (`http://tedxmidatlantic.com`); and The Maryland Internet Marketing Group (`http://www.meetup.com/The-Maryland-Internet-Marketing-Group`) attract social media savvy members of the community.

Figure 3.18 Ignite Baltimore

Meet Your Peers on Twitter

For executives from all sectors, Twitter serves as a peer-to-peer connecting device that wields perhaps more power than the current leader in business connections, LinkedIn. Twitter's no-boundaries access to users means that Twitter makes it easier for even C-level executives to connect as they never have before. I may know and have access to peers in my industry but, prior to Twitter, getting the ear of a CEO in a completely different industry or with a major brand was nearly impossible. One of the beautiful features of Twitter is that it evens out the currency of hierarchy and, theoretically, makes anyone on Twitter accessible to others.

A few compilations have made it even easier to locate C-level executives on Twitter:

- *BusinessWeek* compiled a list of more than 50 CEOs using Twitter: http://images.businessweek.com/ss/09/05/0508_ceos_who_twitter/index.htm.
- Systemic Marketing maintains a list of the Top CMOs on Twitter (as ranked by number of followers): http://www.systemicmarketing.com/top-cmos-on-twitter.
- CTOList.com (http://ctolist.com) is a community of CTOs using Twitter.
- Vistage, a global organization of CEOs of mid-level companies, has a Vistage Twibe: http://www.twibes.com/group/Vistage.
- ExecTweets (http://www.exectweets.com)is a type of Twitter community or aggregator of tweets posted by executives.

Outreach

One of the words you most often read or hear about among Twitter best practices is "transparency." Whether you're entering Twitter as a brand or as an individual (or as a little bit of both), you must be prepared to be transparent. *Transparency* does not mean that you have to give away all your corporate secrets, financials, and marketing plans. Transparency does not mean that all of a sudden your company is a total open book. Transparency, in this case, means that the brand strives for honest, open, and *humanized* communications with the people who are communicating with them. In other words, cut the BS. People on Twitter are not attracted to robotic responses any more than they're attracted to scripted corporate ones.

On Twitter, brands and people intermingle, talk to each other in an open forum, and build mutually beneficial relationships. Twitter is like the Main Street USA of old, where the guy who owned the bank knew what was going on in the life of the grocery store checkout clerk and, because he cared enough to know, she brought her banking business to him. Some of the best ways I've seen Twitter used is when the brand shouts out to its regulars via tweets. "How was your weekend?" or "How did you like that new menu item?" What better way to make a consumer feel like your brand cares than someone taking the time to reach out to them like this?

On Twitter, not only do people express an interest in your life; people are also helping others in ways large and small—everything from sharing information to finding life-saving organ donors. The exchanges produced on Twitter by any number of sources and thought leaders bring us all outside the boundaries of traditional media and business communications. These statements are not solely in the hands of pundits, politicians, talking heads, or journalists. The whole Twitterverse can be involved and make their thoughts known to anyone who wants to hear them, and Twitter more easily enables these people to be heard than traditional forms of media.

As a business, how do you conduct outreach on Twitter? Let's explore.

Establish a Network

At least in one way, getting to the right person on Twitter is not that much different than in the real world: It's all about who you know. Establishing a network, though, does take time and effort. Once you establish your network, you can do outreach much more easily. Your network can significantly reduce the time it takes for you to get the word out.

Building a network has a few recommended steps:

1. **Follow Twitter and other social media experts.** Follow Twitter creators Evan Williams (`@ev`), Biz Stone (`@biz`), and Jack Dorsey (`@jack`); follow social media blogs and pubs like `@Mashable`, `@TechCrunch`, and ReadWriteWeb (`@rww`); follow Power Users (see Chapter 2) who are developing and reporting on the medium. Don't necessarily follow them expecting that they will follow you back. You're following them so you can be kept informed about what's new.
2. **Start sourcing your audience.** In Part II, we'll go into greater detail on how to attract friends, find followers, and monitor the landscape. Strategically, however, think of this much in the same way as you would if you were trying to identify your traditional market segments (by geography, demographics, psychographics, and so forth).
3. **Find your stakeholders.** Users already vested in your organization in some way or another make prime pickings to become part of your Twitter community. Make sure they're aware your organization is on Twitter and seeking their involvement. You should also be following them to keep tabs on their activities and their opinions, and to gain insight into what makes them tick.
4. **Track your competitors.** Though competitors theoretically could block you from following them, Twitter's such a public space that this is not deemed good practice. Following your competition allows you not only to garner competitive intelligence but to also learn from their comings, goings, successes, and failures.
5. **Mine everyone's own followers.** Now that you've read steps 1–4, keep this in mind as you take action. When you find an interesting Twitter user to follow, you should also look at who they're following (see Figure 3.19). Unless the followers-to-following counts are roughly equal, it stands to reason that the higher the caliber of tweep, the more likely you'll find other valuable users to follow within those that this person follows.

Having built your network, you can use it to help spread the word about all kinds of things, from contest and sweepstakes to deals and specials to fun or interesting pictures, podcasts, or video. Your network becomes your own broadcast mechanism.

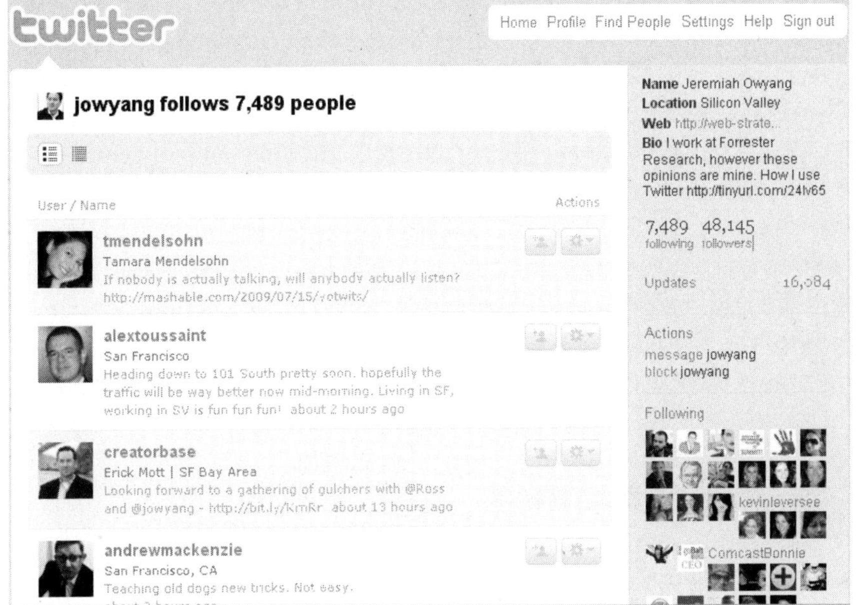

Figure 3.19 Jeremiah Owyang, partner at Altimeter Group, is following these people.

Get in the Conversation

When the people you start following check out your profile in order to decide whether or not to follow you back, it will strike them as odd if you don't have any updates (tweets). At first, your tweets might be more one-way: you tweeting about yourself, your organization, your promotions, and so on. The point is, don't plan on keeping it one-sided for too long. Consumers look for brands on Twitter to be engaged; they want you to reach out to them. In fact, I'd like to see more brands be proactive and **initiate** the engagement rather than waiting for someone to tweet them and be reactive. Getting in on the conversation takes very little effort. Here are some examples:

- **Pose a question.** Don't know what to say? Ask a question instead! Questions are great conversation starters, and these questions don't even need to be related specifically to your business. Ask about current events, favorite sayings, best-ofs, and so forth. Answers to your questions can actually lead to some pretty interesting insights and possibly other new conversations.
- **Seek advice.** Just getting started? Fess up! The Twitter community is a helpful bunch (in fact, they may take pity on you and even help you along in developing your Twitter following). So if you need help with using Twitter and all its various tools and applications, or anything else about Twitter, don't be shy—just ask.

- **Express an opinion.** This is a touchy one for a brand. The more conservative the brand, the less they want opinions expressed other than company-prescreened and -sanctioned ones. Not all opinions have to raise controversy, however. You can always take the optimistic road, and cheer on your followers or share more of your likes than your dislikes (Figure 3.20). Still, the more multidimensional the tweets, the more likely your followers will view you as authentic and truly transparent.
- **Help others.** Of course, if your brand is on Twitter for customer service, helping people will be the mainstay of your responses. More engaged brands, however, will monitor the Twitter stream of their followers and respond to or comment on other tweets in ways that show you can provide insight or expertise.

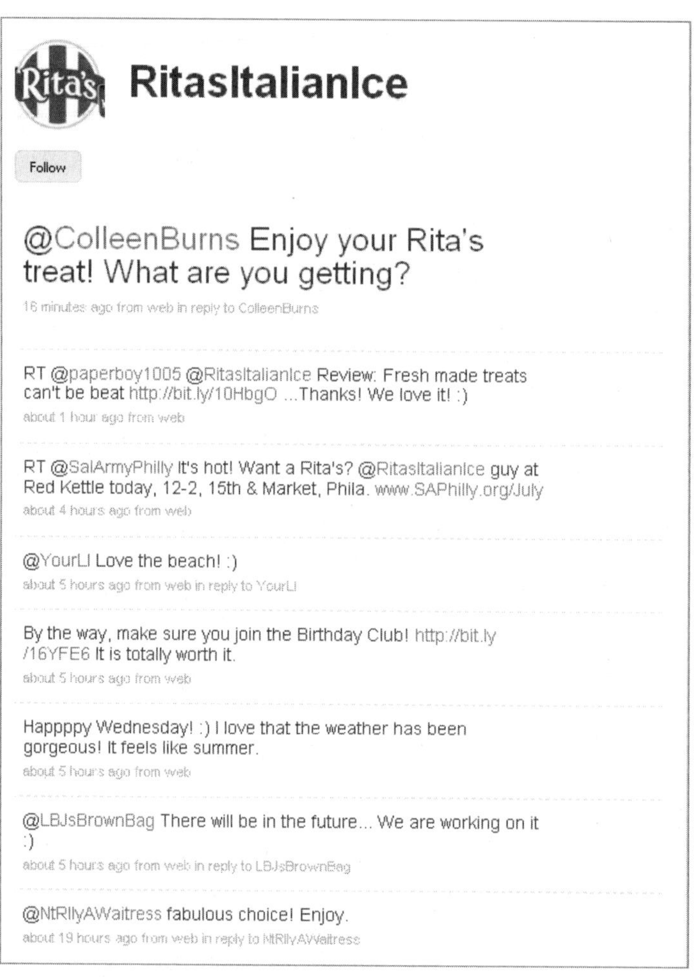

Figure 3.20 Rita's Italian Ice shares positive opinions.

Micro–Focus Groups

Earlier we talked about meeting your Twitter consumers offline. Another form of outreach that you can conduct both offline and online plays on the idea of the focus group. When you have an engaged network, you can recruit their help in evaluating subject matter informally, where you might otherwise go through the expense and time of formal focus groups or research. In the online equivalent of this, you set up a poll or survey for your users to take; in the offline version, you ask people to show up at a location—for example, your offices or someplace central where you can conduct your research without worrying about distraction or disturbance (hence, we do not recommend bars or restaurants for this kind of outreach). You might want to have a sign-up and a cutoff number so you don't attract more people than you need or can accommodate. If the subject matter requires computers, plan on having enough systems available for each of your volunteers, or phase their attendance into shifts. As you'd do with more formal research, you still need to plan and prepare what you'll be asking your volunteers to do and the process by which you want them to do this. You'll also want to determine ahead of time how you're going to sort through and analyze the data you're going to collect.

Results from a Micro–Focus Group

Visit Baltimore (`@BaltimoreMD`) through Twitter specifically contacted local users heavily active on Twitter to come to a happy hour and test their new social media website, VisitMyBaltimore (`http://www.visitmybaltimore.com`). From this test, Visit Baltimore was able to gather feedback and suggestions to incorporate into the site before it went live. The changes resulting from the focus group had favorable results. Visit Baltimore was able to improve the site, engage the local community, educate the community about and promote the new site in advance of its launch, and positively reinforce Visit Baltmore's standing as a local leader in social media. The whole endeavor "cost remarkably less than traditional focus groups," according to Visit Baltimore's director of web marketing, Tom Rowe.

Brand Building

Earlier I touched on brand building and awareness as something brands can gain by using Twitter. Because every touchpoint consumers have with your brand is an opportunity for you to build on the brand, Twitter cannot be ignored. Not having your brand represented on Twitter denies your customers another way to have a positive brand experience. For companies with little or no brand recognition, pay attention. Twitter can help you get there.

Listen! Brands have been accused of not really understanding their consumers. That's kind of hard to do when you're mass marketing. On Twitter, however, you can learn a lot about your brand just by listening and looking for common threads. What do your consumers like or dislike the most about your company? What do they feel you're doing really well or really poorly? What are people saying about your competitors? Are there untapped spaces in your market that no brand is yet reaching? Listening can inform your brand and, from this information, you can not only do a better job taking your company to market on Twitter, but you might actually learn things you can apply to the rest of your marketing efforts as well.

Spread the Touchpoints Around Some brands take a "the more, the merrier" approach to brand building on Twitter. That is, the more that employees are on Twitter, the more possible customer touchpoints. Zappos, Microsoft, Best Buy, and Dell all embrace this approach.

Brand Consistency Existing brands must confront the danger of messaging inconsistent with their brand if they move from traditional marketing to Twitter and other social media. Ultimately, it was the incongruity of helpful, honest, eco-sensitive tweets from a supposed Exxon Mobil representative on Twitter that raised suspicions and led to the exposure of Exxon Mobil's "brand hijacking" (see Figure 3.21).

Figure 3.21 Faux tweets posted by ExxonMobil brand hijacker

Perception Is Reality With the `@ComcastCares` example, we described how Comcast has begun to change customer attitudes with its Twitter efforts. If you own an unknown company with zero reputation, on Twitter you get the luxury of a clean slate. Both your company's personality and reputation can, in part, be built on Twitter. It's like a kid whose family moves across the country and who has the luxury of donning a completely new personality at his or her new school.

Work the Network The time you spend building your network should pay off as you communicate to and with them about your products or services, while at the same time engaging with them about their needs. As your followers tweet, retweet, or reply to your tweets, they help amplify and reinforce your brand. Use your spokespeople as brand ambassadors. If they really believe in your company and what it's doing, don't be afraid to ask them to help you deliver your message.

Integration No kind of brand building can or should exist in a vacuum. That your brand is on Twitter can be cross-promoted through other marketing channels. You can use Twitter to promote other marketing initiatives as well.

NAKEDPizza: Brand Building through Twitter

Much has been written about NAKEDPizza (`@NAKEDPizza`), a lone pizza shop in New Orleans that has so embraced social media that its owners have proclaimed, "We are betting the farm on it." NAKEDPizza has gotten into Twitter in a big way. Its Twitter handle appears on its pizza boxes, carryout menus, direct mail pieces, and website, and in its email newsletters. It has even replaced the giant sign over its location that used to advertise its phone number with a new one featuring the Twitter bird and NAKEDPizza's Twitter handle. NAKEDPizza closely monitors the sales and return on investment (ROI) generated by its Twitter activities, which it can do through trackable Twitter-only specials. Its first Twitter-only promotion drove 15 percent of daily revenues, 90 percent of which were first-time customers. NAKEDPizza has become so proficient and well respected for its Twitter marketing abilities that it's now hosting Twitter Day seminars! All this success and subsequent attention has led it to consider franchising. One criteria, however, would be that franchisees must embrace social media to market their locations.

What NAKEDPizza has done right is everything we've touched on so far regarding Twitter brand engagement. As the NAKEDPizza principals wrote on *Advertising Age's* "Digital Next" blog (`http://adage.com/digitalnext/article?article_id=136957`), "Above all else, Twitter has taught us an obvious but often overlooked lesson of building a new company: The brand is just as much a creation of the end user as it is a product of the ideals and hard work of the founders."

Sales and Lead Generation

The NAKEDPizza story exemplifies sales generation through Twitter. In fact, local businesses, which typically have to operate more nimbly and leaner than their large-brand counterparts, seem to have discovered more early success on Twitter. Much has been written about local businesses, particularly eateries and street food-cart vendors, capitalizing on the low cost and potent marketing power of Twitter. Look up Twitter handles such as `@boloco`, `@caltort`, `@YogiJones`, and `@kogibbq`. These accounts may vary in their number of followers, but all of these food-related entities have had cash-register-ringing success on Twitter. Mashable did a great write-up on Twitter lessons learned from street-cart vendors: `http://mashable.com/2009/07/17/twitter-street-vendors`. Now bars such as the Walrus Saloon in Boulder, Colorado (`@boulderwalrus`), real estate brokers (`@Kevin_Curtis`), local authors groups (`@readinglocal`), and massage therapists (`@truemassage`; Figure 3.22) all work magic through Twitter.

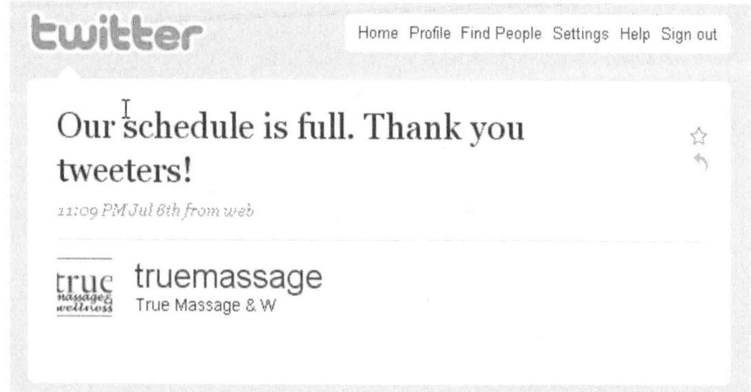

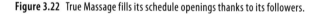

Figure 3.22 True Massage fills its schedule openings thanks to its followers.

One of the most noteworthy examples of "working Twitter magic" to gain sales also involves a pizza shop. I love the title on the blog on which this story appeared: "How Tony & Alba Stole $75 from Jake on Twitter." This whole blog post is a must-read: (`http://www.ryankuder.com/2009/04/how-tony-alba-stole-75-from-jake-on-twitter`). Tony & Alba (`@tonyalba_pizza`) is a pizza joint in Silicon Valley. The blog's author, Ryan Kuder (`@ryankuder`), was actually the beneficiary of Tony & Alba's Twitter savvy. Al, the clever manager at Tony & Alba, figured out that if they tracked their local competitors (in this case Jake's), they might be able to intervene and pick up some business. As Kuder and his friend tweeted about dinner plans at Jake's after the kids' soccer practice, Al picked up on the discussion and—even though the pizza shop was 15 minutes farther away than Jake's—managed to woo Kuder and his party of 12 with no wait and free fountain drinks. "All because of a tweet." Potent stuff!

Featured Case: Kodak and the Risk of Ignoring

When asked why Kodak got involved in Twitter, the company's chief marketing officer and vice president, Jeffrey Hayzlett, starts by explaining, "there's no better way to engage the various audiences that are important to the company." Since Kodak established its first official Twitter account in May 2008, they've found tangible benefits in being able to update quickly and to continuously follow employees, customers, the media, and others who want to know what's happening at the company. The company found Twitter so beneficial that, in the past year, it greatly increased Kodak's presence on Twitter with several more active accounts, including specialized ones for specific business units and special projects such as `@KodakChallenge` and `@IDigPrint`. Kodak has an official company social media policy/rules of engagement for all corporate tweeters. These guidelines help ensure that all employees are totally clear on the appropriate use of this medium. (See Appendix D, "Social Media Guidelines.")

For Kodak, social media helps build the brand organically. It illustrates their relevance and keeps the brand top-of-mind. Hayzlett says, "There's no better feeling than to get an excited response to a tweet by an employee or customer about something they didn't know we did, or to hear about their support of our activities." Kodak does get some negative feedback, but the company treats that as a benefit as well. Hayzlett explains: "With Twitter, I receive negative comments directly, not filtered through people whose job it is to manage feedback. So I get the unvarnished truth, which helps me understand the real concerns of our customers."

The company tracks and attributes all kinds of positive gains from Twitter, such as media coverage, sales leads, increased product consideration, and direct product purchase. It did not enter Twitter expecting or seeking ROI. Instead, Kodak thinks of social media ROI as "risk of ignoring." Hayzlett acknowledges, "in this environment, people are discussing and debating your brand and products, whether you're there or not. All conversations, whether a person has one follower or a million, are worth tracking because we get a chance to hear from our customers, and we learn new things every day."

Small, local businesses aren't the only companies that can attribute direct sales to Twitter, however. It's well documented that Dell credits Twitter with generating at least $3 million in new sales for the company. Also, let's not forget charities that are using Twitter for directing fundraising efforts.

Important Lead Generation Considerations

Twitter is not only a source of immediate sales. Chicago public relations agency Arment Dietrich (whose business was up 26 percent as of summer 2009) attributed 40 percent of its new business leads directly to its Twitter efforts, particularly the active engagement of its CEO, Gini Dietrich (`@ginidietrich`). But getting on Twitter expecting to generate sales or leads without a clear understanding of what's involved is just foolhardy. Like any other marketing and sales tactic from which you want to derive results, you need a realistic framework, a solid plan, and resources to work that plan. Think through some of these factors before you leap:

- What constitutes a lead for your organization, how detailed does that lead have to be in order to be considered qualified, and can leads be obtained through activities on Twitter?
- How will you measure unique leads? If you don't have some unique actions to separate and quantify Twitter leads, what will it take to put such things together and how much time will this take before you're ready to go live?
- How will you track leads from Twitter and attribute them accordingly? Do you have the tools at your disposal already, or do you need to review and consider the options?
- If leads have a higher dollar value, they will most likely require the cultivation of a relationship. Therefore, the company (or company representative) profile and persona on Twitter must firmly be developed before engaging in lead generation activities. Are you there yet, and if not, how much time is the development of this engaged profile going to take?

Customer Service

Most major brands on Twitter have primarily embraced it as another platform with which to deliver customer service. That's OK. Doing so is a relatively safe, benign, and, in some instances, a much-needed solution. It also gives consumers a feeling of comfort: Perhaps there's something more tangible about tweeting your brand and getting a response back than talking to a faceless voice on the phone or typing with a faceless and voiceless representative on live chat. Before you decide to engage in a customer-service approach to Twitter, you'll want to keep the following in mind:

- **People like dealing with people.** Even if your brand is being represented by your logo, try not to make that a nameless entity as well. Identify the people who will be responding to the consumer's questions, whether that's a single person or multiple people servicing a single account. GM (`@gmblogs`), Graco (`@graco`), The Home Depot (`@homedepot`), and Dunkin' Donuts (`@dunkindonuts`) all do this well.
- **Twitter expectations are in real time, baby!** Used to the 24-hour turnaround time afforded by email? Fuggetaboutit on Twitter. Customers will expect some kind of response within minutes or hours, not days. If you think this kind of response rate will tax your resources, ramp up your resources before you start up with Twitter.
    - If you're concerned about response-rate times, you might want to mitigate complaints by adding some copy in your brand's Twitter bio about response-time expectations.

- **Don't just wait for the request for service to come to you.** Users might be more apt to complain than to contact your company for problem resolution. Use Twitter search tools to help you locate users talking either positively or negatively about your brand or products, and empower your Twitter customer service reps to reach out and help them.
  - Convert a negative into a positive. You might even be rewarded by someone tweeting about how these kinds of efforts helped turn their situation around. Both compliments and complaints travel fast on Twitter.
- **Identify consumers in the research phase of buying.** Users posing questions or seeking recommendations about products can also be found through search. Customer-service reps can make themselves available to answer questions, suggest appropriate products, provide helpful links, and even offer discounts or promotions to close the deal. Whatever that rep can do to personalize the interaction will help. Twitter blurs the line between passive customer service and active consumer selling.
- **Promote favorable experiences and encourage future engagement.** Use the positive experience to thank customers for their business now and in the future. Encourage them to return with any future questions or concerns. If all goes well, every now and then, use the experience subtly to toot your own horn ("Very happy to have solved `@[customer's name]` problem with her dishwasher issue.") You never know if, in doing so, you may make another user realize that they can come to you on Twitter about this very same problem.
- **Don't forget to listen and learn.** Develop an internal process for taking in and utilizing the nuggets of wisdom you learn by listening to your Twitterverse.

Key Questions to Consider for Branding

As I've stated before, Twitter isn't going to be for every company. Even if it's right for you, making it work for you requires at the very least the commitment of internal resources, mostly in the form of time. In Part III, "Month 2: Develop and Launch Your Strategic Plan," we're really going to roll up our sleeves and show you how to develop and launch a Twitter marketing strategy. For now, here's a list of questions to get you thinking about what factors to consider.

Do we have an audience on Twitter? How does that audience match our traditional audience? Clearly, if your audience is unlikely to be on Twitter (or at least not right now), Twitter might not be where you want to focus your attention and resources at the moment. If you determine your audience *is* on Twitter (oftentimes verified through some simple searches), then it's definitely worth exploring Twitter's viability for your organization.

What are our competitors doing on Twitter? I'm not one to advocate a "follow the competitors' lead" strategy of marketing. Too many times I see companies hindered by their reluctance to enter into marketing tactics unless their competitors are there first. I do believe, however, that it's wise to investigate the lay of the land with respect to your competitors to get perspective. With regards to Twitter, you'll want to understand if your competitors are currently using Twitter and how. You may choose to differentiate yourself by using Twitter differently—or you may want to take the same course of action and just execute it better. If you find your competitors missing from Twitter, you'll be able to be first to market, which isn't such a poor position to be in.

What is our objective going to be on Twitter? This whole chapter has been devoted to telling you all the ways in which you can use Twitter. Sometimes, those ways can be used in tandem to meet a singular objective (promotions, entertainment, sales, and lead generation, for example), but in other circumstances, one objective might be too far apart from another for you to expect both to be married successfully in a single Twitter account. You need to define ahead of time the purpose of this account's existence so that you can communicate this to the people who will be tweeting on your behalf.

How are we going to measure our Twitter success? What are the metrics we will use to do this? There are a number of criteria you can use to track and measure, but that doesn't mean these measurements are relevant to you and your efforts. For example, there are those who'd advise you to build a huge following because you can amplify your reach. If your objective is to service customers on a one-to-one level, however, your follower count won't come into play. Other measurements aren't as easy to extract without using additional tools. What are some of the things you can measure? Here's a short list:

- Number of followers
- Number of tweets
- Number of @ replies or DMs (also received versus sent)
- Number of click-throughs on trackable URLs
- Number of customers serviced per day/week/month
- Number of those customers retained month over month
- Number of retweets
- Total reach of those retweets (retweets × number of followers of each retweeter)
- Number of times your hashtag is used
- Favorites
- Influence
- Referring website traffic
- Conversions generated
    - Sales
    - Leads
    - Email opt-ins
- Secondary benefits, such as media coverage

Featured Case: FlyCast/Growing a User Base

FlyCast (`http://www.flycast.fm`) is a free service that allows listeners to stream thousands of different channels of music and talk-radio programming to their mobile phones. This includes hundreds of radio stations, terrestrial and Internet-only stations, podcasts (both audio and video), and other specialized content. (Consequently, FlyCast has Twitter handles that correspond to these genres—for example, `@FCTopJazz`, `@FCTopHipHop`, and so on—rather than a single corporate account.) It was looking for ways to promote its service and decided to try using Twitter. Within its application, FlyCast developed and integrated the ability for users to Tweet This Song or Tweet This Program. Listeners can call attention to what they are listening to via FlyCast by tweeting it, and their followers can click on the link to listen, whether the follower has FlyCast installed or not. Rather than jumping into the song or program midstream, the follower gets to hear it from the very start. To avoid copyright issues, these tweeted links are active for only two hours after they are posted.

Immediately after launching this initiative, hundreds of listeners began tweeting the music they were listening to, and hundreds more clicked through and got to share the music their friends recommended. For many, this was the first time they had ever heard of FlyCast, let alone had an immediate interactive FlyCast application on their desktop or mobile device. As a result, FlyCast has found a successful, low-cost way to add thousands of new listeners to its user base. It considers its Twitter initiative its "un-promotion."

What will be our brand personality on Twitter? What is the voice of our brand? If you've read this far, you realize that Twitter demands personality of its users, be that brand or individual. Thought needs to be put into what that personality will be and, as a consequence, how the voice of the brand will come across. Will it be warm and humorous? Caring and concerned? Technical or topical? You get to decide.

What should our Twitter "look" be, and how will that represent our brand? Once you determine your brand personality and voice, how will you want to represent that through the design elements that Twitter make available to you? Simple things such as your page background and avatar will play a role in the first impression your brand makes on someone visiting you on Twitter.

Who's going to oversee our Twitter efforts? Because your Twitter account is going to be the voice of your brand, it cannot just be thrown up there with no oversight or management. Someone needs to be in charge and, if your company doesn't have a social community manager, as the role tends to be called, you'll need to assign responsibility.

Featured Case: University of Baltimore/ Towson University MBA/Communication

Communication is important to any college or university, and it's no different with the unique co-university MBA program offered by the University of Baltimore and Towson University @UBTowsonMBA). The program first joined Twitter as a way to communicate with current students, prospective students, alumni, and other community stakeholders, as well as a way to build brand awareness. They believed that being on Twitter was a way to demonstrate some of their core differentiators by engaging their community of followers and adding benefits for them. The program clearly defined its purpose for being on Twitter, stating as much on their Twitter profile page background: "Topics we tweet" (MBA program news and events; topics of interest to students; the MBA degree; business; and social media). The program "uses a cadre of strategies and techniques to make connections—and not just any connections, but the RIGHT connections." That means @UBTowsonMBA intentionally chose not to amass large numbers of followers but rather a smaller number of focused, critical thinkers.

Though the schools don't have statistical information on increased MBA applications as a result of Twitter, applications are up and they have positive affirmation from students who have said they have better school communication because of Twitter. Says MBA school director, Ron Desi (@rondesi), "All I can say is given our message to the marketplace, we need to be on Twitter."

Do we currently have the internal resources and empowerments Twitter will demand? Just because someone's been put in charge of your brand's Twitter activities doesn't mean that person also had the bandwidth to be active on Twitter. Twitter will require manpower—that is, people to monitor tweets and respond in a timely fashion. Who will those people be? In conjunction with this activity, will you empower these people to manage, update, and respond to inquiries or complaints without prior authorization or concerns from corporate PR or Legal departments?

What is our corporate policy for our employees using Twitter? Has your company already established a social media policy that includes protocol for employees using Twitter? Does this policy delineate between tweeting on behalf of the company and tweeting on company time, or about anything having to do with the company? If a policy has not already been established, it ought to be readied prior to launching any initiatives on Twitter.

How should we organize our Twitter account(s)? As I alluded to earlier, organizations typically approach Twitter by adopting one of three account structure types:

- **Single account/single user:** A single user per account will respond to requests and messages.

- **Single account/multiusers:** In this situation, the brand maintains a single account, but more than one employee at any given time can respond. Managing this kind of approach behind the scenes can be facilitated by a number of multi-user tools on the market.
- **Multiple accounts/multiple users:** An organization might encourage a company-wide Twitter adoption strategy in which multiple users represent the brand through many accounts.

How should we access Twitter to manage our strategy? What applications or devices works best? There is no single cut-and-dry best answer to this question. These days, new applications come to market regularly, and everyone seems to be giving them a whirl. The solution that's best for your organization needs to, in part, be a function of your approach to your accounts and who will be tweeting on behalf of your company. In later sections of this book, we'll be surveying the various tools currently at our disposal so you can begin to assess what's right for your organization.

Are there any products we have to develop to promote our Twitter feed? The more complex your approach to Twitter, the more you'll want to think about additional technology or solutions that you might need to have in order to manage or optimize your efforts. Some of these might not be readily apparent until you become more active on Twitter. Just don't rule anything out going in.

When Times Get Tough, the Tough Get Twittering

It's common knowledge that when times get tough on a business, one of the first budget-line items to get cut is marketing. Businesses know this isn't a wise move, and yet many do it. Twitter, however, is the kind of activity that you could benefit from in the long run, even if it's executed on a shoestring.

Social media is akin to public relations, and most companies will readily acknowledge the benefit of good PR. Twitter can help elevate your brand's visibility, the public's impression of your brand, and better still, their direct interaction with your brand. Also, Twitter can be a way to invigorate and involve your staff. They can help tweet for your brand, listen to what people are saying, come up with suggestions to help your company in all kinds of ways, and provide customer service or relations that helps secure and protect what business you have.

The other day I passed a billboard that read, "Recession 101: Bill Gates started Microsoft during a recession." It seems to me that perhaps a recession might be the ideal time to start using Twitter, too.

Featured Case: ACME Production Resources/Awareness

ACME Production Resources (`http://www.theacmecorp.com`) needed to find a cost-effective way to build awareness of its company among event planners and other potential clients in the local and surrounding community. Marketing assistant Carolyn Fraser started tweeting on behalf of the company (`@acmemilwaukee`) in December 2008. Using Twitter Search to find companies and individuals in ACME's vicinity of Wisconsin and Chicago who were tweeting about events, she followed as many of these people as she could, as well as whomever they followed or tweeted on a regular basis. By adding her name and some information about herself to her profile, Fraser personalized her Twitter account so that other Twitter users could get to know the person behind the Tweets instead of a faceless corporation. She created a Twitter background with a collage of pictures to showcase the lighting the company had done.

Strategically, Fraser tries to `@` reply to at least one post in her stream per day, and to retweet at least one interesting link or post a day. She tries to tweet only when she has something interesting or valuable to add to a conversation, but she doesn't want a day to go by without at least one post. Fraser also posts pictures of the lighting that the company does at events, using tools such as BudURL and TwitPic to keep track of click-throughs. She engages in conversations with members of the media through tweets and direct messages, regularly recommends people on `#followfriday`, and has added the account to multiple Twitter directories.

As a result of these humble efforts, this local small business found that Twitter has helped them with networking, sales, marketing, and PR. Through Twitter, Fraser has been able to build the company's relationships with area photographers who now supply them with free pictures of their lighting for marketing use. Fraser's Twitter followers send her direct messages with contact information for potential leads. She has connected with a job website that will post ACME's internship openings for free. Fraser has also connected with several local reporters using Twitter, and one ended up featuring Fraser on the *BizTimes Milwaukee* blog as Executive of the Week. Fraser says, "We have found Twitter to be a very beneficial marketing tool to grow our small business."

Is a budget available? The answer to the previous questions should make evident what you might need dollars-wise to allocate to your Twitter efforts. More than anything, Twitter will demand time and staff resources. How will this impact other personnel demands that already exist? Will you need to hire staff to offset the imbalance? Other costs may be borne by certain tools and applications your organization chooses to use, or Twitter-only promotions it wants to run.

Where are our points of integration? As I've said before, Twitter is not a stand-alone marketing tactic. It should be considered part of a marketing toolset. Your organization most definitely should consider how Twitter will integrate with the other marketing activities you do and vice versa. Will you want to promote your Twitter efforts through advertising? Wrap it into your other online efforts such as email marketing, Facebook pages, and so forth? Will you want to redeploy users from other marketing initiatives to become involved with you on Twitter?

Do we have buy-in from leadership? Depending on your organization, you may need to find answers to all the previous questions before taking the idea to corporate leadership for approval—or you may want to secure some initial buy-in and then do the legwork to flesh out the details. Either way, at some point, your leadership is going to need to approve this very public effort in which your organization plans to partake. For some companies, this kind of activity can be very unsettling. Be prepared to have a solid game plan.

The Main Points

- Twitter can't be pigeonholed into a single type of solution for every organization. It can serve different purposes depending on the organization's goals and objectives. Twitter's versatility is limited only by imagination ... and 140 characters.
- Speed and the need for immediate gratification go hand-in-hand on Twitter. If you plan to get involved as an organization, be prepared to be committed and respond quickly.
- Successful brands combine responsiveness with proactivity. They don't just wait for people to come to them. They engage first, often enticing people through this engagement.
- There are a lot of factors to consider when determining if Twitter is right for your company. Your initial strategy may end up zigging when you planned to zag because of the needs of your community.

Month 1: Master Twitter Fundamentals

II

Now it's time to learn Twitter basics as an individual user. We'll set up your Twitter account, review the rules of Twitter etiquette, and show you the various tools at your disposal to enhance your Twitter experience so you can move from being a Twitter user to being a Twitter marketer in Part III. As you go through this process, you'll find that using and working with Twitter is cyclical, so we'll pepper you with reminders along the way. Although a lot of your work will be repetitive, repeating these actions will teach you the nuances and best practices of Twitter. You might not think you can learn very much by tweaking a mere 140 characters, but you definitely can—and will!

Week 1: Get on Twitter

This is the fun part. Getting on Twitter is easy. You won't need to agonize over too many decisions at this point. I'm going to give you some good practice exercises and food for thought. Although you'll be taking in a lot of information, Twitter's cyclical "rinse, wash, and repeat" process will give you plenty of practice so you can get the hang of things and test run more than a tool or two. By the end of Week 1, you'll be up and running. By the end of the month, you should be quite prepared to transition your personal Twitter experiences to business marketing ones.

4

Chapter Contents

If you haven't gotten on Twitter yet, don't worry. I'll walk you through the entire process and make sure you get yourself going properly. I'll start with the really easy stuff and move on from there. By the end of the week, you should feel like you're really getting the hang of all this tweeting and Twitter stuff.

Monday: Create an Account

You can't really be anything more than an outsider looking in on Twitter unless you create an account. As we touched on in Chapter 1, "Understand Twitter," creating a Twitter account is both free and easy to do. Your Twitter account will serve as the central hub for maintaining your public (or private) Twitter profile, managing your alerts, and communicating with the Twitter community at large. Your account is an integral part of Twitter's overall user experience and, therefore, careful planning—as well as a bit of creativity—should be put into the account-creation process.

Before getting started, ask yourself these questions:

- Will I be tweeting mainly as myself?
- Will I be tweeting mainly as a representative of my company?
- Will I be sharing Twitter responsibilities with one or more people?

The answers to these types of questions will determine how you go about setting up your account. If you're planning to create multiple Twitter accounts, perhaps one for personal use and another for business, the same fundamentals apply. To get the most out of your Twitter presence, no matter what its purpose, plan on giving each individual account the care and attention it deserves during the account-creation process to build a solid foundation for Twitter success.

Single Accounts

Most Twitter users have just one Twitter account because a single Twitter account suffices—even for businesses. A single account is ideal for almost anyone, be they small-business owners, entrepreneurs, bloggers, marketers, or even CEOs. A cursory look into the Twitterverse reveals users from all walks of life, each using his or her own Twitter account to network, connect, and share on a personal level. (See Figure 4.1.)

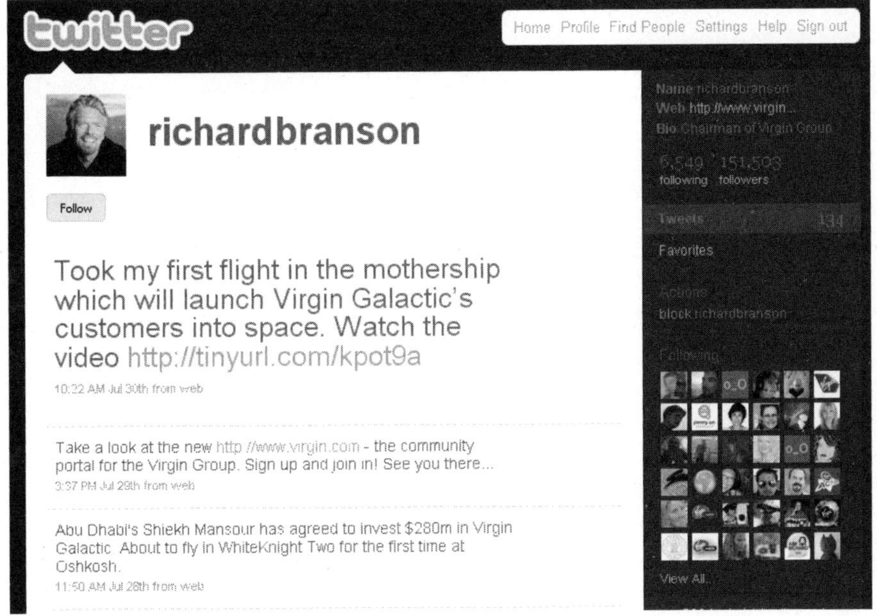

Figure 4.1 Example of a single account: Richard Branson, CEO of Virgin Group

Multiple Accounts

Establishing and maintaining more than one Twitter account is also quite common and is sometimes even a necessity. Multiple accounts are appropriate in the following examples:

- Individuals who want to keep business interactions and personal dealings separate can benefit by setting up multiple Twitter accounts.
- People who want to reduce the *noise ratio* on Twitter by segmenting the types of information they share can do this with multiple Twitter accounts. For example, someone can belong to two very different trade associations and keep an active Twitter account for each, so that the conversations are focused. Someone who has very divergent passions and interests may also want to set up several accounts.
- Companies may decide to maintain one Twitter account solely for customer service and another for official company news and updates.
- Corporations that want to segregate social media marketing efforts by department, region, or revenue stream would need to set up multiple Twitter accounts. (See Figure 4.2.)

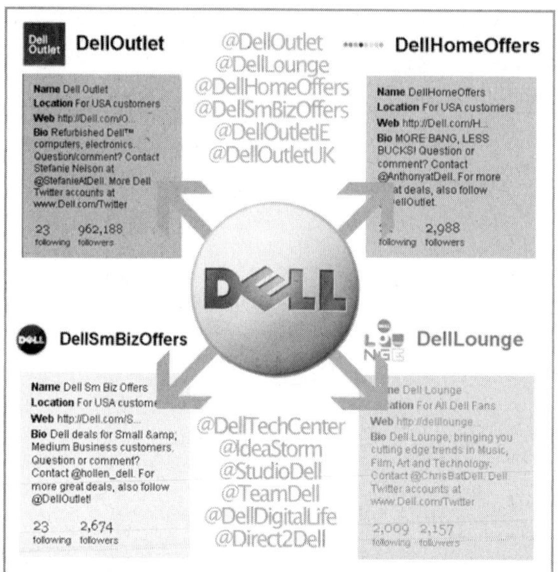

Figure 4.2 Dell's multiple-account scenarios

There is no limit to the number of Twitter accounts you can create. Each Twitter account, however, must be linked to a unique email address. (Currently, Twitter does not validate this email address; however, due to the growing number of spammers exploiting Twitter, this might change in the future.) Maintaining multiple Twitter accounts is not unlike managing multiple email accounts. For example, a business may use one email for general contact inquiries, another for sales, and another for press communications.

Twitter has alluded to creating special services for businesses, but right now, there is only one type of Twitter account. Having multiple accounts simply means creating and maintaining more than one Twitter account. The task of managing and maintaining multiple Twitter accounts is made easier thanks to the Twitter UI or user-interface applications that have this functionality built in. We'll discuss these in depth in Part III, "Month 2: Develop and Launch Your Strategic Plan."

Let's cover the account-creation process in more detail, being mindful that these early actions are the crucial first steps of your long-term Twitter strategy. We're going to proceed at first as if you're only using Twitter for casual, not business, gain so you can get comfortable with the process and ordinary use of Twitter. As we take you through this first week (where you'll set up your account) to the fourth week (where you'll gain an understanding of how to measure, track, and place meaning behind your Twitter activity), you'll learn what you need to know to move on to Twittering on behalf of your business. Keeping your Twitter goals in mind during this process will help you make better decisions each step along the way.

Monday's One-Hour Exercise: Create a Twitter Account

Creating a Twitter account is as easy as 1, 2, 3.

1. Sign up.
2. Find people to follow.
3. Start tweeting!

We're going to walk you through these steps as your exercise assignment. Even if you have previously set up a Twitter account, follow along because you might pick up a tip or two.

1. Using your favorite web browser, head to `http://www.twitter.com`.
2. Under Join the Conversation, click the Sign Up Now button (see Figure 4.3).

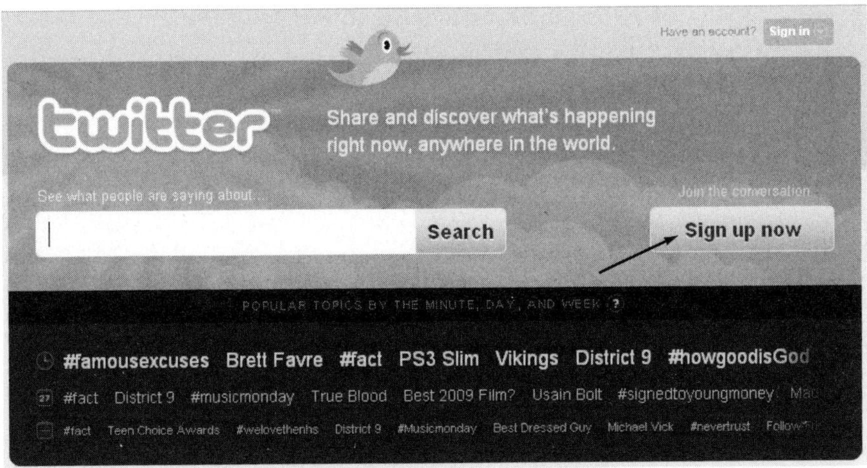

Figure 4.3 The Sign Up Now button on Twitter's home page

3. Fill out the simple Join the Conversation form that asks you for the credentials shown in Figure 4.4.
4. Twitter asks for your first and last names; however, it's not a requirement to complete this field at all, and if you do, you may enter any name you wish.

   This *handle* will be the nickname by which all other Twitter users will know you. Usernames cannot exceed 15 characters. Twitter will reject usernames that are already being used. Your username is the most important part of your Twitter identity. It's the way to tell Twitter who you are: people will identify you, reply to you, and refer to you in conversations by this name. Twitter handles can impact both personal and business branding. These tips will help you create your username:

   - Usernames cannot exceed 15 characters.
   - Usernames cannot contain any special characters, apart from an underscore (_).

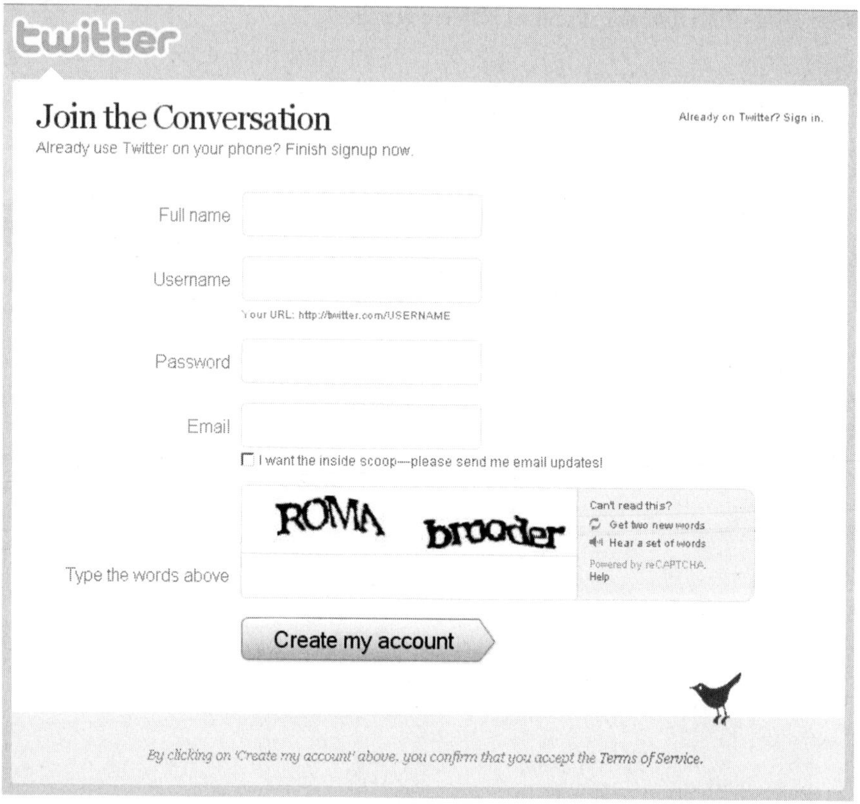

Figure 4.4 Twitter's sign-up form

- Twitter does not distinguish between capital and lowercase characters—e.g., the username `@MyUsername` is the same as `@myusername`. You can change the capitalization in your displayed username at any time.
- Certain words (such as "Twitter," "tweet," and "admin") can't be used in Twitter usernames.
- Long usernames leave fewer characters available for tweeting.
- If the name you choose is accepted, Twitter will display the OK symbol to the right of the Username text box.

If you're stuck for ideas, or if the username you really want is already taken, skip ahead or complete the password and email fields and then come back to username later.

5. Enter the password with which you plan to access Twitter. Twitter passwords can be anything you like, but they must contain at least six characters.
6. Enter the email address you want Twitter to use for your account. This will be the address where you receive notifications about new Twitter followers and DMs as well as Twitter-related updates, should you choose to receive them.

Twitter will not email you unless it receives your permission. As mentioned earlier, each email address must be unique per account, so if you already have a Twitter account and are creating a new one, you cannot use the same email address you used for your other account.

7. A two-word *Captcha phrase* will appear in the image field. Enter the two-word phrase in the Type the Words Above entry box. This verifies to Twitter that you are indeed a human visitor and not a software program.
8. Click the Create My Account button.

Usernames for Individuals

If you will be tweeting as yourself, don't be afraid to use your real name. This is a common convention encouraged by Twitter, and one you will see quite often (see Figure 4.5).

Figure 4.5 Real people using their real names

If your real name is very long, however, or if someone else is already using your name, you might consider using a shortened or alternative name such as the following:

- A nickname
- Initials or abbreviations instead of fully spelling out your name (e.g., if `@trevorjones` is taken, try `@tmjones` or `@trevjones`), a commonplace practice for individuals and brands with long names
- An underscore to separate elements of your desired username (e.g., if `@johnsmith` is taken, try `@john_smith`)
- Alternative spellings, such as removing vowels or using intentional but still easily readable misspellings
- A combination of your first name and something you enjoy doing or something else about you (e.g., `@IrishJames` or `@LisaTeaches`)
- A handle created by appending meaningful numbers to the end of your first name, such as the year you were born, your favorite athlete's number, and so forth

- A username created by adding something witty or clever to your name to make it stand out and give it some personality (e.g., if `@sarahbarnes` is taken, try `@SarahRules`, `@IAmSarah`, or `@HeyItsSarah`)
- Any other modification to your original name that still suits you

Twitter will intervene to reclaim names for celebrities and other distinguished individuals. It created its Verified Account program to authenticate the tweeter for the rest of the Twitterverse. Some well-known people have also turned to using "TheReal" or "The_Real" as part of their usernames to authenticate them.

For people who can't or don't use their real names as their usernames, it's good practice to share their real names in their user profiles instead. It's up to you to decide, however, what you feel is appropriate and what makes you comfortable.

Username Dos and Don'ts

- Do choose a username that expresses who you are.
- Do be creative when choosing your username.
- Do choose something attention-grabbing.
- Do choose a username that is easy to read and pronounce.
- Do keep it simple. (See Figure 4.6.)

Figure 4.6 Well-created usernames

- Don't use profane, offensive, or hateful language in your username. Although not explicitly prohibited by Twitter, these types of names should be avoided.
- Don't attempt to impersonate someone else—it is against Twitter's terms of service and could get you banned.
- Don't choose a username that is hard to understand or is purposefully confusing, a tactic that many spammers favor.

Usernames for Brands

Brands should follow the same "real name" best practices as individuals, although with the boom in Twitter, someone may already have taken your brand name. Twitter does not permit username-squatting, impersonation, or trademark infringement. In these cases, and if you own the rights to that name, Twitter will work with you to regain that name for your use. We provide more information about this in Chapter 8, "Week 5: Develop a Successful Twitter Strategy."

I Created My Account. Now What?

Once you've successfully created your account, Twitter will take you to a screen that says, "See if your friends are on Twitter." At this point you may enter in a Gmail, Yahoo!, or AOL email address and password and click Continue to see if Twitter can find anyone you might know from your address book. We're going to cover this in further detail on Tuesday, so you can choose Skip This Step for now. The next screen also helps you find friends with its "Look who else is here. Start following them!" suggestions. Skip these too for the time being.

After the account is created, Twitter will automatically direct you to your main Twitter profile page (Figure 4.7) and send an email to the email address you provided when you set up your account. This is just a general email welcoming you to Twitter—no further action is required.

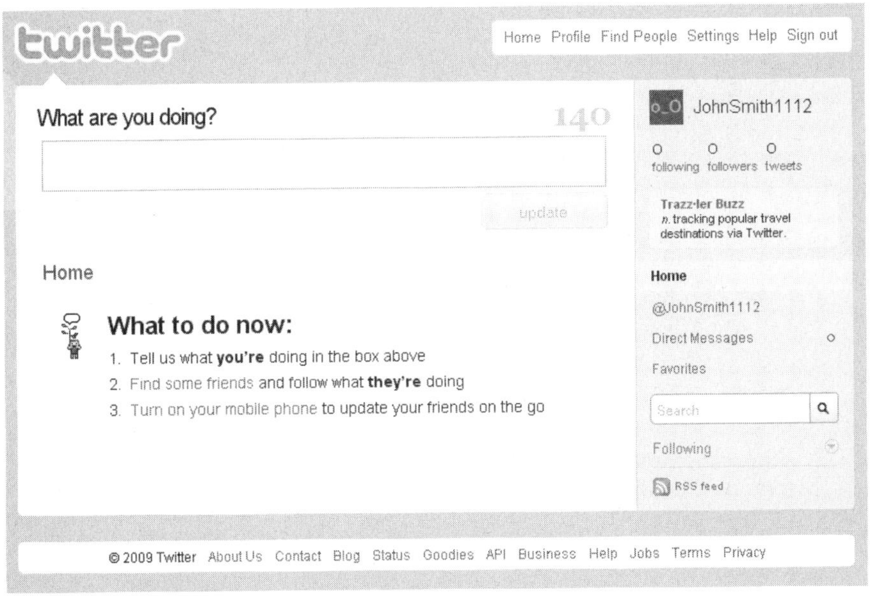

Figure 4.7 A newly minted Twitter account profile page

You may have created your account, but you're not ready to start tweeting just yet! (See Figure 4.8.)

Figure 4.8 Stop before you tweet.

Before You Start Using Your Twitter Account

Before you begin to tweet, add followers, or begin poking around Twitter as a Twitter newbie, you should do a couple of things. Click the Settings link located at the upper right of your profile page (Figure 4.9).

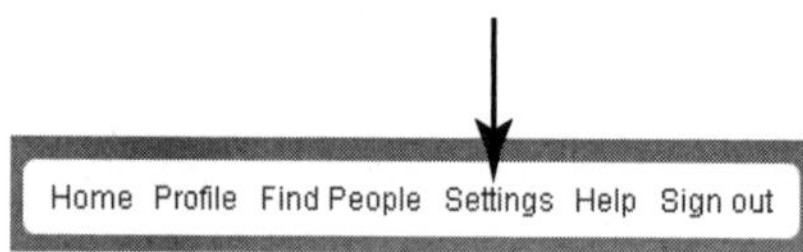

Figure 4.9 Accessing your Twitter settings

The Settings screen contains multiple tabs. Let's go through them, starting with a few of the easiest ones first.

Devices Click the Devices tab. Here is where you can associate your Twitter account with a mobile device for tweeting via text messaging. Doing so is completely optional. If you tweet via text messaging, it's important to realize that standard text messaging rates from your phone carrier may apply.

Recommended Actions for Devices:

1. Enter your mobile phone number into the text box, and then click Save. You must read about and acknowledge that standard text messaging rates may apply.
2. Follow Twitter's on-screen instructions to verify that your number is correct.

Optional Actions for Devices:

1. Select your device updates (On, Off, Direct Message). If you select On, Twitter will send you tweets from everyone you're following and everyone who sends

you a message. That will be a lot of text messages before too long! You can elect to receive just direct messages, which will cut down on the volume of texts you get but will still deliver those more personal messages to your phone.

2. Enable the Sleep feature from *X* time of day to *Y* time of day. This can curtail the number of tweets you get if you choose to enable your device updates.

Notices Notices consist of three options for you to check:

- **New Follower Emails: Email when someone starts following me.** The default setting is On.
- **Direct Text Emails: Email when I receive a new direct message.** (This should really say "Direct Message Emails," because a notification is delivered regardless of the means by which someone sends it.) The default setting is On.
- **Email Newsletter: I want the inside scoop—please send me email updates!**" The default setting is Off.

If you change any of these checkboxes, be sure to click Save before moving on.

The next steps are the most important ones. You'll be completing your Twitter profile (Figure 4.10), which means you'll be personalizing your account the way you want the Twitterverse to perceive you. To personalize your account, Twitter provides additional ways, apart from your username, to tell the Twitter community about yourself. These customizations give potential followers a sense of who you are and what you'll be tweeting about. Established Twitter users tend to be leery of accounts with sparse or suspicious profile information, because this is a characteristic of spammers. Do yourself a favor and complete your profile before venturing into Twitterville.

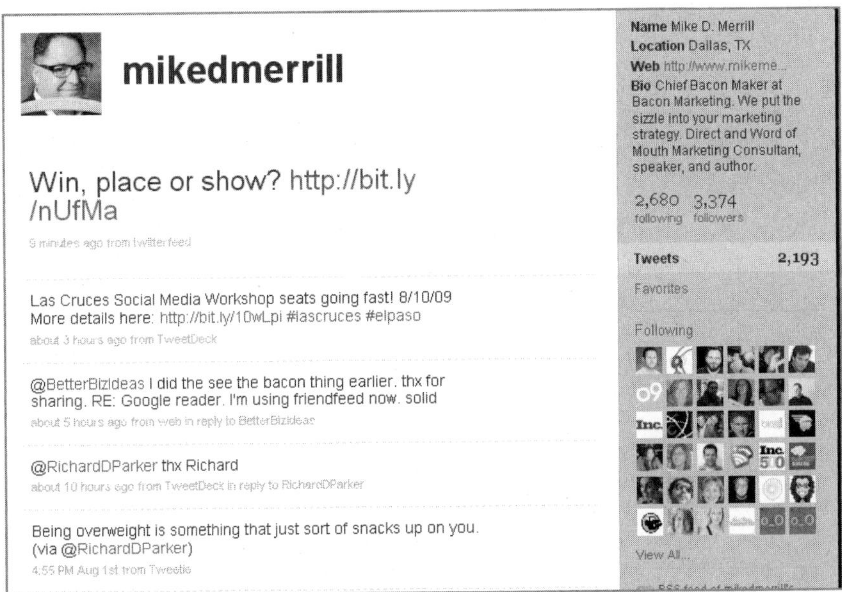

Figure 4.10 A completed profile page

Let's take a closer look at these public elements of your Twitter profile. (Even if your Twitter profile is set to be private, these components are still plainly visible to anyone visiting your profile page.)

Your Twitter account profile is composed of six basic parts:

- Username
- Location
- More Info URL
- One-line bio
- Your photo or picture
- A background image or design

The latter two are the only items not found in the Account tab, so let's deal with the other four first. (See Figure 4.11)

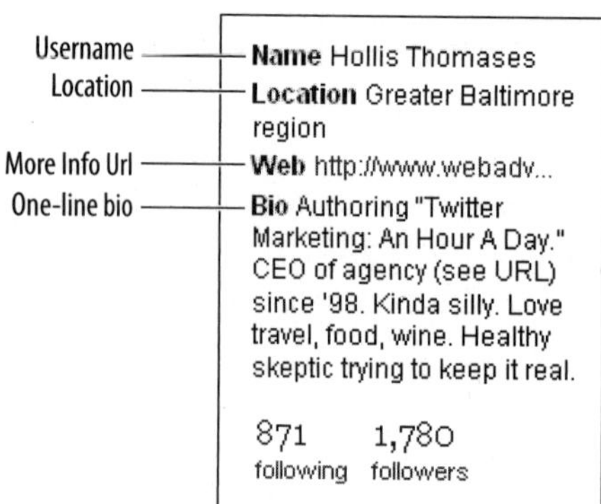

Figure 4.11 Profile parts found in the Account Settings tab

Account

In the Account tab, your username and email will have already been filled in from when you created your account. You'll now want to take the following recommended actions:

1. Fill in your Name. If you're tweeting as yourself, use your first and last name; if you're tweeting on behalf of your company, you can use the company's name. The more you want to use Twitter for marketing, the more you want to avoid pseudonyms or cutesy names.
2. Check to make sure your Time Zone setting is correct. Timestamps are applied to all of your tweets, so it is important to make sure your time setting is correct.
3. In the More Info URL field, enter the URL to which you'd like to direct your profile visitors. This could be your company website's home page or an internal page of that site, your blog, your LinkedIn or Facebook profile, a custom-created for-Twitter page, or any other URL you think is most relevant.

4. The One-Line Bio field gives you a chance to practice the same character-limiting skills you'll be employing for tweeting. Here, you have a 160-character chance to tell your profile visitors something about yourself. It can be all business, all personal, a smattering of both, or none of the above. What you opt to tell the world about yourself is your prerogative, and it can be changed at any time (see Figure 4.12).

Figure 4.12 Different people take different approaches for their Twitter bios.

5. In the Location field, you're doing more than just letting your profile visitors know where you're located geographically. You're also telling search engines and other geo-locator tools what area of the country to associate with you. You can enter any kind of location you'd like or none at all. Some savvy Twitterers update their Twitter location as their physical location changes. For example, throughout the day it might change from the town where they live to the town where they work. To make the most of this field, provide a location with which you want to be associated, or for others to be able to find you. For instance, if you're setting up a Twitter account for your restaurant located in downtown Baltimore, your location should say something like "Baltimore, Maryland," as opposed to a lesser-known area like "Inner Harbor" or too broad of a description, such as "Maryland." Try to pinpoint the best and most appropriate location to use based on your goals. If your mobile device has the capability and you

enable it, it can be used to update your location automatically, providing the GPS coordinates of your whereabouts as you travel (Figure 4.13). If this occurs and you want to change it, you will need to log into your Twitter account settings to change it back to a non-coordinates location.

Name Jaime in da Hood
Location ÜT: 39.499185,-76.336906
Web http://shezcrafti...
Bio 20-something geek girl who doesn't get out much. I heart gaming, horror movies, comics, anime, and all things sci-fi and fantasy. Also kittens.
353 following 431 followers

Figure 4.13 GPS Coordinates for location

6. Under Language, check to make sure the correct language is selected. It should be set to English by default.
7. Under Accounts, unless you want to make your Twitter private (not visible to the public), make sure the Protect My Tweets box is unchecked. (Choosing the Protect My Tweets option is not advised. Doing so means your tweets will be displayed only to people to whom you give permission. The whole point of Twitter, particularly if you want to use it as a marketing vehicle, is to be open and engaging with the Twitter community. Protecting your tweets defeats this purpose.)

Picture

Now let's move onto the visuals. Almost as important as your username is your Twitter profile picture, which is also called an *avatar.* You can usually tell a Twitter newbie because they haven't changed their picture from Twitter's default avatar (see Figure 4.14).

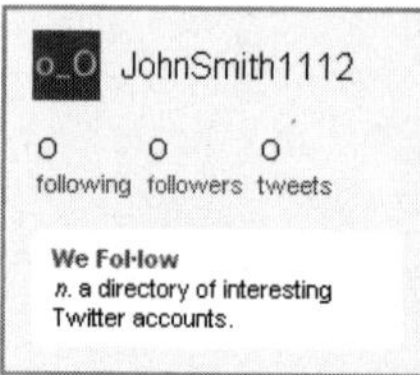

Figure 4.14 Twitter's default avatar

Most individuals use some kind of photo for their picture. It's an important feature of your profile because your photo can be seen by everyone on Twitter, regardless of whether your profile is set to private or not. Like your username, it represents who you are. It can also make a statement. During the Iran elections, tweeps showed their support for protestors by adding a green tint to their photos. There are also all kinds of symbolic cause-related overlays such as borders, ribbons, and bands. (See Figure 4.15.) There are even free site tools like Twibbon (`http://twibbon.com`) that have thousands of designs from which to choose.

Figure 4.15 Tweeps show support through their avatars.

For individuals, the most common type of Twitter photo is a close-up crop of one's face, a *headshot*. For businesses, it depends on how they're being represented: general brands typically display logos or other branded images; individuals representing their brand might have their own headshot.

To upload a photo for your Twitter picture, go into the Picture tab of your Settings. The photo you want to upload must reside somewhere on the computer you're using to access Twitter. Click the Browse button to browse to the desired image file on your computer. Double-click on the image you want, and then click Save. If successful, Twitter will confirm that your photo was uploaded properly (Figure 4.16).

Figure 4.16 Successfully uploading a picture

Here are some valuable photo tips:

- Image file size cannot exceed 700K.
- Twitter accepts JPG, GIF, and PNG image formats.
- Twitter will automatically crop large images to fit its picture window.
- Use a square image to ensure Twitter will crop it properly.
- Use a clear, unblurred image.
- Nude or otherwise obscene images are prohibited by Twitter's terms of services.

You can get creative and have fun with your avatar. In addition to uploading a photo, you can also produce cartoons and caricatures. Some free and for-fee resources to do so include the following:

- Face Your Manga (`http://www.faceyourmanga.com`)
- Meez (`http://www.meez.com`)
- Simpsons (`http://www.simpsonsmovie.com/main.html`); click Create Your Simpsons Avatar
- MadMenYourself (`http://www.madmenyourself.com`)
- My Caricature (`http://www.mycaricature.com`)
- Mrs. Toon (`http://www.mrstoon.com`)

Design

The design is the last thing you need to personalize for your Twitter background. Within the Design tab, you can do three things (Figure 4.17):

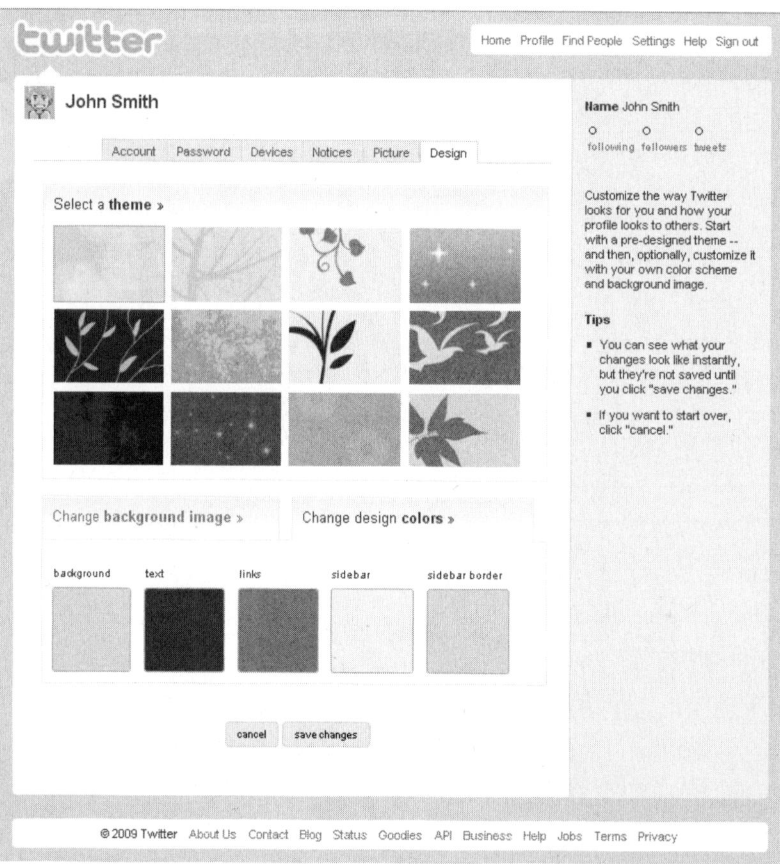

Figure 4.17 Design options

- **Select a theme.** Choose one of Twitter's 12 built-in themes. To do this, simply click on your choice of theme. Twitter will then display the theme in preview mode. If you like the theme and want to keep it, click Save Changes.
- **Customize your design colors.** Twitter enables you to change its default profile design colors, the colors of your background, typed text, links, sidebars, and sidebar borders (Figure 4.18). To customize your colors, click Change Design Colors, click on the element you want to change, and select from the pop-up menu of color swatches or enter in a specific color value.

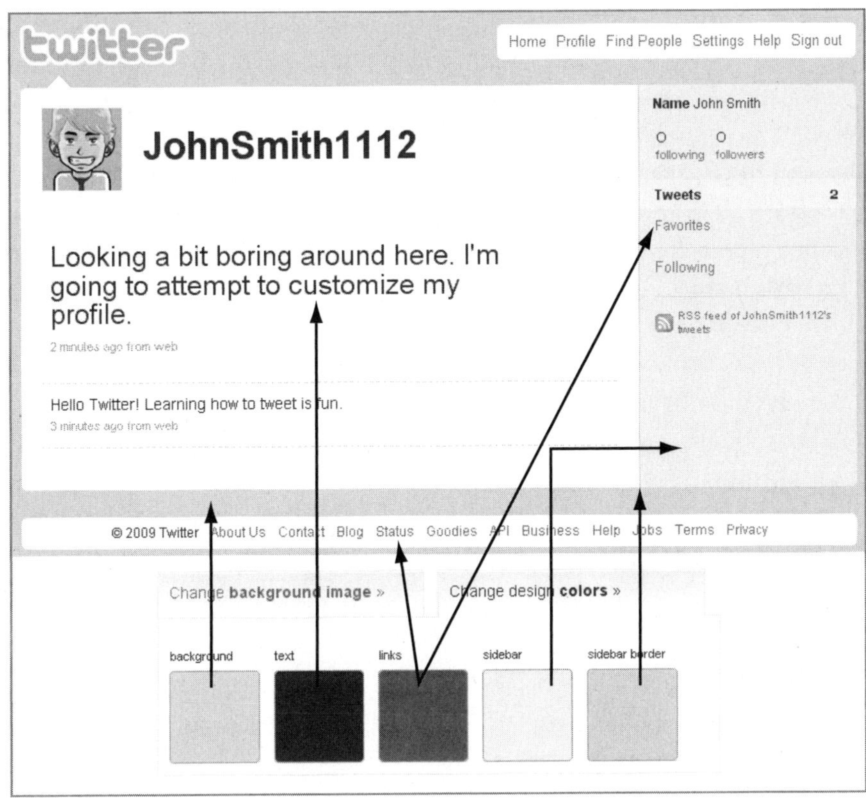

Figure 4.18 Design elements that can be color-modified

Twitter will show the changes in preview mode. When you like what you've created, click Save Changes to update your profile.

- **Change the background image.** Twitter's built-in themes are nice, but to stand out from the crowd and brand your Twitter page effectively, you will want to customize your Twitter design background. Because there's a lot of information on this, let's discuss it in more detail.

Customize Your Twitter Background

Your Twitter background is a great way to incorporate your branding, marketing message, personality, and other elements into your Twitter profile. It's also where you have the most creative freedom to change the look and feel of your Twitter page. You might want to consider incorporating the following into your Twitter background:

- Your contact information
- Additional details about you or your company that do not fit into Twitter's 160-character Bio field
- Additional photos of yourself or business
- Branded design elements

As with your photo, the background image file must reside on the computer from which you'll be accessing Twitter. To customize your background, click the Change Background Image link, and then click the Choose File button to select an image from your computer. You have the option to Tile Background (if you want a patterned background that repeats horizontally and vertically). Once your file is uploaded, click the Save Changes button.

Here are some valuable tips for background images:

- The background image file size must be smaller than 800K.
- Images must be in GIF, JPG, or PNG format.
- Select a background that is aesthetically pleasing and matches your profile's design colors.
- You can design your own background image for uploading. If doing so, follow these general guidelines:
  - Create a main background image that is 2048 × 1707 pixels in size
  - Within the main background image, create a smaller image (or layer) that is 80 × 587 pixels in size. This is where your branded info will go.
  - Align the smaller image so that it is 20 pixels from the left and 14 pixels from the top of the main image.

If the thought of designing your own graphics is daunting, you can find a ton of free Twitter background resources online. These sites offer premade backgrounds, themes, and customizable backgrounds you design online and then download.

Here's a list of some of the most popular online resources for free Twitter backgrounds:

- TwitterBackgrounds (`http://www.twitterbackgrounds.com`)
- Twitbacks (`http://www.twitbacks.com`)
- Twitterbacks (`http://www.twitterbacks.com`)
- Mytweetspace (`http://www.mytweetspace.com`)
- TweetStyle (`http://www.tweetstyle.com`)
- Twitter Patterns (`http://www.twitterpatterns.com`)

In the past, these customized backgrounds lacked the ability to utilize clickable links. A new service called ClickableNow (`http://www.clickablenow.com`) makes incorporating clickable links possible. The solution is still imperfect, though, because users need to install a browser plug-in to make it work.

Of all the setup features for Monday, customizing your background will certainly take the longest, so if you don't get to it during your one hour, don't sweat it. Use a simple solid-color background or an existing photo on your computer.

Tuesday: Find People to Follow

Now that your account is established, you can do two primary things: compose a tweet or find people to follow. Before we talk about tweeting, let's help build your following. The kind of users you seek to follow might be influenced by your reasons for joining Twitter in the first place. You might seek out friends, news makers and breakers, business colleagues, industry experts, companies you like, or brand-new people with whom you'd like to connect.

Twitter offers a number of built-in ways to find people to follow. As we mentioned during Monday's account-setup process, Twitter steers newcomers to its See If Your Friends Are on Twitter screen. We skipped that then, but let's cover it now. Today, instead of taking action as we go, hold off until the end of our review and then follow your one-hour exercise assignment.

Start Building Your Following with Twitter's Help

To ease your way into Twitter, why not start by connecting with people you know with Twitter's help. Click the Find People link on the Twitter menu at the top of your screen.

This opens the Find People screen, which has four tabs (Figure 4.19):

- Find on Twitter
- Find on Other Networks
- Invite by Email
- Suggested Users

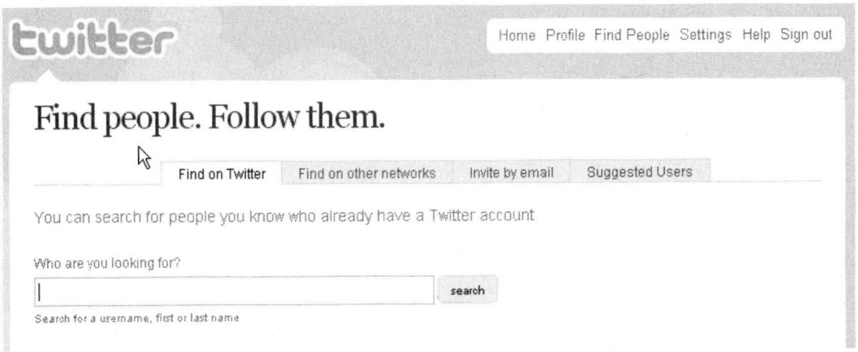

Figure 4.19 The Find People screen

Find on Twitter This is the best option to use if you're looking for someone in particular. Use this search box to find people by username, first name, last name, or both first and last name. Twitter will scour its database and return users it thinks most closely match your query and deliver them in descending order based on their number of followers (Figure 4.20).

Figure 4.20 How Twitter name search works

Find on Other Networks If you have an email account through Gmail, Yahoo!, or AOL, you can use this Twitter feature to look for contacts you may know (Figure 4.21). Choose one of the three available networks by clicking its tab on the left. Enter your email address and the associated password for that account (Twitter does not store this information), and then click Continue. If Twitter finds any user matches, it will display a list of results. In one shot, you can check the boxes of those contacts you want to follow and then click Finish (Figure 4.22). If Twitter finds people by accessing the address book in your selected email account and identifying those who are *not* on Twitter, it will display those people and encourage you to invite them to join as well.

Invite by Email Know some folks who aren't on Twitter or in your email address books? Use the Invite by Email tab to invite them to join Twitter too. Simply enter their email addresses in the box provided, separating the email addresses with commas. You can use this feature to copy and paste from your business contact database to notify customers and colleagues that you're now on Twitter. By clicking on the See What You'll Send Them link, you'll get a preview of the exact message Twitter will mail out on your behalf (Figure 4.23).

Figure 4.21 Using Twitter to find your contacts on other networks

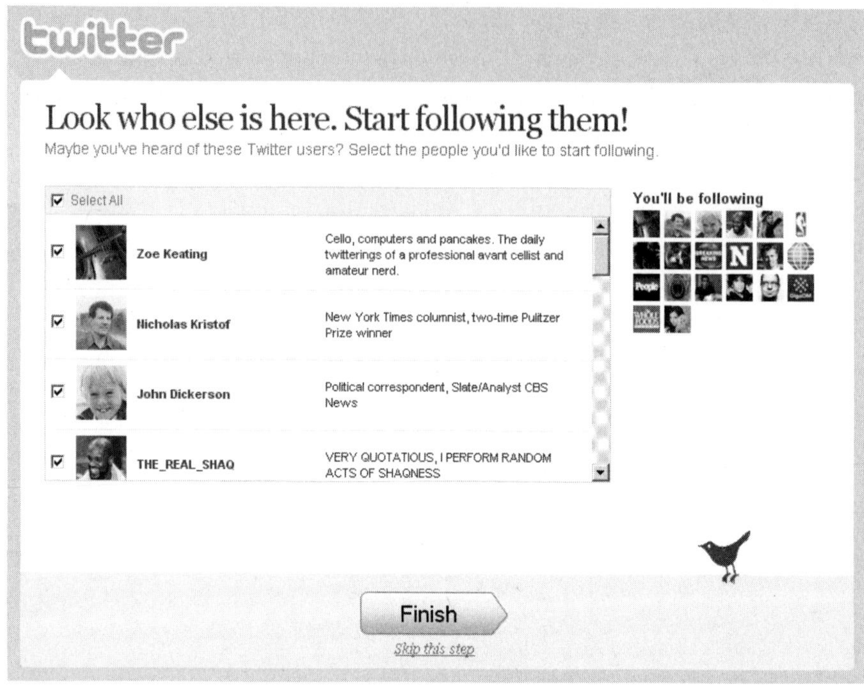

Figure 4.22 Following existing contacts on Twitter

twitter

Home Profile Find People Settings Help Sign out

Find people. Follow them.

Find on Twitter | Find on other networks | Invite by email | Suggested Users

You can invite folks by sending them an email. See what you'll send them.

Enter some email addresses:

Separate multiple email addresses with commas, ex: joe@twitter.com,jane@twitter.com

Invite

© 2009 Twitter About Us Contact Blog Status Goodies API Business Help Jobs Terms Privacy

Figure 4.23 Email contacts an invitation to join Twitter.

Suggested Users If you don't know who to follow, or if you're curious about connecting with new people, Twitter offers its Suggested Users tool to recommend people in whom you might be interested (Figure 4.24). Just scroll through its suggestions, check off any that appeal to you, and then click the Follow button.

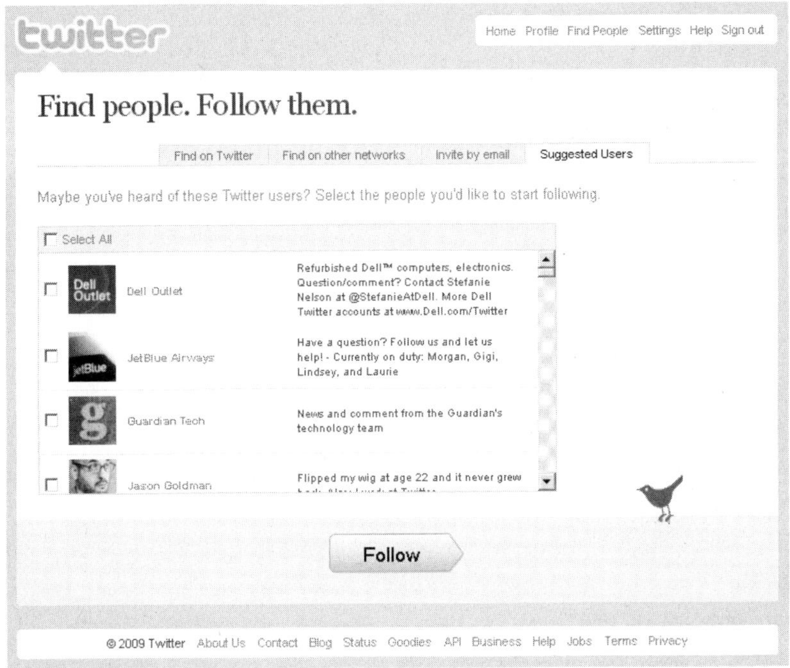

Figure 4.24 Twitter suggests...

Find People to Follow Using Online Resources and Third-Party Tools

Although Twitter offers the previously mentioned ways to get you started, these integrated tools are very limited. Unless you want to follow only people you know, you'll most likely want to use additional resources to help find people to follow and start building your network. We're going to cover this topic in greater detail in Chapter 6, "Week 3: Use Twitter Search and Other Tools to Improve Your Experience." when we flip the conversation around to attracting followers. In the meantime, here are just a few other good resources to help you get started.

Search Engines Google can help you find tweeps when Twitter cannot, particularly if you don't know all the information about a person—for example, their last name or their handle. All you need to do is type in the bits of information you know about this person, and let Google do its thing (Figure 4.25). You can do the same thing with Microsoft's Bing search engine.

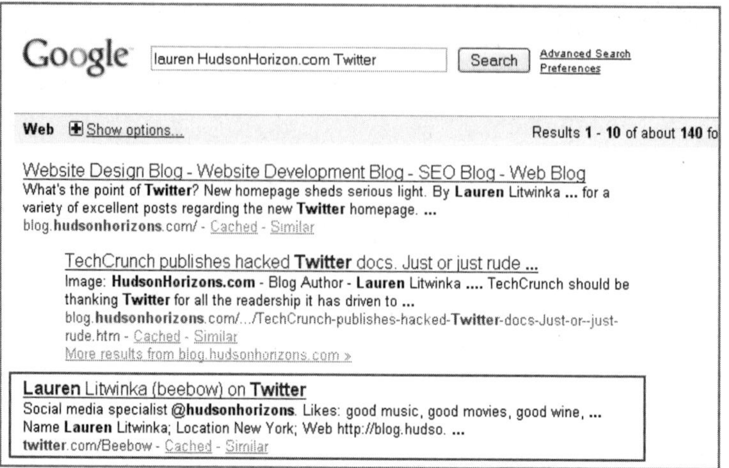

Figure 4.25 Google can find people when Twitter can't.

Web Directories and Tools More than a dozen well-known kinds of these web directories and tools exist to help you find people to follow. In Chapter 3, "Twitter, the Multipurpose Platform," we talked about some geo-locator tools, and next week we'll expose you to even more kinds. To give you a flavor right now, check out TwitDir (`http://www.twitdir.com`), which allows you to search by a variety of criteria.

Twitter Lists and Databases A number of great specialized Twitter lists and databases, created by enterprising individuals who took the time to research and compile listings and were kind enough to share the information with others, are available online. I provided some of these lists in Chapter 3 in the "Meeting Your Peers on Twitter" section. Another useful example is Paul Dunay's "Brands That Tweet" list on his blog: `http://buzzmarketingfortech.blogspot.com/2008/12/brands-that-tweet.html`.

Tuesday's One-Hour Exercise: Start Finding People to Follow

1. Use Twitter's integrated Find People tools to help you locate people to follow. Try using all four methods: Find on Twitter, Find on Other Networks, Invite by Email, and Suggested Users. Spend no more than 30 minutes doing this step.
2. Perform some Google searches to find people you might not be able to find using Twitter's tools. Spend no more than 15 minutes doing this step.
3. Use TwitDir or any of the local search tools from Chapter 3 to find tweeps. Spend no more than 10 minutes doing so.
4. Scan the "Brands That Tweet" list. Follow one or two of your favorite brands listed. Spend no more than 5 minutes.

Wednesday: Learn Twitter Lingo

It's commonplace for technology and web-related systems to develop their own lingo, and Twitter is no exception. Early in Chapter 1, we defined some of these common terms to help explain the whole universe that is Twitter. Let's pull out that mini-glossary again to review.

Twitter Terminology

Handle. A user's Twitter name (e.g., hollisthomases).

Tweet. The 140-character-or-less message sent by a Twitter user. On Twitter, these are tracked in your profile as *Tweets*.

Tweeting or **Twittering.** The act of composing and sending a message.

Retweet (RT). Stands for retweet. When someone "forwards" your tweet, they manually put "RT" in front or use a retweet function to automatically do so to give you proper credit.

@reply. The @ symbol directly in front of someone's name (`@hollisthomases`) indicates you're sending them a public message or responding to a message they sent you. It's a publicly visible type of Twitter messaging between two users or more.

Direct message (DM). A DM sends a private message to another Twitter user. In order for them to receive this private message, they need fto be following you. In order for you to receive a DM back, you need to be following them. To send a DM, use "D," plus a space, plus the recipient's Twitter handle. Do not use the @ symbol when sending a DM.

Tweep. A shortcut word (Twitter + people, *peeps*) to describe a Twitter user (the word "Twitterer" takes up more characters.) "Tweeps" describes more than one tweep.

Follower. Someone who has consciously elected to follow a Twitter user.

Friend. A way to describe someone you've chosen to follow (also known as "Following").

Twitterverse. Describes the Twitter community at large—that is, the Twitter universe.

Hashtag. The hashtag is a way of identifying a tweet related to a particular subject. The hashtag protocol is the hash or pound sign (#) directly followed by the word, words, or characters someone has assigned to that subject, the fewer characters the better. We're using the hashtag #TMHAD for this book.

Now let's explore some of the finer nuances of some of these terms as well as some helpful abbreviations and a few other terms you might want to know about. This will help you look less like a newbie as you begin tweeting.

@Replies, Direct Messages, and Retweets

As you're about to learn, `@replies`, direct messages, and retweets are the fundamental building blocks of Twitter conversation. These kinds of messages take your single, one-way posts and turn them into a dialog with or about others.

@Replies

In Twitter, the at (`@`) symbol is a very powerful character. With it, you can send tweets to other Twitter users, refer to people in conversations (sometimes called *name dropping*), and use Twitter commands to interact with others. When you use this symbol to initiate tweets with other users or reply to an incoming tweet, it is most commonly called an `@reply`. Because the `@` symbol serves two purposes—replying to someone else's tweet or sending a message to a user—I commonly differentiate between the actions when I talk or describe the process verbally. When I'm the originator of a first-time tweet, I say I'm "sending an `@message`;" when I'm replying to someone's tweet directed at me, I say I'm "`@replying`;" and when I'm interjecting myself into someone's conversation where their tweet was not necessarily directed at me or anyone in particular, I say I "`@messaged`" (past tense) this person. A little confusing, huh? Don't worry; you'll get the hang of this because you'll soon see that the actions are different.

The last form of tweeting, `@messaging`, is one of the key things that makes Twitter different than most everything else on the Web, because everything you tweet is in the public domain and anyone can theoretically find and respond to it. (I'd say the closest analogy is commenting on someone's blog post, although commenting is not the same as having a Twitter conversation.) (See Figure 4.26.)

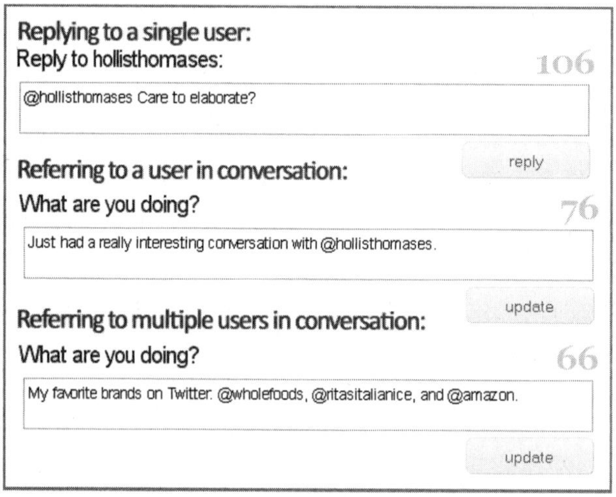

Replying to a single user:
Reply to hollisthomases: 106
@hollisthomases Care to elaborate?
reply
Referring to a user in conversation:
What are you doing? 76
Just had a really interesting conversation with @hollisthomases.
update
Referring to multiple users in conversation:
What are you doing? 66
My favorite brands on Twitter: @wholefoods, @ritasitalianice, and @amazon.
update

Figure 4.26 Various `@reply` syntaxes

To reply to someone's tweet, you need only click the curved arrow within the tweet. Twitter will automatically set up the reply with `@[theirname]` (Figure 4.27). The secondary benefit to utilizing the reply link is that it preserves the conversation thread. Twitter can display the handle of the person to whom the user is replying, and this handle is linked to the unique URL associated with that user's post.

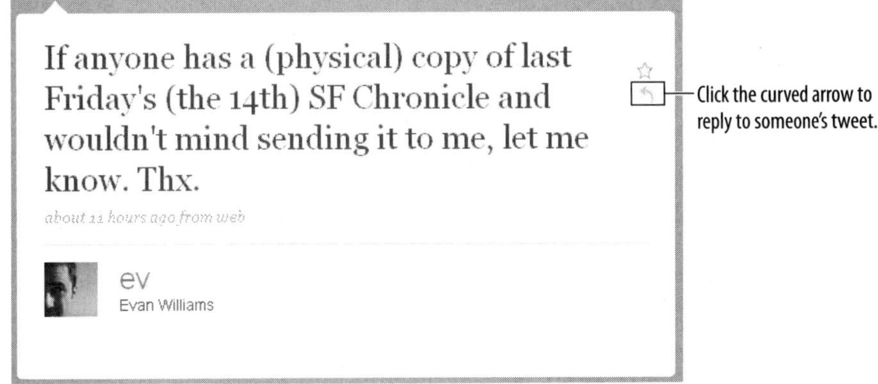

If anyone has a (physical) copy of last Friday's (the 14th) SF Chronicle and wouldn't mind sending it to me, let me know. Thx.
about 11 hours ago from web
ev
Evan Williams
Click the curved arrow to reply to someone's tweet.

Figure 4.27 How to reply to a message using Twitter

All public `@messages` can be searched, viewed uniquely, or marked by anyone as a Favorite by clicking the star that appears to the right of the tweet. Those that are `@replies` in response to someone else's tweet also display and link to the original tweet underneath the message, known as the *conversation thread.* (See Figure 4.28.)

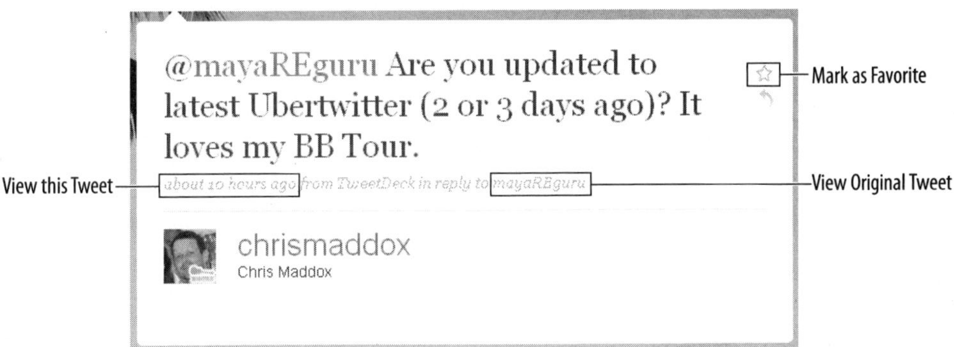

@mayaREguru Are you updated to latest Ubertwitter (2 or 3 days ago)? It loves my BB Tour.
about 10 hours ago from TweetDeck in reply to mayaREguru

Figure 4.28 What you can do inside a single `@reply`

Direct Messages

Because direct messages (DMs) are confidential one-on-one tweets sent to a single user, they do not appear in your public Twitter timeline. Instead, they are stored in your Direct Messages folder that, like email, has an Inbox and a Sent box. Like regular tweets, DMs can be deleted, which in turn deletes the recipient's copy as well. There are a few other key differences between regular tweets and DMs, however.

- DMs cannot be marked as Favorites.
- DMs cannot be located through searches.
- DMs do not follow a conversation thread. (Some third-party applications do make this option available, but Twitter.com does not.)

Direct messages can only be sent to users who are already following you; that is, you cannot send unsolicited DMs to random people. The recipient must "know" you at least well enough to follow you, but it's not necessary that you follow that person back in order to DM them.

Retweets

Retweeting is akin to forwarding an email message. There are a number of reasons you might want to retweet (RT) someone's message, such as the following:

- You like what they have to say and want to share it with your followers.
- They have provided a valuable, useful, or entertaining link to content you want to forward.
- They say something nice to you that you'd like to share with your other followers.

Next week we're going to review some aspects of the etiquette of retweeting. What you should know right now is that if you see the "RT" or "via" followed by someone's `@[username]`, it means it's information being passed along courtesy of someone else as the source (Figure 4.29).

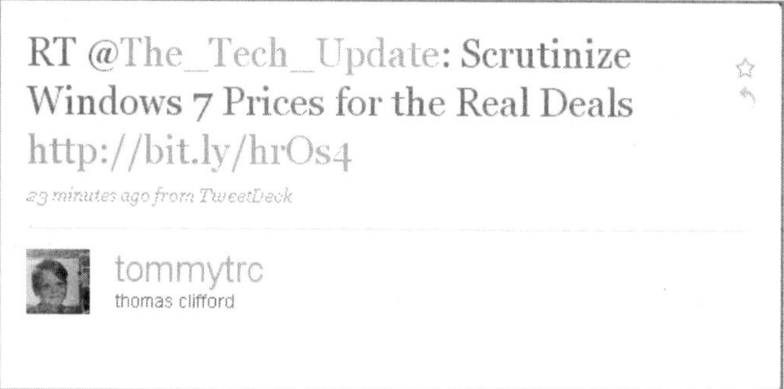

Figure 4.29 A basic retweet

Hashtags

While not an official Twitter command, a hashtag is a convention adopted by the Twitter community used to tag, track, and promote topics of conversation. The pound symbol (#) is used before a word or combination of letters to denote the hashtags. When a hashtagged word appears somewhere in the body of your tweet, it signifies that this tweet is part of a broader conversation or is associated with a particular topic. Hashtags act as the anchor by which users can search for and monitor tweets related to a particular topic, even if they are not following the people doing the tweeting. Hashtags can be tricky to grasp at first, but until something better comes along, they are an essential means of organizing and digesting the tsunami of information that one receives through Twitter.

Other than using the # symbol, there's no standard or protocol to starting a hashtag. Anyone can create one and is free to use it. Popular hashtags tend to spread wings virally throughout the Twitter community, often becoming Trending Topics. Hashtags are a very loosely moderated means of controlled conversation. Sometimes different variations of hashtags exist to flag the same topic, which can make things confusing. If there's an authority figure, such as a conference organizer or conversation moderator, this entity or person can impose some order by dictating the appropriate hashtag to use. Because of the lack of control, scope of use, and relative chaos surrounding hashtags, a little cottage industry has been spawned and taken on a life of its own. There are entire websites and other tools devoted to monitoring and documenting hashtag usage and popularity. We'll introduce you to some of these tools here:

Hashtag Dictionaries/Directories

- `#hashtags` (`http://www.hashtags.org`) is the granddaddy of them all. It identifies, tracks, analyzes, and archives hashtags. You can search the directory for hashtags. Brand-new hashtags might not appear, but well-used or very popular ones definitely make their way into this massive directory (Figure 4.30).
- Twemes (`http://www.twemes.com`) identifies and posts tweets with hashtags in real time.
- Tagalus (`http://www.tagal.us`) lets users define tags so that others can understand what they're talking about. Other users can vote on definitions and decide which one best describes the given tag.
- Tagdef (`http://www.tagdef.com`) tweets new trending tags and even allows you to send a tweet with the hashtag, and they'll define it for you.
- HashDictionary (`http://www.hashdictionary.com`) is a resource similar to Taglus.
- What the Trend (`http://whatthetrend.com`) lets you "find out what's trending on Twitter and why." As with a wiki, anyone can edit the blurbs.

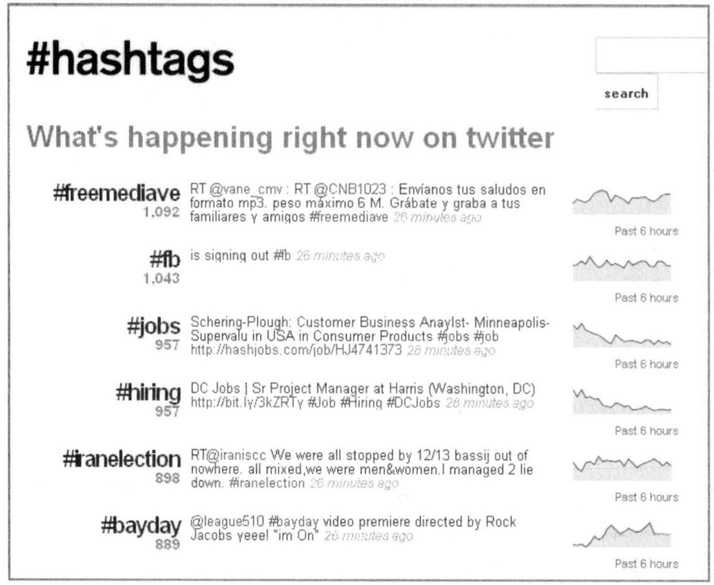

Figure 4.30 The home page of the #hashtags website

Shortened URLs

URL shortening tools have been around a long time—for example, TinyURL (`http://tinyurl.com`; Figure 4.31)—but the advent of Twitter has generated a new breed of tools that make URLs even shorter. These tools take average to long URLs and compact them into fewer characters (usually 10 or more). On Twitter, because every character in a tweet is valuable, the shorter you can make a link, the more room you have to say other things (Figure 4.31).

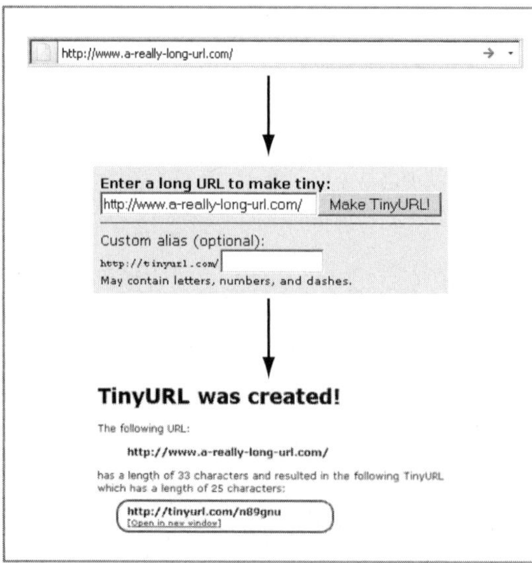

Figure 4.31 A URL before and after it's been shortened

Today, dozens of URL shorteners exist, among them, these:

BudURL (`http://www.budurl.com`)

bit.ly (`http://bit.ly`)

j.mp (`http://j.mp`)

ow.ly (`http://ow.ly`)

tr.im (`http://tr.im`)

is.gd (`http://is.gd`)

su.pr (`http://su.pr`)

awe.sm (`http://totally.awe.sm`), a fee-based build-your-own custom domain

Some of these URL shorteners come with robust tracking and analytics that allow you to see how many clicks you're generating from your tweeted links. Many URL shorteners allow you to log in and tweet directly from their interface, and some have a helpful bookmarklet that you can drag to your browser toolbar so you can click to shorten and tweet more easily. Third-party Twitter clients, which you can use to access Twitter (more on this tomorrow), oftentimes either have a built-in URL shortening solution or allow you to select one from a few they have integrated. For instance, if you don't use a URL shortener and you insert a long URL on Twitter, it might use bit.ly to shorten the URL in your tweet before it sends it.

Other Short Stuff

Twitter's 140 character limitation has also led to all kinds of shortcuts to enable a user to say more with less.

Helpful Abbreviations

As you can probably imagine, Twitter breeds all kinds of shortcuts, particularly abbreviations. Recognizing, translating, and knowing when it's appropriate to use some of these abbreviations makes using Twitter a little bit easier.

Commonly Seen and Acceptable Abbreviations:

ppl = people

2 = to

b = be

u = you

<3 = love

On Twitter, it's also acceptable to drop initial articles and pronouns such as "the" or "I" if it frees up a few extra characters.

Twitter Keys

Sometimes in people's tweets you'll also see fun symbols and characters such as ♥, ☺, or ♫ and wonder how they did that. At `http://thenextweb.org/2008/09/16/twitter-keys-enhance-your-twitter-conversations`, you can drag their TwitterKeys toolbar into your browser, which then easily lets you copy and paste symbols for incorporation into your tweets. If you see someone else using an icon you like that may not be part of TwitterKeys, favorite that tweet so you can copy and paste the icon into a tweet at your discretion.

Fun with Twitter Lingo

Twitter's vernacular has led to a whole slew of "Tw" words to be unleashed on the world. We have listed a bunch in the glossary in the back of this book. For teasers, let's just give you a few now:

Twits. A not-so-nice description of a person on Twitter ("nitwit")

Twitterati. Celebrities and other A-list people on Twitter

Twanker. A person, organization, or company behaving badly on Twitter

Twenius. A tweeting genius

Can't Forget the Fail Whale

The Fail Whale we mentioned in Chapter 1 has become so ubiquitous that now just the hashtag `#fail` carries a similar connotation. You'll also see `#fail` married to other stories of failure, for example, `#CNNfail` when it could not cover the protests during the Iranian elections.

Wednesday's One-Hour Exercise: Simple Tweets

Today you'll begin to compose some simple practice tweets. Perhaps pick a friend with whom you can tweet back and forth before venturing out into the great wilds of Twitter. Try the following steps:

1. Pick a buddy with whom you can practice.
2. Send a simple `@message` to that friend. Remember, there is *no space* between the `@` symbol and your friend's Twitter handle. Ask your friend to send you an `@`message.
3. Reply to your friend's message using the reply arrow.
4. Retweet a basic message from your friend.
5. Create and send a direct message to your friend.

6. Go to What the Trend and find a hashtag trending topic of interest, or go Hashtag.org and search for a hashtag on a subject in which you're interested. Use that hashtag in a tweet to your friend.
7. Visit two to three sites with URL shortening tools. Try them to see how you like them. Then find useful links (like news or links you already have bookmarked) and practice shortening them with the tools you've chosen. Send some shortened links in tweets to your friend.
8. Try composing some tweets to your friend using abbreviations and/or TwitterKey characters. Have some fun!

Thursday: Access Twitter

One of the most appealing things about Twitter is its flexibility when it comes to when, where, and how to use it. You already know that Twittering can be done from the Web or a mobile phone, but that's just the beginning. Because Twitter has an open API, there is a whole host of useful (not to mention free) services that improve how you Twitter and make communicating with those hundreds of followers this book will help you obtain much easier. Many of these services offer multifaceted solutions, so don't be surprised when they crop up in a discussion topic further along in the book. For now, we're focusing on ways besides Twitter.com to access the platform.

Twitter Desktop Clients

There are a number of great desktop-based applications for Twitter. These are independent, third-party applications called *clients* that you download and install on your computer. These clients offer many advantages: they're often faster, more streamlined, and more feature-rich than Twitter's basic user interface (UI). Many of them are compatible with both Windows and Macs.

Some of the more popular Twitter desktop clients:

TweetDeck (`http://www.tweetdeck.com`)

DestroyTwitter (`http://www.destroytwitter.com`)

Seesmic Desktop (`http://desktop.seesmic.com`)

digsby (`http://www.digsby.com`)

Twitter Browser Clients

A browser client plugs into your browser to allow you to tweet and receive tweets directly in your browser. You don't have to launch a separate program and toggle back and forth between it and your browser. One popular browser client is the Firefox extension Echofon (http://echofon.com).

Web-Based Clients

If you prefer to stick to twittering on the Web but are underwhelmed by Twitter's basic UI, you can utilize other web-based Twitter clients. With a web-based client, you don't have to install yet another program on your PC. Some offer unique features not seen in other clients, and the best part is that you can access the same information wherever you connect to the Internet.

Popular web-based clients for Twitter:

HootSuite (http://www.hootsuite.com)

SocialOomph (http://www.SocialOomph.com)

Seesmic Web (http://seesmic.com/app)

PeopleBrowsr (http://my.peoplebrowsr.com)

Mobile Twitter Clients

Technically, mobile Twitter solutions are called *applications* as opposed to *clients*. Many of the mobile applications were developed specifically for smart phones like the iPhone or BlackBerry, although there are others that work across all smart phone platforms. Even if you don't own a smart phone, you can still use Twitter while on the go. As with desktop and web-based Twitter clients, there is no shortage of mobile Twitter applications. No matter what kind of mobile device you have, you can bet there's a Twitter app for it! In Chapter 1, we covered the basics of tweeting from a mobile phone using SMS texting. The mobile Twitter apps discussed here offer features and functionality beyond Twitter's basic mobile commands. Some are free; some charge a basic fee or a fee for an upgraded version.

Mobile apps for general smart phones:

Tiny Twitter (http://www.tinytwitter.com)

twibble mobile (http://www.twibble.de/twibble-mobile)

Mobile apps for iPhone:

Echofon (http://echofon.com)

Tweetie (http://www.atebits.com/tweetie-iphone)

TweetDeck for iPhone (http://tweetdeck.com/iphone)

Twitterific (http://iconfactory.com/software/twitterrific)

Twittelator (`http://www.stone.com/Twittelator`)

Birdfeed (`http://birdfeedapp.com`)

Mobile apps for BlackBerry:

TwitterBerry (`http://www.orangatame.com/products/twitterberry`)

ÜberTwitter (`http://www.ubertwitter.com`)

Current Clients

New Twitter clients are constantly being introduced to the market and, from month to month, the popularity of these clients changes. If you want to see what the most current clients are, visit `http://twitstat.com/twitterclientusers.html`.

Thursday's One-Hour Exercise: Familiarize Yourself with Other Twitter Clients

Clearly, what you choose to work with has to be compatible with your computer system (Windows versus Mac) and the devices you own—for example, a smart phone. Still, there are plenty of Twitter clients from which to choose, so test-drive a few before deciding. Test-driving these tools will take some time. I recommend you select three you'd like to try and assign no more than 20 minutes to each. Try testing one from each category, so you can compare the experiences. Start with a desktop solution, then move to a web-based client, and finally to a mobile client. Don't feel you need to conquer every feature of each—in Week 2, we're going to revisit some of these clients for their advanced functionality. Instead, get the hang of doing the basic things, like reading and replying to tweets and direct messages, retweeting, favoriting, and so on. In other words, try to mimic the same activities you'd be doing on Twitter.com. If you get that and still have time, then probe the advanced functionalities of each.

Friday: From Lurking to Leaping

You've created an account, you've filled out your profile, and you've practiced tweeting back and forth with a friend—I'd say you're ready to venture out into the Twitterverse now! What will you tweet about? What *should* you tweet about? (The answer isn't "What are you doing?"!)

Twitter is described as microblogging, and if you publish a blog, you want people to read it. To get them to read your blog—or your tweets, for that matter—the content should be engaging, informative, and entertaining. More importantly, your tweets should be a reflection of you or your brand. The twist with Twitter is that you can expect (and should encourage) immediate feedback because, unlike a blog, Twitter is conversational. Sure, most blogs allow you to leave comments and respond to others; but with Twitter the responses are often quicker, more relevant, and, thanks to the 140-character limitation, more to the point.

The Art of Tweeting

What kind of response would a bad tweet get? (Yes, there is such a thing!) Once you start a conversation, how do or should you keep it going?

"Need coffee."

"Sitting in traffic."

"Working."

These are real tweets. Not terribly exciting, are they? Unless you're `@BarackObama` or `@Oprah`, it's a safe bet that your followers won't be interested in every little thing that you do. Likewise, honestly ask yourself, "Do I want to know every little thing the people I follow are doing either?" I know you said no! Your followers want more. In a way, they're very needy . . . or at least thirsting for something of interest to keep them coming back. In the beginning, before you have many followers and before you truly find your "voice" on Twitter, it may seem challenging to know what to tweet about.

Engaging Tweets

Don't start out on Twitter blatantly promoting an agenda. You turn people off instead of attracting them. Instead, here are a few ideas for some good first tweets:

- Introduce yourself. What's your best 140-character-or-less introduction? That's something you can continually practice.
- Say hello to the Twitterverse.
- Welcome any early followers.
- Share your expertise.
- Tease what you'll be tweeting about in the future.

Reminder Unless you delete a tweet, it will live on in Twitter and be visible for as long as your account remains active. It will also probably live in in perpetuity in search engines like Google and Bing. This is something you should keep in mind for all of your tweets.

When you start out with Twitter (and even later on), it may seem like you're talking to yourself at times. Not very much fun, I know, and perhaps this is why many users abandon Twitter after their initial experience. The idea, however, is to build up a nice repository of quality tweets in the beginning to attract people and give them an incentive to follow you. As you start to use Twitter regularly, you may notice that certain types of subject matter prove to be popular tweets:

Entertainment and Humor Sharing links to cool or funny stuff you find on the Web, such as photos, YouTube videos, games, and interactive quizzes.

News People have described Twitter as their "new front page news." Breaking news spreads like wildfire on Twitter, but you can do your part to share more ordinary news you learn firsthand as well. Your followers will appreciate being kept in the loop. Because Twitter is still a cutting-edge social media technology, tech- and social media-related news is especially popular.

Help With time on your hands in your early Twitter days, why not provide help or advice to users who ask for it? It's a great way to earn new followers and a solid reputation.

Support Tweeting words of encouragement, well wishes, or congratulations is common fare on Twitter. It's part of being a good Twitter netizen.

Participate and Contribute

If you're still not sure what to tweet about, there are plenty of ways to contribute to Twitter, as well as encourage conversations.

Reply. Find a tweet that interests you, and simply reply to it! Try asking a question about it, agreeing (or disagreeing), or making a statement that adds value to the conversation. This kind of tweet might be intimidating at first, but it's also a surefire way to attract new followers.

Start a conversation. Starting a conversation can be as simple as posing an open-ended question to the Twitterverse. For example, "What do you think about _____?" Then sit back and see what kind of responses roll in.

Inject yourself in the middle of a conversation. Sometimes called *tweavesdropping*, this is when you watch a conversation unfold between two (or more) other Twitter users, and then reply to join in yourself. Don't feel awkward or out of place doing this—on Twitter, it's a common method of networking!

Tweeting Tips

- Finding your Twitter voice involves a good amount of trial and error. Don't be afraid to try something new! If your tweets aren't getting the attention they should, don't get discouraged—try a new direction.
- Try to find unique content to contribute, but don't be afraid to tweet about what others are tweeting about, especially if you can add your own unique spin.

Twitter Etiquette Dos and Don'ts

Twitter etiquette, or *twetiquette,* will be mentioned throughout this book because it's an important topic, particularly as you migrate from tweeting for yourself to tweeting for your company. Regardless of what, how, and for whom you tweet, always keep in mind that Twitter is a community of real people. Your words have meaning and consequences, and the larger the consequence, the more is at stake.

I personally I have an interest in Twitter etiquette and people's behaviors on Twitter. As a "twanthropologist" of sorts, I've conducted multiple insta-polls and surveys to try to get a better understanding of Twitter user preferences and expectations. From what I learned doing this research, combined with common knowledge of best practice, here's a helpful starter list of what you should and shouldn't do and what you should expect in return:

Do:

Use your real name (or real company name) to let the Twitterverse know you're a real person.

Take an active interest in conversations between others and join in if appropriate.

Try to give new (legitimate) followers a chance, and treat other users with respect.

Give credit where credit is due. Don't try to pass off unoriginal tweets as your own.

If someone scratches your back, scratch theirs in return.

Use as much of your 140 characters as possible, minus 15 characters or so to leave room for retweeting when `@messaging` so that whoever's retweeting you can include the "RT" plus your user handle, but still get the full gist of your message.

It's OK to steer your followers tactfully toward promotional content, as long as that's not all you're doing.

When you disagree with another Twitter user's tweet, it's OK to disagree politely and respectfully with them.

Don't:

Hide behind a fake persona.

Brag about the number of followers you have; it's usually considered arrogant.

Ignore new followers completely.

Try to derail others' conversations if you're not contributing anything of value.

Spam or push your agenda too heavily on your followers.

Intentionally Tweet incorrect information. If you do so by accident, correct yourself.

Use curse words, racist remarks, or otherwise offensive language in your tweets.

Turn a disagreement into a public flame war.

"Over-tweet" to one person. Some things are more appropriate in an email—and less annoying to your other followers.

Misrepresent yourself or your company.

Send a public message when you'd expect a private DM in return.

Necessarily expect a thank you for RT'ing someone else's tweet.

Drink and tweet! You might regret it when you sober up.

The Main Points

- When you create your Twitter account, finish the job. Don't just stop at signing up without completing your profile information and helpful user settings.
- Use Twitter's tools to help you find people to follow; just don't rely solely on them.
- Don't be so intimidated to tweet that you don't post anything. The key to attracting followers of your own is to have interesting content on your profile and show that you're willing to carry on conversations.
- When you're ready to begin engaging with others in earnest, know that Twitter already has a culture that calls for certain rules of etiquette. This etiquette is even more important to practice when you're representing a brand.

5

Week 2: Find and Attract Followers

In Chapter 4, "Week 1: Get on Twitter," we covered the basics of how to find people to follow. Now we want to help you attract people to follow you. There's still a lot of "finding" involved, but the point of this kind of searching and seeking is that it's purposeful. You'll want to seek out and try to connect with people who'd benefit you the most if they followed you in return. Though deliberate on your part, there's a whole lot of finesse and subtlety in how you go about this. You can't just find someone and tweet them, "Hey! I think you'd find me a great person to follow, so you should!" and expect them to do so. In this chapter, we'll cover how you can do your best to attract and motivate people to follow you.

Chapter Contents

Followers and Following

As you know by now, your Twitter universe will consist of three primary components: you, your followers (those who follow you), and your following (those you follow). The fourth component of this universe is "everyone else." Because your tweets are part of the searchable public domain, theoretically, anyone can find you by way of what you have to say. In other words, everyone has a voice, but it's by attracting followers—the right kind of followers—that your voice gets heard. How you define "the right followers" for you is somewhat subjective. It harkens to the question of why you're on Twitter, what you hope to gain, and how much effort you're willing and able to put in to nurture and attract followers.

Don't, however, get too caught up in your follower count. Doing so can too easily distract you from the more important aspects of using Twitter, what you're tweeting about, and with whom you're holding conversations. Keep in mind that you want to *earn* your followers through the substance of your tweets and the relationships you build. Earning anything, particularly people's interest and trust, isn't easy. Just as earning money the old-fashioned way takes hard work and devotion, so does building a good Twitter follower base. If you take a shortcut to gain followers, you really don't gain anything but a number. Some of the most interesting people with whom I have Twitter relationships have few followers and follow few people. I'm actually more honored to have them as followers than I am to have those who follow anyone and everyone, because it says to me that what I have to say really has an impact on them. That's my priority on Twitter; however, it might not be yours, so you need to define what's right for you.

Motives for Attracting Followers

People who use Twitter have all different kinds of agendas—and some people have multiple agendas. We all have to play in the same sandbox though, so even if you don't agree with someone's motives, it's a good idea to understand their actions on Twitter and why they do what they do.

Socialize

As I mentioned in Chapter 1, "Understanding Twitter," some people just use Twitter to socialize by connecting with friends and making new ones. If that's one reason you're joining Twitter, seeking out these kinds of people makes sense. On the other hand, if you're joining Twitter to market your business, the user focused mostly on socializing is probably not right for you. This person won't be seeking brand messages and offers, but that doesn't mean that they mind hearing them from their friends!

Motives for Attracting Followers *(Continued)*

Network

Some people like to socialize, but with a purpose in mind: to connect or get connected with others. For networkers, it's all about engagement. Networkers have an unusually high number of `@messages`, and conversations with networkers might not run too deep or be very informative. Marketers should keep their eyes out for networkers, however, because of their power to expose you to their widely cast net.

Provoke Thought

People who like to provoke thought can stray toward opposite ends of the spectrum: they either just want to postulate without necessarily engaging, or they get highly engaged, sometimes to the point of contention. A user with this agenda may be great for your brand if they agree and like what you're doing, but be prepared for some bruises and scrapes. You might, though, come out better for the wear because this kind of user probably also generates great ideas.

Inform

People who join Twitter to genuinely help educate and inform the masses, their peers, the industry, or their friends truly tap into the power of the Twitterverse. These are people who read, filter, and share news or who create the news through their research, analysis, and/or writing. It's a bit sticky to try to market to someone who's on Twitter to inform, because that person may feel there are ethical lines they don't want to cross, but informers can also be objective and fair. Seek out these types because they can help convey your message.

Lead/Influence

You'll easily recognize leaders and influencers, even if they don't have tons of followers. This type of user has no problem expressing an opinion—and often does. They're the enthusiastic, passionate types who love telling the world about things they find exciting. They are equally quick to criticize when they've been wronged. People trust and respond to leaders and influencers. Influencers tend to be very brand loyal. Win them over and consistently treat them well with excellent products and service. You'll not only get a fan for life, but they'll help you convert more people into fans.

Publicize

You can pick out from their tweets those who are using Twitter as a mere vehicle for publicity or self-aggrandizement. They're not a target follower for a marketer.

Motives for Attracting Followers *(Continued)*

Activate (Cause-Related)

Twitter can be used very effectively to motivate people to take action. President Obama realized this potential early in his presidential campaign. Users with the primary purpose of motivating action probably won't be receptive to ordinary brand messages, unless the message ties in to their cause or to related ones in some way. That's not a bad marketing tie-in idea right there, eh?

Entertain

Entertaining tweeps are great. They make everyone laugh or react in some kind of visceral way. They are not, however, very relevant to marketers unless they are marketing entertainment. I do advise following a few entertainers because you can learn a lot from them about effectively incorporating entertainment into your own Twitter marketing efforts.

Build Awareness

Be it on a personal or business level, some people just want to bring attention to themselves, their cause, their product, or their service. They may do so by deploying a mix of the previous methods, or they may have a unique way of calling attention. Marketers should observe those whose motive seems to be building awareness and learn from those who do it well (and those who do not).

Drive Traffic

Most marketers fall into this category. By "traffic," I mean website traffic, in-store traffic, or even call-in traffic. If your purpose is to drive traffic, you are most likely trying to achieve one or more of the following objectives: publishing, promotions, sales, or list building. Depending on the kind of marketing entity you are, you're probably not too interested in attracting other users with the same motive for using Twitter. If you're a leader in your field, however, you probably will be followed by other marketers so that they can keep tabs on what you're doing and how you're getting it done.

Preliminary Exercise

Now that you know the motives for attracting followers and have probably identified a few that resonate best with you, you should start thinking about how to attract the kind of followers suited to meet your objectives. You'll likely attract most tweeps with your content—your tweets. As a preliminary exercise, let's have you think deliberately. Come up with a few initial content ideas that you can tweet about and enter them in the following list. These content ideas should relate to the kind of follower you're trying to attract.

1. ____

2. ____

3. ____

4. ____

For each content idea you came up with, list a handful of keywords or keyword phrases you feel are related to that topic:

1a. ____

1b. ____

1c. ____

2a. ____

2b. ____

2c. ____

3a. ____

3b. ____

3c. ____

4a. ____

4b. ____

4c. ____

Monday: Use Basic Search to Find Followers

Your preliminary exercise should result in a few practical ideas you can use to get the week started. Today we're going to show you how you can use the elements of Twitter Search to find followers. For the time being, we're going to limit this instruction to web-based Twitter use (as opposed to going into the search functionality that you might find through third-party applications). It will keep things simple and everyone, regardless of the application they use, can follow along.

Twitter's Search Tools

There are two ways to access Twitter Search via the Web:

- **Within your Twitter profile.** Twitter has a built-in search bar on the right-hand side of your profile (see Figure 5.1).
- **On Search.Twitter.com** (`http://search.twitter.com`). (See Figure 5.2.)

Figure 5.1 The search bar within your Twitter profile

Figure 5.2 Stand-alone search at Search.Twitter.com

Both searches deliver results in reverse chronological order: the most recent tweet containing your search term(s) will appear first. When you use the search bar within your Twitter profile, the results will also be delivered to your profile page (Figure 5.3). When you go to Search.Twitter.com, you will be outside of your profile. Search.Twitter.com's advantage is that it doesn't require you to be logged into your Twitter account to perform a search (Figure 5.4). On the other hand, it's a little more convenient to use the search bar within your profile page because doing so lets you save a click or two by accessing users directly from within your profile.

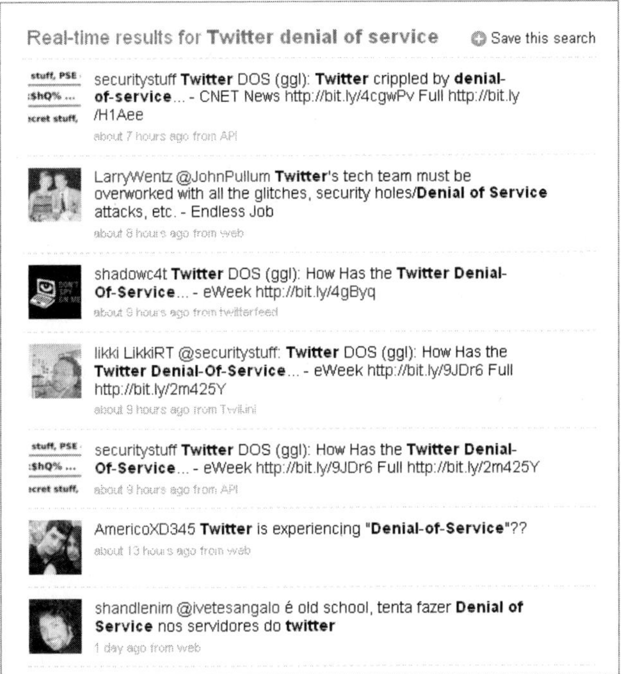

Figure 5.3 Search results from within your Twitter profile

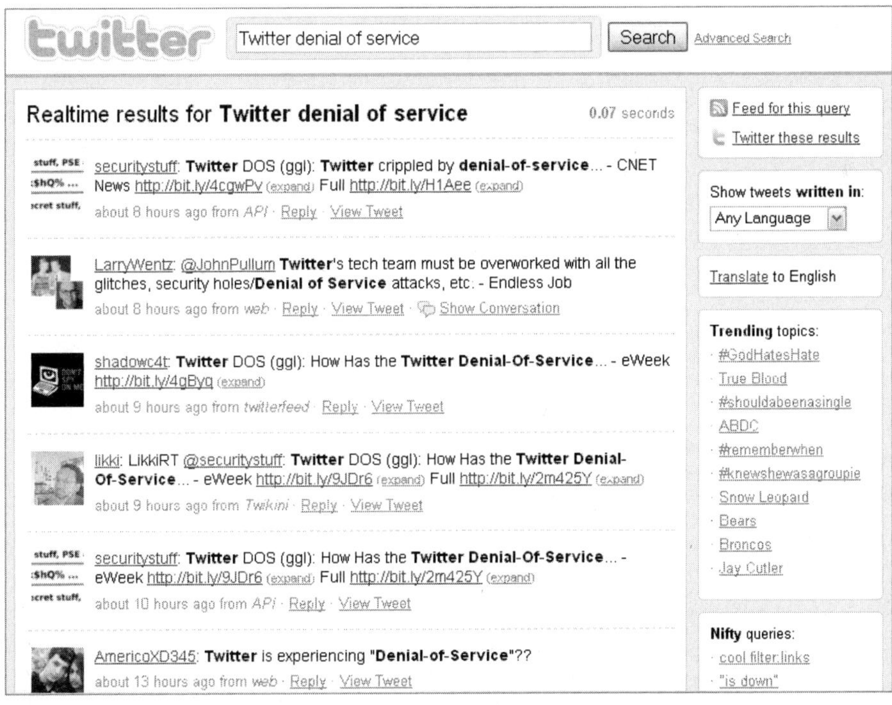

Figure 5.4 Search results on Search.Twitter.com

Note the handy Save this Search feature. Saved searches are helpful when you know you'll want to repeat a search frequently. They appear below the search bar in your Twitter profile (Figure 5.5).

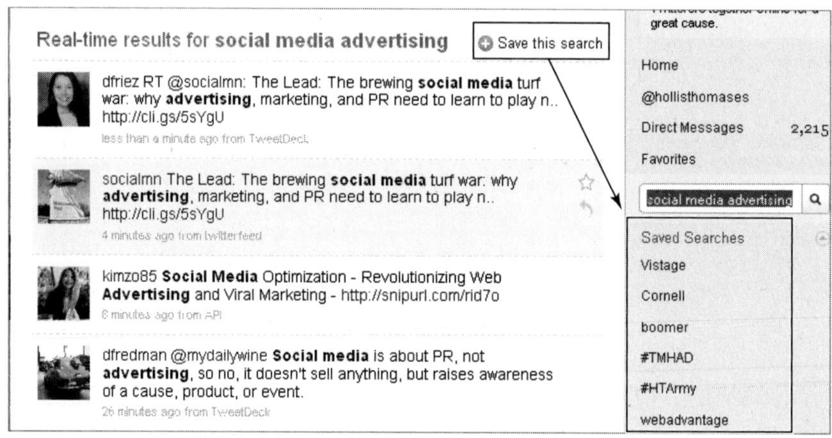

Figure 5.5 Saved searches

Twitter also enables you to subscribe to searches via an RSS feed. Doing so will let you check for search query updates through your RSS reader. Just click the orange icon underneath Following in the Trending Topics list on your search query results page ("RSS feed") (Figure 5.6) and indicate how you want to subscribe to it.

Figure 5.6 Subscribing to a search query via RSS

Either way you search, Twitter will return results that show you people's tweets that include your search keyword or phrase. By reviewing the tweet, you can usually get a sense of whether that person's tweet really relates to your defined subject matter or if they were using that word or phrase in a different context. If the tweet seems relevant, you might want to check out that user; if the tweet was out of context, you will probably skip that user and move on.

Understanding the context of people's tweets is very useful in learning how to attract followers of your own. Pay attention to what people are saying about the subject matter that's important to you. It's likely that if you're interested in searching for this subject matter, other like-minded people are performing similar searches. Learning how to craft your tweets in a context that relates to your subject matter will be useful in attracting followers.

Evaluate Users as Potential Followers

In Week 1, we introduced you to finding people to follow; in Week 3 we'll dive deeper into how to find more information and people through advanced tools. Right now, however, let's spend some time talking about attracting followers. The nuances between finding people to follow versus attracting people to follow you might be subtle. Ask an ordinary Twitter user, and they really don't distinguish between the two. They just go out, find people to follow, and organically grow their following through interactions with these followers.

Businesses, however, probably want to take a more deliberate approach, particularly the more specialized their audience. Businesses should think about this audience ahead of time and determine some criteria by which to evaluate whether or not a user might also make a good follower. Armed with this information, you can take the next steps to attract followers.

It's important to note that the follower evaluation process is not the same marketer to marketer. Based on your organization's agenda, the evaluation process may be very different. You might be fairly nondiscriminatory: you're a mass marketer or a media organization and, therefore, interested and open to attracting anyone and everyone as followers.

On the other extreme, your business might be the type that seeks a limited but very niche-focused group of followers. In this case, it's not about collecting huge numbers of followers: you're largely content to have a finite and well-defined small group of tweeps with whom you can be very actively engaged.

The in-between category is where the majority of users and businesses fall: you're seeking followers with whom you can connect on some fundamental business level, build relationships, exchange information, network, and share insights. In the process, you're working toward the kinds of objectives we covered in Chapter 3, "Twitter, the Multipurpose Platform."

As an individual deliberately seeking to attract followers on behalf of your business, you'll probably find yourself considering the following evaluation criteria:

- What do their bios (or custom background images) reveal about them and their interests? Is there anything that might indicate they'd be likely to follow you?
- What's the ratio of their followers to following? The higher the disparity between their following versus their follower counts, the harder you will probably have to work to attract them as followers.

- Who's following them? Are their followers also potential followers for you, such that engaging with them helps expose you to whole new audiences?
- Who are they following? Might you also want to reach out to any of their friends?
- How recent are their tweets and how frequently do they seem to be on Twitter?
- What are they tweeting about? Do their posts indicate that what you tweet about might be of interest to them?
- Do their tweets display the kind of engagement you're looking for?
- Is there anything in a recent post that you might want to respond to directly and, therefore, attract them to you?

You might actually find the follower evaluation process a bit like dating. Once you determine a tweep is worth trying to attract as a follower, you might need to court this person to earn the follow. How much effort you put into this courtship could be directly related to how much you desire this person as a follower. During your courtship, you might also pick up people who find you "attractive." You'll also find yourself in competition for your target's attention.

Monday's One-Hour Exercise: Searches to Find Followers

Now that you've been shown the basics for conducting Twitter searches and the criteria by which to evaluate tweeps as followers, return to your preliminary exercise.

1. To get a feel for each form of Twitter Search, practice some searches using the keywords you selected in your prep work within your Twitter profile and do some other searches using Search.Twitter.com.
2. When you generate search results, review them for people you think might make relevant followers.
3. Check out the Twitter profiles of potential followers and start to evaluate them. You'll quickly get the hang of the evaluation side of finding followers: your eye will swiftly glance over their tweets, bio, background image, and stats, and you'll assess whether or not you want to try to establish a relationship or court them as followers.
4. If any particular searches regularly seem to yield the kind of followers you're looking for, save the search using Saved Search and the RSS feed for this query.
5. If you find a tweep you want to try to recruit on the spot, try sending this person an `@message`. You might want to make it relevant to something he or she said or you might want to tweet them something you think they'd find interesting. You do *not*, however, want to tweet them a disconnected sales pitch message. This is *not* how to attract quality followers.

Reminder As you go through this process, constantly reevaluate the ideas you originally developed. You might want to change your direction based on the results of your searches.

Tuesday: Add New Friends

"Friends" is an easy way to describe those people you follow, your *following*. It's important to know that you cannot just follow people ad infinitum. Twitter allows anyone to follow up to 2,000 people without limitation, but once you're following 2,000 people, Twitter imposes limits. If 2,000 people or more follow you in return, Twitter allows you to follow more people based on a ratio of the number of people following you.

Reminder The word "friends" is beginning to have two distinct meanings: (1) It is used in place of "following" (people who you follow) because the term "adding new followings" is awkward and is not natural English; and (2) some people now use "friends" to explain that there's a mutual follower/following relationship between two people. For this book's purpose, we will refer to "friends" in the latter context of this definition (see Appendix A, "Twitter-Related Glossary."

The criteria by which you evaluated a potential follower likely also applies to your decision to follow them yourself. As an individual, you might have all sorts of reasons to follow someone, but as a Twitter marketer, the same reasons might not apply. However, this chapter is about getting you acquainted with Twitter as an individual before you start strategizing as a business, so let's keep the funnel wide open.

In Chapter 1, we covered some of the key starting points to finding people to follow, and in the previous section we showed you how to use some of your own important or topical keywords to locate people through Twitter's basic search. Now let's review some other ways to find new friends.

Ask! The simplest way to find and add a new friend is to ask them for their Twitter handle. Be sure to do this when you meet people face-to-face at business networking events, as Twitter handles aren't commonly found on business cards. If you know someone's Twitter handle, you can just append it to the main Twitter URL. For example: `http://www.twitter.com/hollisthomases`. That will take you to their profile page, where you can then click the Follow button and you're off!

Mining Your Following If you follow someone whose tweets really appeal to you, take a look at with whom they're engaging. Who is this person `@replying` to? Who is she or he following? Allow yourself to be curious and explore these other tweeps and determine if they might be good for you to follow too.

Along these lines, there are a few other more direct ways to mine your following. One popular practice started in early 2009 by Twitter user Micah Baldwin (`@micah`) is called FollowFriday (`#followfriday`). On Fridays, using the `#followfriday` tag and Twitter handles, users recommend people to follow. Though oftentimes you'll just see huge run-on lists of `#followfriday` recommendations, the preferred approach is to explain why someone might find the recommended user(s) worth following (see Figure 5.7).

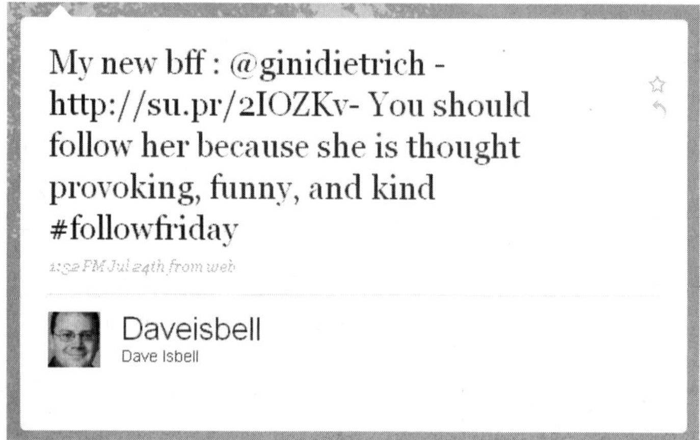

My new bff : @ginidietrich - http://su.pr/2IOZKv- You should follow her because she is thought provoking, funny, and kind #followfriday
1:52 PM Jul 24th from web
Daveisbell
Dave Isbell

Figure 5.7 A FollowFriday recommendation

If you like `#followfriday`, you might also find the website Top Follow Friday (`http://www.topfollowfriday.com`) helpful in locating new or frequently recommended tweeps.

Along the lines of `#followfriday`, `#TweepleTuesday` was created by Sarah Robinson (`@SarahRobinson`) so that on Tuesdays, Twitter users could specifically introduce two tweeps they think should meet (Figure 5.8).

@jenniferbourn meet @StephanieFrank you are both amazing biz women and fabulous people! #tweepletuesday thx 4 the RT!
8:02 PM Jul 21st from TweetDeck
AnnEvanston
Ann Evanston

Figure 5.8 How `#TweepleTuesday` works

Web Directories and Tools In Chapter 3, we went over some web directories and tools to help you find locally based tweeps. Web developers are constantly creating new Twitter tools for us to test and use, and the category of Twitter directories and people-finding tools is a popular one. There are many people-finding tools. Let's cover some relevant ones now, with more to come in Week 3.

Directories and Tools

Twitter tools abound and their uses sometimes overlap, so don't be surprised if they appear more than once in this book. Because of security issues, we will not be listing any sites that both lack a privacy policy and bypass Twitter's OAuth security access.

TwitterCounter TwitterCounter (`http://twittercounter.com`) gives you all kinds of data. You can look up your own Twitter account to see how many people have added you, you can compare your profile to others, or you can locate people who are similar to someone you enter ("If you are interested in *`@handle`* , you might also like these people:").

Twitterholic Twitterholic (`http://www.twitterholic.com`) tracks the top 1,000 Twitter users based on their number of followers. As with TwitterCounter, you can also enter a user's handle to get their stats and see their followers.

FriendorFollow FriendorFollow (`http://friendorfollow.com`) is a nifty service, particularly once you amass some friends and want to see if they're following you back or not. Just enter your Twitter handle, and FriendorFollow will do its little "gap analysis" and identify those people with whom you're not connected. FriendorFollow can also tell you the reverse, namely who's following you without being followed back. Even more helpful, FriendorFollow lets you export the information as a CSV file. Like some of the aforementioned tools, FriendorFollow also provides Twitter Top lists.

WhoShouldiFollow WhoShouldiFollow (`http://www.whoshouldifollow.com`) has you input your username to find relevant people you don't follow. Its adjustable finding scale is a nice feature: you can find people more or less popular and closer or farther away from a particular geographical location (Figure 5.9).

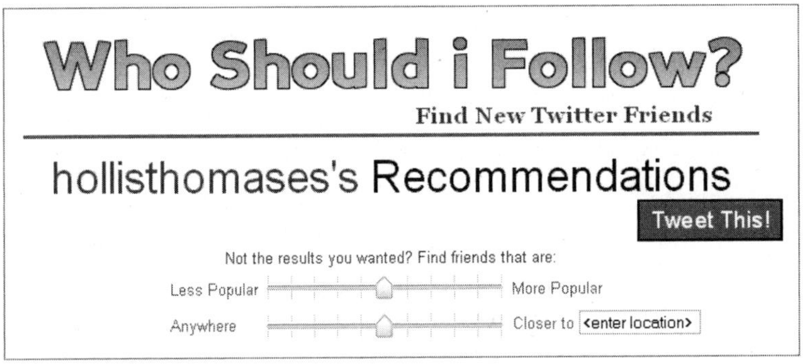

Figure 5.9 WhoShouldiFollow's adjustable scale locates new friends.

Twittersheep Enter your username into Twittersheep (`http://www.twittersheep.com`), and it will create a tag cloud from the bios of people who follow you (Figure 5.10).

Figure 5.10 Twittersheep tag cloud for Marivic Valencia (`@techpr`)

Mr. Tweet Mr. Tweet (`http://mrtweet.com/home`) is similar to WhoShouldIFollow. Although it requires you to be signed in to Twitter and first follow Mr. Tweet, it provides a lot of rich information about the people it recommends for you to follow and it allows you to recommend your followers to others.

WeFollow At WeFollow (`http://www.wefollow.com`), users select up to three categories to assign themselves to using hashtags. The user list in each category is arranged in descending order of users based upon the number of followers each has. Anyone can search the WeFollow directory for any hashtag.

TwitR TwitR (`http://www.twitr.org`) works a lot like WeFollow. Users add themselves using up to three different hashtags. If you're going to add yourself to WeFollow, be consistent and use the same hashtags in TwitR.

TwitDir TwitDir (`http://www.twitdir.com`) is a directory that lets you search for Twitter users by name, username, location, description, or "everywhere."

TweetFind TweetFind is a live Twitter directory (`http://www.tweetfind.com`) with an integrated Twitter News column.

Twibs Twibs (`http://www.twibs.com`) is a directory skewed toward business listings on Twitter. If you're looking for a specific firm, you can also use its alphabetical listing.

twit4 In their own words, "Twit4 (`http://www.twit4.com`) enables companies to organize business-related Twitter accounts all in one spot." You can also submit your company, school, or organization, but you must have an associated website.

ExecTweets I mentioned ExecTweets (`http://www.exectweets.com`) in Chapter 3. It's not the most user-friendly or intuitive site, but you can use it to source business executives, nominate others, or add yourself to its directory (Figure 5.11).

Figure 5.11 ExecTweets

TweepSearch Looking for people just by some criteria of their Twitter bios, a location, or stated interest perhaps? TweepSearch (`http://www.tweepsearch.com`) is an invaluable tool for locating people based on their bios alone. Not only will you find TweepSearch helpful for finding people to follow; it's helpful for other forms of research down the road.

Tweet Scan User Search Like TweepSearch, Tweet Scan User Search (`http://www.tweetscan.com/usersearch.php`) identifies users based on their Twitter bio; but unlike TweepSearch, there is no way to know how many results matched your search or to skip ahead to the next screen.

Note For easy reference, here are the geo-local tools mentioned earlier in the book that you can also use to find people to follow:

- Twellow (`http://www.twellow.com`)
- Tweetmondo (`http://www.tweetmondo.com`)
- monitter (`http://www.monitter.com`)
- Localtweeps (`http://localtweeps.com`)
- ChirpCity (`http://www.chirpcity.com`)
- Twibes (`http://www.twibes.com`)
- TwitterLocal (`http://www.twitterlocal.net`)

Other Kinds of Tweeps to Follow and Why

To get yourself primed for using Twitter for business, don't just think of Twitter as a platform for socializing. By following the news media and your industry publications, you can use Twitter to keep yourself in the know. Opposing viewpoints can add perspective to political and social discussions, so follow people who are different from you. Twitter can also be a great source for competitive intelligence. Follow your competitors, so long as you don't mind them following you back (unless you've created a distinct, unidentifiable account solely for this purpose). Consider following people earlier and further along in their careers than you are. Mentor and be mentored.

News Media Professional journalists mine Twitter for trends and feedback, oftentimes incorporating other people's tweets into their own Twitter streams, even using them on-air and on-site. Find these news outlets (or the faces representing them) through Twitter or Google searches. You can also refer to the journalist databases I referenced earlier: JournalistTweets (`http://journalisttweets.com`) and MediaOnTwitter (`http://www.mediaontwitter.com`).

Industry Publications Almost every industry trade publication is now on Twitter. Following them on Twitter helps you get their latest news…fast.

Mashups A *mashup* is a web application that combines data from two or more sources into a single, integrated tool. Many of the tools mentioned in this book are mashups combining the Twitter API and other bits of data. Once a tool is created, you can often find and follow it on Twitter, which may or may not be helpful to you (although you won't know until you try). Curious to see what's out there for Twitter mashups? Here's a great database from Programmable Web: `http://www.programmableweb.com/mashups/directory/1?apis=twitter`.

Tuesday's One-Hour Exercise: Test Drive Directories and Tools

I've given you more than enough examples of sites and tools to test. It's very easy to get sucked into these directories and tools: one minute you're logging in, and before you know it, 30 minutes has gone by. For Tuesday's exercise, test-drive the various tools and sites we've discussed. Get acquainted with how they work, see what kind of information they deliver, and determine whether they are valuable to you or not. Try to impose some discipline as you conduct these test drives. Don't hesitate to follow good people if you find them—just don't spend more than an initial five minutes on any one site or application. If you like what you see, make a notation in the book or bookmark it in your web browser to come back to another time. This will allow you to draw your own conclusions about what's best for you and why. We'll remind you to come back and revisit these tools when you have time.

Wednesday: Attract Followers

Now that you've learned how to locate and add new friends, you've got the easy part covered. You found and you followed. Authentically attracting followers requires more skill, finesse, communication, and content. Studies have shown that the more you tweet, the more likely you are to attract followers. Sysomos found that people with 100 followers send out an average of 2.5 tweets a day, but those with 1,800 followers, tweet an average of 10.2 times a day. Of course, if everything you tweet is trivial and rather useless to anyone but yourself, not many people will want to follow you.

So, what can you tweet about? If you're being strategic about your tweeting, you should really go back to your motives for attracting followers and your preliminary exercise. Consider the guide in Table 5.1 for starter ideas.

► **Table 5.1** Motives and Tweet Ideas

Motive	Tweet Ideas
Socialize	Events and happenings
	Personal news
	Local news
	Entertaining tidbits

Continues

► **Table 5.1** Motives and Tweet Ideas *(Continued)*

Motive	Tweet Ideas
Network	Friendly or "Do you know" tweets
	Follow-ups
	Asking for help
Provoke Thought	Pose questions
	Write and link to blog posts
	Quote others
	Make a prediction
Inform	Read and filter
	Share information
	Listen and interpret
Lead/influence	Research; share findings
	Conduct interviews
	Make bold statements
	Provoke thought
Publicize	Create and distribute news
	Associate with buzz-worthy topics
Activate (cause-related)	Claim a cause
	Appeal to passions
	Ask for help
Entertain	Share a joke
	Link to videos, photos, or games
Build awareness	Events and happenings
	Industry news/information
	Local news/information
	Write and link to blog posts, videos, podcasts, online presentations, webinars
Drive Traffic: Publishing	Tease an article
	Publish a headline
Promotions and sales	Tweet a coupon code
	Offer a deal or discount
	Twitter-exclusive activities
List building	Stay in the know
	Push future events
	Offers for first XX sign-ups

Principles of Engagement

When you engage people to attract them or others as followers, you should follow the same rules of Twitter etiquette we reviewed last week. You should also try to follow these key rules of engagement:

- **Listen and learn.** Don't feel obligated to dive in both feet first. It's OK to start following people first. Learn how they converse and what they're interested in before you start up a dialog with someone. This way, when you do tweet them, it's more likely to be of greater substance, which will be more attractive to them as well as other followers.
- **Join the conversation.** Most individuals join Twitter and expect to have a two-way dialog. After all, it's no fun talking to a wall.
- **Share first; grow followers as a result.** A strong following is usually the result of a lot of hard work—engaging users, writing blog posts, sharing links, and so on—on the part of the tweep. Consequently, avoid tweeps who have gobs of followers and few updates—they're probably not legit.
- **If someone follows you, do not feel obliged to follow them back.** Twitter should not be reduced to a tit-for-tat platform.
- **Do not set up auto-DM for new followers.** Nothing is worse than getting an auto-DM from someone who just engaged you in a six-tweet conversation, only to get an auto-DM from them 30 minutes later with a message like, "Thanks for the follow. Please tell me why you decided to follow me." Duh! Worse still is someone who uses the DM as a shill to try to get you to do something. "Thanks for the follow. Buy this great guide on how to get 1,000 more followers; just click this link!"
- **Welcome new followers with a personalized tweet.** (See Figure 5.12.) In the beginning, when you have fewer tweeps, this is much easier to do. Imagine, however, how the tweet makes your new follower feel. It's a great way to start the relationship off on a positive note.

@roguepixel99 thanks for following. Sorry that I missed you when I went scouring for Victoria BC #yyj tweeps to follow. Welcome on board.
4 minutes ago from web
yyjtwestival
Twestival Victoria

Figure 5.12 Welcoming a new follower with a customized tweet

- **If someone tweets you, reply to them.** It's not only polite, but it could encourage a whole new branch of conversation from other people catching your thread. (Although DMs are not public, you should reply to them in the same courteous fashion.)
- **When you reply, be mindful of context.** Imagine a perfect stranger reading your solitary tweet in isolation: can they make some sense of it? If they can't, add better context or rewrite the tweet.
- **Be mindful of your Twitter stream.** Imagine you are a first-time visitor to your profile. Would your stream accurately reflect who you are and what you're trying to accomplish on Twitter? Try to post deliberately—that is, do you have a solid balance between `@replies` and original tweets?
- **Be brave.** Reach out to a leader in your industry. If you've been following them a while, one way to start the conversation and get their attention is to comment on a theme you see them working.
  - If you're `@replying` or tweeting a popular power user, don't expect them to reply and don't be offended if they don't. They have a lot of noise in their @ box. If you want to get their attention, write a powerful message or tweet them during off-hours when you see they're online but Twitter has less traffic.
- **Help the community.** Answer questions and be a resource. People will appreciate the help you've provided and will likely be more loyal followers and retweeters as a result.
- **When linking to someone else's content, give that source credit within your tweet.** For example, CNN will give NBC credit if airing a clipping of NBC's film footage, so on Twitter, you should do likewise. (See Figure 5.13 and Figure 5.14.)

Figure 5.13 The right way to credit the content source (MediaPost)

Figure 5.14 Less-properly tweeting the same article

- **Leave room for retweets.** When composing a tweet you think is retweet-worthy, try to leave enough blank spaces for `RT+@yourusername`, so others won't need to edit your tweet.
- **Give credit for retweets.** When retweeting someone's post, give them credit, even if you have to edit their original tweet slightly. Credit can be in the form of a direct copy and paste of their tweet with `RT` in front of their *`@username`*; it can be a lead-in, such as "And another gem from *`@username`*" (Figure 5.15); or you can use "via *`@username`*" when referencing them as an original source.
    - If what you're retweeting has a link, it's proper to retain the original link. The user might be tracking through that link, and changing it will break their tracking chain.
    - If a retweet has too many people to properly credit in 140 characters, give credit to the most recent and the original tweeps.
    - It's OK to use a retweet to add your own commentary or direct it to a specific tweep's attention. This helps add to the conversation.
- **If you don't have something meaningful to say, say less of it.** Posting pointless tweets won't win you many new friends.

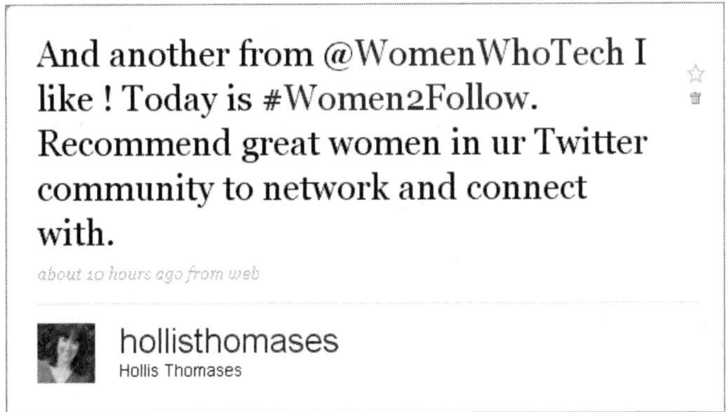

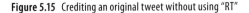

Figure 5.15 Crediting an original tweet without using "RT"

- **Don't tweet points in endless rapid succession.** Most tweeps will find that a turn-off and view it as clutter in their Twitter stream. If you have that much to say, write a blog post and direct users there.
    - If you don't have a blog, quick-and-easy tools such as Posterous (`http://www.posterous.com`) or Tumblr (`http://www.tumblr.com`) make versatile blogging a snap.
- **It's OK to tweet the same thing more than once over time.** People have so much going on in their Twitter streams that the odds are slim that they'll catch your one and only tweet about an important subject. If it's important to you, particularly if you're trying to generate action, tweet it more than once and at different times of day. Just don't tweet the same thing over and over or tweet the same thing too close together timewise.
- **Heed your friends when integrating your Twitter stream into your Facebook profile.** Divergent opinions exist on the better practice. One school of thought says not to integrate your Twitter stream into Facebook if you plan on tweeting a lot. The other says it's no big deal. I believe, however, that it varies by individual. You should listen to the feedback you receive from your Facebook friends. If they tend not to comment positively on your tweets, you should consider disengaging the feed.
- **Don't overdo it on SMS lingo and abbreviations**. Twitter may limit you to 140 characters, but unlike text messaging, Twitter's culture isn't as accepting of language shortcuts, particularly if an entire tweet is composed that way. It's OK to substitute a "u" or a "2" here or there for a "you" and "to," but too many abbreviations can make your tweet difficult to decipher.
    - The more you tweet for business, the less socially acceptable are shortcuts and abbreviations.
- **Similarly, don't overdo it with hashtags.** In general, the maximum number of hashtags in any given tweet shouldn't exceed three.
    - That being said, hashtags can be very useful to bookmark or flag a tweet for someone searching on that particular subject matter or seeking a common thread. You'll often see hashtags appear in Trending Topics because they're easy to find and they catch on quickly.

Reminder If you have a lot in common with a group or are based in the same vicinity, consider continuing your conversation off-line either by email or by organizing a tweetup. Meeting people face-to-face is one of the coolest outcomes of Twitter.

Hashtags in Tweets

Follow a Topic

In their simplest forms, hashtags are bookmarks: a way for anyone looking for that topic or tag to find your tweet. If someone you follow and respect uses a hashtag that strikes your curiosity, do a Twitter search to see if you can find out what it's about. You might want to follow that hashtag too.

Live-Tweet an Event

At most interactive industry conferences these days, the organizers will indicate the hashtag for the conference and the various sessions so that Twitter users can post and others can follow along. Long after a conference has ended, you'll likely still find people tweeting about some topic or another.

Congregate as a Twitter Group

There are now groups (for example, `#smallbizchat`, `#pr20chat`) that have formed and regularly meet each week to discuss a topic.

Debate or Interview

Tweeps can come together for a short, one-off debate, participating via the use of a hashtag.

Flag, Alert, or Show Solidarity

Hashtags can be used to call attention to something, be it trivial like the winner of a reality television show (`#bachelorette`) or serious like the Iranian election protestors (`#IranElection`).

Collective Mentality

As we discussed in Chapter 1, Twitter manifests the notion of crowdsourcing. When it comes to attracting followers, there's a similar coming together of people to form a collective mentality. Even though all of us are isolated in front of the devices through which we tweet, like typical human beings, we have a propensity to form groups. Because of this, a few things could happen to help you build a following.

You might find people from groups or communities of which you're already a member. Connect with others in these groups on Twitter. Twitter's *multiplier effect* means that tweets between you and a member of this group will not only expose you to other members but also to anyone else following those tweeps.

People like to "get in on the action." It's one of the reasons that Trending Topics take off in the first place. Tweeps can congregate virtually around a topic like a flash mob, or they can come together slowly, gathering momentum over time. In the latter instance, you're much more likely to meet, follow, and be followed by other users. In actuality, a new type of group is formed.

If you're a real data wonk, you might be interested in reading HubSpot analyst Dan Zarrella's (`@DanZarrella`) "The Science of ReTweets" on Mashable (`http://mashable.com/2009/02/17/twitter-retweets`). It is chock-full of retweet data analysis, and it has a formula for calculating the *retweetability* of a user.

Timely Tweets

Believe it or not, there are actually better times of day and days of the week to tweet. People tweet the most on Tuesday through Friday, so if you want to reach an active audience, you probably want to tweet on those days. There is conflicting information about the most popular day for tweeting. HubSpot reports Thursday as the most popular, and Sysomos finds that Tuesday is (Figure 5.16 and Figure 5.17).

As for the heaviest tweeting hour of the day, HubSpot found spikes at 10:00 AM, 5:00 PM, and 10:00 PM (EST); while Sysomos found tweeting between 11:00 AM and 3 PM (EST) to be the most popular (Figure 5.18 and Figure 5.19). Dan Zarrella's findings showed retweets most likely to occur between 8:00 AM and 7:00 PM, with the peak being at 2:00 PM (Figure 5.20).

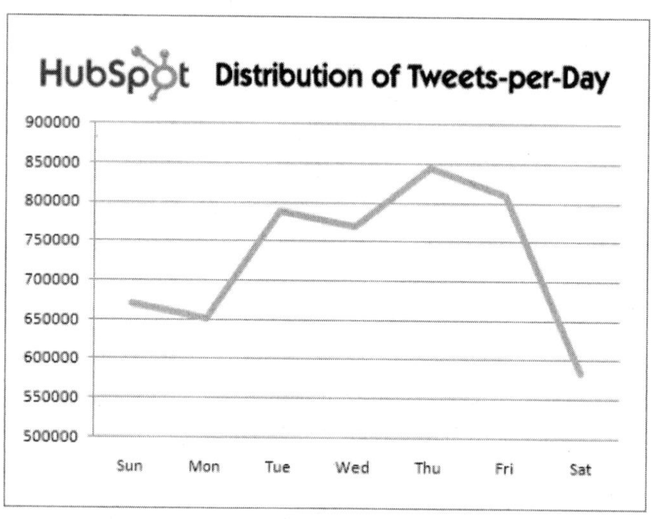

Figure 5.16 HubSpot's days-of-the-week tweeting analysis 2009

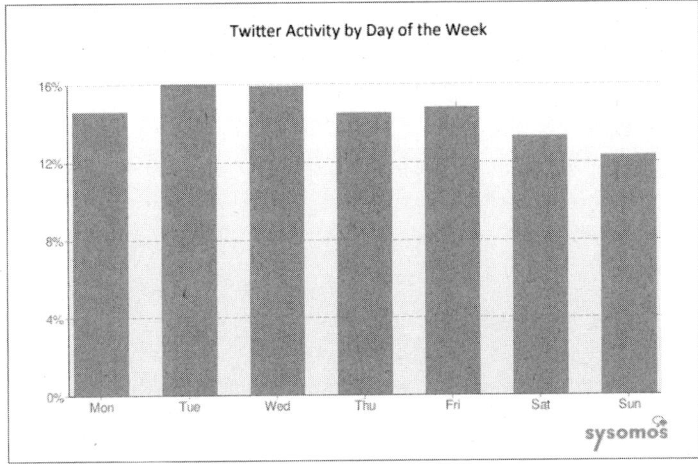

Figure 5.17 Sysomos' days-of-the-week tweeting analysis 2009

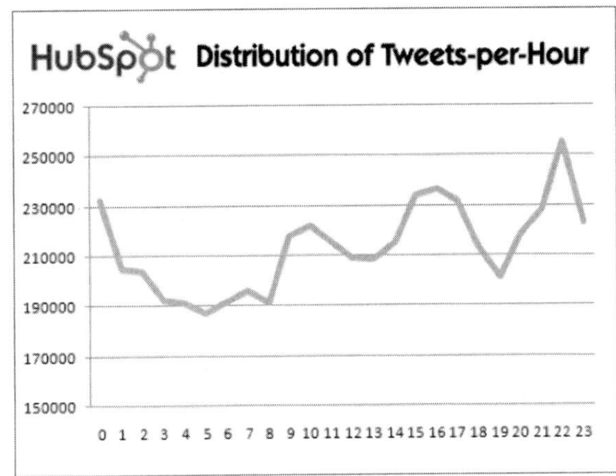

Figure 5.18 HubSpot's time-of-day tweeting analysis 2009

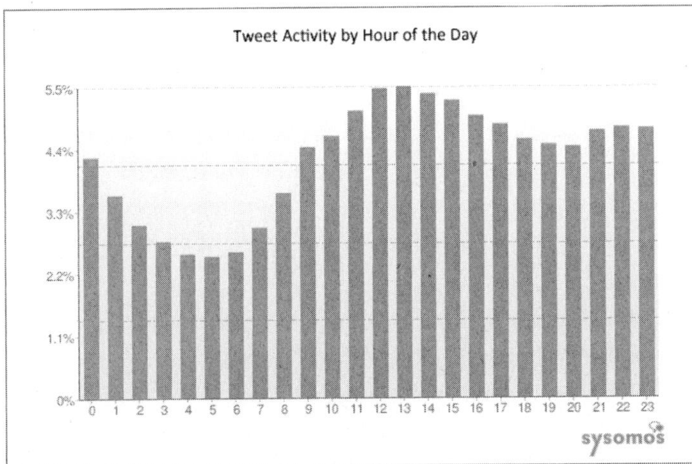

Figure 5.19 Sysomos' time-of-day tweeting analysis 2009

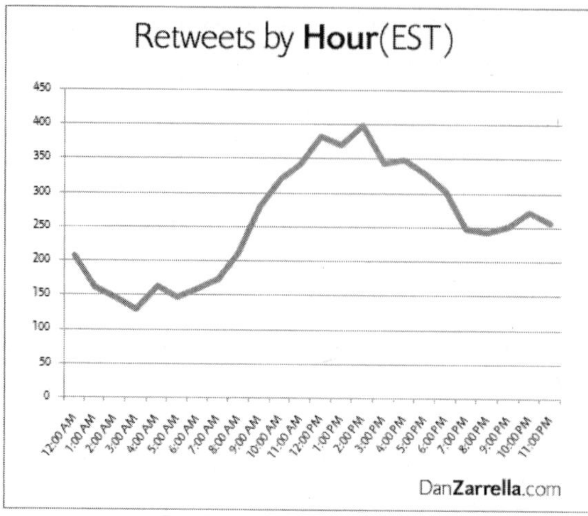

Figure 5.20 Dan Zarrella's time-of-day retweeting analysis 2009

With Twitter, however, everything is in the moment. Have a great thought? Tweet it now, and it'll be posted now for the world to see. You don't want to wait to post your tweet for the right time because the opportunity might pass or the thought might escape you. Fortunately, tweet scheduling tools are available to cleverly let you tweet now but post later. Two such tools are HootSuite (`http://hootsuite.com`) and SocialOomph (`http://www.Socialoomph.com`). (See Figure 5.21.)

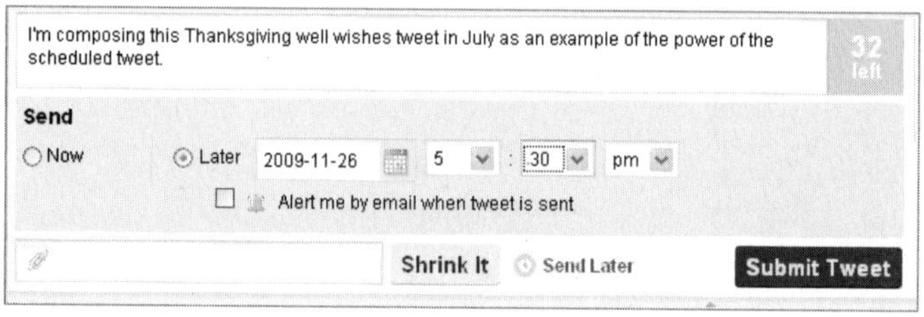

I'm composing this Thanksgiving well wishes tweet in July as an example of the power of the scheduled tweet.
32 left
Send
Now
Later 2009-11-26 5 : 30 pm
Alert me by email when tweet is sent
Shrink It
Send Later
Submit Tweet

Figure 5.21 A scheduled tweet via HootSuite

All this being said, when everyone is tweeting at the same time, your messages might get lost. So use the rule of well-executed frequency to help get your word out, and don't be surprised if you also have success in off-peak hours. There might be fewer people to reach, but your message might better resonate with those who receive it.

Auto-Follow and Auto-DM

In the rules of engagement, I advised against using an auto-DM solution. It's inauthentic and can nip even the best tweeps in the bud. As your popularity grows, however, it's not unreasonable to consider using an auto-follow solution. You might intend to keep up with your new followers and determine manually whether or not they're worth following, but your volume of followers just might get out of control so you won't be able to keep up with them. This isn't necessarily a bad problem to have!

Yet too much volume can be a problem. During the summer of 2009, some power users received so much spam and so many unwanted messages that they had to act. Chris Brogan discontinued his auto-follow practice, and Robert Scoble discontinued auto-following and completely unfollowed everyone he was following. You can read about this on Brand Republic: `http://www.brandrepublic.com/News/925403/Tech-blogger-Robert-Scoble-unfollows-thousands-Twitter-spam-onslaught`.

To manage the flow, you can use a third-party auto-follower solution such as Twollow (`http://twollow.com`), SocialToo (`http://www.socialtoo.com`), or SocialOomph (`http://www.Socialoomph.com`). I should caution you against a little snafu that can result from auto-following. Twitter scam artists send out *phishing bots* to try to identify users who are set up with auto-follow. Once you follow them, their junky messages will clog up your feed, they can DM you the same junk, and it will feel even more offensive. If they're doing so for the purpose of identifying and compiling a database of "ready-prey" users with auto-follow, you can bet they'll be resell those names to other spammers.

Wednesday's One-Hour Exercise: Practice Rules of Engagement

The only way to really get comfortable with these common Twitter best practices is to regularly utilize them. Today's exercise is designed to give you a head start.

1. Using the rules of engagement presented today, try to execute each one that specifically addresses an action. See which one generates the best reaction for you, and make a note of it for future reference.
2. Set up a HootSuite or SocialOomph account. Develop, compose, and schedule some future tweets.

Reminder Practice initiating a conversation or skillfully inserting yourself into someone else's.

Thursday: Syndicate Your Tweet Content

Once you get the hang of tweeting, it's a good idea to leverage your tweet content for greater exposure. For example, if you see someone's Twitter stream while visiting their blog, that blogger is probably using a widget to interface between Twitter and the blog and pull the blogger's tweets to be displayed simultaneously on the blog. Also, you might be logged into your Facebook account and see your friend's posts from Twitter in their newsfeed. This feature was enabled by installing a Facebook application. You can also post to or post through other third-party applications to deliver more content to your Twitter stream. Because you already have a Twitter account and you're trying to attract followers through your tweets, you might as well use this content to improve your chances.

Twitter Widgets

The term *widget,* when used with Twitter, generally means some code that allows your tweets to be pulled into and be displayed graphically on a location other than Twitter .com. Many blogging platforms, such as WordPress, provide links to the widgets (*plug-ins*) that have been written to work for their platforms. Dozens of Twitter widgets have been developed, and most require just a simple copy and paste of their code to get started. Twitter even offers versions to get you started (`http://twitter.com/widgets`), or you can find ones more to your liking through a simple search (Figure 5.22).

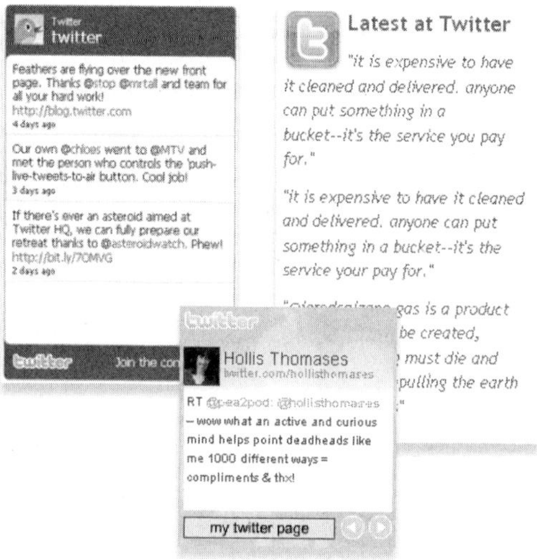

Figure 5.22 Various Twitter widgets display tweets.

Specialized Feeds

A feed formats content for distribution and subscription. Unlike widgets that display your Twitter stream graphically, feeds do not. To view a feed, you must subscribe to it and view it through a third-party reader. One solution for creating a feed from your Twitter stream is Twitterfeed (`http://twitterfeed.com`). Twitterfeed prepares your tweets in an RSS format so that people can, usually with a single click of an icon, subscribe to it. Twitterfeed also provides statistics about subscriptions to your feed.

Push Tools

Got something to say that you want to tweet about? In some circumstances (for example, when broadcasting or sharing news), it might be more worthwhile to post your news to an application that instantaneously broadcasts to all your social networks, including Twitter, at once. We define these solutions as *push* tools, because they're really meant to push out information, rather than be used to carry on conversations. Some examples of these applications include Ping.fm (`http://ping.fm`), FriendFeed (`http://friendfeed.com`), and HelloTxt (`http://hellotxt.com`). These tools are helpful when used in conjunction with Twitter, but are not a replacement for it.

Thursday's One-Hour Exercise: Get Comfortable with Content Tools

Working backward, check out the push tools mentioned in this section. Using any of these solutions is free, so why not sign up for an account or two? Then do a little research on TwitterFeed and Twitter widgets that you can incorporate into your blog or website. You may not be ready to take the plunge yet, but at least you'll have your homework done when you are.

Friday: Tools to Help Build and Manage Followers

Many of the tools we discussed on Tuesday to help you find followers are the very same tools you'll want to use over and over again to help build your followers. Just because someone's not following you now doesn't mean they won't be in the near future. Some of these tools have advanced features. Additionally, several of the more advanced third-party Twitter applications have follow-management features. It'll be hard to mention them without stepping on their thunder in Week 3, but if nothing else, we can prep you with a little sneak preview.

Reminder It's FollowFriday (`#FollowFriday`)! Check out who your friends are recommending, and practice by recommending some tweeps on your own!

The Advantages and Disadvantages of Tools

Tools can be very helpful by simplifying and automating a lot of the maintenance for your Twitter account:

- Tools can be very helpful for newbies just getting started.
- Tools can help busy people with the sourcing and daily management of followers and tweet streams.
- Tools can reveal more information about a follower and allow you to do more activities in a single place than can Twitter.

Of course, there are also disadvantages to using them:

- I've already given you my advice and cautions about auto-follow and auto-DM tools. Many tweeps can see right through your high-tech solution, and they may not like it. Because Twitter makes forming perceptions so rapid-fire, you may not have a chance to undo an initial faux pas if that's how your follower views it.

- Auto-follow tools in particular can lead to high-quantity but low-quality followers. Is that helping you?

Follower Identification and Management Tools

Some tools help you connect the dots, clarifying the relationship between you and another Twitter user.

Tools to Help Identify Tweeps

With millions of Twitter accounts and dozens, hundreds, thousands, or even millions of followers, it's not hard to lose track of whether someone is following you or not.

DoesFollow DoesFollow (`http://www.doesfollow.com`) is a simple yet extremely useful application to address this problem. Just type in the username of the person you want to identify as a follower or nonfollower, and DoesFollow will give you a quick Yup or Nope response (Figure 5.23 and Figure 5.24).

Figure 5.23 DoesFollow's simple solution to a tough question

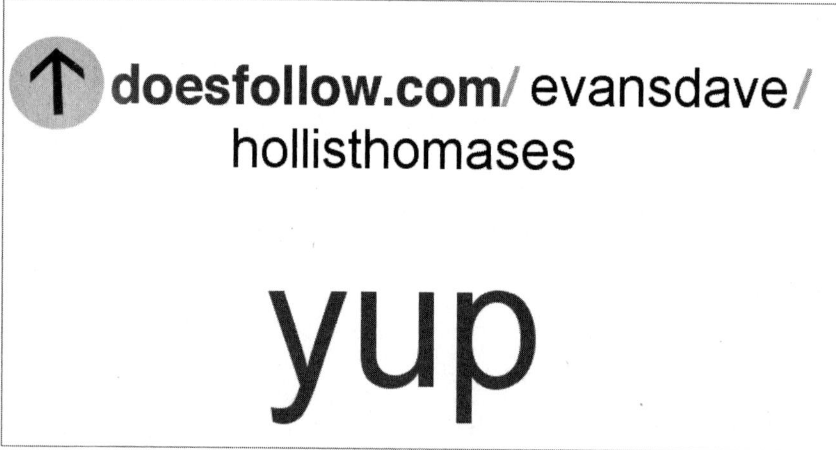

Figure 5.24 DoesFollow offers a simple response.

FriendorFollow Mentioned previously, FriendorFollow (`http://friendorfollow.com`) helps you identify people you are following (following) but who are not following you back—and vice versa (fans). it also shows you mutual following relationships (friends). FriendorFollow shows all of these relationships as a collage of their avatars, which can make it easy to visually identify particular tweeps for whom you might be searching. You can also change the sort options from their username to their name, location, followers, following, last tweet, and account age. Each avatar is a direct link to their Twitter account. This whole application is streamlined and very user-friendly.

Tools to Help Manage Tweeps

In a moment, we're going to discuss what commonly comes to people's minds when they think about managing tweeps: their Twitter client. The most robust Twitter clients definitely offer ways to manage tweeps as well as tweets, but these next tools are not full-blown Twitter clients, which sets them apart.

Twitter for Busy People This is a very cool web-based application that also displays tweeps by their avatars, but in this instance, it's only people you're following. Twitter for Busy People (`http://t4bp.com`) lists people in chronological order, with their most recent tweet first. Hover your cursor over a tweep, and their most recent tweet will appear; if the tweet was in response to another user, you can drill down into the conversation (Figure 5.25).

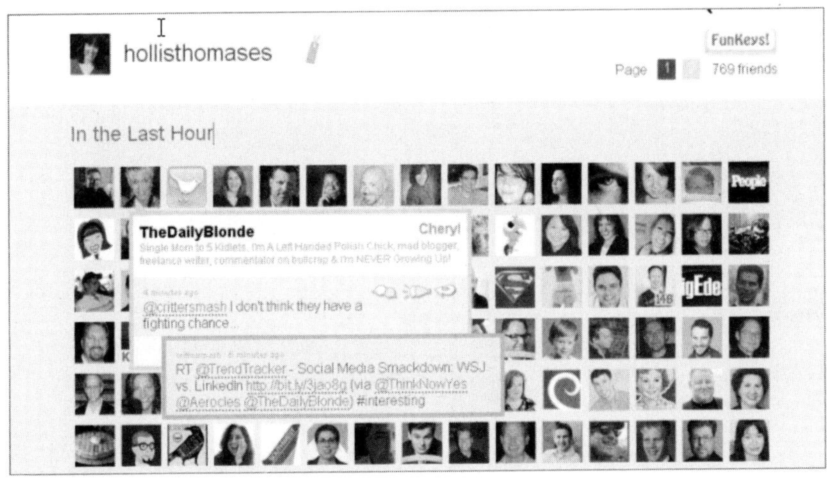

Figure 5.25 Twitter for BusyP eople

Twitter 100 Kind of like a lighter version of Twitter for Busy People, Twitter 100 (`http://twitter100.com`) displays up to 100 of your tweeps who have made recent posts. Unlike Twitter for Busy People, however, Twitter 100 has an auto-refresh feature, which is quite helpful (Figure 5.26).

Figure 5.26 Twitter 100

TwerpScan Billing itself as "anti-fool contact management," TwerpScan (`http://www.twerpscan.com`) performs a computation that checks the number of followers of all your contacts (following) and the number of people they are following, and then computes the ratio between these two pieces of data. From the output, you can sort the list and make follow, unfollow, and/or block decisions on the spot (Figure 5.27).

TWERP SCAN

Welcome,

Home → Manage Contacts You're Following

Screen name	Name	F'ers	F'ing	R	#T	Last
loudHIVE	loudHIVE	3631	4037	1:1	756	2009-01-25
PLVistageChair	Philip Liebman	540	571	1:1	466	2009-04-02
waldosimon	Simon Schanche	282	294	1:1	54	2009-04-22
ematlick	Erik Matlick	34	37	1:1	5	2009-04-28
socialHigh	Laura	1501	1969	1:1	114	2009-04-29
RichardSHearn	Richard Hearn	447	520	1:1	97	2009-05-16
jjbugs	Jayla Boire	17	16	1:1	35	2009-05-18
BaltimoreLives	Baltimorelives	177	101	2:1	309	2009-05-26

Figure 5.27 Managing your following with TwerpScan

Twitter Karma A bit like TwerpScan, Twitter Karma (`http://dossy.org/twitter/karma`) fetches your friends and followers from Twitter when you click its Whack! button. The results are ordered based on the most recent tweet, and simple symbols/text indicate your relationship to this person. You can re-sort the list by user handle or filter it to show only one kind of relationship. Once the results are displayed as you'd like, scroll all the way down to the bottom of the page where you can checkmark the users on which you want to perform the following actions: Bulk Follow, Bulk Unfollow, or Bulk Block. This feature is very handy, particularly to get rid of useless bottom feeders (Figure 5.28).

Figure 5.28 Managing your Twitter relationships with Twitter Karma

Twitter Clients Help Manage Tweeps

In Chapter 1, I listed some popular third-party applications called *clients* that can manage your Twitter use. Now that we're into your Hour-a-Day work, we'll discuss some of these clients and their features in more detail. For example, some of the advanced applications—TweetDeck (desktop and iPhone), Seesmic (desktop and the Web), HootSuite (the Web), PeopleBrwsr (the Web)—give you tweep-management controls such as the ability to sort people into groups, one-click RTs and DMs, timing the frequency of your Twitter stream refreshes (how often you'll receive new tweets), and more. You should give a few of these clients a test drive to compare them.

Four clients are worth touching on because they perform more unique functions:

TweetDeck TweetDeck (`http://www.tweetdeck.com`) offers many powerful features, but here are the ones I want to emphasize:

- TweetDeck allows you to register for syncing so that no matter how many computers you install TweetDeck on, you do not have to remember all of your customizations, such as groups, members of groups, or saved searches.
- TweetDeck has a handy one-click Spam button. With just one click of this button, TweetDeck deletes the unwanted message from view, blocks the user, and reports them to Twitter. It's TweetDeck's version of the Easy button.
- TweetDeck also has an iPhone application that allows you to sync from your desktop to your iPhone and vice versa. This gives you TweetDeck's powerful grouping feature (columns) on the go.

HootSuite Web-based HootSuite (`http://hootsuite.com`) enables you to easily manage multiple Twitter user accounts from a very clean interface. Like with TweetDeck, you can create and move groups and saved searches into columns, but HootSuite also lets you add tabs for additional columns. HootSuite has a built-in URL shortener (ow.ly) with a statistics dashboard, and you can pre-schedule tweets for future dates and times.

twalala twalala (`http://twalala.com`) describes itself as "Twitter with a mute button." It's a Twitter client that allows you to control what you see and what you don't see in your Twitter stream. You can filter tweets out of your stream by keywords and phrases, or you can mute individuals who get a bit too chatty.

DestroyTwitter With such an imposing name, you'd think DestroyTwitter (`http://www.destroytwitter.com`) was something working against Twitter, when in fact it's actually another powerful third-party client. It has many of the same advanced features of TweetDeck and others, but DestroyTwitter also has some nifty added features that help with tweep management. I like the include/exclude rules that put you in control of whose tweets are displayed in the application's window. You can follow someone and not necessarily have to view their tweets all the time. I also like the Quick Friend Lookup feature, which attempts to auto-complete a Twitter handle as you type it. DestroyTwitter also has an Away mode that freezes all the tweets in your window so that you don't lose your place if you need to step away from your computer.

A Word about Unfollows

It's going to happen. People are going to stop following you. They follow you on Twitter for various reasons. Those reasons may not have a lasting purpose, so you should expect this to happen. Don't lose any sleep over it, and if you notice someone in particular who's no longer following you, don't harass them about it. That's definitely poor twetiquette.

Is there a way to identify who's stopped following you? Yes, you can use several of the tools listed previously, which inform you of the relationship you have (or don't have) with a tweep. Two applications are specifically designed for the purpose of notifying you about unfollows: Qwitter (`http://useqwitter.com`) and Twitterless (`http://twitterless.com`). I don't encourage you to use either tool, because spending a valuable one hour to review specific unfollows is, in my opinion, not worth it, particularly if many of them are likely to be bots or spammers who followed you just to get you to follow them back. Instead, you should focus on whether you're steadily trending downward in the number of your followers rather than upward. If this is the case, you have bigger problems that need your attention.

Friday's One-Hour Exercise: Start Managing Your Tweeps

The more tweeps you get, the harder they will be to manage; so it's better to test-drive these management applications now. Here's what I want you to do:

- Play around with the features particularly related to user management—that is, create groups or columns, add and remove people from these groups, and apply other filters or rules I've told you about that seem of interest. Spend no more than 30 minutes on this exercise (5–10 minutes per application). *Once you install these applications, do not have them all open at once. Each of them has to place a server call through the Twitter API, which has hourly limits. By having more than one Twitter application calling the server at the same time, you might exceed your limit and have to wait for the next refresh to do anything.*
- In the remaining 30 minutes, try out some of the other tools we talked about today such as FriendorFollow, TwitterForBusyPeople, and TwerpScan. You can also add, unfollow, or tweet users while you perform this exercise. Just be mindful of your time. It's going to fly very quickly!

The Main Points

- Accumulating quality followers doesn't just happen. You need a game plan, an understanding of what motivates various Twitter users, and a willingness to put in a lot of hard work.
- A lot of tools are available to help you find and manage your followers. Put them to good use, but be forewarned that some of them, the follower-finding tools in particular, can suck up a lot of your time. Proceed judiciously.
- Tweet deliberately and strategically. Put the rules of engagement into regular practice. Revisit them and remind yourself of them frequently. Consider tweeting (or pre-scheduling tweets) during the best times of day and days of week to attract those you most want to reach. Above all else, remember that your tweets will be part of the public record—period.

- Hashtags and retweets are an important part of positive engagement. Plan to use them regularly.
- If you can avoid it, don't auto-DM. It doesn't come across as personal, and your auto-DM message could be contrary to a conversation you've already had with the recipient.

Week 3: Use Twitter Search and Other Tools to Improve Your Experience

Twitter can be a virtual goldmine of information for brands. To help you monitor conversations and parse through data, Twitter and other third parties provide tools that let you search on particular keywords and receive alerts when someone mentions you. The results can help you understand how people use twitter and how you tweet in relation to these tweets which help you define and create a Twitter strategy. Perhaps you can unearth a great idea, a new business opportunity, or new potential customers from these searches.

Chapter Contents

Search and Other Tools for Twitter

Today you're going to learn the ins and outs of using Search to make you a more proficient user and ideally a more proficient Twitter marketer. Why is Search so important? With over three million tweets a day by some estimates, in order to make sense of the clutter, you will need to develop a strategy to find the information you're seeking. So what should you search on? Obviously that depends on your goals, but finding the right keywords and being at the right place at the right time can help you identify someone's need and be there with an instantaneous solution.

Real-time searching is a powerful tool for a business. Let's say, for example, you own an email marketing company. You would want to search on your company's name, any misspellings and abbreviations of your company name, your competitors' names, and certainly the terms "email marketing" and "email ASP." Over time, you can add or subtract search terms to your queries based on what you are seeing or what's happening in your marketplace. This is the incredible listening power that happens on Twitter. Hear what potential customers are talking about, and then figure out how to get in front of them.

The fundamental Twitter Search is easy. Knowing about, using, and mastering all of the additional tools at your disposal can be the challenging part. That's why this week's lesson is important.

Monday: Master Twitter Search

If you plan to use Twitter for marketing, you'll find Search an invaluable tool. Let's walk through the learning process from the fundamentals to advanced techniques.

Monday's Preliminary Exercise

In preparation for your Twitter Search education, do this exercise and keep it handy:

1. Write down your company's name and any of its common misspellings or unique abbreviations.
2. Write down your top three to five competitors' names and their common misspellings or unique abbreviations.
3. Write down your top half-dozen most important products or services by name.
4. Write down associated modifiers or descriptors relevant to the previous products or services—for example, geographical focus, audiences, industries, colors, flavors, and such.
5. Write down five keywords that people would search for on Google in order to find your website (you can repeat keywords from Week 2 here).

Using this list, you are going to put Twitter Search through its paces.

Twitter's Built-In Search

In Week 2, you saw how Twitter has made search a lot easier by integrating the ability to search directly from within your profile on Twitter.com. (Remember, you must be logged in to do so.) You learned how to save a search to retrieve refreshed results in only one click and how to subscribe to a search query via RSS. Eliminating a saved search is as easy as saving it. Merely click the link to the saved search and, at the top right of the query results, click Remove This Saved Search to eliminate the search from your list.

Advanced Twitter Search

Sometimes, a basic Twitter Search just isn't enough. The results may be too voluminous or too broad, and you need something more robust. For example, if you are a local Boston-based business and don't want to know when *everyone* on Twitter types "pizza," you only want to see when people in Boston type "pizza," you can use the Advanced Search option of Twitter Search (`http://search.twitter.com/advanced`). (See Figure 6.1.) Advanced Search can be invaluable; you might want to save it as a button on your browser's toolbar. Because of its importance, many people believe that Advanced Search will soon be integrated directly into Twitter.com, rather than exist as separate website.

twitter
Search
Advanced Search

Advanced Search

Use this form to automatically construct your query. (Alternatively, you can type search operators directly into the search box.)

Find tweets based on...
Search

Words
All of these words
This exact phrase
Any of these words
None of these words
This hashtag
Written in: Any Language (persistent)

People
From this person
To this person
Referencing this person

Places
Near this place
Within this distance: 15 miles kilometers

Dates
Since this date
Until this date

Attitudes
With positive attitude :)
With negative attitude :(
Asking a question ?

Other
Containing links
Results per page: 15 (persistent)

Search

Figure 6.1 Twitter's Advanced Search

Advanced Search gives you the option to filter your search by specific criteria:

- Keyword inclusion/exclusion
- Hashtags (When entering a hashtag in the hashtag field, do not use the # symbol.)
- Language
- To, from, or referencing a person (Use handles rather than people's full names to get the best results.)
- Locations, optionally narrowed by distance
- Date ranges (They can be an extremely helpful feature, but Twitter does not have an extensive public archive currently. It allows applications to access up to 3,200 of any user's tweets. Tweets can disappear from view prior to the 3,200 count, so don't expect results to appear that are more than about 30 days old.)
- Attitudes or questions, as indicated by punctuation
- Containing links

Just complete the fields that are relevant to you and leave the others blank. Do you want to take search filtering up another notch? Try incorporating Twitter *search operators* where appropriate (Figure 6.2).

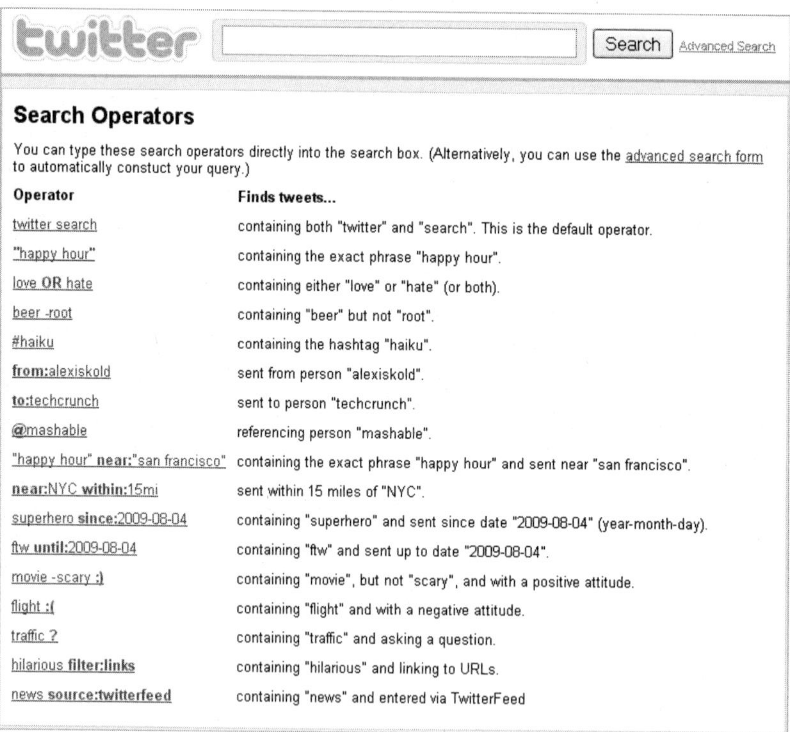

Search Operators

You can type these search operators directly into the search box. (Alternatively, you can use the advanced search form to automatically constuct your query.)

Operator	Finds tweets...
twitter search	containing both "twitter" and "search". This is the default operator.
"happy hour"	containing the exact phrase "happy hour".
love **OR** hate	containing either "love" or "hate" (or both).
beer -root	containing "beer" but not "root".
#haiku	containing the hashtag "haiku".
from:alexiskold	sent from person "alexiskold".
to:techcrunch	sent to person "techcrunch".
@mashable	referencing person "mashable".
"happy hour" **near:**"san francisco"	containing the exact phrase "happy hour" and sent near "san francisco".
near:NYC **within:**15mi	sent within 15 miles of "NYC".
superhero **since:**2009-08-04	containing "superhero" and sent since date "2009-08-04" (year-month-day).
ftw **until:**2009-08-04	containing "ftw" and sent up to date "2009-08-04".
movie -scary :)	containing "movie", but not "scary", and with a positive attitude.
flight :(	containing "flight" and with a negative attitude.
traffic ?	containing "traffic" and asking a question.
hilarious **filter:links**	containing "hilarious" and linking to URLs.
news **source:twitterfeed**	containing "news" and entered via TwitterFeed

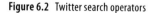

Figure 6.2 Twitter search operators

You can use search operators in the form or, if you become familiar enough with them, use them when you conduct basic Twitter searches, as they'll yield the same results. For example, if you want to search on "ice cream" in New York City, you can complete the Advanced Search form, or you can just enter **"ice cream" near: "New York City"** in the search box in your Twitter profile. (The quotation marks tell Twitter that you're looking for an exact phrase.) Look how this kind of search might help a local street vendor (Figure 6.3).

Peddling ice cream at Greene & Prince,12-8p W. 13th & Washington st.12-11p, Bedford & N 7th.12-12p and University and 12th from 8p-11p enjoy
VLAIC
Van Leeuwen Artisan

Figure 6.3 One New York City ice cream vendor's tweet

If you're using Advanced Search for business, try to put yourself in your customers' shoes. What kinds of questions might they be asking related to your or your competitor's products or services? Using the email marketing example from earlier in this chapter, if you searched on **"do you" "email marketing"**, you would get an incredible list of people asking questions about email marketing (Figure 6.4). What a super way to see what people are currently talking about as it pertains to your company and to be able to engage with potential customers and answer their questions. Talk about getting a chance to make a great first impression!

Figure 6.4 Twitter search results can open the door to opportunity.

Once you have found searches that provide relevant search results for you, you can create an RSS feed to monitor your results on a daily or hourly basis so you can respond quickly.

Other Search Tools

In addition to Twitter.com and Twitter Search, there are many other ways to search. Some of these tools were covered in other sections because activities such as finding followers or locating geo-targeted users are so intertwined with search. We'll discuss those tools now in the specific context of Search. It's also worthwhile to note that many of these applications let you save searches as RSS feeds.

Third-Party Twitter Clients Most of the advanced third-party Twitter clients such as TweetDeck, Seesmic, HootSuite, DestroyTwitter, and most mobile applications let you save searches within the application and even notify you when new searches have been generated so you can monitor and respond without leaving the application.

Twoquick A lovely, light, yet powerful application, Twoquick (`http://www.twoquick.com`) enables you to search Twitter and Google simultaneously for the same query, which often leads to quite different results. You can search "everywhere" or "nearby," and Twoquick delivers your query results in one single screen (Figure 6.5).

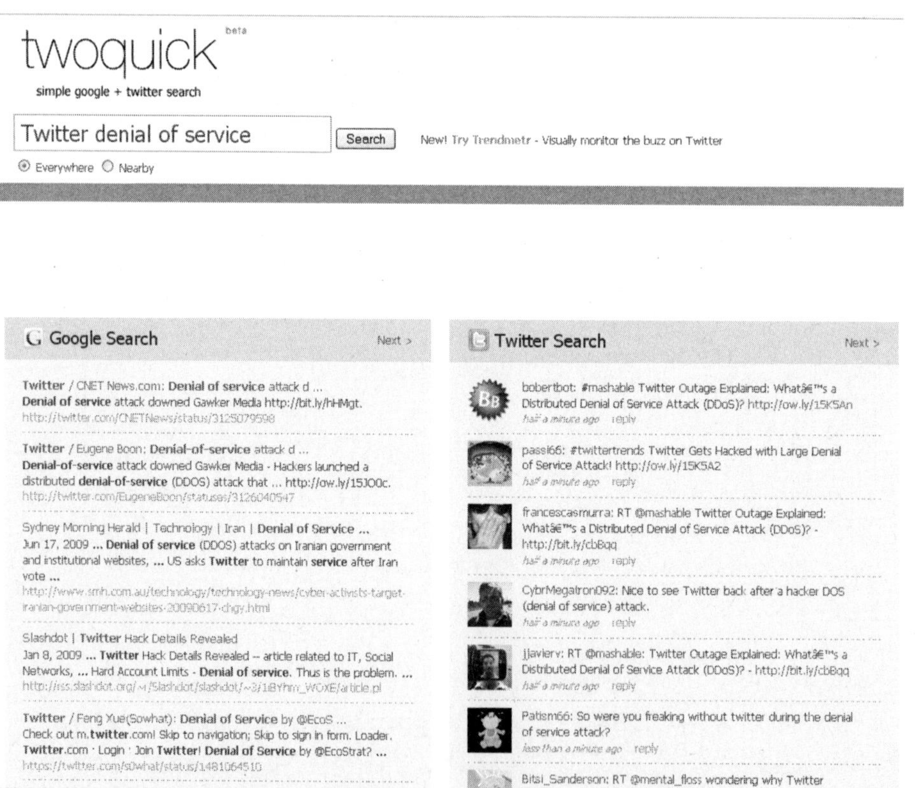

Figure 6.5 Twoquick's results for the query "Twitter Denial of Service"

SiteVolume With SiteVolume (`http://sitevolume.com`), you enter the kinds of keywords you want to search for and select the social media site you want them tracked on (DIGG, MySpace, YouTube, Flickr, or Twitter), and you'll learn how many times your keywords appear on your selected site.

Twazzup Twazzup (`http://www.twazzup.com`) is not a widely used application, but it should be because it shows you the overall landscape of your searched topic rather than just individual tweets. It not only shows real-time tweets, but also shows the people who tweet most about the topic, photos, and the most popular links (Figure 6.6).

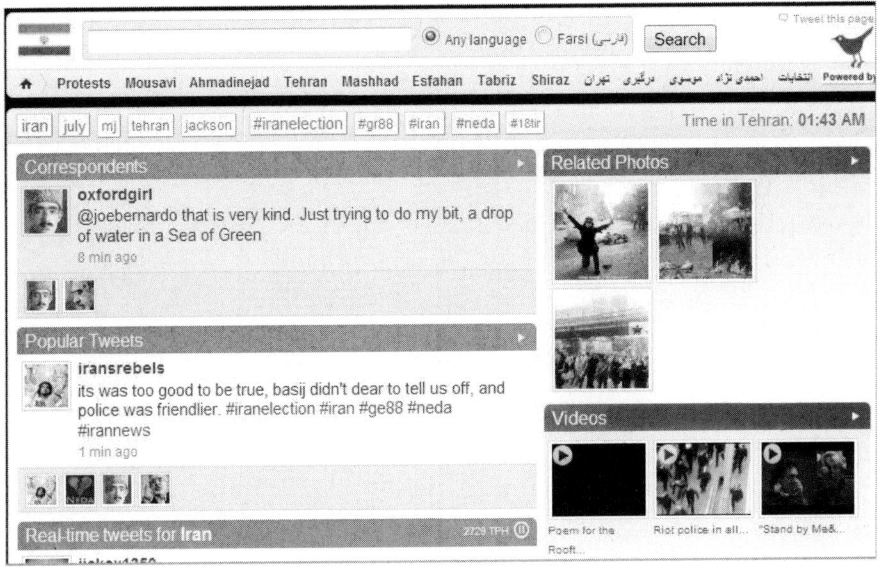

Figure 6.6 Twazzup search results for Iran

Tinker Follow the latest buzz on your favorite topics by creating a keyword-based *event stream* on Tinker (`http://www.tinker.com`). Tinker pulls in all relevant tweets surrounding that keyword, which you can even embed on your website and upon which people can comment (though you maintain comment control).

Twitterfall This tool provides a fun way of viewing the latest tweets, as they *fall f*rom the top of the screen in real time. Twitterfall (`http://www.twitterfall.com`) gives you a lot of control over the process with pause and resume links, filters, trending topics, the ability to hide panels, and more. Twitterfall is also useful at an event or conference when you want to track and display hashtagged tweets on a computer screen for the entire audience (Figure 6.7).

monitter and TweetGrid Monitter (`http://www.monitter.com`) was introduced in Chapter 3, "Twitter, the Multipurpose Platform," when we discussed locating people by geography. It's limited to a few keyword searches at a time and only three columns' worth. TweetGrid (`http://www.tweetgrid.com`), though not as clean or intuitive as monitter, lets you perform and view more searches simultaneously. You pick the number of search grids you want to view (up to three wide by three high), which allows you to search on an equal number of terms (Figure 6.8). The more grids, the less you'll see in the window, but you can scroll down through each grid to expose more tweets. You can even tweet from TweetGrid, much as you would any other web-based third-party Twitter client.

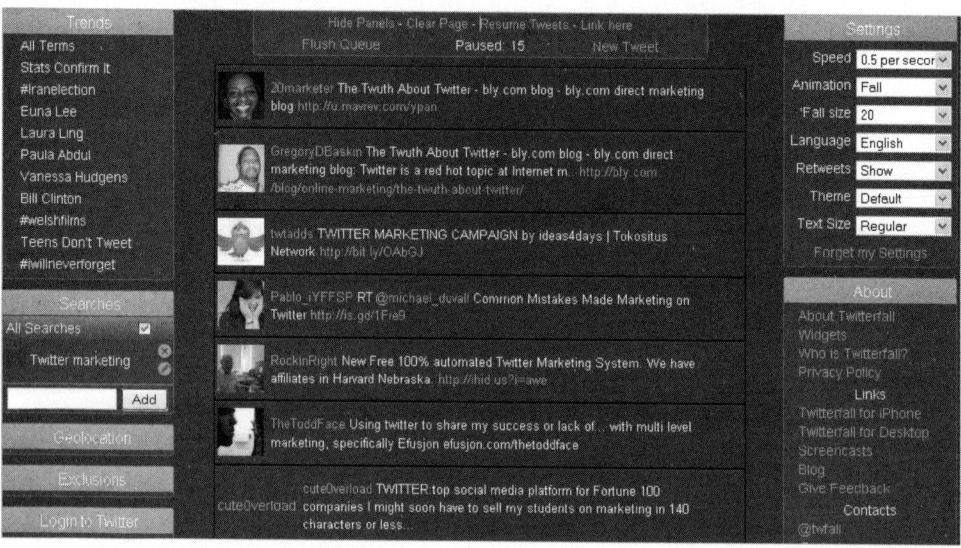

Figure 6.7 Twitterfall results for "Twitter Marketing"

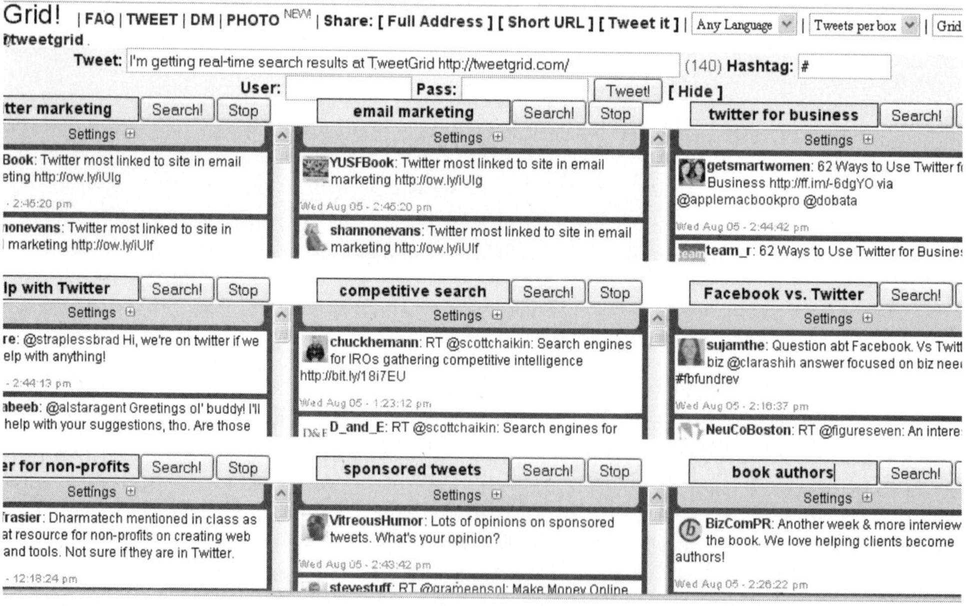

Figure 6.8 TweetGrid at maximum capacity: nine separate simultaneous searches

backtweets If you were to set up a saved search of a URL, one shortcoming is that you wouldn't capture tweets that refer to that link in a shortened URL. backtweets (`http://www.backtweets.com`) lets you search a URL and expose tweets containing shortened versions of that same URL (Figure 6.9). This gives you more of an opportunity to interact with people who are tweeting about your website. Someone may, for example, tweet about your blog post but not know that you are on Twitter or your Twitter handle, particularly if they saw your post in their RSS reader. By reaching out to them, you can not only make a personal connection, but you also may earn a valuable follower. You can even set up an RSS feed for these searches.

BackUpMyTweets, TweetBackup, The Archivist Not to be confused with backtweets, BackUpMyTweets (`http://backupmytweets.com`) solves the problem of trying to back-search your own unarchived tweets. Not only does BackUpMyTweets save your tweets, but it also lets you view or download your archived tweets in multiple formats (HTML, XML, JSON). TweetBackup (`http://tweetbackup.com`) performs a similar function. The Archivist (`http://flotzam.com/archivist`) is a Windows application that must be installed on your computer (as opposed to running off the Web), but it only provides some of the functionality of the other two solutions.

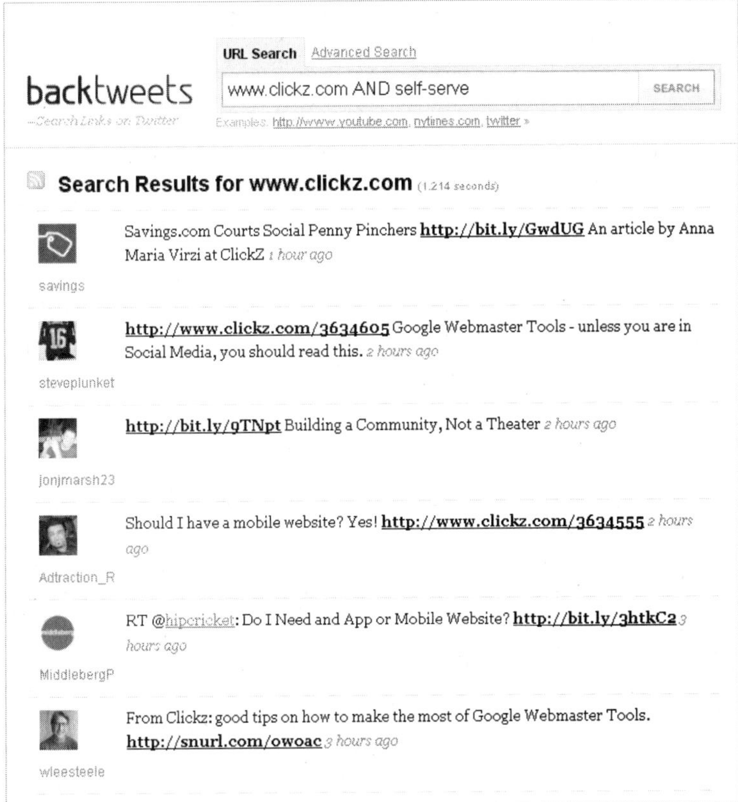

Figure 6.9 backtweets exposes shortened URLs.

Twithority Twithority (`http://www.twithority.com`) allows you to search on a particular topic and view the tweets based on a user's "authority," as defined by their number of followers (Figure 6.10). People have, however, questioned the validity of authority based on the number of followers.

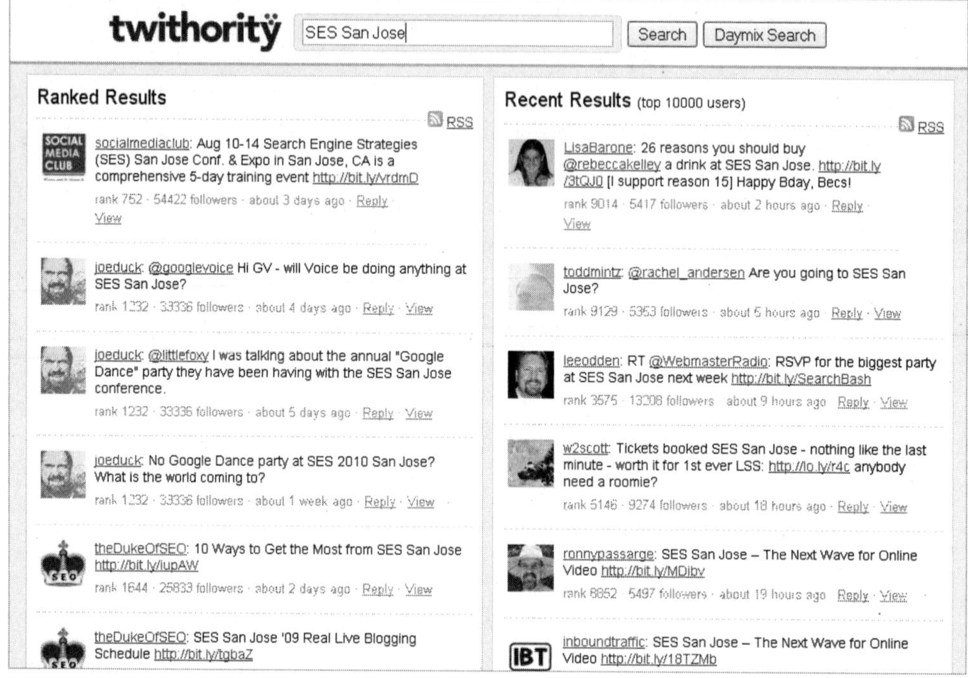

Figure 6.10 Twithority search results for "SEO San Jose"

#hashtags Because Twitter's archives are limited, you might want to head over to #hashtags (`http://www.hashtags.org`) to find any tagged tweets from long ago.

Table 6.1 conveniently summarizes the Twitter Search tools.

► **Table 6.1** Twitter Search Options at a Glance

Search Option	Description
Twitter's Advanced Search	Refine searches by filters and search operators.
Tweetdeck, Seesmic, HootSuite, DestroyTwitter	Desktop- and Web-based Twitter clients that enable management of your Twitter use without needing to use Twitter.com.
Twoquick	A side-by-side comparison of Google and Twitter search results.
SiteVolume	Compares keyword appearance in social media.
Twazzup	For a one-time search on a visual topic.
Twitterfall	Use at events on a projection screen.
TweetGrid/monitter	Use to watch and check in on a few keywords at once.

Continues

► **Table 6.1** Twitter Search Options at a Glance *(Continued)*

Search Option	Description
Backtweets	Allows you to see URLs you want to track that others have shortened and tweeted.
BackUpMyTweets, Tweet Backup, The Archivist	Use them to save and view past tweets.
Twithority	Use to determine if people of "authority" are tweeting on a topic.
#hashtags	Locate older hashtagged tweets that Twitter Search no longer archives.

Monday's One-Hour Exercise: Make Search Relevant

Using your preliminary exercise sheet, perform these steps for today's exercise:

1. Using the criteria you jotted down, perform at least one search on each tool listed in Table 6.1. (Try to avoid searches you may have already performed in Week 2.)

2. Identify five or six users legitimately tweeting your topic. Filter through to find someone posing a question you can answer.

3. Compose and send a tweet with that response. Send the tweet and see if they respond and if they begin to follow you. You might need to wait 24 to 48 hours (or more) for their response, depending upon how frequently they use Twitter.

Tuesday: Use Tools to Enrich Your Tweets

Today you're going to learn how to add some razzmatazz to your tweets and make your "140 be so much more than 140." What that means is that there are many ways to get more out of your 140 characters by structuring your tweets in certain ways or using other Twitter-related tools. You'll accomplish this mainly through some kind of a link—be it a link to a blog post, website, event invitation, survey/poll, video, photo or audio content, longer tweets, maps, chat rooms, or hashtags. (Whew, that's some list!) These links make you and your tweets more interesting, and they further engage your followers.

Tuesday's Preliminary Exercise

In preparation for Tuesday's section, jot down a few notes about content, such as the items listed in Monday's preliminary work that your company may want to share but that wouldn't fit into a 140-character tweet without a link.

What's in a Link?

Links are the most common method for enhancing a tweet. You can link to either something you have created or something you have seen that someone else has created. You can actually develop a whole strategy about a diversity of linked content.

When you're linking to your own content, get the most out of your 140-character limitation by remembering to shorten your URLs, as we discussed in Week 1. Even if you don't need to shorten the link to fit your tweet into 140 characters, you should use a URL shortener for two reasons:

- You can track the number of times your link gets clicked if you use a robust URL shortener with tracking capabilities (though you can also use backtweets to help you identify even more of your links).
- A shortened URL might be more likely to be retweeted, and certain URL shorteners, such as bit.ly or awe.sm, allow customization.

When you're linking to someone else's content, if that person has already tweeted a shortened URL, proper etiquette encourages you to retain their link so they can continue to track the pass-along value of their tweet.

Links for Verbosity

Although some might argue that the whole point and appeal of Twitter is its brevity, you can actually work around the 140-character limitation if you really have something important to say.

Uneditable Tweets Do you have a tweet that just can't cut it in 140 characters, even with a shortened URL? Try tools such as Twtlong (`http://www.twtlong.com`), TwitLonger (`http://www.twitlonger.com`), RichTweets (`http://richtweets.com`), or shortText (`http://www.shorttext.com`). As contrary as it may seem to Twitter's premise, these tools allow you tweet longer content that is then saved and reduced to a shortened URL. Clicking on that URL takes the reader to the longer tweet content saved on the tool's website. All these solutions are simple to use, and shortText, RichTweets, and Twtlong let you add images and videos as well.

Blogs These days, much of the linked content on Twitter is directed to blog posts. On a blog, a company or an individual can be as wordy as they want to be, and there's nothing wrong with that.

Want to write a missive but don't have a blog? Try Posterous (`http://www.posterous.com`) or Tumblr (`http://www.tumblr.com`). Both applications allow you to blog via email (among other means). All you need to do is compose your email, send it to the designated Posterous or Tumblr email address, and a blog post will automatically be created and immediately tweeted.

Surveys and Polls

People never seem to get sick of data. People love percentages, statistics, mass quantities...heck, that's why people get so wrapped up in follower counts. On Twitter, you have a ready-made audience of survey and poll participants. Surveys and polls are a great way to generate the kind of content people hunger for, and, at the same time, give users a more direct means to have their opinions matter. It's a great form of user engagement. There are some very simple web tools to gather data, some of which have been specifically created for Twitter.

Twitter-Specific One poll application specifically designed for Twitter is Twtpoll (`http://www.twtpoll.com`), which allows you to set up simple multiple-choice-question polls (Figure 6.11). Twtpoll also asks for the Twitter names of the survey creator and completers so people can connect. A Twtpoll can be set up and launched in seconds, and you can embed the survey and survey results into a website. Twtpoll's simplicity also is its downside because it's very limited: you can't edit surveys or create open-ended questions.

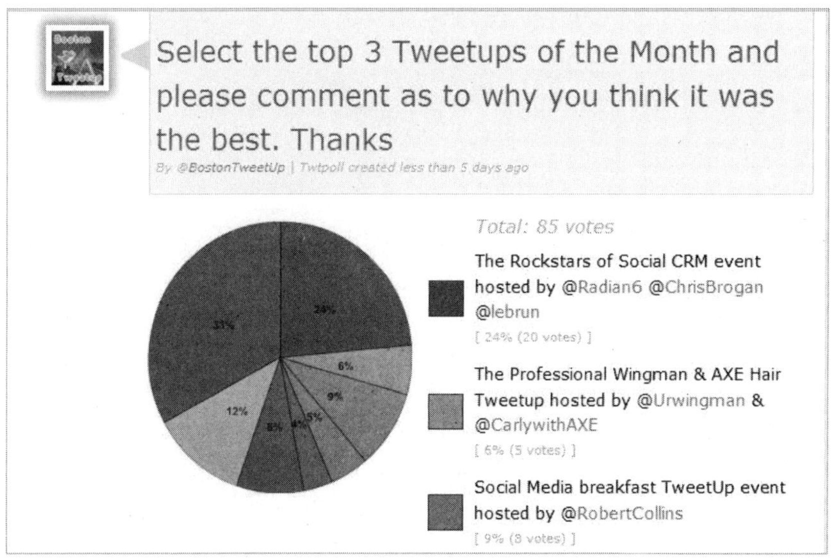

Figure 6.11 An @BostonTweetUp Twtpoll

Poll Applications Zoomerang (`http://www.zoomerang.com`), SurveyMonkey.com (`http://www.surveymonkey.com`), and Poll Daddy (`http://www.polldaddy.com`) are very similar poll applications, but none were specifically created for Twitter. They're beneficial to create longer, more in- depth surveys whose for-fee versions give you more survey control—that is, limitations on the number of responses, custom branding, question limitations, survey rules, defining required answers, and more.

Simple Forms Google Docs has a poll feature called a *form*. (See Figure 6.12.) It's easy to use, and it can be embedded on your website, linked to, or emailed. If you use the blogging software WordPress, it also offers a basic plug-in (`http://wordpress.org/extend/plugins/wp-polls`). Both of these solutions are very basic and limited, however.

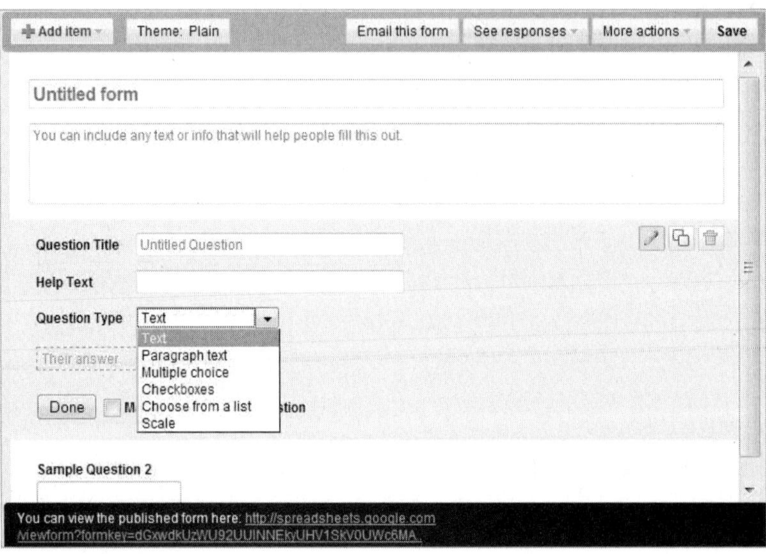

Figure 6.12 Google Docs' poll form

Multimedia

Spice up your tweets by bringing the words to life using multimedia. Here are some options and solutions.

Photos The most commonly used application to link to a photo is TwitPic (`http://www.twitpic.com`) because it's already been integrated into most desktop, web, and mobile Twitter clients. When using a mobile device with a built-in camera, you can usually tweet the photo directly from your mobile application. If you're using a computer, you just go to the TwitPic website, log in to your Twitter account, browse to the location of the photo on your computer, add a message to tweet, and TwitPic automatically uploads, links, and tweets it for you (Figure 6.13). (You can also upload photos but choose not to tweet them.) yfrog (`http://www.yfrog.com`) is another popular service similar to TwitPic. Both of these applications are tied to your Twitter profile so people can look up the photos you've posted, but neither has the capability to upload multiple photos at one time.

Figure 6.13 Uploading a photo to TwitPic

Flickr (`http://www.flickr.com`), on the other hand, allows you to post more than one photo, so people typically use it to upload photos from an event or seminar. The photos can be tagged, which has benefits for search engine optimization (SEO). You'll need to create a Flickr account, but for Twitter purposes, you'll want your Flickr photos publicly searchable. (You can set your permissions, however, to private if you do not want anyone else to see your photos.) Flickr does not have a post-and-tweet feature, so you'll need to generate a shortened URL of your own.

Audio Audio recordings bring tweets to life and create personality. Hearing someone's voice is a much more meaningful way to connect than reading 140 typed characters. Why not create, upload, and link to a recording from your CEO and his or her thoughts on a particular topic? You could also interview a customer about why they do business with your company. You could even record part of a seminar you attended to give people a sense of your world.

Chirbit (`http://www.chirbit.com`), Utterli (`http://www.utterli.com`), and TwitterFone (`http://www.twitterfone.com`)—not to be confused with the iPhone application TwitterFon—allow you to upload audio files or record and post directly to Twitter. iPhone applications TweetMic (`http://www.tweetmic.com`), which has no limit on the length of your recording, and AudioBoo (`http://www.audioboo.fm`), which lets you record five-minute "Boos" along with a photo, both let you record and tweet. AudioBoo describes itself as audio blogging—it even has an integrated text transcription. A good example of this use was when Leo Laporte (`@leolaporte`) traveled to China, where he recorded and tweeted from his trip. It gave his followers a good sense of what he was up to on his trip.

Another audio-based Twitter application is trottr (`http://trottr.com`), which just requires you to set up an account and have a phone. Any time you want, you call one of their access phone numbers, hear a welcome message and beep, and can record your message—in 140 seconds or less. trottr posts your audio message to its site, but you can change your settings to have it tweet your recording as well.

Video Let's face it: social media is for voyeurs, and video's a huge part of this phenomenon. Video literally brings to life all this otherwise static content, and it works as well for businesses as it does for individuals. Video can announce, educate, update, instruct, and even humanize you as a company (Figure 6.14). Research has shown that Twitter users are more engaged with video than those using any other social network.

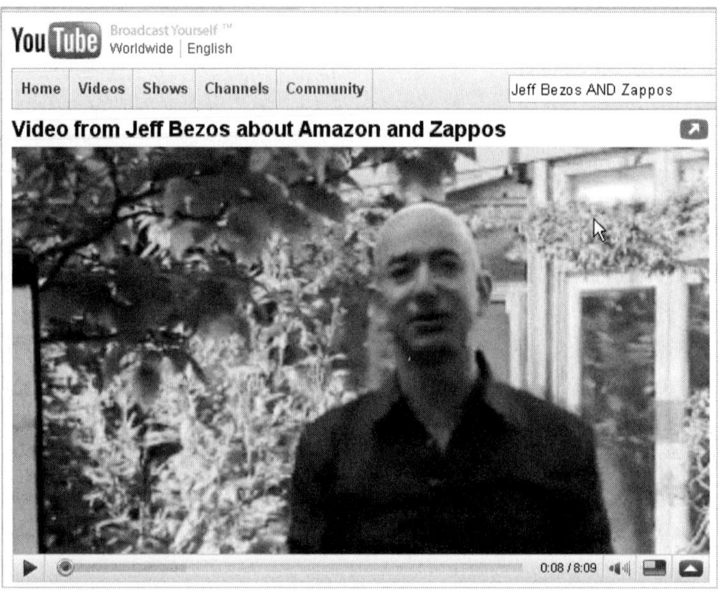

Figure 6.14 Amazon CEO Jeff Bezos talks about Amazon's acquisition of Zappos.

With webcams being integrated into most laptops and some phones these days, recording video is simpler than ever and gives followers an even better sense of who is actually behind the written words. One of the most popular Twitter users of video is iJustine (`@iJustine`), who video blogs (vlogs) much of her life. You can record something in the here and now quickly; or you can vlog a longer recording. When you're done, you just upload and post to Twitter.

There are several Twitter video tools. Qik (`http://www.qik.com`), which works only with select cell phones so consult its site, streams live video recordings from your phone or video camera. When you start recording, Qik posts a tweet to let your Twitter followers know you are streaming live. Watchers can chat with each other, and even make comments to the person taking the video. It makes for a very interactive, live experience. Many people click in to watch just to see who the face behind the profile photo is in real life.

Ustream (`http://www.ustream.tv`) also streams video live. It's similar in functionality to Qik but generated from a computer rather than a video camera. You can also take a live poll of your viewers. Darren Rowse (`@problogger`) uses Ustream to host question-and-answer sessions with his followers (Figure 6.15). He announces on Twitter that he's going to be live on Ustream, and people log in to ask him questions and listen to his responses. Darren answers on the spot. It's a great way to interact with people and increase his brand equity.

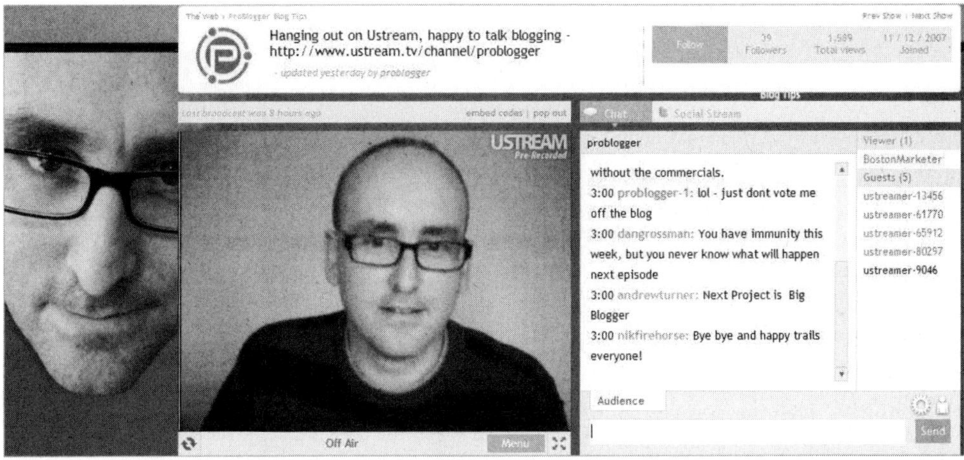

Figure 6.15 Darren Rowse's Ustream questions and answers

There's also TwitVid (`http://www.twitvid.com`), which likewise lets you upload and tweet a video. TwitVid uploads from a phone, a computer (live via webcam or from a saved file), or TwitVid's API.

Bubbletweet (`http://www.bubbletweet.com`) is meant to be used to enhance your Twitter profile. It records a 30-second video message delivered through Bubbletweet's proprietary player. Bubbletweet videos make a profile much more personable because they allow you to say more than what you can type in the 160-character bio. In order to see the video, the visitor must somehow click on your custom Bubbletweet URL. Here's the Bubbletweet URL for Lauren Litwinka (`@beebow`), for example: `http://www.bubbletweet.com/showBT.php?id=edk9e`. You can, however, insert this URL in your profile's URL under Twitter Settings. To promote it, you can also tweet your Bubbletweet URL or list it in other contact lists, such as email v-card or Facebook.

If you have very little to say, you may want to use 12seconds.tv (`http://www.12seconds.tv`), which lets you share short videos up to 12 seconds long using your webcam or mobile.

Chat Segueing from video to chat, consider Tinychat (`http://www.tinychat.com`), an application integrating old-fashioned chat capability with live video feeds (Figure 6.16). When you log on (warning: adult content may be displayed), it sends a Tweet saying that you are chatting in the room. Up to 12 people can simultaneously use video and audio, while up to 200 people can chat by typing. It's a great way to get a group of people together quickly to discuss a particular topic. Just beware that because it does send a tweet, it's not going to be a private chat—anyone can log on at any time.

Figure 6.16 Tinychat in action

TweetChat (`http://www.tweetchat.com`) is a simple application that makes communicating around a topic's hashtag easy. You sign in and enter a *room* by typing in a hashtag—for example, `#journchat`. What you will see is all the tweets that are in progress with that hashtag in one list. TweetChat automatically appends your tweet with the hashtag, so you don't have to enter it each time—a major timesaver. This is great to use at conferences or on webinars so that you can keep up with what people are saying and not get slowed down by entering the hashtags. Tweets posted through Tweetchat are fully searchable and are archived along with your other tweets, so you won't lose any content by using TweetChat.

If you don't want to deal with hashtags at all, check out Tweetworks (`http://www.tweetworks.com`). Less of a chat tool and more of a discussion group tool, Tweetworks has multiple functions—public, group, or private discussions; link-appending options for posts; and URL shortening. (See Figure 6.17.) Its nicest feature is probably threaded conversation, which means that there's no need to click through countless "in reply to" links, no need for hashtags, and no need to write queries on a search tool to get the whole conversation.

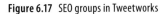

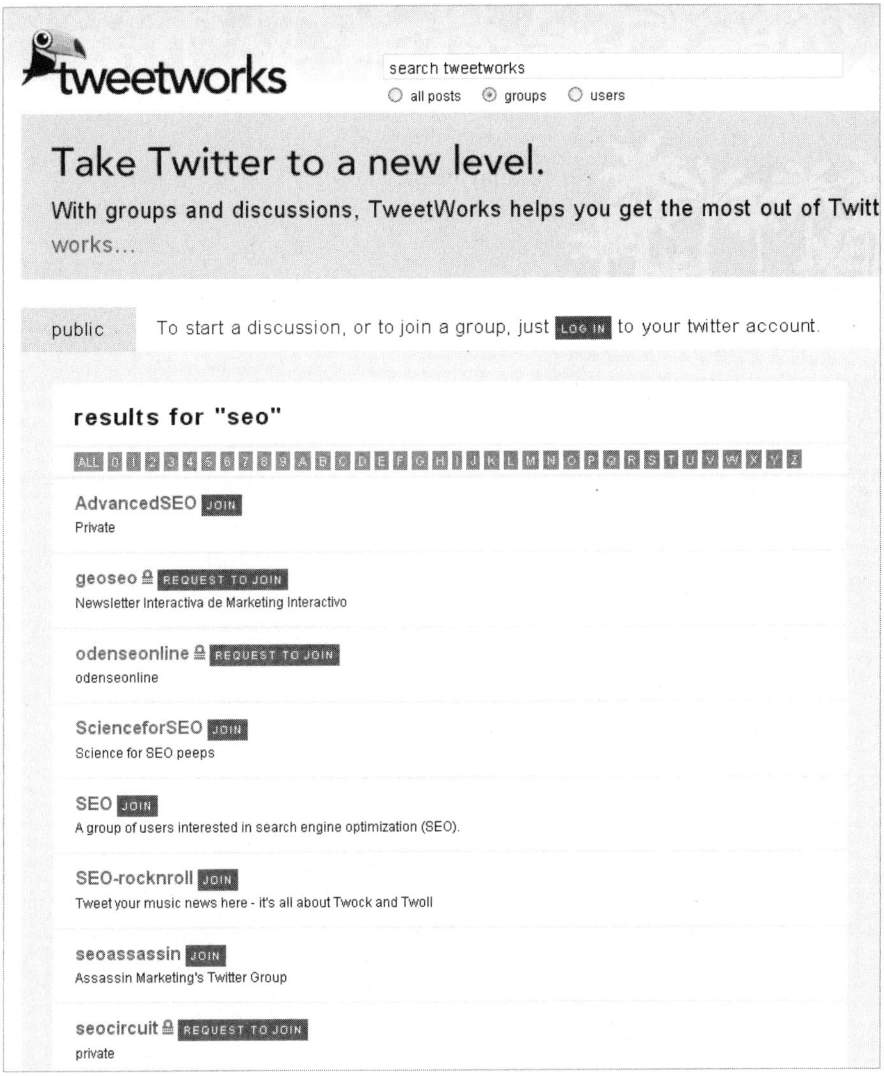

tweetworks

search tweetworks

all posts groups users

Take Twitter to a new level.

With groups and discussions, TweetWorks helps you get the most out of Twitt works...

public To start a discussion, or to join a group, just LOG IN to your twitter account.

results for "seo"

ALL 0 1 2 3 4 5 6 7 8 9 A B C D E F G H I J K L M N O P Q R S T U V W X Y Z

AdvancedSEO JOIN
Private

geoseo REQUEST TO JOIN
Newsletter Interactiva de Marketing Interactivo

odenseonline REQUEST TO JOIN
odenseonline

ScienceforSEO JOIN
Science for SEO peeps

SEO JOIN
A group of users interested in search engine optimization (SEO).

SEO-rocknroll JOIN
Tweet your music news here - it's all about Twock and Twoll

seoassassin JOIN
Assassin Marketing's Twitter Group

seocircuit REQUEST TO JOIN
private

Figure 6.17 SEO groups in Tweetworks

Other Uses of Links

One clever way to get more out of a tweet is by linking to someone else's tweet. This is different than a retweet. As pointed out in Week 1, each tweet has its own unique URL associated with the time it was created that you can navigate to from the bottom of the original tweet. If someone is `@replying` to another tweep, you can also navigate to the original tweep's tweet by clicking on the "in reply to [user's name]" which is linked text; or, if you're looking at an original tweet, you can click on the link text date/timestamp (Figure 6.18). Both of these methods will take the single tweet made by the user you're trying to reference, and this single tweet has its own unique URL. If you think the original tweet is worthy of citing, you can shorten the original tweet's URL and direct your followers to it via the newly shortened URL.

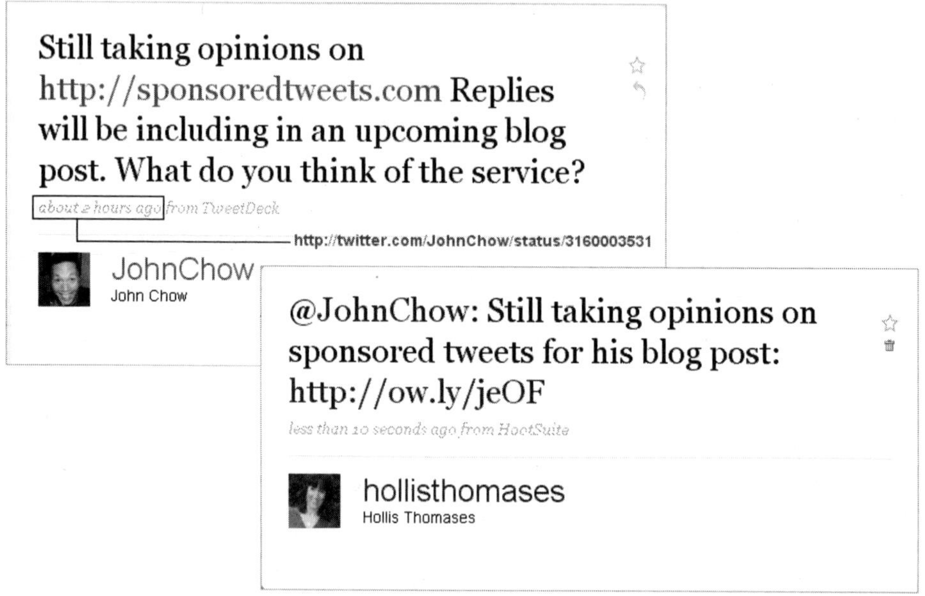

Figure 6.18 Constructing a new tweet from other tweets

Use or create hashtags to give topical relevance to your tweet or attract curious tweeps to investigate and possibly become engaged in your subject. People often include hashtags from original tweets when they're retweeting so you can see what kind of "legs" your hashtag has without your involvement.

Linking to an event invitation like a tweetup, for example, via Twtvite (`http://www.twtvite.com`) or webinar is a common and effective use of links. (See Figure 6.19.) Does your company host events? They are great ways to introduce the Twitter community to your brand.

Create a Twitter-exclusive coupon through twtQpon (`http://www.twtqpon.com`), which will require that you do some advanced planning, but once the offer/coupon code, optional associated URL, and image are in place, creating your coupon is a piece of cake (Figure 6.20).

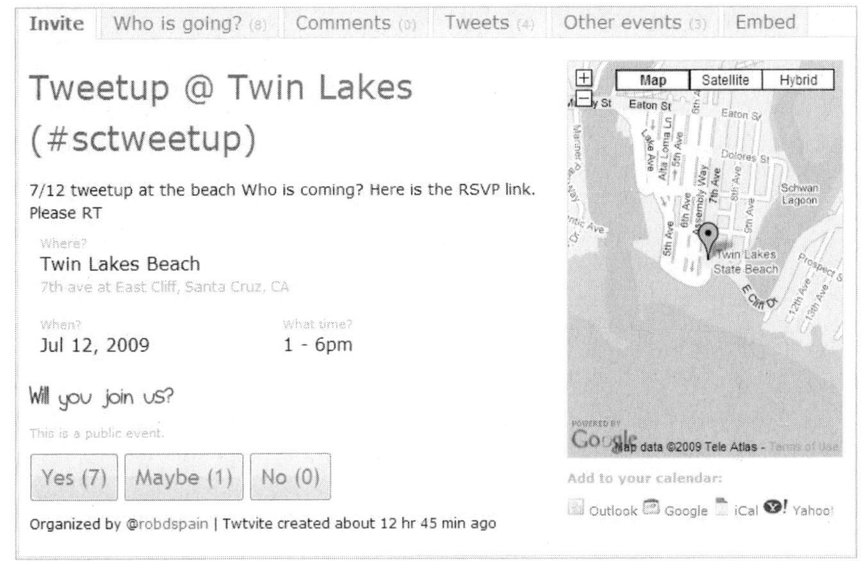

Figure 6.19 Twtvite for a Boston tweetup

twtQpon
Offer exclusive deals on Twitter!

branded twtqpon | follow @twtqpon | contact us

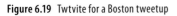

Create a Twitter Coupon | Search/Browse | My twtQpon

Create Twitter Coupons.
Share them with your followers!

Twitter name? @your_twitter_name

Coupon title?

Coupon details? Tell us about your exclusive offer in 140 chars. 140

Image? (2MB) (GIF, JPG, PNG) Suggested size: width: 700px, height: 300 px Browse...

Coupon code?

Redirect URL? http://

Valid until? Leave it in blank if it does NOT expire (mm/dd/yyyy)

Create a Twitter Coupon

Figure 6.20 To create a coupon, use twtQpon's simple form.

Tuesday's One-Hour Exercise: Create Enhanced Tweet Content

- (15 minutes) Think of a good chat topic that you think will interest people. Create a hashtag that relates to this topic. Go to `http://www.hashtags.org` to see if that hashtag is already being used. If it is not, keep the hashtag; if it's already being used, create a new one.
    - Compose a tweet to send your followers that lets them know you will be hosting a chat on TweetChat about this topic in 45 minutes. Use your hashtag. Ask your followers to retweet about your upcoming chat. Repeat this tweet, or a variation of it, every 5 minutes for the next 45 minutes until it's chat time.
    - Now jot down some important points you want to bring up in a chat about that topic (news and information, opinions, questions, and so on). Set these points aside and move on to the rest of your exercises.
- (5 minutes) Take Tuesday's preliminary exercise and, with one idea, create a longer tweet using Twtlong or TwitLonger. With another idea, create a Posterous or Tumblr account to email, post, and tweet your content.
- (5 minutes) Write down three areas you would like to know more about from your consumers or customers. Do you have just one question for each area, or more than one question? Is it a simple question, or a more complex one? Your answers will determine if you can use a simple polling application or need a richer survey tool. Try to narrow down your questions to one that can be delivered in a poll. Once you have it, set up a quick poll in Twitpoll and tweet about it.
- (5 minutes) Take a photo or use an existing photo on your computer. Try to make this photo somehow relevant to your business or your customers. Using Twitpic, log into your Twitter account, upload your photo, compose your tweet, and send.
- (10 minutes) Think of two or three ways you could use audio on Twitter in an enriching way, preferably related to your business. Write down these ideas and determine what would need to be done in order for you to produce this audio. For example, does a script need to be written? Do you need to interview someone? Do you need to draft how-to instructions?
    - If you have audio that's already prepared or an idea that you can simply execute, use one of the audio tools to upload and tweet the content.
- (5 minutes) Have a webcam? Try recording a simple Bubbletweet. Share it with all or a select group of your followers and gather their feedback.
- (15 minutes) When your chat time arrives, log into TweetChat to kick things off. Welcome everyone, remind them about your topic, and introduce the agenda of discussion points you'd like to cover. (Tips: Be prepared! In the beginning, you'll

probably find that you're doing most of the tweeting until your participants feel comfortable and warm up to the topic. Also try to engage your participants by responding directly to points they're making or encouraging others to respond to someone else's tweet—for example, "What do you all think of John's view on this?")

Wednesday: Analyze Your Twitter Activity

Understanding your Twitter activity is an important step in the process of Twitter marketing. You want to learn from your analysis (as well as the analysis of others) and make corrections as you go forward. For example, you'll want to know if you tweet a higher percentage of links than most other Twitter users and affirm that this is the strategic direction you want to make. Does your Twitter stream consist mainly of replies to other people, and is that OK with you? Many people dislike coming upon such Twitter streams when considering new people to follow, while others seek very active `@replying` as a sign of strong engagement. What's your motive for using Twitter, and who are you looking to attract? How about ascertaining why someone followed you or the kind of tweets you posted to attract a large influx of followers (versus a time or topic when you seem to lose an unusual number of followers)? There are applications to help answer these questions —you just have to know where to look.

Wednesday's Preliminary Exercise

Before you get started, write down your guess for where you think you rate on the following parameters based on averages (more than, less than, or on average):

- Number of tweets per day
- Percentage of links in tweet
- Percentage original tweets
- Percentage retweets
- Percentage `@replies`
- Time of day when you tweet the most

Twitter Statistics

One of the most common themes you'll see among Twitter tools is that many of them track and crunch Twitter data for you. None are exactly alike, so if you want to get a feeling for what they have to offer, you need to go through each one individually.

TweetStats TweetStats (`http://www.tweetstats.com`) shows you your average number of tweets per day, when you typically tweet, tweets per hour, who you tweet with, who you retweeted, and what you typically tweet about (Figure 6.21). Understanding your own statistics can help ensure that you are tweeting the way you want to be tweeting, but you can also view these same statistics for any Twitter user. You can then compare yourself to that person or gain a clearer sense of how or when to contact a particular person.

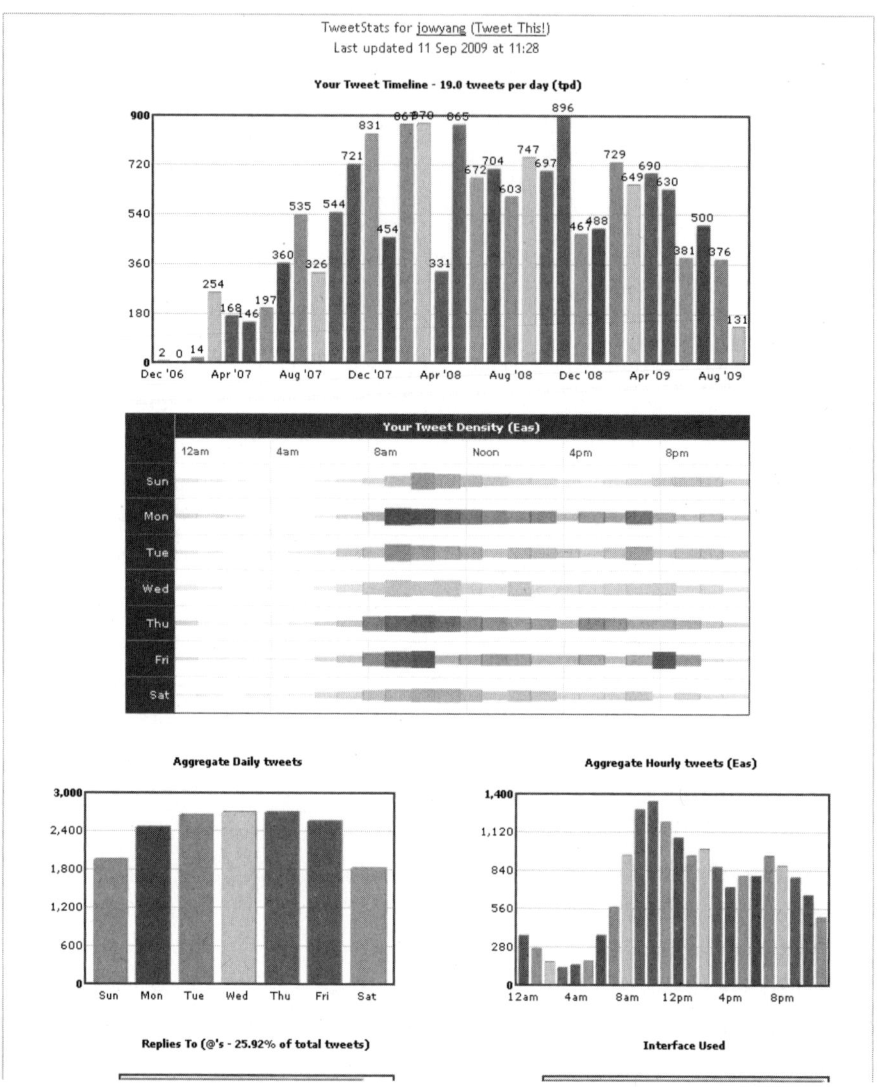

Figure 6.21 TweetStats' analysis of Jeremiah Owyang's tweets

TwitterCounter TwitterCounter (`http://www.twittercounter.com`), which was introduced in Week 2 as a tool to gain insights on other followers, is also helpful in understanding your own Twitter history over time. Based on your growth trends, TwitterCounter can even estimate the number of followers you will have on the following day or month (Figure 6.22).

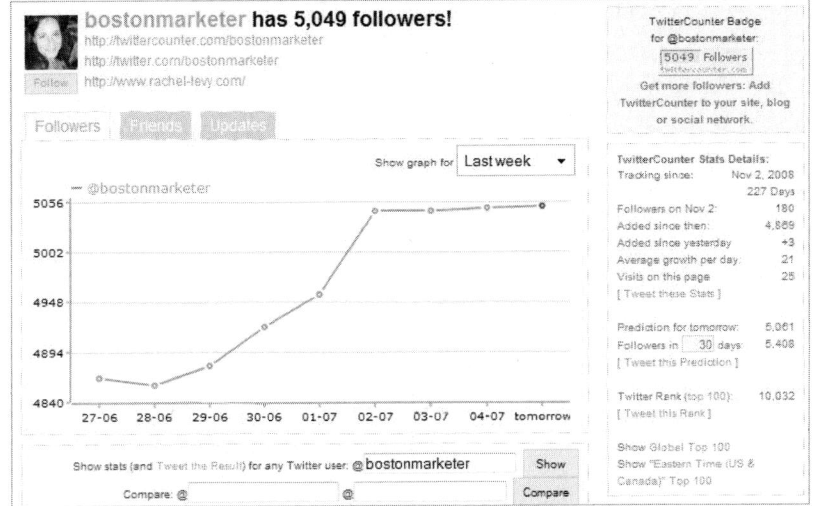

Figure 6.22 TwitterCounter trend and forecast for @bostonmarketer

Trendistic Looking for a longer-range view of trending topics on Twitter or an analysis of any keyword at all? Check out Trendistic (`http://trendistic.com`), which can give you data from the last 24 hours to 180 days (the latter requires logging in). You can also get code to embed a trend chart on your website.

SocialToo Understanding why people follow or unfollow you can give you insights into how well you are tweeting. SocialToo (`http://www.socialtoo.com`) is an application that will email you each day with the previous day's followers and unfollowers and the tweet that happened immediately before they followed or unfollowed you. It obviously doesn't mean that there was a cause/effect relationship there, but it's helpful to see trends from your tweets.

URL Shortener and Other Tool Stats Monitoring shortened URL click-throughs will also help you understand your Twitter activity and the kinds of links that have the greatest impact. Let's say you tweet about an article you find interesting. Using bit.ly (`http://bit.ly`) or its alternate version, j.mp; (`http://j.mp`), a common URL shortener, you can track the number of clicks that URL got, plus all kinds of additional information such as referrers and location of users who clicked on the link (Figure 6.23). These kinds of stats also let you test the impact of tweeting the same article at different times of day with different shortened URLs to measure their respective impact. If you find a pattern after multiple tests, this might indicate the best time of the day you'll want to tweet your links.

Many multimedia applications, such as TwitPic and yfrog, also show you the number of clicks or views, so you can measure the effect of your links.

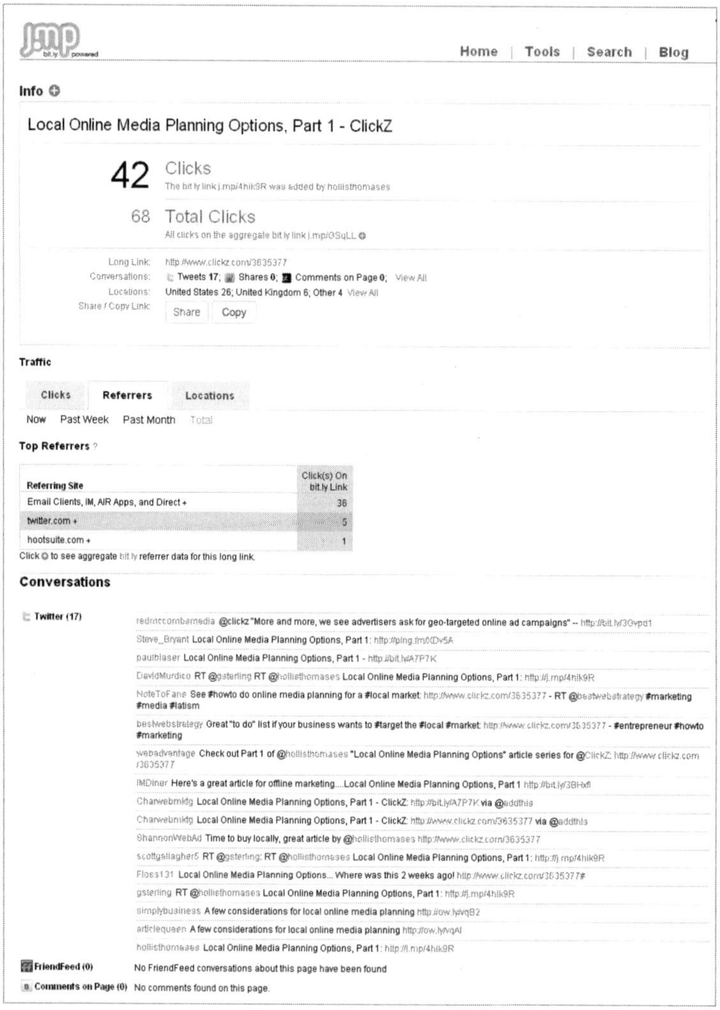

Figure 6.23 Some statistical breakdowns from URL-shortening tool j.mp

Twitter Rank and Impact

People love data, especially data about themselves. Many tools have been developed to help assess people's ranks or scores in Twitterdom, and people tweet their scores with pride. Let's look at some of the tools out there for Twitter ranking, grading, and impact.

Twitalyzer (`http://www.twitalyzer.com`) This grading program ranks based on such factors as generosity, clout, velocity, influence, and signal-to-noise ratio (Figure 6.24). It defines these criteria this way:

- *Generosity:* your propensity to retweet someone else, thereby creating awareness of your work and ideas among your own followers

- *Clout:* the likelihood that other people will reference you in Twitter; the number of references to you divided by the total number of possible references (as governed by the Twitter Search APIs); the more people who reference you, the higher your clout
- *Velocity:* the number of tweets you publish over a seven-day period
- *Influence:* a weighted calculation based on relative reach (number of followers), relative authority (number of times you are retweeted), relative generosity, clout, and velocity
- *Signal-to-Noise Ratio:* the tendency for people to pass information, as opposed to anecdotes, as measured by references to other people's Twitter handles, links, hashtags, and retweets

Twitalyzer gives you countless other statistics and graphs depicting these factors changing over time. Use Twitalyzer to analyze your own Twitter use or the Twitter use of others (including competitors).

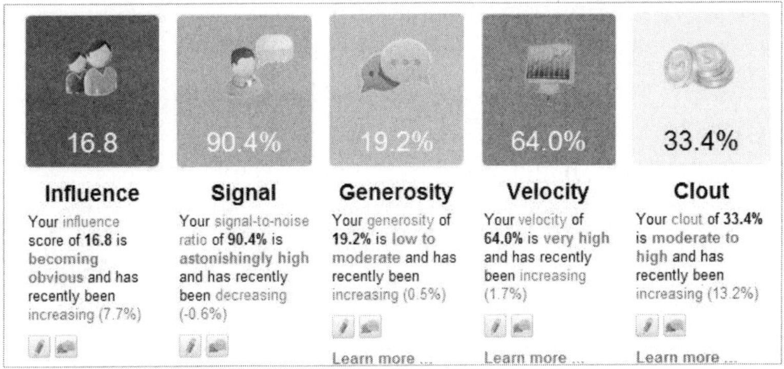

Figure 6.24 Twitalyzer's analysis by criteria

Twitalyzer also offers its powerful brand analyzer (`http://www.twitalyzer.com/brand/index.asp`) that shows brand strength, signal, favor, passion, and clout. This elevates you above the granular analysis of individual tweets, to give you a way to view your overall brand health on Twitter and track it over time.

Twitter Analyzer Not to be confused with the aforementioned Twitalyzer, Twitter Analyzer (`http://twitteranalyzer.com`) analyzes and graphs a user's Twitter activity, including total tweets, total retweets, percent of retweets as a function of the total, unique users retweeting, total readers reached, and unique readers reached.

Klout View your Twitter influence another way by using Klout (`http://www.klout.net`). Klout requires that you create an account to see your analysis. It uses descriptions to articulate what kind of tweeter you are and shows analysis of your engagement, reach, velocity, demand, network strength, and activity. It shows who influences you most as a result of analyzing your tags, retweets, and shared URLs.

Twinfluence Twinfluence (`http://twinfluence.com`) calculates two types of ranks: Reach Ranking, an absolute number and percentage that compares you to all analyzed Twitter users to date, and Relative Score, a value and category relative to other Twitter users that have more or less the same number of followers as you do.

Twitter Grader Put out by Hubspot, Twitter Grader (`http://twitter.grader.com`) is the most popular of the ranking applications. It assigns a user's ranking on a scale from 0 to 100, using factors such as number of followers, power of followers, number of updates, update recency, followers/following ratio, and engagement (a retweet analysis). The analysis also tells you your rank versus all other Twitter users. In addition, you can see the rankings of top users in your city or state, which is another way for you to find new people to follow.

Twit Truth Twit Truth (`http://www.twittruth.com`) shows you a variety of statistics about users' accounts, breaking tweets down into three groups: direct replies (replies to other people), no engagement (not sent to anyone), and contains username (Figure 6.25). This gives you a good snapshot of someone's engagement with others. It also shows you the number of messages per day they receive, and your chances of receiving a reply. It really puts in perspective how many tweets these heavy users receive, and how difficult it is for them to reply to everyone. If you run the statistics for an individual user, you also see how long it takes them to respond to a DM, an `@reply`, the percent of their tweets sent with hashtags, and many more similar statistics. (The user must first be entered into Twit Truth's directory in order to be analyzed.)

Name	Messages to User per day	Chance of Reply 1 in	Replies Sent Per Day	Direct Replies %	Contains Username %	No Engagement %	Top Contact %
Stephen Fry	5272.31	962.31	5.48	47	5.5	47.5	1
Ben Stiller	3933.37	1419.19	2.77	42.5	2	55.5	2
Tom Fletcher	2643.75	298.63	8.85	50.5	0.5	49	4
Phillip Schofield	2050.56	133.96	15.31	67.5	2.5	30	1
JohnCleese	1780.11	5591.28	0.32	38	11	51	2
Alan Carr	1636.76	327.78	4.99	56.5	0	43.5	0
Jonathan Ross	1254.99	39.44	31.82	79	2	19	2
Marcelo Tas	1093.2	2625.32	0.42	8.5	28.5	63	8
John Mayer	894.44	356.58	2.51	19	13.5	67.5	4
Sherri Shepherd	861.68	84.11	10.24	44.5	17.5	38	1.5
Russell Brand	655.29	171.05	3.83	61.5	2	36.5	4
Jimmy Carr	521.86	2344.97	0.22	6	1.5	92.5	0

Figure 6.25 Twit Truth stats for commonly followed users

Retweet Statistics

Being retweeted has been noted as a powerful measurement of your value within the Twitter community. It means people find your tweets interesting, valuable, or useful in some way. Being retweeted, particularly by influential people, is an indication of your own Twitter influence. If you look at someone like Chris Brogan (`@ChrisBrogan`), probably about half of every tweet he makes gets retweeted at least once; hence he's considered extremely influential and a retweet *from* him is incredibly powerful. Like almost everything else on Twitter, there are a few applications that track your retweet statistics.

Retweetrank A simple application, Retweetrank (`http://www.retweetrank.com`) shows where you rank in terms of the number of retweets you receive versus everyone else on Twitter. It provides an overall rank and a percentile one, and lists a retweet feed for the user you entered (Figure 6.26). You can even subscribe to an RSS feed of a particular user's retweeted items.

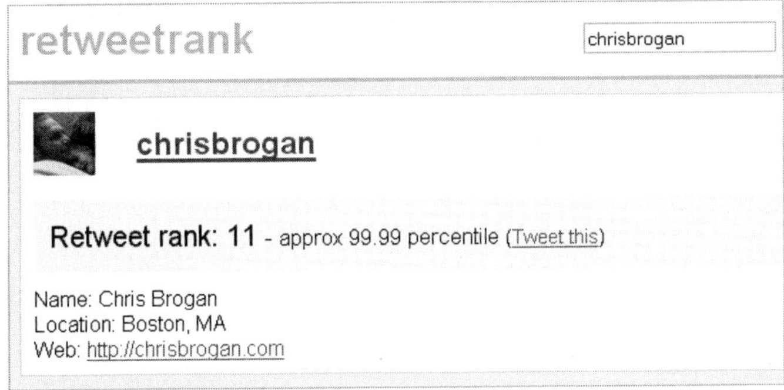

Figure 6.26 Retweetrank score for Chris Brogan

***Re*Tweetability Index** The *Re*Tweetability Index compiled by Dan Zarrella (`http://www.retweetability.com`) measures the *re*tweetability of someone's tweets as a consequence of the number of the user's followers and overall tweets (Figure 6.27). Users with a high *Re*Tweetability Index have a greater percentage of their content spread by a greater percentage of their followers: people like the user's tweets. A low *Re*Tweetability Index score probably indicates that what you're tweeting doesn't resonate with your followers.

Get a specific user's rank:

bjmendelson [Find User]

Rank	User	Followers	Updates	ReTweetability
2937	BJMendelson	624083	7037	25257

Figure 6.27 The *Re*Tweetability Index Score for `@bjmendelson`

Retweetist and Tweetburner Want to gain insight on retweeted topics? Head over to Retweetist (`http://www.retweetist.com`), where you cannot only view the most popular retweets, but the top retweeted people and URLs as well (Figure 6.28). Tweetburner doesn't track retweets per se but it does shorten URLs and publicly posts the most popularly clicked ones, another good insight into trends.

Figure 6.28 Retweetist

Return on "I" Twitter Metrics

As with any marketing activity, you probably want to understand your Twitter marketing return. Businesses normally look at this return in terms of an investment (ROI). In Twitter's case, however, it's been argued that investment might not be the right analysis. Depending on your Twitter strategy, which we'll get into more in Chapter 8, "Week 5: Develop a Successful Twitter Strategy," you might instead want to consider other "I's," such as *influence* or *ignorance* (as in, how much damage are you doing to your company by *not* participating in Twitter) as your rate of measurement. In this case, you're still measuring an ROI; it's just a different ROI.

If you do choose to track return on investment, because Twitter's biggest expense is the time it takes to use the platform effectively, you'll want to look at your time invested on Twitter compared to the actual business you have generated from it. Depending on your business, that may be easy or difficult to measure. You'll need to determine what you can accurately and effectively measure and attribute to Twitter before you can assume to be able to calculate some kind of ROI. Besides direct sales, however, you can track things like traffic driven to your website from Twitter, time spent on your site, and conversion funnels from Twitter-driven web traffic.

If you decide to track Return on Influence, you can also consider factors like positive, neutral, and negative mentions of your brand, which tools like Twitrratr (`http://www.twitrratr.com`) or Twendz (`http://twendz.waggeneredstrom.com`) help you measure. (See Figure 6.29.) In Twitrratr, you can look at how far these opinions have reached (the number of followers of an opinionated user and the number of retweets his or her tweet received), brand awareness, impressions, brand engagement (how much tweeters are interacting with you), negative situations turned around or handled, or money saved replacing other activities by leveraging Twitter. Twendz looks at up to 70 of the most recent tweets about a keyword and analyzes the content of those tweets to try to gauge sentiment.

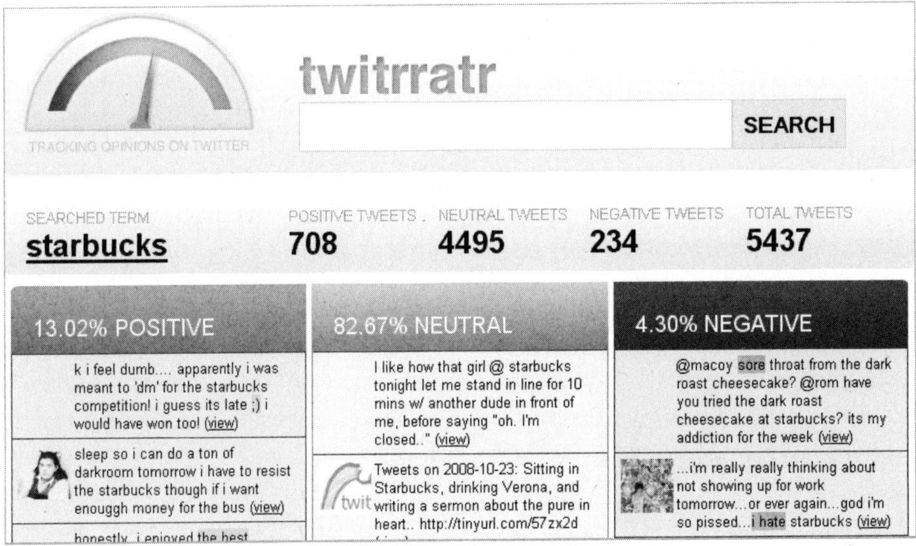

Figure 6.29 Twitrratr's score for Starbucks

Wednesday's One-Hour Exercise: Practice Measuring and Analyzing

Since using these measurement applications is the best way to help determine if they're going to yield you the kind of information you might be looking for specifically, today's exercise will take you through several of them. Feel free to venture out beyond those on the below list if you want additional perspective.

1. Run Twitter Grader on yourself, and then click through to the highly ranked tweeters in your area of the country. Follow any who seem interesting to you. You can even send them a tweet explaining that you found them on Twitter Grader and why you are looking forward to reading their tweets.
2. Go to the Klout application. Create an account and run the statistics for yourself. What do you see? Are you engaging with people? Are you sharing informa-

tion? Is anyone you are influenced by someone with whom you want to interact? Does this give you any ideas for some goals? If so, write them down.

3. Go to Twit Truth and run statistics for `@ChrisBrogan`. Then add yourself and run your statistics. What do you notice? What can you learn from viewing Chris's stats? Write down two action steps for you to change about your tweeting, and plan on implementing these changes and testing them over the next seven days.
4. Try running your Retweetrank statistics. Run them for a few other users you know. How do you compare? Who gets retweeted more? Is there anything you learned here that you can add to your previous two action steps to test for the next seven days?
5. With regards to measuring ROI, are there any methods your company can use to attribute sales or leads directly to Twitter? Document them and start tracking those actions.
6. Develop a plan for regularly monitoring your twitter activity over time. For example, create a spreadsheet for your key statistics and monitor it each week.

Thursday: Experiment with Other Useful Twitter Tools

Welcome to Thursday. By now you might be feeling overwhelmed by all the tools you've been introduced to so far—and there are still plenty more to go! Don't worry too much. Keep in mind that you're not going to need to use all these tools all the time. You just should understand what functionality these tools can bring to you and how they can improve your Twitter experience. By picking the tools that work for you, you can get out of Twitter what you want to get—and get it in your own way. This is both the benefit and the downside of Twitter's open API. The good news is that developers can create a multitude of applications, but the bad news is that you have to sort through them and figure out what to use. With new tools being added every day, it's tough to keep up. You'll find yourself feeling like Twitter has more tools than The Home Depot!

Here are some more useful tools, and come Friday, you'll see how you can use some plain ol' fun ones.

Topify Twitter's email notifications of new followers, though richer than they once were, still leave a lot to be desired for at-a-glance decision making. For a richer solution, try Topify (`http://www.topify.com`). Still in beta as of this writing, Topify requires that you apply for an invitation, and there is currently a waiting list to get a Topify account. Once you're able to create a Topify account, however, it becomes your de facto Twitter email notification service. A Topify email gives you more relevant information about a new follower, such as his or her followers and following counts, a following/followers ratio, statistics from Mr. Tweet, the user's bio, most recent five tweets, location, and URL (Figure 6.30). Then, if you decide you want to follow this user, all you have to do is reply to Topify, who processes your follow request.

Figure 6.30 A Topify notification

Unlike when using Twitter, you can respond directly to a DM that comes via email from Topify. Not only does this require fewer steps to reply to DMs, but it also allows for a more searchable record of your DMs, a feature that is not currently available in Twitter.

FileTwt and FileSocial FileTwt (`http://www.filetwt.com`) gives you public or private file-sharing (up to 20MB) capabilities through Twitter. If you want to share files privately, both sender and recipient must have FileTwt accounts. FileTwt limits your tweet to 114 characters, considerably less than Twitter's 140. Similarly, FileSocial (`http://filesocial.com`) lets you publicly share all kinds of files up to 50 MB. You provide a brief message to tweet along with your file, and FileSocial uploads your file, converts it into a link, and sends out your tweet.

Twibes and Twubs These two somewhat similar tools allow you to join or create your own groups. Twibes (`http://www.twibes.com`) organizes existing groups by topics. You can also search for a Twibe by name. If none already fit your needs, you can create up to three of your own. For example, to help gather information for this book through crowdsourcing, I created a Twibe called "Hollis Twitter Army" (`http://www.twibes.com/HollisTwitterArmy`). Using the hashtag `#HTArmy`, I could flag twibe members with missions, and over time, the most active members formed Twitter relationships of their own.

Conversely, Twubs (`http://twubs.com`) takes hashtags and aggregates groups around them. They also have a solution suite to help conference and meeting planners leverage Twitter before, during, and after an event.

Tweetbeep, Tweet Scan, and Twilert If you use Google Alerts, you'll find these similar Twitter alert tools helpful. TweetBeep (`http://www.tweetbeep.com`), Tweet Scan (`http://www.tweetscan.com/alerts.php`), and Twilert (`http://www.twilert.com`) all enable you to track keywords or important links and be notified of these mentions by email (Figure 6.31). These alerts mean you don't have to rely on checking your search results or RSS feed often, which requires proactive action on your part. The results are delivered to you (passive action, which is much easier for you). It's handy to use these solutions to inform you of mentions of your Twitter handle, especially if you plan to step away from Twitter for a few hours, so you can still respond in a timely manner (a few hours' delay is an eternity in the Twitterverse!).

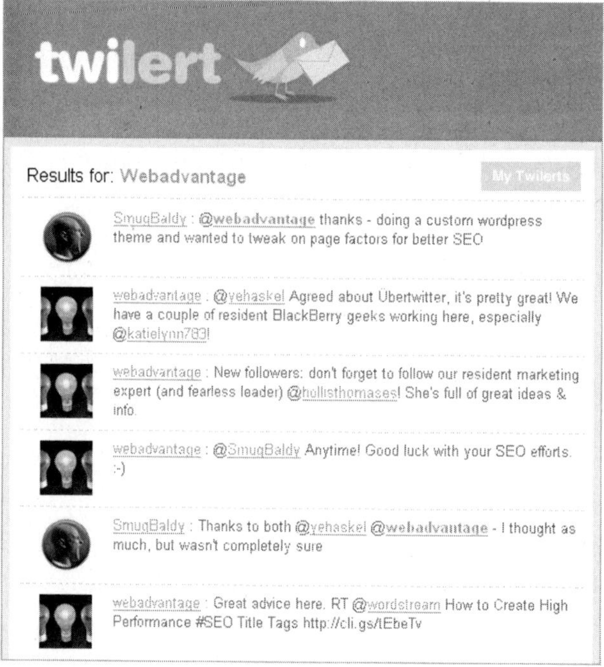

Figure 6.31 An email notification from Twilert

Brizzly or DestroyTwitter Need a break from a particular user for a few days or when they're tweeting a lot at a conference? Consider using the mute feature third party Twitter client Brizzly (`http://www.brizzly.com`) or the suppress feature of DestroyTwitter, mentioned earlier.

Twitter Buttons and Web Designer Depot Want to promote your Twitter ID on your website in a more interesting way? Twitter Buttons (`http://www.twitterbuttons.com`) and Web Designer Depot (`http://bit.ly/webdesignerdepot`) have a variety of buttons you can use and customize for your website (Figure 6.32). These buttons call attention to your presence on Twitter and encourage new followers.

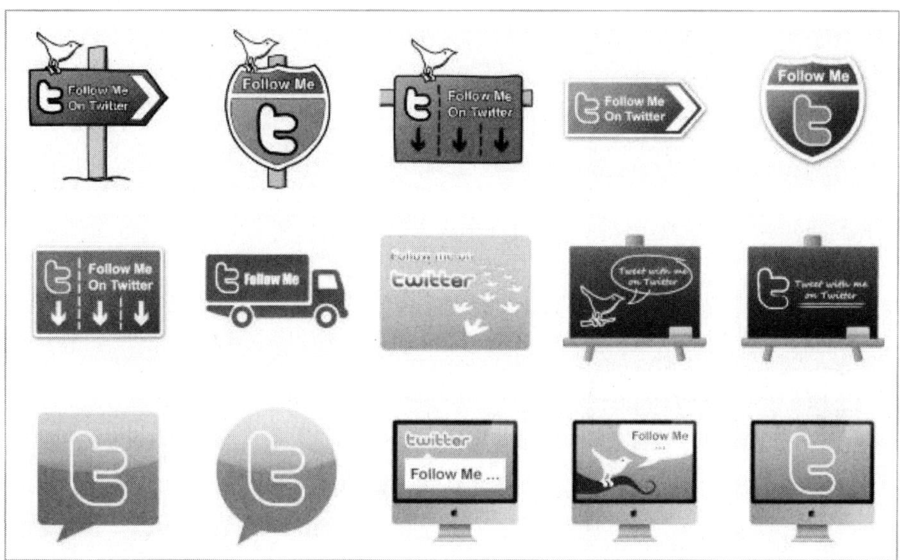

Figure 6.32 Twitter Buttons

CoTweet, ChatterBox, and TweetFunnel As a business user of Twitter, you should know about CoTweet (`http://www.cotweet.com`). Fee-based CoTweet's interface allows a single Twitter account to be managed by multiple internal users. Tweets can be assigned to respective internal users and marked as "archived," so everyone knows they have been handled.

ChatterBox (`http://www.chatterboxhq.com`) is a similar multiuser management tool. Within the ChatterBox dashboard, you can categorize, tag, prioritize, and assign tweets for follow-up as well as monitor and respond to tracked keywords and usernames. You also can collaborate in a chatterbox with anyone to help sort through your target keywords on Twitter.

Lastly, TweetFunnel (`http://www.tweetfunnel.com`) performs similar Twitter team management tasks. You can approve and post or approve and schedule tweets, hold them for later, or reject them altogether. Administrators can retain editorial approval rights, and like many other Twitter clients, it also automatically shortens and tracks URLs (Figure 6.33).

Figure 6.33 TweetFunnel's dashboard

iPhone and BlackBerry Twitter Clients I've presented multiple tools built specifically to enhance tweets delivered by iPhone or BlackBerry, but how about accessing Twitter itself? Though new applications keep cropping up, some of the more popular Twitter clients to date include the following:

- For iPhone: Tweetie (`http://www.atebits.com/tweetie-iphone`), Echofon (`http://echofon.com`), Twittelator (`http://www.stone.com/Twittelator/index.html`), and Birdfeed (`http://birdfeedapp.com`)
- For BlackBerry: UberTwitter (`http://www.ubertwitter.com/bb/download.php`) and TwitterBerry (`http://www.orangatame.com/products/twitterberry`)

TwitterGadget If you're a big Google applications user, you might appreciate TwitterGadget (`http://www.twittergadget.com`), an add-on for your Gmail or iGoogle accounts. A light third-party client, TwitterGadget places a box right on your Gmail page that allows you to see your Twitter activity and tweet from there (Figure 6.34).

Figure 6.34 TwitterGadget

Thursday's One-Hour Exercise: Use Tools

Spend about 30 to 45 minutes testing a variety of the previously mentioned tools. Pick three that you like the best, and spend the next 15 minutes composing and posting tweets about them. Do you get any responses? Talking about Twitter tools typically strikes up some kind of response or retweet.

Friday: Fun with Twitter Tools

TGIF! Today we're going to have some fun. As we've discussed, having variety in your Twitter stream is a great way to engage your followers and continue to keep them interested. Twitter isn't just all about business, and business shouldn't be boring, so sometimes it's enjoyable to explore some off-the-beaten-path tools or applications and get others to do the same. Who knows; it might lead to a great Twitter marketing idea!

Some Twitter Applications

A word of caution with these applications: be careful when providing your password to any Twitter application, particularly those that post no privacy or security information. Twitter implemented OAuth, which gives the application authorization directly through Twitter without requiring your password. This makes it safe for you, as the application does not actually have access to your password. There are still some applications that do not use OAuth, so before you blindly play around with them, see if they have proper privacy policies and contact information posted on their site. You might also want to do a Twitter search to see if there is any positive or negative talk about the application.

My First Follow For some silly reason, you're going to find this a handy tool when you try to recall the early days of your Twitter experience. You have to be logged into your Twitter account already, and then enter the username you want reviewed. My First Follow (`http://www.dcortesi.com/tools/my-first-follow`) then displays the first person you (or any username you enter) ever followed on Twitter (provided this person is still being followed) along with some other bits of information about them and the username you searched.

TweetPsych Using linguistic-analysis algorithms, TweetPsych (`http://www.tweetpsych.com`) builds a psychological profile of a user based on the content of their last 1,000 tweets. The application scores the user on criteria such as cognitive processes, sensations, future tense, similes, insight, and such.

Twanalyst Twanalyst (`http://www.twanalyst.com`) analyzes your Twitter personality and style (talker, sharer, newbie, networker, writer, and 10 other types) based on your tweets and follower numbers. The analysis also gives basic statistics on the user, how readable are his or her tweets, and a breakdown of the types of tweets posted. It actually tells you what percentage are conversations, retweets, links, hashtags, and content (Figure 6.35).

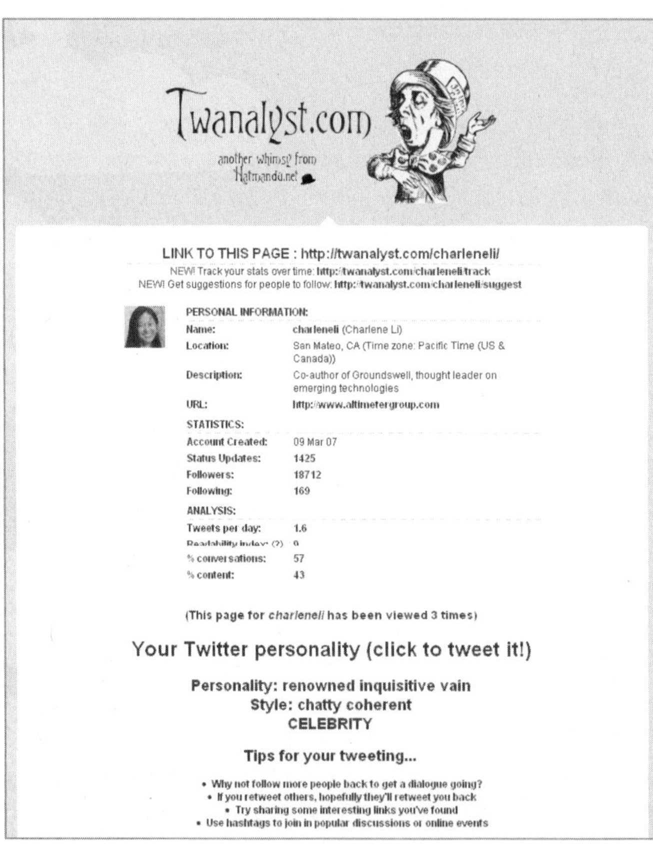

Figure 6.35 Twanalyst for analyst Charlene Li (`@charleneli`)

Click&Win It's a simple Twitter lottery-type game. All you need to do is follow Click&Win's (`http://clickandw.in`) Twitter account (`@ClickAndWin`) and, if you happen to catch when they tweet about a new lottery, click on the link and you'll be entered to win. (Right now, the site gives away Amazon gift cards, but I could see other advertisers using this tool in their promotions.) Can you imagine anything simpler?

Twrivia Follow `@Twrivia` (`http://www.twrivia.com`) and, when it tweets a trivia question, tweet back the answer. If you get it right, you earn points and you could win a prize (Figure 6.36).

Figure 6.36 A Twrivia question

TwitLOL Want to add some humor to your tweets? Go to TwitLOL (`http://www.twitlol.com`) and search for funny quips. Click the Twitter icon to tweet them.

Die Fail Whale For anyone ever frustrated by Twitter's infamous outages (the dreaded Fail Whale) Die Fail Whale (`http://www.diefailwhale.com`) might be a humorous way to blow off some steam.

The Oatmeal Twitter Addict Quiz If you are a Twitter addict, the questions on this quick 15-question quiz alone will make you laugh out loud (`http://theoatmeal.com/quiz/twitter_addict`). (My score is 87 percent addicted, by the way.)

ChessTweets If you're into Twitter and chess, ChessTweets (`http://chesstweets.com`) might be right up your alley (Figure 6.37). This application uses the Twitter API to send your chess moves to your opponent by just updating your Twitter status. You can play against a friend or start a correspondence game.

Spymaster One of the most successful Twitter-based games to date, Spymaster (`http://www.playspymaster.com`), grew virally by its premise: participating Twitter users need to complete jobs to raise money to buy equipment or order assassinations. The more of a participant's followers involved in the game, the more power that participant has. The game can be set to tweet game posts automatically so the more you play, the more the game's messages are posted to Twitter, and the more it gets promoted. Obviously, overexposure has its downside in tweet fatigue. Still, Spymaster's clever, inventive approach shows yet another way Twitter can be used.

Figure 6.37 ChessTweets' Twitter board

***ouT*WIT.me** This is a whole site of Twitter games. You can also click on their cloud navigational link (`http://www.outwit.me/twitter-cloud/cloud.php`), type in a word or Twitter handle, and *ouT*WIT.me produces a clickable cloud of keywords. Click on a keyword in the cloud, and it takes you to yet another cloud based on that keyword.

twittervision A cool mashup between Twitter and Google Maps, twittervision (`http://www.beta.twittervision.com`) shows random and fleeting real-time tweets on a visual map of the world. It's proof positive that people are tweeting all around the world.

Tweetwhatyouspend and Xpenser Two Twitter tools to help you manage your everyday expenses, Tweetwhatyouspend (`http://www.tweetwhatyouspend.com`) and Xpenser (`http://www.xpenser.com`), let you tweet from the cash register to upload your regular expenses to the Web, where you can then analyze and manage your money further.

FlipMyTweet.com Just a fanciful little gimmick, FlipMyTweet.com (`http://www.flipmytweet.com`) flips the letters of your tweet upside down and backward before tweeting it (Figure 6.38). It's clever, but you probably won't want to use this one too much, or you're likely to get unfollowed. (Although it works fine using Twitter.com, it doesn't necessarily work with third-party applications.)

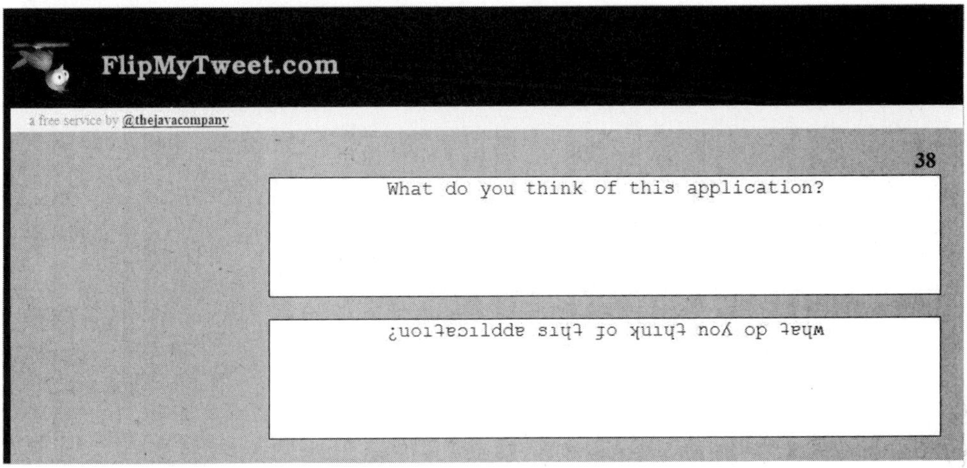

Figure 6.38 A flipped tweet

Twecipe Follow `@twecipe`, visit the Twecipe website (`http://www.twecipe.com`), or send `@twecipe` a tweet with your Twitter handle, tell them what you have in your refrigerator, and the application will give you a recipe to make with your ingredients. It's fun and useful!

Twitterlit Follow `@twitterlit` on Twitter and watch for its tweets at 9:00 AM and 9:00 PM, Eastern Time, when it tweets the first line of a book. The tweet excludes the author's name or book title, but has a link to Amazon so readers can see what book the line is from. It's a quick tease to see if you can figure out the book, *and* Twitterlit smartly uses its Amazon affiliation in every tweet, so it gets paid for every sale resulting from one of its teaser tweets. This is a very interesting business model that larger brands might want to emulate.

Didn't have enough fun today? For more fun Twitter applications, check out these other links:

- `http://techxav.com/2009/07/05/30-funny-weird-twitter-applications`
- `http://twitdom.com/tag/games`
- `http://mashable.com/2009/08/21/13-twitter-tools`
- `http://featuredusers.com/publishers`

Friday's One-Hour Exercise: Some Fun, Some Practice

After going through some of the fun or interesting applications we've listed today, you're also going to go through some of the exercises you've done in the past. It's good to get these kinds of patterns built into your Twitter routine.

- Spend 30 minutes having fun with some of these applications.
- This is your first `#followfriday`, so don't forget to tweet some of your favorite recommendations (about 5 minutes).
- Spend 20 minutes re-visiting some tools you were introduced to this week that you either didn't get to test out or that you want to go back and use again. During these 20 minutes, though, think about how these tools specifically can help you meet some of your early Twitter objectives.
- Spend the last 5 minutes using one of the scheduling applications to line up some tweets for Monday morning so that you can start next week off with a tweet even if you're not yet logged in!

The Main Points

- You can gain a vast amount of information from the various means used to search Twitter. Next to tweeting, searching probably will be the thing you do the most on Twitter.
- Tweets can be so much more than flat statements. Create enriched content through tools and links that'll keep your followers coming back for more.
- The constant flow of information and activities you and others connected to you can do with Twitter leads to rich data to parse and analyze. Don't overlook this important step to help justify your Twitter-for-marketing initiative.
- Twitter tools abound. You will never be able to keep up with them all *and* do an efficient job focusing on your marketing efforts. Just try to vet them as relevant or not for your business and move on.
- Twitter can be fun, so have a good time out there!

Week 4: Track and Monitor What Twitter Generates for You

You're probably wondering how to derive meaning from all of this Twitter activity, particularly in the context of marketing. In this chapter, as we turn our focus to the topic of tracking and monitoring, keep in mind that so much of Twitter is "of the moment" that you almost have to be in this mindset continuously. Listen *to what the Twitterverse is saying. It might open your eyes to a whole new benchmark to consider or an idea to develop, which will then need its own metrics. Numbers are great, but on Twitter, it's not always about the numbers.*

7

Chapter Contents

Twitter Metrics

If you're following this book, you've been on Twitter for almost a month now. During your first month on Twitter, like most people you were concerned with what to tweet about, finding people to follow, and attracting a following. The process takes some time to get used to, so you've hardly been able to think about what all this Twittering is doing for you. Now that you've gotten into a groove, you'll find yourself wondering if what you're tweeting about is having an impact on the Twitterverse and on your business. That's where tracking and monitoring come in. In Week 4, we're going to focus more on the metrics you might care about as an individual so you can get used to conducting this analysis. Later, in Week 8, we'll focus on measuring as a business, so we'll expand the data points and go deeper with the analysis.

Prelimary Exercise: Define Objectives

With the information you've obtained and the effort you've exerted to date, you should have formulated some ideas about what you can do with Twitter. Because you're reading this book to help you market your business, you're thoughts and goals probably stray toward business. That's OK, but for the sake of this week's curriculum, let's have you separate some individual goals from some business ones.

Take out a piece of paper and divide it into two vertical columns. On the left side, write the column header "Individual Objectives," and on the right side, write "Business Objectives." The right side is where you'll record all the ideas that come to your mind now that do not pertain to your individual objectives; you're going to save them for later. You don't need to brainstorm about them right now. Instead, focus on the left column, write down one to three goals you can refer to throughout the week, and keep them handy.

Monday: Understand What to Track and How to Review It

To understand what to track and what it means to you, put tracking into perspective apart from you individually: let's look at the Twitterverse at large. We all know the data points that pretty much everyone visiting your profile will look at:

- Number of followers
- Number of people following
- Number of tweets

What do these stats tell someone about you?

It's almost inevitable, and perhaps a flaw in the Twitter system, that everyone's eye is drawn to the number of followers someone has. It's then a quick-second hopscotch to draw the conclusion, "Oh, this person has thousands of followers so they must be important, smart, helpful, and worth following." On the other hand, you might draw the opposite conclusion about someone who doesn't have a lot of followers;

"This person must be a 'nobody' with nothing useful to share with me." Are these assumptions accurate and fair? What you don't know from that first glance includes the following:

- How did that person acquire their followers?
- How long did it take that person to acquire their followers?
- How many people is this person following, what's their followers-to-following ratio, why might it be what it is, and what might this mean to you?
- What is that person's agenda when it comes to acquiring followers? For example, what's their purpose in being on and using Twitter? How much time are they devoting to "work" their Twittering?

In order to ascertain this information, you need to look a little further.

How Do Users Acquire Followers?

The answer to this question lies in that person's tweets, so that's the first place to look. For starters, how many tweets does this person have in total? You've already been told how to identify shady tweeps, such as those with thousands of followers or followings yet only a handful of tweets. If the user doesn't look suspicious from this perspective, then take a look at their tweets. How frequently is this user tweeting? Is it multiple times an hour? Multiple times a day? Every day of the week? Sysomos' *Inside the Twitter World* study found a direct correlation between the number of followers a user has and the volume of that user's tweets (Figure 7.1).

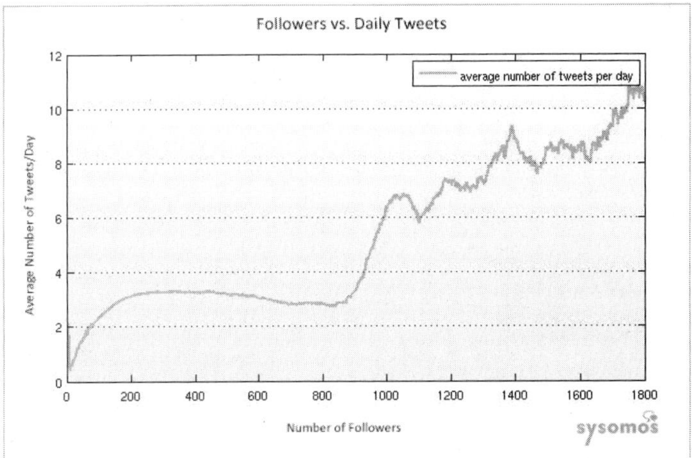

Figure 7.1 Sysomos' findings show a direct correlation between the number of followers someone has and their volume of tweets.

Sysomos went on to analyze the most active 5 percent of Twitter users; it had found earlier that they account for 75 percent of all Twitter activity. Sysomos found that "32 percent of all tweets made by the most active Twitter users were generated by machine bots that posted more than 150 tweets per day," which correlates to nearly 25 percent of *all* tweets posted per day. Some other fascinating study results include the following:

- 88 percent of the most active Twitter users have never missed a day without making at least one update, while another 2.1 percent have been inactive for only one day.
- 33.7 percent of the most active Twitter users have joined Twitter this year (2009), compared with 72.5 percent of overall Twitter users who have signed up this year.
- The most popular keywords within the bios of the most active users are *Internet marketing, music lover, web designer, video games,* and *husband/father.*

This all just goes to show you that if you happen to find someone with a lot of followers, there's a good chance that this person is a tweeting fiend. But is there value to these tweets? To determine this, read a few pages' worth of their tweets. What do you see? Are their tweets random blathering? Are they a never-ending list of retweets? Are they an equally never-ending list of `@replies`? Come to your own conclusion, and then hold that thought.

How Long Has Someone Been on Twitter?

Most people don't really use how long someone has been on Twitter as a factor in determining whether or not to follow them. But having this piece of information can help shed some light on their methods and motives for attracting followers. For instance, it would be odd if an ordinary Joe or Jane joined Twitter two months ago and already had tens of thousands of followers.

How can you determine how long someone has been on Twitter? There's a nifty little application called When Did You Join Twitter (`http://www.whendidyoujointwitter.com`) that can answer this question for any Twitter user (Figure 7.2). The application even has a handy little bookmarklet you can drag to your browser's toolbar so that you can find the answer to this question quickly. Either select some text with an `@username` and click the bookmarklet, or just click it when you're looking at someone's profile.

Figure 7.2 Juli Barcelona (`@julibarcelona`) has been on Twitter since November 12, 2008.

You can also turn to tools like TwitterCounter, which has this stat built in.

Find the Number of People a User Is Following

A quick glance at a user's Following count can tell you a lot, too. Someone who has a lot of followers but not an equal amount of following is probably not using auto-following software. This person is probably not very motivated or focused on attracting a large number of followers (the reasons for which we'll discuss in a moment). If you decide to follow such a user, you should do so because you're interested in what that person has to say more than you're interested in attracting them as a follower of your own. Some people actually calculate this likelihood as a ratio:

[(Number of Followers – Number of People Following) ÷
Number of Followers] × 100 = Likelihood to Follow Back

If the answer to the equation is less than 50 percent, your chances of being followed back are less than 50 percent, and so on. There is no single specific reason why a user maintains this ratio, or even a way of telling if she or he does so intentionally. Some users attract a lot of spammers, yet they don't block and remove them from their followers. Some users want to be more of a broadcaster type than a conversationalist. Other users want to be so engaged in conversation they follow only users they think they can actively engage. Still others feel the lower the ratio, the more elitist their standing, a perception they want to encourage. Then again, perhaps they can't find the time to filter through their new followers manually on a regular basis.

What's Your Twitter Agenda?

In previous chapters, we covered the plentiful reasons why people use Twitter. You'll find that people's level of Twitter activity is likely to relate directly to their roles and responsibilities in life. Those more active on Twitter are likely to be people whose job it is to engage in or analyze social media (this includes bloggers); to coach or perform business consulting; to carry out corporate communications; to perform public relations or marketing functions for their companies; to do business development, sales, or fundraising; to sell products from home; or to do public speaking. These people hope to see some *direct benefit* or *profit* from their Twitter activities. If your responsibilities don't fall into one of those job categories, however, don't try to compete with the others, because you might wind up feeling supremely inadequate.

If, on the other hand, your motivation for being on Twitter is primarily to find new friends with whom to cyber-socialize, gangs away! You're looking for chatty, friendly tweeps who from time to time might also steer you in the direction of helpful tips and answers to your questions.

There is no wrong or right answer to the agenda question. As with everything in life, people have different motivations and agendas. Is there a way to tell what people's Twitter agendas are? Yes. Start by looking at user's bios, which reveal a lot about them.

The content of their tweets, their profile URLs, and the associated About pages to which the URLs lead also reveal a great deal (Figure 7.3). Background designs can also literally or interpretatively provide insight.

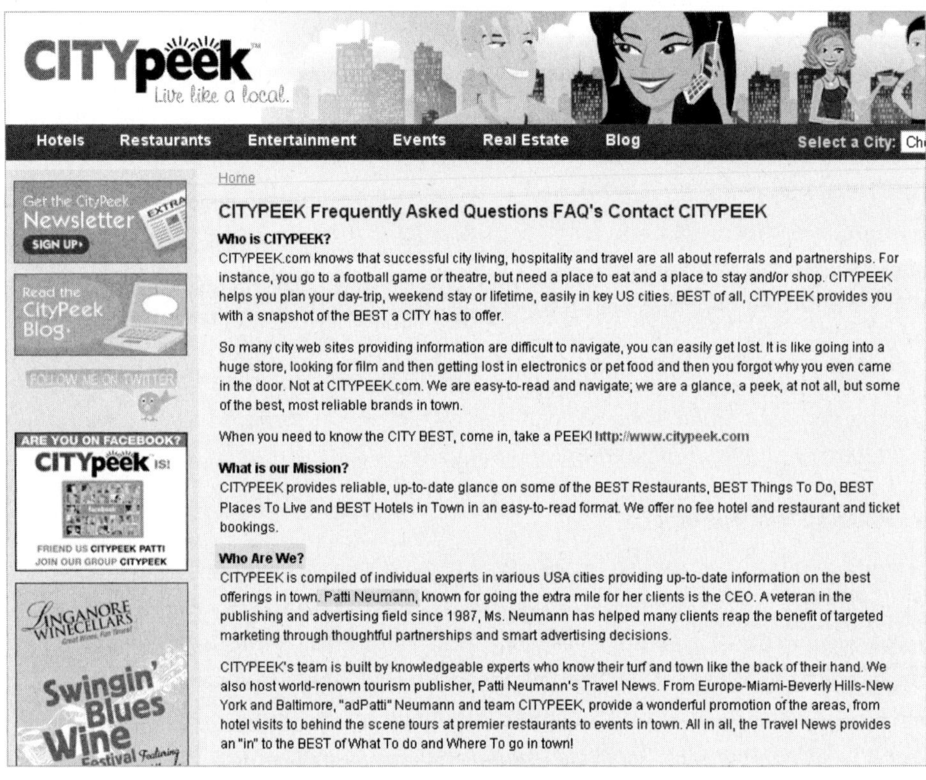

Figure 7.3 Learn more about @CityPeekPatti by clicking on her profile link.

You can also use many of the tools we reviewed in the previous weeks to find information about people. For example, go to some of the self-identified directories such as WeFollow or TwitR, search for a hashtag, and see who's listed under what categories. You can also pay attention to who's advertising themselves as a "Featured User" on various applications. (See the "What Is Featured Users?" sidebar.) The fact that users are paying to promote themselves should tell you something about their intent.

What Is Featured Users?

If you spend time on any of the many free Twitter tool and application sites, you'll probably notice display advertisements showing you users to follow. These ads are served by Featured Users (`http://featuredusers.com`), a clever win-win-win way to help users build followers. Unlike surreptitious services that "sell" followers, Featured Users is a legitimate service by which the user pays to be advertised. The ads give app developers a way to monetize their traffic, which in turn can help them support their applications. So users win by obtaining new followers through opt-ins; apps developers (publishers) win because they make money; and Featured Users wins because it too makes money. It's a more wholesome way to support the Twitter ecosystem.

You should follow @shortformblog on twitter here.
Bio: Writing a little. Saying a lot. We give you news that's really short. It's pretty sweet.
Location: Washington D.C.
Become a sponsor at FeaturedUsers.com

To date, Featured Users has caught on primarily with individual tweeters. Some businesses, such as `@140tc`, `@Uncrate, 6s_marketing`, and `@TacoBellCanada`, have tested the ads, although I expect to see more as Twitter continues to catch on.

Agenda + Action = Measurements

When you have clearly established your agenda, or goals, for being on Twitter, you will probably be able to see more clearly what you need to do to reach those goals. Once you understand those actions, you'll be able to define the things you want to measure. Obviously, different measurements will be appropriate for different goals, and your goals as an individual tweeter will probably be different from your company goals. This week, we're going to focus on the measurements most relevant to an individual; later we'll cover additional measurements that pertain to businesses.

What You Can Track

You can track a lot of activity besides your followers and following. Last week, you learned some ways to track your own Twitter activity; they primarily related to the composition and timing of your tweets and how people act on your tweets. Let's review those benchmarks for a moment:

- Number of tweets per day
- Percentage of links in tweet
- Percentage of original tweets

- Number of retweets
- Percentage of retweets
- Number of `@replies` or DMs
- Ratio of received versus sent replies or DMs
- Percentage of `@replies`
- Time of day when you tweet the most

Here are some other things you can measure for yourself:

- Click-throughs on shortened and/or trackable URLs
- Total reach of retweets (retweets × number of followers of each retweeter)
- Number of times your hashtag is used
- Referring website traffic (via web analytics)
- Actions, such as event registrations, email subscription sign-ups, or form completions
- Secondary benefits, such as media coverage

Later in the week we're going to review how to crunch all this data and make sense of it; but for now, let's evaluate the items on these lists, noting those that seem be of greatest interest to you as they relate to the Twitter goals you established at the beginning of the week.

Monday's One-Hour Exercise: A Study in Goal Setting

Today, you're going to put some of the skills you've already learned to work for you in Monday's assignment.

1. Take the list of Individual Objectives you laid out in the beginning of the week.
2. Perform a search related to one of those goals to find users tweeting about that topic.
3. Based on how their tweets on your topic resonate with you, select a few users from the bunch. (If your first search didn't generate useful results, perform a different search.)
4. Go to the first user you selected, and see if you can identify the following things:
   - **a.** How long have they been on Twitter?
   - **b.** How do they seem to be acquiring their followers?
   - **c.** What seems to be their agenda for being on Twitter?
   - **d.** Based on their agenda (their motives or objectives), what criteria in the "What You Can Track" list do you think matters to them? Can you find out some of these measurements?
   - **e.** Of those measurements you can determine, document them for that user and then set that information aside. Go to step 5.

5. Repeat step 4 two or three times or until you feel as though you've got the hang of this kind of assessment.
6. Using the goal you selected from your list of Individual Objectives at the beginning of this exercise, perform the same analysis in step 4 on yourself.
7. Compare your own analysis to those of the users you reviewed. How do you compare, contrast, and stack up against them? Do you see room for improvement in certain areas? If so, note them and add them to your Twitter objectives.

Reminder Do you have contrasting objectives that don't really belong together in the same Twitter account? Consider establishing another Twitter identity to serve the separate objective. Many third-party Twitter clients make it easy to manage multiple identities, but just remember that this could mean more work for you.

Tuesday: Alerts—Simple Tracking Tools

The simplest Twitter tracking tool is the Saved Search, which you studied in previous chapters. You've also seen how to set up an RSS feed for your saved searches so they are pushed to you, so you don't have to look up your saved searches. Robust third-party applications such as TweetDeck, Seesmic, HootSuite, and DestroyTwitter go one step further by notifying you when your saved search has been refreshed.

Still, if you're not online at the time or if you're too busy at the moment to delve into search notifications, you might miss something important, which you especially don't want to do if your reputation is on the line. This is where an "old-fashioned" form of notification may help: email. If you use Google Alerts in any capacity to keep track of crucial keywords or topics, you'll find these similar Twitter alert tools helpful.

Twilert Twilert (`http://www.twilert.com`) is probably the simplest of the free email notification applications. You create an account, create and name an alert, and Twilert will deliver it to you via email (Figure 7.4). Twilert can deliver this email once a day, once a week, or once a month. You can edit or delete alerts at any time through Twilert's interface.

TweetBeep TweetBeep (`http://tweetbeep.com`) has both free and paid versions of its application. TweetBeep's free version offers up to 10 saved ad-supported email alerts, which are delivered on an hourly or daily basis. You can track `@mentions`, `@replies`, keywords, or URLs. It reveals shortened URLs (like bit.ly or tinyurl.com) of the full URL you might be tracking, so you won't miss them either. TweetBeep also has paid versions, so you can have domain-wide searches performed and you can save more searches (30, 75, and 200) about which to be alerted. The latter Premium level provides ad-free alerts with the option to have them delivered every 15 minutes.

Results for: Webadvantage   My Twilerts

SmugBaldy : @webadvantage thanks - doing a custom wordpress theme and wanted to tweak on page factors for better SEO

webadvantage : @yehaskel Agreed about Ubertwitter, it's pretty great! We have a couple of resident BlackBerry geeks working here, especially @katielynn783!

webadvantage : New followers: don't forget to follow our resident marketing expert (and fearless leader) @hollisthomases! She's full of great ideas & info.

webadvantage : @SmugBaldy Anytime! Good luck with your SEO efforts. :-)

SmugBaldy : Thanks to both @yehaskel @webadvantage - I thought as much, but wasn't completely sure

webadvantage : Great advice here. RT @wordstream How to Create High Performance #SEO Title Tags http://cli.gs/tEbeTv

webadvantage : Thanks @bandhphoto & @jasonrashaad for the RTs! We'll keep our cool finds coming.

webadvantage : We're following @MLMboomers for a diverse stream of boomer-related links & resources.

AgentKyle : @webadvantage Thanks! We love @Twelpforce, too. It's fun being on the "bleeding edge" of customer service =)

webadvantage : Tip for domain owners: be wary of a Chinese email scam soliciting to "protect" your "internet brand" by selling you similar domains.

jasonrashaad : RT @webadvantage: Want to find tweets containing shortened URLs that link to your website? Check out http://bit.ly/16lfXe

webadvantage : Our favorite browser is still "Farfox" -- that's Firefox, spoken with a Baltimore accent. ;-)

webadvantage : @SmugBaldy They are weighted in order of importance: H1, H2, H3, and so on.

webadvantage : We're loving Best Buy's @twelpforce angle. Great Twitter strategy + customer service in action! Smart accompanying TV ad, too.

webadvantage : Want to find tweets containing shortened URLs that link to your website? Check out www.BackTweets.com

bandhphoto : RT @webadvantage This is a pretty cool real-time social search mashup tool: http://collecta.com/

webadvantage : Web Advantage Poll: What's your preferred way to handle shortened links when Retweeting http://bit.ly/wz9ah

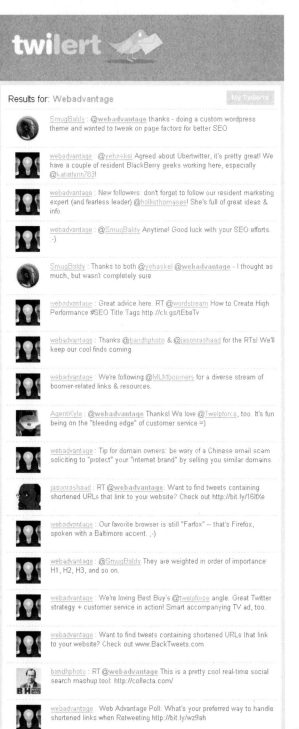

Figure 7.4 An email notification from Twilert tracking Webadvantage

Setting up an alert on TweetBeep looks exactly like performing a search on Twitter's Advanced Search, although you name the alert and determine the frequency with which you want (Figure 7.5). TweetBeep has taken the added precaution of requiring an email confirmation for the account before it will deliver any alerts.

Tweet Scan A few things differentiate Tweet Scan's (`http://www.tweetscan.com/alerts.php`) email alert system from TwitBeep's and Twilert's. Tweet Scan not only scans tweets; it also scans user profiles for your keyword(s) of choice and alphabetizes the results (Figure 7.6). This feature would be handier if there were an easy way to scroll through the results, but there isn't. It also indexes other Twitter-like public timelines built with another micro-blogging platform, StatusNet.

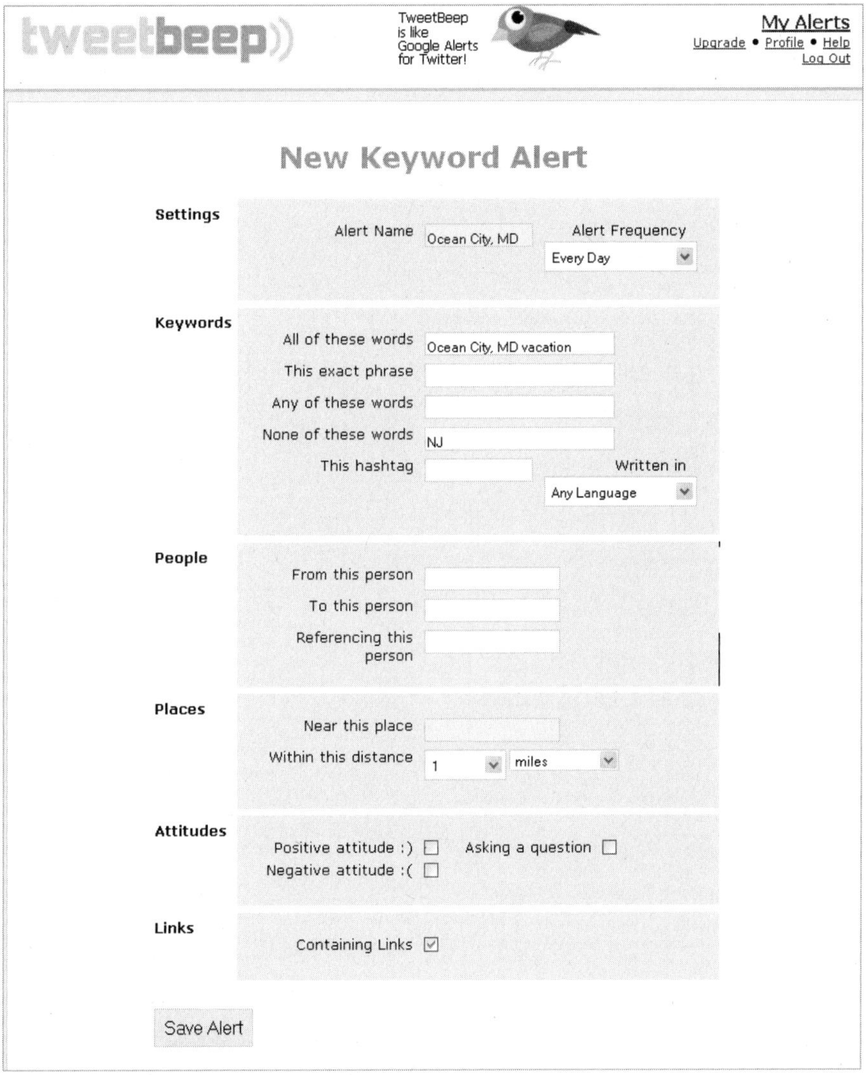

Figure 7.5 Setting up a TweetBeep alert for an Ocean City, MD vacation

TWEETSCAN What is this? Sign in Download Advanced Find People
jockey Search

Jockey
Shop for Jockey Underwear. Free Shipping All Orders. Shop Now!
www.BareNecessities.com

Ads by Google
Twitter this

adammcmillan Location The Jockey Club Estates, Georg - Bio Web

adirondackangel Location - Bio Daughter, Photographer, Girlfriend, Desk Jockey Extrordinaire and Heroine in my own Mind.

boxspring Location Hollywood, CA - Bio Computer jockey in the service of science.

brew Location UK - Bio Designer / Developer / Champion Jockey Web

CemPorCento Location Brasil - Bio 100% é o blog de Brayhan, Forattini e Kowalsky. Música, cultura disc jockey e afinidades. Muitas festas 100% virão. Visite, leia, ouça e participe. Web

clarocine Location Rio de Janeiro - Bio Maior evento de cinema a céu aberto do país vai ocupar o Jockey Club entre 19 de novembro e 7 de dezembro com seleção de 20 filmes e 26 atrações musicais Web

codingbytes Location Clarkston, MI - Bio Husband, Code Jockey, Puppy Tamer, Blogger, Twitterer (?) Web

djCarol Location Manhattan, NYC - Bio Disc Jockey, Music Producer Web

djquest95 Location Cleve/Chicaga - Bio Full Moon Productions is a full service mobile entertainment company, offering your company 22 years of disc jockey and entertainment experience. Founded in 199 Web

djspeede Location Michigan U.S.A. - Bio Part Time Disc Jockey and Full Time Music and Science Fanatic, Animal Lover and Friend of the Democratic Party

dj_dead_serious Location San Diego, CA - Bio disc jockey Web

Dourgrim Location Wisconsin - Bio I'm a loan officer AND a disc jockey AND a freelance game designer... weird, huh?

EricScherer Location Paris - Bio grey surfer, newsosaur, netocrat, old media refugee, information environmentalist, mediawatcher, news jockey Web

estcla Location Providence, RI - Bio Art jockey for the conceptual corral.

fightdesigner Location Seattle - Bio Fight Choreographer, Props Rentals, Day Job Desk Jockey, Student, Father, Husband. Just not neccessarily in that order. Web

GalaxyNewsRadio Location Washington, DC - Bio I am Three Dog Jockey of Discs and teller of Truths, Lord and Master over the finest radio station to grace the wastes. --Galaxy News Radio Web

grantrandom Location Washington, DC - Bio I'm a satellite radio disc jockey, a basement dweller, and quite possible an idiot. Web

HeavyHeavyHeat Location - Bio insomniac. future disc jockey. enjoys sharing altoids on the outskirts & sticky notes in the midst of algebra tests.

hyperactive Location Gainesville, FL - Bio MBA Candidate at University of Florida. T-Shirt jockey. Digital Media freak. Breakdancer extraordinaire.

ianclarke Location UK - Bio ex jockey - Horse Racing Tipster Free Racing Tips Web

jalynhenton Location Alexandria, VA - Bio Disc Jockey! Put on some Al Green!

jayfajardo Location Manila - Bio Tech entrepreneur, startup junkie, code jockey, and Web 2.0 fan Web

jefbot Location iPhone: 34.087723,-118.384918 - Bio writer, artist, actor, ostrich jockey. Web

jerry Location 398 E Wildwood Dr, Warsaw, IN - Bio Rails-jockey by day and a Dad by Night. Web

jesshickey Location The Jockey Club Estates, Georg - Bio Just a poor dirt farmer

jkwatson Location Portland, OR - Bio Code jockey and wine enthusiast from PDX Web

jodepoley Location Lincoln, NE - Bio Computer Jockey who believes Jesus is the only hero who can save us

kirbostic Location Los Angeles - Bio illustrator and office jockey Web

Figure 7.6 Any Tweet Scan user query can be delivered by email.

Use these solutions so you won't miss any tweets about your brand or products. They provide a helpful alternative to saved searches and RSS feeds, with an added benefit—unlike Twitter's archives, you can save these email notifications for as long as you'd like in your email system. You should use any mentions of the items you're following as a way to identify new potential followers and to reach out and strike up conversations with anyone of interest. We will discuss this again on Friday.

Tuesday's One-Hour Exercise: Set Up Twitter Alerts and Practice Tasks

Tuesday's an easy day. After you complete the alert assignment, you'll do a set of tasks you'll find yourself doing over and over again in Twitter. Why not get you used to this process now?

Alert Setup

1. (10 minutes) Using each of the three free services, set up the following:
    a. An alert for the same keyword or phrase
    b. Three different alerts (one with each service)

    Do this step so you can compare what each service delivers and how they perform. After you receive your alerts and make your evaluations (give yourself a full 24-hour period at least), you'll be able to determine if you prefer one service over the others. Then you can delete the services you don't care for and migrate your alerts over to your preferred solution.

Practice Assignments

1. (15 minutes) Perform some searches on your critical keywords using any of the many tools we've discussed to identify potential new people to attract as followers. Send five to ten tweets to these people with something you think will get their attention. Track whether or not they respond to you and/or if they also start following you.
2. (10 minutes) Read your Twitter stream. Identify at least two to four tweets worthy of retweeting. On each tweet, use a different method of acceptable retweeting.
3. (15 minutes) Compose and/or prepare some enhanced tweets that contain links of one form or another. Send any that don't require more than 15 minutes to enhance.

Reminder It's `#TweepleTuesday`. Introduce two of your Twitter friends to each other and explain why you think they ought to meet. Use the `#TweepleTuesday` hashtag.

Wednesday: Advanced Tracking Tools

As you become more sophisticated with your Twitter efforts, you should see how much they tie into your other social media efforts: blogging, tagging, news voting, photo and video sharing, discussion boards, mobile activities, audio posting/podcasting, Facebooking, and the like. What you might find blossoming from all of this activity is a need to track how your efforts resonate throughout the social media sphere at large. That's what advanced tracking tools can tell you.

Social Media Tracking for Anyone

There are many advanced tools with varying capabilities. Let's outline some for you so you know what to look for and can determine which tools might be right for you.

Social Mention Like the email alerts mentioned yesterday, Social Mention (`http://socialmention.com`) sends email alerts for *all* things social media: blogs, Twitter and other microblogging platforms, bookmarks, comments, events, images, news, videos, audio, questions and answers, and anything else.

Trendrr Trendrr (`http://www.trendrr.com`) allows you to track the popularity and awareness of trends across a variety of inputs, ranging from social networks (including Twitter) to blog buzz and video views and downloads, all in real time. You can automate tracking and reporting and garner real-time return on investment (ROI) and actionable data. You can even automatically compare trends to one another, monitoring and evaluating the comparison across the various sources. Trendrr has a free version and a paid version with added features (such as Executive Reporting), alerts across all data sources (as opposed to the 10-source limitation with the free version), more data tracking, competitor tracking, and API integration.

socialseek For individuals or businesses, social seek (`http://www.sensidea.com/socialseek`) is a downloadable application that tracks a wide variety of social media sources and topics. The application generates real-time notifications, charts, graphs, and topic comparisons that you can export for further use or manipulation (Figures 7.7 and 7.8).

Filtrbox Filtrbox (`http://www.filtrbox.com`) offers two levels of solutions: Basic and G2. The free Basic version should appeal to individuals. It has a nice set of features to find, aggregate, filter, and deliver social media results directly to you. The G2 version has more robust tools, much like those listed in the next section, and is therefore more appropriate for businesses.

socialseek by sensidea

socialseek starbucks City SEEK Charts | Save | My Seeks | Export

All (280) Blogs (40) Twitter (99) Videos (50) Images (91) Events (50) My Feeds

Fri Jul 3 2009 11:37:03 AM
bychadmccool: In line at #Starbucks. Started one load of laundry, going to write!

Fri Jul 3 2009 11:37:02 AM
turner: Enough sitting around... Time to pick up the boy from his grandparents. Beautiful morning to sit at Starbucks though.

Fri Jul 3 2009 11:36:55 AM
lauradye: Reminder: bake sale tomorrow at the OC starbucks. Since its 4 breast cancer research, can I call it "bake sale for

Fri Jul 3 2009 11:36:51 AM
nephie: Hey lady. You wanted something southern to hive as a gift. Showed you our soap from RALEIGH. What did you buy? A

Fri Jul 3 2009 11:36:36 AM
NicoyaBoy: Good morning all ! Pura vida !
Off to starbucks , BBQ food run, pool party items! Plan to watch the second men's semi. Wimbledon !

Fri Jul 3 2009 11:36:31 AM
SarahLee27: Ughhhhh I need some starbucks right now!!!!! But I'm in like one of the hoodest parts of jamaica queens...no

Fri Jul 3 2009 11:36:23 AM
DeJota712: StArBuCkS WiTh fRaNk!!!!!!

Filter: Include: Blog Twitter Videos Images Events

Next update: 21

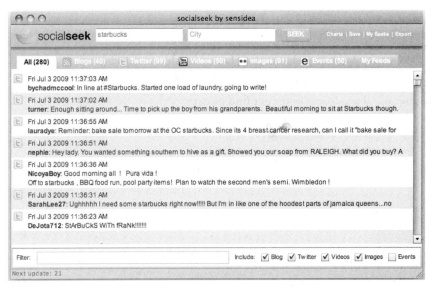

Figure 7.7 The socialseek application tracks all mentions of Starbucks.

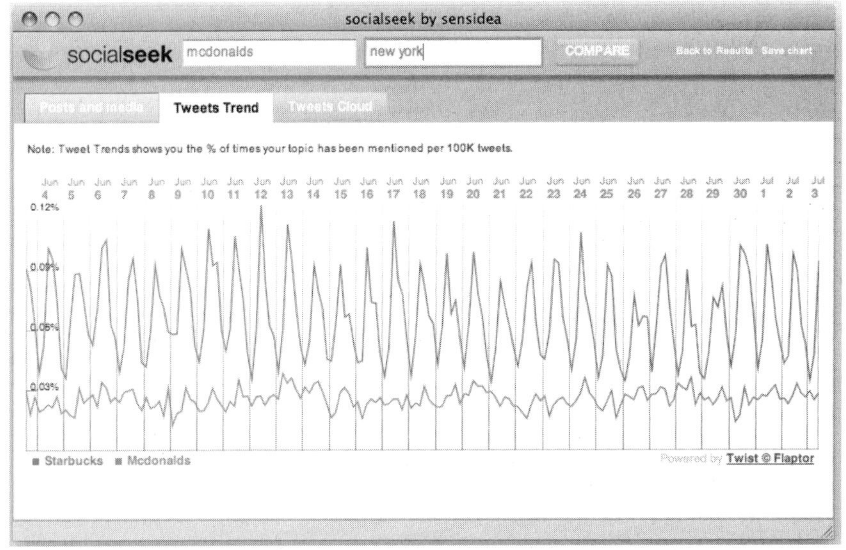

Figure 7.8 The socialseek application compares Starbucks and McDonald's tweets.

Viralheat Viralheat (`http://www.viralheat.com`) enables tracking for a variety of subject matter. Users can also publicly share "profiles" they set up to track. Although Viralheat is not free, it is inexpensive. It does let you view stats of the Top Five mentions in any profile category for free—or you can search for by a profile name and view the results: (`http://www.viralheat.com/social_trends`). (See Figure 7.9.)

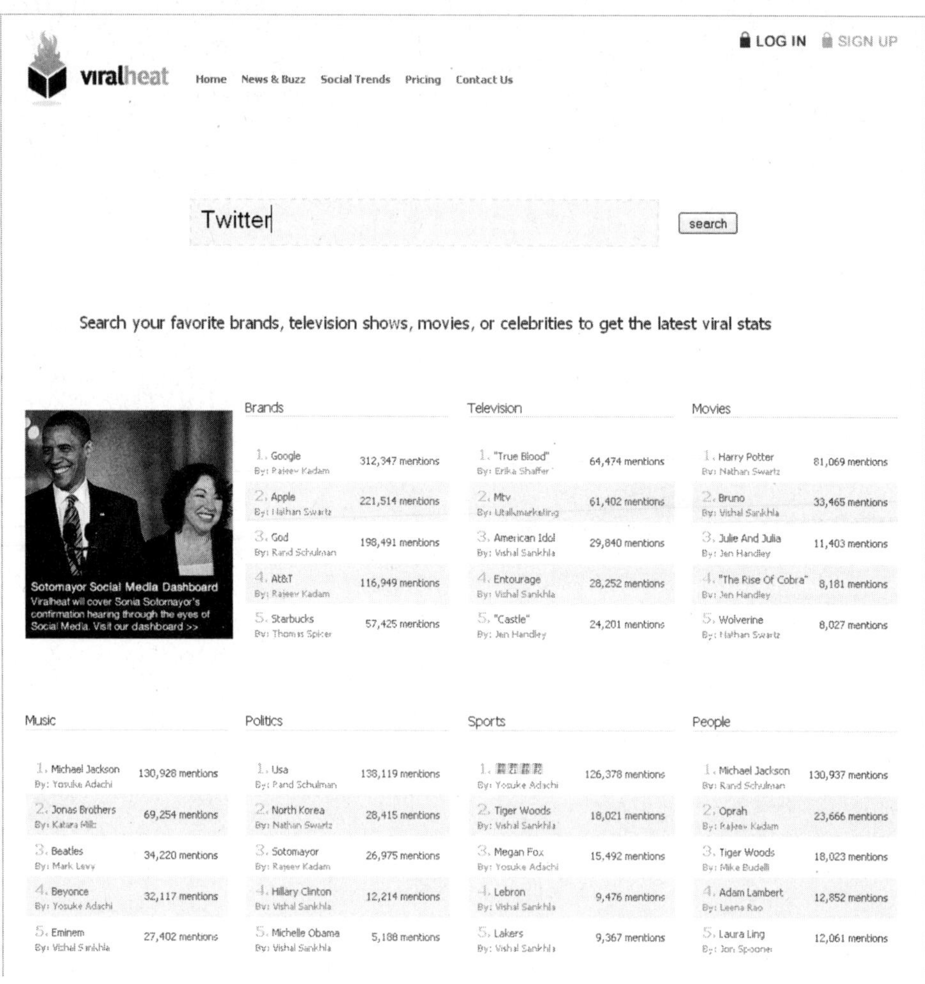

Figure 7.9 Viralheat's Social Trends tool

Social Media Tracking for Business

Many of these tracking solutions could be used by any medium-to-large-size brand, business, or agency on Twitter.

Radian6 Radian6 (`http://www.radian6.com`) is one of the more well-known solutions in the industry. It has both corporate and agency solutions. Through its real-time executive dashboard, companies can track and be alerted to who their influencers are and what they're saying and sharing about the brand. Captured data can be aggregated or filtered and sliced and diced based on relevant post metrics, conversation metrics, and web analytics. Radian6 offers a workflow module that enables companies to engage directly with influencers, prioritize and route assignments internally, and tag conversations (Figure 7.10). Radian6 also ties in with software such as Salesforce.com and Web Trends.

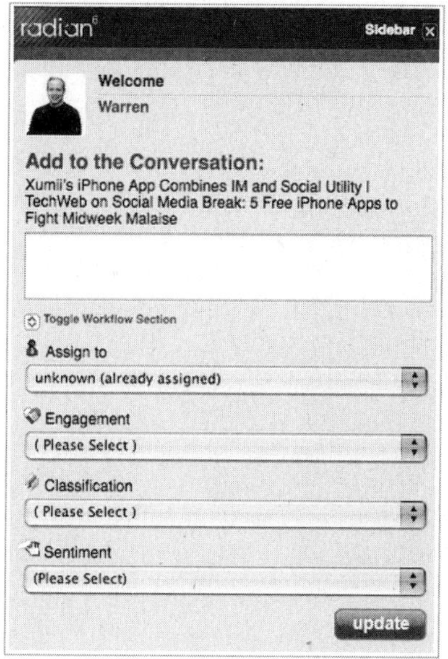

Figure 7.10 Radian6's workflow assignment

SM2 Commonly referred to as Techirgy, the company that built it, SM2 (`http://www.techrigy.com/what_is_sm2.php`) is a social media monitoring and analysis solution designed for public relations and marketing professionals. It tracks social media conversations, reviews, and positive/negative sentiment for brands, clients, competitors, and partners. Like Radian 6, SM2 has real-time tracking and alerts and customized reporting. SM2 also provides *sentiment analysis*, which uses natural-language processing and Bayesian analysis to uncover and aggregate the sentiments around each discussion, and *discussion clustering*, which provides a graphical analysis and clustering of similar conversations so you can quickly target a particular discussion thread. (See Figure 7.11.)

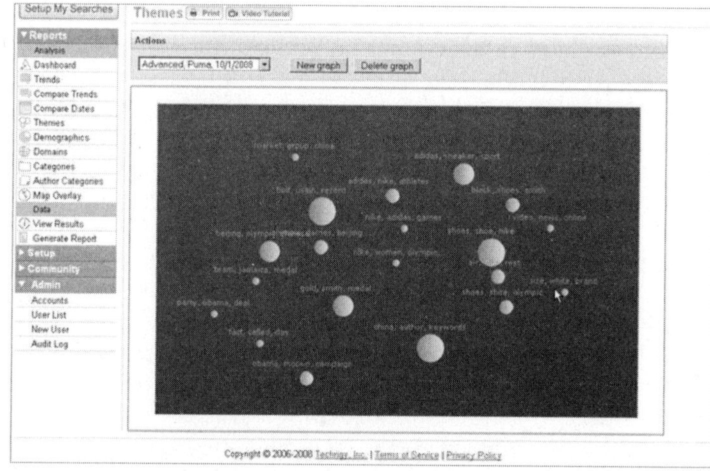

Figure 7.11 SM2's dashboard displays discussion clustering.

Sysomos The name Sysomos (`http://www.sysomos.com`) should already be familiar to you. Like the two companies mentioned previously, Sysomos' Web solution, MAP, provides real-time robust tracking, notifying, aggregating, analysis, and data reporting options (Figure 7.12).

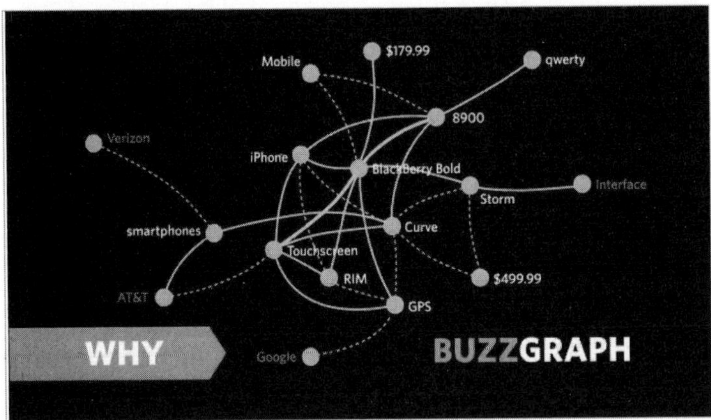

Figure 7.12 Sysomos's Buzz Graph

ListenLogic Focused on the enterprise sectors such as sales and prospecting, marketing, customer service, research and development, public relations, corporate monitoring, and competitor intelligence, ListenLogic's (`http://www.listenlogic.com`) *listening platform* tracks and analyzes online chatter.

Spiral16 Labeling its "informatic software" solution Spark, Spiral16's (`http://www.spiral16.com`) virtualization engine enables businesses to discover patterns and relationships among large data sets by organizing them in interactive displays.

ObjectiveMarketer ObjectiveMarketer (`http://objectivemarketer.com`), a social media campaign management and analytical solution, offers separate programs for enterprises and agencies.

Infegy Marketing a monitoring, tracking, and analysis solution called Social Radar, Infegy (`http://www.infegy.com`) provides "instantaneous insights and measurement into online chatter."

RapLeaf RapLeaf (`http://www.rapleaf.com`) gathers and analyzes people information, such as demographics, personal interests, friend networks, and someone's social media footprint across the Social Web.

Scout Labs A solution priced to accommodate even small businesses, Scout Labs (`http://www.scoutlabs.com`) delves into searches, sentiment tracking, buzz tracking, email alerts, collaboration, and conversation digests, among other offerings.

Compete PRO Enterprise Though Compete (`http://www.compete.com`) provides useful free tracking "for every site on the Internet," such as site traffic history and competitive analytics, it offers even more robust tracking and analytics such as industry profiles and behavioral segments, including engagement metrics, in its paid PRO Enterprise version.

Sentiment Metrics Doing business internationally? Sentiment Metrics (`http://www.sentimentmetrics.com`) offers its social media data analysis tool in multiple languages: Dutch, English, French, German, Italian, Norwegian, Portuguese, Spanish, and Swedish.

Reputation Management Tools

Skewed more toward public relations professionals or brands with their own corporate communications departments, these tools specifically market themselves as reputation or buzz tracking and management tools.

TruReputation TruReputation's Monitoring service (`http://www.trureputation.com/internet-monitoring-services.htm`) reads much like the above solutions, but with the focus instead being on public relations, corporate and crisis communications, and customer experience.

Trackur Trackur (`http://www.trackur.com`) describes itself as "60-Second Reputation Monitoring" (Figure 7.13) and welcomes individuals, companies, and agencies to its tool. Trackur has some nice additional social media tracking features, though it might do well to emphasize the social media monitoring message in order to attract a wider audience.

BrandsEye With packages for individuals through enterprises, BrandsEye (`http://www.brandseye.com`) positions itself against Google Alerts and Trackur with more functionality and value-added services.

Visible Technologies Among its suite of social media listening and monitoring solutions, Visible Technologies (`http://www.visibletechnologies.com`) offers its truREPUTATION product.

Cision Powered by Radian 6, Cision's social media tools (`http://us.cision.com/products_services/cision_social_media/overview.asp`) like its Social Media Dashboard or its Social Media Daily Reports are designed for PR professionals and brand managers.

Cymfony Truly a high-end PR pro's solution, Cymfony (`http://www.cymfony.com`) tracks and combines traditional and social media to capture a more complete picture of which strategies are producing the best ROI.

Social Media Monitoring Tools

Online Reputation Monitoring in 4 Steps!

We believe Trackur is the easiest online reputation monitoring tool in existence. In fact, it's so simple to use, we debated whether you'd even need a walk-through of how it works.

How simple is Trackur to use? We'll show you.

1. Enter the main keyword you want Trackur to automatically monitor for you.

keyword search

Enter a Keyword

apple

Exact Match

2. Let Trackur know of any filter keywords that a story "must include" and those that it "does not include." Trackur will then filter the results for you. (You can also leave this blank and filter later).

Optional Filters

Must Include:

iphone

ipod

[Add +]
[Remove -]

Does Not Include:

mac

itunes

[Add +]
[Remove -]

In the example above, you can see we've included only those items that include "iphone" and "ipod" and filtered-out any items that we're not interested in ("mac" and "itunes").

3. Now click "Search Articles"

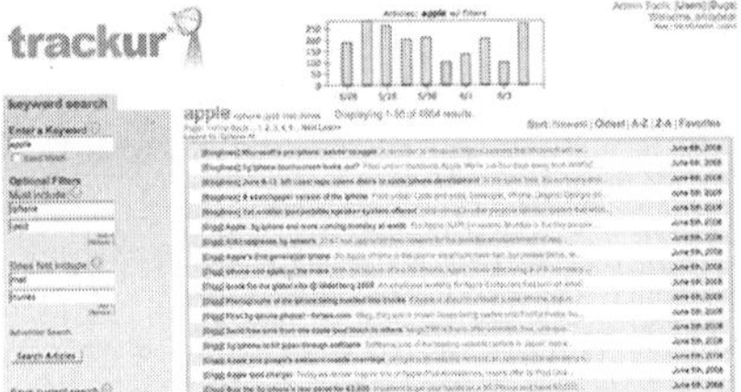

Trackur shows you all of the matching items and lets you expand each one, save items for future reference,

Trackur shows you all of the matching items and lets you expand each one, save items for future reference, and sort them the way you want.

Note: When you first run Trackur, it displays a selection of relevant items. As it continually monitors the web, it will show you ALL items that match your search criteria. In other words, Trackur does better at monitoring future items, than digging up the past.

4. Save, and Subscribe!

Save current search

apple | Save

search list

marketing pilgrim (1)

andy beal (1)

Now that you've created your first search, you can save it and either check back with Trackur for updates, or subscribe by RSS or email.

Didn't we say it was one of the easiest online reputation monitoring tools you've ever used? If you happen to have additional questions, check out our FAQ.

Figure 7.13 Trackur's "60-Second" setup

Wednesday's One-Hour Exercise: Social Media Tracking

Now it's time to see the larger impact of your tweeting. In today's exercise, you'll work with some of the tracking tools:

1. Review each of the solutions listed under "Social Media Tracking for Anyone." Sign up for any that are free or offer free trials.
2. Using your name, company name, keywords, competitors, or any of the other items you've come up with previously that you might want to track with these tools, create alerts or profiles to track.
3. If you still have time, explore the business and reputation management tracking tools, noting any you think might be relevant for your business needs.
4. If you have the authority and are prepared to obtain tracking data on your company, sign up for any of the commercial versions you find worthwhile.

Thursday: Compile Tracking Data

Today is going to be more of a roll-your-sleeves-up-and-work than read day. Compiling data can *easily* take more than an hour, especially now that you've seen just how much data you can generate! So consider this entire section for Thursday as your exercise.

Do you remember the list of Twitter-specific measurable items we reviewed on Monday? Do you recall the tools you learned about last week, many of which help you to locate and review this data? In today's exercise, you're going to collect your stats on *all* of these items (or as many as you complete within the hour). You'll do this for two reasons: it's great practice to do this all thoroughly at least once, and it's helpful to establish a documented baseline by which to compare your activity over time, especially because a lot of these tools give you only a snapshot in time.

Metrics, Metrics, and More Metrics

Take a look at Figure 7.14. You'll notice many of the metrics you've read about before, as well as some new ones. This list is as comprehensive as possible, given all the measurements the tools spit out. You may have some measurements or metrics specific to your business you'd like to add. We're going to cross over into Twitter for business data analysis in Chapter 11, "Week 8: Monitor, Measure, and Valuate," but you can always jot down these measurements now so you don't forget the idea.

The chart also indicates which tools can deliver what data to you. Sometimes only one tool can deliver a data point; sometimes multiple tools can. When multiple tools deliver data, you can choose which one to use.

ITEM TO TRACK	Your Stats	ANALYSIS TOOLS TO USE Twitter	"Tweet Stats"	"Twitter Counter"	bit.ly	Twitalyzer	Klout
	Date:						
# of Followers		•		•			•
Changes in # of Followers				•			
# of Following		•		•			•
Changes in # of Following				•			•
Follower/Following Ratio							•
# of Friends (each of you follow each other)							•
Total # of Tweets		•		•			•
# of Tweets per Day							
# of Tweets per Hour			•				
What You Tweet About (keywords; hashtags)			•				
Who You Commonly Tweet With			•				
# of Links in Tweets			•				•
% of Links in Tweets							•
% of Tweets Containing Hashtags							
% Original Tweets							
# of Retweets You Make							•
# of Retweets You Receive							•
% Retweets							
Who You Commonly Retweet							
Who You Influence			•				•
Who You're Influenced By							•
# of @replies							•
% @replies							
# of DMs		•					
# of Questions Asked							•
% of Tweets Containing Questions							•
Avg # of Replies Per Question							•
Time It Takes To Read & Respond To Messages							
Time Of Day When You Tweet The Most							
User Comparisons			•	•			•
Influence						•	•
Generosity						•	
Clout/Reach						•	•
Signal-to-Noise Ratio						•	
Engagement							•
Reach							•
Velocity							•
Demand							•
Network Strength						Pro Version	•
Activity							•
Twitter Rank (# of out ?)/percentile							
Retweet Rank (# & percentile)							
Positive Tweet Sentiments							
Neutral Tweet Sentiments							
Negative Tweet Sentiments							
Common Tags:							•
Click-throughs on Shortened And/or Trackable Urls By Day			•		•		
Click-throughs on Shortened And/or Trackable Urls By Week, Month, Total					•		
Click-throughs Related to The Aggregated Total for That Shortened URL					•		
Geographical Source of Click-through on Shortened URL					•		
Referring Site or Tool Used to Click-through on Shortened URL					•		
Conversations Generated by Shortened URL					•		
Referring Web Site Traffic							
Secondary Benefits, Like Media Coverage							

Figure 7.14 Data-compilation Chart

ANALYSIS TOOLS TO USE							
"Twitter Grader"	Twit Truth	"Retweet rank"	"ReTweet ability Index"	Twitrratr	filtrbox	Your Website Analytics	Social Media or PR Tools
•			•		•		some
•					•		some
•							
			•		•		some
							some
	•						
	•						
	•						
	•						
	•						
	•						
							some
•							
		•					
				•			•
				•			•
				•			•
							some
						•	
							•

Thursday's One-Hour Exercise: Compile Tracking Data

Now it's time to go down the list and complete the column labeled "Your Stats." Don't forget to fill in today's date, so you can determine how much time has elapsed between when you do this exercise and when you do it next, and to pace out the change in your stats. If a tool tells you something that isn't listed here, add it in the blank spaces of the chart if you'd like.

Ready to begin? You have one hour. Go!

Friday: Review, Analyze, and Respond to Tracking Data

Now that you have compiled your data, let's derive some meaning from it, particularly with respect to your objectives. Pull out your preliminary exercise list of Individual Objectives. Remember we're going to cover business-specific ones later so you can review them against the data you compiled.

Because different readers are going to have different objectives, not every part of this section will pertain specifically to you. If something isn't pertinent, skip it and move on if you like—or you can read and absorb another perspective. Understanding different perspectives will help you realize why people undertake the activities they do on Twitter. This section skips over the "to socialize" objective, because if that's your motive, you're probably not focused on any kind of metrics except maybe your follower count.

What are some common objectives and what measurements are used to focus on those objectives? You've seen these objectives before, so let's cover the analysis.

Information Dissemination

If your primary objective is information dissemination, and this includes branding and awareness efforts, you'll want to focus on building a large following (in Twitterspeak, that means you want more followers) because the larger your following, the greater the chance for your message to get out there. That's called *reach.* When this is your objective, you'll want to focus on metrics related to your followers and how many people are retweeting your message. Locate these data points on your chart. If you've just started out on Twitter, your follower counts might not be large, but that's OK. Just keep striving to grow your followers by fulfilling your objective: creating and/or sharing information. Do monitor your followers over time, however, so you can measure your growth.

You can measure a few things right now, starting with your retweet figures. Is your content being retweeted? How often does this occur in relation to your total tweets? You can also look at the click stats on your shortened URLs. Are people clicking on your links? At what rate? Figure out what you're tweeting that gets a lot of retweets and link clicks. Do more of this. If your figures are low, it might indicate that your content isn't very appealing to your followers. You might risk losing followers if you continue down your course, but at the very least, you should rethink your content strategy if it's not working to meet your objective. Finally, pay attention to the time of day you're tweeting and how this impacts your responses. You might think you should be tweeting Tuesday through Friday, 9:00 AM to 5:00 PM, when in fact you should be tweeting Sunday evening 8:00 PM to 11:00 PM and Monday through Thursday 10:00 AM to 6:00 PM.

Publicize

People who use Twitter to generate publicity have similar objectives to those who are on it to disseminate information, so the data you want to analyze is very similar. There are also many differences. For example, publicity seekers might want to attract an even larger pool of followers and be less discriminating about who these followers are and whether or not the content they're tweeting keeps a follower around. Publicity types, particularly those on the general agency side, realize that their clients are diverse and that, at any given time, they'll need to promote varying messages. If you work in corporate PR or for a specialized agency, this doesn't apply.

If you're using Twitter for publicity you ought to track almost all of the Twitter stats available to you but also the reverberation of your message throughout social media (this is why specific tools are designed for the agency type).

Lead/Influence

One could say this type of user is the most powerful on Twitter. He or she typically has a large audience of followers who eagerly read and retweet the influencer's posts. Leaders have influence far beyond the Twittersphere, in no small part thanks to prolific writing and the power of their ideas. If you fall into this category, you'll want to use a social media tracking tool, in addition to Twitter analysis ones, to keep track of where and how you're having influence. You'll also want to monitor your engagement, as the best influencers are also highly engaged with their followers (it's part of their appeal). You'll want to measure a lot of the same statistics as the previous groups, but pay attention to your tweet counts (total volume and by the day) and velocity. Some people criticize (and unfollow) people who tweet too much, even leaders. Influencers tend to create and participate in hashtagged content and events, so watch these as well as your keywords (Figure 7.15).

Figure 7.15 Tweet Stats' hashtag cloud for Jason Baer (@jaybaer)

Network

If you're on Twitter for networking purposes, you're probably less concerned about a large follower count than *the right* follower count. This means identifying people who are either in your industry, know a lot of people, or have a propensity to connect people. You should also work to get introduced to those on Twitter who have influence or clout, as they can help you find who you're looking for more quickly by their own network and reach. Depending on the kind of networker you are, you might meet someone briefly to get your introduction or you might cultivate a long-term, active dialog with them. Monitor how you share links and your generosity—do higher stats in these areas correlate to faster or better introductions? People like you should examine your `@reply` stats, with whom you commonly tweet, what you commonly tweet about (keyword clouds; tags), tweets related to questions, and a user character comparison such as Klout's Neighborhood Comparison Graph to see where you fall in relation to your following, who you influence, and who might influence you (Figure 7.16).

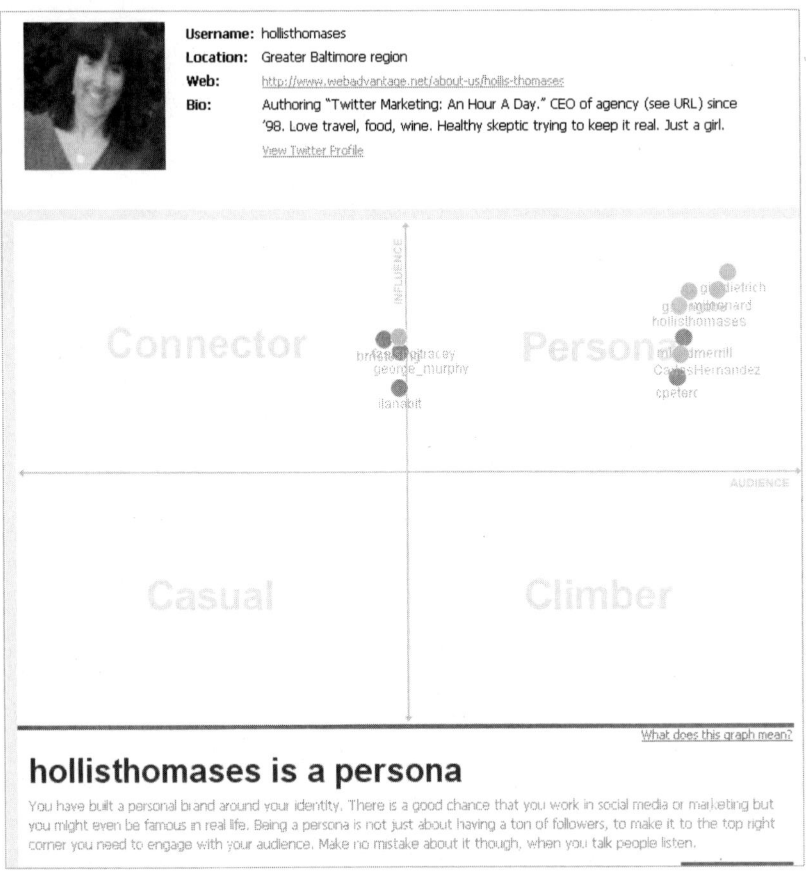

Figure 7.16 Klout's Neighborhood Comparison Graph

Provoke Thought

If you're on Twitter to stir the pot and provoke thought, you're trying to generate reactions. Therefore, to you, `@replies` and direct messages count. Look at these data points. How many `@replies` and DMs do you have? How do they compare to your number of tweets?

For you, your followers and retweets count for the same reason as the information disseminator's motives, but you're really seeking to be engaged. That engagement is a sign that someone's hearing your opinion. People might not agree with your opinion, but that's OK with you—you're just trying to get them to think. What are your engagement scores? What are your sentiment scores?

Entertain

People who entertain might also provoke thought...or laughter, or shock, or other emotions. They're sort of like emotional information disseminators. If you're using Twitter to entertain, you still might have varying degrees of motive: you might want to entertain the few rather than the many. Whatever their motives, most entertainers like to have a large audience, so your followers and reach will be important to you (for most, the bigger and broader, the better), as will the number of times your messages are retweeted, which is a sign your audience found you entertaining. If you're the analytical type, drill into your shortened URL stats to see which remarks generated the highest clicks—you might want to stay the course on that topic for a while. You probably do care about sentiments expressed by and about you, although you might care less about your engagement scores. If you're a comedian, chances are you present your humor in the form of a question, so check out your stats related to tweets with questions. Last but not least, entertainers *do* care about their influence, so look at these ratings as well (Figure 7.17).

Drive Traffic, Sales, Promotions, Leads, and List Building

When your mission is to drive traffic and other subsequent actions, you'll definitely need to approach Twitter with more deliberate intent and a tracking plan in mind. People seeking to drive traffic run the gamut from "get-rich-quick" schemers to bloggers to legitimate organizers and salespeople. To analyze for this objective, you'll absolutely want to refer to your web analytics to measure such things as traffic referred by Twitter or Twitter-related tools and the subsequent action taken by these visitors. You'll want to try to backtrack to understand the drivers of this traffic. Clearly, it will be from some kind of direct link, but which one? Can you tell by comparing high-volume spikes in traffic to particular subject-matter tweets and shortened URL stats? What keywords are drivers to your site in general and how does this correlate to the subject matter of your tweets and your success with those tweets driving traffic? Also, look at who you're commonly engaging—are they the same people who are retweeting you, and are those retweets helping you reach your objectives? If so, how do you keep cultivating these relationships?

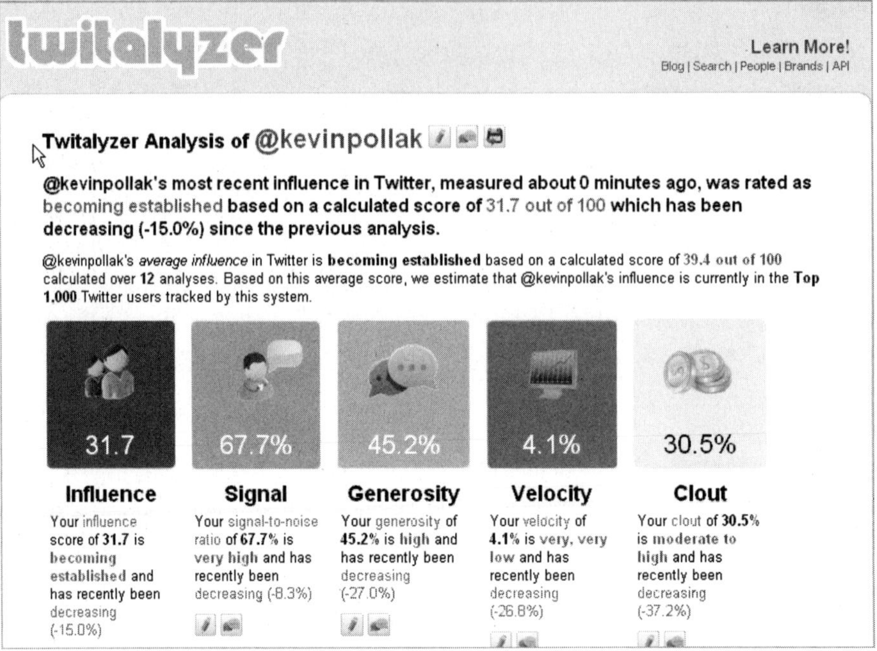

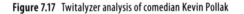

Figure 7.17 Twitalyzer analysis of comedian Kevin Pollak

Activate

If you're using Twitter for cause-related purposes, you're sort of a blend of several intents: information dissemination, publicity, thought provocation, and direct response. You need to spread information to help get the word out (publicity) that gets people excited or passionate enough (provocation) about a cause or event as to get them to attend (action/direct response). As a result, you have a larger monitoring task at hand. You'll want to monitor all the metrics the other users would to determine what Twitter's generating for you.

Respond and React to Your Analysis

As you perform your analysis, you're probably already coming to certain conclusions along the way. "Oh, this is working! I need to do more of this;" or, "Gee, this isn't generating what I expect or need it to. I'd better change course a little here;" or, "Working in tandem with this user to tag-team on retweeting really generated good results;" or, perhaps you don't want to take any action at all and instead treat the analysis as a lesson in general observation. What is important, however, is that you purposefully perform these analyses in some kind of cycle that's right for your objective(s). The act of analysis lends itself to questioning and thinking, which in turn helps to formulate the next steps in your plan. Have patience and give yourself breathing room to learn. No one should tell you there's an exact science to achieve your goals, because everyone's situation might be different. You can't learn, however, unless you do the analysis.

Know, too, that performing the kind of deep analysis we did today can be onerous, and perhaps not wholly necessary for your particular objective. Pay attention to the stats that matter to you repeatedly over time. The next time you go to do your analysis, it should be easier as you hone in on only the data you'll need to collect. Time your analysis according to your objectives. For some stats, like shortened URLs, you might want to check them daily; for others, once a week or once a month might suffice. The point is, you can be exposed to a much bigger picture of your Twitter marketing-effort impact when you compile, review, analyze, and respond to your data measurements.

Reminder It's `#FollowFriday` again. Who will you be recommending this week? You don't need to recommend gobs of people in a run-on list. Try just recommending a few, but give the reason why they're being recommended this week.

The Main Points

- Twitter can be used for fun to socialize and build relationships or for business objectives. Defining your objectives up front will help you determine how you'll use Twitter and what you'll want to measure.
- There are probably more things to measure on Twitter than you ever imagined. Not every data point is essential to every user, but knowing how to measure them is useful.
- There are both simple and robust types of measurement tools. Get acquainted with them all, so you'll know which ones are best to use when you start planning your business objectives.
- Don't let yourself become overwhelmed or frustrated. It's still early, and this is a learning process.
- Be forewarned that, just when you think you've got everything down, Twitter will up and change on you! The important thing is that you'll have some baseline measurements so that you can react or respond accordingly.

III

Month 2: Develop and Launch Your Strategic Plan

By now, with a month or more of Twittering under your belt, you should feel pretty comfortable with Twitter basics.

It's time to sew all the pieces together and get serious about Twitter marketing for your business. This month, we'll help you lay out your Twitter marketing strategy and tackle some of the unique questions and issues facing businesses. We'll draw on the subject matter we've already covered and show you how to use it in a business capacity. We're going to give you more helpful case studies from which you can draw useful parallels, and once again we'll provide practical, hour-a-day exercises to manifest this knowledge for you.

Week 5: Develop a Successful Twitter Strategy

Twitter's versatility poses an interesting dilemma to companies looking to utilize it for marketing: What should be your Twitter strategic objectives? Do you want to utilize it for customer service? For audience outreach? To broadcast company information and news? Specifically to drive direct sales? There is no single answer to this question.

In this chapter, you'll be exposed to some more real-life brands using Twitter. You'll see what they've done and the kinds of strategies and approaches they've used, the internal (or external) resources you might need, and the kinds of pitfalls to avoid.

Chapter Contents

Monday: Study Brands Succeeding with Twitter

Every day we're hearing about more and more companies embarking on their Twitter journey, and the press seems to be placing bets on whether Twitter or Facebook will come out the victor in battle of sustainable social media tools. If you're the type of organization that doesn't want to wait for everyone else to figure it all out, then this chapter will help you make some critical decisions and move forward.

ENGAGEMENTdb, a 2009 study produced by social media analyst Charlene Li of the Altimeter Group and Wetpaint, ranked the top 100 brands by social engagement (`http://www.engagementdb.com/Report`). Topping the list were some well-known brands on Twitter: Starbucks, Dell, Nike, and Amazon. The report also brings to light some business-to-business (B2B) companies you might not normally think of as progressive, such as Thomson Reuters, SAP, and Intel (all of which have multiple Twitter accounts). The top-ranked brands received their rankings because they were found to be "very engaged" across multiple social media channels. The report breaks down how each of these companies engages in social media, including Twitter, and what they hope to accomplish by doing so.

In previous chapters—Chapter 3, "Twitter, the Multipurpose Platform," in particular—we listed many companies and organizations using Twitter and how they are using it. Today, let's dissect how brands have approached Twitter and what they're using it for.

Deliver Customer Service

Many newcomers to Twitter marketing assume that Twitter is being used primarily for customer service. The press has probably contributed to this impression, because many brands commonly showcased for their use of Twitter have customer service as the focal point of their strategy. This impression isn't harmed by the fact that Twitter is very conducive to delivering certain aspects of customer service, so a Twitter customer service strategy is a sort of path of least resistance.

For any company that relies on a call center to handle customer service, Twitter can be a helpful alternative solution, particularly for tech-savvy customers (think `@ComcastCares` but also multichannel marketers like `@verabradley` and `@americanapparel`). For companies with fast-changing service situations, such as airlines and other travel-related companies (`@JetBlue`; `@SouthwestAir`; `@ConnectByHertz`) or restaurant and fast food companies (`@PFChangs`; `@Starbucks`; `@kfc_colonel`), Twitter has proven to be an invaluable tool. Brands like `@wholefoods`, `@toyota`, `@palm`, and `@Quicken` all deliver customer service through Twitter as part of their company's Twitter strategy (Figure 8.1).

Figure 8.1 A wide variety of companies deliver customer service via Twitter.

Build Awareness and Solicit Feedback

You might think that well-established brands would hardly resort to a 140-character-limited medium to help build awareness, but even large brands like `@pepsi`, `@cocacola`, Dell, or HP (the latter two of which each maintain multiple Twitter accounts to serve different purposes) see Twitter's value in helping to reach new audiences or in reaching a loyal audience with new and different messaging. Even more valuable to brands is the instant feedback Twitter provides, so much so that Twitter can prove to be a great testing laboratory. Thinking of a new ad slogan, new product flavors, or new promotional ideas? Put them out there and see what people think (Figure 8.2).

@eric_andersen We certainly hope so Eric. The Freestyle machines we've installed in SoCal & ATL are becoming mini-celebrities of their own.
10:43 AM Aug 19th from CoTweet in reply to eric_andersen
CocaCola
Coca-Cola

Figure 8.2 Coke gets feedback from one of its followers.

Brands have also begun to take an interesting tack to awareness building: integrating Twitter into their advertising. Offline advertising has primarily been limited to making the consumer aware of the brand's Twitter existence by providing the Twitter handle in print or on broadcast ads. The cleverest of campaigns, such as Best Buy's Twelpforce television ads (Figure 8.3), while enlightening, can really only broadcast the Twitter handle for that brand.

twitter.com/twelpforce

Figure 8.3 Best Buy's Twelpforce television ad campaign helped to build awareness of the Twelpforce's existence on Twitter.

Online, however, advertisers have innovatively integrated their real-time Twitter streams directly into their ads. For example, Volvo touted its new model, the XC60, during the 2009 New York Auto Show by launching an associated Twitter account (@VolvoXC60) and taking out a massive, rich media ad on YouTube into which its Auto Show tweets fed live (Figure 8.4). Rehava.com, a real estate listings site, similarly integrated its live tweets into its online banner ad campaign. We'll probably be seeing more of this kind of tying together of paid ads and live free tweeting. It's an interesting and interactive way to leverage two channels at once.

Figure 8.4 Volvo's jumbo YouTube ad with Twitter integrated live feeds

Progressions through Social Media

Some brands have joined Twitter as a natural extension of their foray into social media. What might have begun as a customer relationship through email years ago progressed into richer communications, such as blogs, and finally reached a stage of more direct customer contact through social media.

Such is the case for e.l.f. cosmetics (http://www.eyeslipsface.com). e.l.f.'s chief marketing officer, Ted Rubin, describes their Twitter entry this way:

> "*We built e.l.f on what I call social media 1.0...email, blogs, and product reviews, then moved onto MySpace and Facebook, after which we felt that the obvious next step was moving into the more scaleable environments that interact with and take advantage of the viral nature of the social graph. I had been observing the growth [of Twitter] and how the community operated for a few months. I had serious brand and interaction conversations with a number of specialists and then decided to begin our involvement with one account,* @askelf *[(which is tied to e.l.f.'s social engagement site,* http://askelf.com*)], with the plan to launch* @eyeslipsface *a few months later after working with and getting a better understanding of the dynamics and reach of the community. We created* @askelf *and started tweeting daily, throughout the week including weekends, with makeup tips, beauty tips, coupons, contests, promos, fun, engaging content [Figure 8.5]. We also made it our point to respond to all who engaged us through Twitter.*"

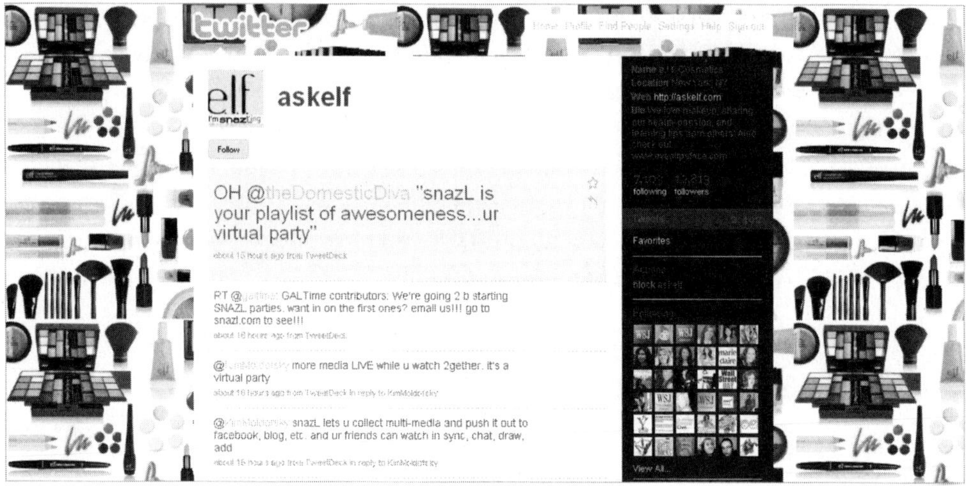

Figure 8.5 `@askelf` focuses on beauty tips.

e.l.f. has not only succeeded in its Twitter efforts with an ever-growing follower base; it has also embraced its followers so that the company now shapes its product strategy around feedback it gets from Twitter and has even developed new colors from recommendations received through Twitter. When the company eventually did launch its `@eyeslipsface` account, it populated it with content followers of `@askelf` were looking for—for example, the product of the day, product reviews, links to mentions of the company in the press, and comparisons to competitive products (Figure 8.6).

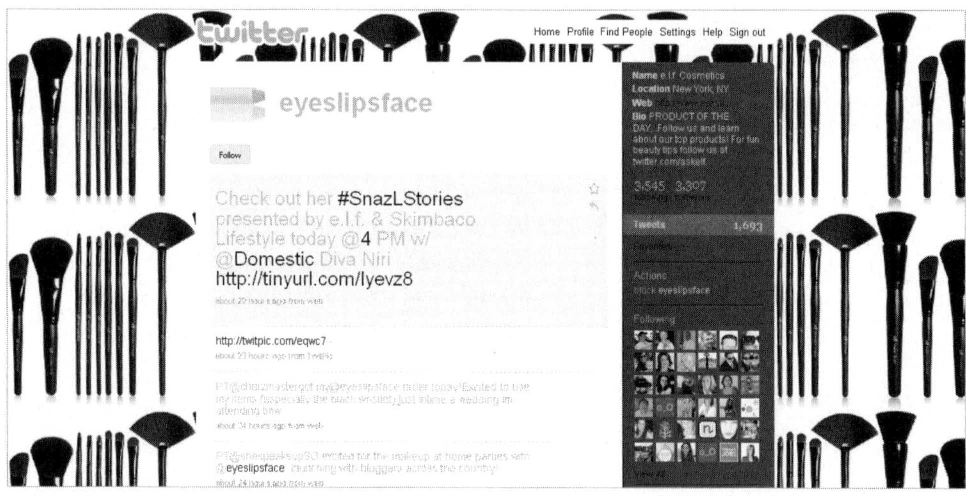

Figure 8.6 `@eyeslipsface` focuses on products.

e.l.f. maintains no official corporate tweeting policy. "It evolves as we move forward and is very fluid," says Rubin. What e.l.f. does see is positive outcome from its efforts. "We have directly incentivized and created sales with the tweeting of coupon codes and contests, all of which we can measure, and every month the referrals to our site from Twitter grow, as do our Twitter visitor-to-customer conversion rates." The company also monitors the chatter about its brand, which is also growing at a rapid pace fostered by its combined social media efforts.

Twitter, as an extension of social media experimentation, doesn't only work for direct retailers, though. Pioneer Credit Union (`@pioneercu`) in Wisconsin primarily targets the 25-to-35 demographic. As a result, in 2008 it had been dabbling in social media when its marketing specialist, Michelle Kozak, attended an industry conference in which a speaker affirmed Kozak's suspicions that she was on to something. "After that conference, we went from experimenting to full-on strategic planning." They began focusing tweets around specific topics relevant to the target demographic in their geography, throwing in a few technology and Twitter tips (not to mention tweets about their beloved Packers) to help attract and retain followers (Figure 8.7).

Kozak tracks the timeline of Twitter-to-conversion activity, demonstrating how in this example:

> *Jan/08: Because of Twitter conversations, Person X became a credit union member, opening two accounts.*
>
> *June/08: Person X brought over his mortgage; appointment set via Facebook Chat.*
>
> *June/09: Person X got his aunt to switch from Chase Bank to Pioneer CU; he tweeted about it.*
>
> *July/09: Person X contacted us on Twitter asking who he should talk to about his car loan because his lease is almost up. We told him we'd be happy to set up the appointment with whichever branch he is closest to. He tweeted back his location, so we told him to ask for a particular regional manager. Thanks to conversations on Facebook and Twitter, we know that Person X has a young daughter so we conveyed to the same regional manager that he may want to open up conversations with Person X about the daughter's future in addition to discussing the car loan.*

"I have had very few 'financial' related conversations with this member," discloses Kozak, "but because we are on Twitter and Facebook and demonstrate that we are a credit union with a personality, he has decided this is the place he wants to deal with. We are building the relationship just as if he were in front of us face-to-face."

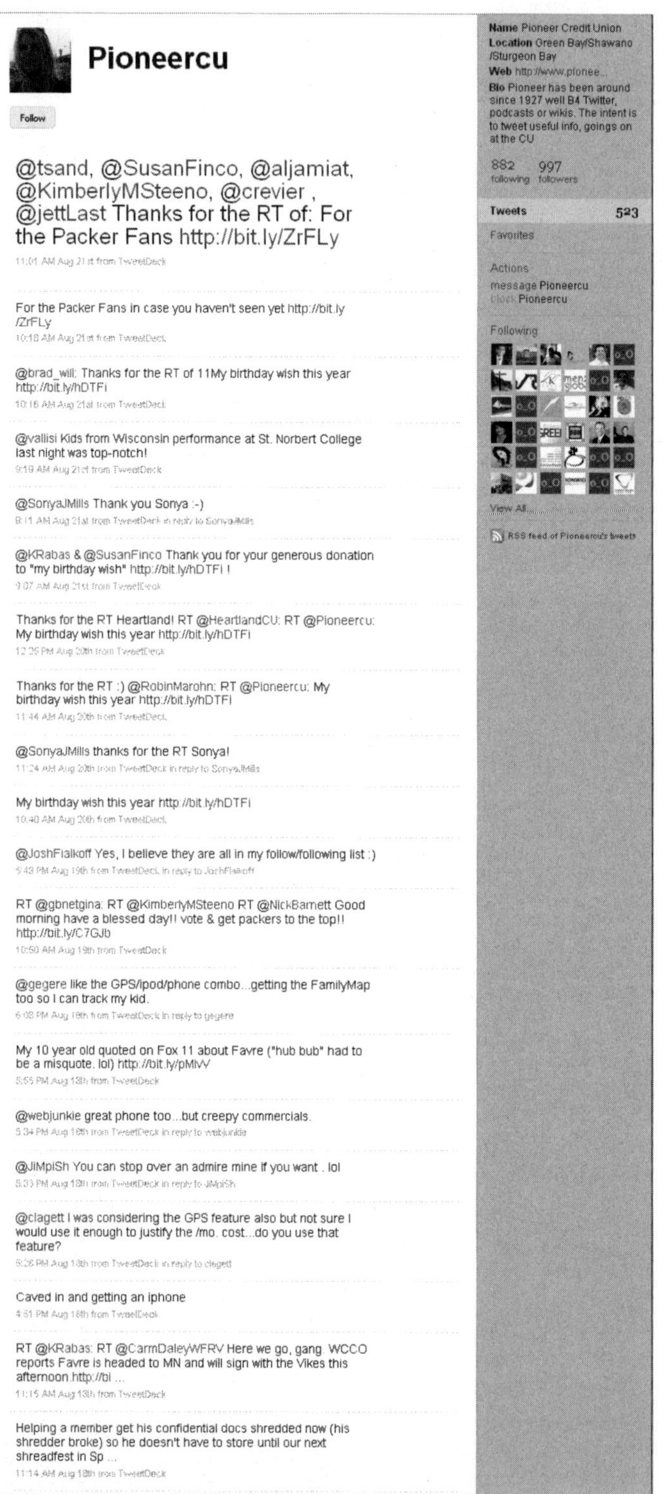

Pioneercu
Follow
@tsand, @SusanFinco, @aljamiat, @KimberlyMSteeno, @crevier , @jettLast Thanks for the RT of: For the Packer Fans http://bit.ly/ZrFLy
For the Packer Fans in case you haven't seen yet http://bit.ly/ZrFLy
@brad_will: Thanks for the RT of 11My birthday wish this year http://bit.ly/hDTFi
@vallisi Kids from Wisconsin performance at St. Norbert College last night was top-notch!
@SonyaJMills Thank you Sonya :-)
@KRabas & @SusanFinco Thank you for your generous donation to "my birthday wish" http://bit.ly/hDTFi !
Thanks for the RT Heartland! RT @HeartlandCU: RT @Pioneercu: My birthday wish this year http://bit.ly/hDTFi
Thanks for the RT :) @RobinMarohn: RT @Pioneercu: My birthday wish this year http://bit.ly/hDTFi
@SonyaJMills thanks for the RT Sonya!
My birthday wish this year http://bit.ly/hDTFi
@JoshFialkoff Yes, I believe they are all in my follow/following list :)
RT @gbnetgina: RT @KimberlyMSteeno RT @NickBarnett Good morning have a blessed day!! vote & get packers to the top!! http://bit.ly/C7GJb
@gegere like the GPS/ipod/phone combo...getting the FamilyMap too so I can track my kid.
My 10 year old quoted on Fox 11 about Favre ("hub bub" had to be a misquote. lol) http://bit.ly/pMlvV
@webjunkie great phone too...but creepy commercials.
@JiMpiSh You can stop over an admire mine if you want . lol
@clagett I was considering the GPS feature also but not sure I would use it enough to justify the /mo. cost...do you use that feature?
Caved in and getting an iphone
RT @KRabas: RT @CarmDaleyWFRV Here we go, gang. WCCO reports Favre is headed to MN and will sign with the Vikes this afternoon http://bi ...
Helping a member get his confidential docs shredded now (his shredder broke) so he doesn't have to store until our next shreadfest in Sp ...
Name Pioneer Credit Union
Location Green Bay/Shawano /Sturgeon Bay
Web http://www.pionee...
Bio Pioneer has been around since 1927 well B4 Twitter, podcasts or wikis. The intent is to tweet useful info, goings on at the CU
882 following
997 followers
Tweets 523
Favorites
Actions
message Pioneercu
block Pioneercu
Following
View All...
RSS feed of Pioneercu's tweets

Figure 8.7 Pioneer Credit Union's experiments led to a full-on embrace of Twitter.

Build Relations/Hold Conversations

Pioneer Credit Union is a great example of how brands have used Twitter to help humanize their efforts. Many companies enter Twitter because it's an ideal way to reach their audience and build that true one-to-one brand-to-consumer relationship. Brands we've already explored (such as Kodak, Planet Hollywood, and 1st Mariner Bank) often describe the rationale for this effort as "communications" or "outreach," but the brands soon find that this relationship building leads to a lot more. Sometimes the consequences, like inspiring purchases, were intended; other times, the outcomes take the company by surprise.

When eclectic, irreverent online retailer ThinkGeek (`@thinkgeek`) first came on Twitter in January of 2008, they saw it as merely another way to "keep in touch with our fellow geeks, as only one arm of our top-secret special-ops geek world domination machine." They credited themselves with being early to the game because, "our customers (like ourselves) are quick to pick up on new technology and web trends. Resistance was futile." (Gotta love a modest company and one that takes itself so seriously.) ThinkGeek initially used Twitter as mainly a one-way channel. They delivered their product-update notices through Twitter as a feed and occasionally threw in "non-robot interjections." After they discovered, however, that their followers wanted a higher human-to-feed ratio, ThinkGeek reorganized its Twitter strategy, moving product updates to `@thinkgeekspam` in October 2008 to free up its mainstay `@thinkgeek` for more direct interactions.

Now the company uses `@thinkgeek` to provide rapid and convenient customer service, geeky news, links, contests, and funny stories from around the office (Figure 8.8). In return, its followers give the company "invaluable (and generally friendly, positive) feedback on our products, as well as generating conversation we release back into the geekosphere via replies and retweets." They also use Twitter during Ustream broadcasts to ask questions or alert followers that they are streaming live at the moment.

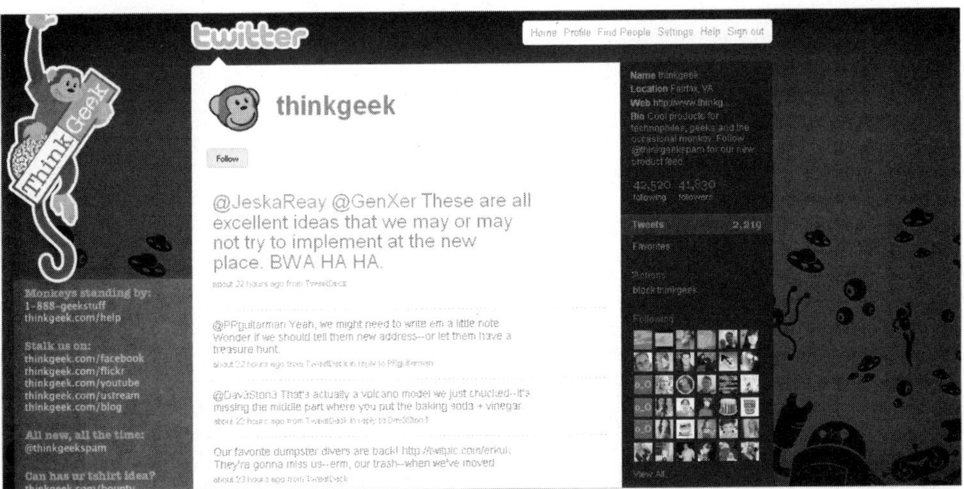

Figure 8.8 ThinkGeek's Twitter stream reflects its irreverent approach to customer relations.

When ThinkGeek entered Twitter, it wasn't completely sure what would happen, and they say, "we've met that goal of not knowing." They have, however, been pleasantly surprised to find that their Twitter followers are "ready to listen and talk to us as people, with respect and humor, not just as a company. We aim to keep it that way."

Promote/Boost Sales

While a few large brands have sales strategies for entering Twitter (the deals and outlet angle has been particularly embraced, for example, with `@DellOutlet`, `@BestBuy_Outlet`, and `@amazondeals`), more often we see Twitter being used to promote rather than to sell directly. As ThinkGeek and e.l.f. cosmetics discovered, Twitter users seek out brands that engage and not those that just deliver a Twitter stream populated by a product feed. Instead, interspersing consumer engagement tweets with mentions of contests, loyalty programs, promotional kick-offs, coupon offers, and more marks the pattern for successful brands on Twitter. This way, Twitter can help feed brand sales instead of being directly responsible for generating them.

For example, when JetBlue Airways offered its groundbreaking flat-fee All You Can Jet Pass (Figure 8.9) in the summer of 2009 "while supplies last," all it took was a single tweet for the word to spread rapidly on and offline. The press, which also received the news, picked up on the potency of the offer and soon the story was all over the media. The offer, which was to end August 21, 2009, actually sold out 36 hours early, clearly a success story.

Figure 8.9 JetBlue's All You Can Jet Pass tweet was heard 'round the Twitterverse.

Note Interested in following the airline industry's foray into Twitter and social media at large? Here's a helpful list and analysis: `http://www.centreforaviation.com/news/2009/08/27/airlines-and-social-media/page1`.

Marketing on a Shoestring: Why Small Businesses and Nonprofits Use Twitter

Some of the earliest Twitter adopters weren't big brands at all—they were smaller companies and even one-person shops—the kind that don't have big budgets to do national advertising and yet still want to get maximum exposure for their efforts. For these companies (and later, not-for-profits), social media and Twitter is a no-brainer: it requires little to no hard-dollar costs, only one's time. The primary Twitter strategy with smaller entities, if an intentional strategy exists at all, usually centers first around raising awareness and communicating information, with the desired outcome of generating inquiries, foot traffic, and ultimately sales.

There are probably more remarkable small business success stories than large brand ones; however, because the companies are small, you might not hear of them as often. Let's give them their due and feature a few here, along with the thought process that went into their efforts.

Featured Case: CakeMail

CakeMail is a small startup email marketing platform, competing against established heavy hitters. They needed to promote their white label, open API solution to agencies and web developers to build a reputation. Twitter was the perfect place to reach both targets, as well as an additional channel for customer support.

Starting out in July 2008, the company set up three accounts: for the brand (`@cakemail`), the CEO (`@cakemail_ceo`), and the sales director (`@stevesmith_cake`). They used the brand account to promote blog posts, field general questions, redirect specific questions to the internal team for follow-up, and retweet important CEO tweets. For the brand account, they also used Twitter search tools to identify prospective targets and began following them. For anyone who followed the branded account, CakeMail maintained a no-spam, no-generic DM introductory messages policy. They kept their tweets discreet and informative (with multilingual tweets, even!). They called out positive tweets by asterisking them for testimonial purposes.

The CEO and sales director accounts were used to ensure that CakeMail had a name and a face, with tweets moving from business to personal. CakeMail's CEO, François Lane, is particularly involved in exchanges with the developer community, offering and soliciting advice.

CakeMail now estimates that at least 5 percent of its business is generated through contacts made through Twitter.

What did CakeMail do right?

- They correctly judged their audience to be on Twitter already and used tools at their disposal to identify and connect with them.
- They had a very deliberate plan of entry.
- They predetermined their approach to tweeting.
- They put real people and faces behind tweets.

Featured Case: Rogers Fine Woodworking

Shannon Rogers is the master craftsman behind Rogers Fine Woodworking (`@RenaissanceWW`). He'd already been blogging and podcasting when he joined Twitter in July 2008. He intended to use social media to inform a broader audience that he would take on any woodworking project, not just chairs or keepsakes. His ultimate goal was to capture some new customers and learn from those "in the biz" who were already successful with Twitter.

He started out by searching for interior designers and woodworkers who could help him find Twitter prospects, and then he began asking questions about what they wanted to see or the kinds of products in which they were interested. He coordinated his blog and podcast posts with his tweeting, oftentimes `@mentioning` the user who had suggested the topic or had posed the original question leading to the post. He further tied his efforts together by starting to reference Twitter in his podcasts, mentioning it as a place to discuss a technique or furniture style. He also tweeted links to sites of interest or similar topics, hopefully to get those site owners to notice his presence and drive more traffic back to his site.

Through these efforts, Rogers landed several new custom-built furniture customers and drummed up additional business from existing customers who professed, "We didn't know you could do that [different style]." His Twitter efforts have significantly increased his website traffic, as well as the volume of links back to the site. His efforts have also garnered him such positive publicity that he qualified for press-pass invitations to the two largest woodworking conferences in the United States.

What did Rogers do right?

- He determined ahead of time what kind of message he wanted to deliver and to what market.
- He leveraged all of his social media assets into one solid closed-loop system.
- He utilized focused tweeps within the Twitter community to get him connected to relevant prospects.
- He gave credit to others.
- He baselined his website traffic and inbound links prior to his efforts so that he could measure the impact accordingly.

No Strategy at All

The idea that you'd approach Twitter marketing with no clear strategy might not be something you expected to read in a book like this. The idea may not hold any appeal for you, but in multiple instances the companies interviewed for this book described *intentionally* coming on Twitter with no strategy. These companies, both large and small, don't want to try to steer interactions; they want to see where interactions can lead. People might see their approach as radical or nonconformist, and that suits these organizations just fine. They wear this badge with pride.

Take, for instance, the case of technology company AMD (`@AMD_Unprocessed`). For AMD, Twitter is one piece of a social media strategy that enables them to "engage in two-way conversations, emphasize relationship-building on a more personal level, help spread messages and expand influence, and support messages from all corners" of their brand. They see Twitter, and social media in general, as being "less about solving a problem than about engaging in new ways of communicating" and, as a result, they took a different tack.

"One of the things we learned quickly is to ignore the suggested 'rules' of the Twitter road," shared Andrew Fox, AMD's senior public relations manager. "Being transparent and authentic are keys to credible social media engagements, and AMD believes it isn't authentic to mechanically follow someone else's rules about how to engage. So we set about to define guidelines that work for AMD. The beauty of all of this is that it's an organic process that doesn't have one fixed outcome. For AMD, we have found Twitter to be very useful as a way to leverage our core competencies to reach new audiences and deepen our relationships with existing audiences."

AMD also takes a nonconformist approach to team tweeting. They do not unnecessarily limit corporate tweeting to a single employee or small set of them. They encourage people from across their team who are driving a variety of projects that merit outside interest to tweet about them on a regular basis.

For AMD, the key takeaways from Twitter so far have been as follows:

- You need to know who your audience is.
- You need to be aware of the format. Twitter isn't for substantive business conversations, for instance, and although 140 characters does have a "slimming" effect, at the end of the day it's still all about content. What is new is how the content needs to be optimized for the Twitter audience and channel in somewhat new and different ways.
- You need to maintain your integrity by being at all times honest and transparent.
- You need a coherent approach, which includes leveraging measurement tools and adjusting your approach accordingly.
- You need to remember that it's about your brand, and you need to preserve your brand attributes accordingly.
- You should be having fun!

AMD's experience echoes what many companies have described: Twitter, and social media at large, is a learning process. It's like a great experiment or human laboratory for learning. Admitting that you don't have it figured out seems perfectly alright. Instead of stressing out about getting it all right the first time, brands with this approach seem to flourish from how open they allow themselves to be. These intangible gains, they believe, can over time turn into tangible ones; they're just not tangible in a way they originally imagined.

Monday's One-Hour Exercise: A Study of Brand Strategies

Monday's exercise will help you prepare for Tuesday's lesson. Chapter 2, "Who's Using Twitter for What?" provided a lengthy list of brands on Twitter you can use, or you might have your own favorite brands you're following or want to follow. Regardless of where you source your brands on Twitter, spend the next hour looking at a wide variety of brand accounts on Twitter. Can you identify their Twitter strategy from what you see? Does it seem to be effective? What do you like about how these brands are using Twitter? What don't you like? Are there any things in particular you can observe about how they present themselves on Twitter or tools they use that you like or dislike? What else do you see?

Be open-minded during this exercise. Although you may think you know what your own Twitter strategy should be at this point, perhaps something you see will change or modify your perspective.

Tuesday: Different Approaches to Develop Your Strategy

This might be the day you've been waiting for: defining your Twitter marketing business strategy. Hopefully, by now, you have so much to think about that you're ready for this step. Whether you *think* you have it right or not, take heart: you've already seen that even the biggest companies admit they got it wrong at first or intentionally started with no clear strategy in mind. That said, let's lay some foundation and walk through the process.

Validate Your Typical Customer's Use of Social Media

If your strategic considerations for getting involved in Twitter revolve around reaching your customer (as opposed to, say, helping your search engine visibility or establishing a leadership position in your industry regardless of whether your customers are on Twitter or not), you might want to first validate your customer's use of social media. One way to do this is to use Forrester Research's Technographics Social Technology Consumer Profile Tool (`http://www.forrester.com/Groundswell/profile_tool.html`) or the B2B Profile Tool (`http://www.forrester.com/Groundswell/b2b_profile_tool.html`). In Chapter 2, we discussed the Technographic profiles: Creators, Critics, Collectors, Joiners, Spectators, and Inactives. Whether you use the Consumer or B2B Profile Tool, you can identify, for certain filters, the breakdown of your market and, therefore, how likely or unlikely your audience is to be using social media, including Twitter. Most marketers might want to avoid a profile high in Inactives; however, if you're a packager of prepared meals sold in United States grocery stores and targeting older females, you might be just fine with a high level of Joiners and Spectators (Figure 8.10).

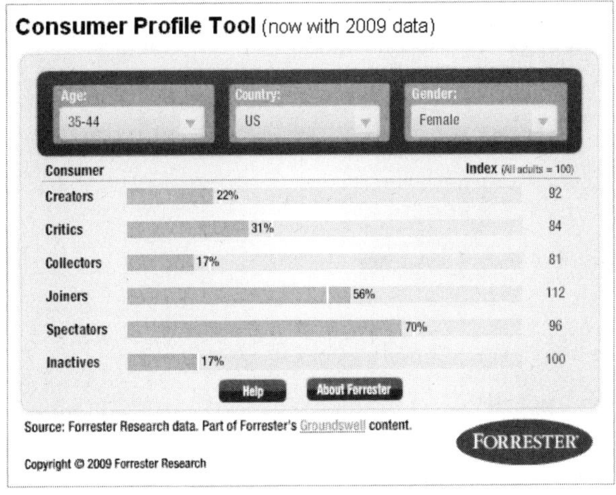

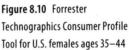

Figure 8.10 Forrester Technographics Consumer Profile Tool for U.S. females ages 35–44

Manage Twitter Communications

Early on, even if you don't have a formal strategy, you'll need to figure out who will be monitoring and responding to tweets on your company's behalf. The answer to this question has nothing to do with the size of your brand or how many people follow you. Some of the largest brands on Twitter—Southwest Airlines (`@SouthwestAir`) and Ford (`@ScottMonty`), for example—rely on a sole individual to manage the company's tweets. Let's review the most common three approaches to managing Twitter communications for your consideration.

Single User

As daunting as it might seem, sometimes a single person represents the company's voice on Twitter. As a company gets started on Twitter, the demands on a single user and volume of tweets might not be too high. In fact, at first managing Twitter communications isn't likely to be someone's only job. If, however, you adopt the single-user approach and your Twitter popularity grows, you might need to reassess the situation. Twitter might become your designee's full-time job, or you might want to bring others in to help.

Another example of a brand relying on a solitary individual to manage all the company's tweets is Starbucks (`@Starbucks`). Imagine Brad Nelson's job, the man responsible for Starbucks's Twitter identity. Tens of thousands of lattes a day, happy and unhappy customers, people who just want to chat, all the while also mixing in promotional and informational tweets (Figure 8.11). Clearly, this kind of job requires inside knowledge of the company, as well as tremendous customer service, communications, and people skills.

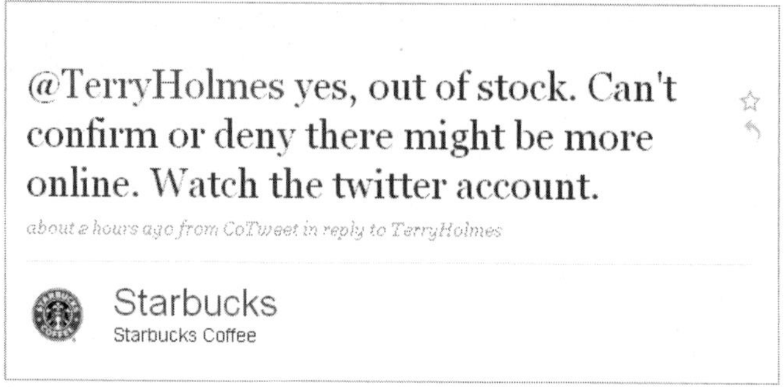

@TerryHolmes yes, out of stock. Can't confirm or deny there might be more online. Watch the twitter account.
Starbucks
Starbucks Coffee

Figure 8.11 One tweet of many for which @Starbucks's Brad Nelson is responsible

Multiuser

If customer service burdens will weigh too heavily on a single individual, or different kinds of inbound tweets demand responses or know-how from different segments of the company, or you just don't want to rely solely on a single individual for the company's tweets, then you ought to consider a multiuser approach. With this method, two or more people manage Twitter on behalf of the brand. These people might work in tandem, in shifts, or by area of expertise. A multiuser approach ensures Twitter coverage should someone be out sick, on vacation, or leave the company, and it's an easy approach to scale. Brands such as Pepsi (`@Pepsi`), The Home Depot (`@HomeDepot`), and Network Solutions (`@NetSolCares`) use the multiuser, Twitter team approach (Figure 8.12).

pepsi
Name Pepsi™
Bio Your direct line to the Pepsiverse. Currently serving: Ana and Rachel

Figure 8.12 Pepsi's Twitter team

Enterprise-Wide

Perhaps your organization loves the idea of Twitter so much that you want not only to embrace it as a marketing channel, you also want to encourage everyone in your company to tweet on your behalf. That's the idea behind the enterprise-wide approach to Twitter marketing. Though there may be a mainstay account, in the enterprise-wide approach either many individuals in the company have Twitter company accounts from which they can tweet, or a single Twitter account might respond to and feed many individuals who typically manage this execution through a multiuser backend dashboard like CoTweet or Tweet Funnel. Examples of brands using the enterprise-wide model include Zappos, Oracle, Virgin Group, and Best Buy's Twelpforce.

Which of these three approaches seems right for your organization at this point? Not sure yet? Maybe starting to lay out your strategy will help make the decision for you.

Lay Out Your Strategy

Those companies that entered Twitter without a strategy aren't the norm. As Forrester analyst Jeremiah Owyang reminds us, with respect to social media, "Remember: 80% is Strategy and only 20% is Technology," and, "success is dependent on understanding customers, defining an objective, and assembling the right strategy that encompasses plans, roles, process, budgets, measurement, and training."

With that in mind, let's set you on your course. In Chapter 7, "Week 4: Track and Monitor What Twitter Generates for You," you listed your individual objectives and noted any business objectives that came to mind as you worked on the exercise. Please pull that list out now.

Tuesday's One-Hour Exercise: Map Your Strategy

Bearing in mind that you might have multiple audiences you're trying to reach simultaneously but with different objectives for each audience, it's a good idea to map it all out to help clarify all this for you. Referring to Table 8.1, look at these components.

▶ **Table 8.1** Strategy Worksheet Template

Audience (Who)	Objective (What & Why)	Plan (When/Where/How)	Role (By Whom)	Measures	Concerns/ Limitations

1. Who are you trying to reach? Indicate each of your target audiences on separate lines.
2. What do you hope to gain and why? By each target audience, list your Twitter objectives (if your objectives overlap for different audiences, that's fine).
3. When, where, and how do you plan to reach each particular target audience through Twitter to achieve the objectives you've laid out? Try to articulate your plan.
4. By whom? What kind of individual (or specific individual by name) do you see being able to fulfill your Twitter marketing plan(s)? If multifaceted, will a single person do or do you need/want multiple people involved?
5. How will you measure your strategy's success? Given all the means provided to you last week to track and measure benchmarks and metrics, list those you feel are relevant for the objective and plan you've listed.

6. Indicate any concerns or limitations you might have, like resources, manpower, time, costs, and the like.
7. Fill in as many lines on this worksheet as you feel matter to your business.
8. When you're done, rank your combined line items by priority. Which one(s) would you definitely want to pursue first?

Now take a look at Table 8.2, the Strategy Worksheet example, to give you an idea of what your worksheet might look like. This exercise should help you sort out initial ideas and a direction to follow for your Twitter marketing strategy.

► **Table 8.2** Strategy Worksheet Example

Audience (Who)	Objective (What & Why)	Plan (When/Where/How)	Role (By Whom)	Measures	Concerns/ Limitations
Women 35–55	Product Awareness	Q4/Nationally/Ask for mix & match outfit ideas. Use hashtag.	Marketing Asst	# of RTs; # of hashtags in Search; website traffic to product pages; Web & in-store sales	Lead time; internal Twitter education curve; manpower time
Women 35–55	Sell Web clearance items	Year-round/ Nationally/Sale Item Product Feed	API	Clicks on product links; Web sales revenue	Setting up feed

Wednesday: Study Strategies for Market Verticals

If you're not a big consumer brand targeting a large mass market, as with all your other marketing efforts, you probably need to focus more narrowly with your Twitter strategy. There are too many market verticals (the segment of industry your company focuses on) to explore them all, but let's cover some now to give you a sense of the diversity (and similarities) of their strategies.

Technology

You probably think technology companies would be very likely to embrace Twitter... and you'd be right to do so. The success Twitter has generated for companies like Dell, Microsoft, Oracle, Sun Microsystems, and IBM has been documented, although their approaches to Twitter might vary. For instance, Sandy Carter (`@sandy_carter`), IBM's vice president of Service-Oriented Architecture and WebSphere, says the company has been incorporating social media into IBM's marketing since 2006, but in an interview with *Marketing Sherpa* revealed, "a key lesson learned is that using social media channels is not a strategy unto itself." All of IBMs campaigns involve a combination of traditional marketing plus social media, not social media as a stand-alone.

Smaller technology companies don't act much differently. AVIcode (@avicode), a provider of application monitoring solutions for the Microsoft .NET Framework, initially turned to Twitter for public relations and message positioning in the hopes of "surrounding perspective customers with our messaging." AVIcode foresaw the rise of Twitter among their predominantly technical audience such that it almost necessitated their adoption of the platform. Early on, they adopted an information delivery strategy, mainly just tweeting company news and links to press releases. Twitter use increased, however, as did AVIcode's reliance on the channel, and soon the company found itself incorporating Twitter into major trade show marketing initiatives.

Their LickTheBugs microsite, specifically launched at a trade show and tied to their Twitter stream, enabled the company to attract visitors to their booth and follow other social media initiatives. Within two days of the microsite's launch, they had over 2,000 unique visitors to the site, four times as many people as visited their trade show booth. In the first week of the microsite's launch, the company had identified three qualified sales opportunities and, through Twitter, they were able to schedule a demo and proof of concept for their technology (Figure 8.13).

@Rass30 : we'd be happy to provide you with references. Please let us know.
1:41 PM Jul 10th from web in reply to Rass30
AVIcode
AVIcode

Figure 8.13 AVIcode conducts direct sales through Twitter.

Retail

Retailers of all kinds—large, small, brick-and-mortar, or Internet pure-plays—have found Twitter to be an effective marketing tool. How they've gone about using it is where the diversity comes in. Some sell, some share tips and information, others just try to create advocacy or community.

Retail pet supplier PETCO (@PETCO) saw Twitter as a way to understand their customers better: what's important to customers, what products they and their pets like or need, and how to take in-store customer relationships and strengthen them by also moving them online (Figure 8.14). PETCO first began tweeting in late 2008 by asking general questions like "What are better: Dogs or Cats?" and sharing important content and articles, such as "Why You Should NEVER Feed a Dog Chocolate." PETCO then branched into Twitter promotions by holding contests, gift-card giveaways, and exclusive Twitter-only coupons. The results so far have not only given PETCO a means to learn more about their customers, but the door they opened for direct customer communications has led from ordinary to fun and fascinating insights. They even discovered a propensity for people to tweet frequently as their pets' personas!

Time to update our Twitter background picture. Send your cute pet pic to @petco and I may put it up.
2:41 PM Aug 18th from web
PETCO

Figure 8.14 PETCO has been able better to engage with customers through Twitter.

Are you curious about other retailers approaches to Twitter? Here's a great compilation of retailers on Twitter: `http://www.shoppingblog.com/twitterstoredirectory`.

Travel/Tourism

Twitter's word-of-mouth, of-the-moment format is perfect for travel and tourism. All you have to do is a quick Twitter search to find locations about which other people are tweeting (good and bad) (Figure 8.15). Many in the travel and tourism industry have done a fine job of embracing Twitter, including hotel chains, airlines, travel destinations, or travel destination management organizations. Some in the industry just want to get on Twitter while others have a more deliberate strategy.

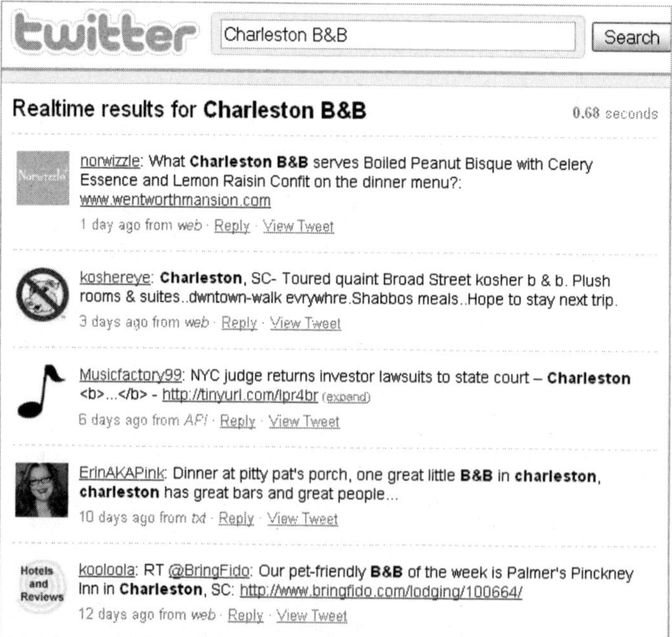

Figure 8.15 What a quick search for Charleston B&B yields

Featured Case: Visit Baltimore

The Baltimore region faced a problem. After several focus group sessions in Ohio, a nearby market, Baltimore's Destination Management Organization, Visit Baltimore (`@BaltimoreMD`), had their assumptions confirmed: pretty much all Ohioans thought about when it came to Baltimore was its Inner Harbor, crab cakes, its sports teams, the Ravens and the Orioles...and maybe the infamous HBO series *The Wire*. This was not necessarily the kind of awareness Visit Baltimore was hoping for. How could Visit Baltimore, with its relatively small budget compared to neighboring regions, work smartly to spread the word about Baltimore's thriving culinary scene, unknown attractions, its rich multicultural heritage, the wealth of art institutes, and all the other facets of Baltimore that could interest visitors beyond those of the Inner Harbor?

As one solution the agency turned to Twitter. It saw Twitter as a way to give Baltimore personality, to create awareness among new and potential visitors, and to spread the word about all kinds of Baltimore happenings, from the most minor to the most grand, far beyond what their traditional advertising buys could convey. Honing in on specific geographies that were the region's sweet spots, director of web marketing Tom Rowe started following people in those markets, listening to what they were saying, and jumping in on the conversation. Rowe also followed locally active Twitter personalities who could help amplify reach and spread the word. Rowe regularly attended local tweetups to forge further bonds, encouraging local tweeps to become personally invested in helping promote Baltimore through retweets, positive perception building, and assisting with focus group testing. Though Visit Baltimore's ultimate objective is to "put heads in beds," using Twitter, says Rowe, "We want to have fun because we're a fun city" and we want to drive that perception.

Visit Baltimore has seen success through active engagement in the community with personal interaction, polling, contests, and event posting, but their biggest claim to fame came about rather haphazardly. Rowe caught a chance *dueling tweet* about two other cities: "Who will get to 3,000 followers first, `@travelportland` or `@visitchicago`?" Those two cities had approximately 2,700 followers a piece, but rather than be left in the dust altogether, Baltimore, with 1,700 followers, reacted. Rowe contacted a good friend who also happened to work for Visit Baltimore's PR agency, and a challenge was born: If Baltimore could reach 3,000 followers before the other cities and before 1:00 AM the next day, the intrepid PR rep would get tattooed with a large, iconic Fail Whale. Starting at 4:00 PM, they began spreading the word through their various accounts, with people latching on for the fun and absurdity of it all. Baltimore became a trending topic throughout that evening, and the whole thing was video-streamed for all to see. Baltimore began connecting not only with people all around Baltimore, but throughout the country, and even the world. By 11:00 PM, well ahead of schedule, they had their 3,000 followers, and the PR rep got his tattoo as a *Baltimore Sun* reporter watched locally and the world watched via Ustream.

Continues

Featured Case: Visit Baltimore *(Continued)*

The story spread like wildfire across the Internet, and print and television soon followed. The resulting press coverage dwarfed the 3,000 followers and made it an enormous event. Visit Baltimore can't even quantify the value in ad dollars, but it was certainly nothing they could have been able to afford. Baltimore has only grown its following since, and now holds a revered spot among the top of destination marketing organizations on Twitter.

Restaurants/Franchises/Localized Businesses

Localized businesses often have the same ambitions as travel and tourism entities, but they might suffer from even less awareness...perhaps as in none. Great stories abound, including some already featured in this book, about how these "little local guys" have made good using Twitter.

Strategically, you can find some helpful advice from blogger Ian Orekondy, who relays the following tips:

- Provide frequent updates—at least once a day.
- Utilize employees, and not just your marketing team, to monitor and respond to tweets.
- Ask if any of your customers are on Twitter and then follow them. Repeat this systematically, as new people join Twitter every day.
- Put a sheet by your cash register to collect customers' Twitter handles. Follow them.
- Post your Twitter handle in strategic locations throughout your premises. Ask your customers to follow you.
- Announce new products, menu specials, sales, events, and seasonal topics.
- Tweet at strategic times of the day relevant to when your typical customer might be getting ready to shop.
- Be creative and playful. If you own a restaurant, for instance, add a side dish, "Cole Slaw: 1 tweet."
- Provide loyalty incentives for your customers to tweet about you.
- Pose a "Twitter Question of the Day," and see if you can create some dialog with your customers as well as with each other.
- Develop a store hashtag for easy finding.
- Use Twitter as another way to assist with lost and found.
- Advertise and recruit for job openings.

Healthcare

Due to regulatory and privacy concerns, whole sections of the healthcare industry have avoided all forms of social media. If on Twitter, healthcare entities tend to use it as an informational broadcast channel. Some entities that support the industry (personnel, technology, and trade groups) are more inclined to tweet, though healthcare service providers from hospitals and healthcare systems (`@RIHospital`, `@HasbroChildrens`, `@Aurora_Health`) to doctors themselves (`@kevinmd`, `@DoctorRobin`) have more freely embraced the medium. Even the Centers for Disease Control has gotten in on the act, creating three separate Twitter accounts, including one for emergency broadcasts (`@CDCemergency`), which has nearly 800,000 followers as of this writing. Though discussions (search for the hashtag `#hcmktg`), articles, conference panels, and blog posts (for example, see the blog of industry evangelist Phil Baumann: `http://philbaumann.com`) have been swirling about the subject of how Twitter could be used by the healthcare industry, no clear-cut strategy seems to as yet have been embraced or endorsed.

Philanthropy and Nonprofit

Always looking to do as much as they can with as little expense as possible, the nonprofit sector has been scrambling to figure out Twitter. Some do it very well; others have shunned it as a black hole for time and resources. The diversity of the nonprofit sector makes it just as hard to pinpoint a single Twitter strategy as it is in the private sector. For example, trade associations or councils, charities, and not-for-profit educational institutions would all likely have vastly different Twitter strategies.

One approach we can explore is that of a unique association, an association for philanthropies known as the Association of Baltimore Area Grantmakers, "ABAG." (`@ABAGrantmakers`). Though ABAG made a conscious decision years ago not to enter the blogosphere, they did decide to jump on the Twitter bandwagon. Rather than use Twitter to communicate with members, however, ABAG uses Twitter to communicate *about* the good work of their members, thereby advancing ABAG's mission of promoting philanthropy. ABAG also recognized and wanted to be a part of the daily dialog that takes place on Twitter about philanthropy. ABAG recommends incorporating Twitter usage into the association's overall communications strategy by doing the following:

- Developing a one-page rationale for the use of Twitter—the goals, expected outcomes, and implementation steps.
- Creating and regularly tweeting about subject-matter categories that are appropriate for your organization and why (ABAG categorizes tweets into ABAG-specific, ABAG Members, ABAG Partners, Regional Philanthropy, and National Philanthropy).

- Mapping your daily/weekly/monthly tweets in advance as much as possible, identifying opportunities based on seasons, holidays, upcoming events, ongoing national news, and so on.
- Ensuring your board knows that you are using Twitter and why.
- Working with staff members to obtain tweets that support your mission and rationale for use.
- Reaching out to members/partners/others to invite information submission for tweets.
- Being clear about who you are following and why in order to obtain the best and most relevant ongoing information.
- Devising a Twitter evaluation plan that works for you and assessing this against your goals and outcomes.
- Adding a Twitter tagline on your email, website, and other communication vehicles.

Wednesday's One-Hour Exercise: Analyze Your Industry

If your business occupies an industry vertical, locate the Twitter accounts of leaders in your vertical, market, or industry, and try to identify their Twitter strategy. In particular, dive into their tweets to see what they're tweeting about, and with whom and how they are tweeting. Refer back to Tuesday's exercise for help.

Thursday: Twitter's Role in Your Overall Marketing Strategy

In reading through the case studies, examples and, most recently, industry verticals, you might have caught a recurring theme. For most companies, large and small, Twitter plays only a fractional role in the overall communications or marketing strategy. So then, how do you go about defining its priority and figuring out how your Twitter marketing strategy will affect the allocation of internal resources?

Important First Impressions

As exciting as it may be, Twitter reaches only a fraction of the mass market, so if you're a mass marketing, your Twitter reach will only carry you so far. If, on the other hand, you're a niche marketer, Twitter might be extremely effective in helping carry your message to your audience. Using Twitter also helps set a tone for your brand. Twitter users who don't know you will be making split-second judgments about your brand just from visiting your profile and seeing how and what you tweet. It all comes back to objectives.

Thursday's One-Hour Exercise: Compare Strategies

Presumably, if you're going through the trouble of building a Twitter marketing strategy, you also have an overall company marketing strategy. Time to take out that document as well as your homework assignment from this past Tuesday, and answer these potentially tough questions:

- How do my top-priority Twitter objectives align with my overall marketing ones?
- Where can Twitter support overall marketing objectives? Do you have any overall objectives that are performing weakly or for which you haven't quite found the right means to carry out? Would Twitter fit the bill to help?
- Where would Twitter play a completely new, different, or unique role in your overall strategy? What would your expectations for it be?
- How might time tables for your overall objectives mesh or conflict with Twitter marketing ones? How will you reconcile the two?
- To what degree would you expect Twitter to "move the needle" on a marketing objective? If the answer is something like "significantly," do you have the resources to dedicate to Twitter in order to make the desired impact?
- Have you even evaluated what those Twitter marketing resources might look like? Do you need to hire and train people or do you have ready-made talent? What does that talent look like within your organization? Who, if anyone, will be responsible for these tweeters?
- What other tools, guidance, or empowerment do you need to give your official tweeters?
- How do you measure your overall marketing objectives, and is there an appropriate and relative means to measure your Twitter efforts?

If answering these questions crystallizes that your company is not yet ready for Twitter, that's fine. The purpose of this book isn't to cram Twitter down your throat as a one-size-fits-all solution for every single company out there. It's to help you navigate the waters. If anything, having a more complete understanding will help you avoid potential Twitter pitfalls that lie ahead.

Friday: Avoid Pitfalls

These are still the relative early days of Twitter. It's not completely the Wild West, but brands still need to be mindful of what they're doing, or not doing, with the medium. Let's have you avoid some common pitfalls and instead focus on best practices.

Name Squatting

In the early days of the Internet, tech-savvy people scooped up big brand-name domain names in the hopes of reselling them for oodles of money. Ambitious and unscrupulous types have also done this with Twitter. Luckily, learning from mistakes of the past, rather than pay these Twitter "name squatters," if brands identify these nefarious types, they can file a complaint with Twitter by sending an `@message` to `@spam` and include the username along with the word "squatter," and Twitter will investigate it. Twitter also makes it clear in its Rules section that, "selling free user names is against the Twitter Rules. If someone has tried to sell you a Twitter user name, please let us know."

Nevertheless, if you have a well-known brand, it's best not to sit around and wait to decide if or when you're going to have a Twitter strategy. At the very least, you're entitled to your brand name, so set up your Twitter account and claim it.

Trademark Infringement

Twitter also has a policy for trademark infringement (`http://help.twitter.com/forums/26257/entries/18367`), which says:

> *"Using a company or business name, logo, or other trademark protected materials in a manner that may mislead or confuse others or be used for financial gain may be considered trademark infringement. Accounts with clear INTENT to mislead others will be immediately suspended; even if there is no trademark infringement, attempts to mislead others is tantamount to business impersonation."*

Twitter's policy seems to indicate that it believes that most trademark infringement situations are unintentional, and therefore they try to work "with most account owners to remove infringements so that the person may keep the account." It further goes on to define three specific situations of possible infringement:

- **If there is a clear intent to mislead people** into believing this account is affiliated with the company/business in question, the account will be permanently suspended.
- **Accounts created to help a community** or provide information will be contacted with the appropriate steps to take to keep the account.
- **News feed accounts** will more clearly designate that they are aggregating news about a company to resolve confusion. (News feed aggregates are welcome, but must not use logos or copyright-protected images, and must clearly designate nonaffiliation with the entity represented in the news feed to avoid suspension.)

If you find your trademark infringed upon, Twitter says to report the violation by submitting a web request from the Twitter Support home page. You should receive an immediate email confirmation number and be contacted by Twitter's Support team within 24 hours. Such statements, however, do not mean trademark infringement doesn't happen or that the process of correcting the situation will be swift. It took Twitter four weeks to shut down a rogue American Airlines Twitter profile. All the more reason, therefore, to be sure to register your brand name's Twitter account and keep careful watch on your brand name mentions on Twitter.

Impersonation/Brand Hijacking

Worse than name squatting or trademark infringement is someone who registers an account, sets up a profile in your brand's name, and then begins tweeting, posing as your brand. As mentioned in the trademark infringement policy, such activity *if identified*, will not be tolerated by Twitter. Many violators have tried to impersonate celebrities, so much so that Twitter developed its "Verified Accounts" to help identify clearly the real person (Figure 8.16).

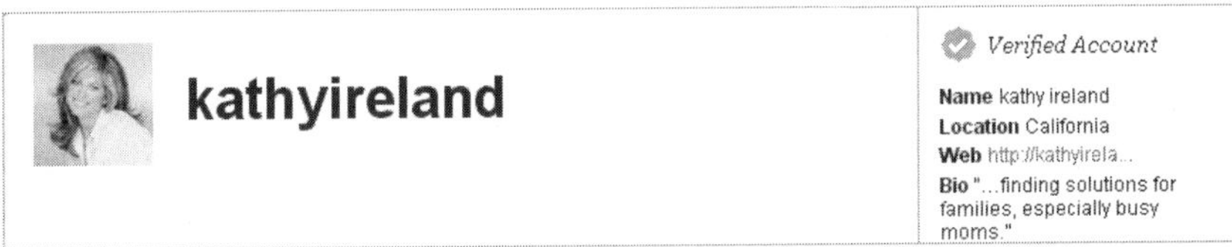

Figure 8.16 Kathy Ireland's Twitter account has been verified.

If a corporate brand has been impersonated, or hijacked, the impact could be just as damaging, particularly from a pubic relations perspective. The most infamous brand hijacking case has to be the Exxon Mobil fraud perpetrated in 2008. Using the handle `@ExxonMobilCorp` (Figure 8.17), a very candid, sympathetic spokesperson, "Janet," tweeted on the company's behalf only to be revealed soon after as an imposter. The situation left egg on Exxon Mobil's face, however, as not only did it have to admit that it was pretty clueless about Twitter and certainly not monitoring its brand, but then it also had to "unendorse" the compassionate, appealing statements made by "Janet" as inconsistent with its brand. The whole incident proved how vulnerable big brands can be that don't pay attention to social media. Though the "Janet" account was shut down, it was not the last time Exxon Mobil encountered this kind of misrepresentation. Almost one year later, it identified yet another unauthorized account in its name. Perhaps it caught this offender sooner?

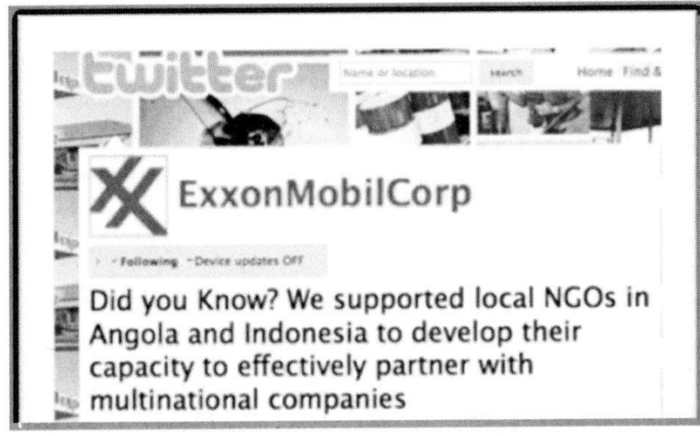

Figure 8.17 Hijacked `@ExxonMobilCorp` account

Dormant and Unresponsive Accounts

Most Twitter users don't want to seek out their brands, find an account, and then find that no one has tweeted from that account in six months. That not only leaves a poor impression with the user, but it might also mean you're completely oblivious to the goings on with respect to your brand on Twitter. As Michael Estrin wrote in an iMedia Connection article, "an unchecked Twitter account isn't an email gone unanswered, it's more like a wide-open storefront without the staff to respond to the customer." This is definitely not good for business.

Twitter users also don't appreciate brands that merely post a promotional feed. A quick review of that kind of Twitter stream tells the user that you're essentially "closed for business" when it comes to dialoging and seeking their feedback. It conveys a message of disinterest and sheer self-promotion. This too is a turn-off to customers (Figure 8.18).

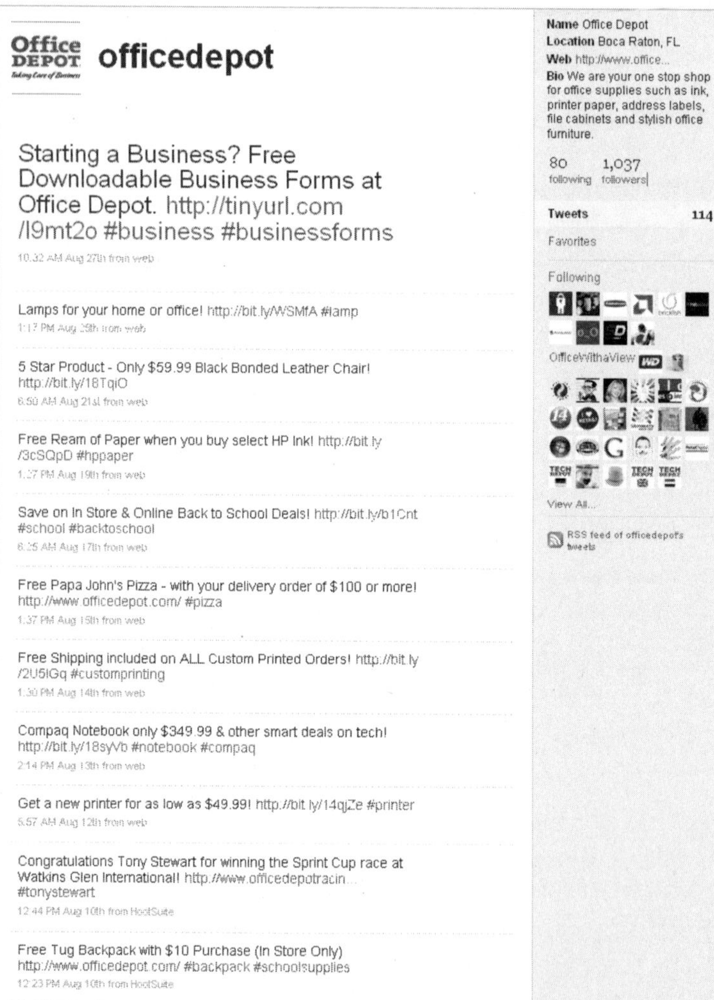

Figure 8.18 Office Depot's tweet stream shows zero consumer engagement and its Followers count has scarcely changed in four months.

Nor does a user want to find your brand on Twitter, send you a message, and never receive a reply. Twitter, in particular, is a demand-response medium. People tweet the brand mainly *because* they want some kind of response. Even if the tweet might be negative, it's really the brand's duty to respond to its audience. Not doing so communicates false intent for being on Twitter.

Overpromising

Brands truly eager to engage with their customers on Twitter could fall prey to a different kind of pitfall: overpromising. In the excitement of joining the discussion and having direct access to customers, overzealous brand tweeters might feel inclined to "tell customers what they want to hear," but on Twitter that's the wrong answer. As easy as it is to tweet you, a dissatisfied or misled customer will tweet *about* you, and what they have to say might not be nice. It's better to meet or beat their expectations so they can rave about you! (See Figure 8.19.)

@WHCCpro Your customer service rocks. Hopefully the canvas I ordered will, too. I've seen some ordered by friends so I'm sure it will.

about 3 hours ago from web

danielbartel

Figure 8.19 Clearly, a happy customer

The Main Points

- State your Twitter marketing objectives, even if at first they are as nebulous as, "We want to join Twitter to learn how we can best use it for our company." Objectives can be modified over time.
- Business Twitter marketing strategies vary by objectives, but sometimes the strategy is intentionally to leave things open and see what develops throughout the process.
- There's more than one way to manage a Twitter account. Refer back to your objectives to help determine what approach is best for your organization.
- Your Twitter marketing strategy can be molded to your industry vertical, just as your overall marketing strategy might be molded to it.

- Review your overall marketing strategy before deciding upon your Twitter strategy. Twitter might be able to fill some gaps or provide support where your current plan is weak.
- Avoid the common pitfalls of first-time brands on Twitter. If you're not confident in your ability to avoid these pitfalls, perhaps it's not yet time to get started on Twitter.

Week 6: Establish Goals and Get Corporate Buy-In

9

Chapter 8, "Week 5: Develop a Successful Twitter Strategy," demonstrated the importance of determining your Twitter objectives. Hopefully, the analysis and exercises helped clarify important objectives for you. These objectives, both short-term and long-term, will steer what you do as you deliberately plan your Twitter marketing strategy and how to execute it.

Chapter Contents

Monday: Establish Objectives

The topic of establishing your objectives may look familiar: you've been jotting down your ideas for objectives and thinking about ways to utilize them for a while now. This week you need to look over the objectives you've come up with on your own and begin the process of finalizing them.

Monday's Preliminary Work: Think about Twitter Achievements

Referring back to your starter list of Twitter marketing for business objectives, let's ask the question another way: What do you want your company to achieve with Twitter? Don't limit your thinking. We'll discuss how to be realistic and refine your list later. Here's a way of describing those achievements you may or may not have already run through on your own:

- Improve customer service
- Increase customer retention
- Develop thought leadership
- Position for expertise when prospects are deciding between us and our competition
- Launch or build a brand
- Develop brand loyalty through engagement
- Improve positive brand sentiment or image
- Find donors
- Develop relationships with reporters and bloggers
- Prospect for warm leads
- Monitor competition
- Search engine optimization
- Social marketing optimization
- Stimulating viral activity and buzz
- Recruit talent
- Direct promotions
- Drive traffic to our website and/or blog
- Drive sales
- Affiliate marketing

Think through the company's goals and add anything else you can think of to your list. As you did in Chapter 8, spend a few minutes prioritizing the list to come up with one primary goal and two or three secondary goals to achieve during the next six months. They may change as you start to use Twitter in different ways, but this allows you to maintain focus.

Case Studies Analyzed by Target Objectives

Last week we analyzed the strategies of certain industry verticals. Today, let's take a look at some more case studies that show how companies are using Twitter to accomplish their different objectives, namely launching a brand, media relations, thought leadership, and monitoring competition to capture new business.

Twitter for Brand Launch

Ventureneer (`@Ventureneer`) is a uniquely positioned membership-based startup provider of online education and peer support. Launched in late Spring 2009 with it first classes premiering in Fall 2009, Ventureneer needed to build a following quickly and on a shoestring budget. Their goal was "to establish Ventureneer as a support resource for leaders of social impact organizations, both nonprofit and for profit." As an online-only entity, Ventureneer determined ahead of time that all its marketing efforts would be executed online. President Geri Stengel started tweeting almost immediately.

Stengel describes her Ventureneer tweets as a mix of links to news on other sites, Ventureneer blog post announcements, webinar promos, survey requests, and personal comments such as thank-yous to guest speakers or updates on interesting events she attended. She rapidly built a follower base, achieving over 1,500 followers in three months. Twitter accounts for about 5 percent of Ventureneer's website traffic, accounting for between 125 and 150 visitors per day. When she promotes webinars through Twitter, Ventureneer receives 25 to 50 sign-ups.

A few noteworthy items Stengel points out that other start-ups might want to take into consideration:

- Initially, tweeting, list building, and maintenance take about two to three hours per day.
- Stengel uses someone to do this legwork and *ghost tweet* on the company's behalf (Note: ghost tweeting is a controversial practice, and not one that this author necessarily endorses).
- The company still maintains the need do most everything related to Twitter manually because they're seeking quality, not quantity. (Though I did notice they use auto-DM for new followers.)

Despite the time the company has invested in Twitter, Stengel says, "I feel the time is well worth the effort."

Twitter for Media Relations

More and more reporters are joining Twitter and using it to develop relationships with contacts, including company leaders, public relations professionals, and other influentials. Media relations has always been about developing and fostering relationships with reporters, but Twitter now allows the dialog to be both direct (corporate user to journalist user, or vice versa) and unobtrusive (journalists can follow and monitor your company daily without fear of necessarily being bombarded with inappropriate pitches…though those still happen too). As a company, if you're looking to improve your visibility in the press, you can utilize Twitter as a media relations tool.

As a case in point, Del Jones (`@jonesdel`), a reporter at *USA Today*, uses Twitter daily as part of his job. He started using it March 5, 2009 to see if he could understand it and use it as a traffic driver to his stories on *USA Today*. Jones's opinion of Twitter today is, "The more I use it, the more I see it as a relationship builder. I compare it to the Lions Club of old, where everyone attends a lunch knowing that everyone else there is trying to sell them something. But no real selling goes on at the Lions Club luncheon. That would be too crass. Instead, the luncheon is a place to make acquaintances and get to know each other to grease the wheels for actual business transactions down the road."

Jones also cleverly uses Twitter to write articles and garner new readers for past stories. For example, on May 28, 2009, he reported an entire story on Twitter. Entitled, "CEOs Tweet in News Story Reported Completely on Twitter," Jones used his CEO network to ask questions and receive answers via Twitter. Imagine receiving this tweet and juicy PR opportunity from a reporter so easily:

> *@jonesdel: Reporting USA TODAY cover story entirely on Twitter. Topic: Is U.S. economy evolving away from capitalism? Your thoughts please.*

Jones received responses from various CEOs, subsequently including many of their responses in his story. He also "outed" CEO duds, such as Barry Diller, CEO of IAC/InterActive (who also started FOX Broadcasting), who never responded. Had Jones known of your company, he might have contacted your CEO to respond to his article request, and therein lies your chance for some highly visible PR.

Jones also monitors people tweeting his stories, even if the tweet happened in the past. He then publicly tweets those people, oftentimes thanking them and specifically linking back to the original article and, in so doing, probably attracts a group of new readers to the piece (Figure 9.1).

@lacherig Discovered on backtweets that you tweeted my best friend at work story long time ago http://bit.ly/12YU6w U have new follower
1:33 PM Aug 27th from TweetDeck
jonesdel
Del Jones

Figure 9.1 Del Jones's clever tweet-thank-attract tactic

Twitter for Thought Leadership

ING DIRECT's (`@INGDIRECT`) approach to Twitter has been "intentionally not what you'd expect from a bank," admits head of marketing John Owens. "Customer service would have been the easy thing to do, but from Day One, we wanted to differentiate ourselves from other banks using Twitter." Because ING DIRECT sees itself as a "challenger brand," they wanted this same viewpoint and its passion to come across on Twitter (Figure 9.2). The bank endeavors to attract information seekers, and its team approach to tweeting strives to find topics about which to take a stand or support a cause, be passionate, while at the same time encouraging Americans to save. It maintains very few "rules of Twitter," other than to tweet with a voice consistent with the brand and spend a lot of time listening.

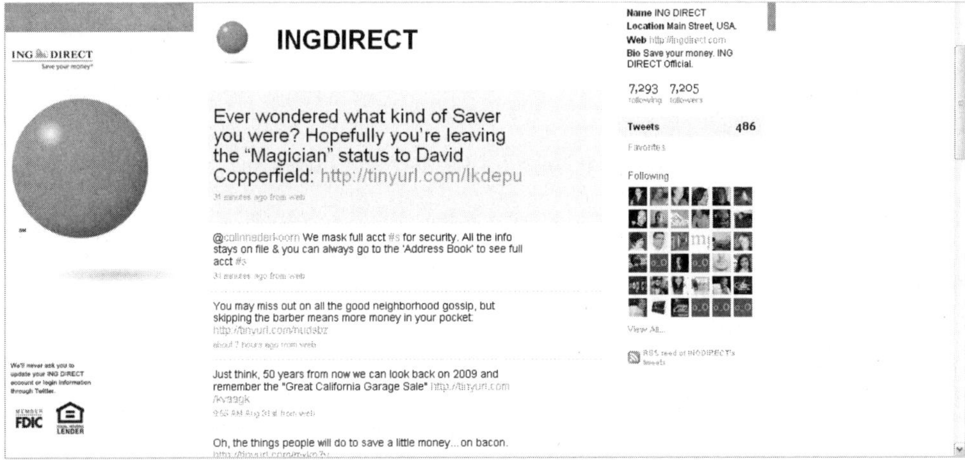

Figure 9.2 ING DIRECT tries to use Twitter as an extension of its brand position.

Those who listen and tweet on behalf of ING DIRECT use multiple tools to accomplish their objectives—TweetDeck, TweetGrid, ListenLogic, CoTweet, and plain old Twitter Search—and by listening, says Owens, they've learned a lot:

- There are people who absolutely love the brand.
- ING DIRECT feels that Twitter is best used for creating conversation, not for pushing out its message.
- There is no universally applicable "right way" to tweet...at least not yet.
- People want to feel the human element coming through your brand on Twitter.
- Twitter is also a way to *drive a company's culture*. By embracing Twitter the way it has, Owens believes ING has inspired and energized the workforce.

If that's not a leadership attitude, I don't know what is.

Twitter to Monitor Competition and Win New Customers

This is a great story about how monitoring your competitors and tweets about your competition can lead to new business. Two weeks before Memorial Day 2009, Gini Dietrich (@ginidietrich) needed to rent a car at the Denver International Airport. A long-time Avis customer and one of its Preferred Service members, Dietrich called to book a reservation during the week leading up to the holiday. The company had no available cars, but instead of contacting other Avis locations to see if they could secure a car for her, the phone representative told Dietrich to "take a cab." Not pleased, Dietrich hung up and immediately tweeted Avis (@aviswetryharder) to say, "No, you don't try harder…at least not in this case."

Avis never responded but within **two minutes**, Hertz (@ConnectByHertz) tweeted Dietrich, apologized for her poor Avis experience, offered up cars available in Denver, and gave her a 20-percent-off coupon. Needless to say, Dietrich booked with Hertz and, because the company was monitoring its competition, Hertz won a new loyal customer who rents a car multiple times each month.

Monday's One-Hour Exercise: Finalize Your Initial Twitter Marketing Objective

After completing Monday's preliminary work assignment, reading these case studies, and thinking back on the other case studies and examples you've studied so far, do you think you can narrow down your Twitter marketing objective to one key selection? Feel free to spend this time going back over previous case studies and daily exercises, particularly last week's Strategy Worksheet. You need to feel comfortable with your decision because it's ultimately going to be the one you pitch to management (or justify to yourself if you *are* management).

Tuesday: Measure and Report Upon Your Objectives

Now that you have narrowed down your goal, it's time to define your benchmarks in order to create timelines and metrics. Let's once again refer to the Strategy Worksheet. For the objective you've selected, what have you indicated as the measures to achieve this objective? Not sure? Now is also a great time to refer back to Monday in Chapter 7, "Week 4: Track and Monitor What Twitter Generates for You," and put to use for your business the same exercises you did for yourself as an individual.

As an easy reference, here is a compiled list of the factors you'll most likely want to track. Determine which ones best serve your primary goal:

- Number of times your crucial keywords appear in tweets
- Number of times your brand name appears in tweets
- Number of times your competitors' brand names appear in tweets
- Number of tweets per day
- Percentage of links in tweet

- Percentage of original tweets
- Number of retweets
- Percentage of retweets
- Number of `@replies` or DMs
- Percentage of `@replies`
- Time of day when you tweet the most
- Click-throughs on shortened and/or trackable URLs
- Total reach of retweets (retweets × the number of followers of each retweeter)
- Number of times your hashtag is used
- Your Twitter grade, score, or rank
- Referring website traffic (via web analytics)
- Actions, such as event registrations, email subscription sign-ups, poll/survey/form completions, coupon redemptions, call-ins, requests for information, or direct sales
- Secondary benefits, such as media coverage

Define and Measure Baseline Metrics

Once you determine the measurement criteria most appropriate for your key objective (your *success metrics*), it's time to establish the baseline measurements for them. The baseline indicates where you are now and gives you perspective on where you want or hope your objective takes you to in the future.

If you are truly just starting your brand out on Twitter, many of your baseline readings will be low or nonexistent. The good news is that you have a great opportunity to make a huge impact during your first three to six months on Twitter. The bad news is that without any history, you don't know how to place context on your goals, so consider these factors:

Brand Recognition If you're a large brand conducting all kinds of marketing initiatives, you have the benefit of your brand name alone attracting visitors to your profile, which in turn can translate into new followers. As a large brand, therefore, you can expect your follower count to grow more quickly than a smaller or no-name brand. For example, at the beginning of 2009, Southwest Airlines (`@SouthwestAir`) had less than 9,000 followers; as of September 2009, the brand had over 570,000 followers!

Twitter's Growth Rate Clearly, Twitter's exponential user growth also impacts the likelihood of follower growth, which makes it even harder to predict future follower counts and other Twitter activity. Since fourth quarter 2008, Twitter has had annualized growth over 2,000 percent, though month-over-month growth stats slowed substantially, with comScore reporting that between April 2009 and July 2009, Twitter only grew approximately 25 percent per month. It's helpful to factor Twitter's growth patterns into your target goals, but don't spend too much time fretting over these precise calculations, because they're in such flux.

Competitive Forces Is your market saturated with competition? Is what you sell widely found and used? The more competitive your marketplace, the more likely you'll have to find ways to differentiate yourself, which in turn will affect what you measure and what expectations to place on those measurements.

Resources We'll discuss this more on Thursday of this week, but how you determine what kinds of resources to allocate to Twitter will also play a role in how your measurements are affected.

The Objective Itself The objective you define will obviously have a direct impact on many of the measurement criteria. If you choose to deliver customer service via Twitter, for example, be prepared to have a lot of tweeting going on, so you may want to track your tweet volume over time. You may also want to track other details besides Twitter activity, such as the most common complaints received (and resolved) through Twitter or the likelihood of a Twitter-handled customer to reorder or remain a customer. These are very different measurements than the ones for a company who enters Twitter to help their search engine visibility. This objective will focus on keyword usage in tweets, baseline rankings for these same keywords in search engines and their movement over time, and website referral traffic from search engines. If questions like "Does Twitter build revenue?", "Does Twitter improve efficiencies or reduce costs?", or "Does Twitter build brand loyalty?" matter to you, then you need to determine how you can track and measure this. The point is, think through the impact you hope your objective has to help you best determine what measurements you should expect to track.

Another interesting perspective on Twitter analysis comes courtesy of an article (`http://www.articlesbase.com/internet-marketing-articles/twitter-metrics-1101391.html`) by Ryan Nokes of Vault Analytics who lays out the following ratios for brands to consider when analyzing their Twitter objectives. Each of the calculations will give you a percentage, with the higher the percentage, the better. (See Table 9.1.)

► **Table 9.1** Calculate Twitter Metrics by Objective

Desired Outcome	Formula to Calculate
Drive targeted website traffic	Tweet Conversion Ratio = Number of Site Visits from Twitter / Number of Twitter Followers (or new Twitter followers)
Build brand loyalty and buzz	Twitter Friends = Number of Twitter Followers over time (watch for upward trends) Retweet Ratio = Number of Retweets / Total Tweets in a given period of time
Obtain opinion data from a diverse group, perform simple market research	Reply Ratio = Number of Replies / Total Tweets in a given period of time

▶ **Table 9.1** Calculate Twitter Metrics by Objective *(Continued)*

Desired Outcome	Formula to Calculate
Direct people's attention to good information or valuable content	Clickthrough Ratio = (Number of Clickthroughs per link) / Total Tweets with Links
Track memes and trends	Number of Tweets in given period vs. Google Trends graph of specific subject/topic
Gather competitive intelligence	Competitive Intelligence Ratio = Number of Tweets about Competitors / Total Tweets about Industry
Manage customer service, create a brand index	(Positive Tweets – Negative Tweets) / Total Tweets
Create a tribe	Number of New Followers per Tweet

Establish a Reporting Structure

As we went over in Chapter 7, the exercise of measuring *everything* you can measure is daunting and impractical. What is important to establish is a system of regular reporting on your metrics. This system does not have to necessitate the measuring of every criterion every single time. You may want to track certain metrics daily, while others are fine to track once a month. You may be able to aggregate the tracking of several of these metrics by using a more robust tool, or you may need to track other metrics manually or individually. Suffice it to say that you need to establish a reporting structure that you and your higher-ups can live with and that continues to support your existence on Twitter. Then you need to build time into your Twitter marketing strategy to perform your analyses so you that can report on them with regularity.

Tuesday's One-Hour Exercise: Establish Baseline Metrics and Report-Generation Schedule

This exercise is the logical next step to help you find a starting point and plan how you will regularly generate your measurement reports.

1. Use the information presented to determine which metrics you'll want to measure given your objectives. Take your baseline measurements.
2. Determine the frequency and timeframe within which you're going to measure these metrics. Create a reporting schedule.

Wednesday: Determine Tweet Topics

Not everyone wants the same things from the people they follow on Twitter, and their reasons for following someone might be very different than why they choose to follow a brand. Even though what you end up delivering to a follower as a brand might ultimately be pretty similar to what they get out of following a person, you still want to consider your followers' motives. Ask yourself, "Why would someone want to follow our brand? What might cause them to find us in the first place? What do they expect from us, and what might keep them around?" Answering these questions will probably help establish the kinds of things you tweet about.

Tweet-Worthy Topics

Let's consider the question previously posed, "What might cause a follower to find us in the first place?" Does the answer give you some clues about tweet topics?

They are brand loyalists. Among a customer base, any successful company has devoted brand loyalists. These people speak highly of your brand to others, are likely to open your emails regularly, and look forward to your new product or service announcements. On Twitter, this translates to an individual who will seek you out and follow your brand just to stay informed and have the opportunity to engage with you more directly. In fact, for brand loyalists, the idea of direct engagement with your brand is both exhilarating and empowering. They're likely to feel that this might be the first time they can really tell you how much they love you and you will hear them. It's kind of a pity it took Twitter to make that happen. After all, how many customers call your hotline just to say "We love you!"?

So what does a brand loyalist want to read? Of course, news that relates to them as a consumer, direct links to items of interest on your website, and Twitter-only promotions and specials; but these people would be thrilled if you sent them an unsolicited shout-out via a public tweet asking how their weekend was or how their child's birthday party went, or related to anything else on a personal level that they may have already tweeted you about. Granted this is tough to manage, but it only helps to reinforce their brand loyalty.

They are brand-curious. The brand-curious could be anyone who's become aware of your company by some other means, such as being exposed to your advertising or seeking you out because they're looking for employment. The brand-curious user doesn't necessarily have a specific reason to follow you, but to this person, your Twitter stream will say a lot about you as a brand. Twitter fulfills to a T the adage, "It only takes a few seconds to make a first impression," because that's what your Twitter stream will do, particularly to someone who has no preconceived notion about your brand.

You told them to follow you. Brands that already have an existing relationship with their customers should be promoting their Twitter handle just as readily as they promote their website URL. (Sadly, the promotion of website URLs still doesn't happen as consistently as it should.) This means every place the brand touches the consumer, it could be promoting its Twitter handle: on company letterhead, on stock statements, in advertising (particularly in print), in email, in brochures, in give-away items, maybe even on product packaging, as Pepsi Raw, a UK-released product, did (Figure 9.3). Why not take advantage of this "free" opportunity to let the world know you're on Twitter?

Figure 9.3 Pepsi Raw's cans have its Twitter handle printed on it.

If you beckon the user well enough to get them to come over, they're probably interested in a bit more of "what's in it for me," or a WIIFM. Get them to follow you and keep them attracted with games, contests, promotions, and plain old-fashioned relationship-building.

They want instantaneous updates and last-minute deals. The airline industry has really figured out a valuable use for Twitter: the instant flight update and the last-minute flight deals to fill seats (JetBlue calls theirs the "Cheeps" (Figure 9.4). Instant deals can also be found through accounts like woot's (`@woot`, `@wootoff`, `@wootshirt`, `@wootwine`, `@wootsellout`) and Amazon.com Deals (`@amazondeals`). These are the ultimate WIIFMs.

Our Monday Cheeps are up! Have a look at @JetBlueCheeps to see this week's fares and destinations! http://bit.ly/cheeps
7:26 AM Aug 24th from CoTweet
jetBlue
JetBlue
JetBlue Airways

Figure 9.4 JetBlue uses its Cheeps to fill seats at the last minute.

Similarly, users follow breaking news and gossip sites for instant news and information. The transportation industry (trains, subway, and mass transit) and traffic- and weather-monitoring sites would do well to capitalize on Twitter by issuing more instant updates. When it comes to these kinds of followers, all you have to do is "Give 'em what they want!"

They read someone else's tweet mentioning you. *Tweet tripping* is a pretty common practice. Someone tweets with or about you and one of their followers reads the tweet. If the tweet strikes them as interesting or curious, they can easily click on your Twitter handle and check out your profile. Tweets like this spread virally, and this kind of user isn't necessarily interested in a WIIFM; there are any number of reasons they may decide to follow you, but probably high on their list is the fact that you show yourself to be engaged with your followers. Nothing is worse than coming to a brand that shows absolutely zero user engagement. They might also be interested in the subject matter about which you tweet, in which case they're interested in receiving this information on a regular basis.

They found you through a search. Whether it was through Google, another search engine, or a Twitter search, this kind of user entered a particular keyword phrase or hashtag and either your indexed tweet or your profile came up. Seeking to find the information for which they're looking, they click through and find you. At this point, if searchers find the answer to their questions or view your tweets as generally informative, the chances are good that they'll begin following you.

They have a problem. The larger the brand, the more likely that when a Twitter-savvy individual has a problem, they'll seek you out. They may want to inform you of the problem; they may want to lodge a complaint; they may be seeking restitution; or they may just want the rest of the Twitterverse to know they have an issue with you. This is probably one reason large brands have shied away from Twitter so far: they figure what someone can't tweet won't hurt the brand. Sadly, when Twitter users are angry, they'll tweet poorly about your brand regardless, and you just won't be there to see it and defend yourself.

These kinds of users are not initially following you for any reason other than problem resolution. It's a clever tactic, however, to ask them to follow you so that you can work to resolve their problem offline through direct messaging rather than by publicly battling it out. The follow may be short-lived, however, if they're happy with the solution, or they may continue to follow you out of gratitude and retained loyalty. That would be called turning lemons into lemonade.

Define Content Goals and Production Expectations

Now that you've put yourself in your followers' shoes, based on your Twitter objectives, it should be easier to come up with some content goals. Twitter is such a versatile platform and tweets are so easy to enrich (as detailed in Chapter 6, "Week 3: Use Twitter Search and Other Tools to Improve your Experience,") that you really shouldn't be at a loss to come up with good content. In many cases, such as customer service, the content will come to you. I've often said, "When hard-pressed to find something to tweet about, dive into your Twitter stream. I'm sure something someone in there has to say will be reply-worthy, and then you'll have a conversation starter."

Still, it doesn't hurt to define some content goals, particularly to get you thinking long-range. Sometimes, to get at the good content, you'll need to do some advanced planning or at least plant some seeds. Let's recap some things you can tweet about and place some production expectations on them (Table 9.2).

► **Table 9.2** Content Goals/Production Expectations

Content Goal	Production Expectation
Instant updates or deal	Little to no lead time—just tweet the instant update or deal. You just need a means to determine what it will be.
News	Little to no lead time—just get the news from the media department and tweet.
Helpful links	Little to some lead time—can be in the form of a retweet, or someone can spend time reading news and/or researching for link material. If you plan on writing and posting articles yourself, this will take additional lead time to fully execute.
Posing one-off questions	Little to no lead time—someone thinks of the question and you tweet it.
Posing polls or surveys	Little to some lead time—polls are easier to produce than surveys, but both require some advanced thinking to create appropriate questions and answers.
Hosting an interview, chat, or debate	Some to longer lead time—to host interviews, chats, or debates, you want to research subject-matter material and recruit attendees. With neither of these, you won't have much to host.
Tweeting an event	Little to longer lead time—depending on the extent to which you want to utilize the event, you can just live-tweet to your stream or you can develop an entire integrated plan, like integrating your tweet stream into online ads. This concept will involve advanced planning.
Offers, discounts, contests, sweepstakes, and other promotions	Little to longer lead time—though pushing a promotion can be as easy as a tweet, you do need time to plan the back-end, such as redemption, rules, and other possible support materials.
Job recruitment	Little to some lead time—although it only takes a quick tweet to say you're looking to fill a position and provide a link to that position, the link still needs to lead to a viable job listing, and that job listing needs to be posted to the Web.
Entertainment	Little to longer lead time—entertaining tweets can range from tweeting a joke (takes little time) to linking to your clever or funny video (takes more time).

Wednesday's One-Hour Exercise: List Your Content Goals

Table 9.2 might feature a few of the content ideas you had in mind to help promote your company. Using a format similar to the chart, list your own content goals and indicate what kind of production expectations you think they'll require.

Thursday: Assign Resources

This is your brand. It is your reputation. It is your public perception. In most cases, you've spent years and thousands, if not millions, of dollars creating your image. So how do you know who is the right person to create and execute a Twitter campaign?

Tweeting Interns

A lot of people want to give their Twitter campaigns to interns because "they've been using social networking their entire lives." Interns, however, don't have any business experience. Most interns have been using social networking only for personal use, and very few have much business or PR savvy. Would you ask an intern to make a presentation in your biggest new business meeting of the year? Would you ask an intern to meet with the bank? Would you ask an intern to lead your organization? Entrusting your brand to someone who has business experience and knows what it is you're trying to achieve is just as important with Twitter as is it with these things.

There are companies out there who are using interns for Twitter campaigns, and it's working relatively well. Take Pizza Hut, for instance, which is not the only big company that has tasked an intern with the role of Twitter, but perhaps it's the one most comfortable with admitting it. Their profile even proclaims, "The Twintern & the Twitter Team are on it" (Figure 9.5). The intern's only responsibilities are to develop new followers, engage with customers, and become a megaphone for the brand. She's been able to build Pizza Hut's followers to (as of this writing) more than 15,000, and she held an apparently successful Fourth of July Twitter sales promotion. Had her efforts gone awry, however, this intern held the keys to produce a public relations disaster.

To demonstrate the downside of letting an intern tweet for your brand, consider the case of London-based home-furnishings retailer Habitat. There, a twintern got in big trouble when he tweeted company information and manipulated users by including topical hashtags such as `#Iran` and `#Mousavi` in his company tweets so that people who searched for information about the Iranian election protests would see his company's promotional tweets as well (Figure 9.6). A (more professionally trained) company representative, trying to quell the public relations crisis, said in a statement, "We were shocked when we discovered what happened and are very sorry for the offence that was caused." (For more on handling a crisis via Twitter see Chapter 13, "Week 10: Prepare for Crisis Management.")

If you still think an intern should be the one tweeting on behalf of your brand, consider this: An intern typically is employed by you only 90 days. Who will pick up the brand message and voice when this person leaves? Would you want your Director of Media Relations position to be a revolving 90-day door?

Figure 9.5 Pizza Hut's tweeting intern has been successful in her mission, and her success got Pizza Hut an interview and free PR.

BBC Low graphics Help Search Explore the BBC

NEWS ONE-MINUTE WORLD NEWS

Page last updated at 15:11 GMT, Wednesday, 24 June 2009 16:11 UK

E-mail this to a friend | Printable version

Habitat sorry for Iran Tweeting

Furniture store Habitat has apologised for causing offence after accusations it exploited unrest in Iran to drive online Twitter users to its products.

Keywords - called hashtags - such as 'Iran' and 'Mousavi' were added to its messages so people searching for those subjects would see the firm's adverts.

Twitter users have not been impressed with the strategy

Users of the networking site reacted angrily and the posts were removed.

The retailer has said the use of the hashtags was "not authorised", but declined to say who was responsible.

Contributors to Twitter posted messages claiming Habitat should be "ashamed" and saying it was "piggy-backing" on the political situation in Iran.

One of the controversial messages - called tweets - which appeared before being removed by Habitat, read: HabitatUK: #MOUSAVI Join the database for free to win a £1,000 gift card.

In a statement Habitat said it had "never sought to abuse Twitter".

> "This was absolutely not authorised by Habitat - we were shocked when we discovered what happened"
>
> Habitat statement

One online communication expert told the BBC it was hard to imagine how such a "serious misjudgement"

SEE ALSO
- Following Iran online 15 Jun 09 | Middle East
- Twitter responds on Iranian role 17 Jun 09 | Technology
- Internet brings events in Iran to life 15 Jun 09 | Middle East
- Twitter hype punctured by study 09 Jun 09 | Technology
- Guide and tips for using Twitter 29 Apr 09 | Click

RELATED BBC LINKS
- Iran crisis

RELATED INTERNET LINKS
- Twitter
- Nielsen Online

The BBC is not responsible for the content of external internet sites

TOP UK STORIES
- UK contractor killed in Baghdad
- Ministers deny torture collusion
- Badminton team quits after threat

News feeds

News Front Page | Africa | Americas | Asia-Pacific | Europe | Middle East | South Asia | UK | England | Northern Ireland | Scotland | Wales | UK Politics | Education | Magazine | Business | Health | Science & Environment | Technology | Entertainment | Also in the news | Video and Audio | Programmes | Have Your Say | In Pictures | Country Profiles | Special Reports

Figure 9.6 Habitat's PR disaster spiraled so out of control that the BBC covered the story.

Who Should Tweet?

Aside from dismissing the idea of a tweeting intern, there are multiple options for who should tweet for your organization. It should, however, be someone, or more than one person, who is already infused with your company's culture, attitude, brand experience, and product knowledge. JetBlue's (`@JetBlue`) manager of corporate communications initially led its charge into Twitter. (JetBlue now has a team of corporate tweeters.) McDonald's (`@mccafeyourday`) leaves it official tweeting to its manager of U.S. communications. Starbucks' (`@Starbucks`) Twitter feed isn't manned by an executive, but a former barista who has developed a good sense of what its customers are seeking. Zappos, with its unique corporate culture, meanwhile, encourages all of its employees to tweet.

Assign Roles

Whether you assign corporate tweeting to a single person or to a team, the effort should be overseen and appropriately coordinated. If you use a multiuser management tool like those we reviewed in Chapter 6, who, when, and how your representatives respond should be defined to avoid confusion. You should also spell out how you want people to respond in your company's Social Media Policy (see Appendix D, "Social Media Guidelines" for an example).

As to what goes into the production requirements for your intended tweets, remember that some kinds of tweets demand longer-range planning and potentially additional resources. Let's move on to your daily one-hour exercise to demonstrate.

Thursday's One-Hour Exercise: Assign Resources

Now refer back to your exercise assignment from Wednesday. Add a third column to the right, labeling it "Assigned To."

1. Taking into consideration the knowledge and capability requirements of the kind of person who could respond to or post the kind of tweet you've indicated, who comes to mind? Write down the names of potential candidates.
2. Consider if each person is solely capable of producing the content related to this tweet. Also consider if he or she will need support. If so, who is then capable of providing this support? Write down these names.
3. Are your top preferences *available* to be engaged with or provide support for Twitter or is their time already maxed out elsewhere? If so, do you need to bring on other resources to enable them to shift over or perhaps shift or outsource some of their current duties in order to make them available for Twitter? What does this Twitter organizational chart look like?

This exercise might initially seem over the top, but it will help reveal where your potential weaknesses are and what considerations you'll need to be thinking about ahead of time in order to minimize Twitter management failures.

Friday: Get Company Buy-In

There are two typical ways you can get company buy-in for Twitter, and they aren't unique to Twitter:

- Tie results to the Profit and Loss (P&L) statement.
- Tie results to improved customer service and better efficiencies.

If your CEO is an entrepreneur, he or she is likely to want to hear new ideas. If you can explain how you think Twitter will improve the P&L or customer service, the CEO will likely want you to run with it. If your CEO is a hired gun, there may be more process behind what you present and how you execute it, but the strategy is the same.

Prepare the Pitch to Management

Right now, create a list of everything your company is doing to build brand awareness, develop thought leadership, recruit talent, engage and support current customers, communicate internally, and prospect for new business. The list might include the following:

- Trade ads
- Trade shows and conferences
- TV, radio, print, outdoor, online, or other forms of advertising
- Public relations
- Email marketing
- Internal and external newsletters
- Marketing brochures
- Customer service department
- Call centers
- Event marketing
- Client dinners
- Promotions, contests, and sales
- Discounts
- Mobile marketing
- Working with a recruiter

What if you can still do all of this, but have a new way of distributing the information, getting feedback, listening to what your clients have to say, and making changes immediately, instead of when someone becomes unhappy or you have a crisis on your hands? What if you can talk to your customers every day to build loyalty, without having to depend solely on client dinners and golf outings? What if, right now, your customer service department or your sales people are hiding an issue from you because they want to try to fix it before you hear about it?

For hypothetical purposes, let's say this is happening. What if you learn about it the instant it becomes an issue, because you or someone else in your organization is talking to your customers every day, one-on-one, in an informal and easy fashion? Don't you think a lot of your issues could be solved pretty quickly and cost-efficiently?

If you begin your presentation to the executive team with these types of scenarios (even better if you have real issues that are happening within your company), and then you show how a social media program can fix a customer service issue quickly—before you lose that customer for good—you'll have their attention.

Improved customer relations certainly has an impact on the bottom line. Do you know the average length of time you retain your customers? What if you extended that value by months or years? What impact would that have on the company's revenue? What if your company lost customers at a higher rate than normal? How would this negatively impact revenue? Do the math and projections for senior management. This will be another way to get their attention.

You can also try to forecast such things as the following:

- An uptick in sales driven by Twitter-only promotions (project the percent and dollar values)
- An impact on new product launches thanks to Twitter (project lift and dollar value)
- An increase in the number and value of leads generated for the company via Twitter
- The impact to your website traffic from tweeting that consequently translates into more transactions for your company (forecast percent increase in traffic and transactions over current figures; predict the dollar value of those new transactions)
- A decrease in call center expenses (by percent and dollar value)

I'm sure you can come up with other criteria that will ring your upper management's bells. After you've come up with appropriate ones, space them out over 30-day, 90-day, 6-month, and annual terms to give an even broader view of Twitter's potential impact. Be sure, however, that all of these projections tie into your key objectives. Don't use projections for new product launches, for example, if you're planning on using Twitter primarily to deliver customer service.

When you feel you have enough ammunition to present your Twitter marketing program to upper management, go and show them why the company cannot afford *not* to participate! If that still doesn't work, tell and *show* them how Tony Hsieh, the CEO of Zappos, does it and how Zappos debuted on the Fortune 100 Best Companies to Work For 2009 list at Number 23 (`http://money.cnn.com/magazines/fortune/bestcompanies/2009/snapshots/23.html`), in large part because of their involvement in Twitter and using it to grow the business...not to mention gaining the attention of Amazon, which instigated its acquisition of Zappos in the Summer of 2009.

When Twitter Is Not Right for Your Business

If you're reading this book, and you've gotten this far, you more than likely think Twitter is the right technology to begin to develop new relationships with people around the world. There are, however, some reasons a company should not be on Twitter, and you should be aware of them so you don't go pitching a lemon to upper management.

You have legal reasons. If you have a corporate legal department that doesn't allow you to distribute anything without their approval, this will present a huge hurdle for using Twitter. Twitter is a social network where conversation is quick and in real time. Waiting for legal council's approval doesn't bode well for this medium.

You plan to do hard-core marketing. As we've often discussed, if you plan to use Twitter solely as one more channel to deliver one-way broadcasts of your marketing materials or press releases, then it's not the right place for you or your company. Twitter users want to engage directly with you. It's why they're on Twitter and not some other platform. Merely blasting out self-centered tweets will not appeal to Twitter users, and you're not likely to succeed, so why waste your time?

You have something to hide. The Twitter community isn't very tolerant of disingenuous, inauthentic, or nontransparent tweeting, and they can sniff a rat pretty quickly. Being outed on Twitter for this kind of behavior is risky—it has the potential to damage your brand image, particularly if the crisis thereafter isn't well-managed. Also, if your CEO doesn't want to tweet and you think he/she should, don't create a Twitter account and pretend to be that person. It won't work. Someone other than the CEO can tweet for your company; they just can't pretend they are the chief executive.

Similarly, if you want to lock down your tweets because you're unwilling to make them available for public viewing, don't bother using Twitter for business marketing. It's completely contradictory to the whole premise. Enough said.

You're unwilling or unable to respond in a timely fashion. For heavy Twitter users, Twitter can easily and quickly replace email. Tweeting 140 characters is so much easier than composing a whole email, and the notion of being able to get through to someone more quickly who can also respond to you more quickly is very enticing. If you don't plan to respond when people tweet, or worse still, direct message you, stay away from Twitter. Receiving a DM or `@message` demands your timely reply.

You have no patience. Twitter success doesn't happen overnight. It builds like a crescendo with your tweets and followers, helping you grow your Twitter visibility. Twitter for business success does not come about by buying your way in. Paying for followers so you can get to thousands of followers overnight or sending out auto-DMs is not going to shortcut you to glory. Twitter is like the best bar ever. If you go to the bar and talk to no one, but before you leave you steal all the business cards out of the fishbowl so you can add these people to your contact database, don't you think they'll know you're spamming them if you send them an eblast? At best, they'd unsubscribe from your blast; at worst, they'll report you as a spammer. Focus instead on quality: the quality of your tweets, the quality of your followers, the quality of those whom you choose to follow. Quality always trumps quantity on Twitter.

Friday's One-Hour Exercise: Draft Your Pitch to Management

Refer back to all the points raised today. Have you thought about what matters most to upper management and also what makes sense for you to expect from executing your Twitter strategy? Write down these points and then try to provide projections and rationales that your executives can buy into.

The Main Points

- Twitter, like ordinary marketing, requires objectives. Define your primary and secondary objectives, realizing too that over time they might need to change as you continue to learn.
- Based on your objectives, determine what metrics apply, and then take baseline measurements so you can measure your progress over time.
- There are so many things your brand can tweet about in addition to answering `@messages`. Think through the kinds of tweets that relate to your objectives, what will be involved in creating these tweets, and who'll be responsible for the production—start to finish.
- Who tweets for your brand is probably just as important as, if not more important than, what they tweet about. Put your best foot forward, not just any old (or young) foot.
- Because upper management speaks a different language than you do, don't expect them to jump up and down over Twitter just because it's cool. Help yourself get buy-in by quantifying what's in it for your company.

Week 7: Get Your Brand Started on Twitter

By now, you should be completely prepared to get your brand on Twitter. You've worked through the elements of Twitter marketing strategy, how to establish your goals, and how to sell your whole Twitter marketing plan to upper management. You've practiced tweeting as an individual, so you should really have the hang of this thing. Now it's time to take the plunge and get your company started on Twitter.

Preparation-wise, you're on the downhill side. A lot of what we'll review should be old ground for you. It's much of the same work you've done already as an individual; you'll just apply it to your brand instead. You're going to set up your brand's Twitter account, plan your first tweets, discuss ways to attract and engage brand followers, and sum it all up by reviewing best practices. Let's get going!

10

Chapter Contents

Monday: Claim Your Brand's Twitter Name

When Twitter first started, the trend was to create clever and catchy handles and to change them every couple of months. One of this book's contributors started out as @BearsFan07, just to figure out how Twitter worked, what it meant to her personally, and how she could use it to communicate a passion—the Chicago Bears. As time moved on, she changed the handle to her real name in order to communicate for her business.

Now that more businesses are using Twitter as a means of communication, it's important to own the handles that are your corporate name and any product or brand names you own. Even if you only use one of them, you'll prevent others from stealing them or name squatting (see Chapter 8, "Week 5: Develop a Successful Twitter Strategy," for more on this topic). Think back to the early days of the Internet when companies that failed to purchase their own corporate or brand domain names ended up either paying exorbitant fees to reclaim them or acquiring a completely different domain name, hoping users would ultimately find them. These days, cyber squatting laws and Twitter's policies protect trademark holders from this kind of extortion, but why run the risk of still having to fight for your name?

Free versus Fee?

At the time of this writing, Twitter is considering charging for corporate accounts. Keep that in mind if you pursue and/or name squat branded Twitter accounts. It's much easier to justify registering dozens of Twitter brand handles when you don't have to pay anything for the privilege of doing so.

Select Your Twitter Name

When it comes to choosing a Twitter name for your business account, there are three different schools of thought:

- Twitter is only for people connecting with people, meaning your customers, current and prospective, want to have a relationship with a person, not a representative of your company posing behind the company logo. Under this school of thought, you represent yourself transparently on Twitter and you may or may not tweet about business-related topics. For example, Jeffrey Hayzlett (@jeffreyhayzlett), Kodak's chief marketing officer, tweets as himself *and* as his company's representative (Figure 10.1).
- It's okay for brands to present themselves as brands so long as the brand exposes the human beings representing them. For example, Marriott Hawaii's (@marriotthawaii) Twitter profile tells us that Poe and Drew will be tweeting us (Figure 10.2).

- Big brands add value to the Twitter community, regardless of who the human is behind the logo. With this approach, we don't know who's representing the brand; if that person, or team of people, are consistently there to help us; or much else about the brand other than that it is a brand (Figure 10.3).

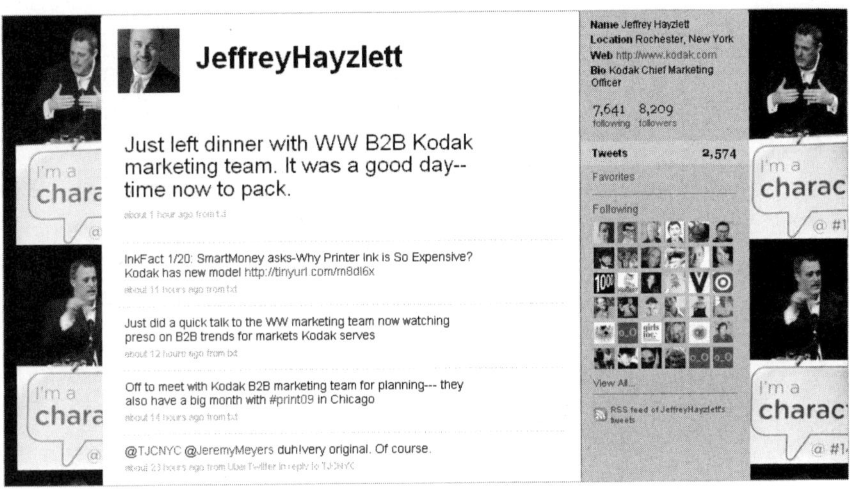

Figure 10.1 Jeffrey Hayzlett on Twitter

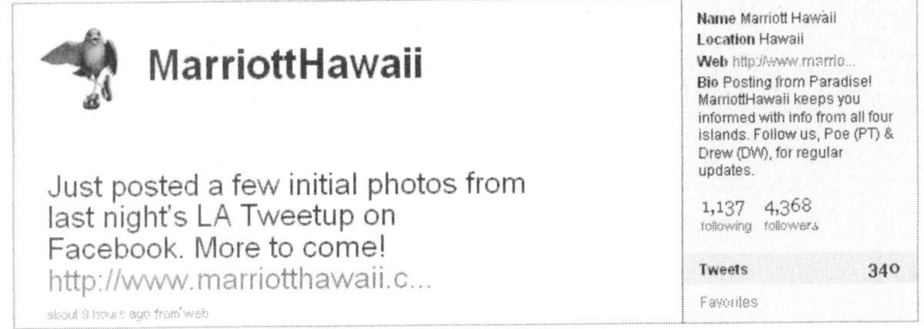

Figure 10.2 Marriott Hawaii on Twitter as represented by Poe and Drew

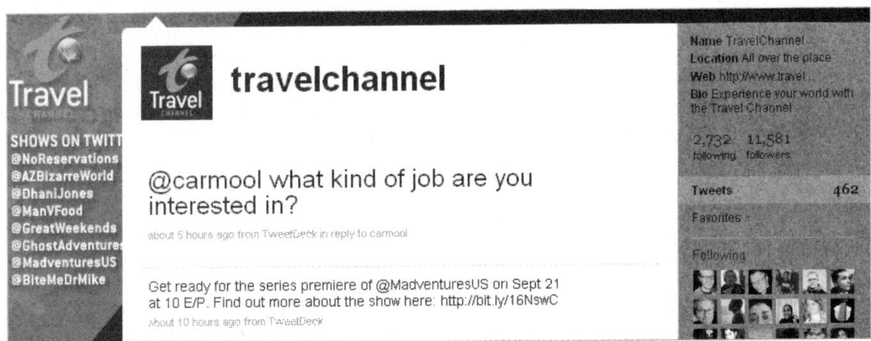

Figure 10.3 We don't know who's tweeting on behalf of the Travel Channel.

Still, the fact of the matter when it comes to social media is that people like connecting with people, even if people are behind the brands. Even if your company is a big brand, you might want to stick with one of the first two schools of thought.

Create Your Brand Account(s)

Just as you did in Chapter 4, "Week 1: Get on Twitter," go through the process of setting up your brand's Twitter account. Start with the obvious: if you can, register your top-of-mind brand name. Remember too that Twitter limits handles to no more than 15 characters, so you may need to use abbreviations to accomplish this. If you do, make sure they make sense to someone searching for your brand without knowing your Twitter handle. If you've been slow on the draw and someone else has registered your brand name, you might choose to create an alternative name rather than wait to have Twitter resolve the dispute. Although the following Twitter handles are clever renditions of their brand names, they're not going to be the first things consumers think of when seeking out these brands:

`@PetSmartTLC`

`@LoveMyPhilly`

`@QuiznosToaster`

`@QuakerTalk`

`@MotoMobile`

`@subwayfreshbuzz`

After you register your primary company account, feel free to register additional ones related to individual products, services, departments, locations, and other differentiators. This isn't to suggest you create accounts for every combination of names under the sun. Just be reasonable and think a few steps ahead. Even if you never use these Twitter handles, you'll always own them and the brands they represent online. Figure 10.4, Figure 10.5, and Figure 10.6 are a few examples of brands that have registered multiple brand names, all to be used for different purposes.

One final thing you might want to do for your brand once you create your Twitter account is to submit your handle to the tool TwitTruth (`http://www.twittruth.com`), so it can start tracking your brand and give you statistics on your performance.

Monday's One-Hour Exercise: Create Your Brand's Twitter Account(s)

Truthfully, this exercise might not even take you an hour. If you've already registered your brand on Twitter, you get a bye for today. If you haven't, and your brand name is available, go ahead and create your account. If you want to create more than one account, do that as well. Don't necessarily worry about setting up the entire account, such as filling out your profile page, just yet. That'll be tomorrow's exercise.

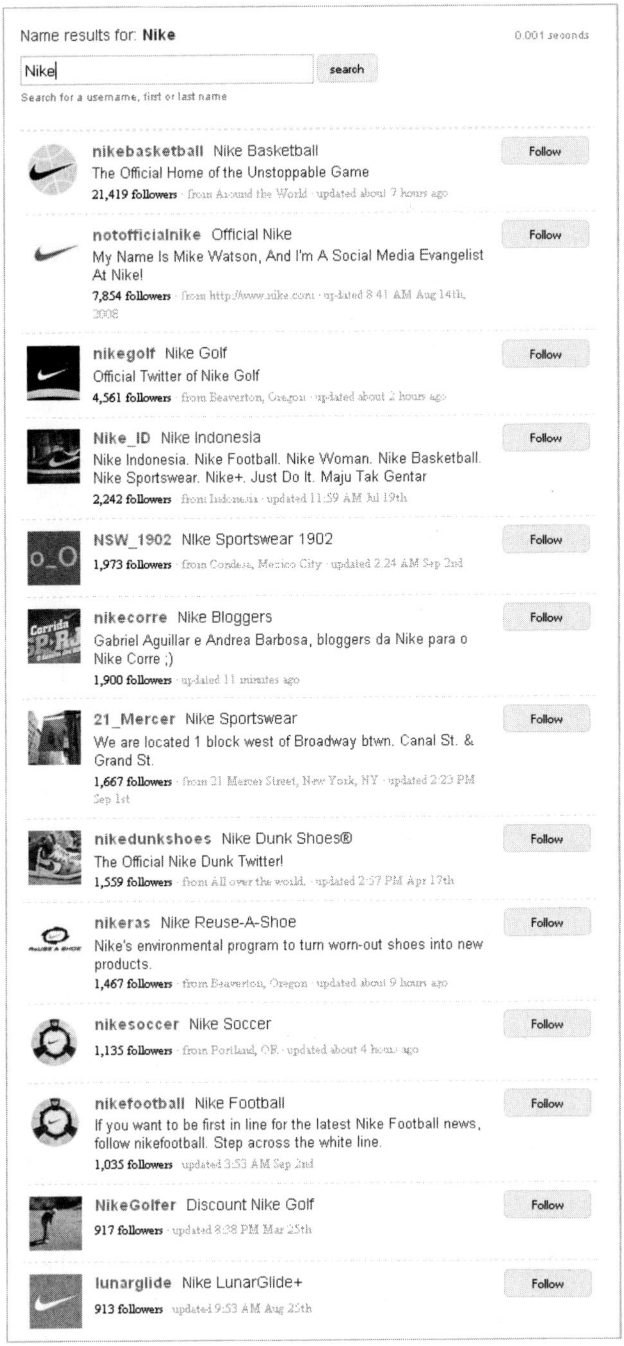

Name results for: **Nike** 0.001 seconds

Nike search

Search for a username, first or last name

nikebasketball Nike Basketball Follow
The Official Home of the Unstoppable Game
21,419 followers · from Around the World · updated about 7 hours ago

notofficialnike Official Nike Follow
My Name Is Mike Watson, And I'm A Social Media Evangelist At Nike!
7,854 followers · from http://www.nike.com · updated 8:41 AM Aug 14th, 2008

nikegolf Nike Golf Follow
Official Twitter of Nike Golf
4,561 followers · from Beaverton, Oregon · updated about 2 hours ago

Nike_ID Nike Indonesia Follow
Nike Indonesia. Nike Football. Nike Woman. Nike Basketball. Nike Sportswear. Nike+. Just Do It. Maju Tak Gentar
2,242 followers · from Indonesia · updated 11:59 AM Jul 19th

NSW_1902 Nike Sportswear 1902 Follow
1,973 followers · from Condesa, Mexico City · updated 2:24 AM Sep 2nd

nikecorre Nike Bloggers Follow
Gabriel Aguillar e Andrea Barbosa, bloggers da Nike para o Nike Corre ;)
1,900 followers · updated 11 minutes ago

21_Mercer Nike Sportswear Follow
We are located 1 block west of Broadway btwn. Canal St. & Grand St.
1,667 followers · from 21 Mercer Street, New York, NY · updated 2:23 PM Sep 1st

nikedunkshoes Nike Dunk Shoes® Follow
The Official Nike Dunk Twitter!
1,559 followers · from All over the world. · updated 2:57 PM Apr 17th

nikeras Nike Reuse-A-Shoe Follow
Nike's environmental program to turn worn-out shoes into new products.
1,467 followers · from Beaverton, Oregon · updated about 9 hours ago

nikesoccer Nike Soccer Follow
1,135 followers · from Portland, OR · updated about 4 hours ago

nikefootball Nike Football Follow
If you want to be first in line for the latest Nike Football news, follow nikefootball. Step across the white line.
1,035 followers · updated 3:53 AM Sep 2nd

NikeGolfer Discount Nike Golf Follow
917 followers · updated 8:28 PM Mar 25th

lunarglide Nike LunarGlide+ Follow
913 followers · updated 9:53 AM Aug 25th

Figure 10.4 Nike's multiple handles by product line

Name results for: **Microsoft** 0.001 seconds

Microsoft search

Search for a username, first or last name

MSWindows Microsoft Windows
Your source for all things Windows on twitter.
37,691 followers from Redmond · updated about 2 hours ago
Follow

Microsoft_Xbox Microsoft Xbox 360
Launch Nov. 22, 2005 (US & Canada). CPU - 3.2 GHz PowerPC Tri-Core Xenon.
30,460 followers · from Worldwide · updated about 6 hours ago
Follow

Microsoft
The official Twitter account for Microsoft Corporate Communications.
21,798 followers · from Redmond, WA · updated about 2 hours ago
Follow

Office_Live Microsoft OfficeLive
Tweets from the team at Microsoft Office Live
7,974 followers · from Redmond, WA · updated about 1 hour ago
Follow

MicrosoftPress Microsoft Press
Publisher of books & ebooks about Microsoft products & technologies (& programming best practices). 2009 is our 25th anniversary!
5,343 followers · from Seattle, enjoying sun · updated about 5 hours ago
Follow

EverythingMS Everything Microsoft
Going Beyond Windows, Aggregating Everything Microsoft
5,013 followers · from C:\Redmond · updated about 2 hours ago
Follow

MSFTResearch Microsoft Research
Microsoft Research is dedicated to conducting both basic and applied research in computer science and software engineering.
4,969 followers · from Global · updated 6:26 PM Sep 2nd
Follow

SharePoint Microsoft SharePoint
The SharePoint Product Group
4,909 followers · from Redmond, WA · updated 7:03 PM Sep 2nd
Follow

Microsoft_EDU
Discovering, highlighting and enabling innovation and achievement among students, teachers and schools
4,588 followers · updated about 4 hours ago
Follow

ch9 Microsoft Channel 9
listen to the cockpit, help us fly the plane
4,425 followers · from Redmond, WA · updated about 3 hours ago
Follow

ch10 Microsoft Channel 10
Channel 10 is Microsoft's online community for the technology enthusiast
3,512 followers · from Redmond, WA · updated 6:14 PM Dec 17th, 2007
Follow

MSLearning Microsoft Learning
We will help you make the most out of your investment in Microsoft technology. Follow us to know what is new w/ Microsoft training & cerfication. :)
3,312 followers · from Bellevue, Washington · updated about 8 hours ago
Follow

PDC09 Microsoft PDC
The definitive Microsoft event for software developers and architects: Nov 17-19, 2009 at Los Angeles Convention Center; pre-conference Nov 16
3,249 followers · from Redmond, WA · updated about 4 hours ago
Follow

bizspark Microsoft BizSpark
The Microsoft BizSpark Program for Software Startups - Software, Support, Visibility for software startups around the world
3,155 followers · from Redmond, Washington, USA · updated about 6 hours ago
Follow

MSMyPhone Microsoft My Phone
The official microblog from the Microsoft My Phone Team
3,125 followers · from Seattle, WA · updated 7:05 PM May 26th
Follow

MSAdvertising Microsoft Ad Team
Microsoft Advertising - Tweeting News and Insight From The Cutting Edge Of Online Marketing
3,142 followers · from Global · updated about 9 hours ago
Follow

microsofthohm Microsoft Hohm
Microsoft Hohm is a free online beta application that helps you save energy and money
2,882 followers · from US · updated 1:08 PM Sep 2nd
Follow

Microsoft_Photo Microsoft Photo Team
Microsoft Photo Community team. We support Expression Media 2 (formerly iView Media Pro), the Icons of Imaging, and the Microsoft Photo website.
2,731 followers · from Redmond, WA · updated 12:15 PM Sep 1st
Follow

msPartner Microsoft Partner
Microsoft Partner Network Digital Marketing Team
2,675 followers · from Redmond, WA · updated about 3 hours ago
Follow

Next »

Figure 10.5 One page of Microsoft's numerous handles listed by product line and usage

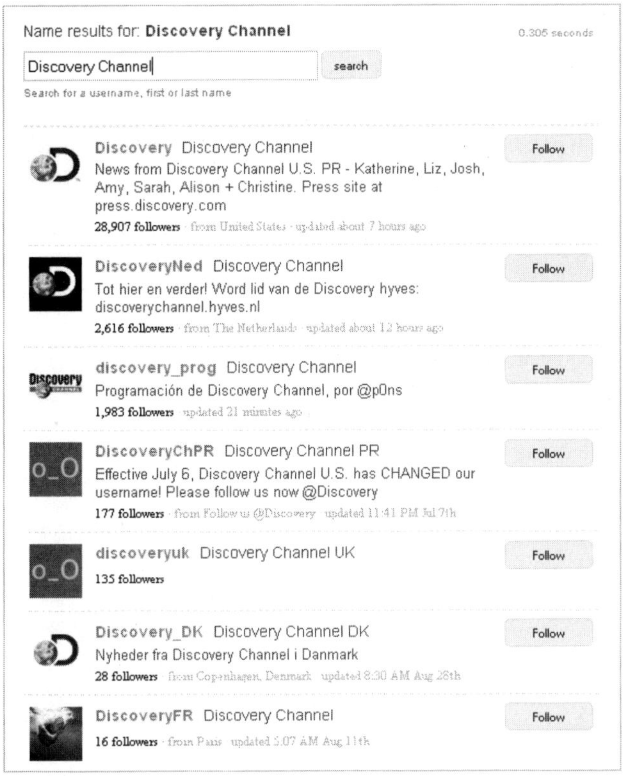

Name results for: **Discovery Channel** 0.305 seconds

Discovery Channel search

Search for a username, first or last name

Discovery Discovery Channel Follow
News from Discovery Channel U.S. PR - Katherine, Liz, Josh, Amy, Sarah, Alison + Christine. Press site at press.discovery.com
28,907 followers · from United States · updated about 7 hours ago

DiscoveryNed Discovery Channel Follow
Tot hier en verder! Word lid van de Discovery hyves: discoverychannel.hyves.nl
2,616 followers · from The Netherlands · updated about 12 hours ago

discovery_prog Discovery Channel Follow
Programación de Discovery Channel, por @p0ns
1,983 followers · updated 21 minutes ago

DiscoveryChPR Discovery Channel PR Follow
Effective July 6, Discovery Channel U.S. has CHANGED our username! Please follow us now @Discovery
177 followers · from Follow us @Discovery · updated 11:41 PM Jul 7th

discoveryuk Discovery Channel UK Follow
135 followers

Discovery_DK Discovery Channel DK Follow
Nyheder fra Discovery Channel i Danmark
28 followers · from Copenhagen, Denmark · updated 8:30 AM Aug 28th

DiscoveryFR Discovery Channel Follow
16 followers · from Paris · updated 5:07 AM Aug 11th

Figure 10.6 Discovery Channel's multiple handles by country

Tuesday: Set Up Your Brand's Profile

People tend to be wary of accounts with incomplete profiles. It's as though the account has something to hide. If you're a brand, users might suspect you're not really that brand if your profile hasn't been filled out completely.

Referring back to Chapter 4, you learned how to complete your account in Week 1. You'll recall that a key step was to fill out your Twitter profile. Let's review the elements of a complete profile:

- Username
- Location
- More information URL
- One-line bio
- Picture
- Design

Username

You can specify something different for your username than what you registered as your handle. Unless your Twitter name specifically represents a program or *brand positioning* you want to take, you may want to consider using your "real" brand name as your username to improve your chances of being found through searches (Figure 10.7).

Figure 10.7 Despite the username `@cherrygarcia`, Ben & Jerry's Ice Cream uses its brand name in the Name field of its profile.

Location

As to completing your location, you can be factual, listing the location of your corporate headquarters, for example. Or you can be playful, as in the case of Philadelphia Cream Cheese, where Kraft Foods says it's located in Philadelphia, despite the fact that it's manufactured at its corporate location in Northfield, Illinois (see Figure 10.8). If you plan to use Twitter for job recruitment, you probably want to list your actual location, as the tools that help you locate someone geographically do so by indexing the Location field of your profile.

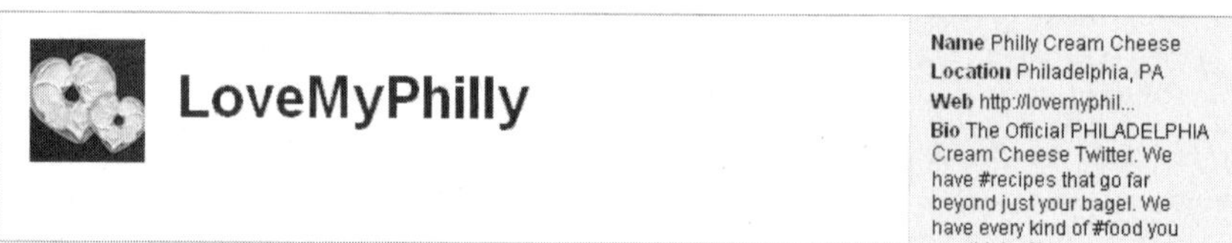

Figure 10.8 Philadelphia Cream Cheese lists its location as Philadelphia, even though the product is not made there.

More Info URL

On your publicly accessible profile page, your "More Info URL" appears as "Web." Therefore most brands merely link to their website's primary domain. Think about this strategically, however. Where do you feel it would most benefit your brand to send people? Do you have a specific message you want to get across where your home page just won't do? Do you have a blog rich with content that might best serve this purpose? Or do you want to take people to a page that aggregates all your social media efforts so users know where to find you throughout the Social Web (Figure 10.9)?

Figure 10.9 L.L. Bean's Twitter profile directs users to its Facebook page.

If you like the idea of directing the user elsewhere, does a web page need to be custom-created and hosted live before you can complete this portion of your profile? You can always insert your primary domain and update the field once the page is live. Just try to think through what you're listing and why. This will help you work Twitter more strategically.

One-Line Bio

Writing this one-line biography (listed as "Bio" on your public profile page) might be harder than crafting your company's elevator pitch because you only have 160 characters with which to work. (Twitter graciously gives us 20 more characters than a tweet.) What do you say about your brand? What do you want people to know?

We've discussed making your brand seem more personal on Twitter. Adding personal flare to your bio is one way to do so (Figure 10.10).

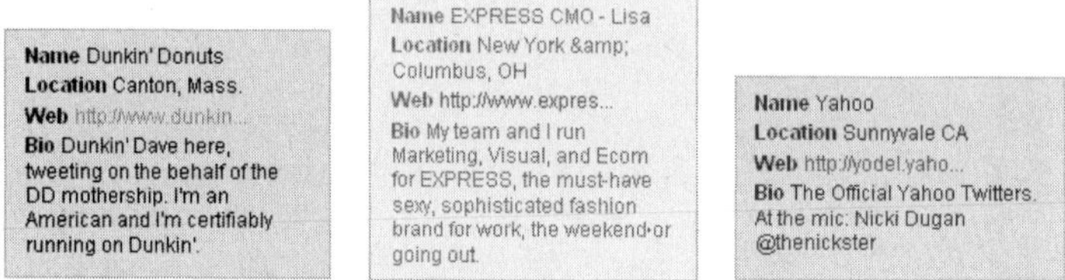

Name Dunkin' Donuts
Location Canton, Mass.
Web http://www.dunkin...
Bio Dunkin' Dave here, tweeting on the behalf of the DD mothership. I'm an American and I'm certifiably running on Dunkin'.
Name EXPRESS CMO - Lisa
Location New York & Columbus, OH
Web http://www.expres...
Bio My team and I run Marketing, Visual, and Ecom for EXPRESS, the must-have sexy, sophisticated fashion brand for work, the weekend or going out.
Name Yahoo
Location Sunnyvale CA
Web http://yodel.yaho...
Bio The Official Yahoo Twitters. At the mic: Nicki Dugan @thenickster

Figure 10.10 Some brand bios with personal flare

Other companies take a more serious approach, emphasizing their "officialness" and reiterating the commonly delivered brand message (Figure 10.11).

Name KFC Colonel
Location Louisville, KY, USA
Web http://www.kfc.com
Bio Official Twitter page of KFC Corp., the world's largest chicken restaurant chain
Name ProFlowers
Location San Diego, CA
Web http://www.proflo...
Bio ProFlowers connects consumers with the highest quality, freshest flowers available. Experience our 7-day freshness guarantee for yourself.
Name AnimalPlanet
Location Silver Spring, MD
Web http://www.animal...
Bio Updates on all things Animal Planet...and then some.

Figure 10.11 Some examples of unembellished brand bios

Finally, we have the companies that have neglected their poor bios altogether (Figure 10.12). It certainly doesn't make the brand feel warm and welcoming to users, and it doesn't help the brand to be found easily. Brand profiles without bios look pretty pitiful.

Figure 10.12 Brands with no bios look sorely neglected and don't maximize the opportunity to attract followers.

Picture

In the space for a picture, some brands display their logo. When an individual tweets on behalf of the brand, it's sensible to display that individual's photo. Does it matter what you choose? It's helpful to have the brand logo somewhere on the page, although it can also appear in the background, which we'll discuss next. Ask yourself this: is having an image of some sort going to enhance the user's understanding of my brand and help to build brand awareness and recognition, or should I place a friendly face with a name? Whatever your answer, put something up. It's inexcusable to leave the default Twitter avatar as your photo (Figure 10.13).

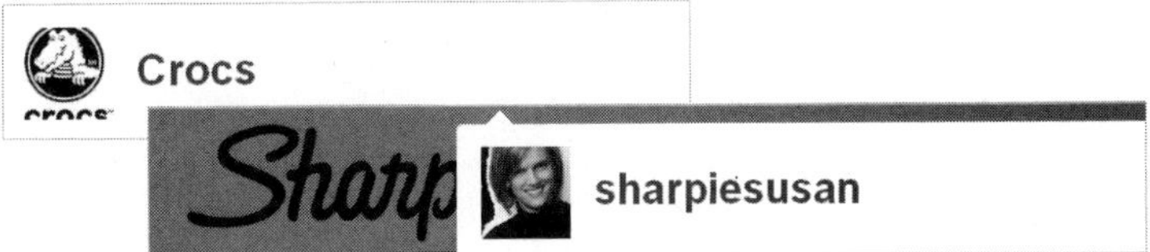

Figure 10.13 The decision to use a logo or a photo should be representative of your overall Twitter brand strategy.

Design

The design is the background image. A lot can be accomplished with a well-crafted background image. More built-out, detailed background images were first utilized by individual Twitter users, such as one early adopter, Rick Mahn (`@rickmahn`), the social media strategist for Land O'Lakes. The enhanced background image gives you a lot more room for expression, brand-building, communication, and visual enhancement. Although links and email addresses listed in a background image are not clickable, the user can type them into their browser and find additional information about your brand or a means to reach you. (There is a third-party plug-in that enables this, but unless both the Twitter account and the profile visitor use this tool, it doesn't work.)

If you plan on enhancing your Twitter background, be aware of screen resolution standards. Many designs have been created for wide screens, though not all users have access to these. If your design doesn't accommodate both standard and wide screens, some users will not be able to see all the information you've worked so hard to present.

Creatively, there is no right or wrong way of designing your Twitter background. Just be creative. Just as you would spend time and energy in choosing a logo and developing product packaging or your brand image, you should spend time developing your Twitter background. It certainly will play a role in forming impressions of your brand.

See Figure 10.14, Figure 10.15, Figure 10.16, and Figure 10.17 for some examples of creative Twitter backgrounds.

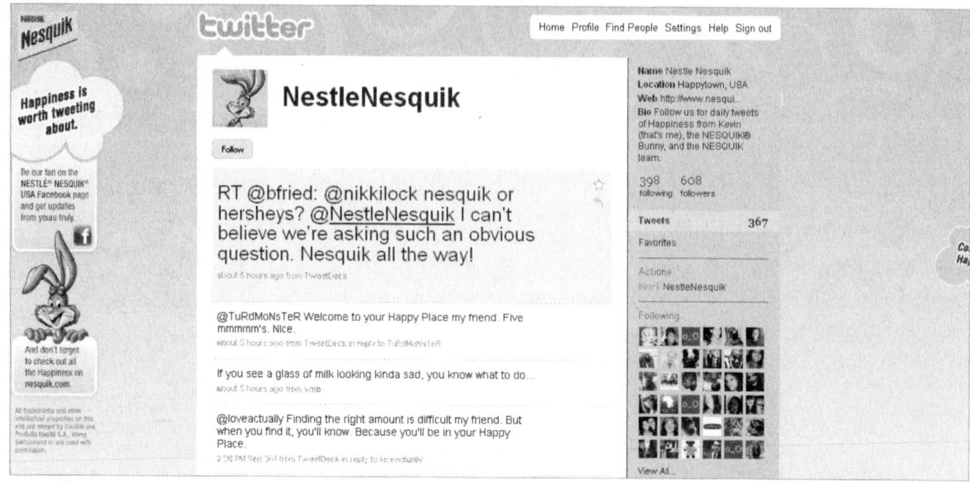

Figure 10.14 Nestlé Nesquik's vibrant, playful background complements their brand.

Figure 10.15 Fast food franchise Church's Chicken makes its background all about people.

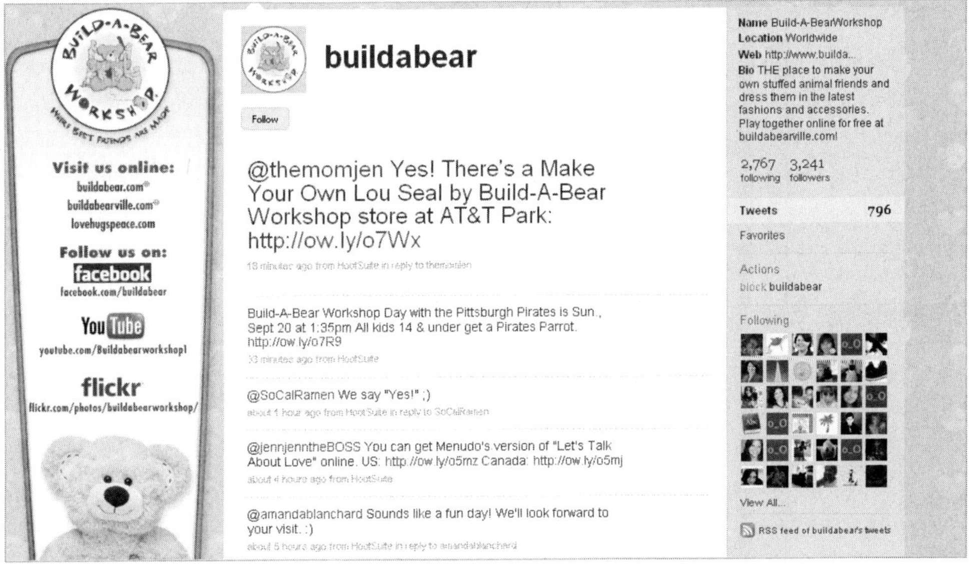

Figure 10.16 Build-A-Bear's background provides links to its other sites and social presence on the Web.

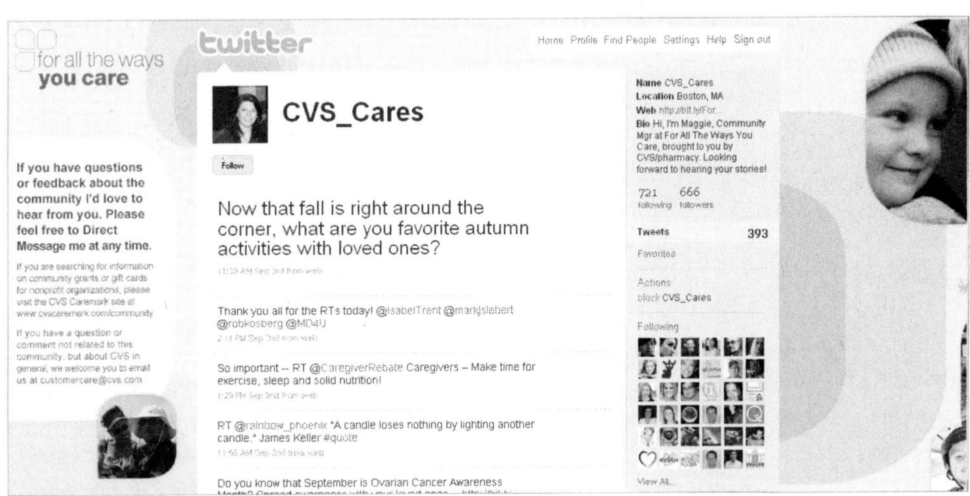

Figure 10.17 CVS Pharmacy presents its caring side in its background.

Tuesday's One-Hour Exercise: Set Up Your Branded Profile

Based on what you've read today, you may have pause for thought. Yes, you can set up your profile pretty quickly, but do you need to get your design team involved for the background and your copywriters for the 160-character bio? If you need to make these kinds of allowances, spend this one-hour time thinking, planning, and coordinating instead of necessarily doing. On the other hand, if you're ready to go, use this hour to complete all the elements of your profile.

Wednesday: Your First Brand Tweets

Throughout this book, we've discussed such matters as whether or not brands belong on Twitter, reserving your personal, brand, and company names and, if you are going to tweet, in what kind of voice are you going to do so and how to manage it all.

With social media in general, and Twitter in particular, how we connect and engage with our customers is changing...and changing rapidly. The static "canned" public relations messages and advertisements that repeat your brand's position over and over again will soon be gone. This kind of one-way, in-your-face communication is dying. In fact, a mid-2009 poll conducted by LinkedIn and Harris Interactive proved just how skewed advertisers' perceptions were from consumers' (Figure 10.18). If you insist on using your Twitter brand in a way that's out of touch with your audience, you'll lose customers and create negative word-of-mouth.

EFFECTIVENESS OF ADVERTISING TYPES
"How effective do you think each of these characteristics of advertising are?"
Percent Saying "Very Effective"
Base: Advertisers and U.S. adults

	Advertisers	Consumers
	%	%
Ads that make me stop and think	53	30
Ads that give me new information	51	29
Ads that are entertaining	41	34
Ads that are informative	37	30
Ads that are funny	32	33
Ads that have a product demonstration	27	20
Ads that are integrated into the feel of the program (i.e. not a product integration into a program, but an ad that has the same tone as the program it's based in)	26	7
Ads that show before/after	24	13
Ads that reinforce a message I already know	21	10
Ads that don't take themselves seriously	14	11
Ads about a serious topic that may leave me feeling slightly guilty	5	6
Ads that are scary	3	3

Figure 10.18 A LinkedIn/Harris Interactive poll showed a disparate opinion of ad effectiveness between advertisers and consumers.

So how do you begin tweeting? First, here are a few things to consider:

- People relate to people.
- Twitter is a place for conversations of all kinds—the good, the bad, and the ugly.
- Twitter builds community, connects people, and fosters relationships. This requires authenticity, which is hard to do if you're not out there being "you." Just what "you" is when you're a brand might require a little soul-searching. That's OK. For social media's sake, it's a good exercise to undertake.

Going back to our bar analogy, you're meeting people at the Twitter bar every day, networking. What would you say to someone the first time you meet them? What would you say to someone at the bar the *fourth* time you see them there? How do you connect with people in person and what kinds of things do you talk about? Do you do all the talking or do you listen too? Do you ask questions so you can learn about the other person? These rules apply on Twitter, as well. If you keep this mindset, you won't be intimidated by what you say or how you engage with others out there.

Refer back to Wednesday in Chapter 5, "Week 2: Find and Attract Followers," for a moment. Review the "Principles of Engagement" section. As advised there, before making your first brand tweets, why don't you start out by listening and giving? Do some Twitter Searches for your company name, your brand names, your own name, and industry terms. Read what people are saying about any of the topics in real time. What's the nature and tone of these tweets? How do you think you can join the current conversation? This little exercise and reflection will help you determine what you do and say first.

Starting out, it's perfectly acceptable for your very first brand tweet to be something like, "Greetings, Twitterverse! We're new here and want to join the conversation. Looking forward to hearing from you." Beyond this kind of announcement tweet, however, you should change gears. Consider this formula for brand newcomers: give about 60 percent and take about 40 percent of your Twitter time. This means that for every 10 tweets you make, six of them should be responses to people who have tweeted you, links to industry information, interesting articles and stats, and retweets of others. The other four tweets can be links to your company's offers, blog posts, news, or other content. Your initial activity will demonstrate to the Twitterverse both how well you "get" the Twitter community and what you're going to give back to it. If you plan to abide by this 60/40 rule, start by giving, not taking.

For today, let's divide your tweets into three parts:

- Retweets
- Provide information, answer questions, join the conversation
- Company/brand information

Retweets

When you determined who you were going to follow during week two, you probably soon stumbled upon a list of Twitter celebrities to follow. These Twitter celebrities aren't necessarily real-life well-known figures, but rather people high up in industry organizations, reporters whose work you admire, social media gurus, or even people in your community. As you begin to follow these people, inevitably they'll be the first people you (or your brand) will start retweeting.

The most basic form of a retweet, as we covered earlier in this book, is to insert an RT in front of someone else's tweet and send it (Figure 10.19). Commonly, and if there's room to do so, however, when users retweet they add their two cents so that their followers understand why they should read the tweet. These retweet comments typically appear before the RT, if the RT is used at all (as we discussed, some people do not abide by this etiquette). Comments can also appear at the end in brackets (`[my comments]`) or even with a typed arrow (<–).

RT @rinkrat: #RedWings Red Wings bloggers' roundtable rolls along: After Winging it in Motown and Snapshots started http://ow.ly/nYjQ

2:14 PM Sep 3rd from HootSuite

Figure 10.19 The most basic form of retweeting

Reminder Twitter is developing a retweet function for web users of Twitter.com. When this functionality is launched, new users, or users who find this form of retweeting easier to perform, will probably default to it. More experienced users will probably want to continue to modify their retweets manually to be more self-expressive, and therefore will rely on third-party Twitter clients if Twitter's retweet function prohibits any alteration.

Provide Information/Answer Questions/Join the Conversation

You've already searched on Twitter for real-time conversations about the industry, your company, or your brand. Now it's time to begin engaging those people. Did someone have a question where you have expertise, even if this expertise is not specifically related to your brand (Figure 10.20)? If so, answer them. Did someone have something to say about your industry, company, or brand where you can add value? If so, make a comment. Did you find yourself fascinated by someone's tweet? If so, tell them. During this phase, however, *do not* tweet articles that are about you, your company, or your brands. Do not be self-serving. You're new to Twitter, so you need to show the Twitterverse that you give more than you take and that you're interested in providing them real value.

@visionspeaks Have you read "10 Best Used Cars for Under $5k" at http://bit.ly/fot1? Need help deciding further?

1:07 PM Sep 2nd from web in reply to visionspeaks

edmunds
Edmunds.com

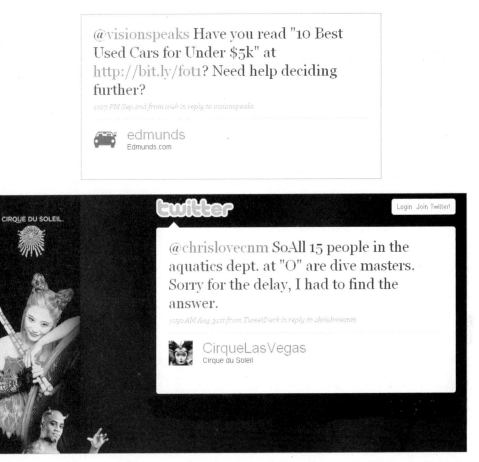

Figure 10.20 If you can't answer someone's question directly, finding and sharing information to help them will help develop brand loyalty and grateful patrons.

Tweet Company/Brand Information

Once you've tweeted for others' benefit, you are entitled to some tweeting of your own. Perhaps this first kind of tweet tells users why you're on Twitter. You can even pose this in the form of a question, which makes it more subtle and more like you're again looking to give back: "We want to help our customers with another means for customer service. Do you have a problem we can solve? Tweet us!" You can also put out a question to the Twitterverse seeking advice. This will make your brand seem more human and humble, and you'll find the Twitter community remarkably helpful, particularly when it comes to Twitter-related questions: "We're trying to decide which third-party Twitter client our Twitter team should be using. Any preferences? Why?"

Another early and obvious brand tweet is to introduce the person behind the brand. Reveal the soul of the Twitter handle and be authentic. What do you want people to know about this person? Begin to build your Twitter personality.

Are you engaged in other social networking sites? Why not tweet a link to your Facebook fan page or your channel on YouTube so people can see and know more about you as a social brand? And yes, you can link to other content of your own now too (Figure 10.21).

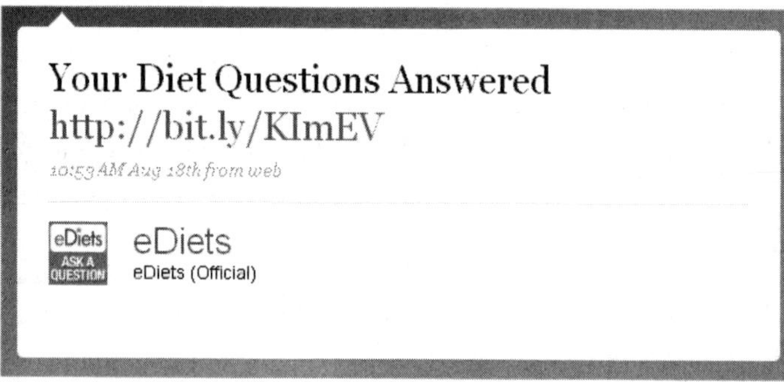

Your Diet Questions Answered
http://bit.ly/KImEV
10:53 AM Aug 18th from web
eDiets
ASK A QUESTION
eDiets
eDiets (Official)

Figure 10.21 Once you help others, it's OK to tweet about yourself.

Remember this important guiding principle rule: *If a Twitter user sends you a message, you must reply.* Even if what they have to say is not something to which you'd like to draw attention, it's important that you demonstrate your brand is listening *and* responding. You can also use the reply as an opportunity to correct a situation or do a little damage control. Without it, users will tweet negatively about your brand, and the only thing that will really be damaged by their tweet is your brand.

Wednesday's One-Hour Exercise: Brand Tweeting

Using the 60/40 rule for this hour, and spend 40 minutes giving (tweeting about or for others) and only 20 minutes taking (tweeting about your brand). Also make sure that your content ratio is equally aligned such that the number of your tweets still skews more heavily toward the giving than taking kind.

- Perform Twitter Searches related to company name, your brand names, your own name, and industry terms. Listen to what people are saying and determine the tone.
- Identify up to three people whose tweets are retweet-worthy and retweet them.
- Through any means (Twitter Search, Google Search, your email newsletters, RSS feeds, blog posts, webinars, events, trade associations, or what have you), find three articles that are pertinent to your brand, your company, or your industry. Tweet them.
- Find up to three people tweeting questions you can answer. Answer them.

Are you at the 40-minute mark yet? If not, keep at the above ideas until you are. Then, with 20 minutes remaining, and if you have built up enough tweets for others' benefit, tweet about your brand.

Thursday: Engage Your Brand's Followers

For today's topic we'll assume you have already begun to attract followers. In reality, this might take a while, but in the meantime you need to learn some valuable practices.

Who Follows a Brand?

Let's be clear: Your followers aren't necessarily your devotees. They may be, but your followers are human beings who have brains and who may choose to follow you for any number of reasons, including the following:

- They like your brand and want to show you their support (Figure 10.22).

Figure 10.22 Fans of M&M's tweet Ms. Green, who in turn thanks her fans. Elsewhere on her profile, she offers chances for free chocolate. What M&M's lover would turn that down?

- They like being able to reach someone at the company in a real one-to-one kind of way.
- They're looking for offers or deals.
- They want customer service (Figure 10.23).

@meducate We were experiencing technical difficulties on the site previously. It should be working properly now. Can you try again?
11:25 AM Aug 31st from twhirl in reply to meducate
BritishAirways
British Airways N.A.

Figure 10.23 British Airways provides a customer with a hopeful problem resolution.

- You provide information of value to them.
- They like how you're using Twitter and want to learn from you.
- Following you makes them feel like smarter, savvier, or more well-informed individuals.
- They like to have conversations, and your profile indicates that you do too (Figure 10.24).

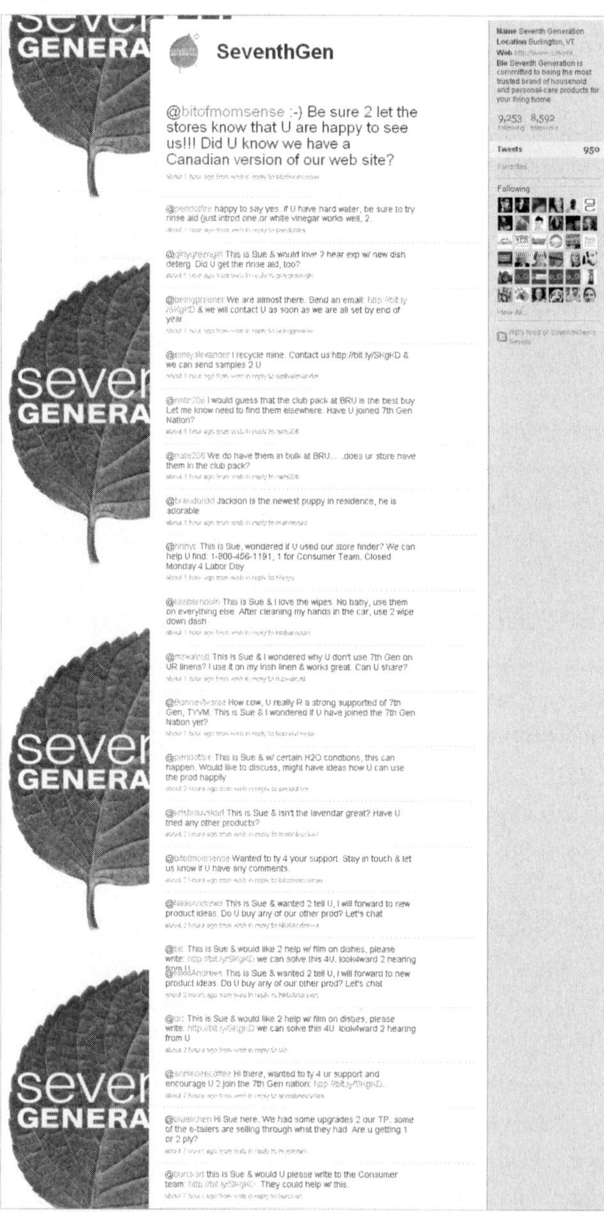

Figure 10.24 Seventh Generation's profile shows it's very chatty with its followers.

Remember not to use auto-DM, particularly if you're a brand. For users with negative attitudes about auto-DM, receiving one from you starts the relationship off on a bad note, and it fools no one into thinking you're treating them personally.

There is one more thing to consider about your followers before you begin engaging. Your followers are not just people you're preaching to; you can't expect them to think you're great every day, all day (as nice as that would be). These people are potential advocates, brand stewards, promoters, and advisers. They can refer business to you without ever having worked with you. They can deliver your messages for you without being asked. These same people, though, can be detractors and saboteurs, which is why it's so important to develop a community and be a real person. You'll always have critics, but your Twitter community can come to your defense if you truly are good to (and for) the community. Think about how you manage your followers so they continue to endorse you, vouch for you, and share you with everyone in their communities. They will influence transactions offline, so never ignore them. Always respond. Always. If you don't, you might as well get off Twitter. Seriously. An unresponsive brand on Twitter is a recipe for failure.

Get Engaged

Reviewing the previous list of reasons why people follow a brand can help you develop ideas for things to tweet about, but your Twitter objectives and strategy should also steer this process. For example, if your Twitter strategy doesn't revolve around providing customer service, you probably don't want to make this the crux of your tweet content. Let's review some basic rules of thumb:

First things first: be human. If your brand is contacted by a human being through any other communications channel, do you have only canned, robotic responses to their questions or concerns? Of course you don't. The things you are asked about through these other channels will likely be the same things that come across on Twitter. Let your voice come through.

Talk about what you're doing during the day. Talk about things that could be of real interest to your followers, not what you had for lunch. What is it like to work for your company? What do you do at work that is unique to your corporate environment? Is there anything newsworthy in your town or surrounding area? What do you do for fun? Did you see any great movies this weekend? These kinds of tweets certainly give your followers a deeper understanding of you as a human being, but remember that what you tweet must add value to your followers, so always keep a professional perspective.

Follow all real people back. If you're tweeting as a brand, you really must follow all of your followers back. It's how you show your awareness of your followers and your gratitude for their involvement with you. It also allows both of you to DM one another, which is appropriate or even necessary in certain instances. This practice does not have to be abided by individual users, but for brands looking to build a convincing Twitter presence, it's a smart idea.

Of course, you should not feel obliged to follow spammers or bots. It's pretty easy to determine spammers, and you should not only *not* follow them; you should block them so they're eventually taken off Twitter.

Join the conversation. Join a conversation, but maintain your professional perspective, which means don't discuss politics, sex, or religion. You can, however, support social causes or commend companies or people that are doing the right thing. Keep your conversations at a level that won't hurt the company, your brands, or your personal brand. If you're unclear about the boundaries, ask your superiors for some kind of guidelines or policy manual to follow.

Tweet win-wins. Earlier we described the 60/40 rule: 60 percent of the time you should tweet to serve others with industry-specific links, newsworthy items, pop culture trivia, answers to questions, and the like. The other 40 percent of the time, your tweets can be more self-serving, such as links to your white papers, blog, webinars, or podcasts, your Facebook fan page, or articles where you've been quoted. Just make sure that your 40 percent adds value for your followers instead of being a blatant advertisement.

The best kinds of "self-serving" tweets, though, are those that are win-wins. They're tweets that help promote your brand while at the same time engage or give something to the user—for example, polls, surveys, information that positions you as a go-to resource in your industry (Figure 10.25), Twitter-only coupons, contests (Figure 10.26) or offers (Figure 10.27), or support for your local community (Figure 10.28), just to name a few.

Figure 10.25 Wegmans, a highly respected supermarket chain, demonstrates the leadership that keeps it on top.

Congratulations to @crazeypoet, the winner of our Friday trivia! Please DM us with your mailing address!

5:18 PM Aug 31st from web

Figure 10.26 Rita's Italian Ice hosts a Friday trivia contest.

A treat for those who tweet: Get 15% off men's & women's styles. Enter TWITTER at checkout, today only, at gap.com. http://bit.ly/x4Vxr

8:45 AM Aug 24th from HootSuite

Figure 10.27 GAP's one-day Twitter-only special

@hungerfighter @FtMyersSoupKtch @mcreative Thanks for what you do to fight hunger & create awareness in SW FL. #followfriday

3:03 PM Aug 28th from Seesmic in reply to hungerfighter

Figure 10.28 Tyson Foods shows its support of the local nonprofits working for the cause of hunger.

Your Twitter Commitment

Now that you've begun engaging on Twitter, keep up your momentum. One of the worst things you can do on Twitter is set up an account, tweet a few times, and then let it sit dormant. (Many of the brands out there have had no tweets in more than a year.) At the very least, commit to tweeting *at least three times every day*: 15 minutes in the morning, 15 minutes at noon, and 15 minutes at the end of the day. In our hour-a-day format, your remaining 15 minutes should be spent screening and following back new followers, finding new followers, or developing new content to tweet. If you can't make this minimum commitment (there are those who believe brands should be tweeting up to eight times per day), don't use Twitter.

This commitment to Twitter will also help establish your Twitter presence, which in turn makes it more reasonable to start promoting to the world that you're on Twitter. You wouldn't expect a store to advertise its grand opening if it didn't have any product on the shelves, would you?

Once you get the hang of your tweeting pattern, you'll really begin to find value in third-party tools that assist you in tweeting, scheduling tweets, and in tracking and measuring tweets (more on this last part next week). Test out a variety of tools to see which ones work best for your brand and/or those involved in tweeting for your brand.

Don't forget your commitment to your followers and those who `@message` you: Always respond back. Always. If you can't keep this commitment, don't use Twitter.

Friday: Summarize Best Practices

We've gone over a lot of information so far on how you can prepare your brand for Twitter and use it as a component of your marketing strategy, so let's sum it all up for you into one central, multipart list.

Get Your Brand Started on Twitter

- Pick a Twitter name that matches your company name or, alternatively, a name that includes your company name, such as `@companyteam`.
- Fill out your profile completely, including a URL. People tend to not want to tweet users with an incomplete profile, including a brand.
- Create a customized Twitter background that matches your corporate brand as much as possible, in which you can provide additional information about your company and its products.
- Include in your bio and/or custom background the names (or *`@usernames`*) of the people tweeting from your company account. It's also a good idea to include additional contact info, such as email addresses.

Get Your Message Out

- Try to tweet between three to eight times per day, and space the tweets throughout the day if possible.
- If you like a particular message, retweet it.
- No more than 40 percent of your tweets should be related to your company or include a marketing or advertising message; the rest of your tweets should be about industry- or focus-related topics that provide value to your followers or show a human side of your company. If you use Twitter exclusively for self promotion, people will stop paying attention to you.
- Most of the tweets you initiate should contain a link to a website, blog post, article, or other noteworthy content not provided by your brand. These types of tweets will establish your Twitter account as being a source of great content and worthy of being followed back.
- Make sure your tweets provide some real value.
- Build up a level of tweets so other users will see you as credible and relevant. The minimum number of tweets that you should accumulate before you start promoting your account is somewhere in the 50 to 100 range.
- Use tracking tools to schedule your tweets and to track your tweet click-throughs.

Follow People

- Use Twitter Search and various other Twitter directories to locate potential users to follow based on keywords —particularly if they mention your company or brand in their tweets or their bios.
- `@reply` to thank people or to just reach out to them.
- Retweet posts that you think are worthy. Generally, the person who posted the original tweet will notice, which improves your chances of adding a new follower.
- Follow back anyone who follows your brand (unless they're a spammer), so they can engage with you directly.
- Always respond to questions or comments addressed to you.

Behavior/Attitude

- Be honest.
- Be responsive and human.
- Be nice.
- Be transparent, authentic, and believable.

Twitter Dos

- Start with a plan, not tactics.
- Listen and observe before engaging; be prepared to address concerns, offer customer service, or thank people for praise.
- Read your community's tweets and glean whatever you can from what they're saying; determine if or how you could use this in your own Twitter efforts.
- Monitor your competitors' Twitter efforts, as well as those of other leaders of industry.
- Understand the real-time nature of Twitter.
- Use a casual, friendly, conversational tone in your messages.
- Give to get.
- Help the community. Answer questions, share your expertise, and be a resource.
- Make each tweet worth reading by *anyone* (remember to add context).
- Credit sources when retweeting or citing someone else's original content.
- Be transparent with intentions.
- Be creative, but not at the expense of clarity.
- Interact, don't just broadcast; welcome participation, feedback, and collaboration.
- Be in it for the long haul.
- Emphasize quality, not just quantity.
- Publicly reply to people you are following.
- Remember that your tweets (even your deleted ones) are being indexed and saved elsewhere online; everything is in the public domain.
- Find tweeps to champion your brand.
- When you offer deals via Twitter, use unique offers or codes so you can track your efforts.
- Tweet the same thing more than once over time, particularly if it's a special offer about which you want to spread the word. Just don't tweet about it over and over and close together in time.
- Commit resources and time to be successful.
- Understand that you do not control the message.
- Build your Twitter equity and credibility, and spread the word about your participation on Twitter once you have.

Twitter Don'ts

- Don't just strategize: execute!
- Don't underestimate your Twitter staffing roles or requirements.

- Don't auto-DM.
- Don't tweet just for the sake of tweeting without adding value.
- Don't tune out when people are tweeting you or about you.
- Don't go overboard with your tweet volume.
- Don't tweet in rapid succession, particularly about the exact same topic.
- Don't be fake, pushy, or overtly "salesy."
- Do not tweet insults about customers, coworkers, or competitors, or anything you would not want a customer, coworker, or competitor to read.
- Do not tweet confidential or nonpublic company information. If you have general counsel, listen to what they have to say about what you should or should not say on Twitter.

The Main Points

- Choose your Twitter name wisely. You want your name to be intuitive to users and you want to be found easily.
- Complete your entire Twitter profile. Failure to do so indicates to savvy users that you don't know what you're doing and must not be taking Twitter very seriously.
- Spend a lot of time listening and planning to give more than you take on Twitter. By so doing, you'll actually be the recipient of far more than you ever imagined.
- Commit to being engaged. A Twitter profile made up of only one-way, self-serving tweets attracts few and retains even fewer followers.
- Familiarize yourself with the common best practices...and then refine this list over time for yourself and your own brand.

Week 8: Monitor, Measure, and Valuate

Welcome to Week 8! By this point, you should be starting to get the hang of "this Twitter marketing stuff" for your company, which means you're at the last part of the equation: measuring the impact of what you're doing. We've discussed measuring previously. In Chapter 7, we reviewed monitoring tools and methods in detail and discussed how you can use them to measure the impact of your Twitter efforts. Then in Chapter 9 you developed and built your case for getting corporate buy-in to Twitter marketing by determining what Twitter objectives you want to measure and report. This week, we'll move the notion of tracking and measuring out of the realm of theory and into regular practice.

11

Chapter Contents

Monday: Review Your Twitter Stats

Let's start this week by pulling out your hour-a-day exercise from Tuesday of Chapter 9, "Week 6: Establish Goals and Get Corporate Buy-In." This was the exercise where you determined which metrics you want to track given your primary Twitter marketing objective. You also determined the frequency and timeframe within which you're going to measure these metrics, take a baseline measurement of these metrics, and create a reporting schedule. Now you're going to be held accountable to this schedule.

In these early weeks of using Twitter to market your business, you need to understand your Twitter activity and impact each week. Over time, you should be able to observe your trends and patterns.

Your Followers

Your followers count is one of the easiest things to measure on a week-over-week basis. Understanding who is following you and the changes in your follower count is one of the most important determinants of your success on Twitter. It's just as with email marketing—if you have five people on your mailing list, or if your open rate is low, you're not really reaching anyone. On Twitter you want to ensure that you have the right target market and the right volume of followers.

Although you want to stress quality over quantity, as a brand, ideally you still want to see an upward trend in the number of quality followers you attract week-over-week. Use a tool like TwitterCounter (`http://twittercounter.com`) to look at the pattern of your follower count week-over-week (Figure 11.1). Have your followers increased each week? Did any one week increase more than another? Is there anything to which you can attribute that? Maybe you reached out to a lot of new followers, ran a contest on Twitter, or posted something that was highly retweeted?

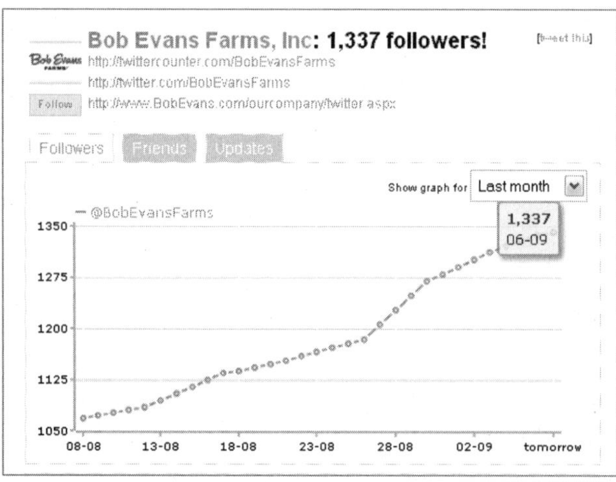

Figure 11.1 TwitterCounter shows Bob Evans Farms steadily increasing week-over-week.

In these early days, make a point of trying to scan your new followers from the past week. Are they the types of people you want to follow you? Do they seem to exhibit demographic or interest types appropriate for your products or services? If not, you may not be sufficiently tweeting *on message,* so you are attracting people inconsistent with your Twitter goals. Getting acquainted with your followers in this way can also lead to tweeting content ideas or even prompt you to `@message` a follower to get a dialog going. Understanding your followers in this way can enlighten you not only in the accomplishment of your Twitter marketing objectives, but for future Twitter marketing plans.

Your Following

Similar to the follower analysis, take a look at your following activity. You can use TwitterCounter to analyze this as well (Figure 11.2). If you're a brand and taking our advice to follow back everyone who follows you, a static count of your following would mean that you're also not adding new followers. What is the proportion of new people you chose to follow yourself compared to your new followers? Even though approximately one-third of Twitter users will auto-follow someone back, in the beginning you might expect this ratio to be negative (more on ratios in a minute), but as time goes on, you want to have at least an equal number of new followers and new followings.

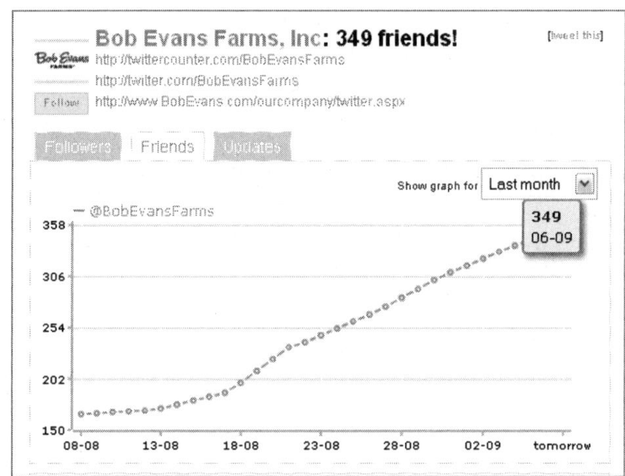

Figure 11.2 Change in Bob Evans Farms' following count over the same time period

Try not to get bogged down by the number of people you're following. You don't have to interact with everyone or read every tweet. Stay on message, and interact with those who are relevant. Use management tools to help you create groups to segment users you'd like to follow more closely. Unless you're `@messaged` directly, you can keep the tweets from those you follow in the background.

Ratios

Something to keep in mind as you're trying to attract followers is what your ratios tell users about your brand's motives and sincerity on Twitter. Normally, for example, users expect that someone with a lot of followers must also have a lot of tweets to attract those followers. It stands to reason, however, that the more well-known your brand, the more likely you won't need as balanced a ratio of tweets to followers because your brand name alone might attract followers (Figure 11.3).

Figure 11.3 Etsy!, a popular online marketplace for buying and selling handmade items, has a significant yet acceptable imbalance between its number of followers and its number of tweets.

Another ratio that Twitter users look at in order to determine if they will follow you back is your *following-to-followers ratio* (F/F ratio).
Even for a large brand, users quickly scan your following-to-followers counts to draw conclusions about you and your purpose for being on Twitter. Is there an imbalance between your following (lower) and followers (higher) count? If so, you're probably not going to be a highly engaged brand or one that's responsive to customer service needs. Do you have a high following count but not an equally high followers count? If you do, you're either just starting out, or you're doing a really poor job using Twitter and not attracting a follow back. At this point, users will check out your tweets to see what you're tweeting about and how engaged you are. People make accommodations for newcomers to Twitter who they judge as making a reasonable effort, but they have little tolerance for misusers or abusers of the ecosystem.

What are your ratios? Are they changing over time, and how? Is the change in a positive direction or one that is appropriate for your Twitter marketing objectives?

Tweet Breakdown

If you took our advice last week, after you set up your account, you submitted it to TwitTruth (`http://twittruth.com`) so that it could start tracking you. It's useful to watch this information change and trend over time. Has your TwitTruth status changed? Are you seeing more `@messages` directed toward you? Are you showing more engagement with users? In sum, are you demonstrating positive change in areas you'd like to see meet your objective (Figure 11.4)?

Can you set some goals for these numbers going forward and aim to get as close to them as possible each week? If you don't succeed, can you explain why? Use this effort as checks and balances to ensure that you are putting out to the Twitterverse the kind of personal and public views you want to deliver.

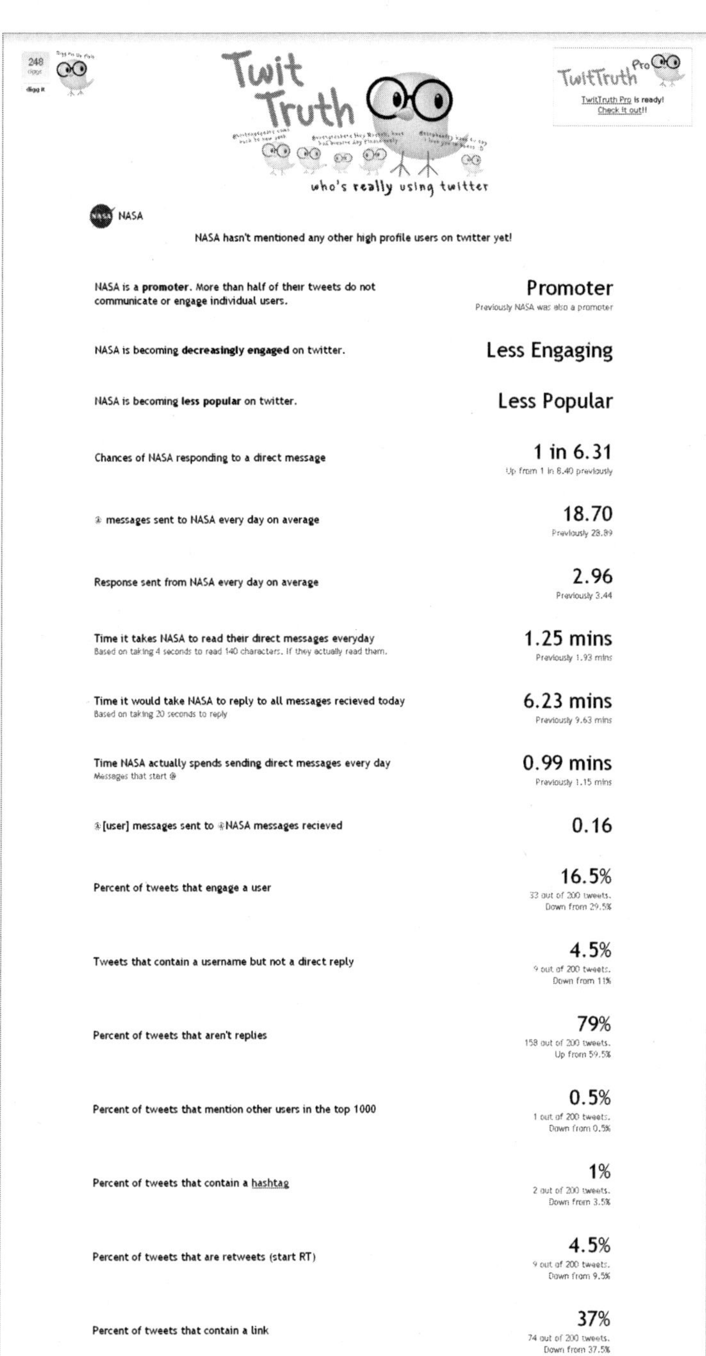

Figure 11.4 NASA's TwitTruth statistics show downward trending data.

Other Analysis

In addition to the previous analyses, there are other benchmarks for your Twitter activity. Klout (`http://www.klout.net`), which we discussed in Chapter 6, "Week 3: Use Twitter Search and Other Tools to Improve Your Experience," is a great application to examine your influence on Twitter. Look again at your data in Klout. Are you engaging people? Are you sharing information? Are the people you are "influenced by" people with whom you want to be interacting? Is your data aligned with your Twitter marketing goals?

We also looked at the *Re*Tweetability Index (`http://www.retweetability.com`). How do your numbers look? Do they align with your goals for how you want to be retweeted? What types of tweets are being retweeted? Are these the types of posts you want to be retweeted? Who's retweeting your posts? Are you following those people and engaging them (Figure 11.5)?

Take a look at TweetMeme (`http://www.tweetmeme.com`) and see if there are any topics that were retweeted a lot in the prior week, which you might have missed, that would be interesting for you or your business. Also check out Trending Topics. You can learn a lot from the topics that are trending. Why are they trending? Is it something you can learn about Twitter or social media in general? For example, when Twitter redesigned its homepage, that topic trended quickly because so many people were tweeting about it the same time. A topic in the act of trending may also be related to your business, industry, or the world.

Remember, it's easy to get caught up in tweeting and amassing followers, but you really need to step back and analyze your numbers, or months could go by before you realize you aren't accomplishing what you set out to achieve.

Monday's One-Hour Exercise: Draw Lessons from Your Analysis

Perform the previously discussed analyses. Write down any major data points you gleaned by doing so and at least three next steps based on what you learned. What will you do more of and what will you do differently? What key indicators do you want to look for the next time you do this analysis and in what direction do you want your measurements to change?

Tuesday: Analyze Your Website Traffic

Another way to understand the impact you are making on Twitter is to see how much traffic Twitter drives to your website and what that traffic does for your business. How many people are going to your site from Twitter? Are these new or returning visitors? What pages are they visiting? How long are they staying? Are they converting to customers by making a purchase, signing up for an event, or joining your email list? This section will help you analyze your site activity from Twitter and determine any changes or increased activity that will help you see a greater ROI.

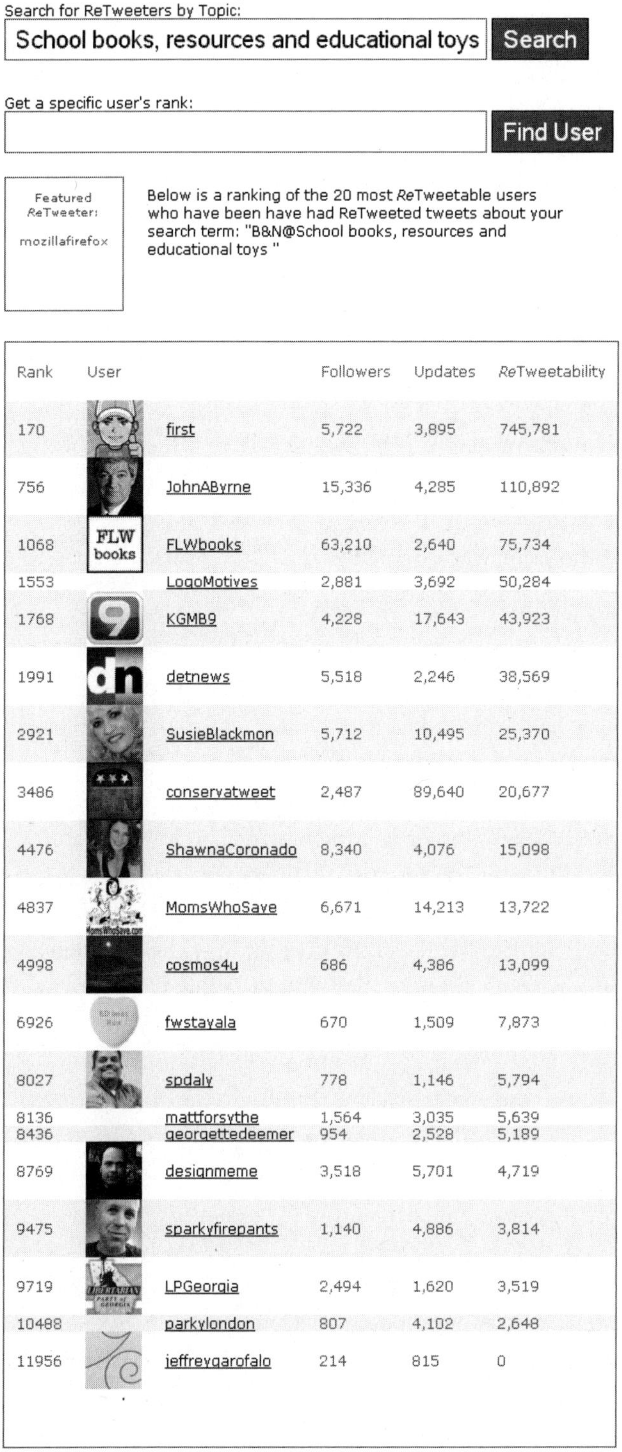

Search for ReTweeters by Topic:

School books, resources and educational toys | Search

Get a specific user's rank:

Find User

Featured *Re*Tweeter: mozillafirefox

Below is a ranking of the 20 most *Re*Tweetable users who have been have had ReTweeted tweets about your search term: "B&N@School books, resources and educational toys "

Rank	User	Followers	Updates	*Re*Tweetability
170	first	5,722	3,895	745,781
756	JohnAByrne	15,336	4,285	110,892
1068	FLWbooks	63,210	2,640	75,734
1553	LogoMotives	2,881	3,692	50,284
1768	KGMB9	4,228	17,643	43,923
1991	detnews	5,518	2,246	38,569
2921	SusieBlackmon	5,712	10,495	25,370
3486	conservatweet	2,487	89,640	20,677
4476	ShawnaCoronado	8,340	4,076	15,098
4837	MomsWhoSave	6,671	14,213	13,722
4998	cosmos4u	686	4,386	13,099
6926	fwstayala	670	1,509	7,873
8027	spdaly	778	1,146	5,794
8136	mattforsythe	1,564	3,035	5,639
8436	georgettedeemer	954	2,528	5,189
8769	designmeme	3,518	5,701	4,719
9475	sparkyfirepants	1,140	4,886	3,814
9719	LPGeorgia	2,494	1,620	3,519
10488	parkylondon	807	4,102	2,648
11956	jeffreygarofalo	214	815	0

Figure 11.5 Barnes & Noble's (@BNBuzz) top retweeters for "books, resources and educational toys" on the *Re*Tweetability Index

Tuesday's Prep Work

In Chapter 9, you took some baseline numbers for your website traffic from your web analytics program. Be sure you have all of these figures handy. What percentage of your traffic comes from Twitter?

For your overall site and for your Twitter visitors:

- What's your number of visits? (Visits represent the number of individual sessions initiated by all the visitors to your site.)
- Your average pages per visit?
- Average time on site?
- Percent of new visits?
- Bounce rate? (*Bounce rate* is the percentage of single-page visits or visits in which the person left your site from the entrance or landing page.)
- Number of pages visited?
- Number of blog comments? (If appropriate.)

Analyze Twitter-Generated Traffic

Let's start by looking at what percentage of your traffic Twitter refers to your site. If your website already has a lot of traffic, it may take quite a while to see any significant rate of traffic coming from Twitter. What did you establish as your goal? Can you begin to forecast how long it might take you to achieve your referral-rate goal? Also, what portion of these are new visits, thus representing non-cannibalized traffic? Did you establish a goal for newly referred traffic? If not, and this is important to you, do so now.

How many pages per visit are Twitter users visiting? Is that more or less than the rest of your visitors? How about time on site? Do they stay for a longer or shorter period of time? Do they bounce more or less?

How are these traffic measurements meeting your initial expectations? If they're off significantly, do you need to adjust your expectations, your Twitter efforts, or both? Spend some time thinking about what you'd like to see in terms of site traffic in the weeks and months to come.

Twitter-Generated Action

Now that you've looked at how much traffic is being driven to your site, it's important to understand what users are doing once they get there. Did Twitter visitors take any actions when on your site? Here are some actions you may want your Twitter-referred visitors to take:

- Register for an email newsletter

- Subscribe to an RSS feed
- Download an e-book
- Register for a webinar
- Purchase a product
- Seek assistance via Twitter versus calling your customer service department
- Comment on a blog post

Did your Twitter visitors take the desired action or do something different? If you're using Google Analytics, which allows you to set up conversion funnels, or some other kind of analytics program that allows you to do likewise, have you set these up to help you track more specifically if people convert as you'd like to see them do? Is the volume of Twitter visitor actions more or less generated by visitors to your site from other sources? How do they compare? How would you like them to compare?

Can you get even more specific and determine to what they are reacting? Did you promote something specific on Twitter that they took action on, or did they come to your site from Twitter, look around, and then take action on something?

If you are using a blog comment plug-in like DISQUS (Figure 11.6) or IntenseDebate, you know if people have come from Twitter. Are the Twitter users engaging with your site by commenting? Was that your goal?

Figure 11.6 DISQUS can identify Twitter as the source of a blog comment.

Obviously, we're posing a lot of questions that we can't answer specifically for you since each business's goals and websites are different, but they are questions you should be asking yourself and then tracking and measuring the data over time, just as you would with any other marketing initiative.

Tuesday's One-Hour Exercise: Analyze Traffic and Plan Your Next Steps

Conduct a thorough analysis of the traffic driven to your website from Twitter, including what actions visitors took on your site. Identify deficiencies and successes as they relate to your Twitter marketing objectives. Come up with next steps for your Twitter marketing efforts based on what you're seeing from your website traffic.

Wednesday: Analyze Actions

In addition to your website traffic, understanding what else your customers or potential customers are doing as a result of your presence on Twitter is important. They may be talking about your product or service or asking for help with it. They may not be talking about your product or service at all but are seeking a solution that what you market can solve, and you want to make them aware of your solution. The interaction you want your prospect or customer to have with you might be something intangible—you may just want them to interact with you and feel good about your brand, so that when the time comes, they choose your product or service over others. How you conduct your action analysis has to do both with the objectives you've set, as well as what you're seeing as a consequence of your Twitter activity.

Measure Actions against Objectives

In Chapter 9, when you developed your objectives and measurements for success, did those measurements include specific actions? It's likely that some did and some didn't, so let's take a moment to help identify actions associated with common objectives. Here again is a list of common Twitter marketing objectives:

- Improve customer service
- Increase customer retention
- Develop thought leadership
- Position for expertise when prospects are deciding between you and your competition
- Launch or build a brand
- Develop relationships with reporters and bloggers
- Prospect for warm leads
- Monitor competition
- Search engine optimization
- Social marketing optimization
- Stimulate viral activity and buzz
- Find donors
- Develop brand loyalty through engagement
- Improve brand sentiment or image

- Recruit talent
- Direct promotions
- Drive traffic to your website and/or blog
- Drive sales
- Affiliate marketing

What kind of outcomes, particularly measurable ones, would you like to see occur as a result of attaining your Twitter marketing objective? Table 11.1, which is by no means a complete list, offers some suggestions. Use your creativity to come up with other ideas for completed outcomes.

► **Table 11.1** Actions Associated with Objectives

Objective	Associated Twitter Outcomes
Improve customer service	Number of `@messages` sent to your company requiring customer service
	Number of `@messages` responded to
	Number of customer service tickets opened
	Number of customer service tickets closed with positive outcome
	Number of positive tweets received as a consequence of satisfied customer
	Number of subsequent orders by this customer post-complaint
Increase customer retention	Number of positive tweets about your brand
	Number of retweets about your brand
Develop thought leadership	Number of positive tweets related to brand impression
	Number of clicks on links you post
	Number of retweets of your posts
	Number of first-time visitors to your site
Position for expertise when prospects are deciding between you and your competition	Number of clicks on links you post
	Number of expertise-related questions you receive
	Number of `#FollowFriday` or Mr Tweet recommendations you receive
	Number of retweets of your posts
	Number of first-time visitors to your site
	Number of white paper downloads or trial offers
	Number of views of your YouTube video or SlideShare presentation
Launch or build a brand	Number of clicks on links you post
	Number of first-time visitors to your site
	Number of participants in brand launch activities
	Number of new email list subscribers
	Number of white paper downloads or trial offers
	Number of views of your YouTube video or SlideShare presentation

Continues

► **Table 11.1** ActionsAssociatedwithObjectives *(Continued)*

Objective	Associated Twitter Outcomes
Develop relationships with reporters and bloggers	Number of your followers who are reporters or bloggers
	Number of tweets from reporters or bloggers
	Number of `@mentions` your brand receives on Twitter from reporters or bloggers
	Number of clicks on company news-related or custom-developed media links you post
	Number of other online mentions of your brand from reporters or bloggers following you
	Number of off-line mentions of your brand from reporters or bloggers following you
	Amount of website traffic that visits your press kit page
Prospect for warm leads	Number of people on Twitter contacting your company for product or service information
	Number of site visitors from Twitter going to your product/service or About Us pages
	Number of white paper, podcast, or video downloads from Twitter-driven traffic
	Number of Sales Inquiry page views and completed forms from Twitter-driven traffic
	Number of completed contacts (direct or electronically) with a Twitter-generated prospect
Monitor competition	Number of times your competitor's brand is mentioned in a tweet versus your own brand
	Number of `@messages` sent to your competitors requiring customer service
	Number of positive tweets your competitor receives as a consequence of satisfied customers
Search engine optimization	Number of keyword-enriched tweets you generate
	Number of these tweets you find appearing in search engine queries
	Number of search engine positions your website increases related to these keywords
	Number of search engine–referred website visitors
Social marketing optimization	Number of click-throughs on links to your other social media efforts (eg Facebook Fan pages, YouTube video, LinkedIn profile blog)

Continues

▶ **Table 11.1** Actions Associated with Objectives *(Continued)*

Objective	Associated Twitter Outcomes
Stimulate viral activity and buzz	Number of click-throughs on your custom-developed links Number of Twitter-referred website visitors to your custom landing page Number of `@mentions` containing your brand name or link (or both) Number of RTs of your posts Number of backtweets mentioning your brand Number of viral-stimulated actions
Find donors	Number of click-throughs on your custom-developed links Number of Twitter-referred website visitors Number of donors self-reporting they found you through Twitter Amount (and dollar value) of donations attributed to Twitter
Develop brand loyalty through engagement	Number of positive tweets about your brand Number of retweets about your brand Number of Twitter-referred members of your brand-loyalty program Number of Twitter-exclusive offers redeemed Number of responses to your Twitter-specific research poll or survey and how quickly you generate responses
Improve brand sentiment or image	Number of positive tweets about your brand (and that these outweigh negative tweets) Number of tweets from others defending or elevating your brand Number of signatures you receive to an online petition promoted exclusively through Twitter
Recruit talent	Number of retweets on your job-posting tweet Number of clicks on job-related links you post Number website visitors to the specific job description you posted Number of applicants to apply to the position Number of qualified applicants determined upon prescreening Number of job offers made to candidates derived from Twitter Number of new hires attributed to Twitter
Direct promotions	Number of click-throughs on your custom-developed links Number of Twitter-referred website visitors to your custom landing page Number of `@mentions` containing your brand name or link (or both) Number of RTs of your posts Number of backtweets mentioning your brand Number of submissions to your Twitter-specific contest or sweepstakes

Continues

▶ **Table 11.1** Actions Associated with Objectives *(Continued)*

Objective	Associated Twitter Outcomes
Drive traffic to your Website and/or blog	Number of click-throughs to your site/blog Number of first-time and repeat visitors to your site/blog
Drive sales	Number of ecommerce sales generated by Twitter-referred traffic Number of repeat ecommerce sales Number of qualified leads that convert into sales Increased average order value of sale Number of sales referred by a Twitter customer Number of sales that used to buy from your competition
Affiliate marketing	Number of click-throughs on your affiliate recruitment links Number of visitors to your company's affiliate marketing information page Number of new Twitter-referred affiliate sign-ups Number and amount of sales generated by Twitter-referred affiliates

Wednesday's One-Hour Exercise: Define Actions to Measure

For the primary objective you have selected, decide on the exact measure(s) for actions you will use to determine if you are meeting those objectives. Think of other actions not listed here that matter to you. Write them down. Decide how frequently you need to measure these actions. Write your reporting schedule next to these actions. Create a means to track and record your progress for each measure over time.

Thursday: Valuate

Now that you have identified how you will measure your objectives and the actions that result, can you quantify the value they've brought to your organization? Do you want to place value on these outcomes? *Value* can be anything from the less tangible (brand sentiment) to the very tangible (product or service sold). Many companies interviewed for this book have actually chosen *not* to evaluate their Twitter marketing efforts at this time. They feel right now that the thing about Twitter is to be part of the conversation with their consumers, rather than to place specific value on it. They don't want to miss the opportunity to learn from these consumers and show their own brand relevance. One could, of course, place value on what has been learned and impressions of relevance as well.

If you do, however, desire to place a value on your Twitter marketing activities, you should try to define those kinds of values important to you based on your objectives. These values must be tied in somehow to your defined actions; otherwise it will be impossible to measure any value from Twitter. For example, if you wanted to measure how many resumes Twitter generated for your company, the value of which would be how much money you saved paying job sites for advertising or executive recruiting firms for finding you talent, you need to be tracking recruitment-related actions.

Reflecting on values, let's list some here that might come to mind:

- Number of Twitter-generated sales
- Average order value of Twitter-generated sales (higher or lower than overall average)
- Value of Twitter-retained customer based on average lifetime value
- Cost of delivering Twitter customer service versus staffing a call center or savings from staffing it with fewer people
- Savings from gathering information or conducting informal research or focus groups via Twitter versus traditional means
- Media mentions from Twitter-related or Twitter-generated activity (how do you value your PR?)
- Twitter-generated gross revenues
- Twitter-generated net revenues
- Higher or lower profits from Twitter-related sales

While you're pondering the other values you can place on your Twitter activity and outcomes, you should also take into account a few other considerations.

Costs

Most people describe social media as free, but are they really? Consider the public relations analogy: sure, you may get your company mentioned in an article or broadcast through no direct effort of your own, but most companies that want this kind of regular, "unpaid" visibility pay pretty substantial fees to professional PR firms to help them. Twitter may be free to use, but you'll still need to account for the cost of someone's time. These costs may not be as high as buying advertising visibility, or even as high as hiring professional firms to provide services to you, but there's still a cost.

Want to quantify it? How about using this book's hour-a-day formula as an example?

> Let's assume you're paying someone $50,000 a year, and this person will be a key member of your Twitter team.
>
> There are 2,080 work hours and 260 "normal" work days per year.
>
> This person is spending *at least* one hour a day Twittering on your company's behalf.
>
> With a $50,000 annual salary, not counting benefits, you're paying this person $24.00 per hour or at least approximately $6,240 per year for your Twitter

initiative, which will scale higher the more hours a day this person spends on Twitter…and this is only counting human capital.

You also need to look at what other expense outlays you have related to Twitter. Did you offer some kind of discount to attract sales? Hold some kind of contest or giveaway for which you had to purchase the award? Produce and host a webinar? Redesign your website or build additional web pages to accommodate your Twitter strategy? Use any kinds of fee-based Twitter-related applications or tools? The list could go on, and all of these costs will begin to add up. If you're trying to calculate some kind of Twitter ROI, you will need to take all of these factors into account in your final calculations.

The Upside

While the costs of your Twitter marketing efforts may end up being higher than you originally expected, so might the benefits. In addition to the tangible things upon which you can place real value, how do you place a value on positive brand sentiment (or negative brand sentiment, for that matter)? What's the cost of a customer complaint or the extent to which this same complaint is spread to other people? Does your company measure "cool," "neat," "cutting edge," "helpful," "informative," or "one of us"?

As we discussed previously, you can also examine the tangible benefits and value that Twitter brings to your company. Naysayers may argue that social media tactics just suck up time and produce little to no productivity, but after reading all the examples mentioned so far, do you still really believe that? You must not; otherwise, you would have given up reading this book long ago. ;)

Thursday's One-Hour Exercise: Place Value on Your Twitter Efforts

This exercise is a series of activities just to help you gain perspective if you want to begin placing value on your Twitter activities:

- Make a list of items for which you want to measure Twitter value. List too what the normal value is for these efforts, so if you do start tracking your Twitter values, you can see if they're higher or lower than what you normally experience.
- Write down all the expenses you have incurred to date from Twitter, including the salaries of anyone working on Twitter. Also add in any estimated costs you expect to see for the remainder of the year.
- Create a list of any intangible values you might see from Twitter.

Friday: Review Case Studies

TGID—Thank God It's Data! We're at Friday; let's keep this interesting and give you a break from your homework for a change. Instead, let's share some Twitter marketing data analysis from case studies to show you examples of companies, large and small, impacting their businesses by using Twitter. They have found more customers, gotten more visits to their website, cut down on customer service costs, increased awareness, and increased revenue.

Dell Outlet

As we discussed earlier, Dell Outlet (`@DellOutlet`) is one of the most publicized "Twitter wins," because they increased revenue by $2 million with their Twitter account. Tweeting only Twitter-exclusive deals (Figure 11.7) on refurbished Dell computers and electronics, it took Dell a year and a half year before it made its first million from Twitter in 2008. Its second million came only about six months later thanks to the growth of Twitter and Dell Outlet's ever-larger follower base. Dell is able to track all of this revenue by using uniquely tweeted URLs and, as one user put it, "in addition to making $2 (some say $3) million on Twitter, Dell got tons of PR probably worth more than $2 million." While it appears that Dell Outlet's follower growth has somewhat stagnated since May 2009 (Figure 11.8), it's still tweeting away.

20% off any Dell Outlet XPS™ One 20 or XPS One 24. Enter at checkout: 9GW7SSVPVXXT2K – exp 7/14 http://ow.ly/gYIf
9:05 AM Jul 13th from HootSuite
Dell Outlet
DellOutlet
Dell Outlet

Figure 11.7 Dell Outlet's Twitter-exclusive deals also provide a means to measure sales and ROI.

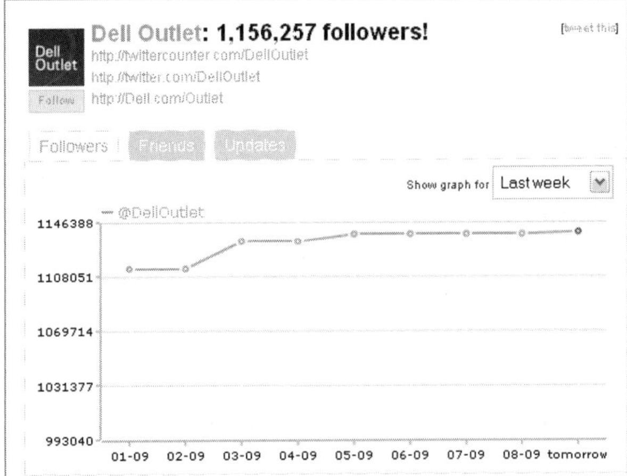

Figure 11.8 Dell's follower growth slowed to nearly a plateau in 2009.

Boloco

Boloco (`@boloco`) is an example of a local business making a sales impact through Twitter. A burrito chain mostly in the Boston area (in fact, Boloco stands for "Boston Local Company"), the company also has a few other locations in New England. John Pepper, the company's CEO, wanting to find a way to better leverage its Boston-area advertising in order to reach its other markets, took a picture of one of its $3.00 burrito print-ad coupons and posted it on Twitter. He encouraged people in any Boloco location to redeem the coupon just by bringing an image of it—by photocopy, printout, or even on a cell phone—into one of its locations (Figure 11.9).

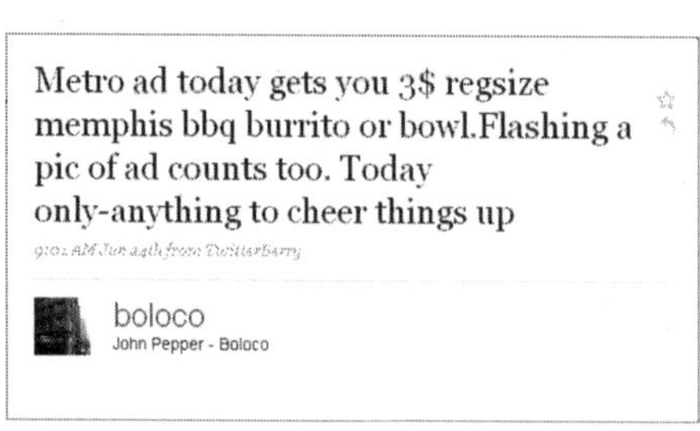

Figure 11.9 Boloco's original tweet, followed by the photographed coupon

What did this harebrained idea yield? Whereas normally Boloco would get 350 coupons redeemed per ad, this time they got 900, a 157 percent increase. On the day Pepper tweeted his coupon, 25 percent of Boloco's business came from the coupon alone.

AMC Fork & Screen

In October 2008, the AMC Theatre in Olathe, Kansas was planning on opening its new "Fork & Screen" concept (Figure 11.10), with casual and premium in-theatre dining and entertainment experiences. Its press release announced, "an entire wing of the theatre has been completely transformed into an enhanced entertainment and dining experience," so clearly this was a big deal. In advance of the opening, and with a goal of generating local buzz a few days before the theatre's grand opening three days later, AMC's social media manager, Justin Gardner (`@jpgardner`), sent invitations to bloggers via Twitter, and those who responded were invited to the pre-opening event on October 28th.

Figure 11.10 AMC's Fork & Screen debut

Using social media tracking solution Spiral16, the theatre was able to track its mentions. The day before the event, only 34 websites mentioned Fork & Screen. Twenty-four hours after the event, this count grew to 73 sites, and within 72 hours, it was up to 155 sites (Figure 11.11). The explosion was attributed to the bloggers who attended the pre-opening event, who then either blogged about it as soon as they got home to their computers, or tweeted about the concept right from the theatre. Buzz-generation mission accomplished.

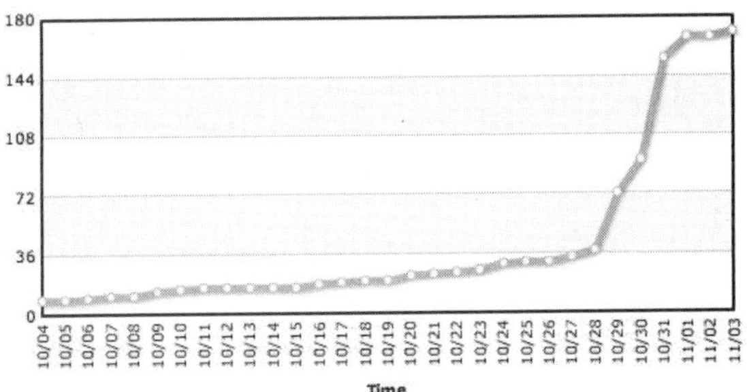

Figure 11.11 AMC's Olathe, KS theatre buzz stats pre- and post-Twitter outreach as tracked by Sprial16

Miller High Life

For the 2009 Super Bowl, Miller Brewing Company determined it would *not* be among the advertisers doling out $3 million for a 30-second television advertising spot. How to attract traffic and stand out from the ad crowd? Why, be creative, of course!

Thinking ahead, it launched a microsite (`http://www.1secondad.com`) featuring a video clip of "rejected" one-second ads, "High Life 1-Second Ads That Didn't Make

The Cut," that featured comedian Windell Middlebrooks. (`http://www.youtube.com/watch?v=K9GwHnU2ESE`). You can't do or say much in one second, but it was clever and got people's attention. In the weeks leading up to the game, the site grew virally, mainly gaining its popularity through social networking.

After analyzing the data, Miller found that 55 percent of online chatter about the one-second ad campaign was on Twitter (beating news organizations as a referral source), with 67 percent of sentiment about the ad coming from Twitter. These statistics made Twitter the most influential domain for conversation about the ad. Why was Twitter so influential? It met all the criteria for Twitter *stickiness:* entertaining, humorous, video, real-time, short, and an easy-to-tweet URL.

Does Twitter Influence Hollywood's Box Office?

There has been increased supposition that Twitter now plays a role in whether or not newly released films will be a boom or a bust at the box office. Whereas Hollywood used to rely on ordinary word-of-mouth to help bolster movie attendance, now they're seeing people tweet about how they liked or disliked a movie immediately after leaving the theatre. If positive, these tweets can help positively influence a film's popularity. If these tweets are negative, a film could essentially be killed its first weekend out. We first saw this kind of correlation drawn when the Sasha Baron Cohen movie *Bruno* crashed and burned its debut weekend, and later films, such as *Inglourious Basterds,* saw a positive Twitter effect.

Whether Twitter will have a lasting effect on Hollywood remains to be seen, but those in the business are definitely taking notice.

San Francisco Kitchen

The San Francisco Kitchen (`@sfkitchen`) is a small Asian-fusion bistro, located in Nashua, NH, with sushi bar and Asian hot pot. The restaurant has been in business for over 15 years. The owners decided to let their son Anthony Liang (`@liangtfm`) work some social media magic in order to increase awareness. Anthony started using Twitter for the restaurant to connect with more people in the area and talk about specials. He started to notice that more people were coming to try the restaurant because they had heard it was on Twitter and saw the tweets about it.

Once San Francisco Kitchen had a good base of followers, Anthony decided to hold a tweetup at the restaurant to generate leads and increase awareness. He created a page on Eventbrite (Figure 11.12) and started tweeting about it. Soon there were so many RSVPs they had to release more tickets. Fifty people attended the event, many of whom had never been to the restaurant. Anthony also had the clever idea of having "tweet tees" created for attendees, with a blank tweet caption, "Hello, My Name Is [*blank so you could fill in your Twitter handle*] and I love @SFKitchen" (Figure 11.13).

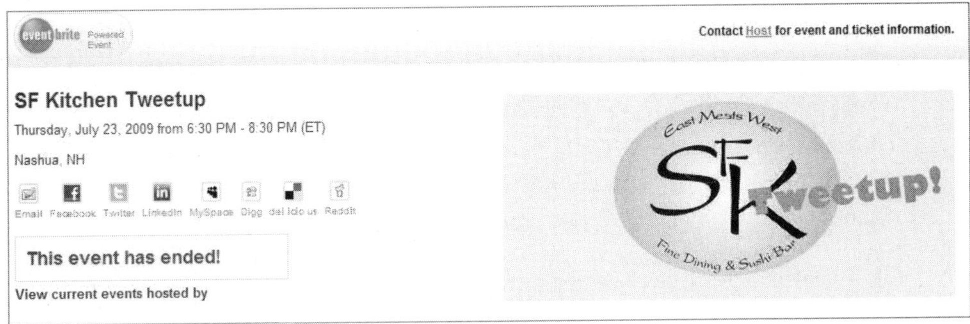

Figure 11.12 Eventbrite invitation for San Francisco Kitchen's first tweetup

Figure 11.13 An attendee wearing the clever Twitter tee

The attendees were impressed with the restaurant and wanted to come back—some even booked reservations for another night right there on the spot. Overall, the tweetup was a success, and San Francisco Kitchen is continuing to use Twitter successfully as part of its marketing mix.

Bob Evans

On April 15, 2009, Bob Evans relaunched its corporate website (`http://www.bobevans.com`) with a completely restyled look, meant not only to play off its farm heritage and utilize important brand cues, but also to upgrade its digital positioning for future initiatives. In the spirit of relaunching its new website, the company developed two primary goals: to heighten awareness that the site had been redesigned and to increase website traffic. Bob Evans chose to target mommy bloggers exclusively online with its social media tactics narrowed to Twitter (`@bobevansfarms`) and Facebook. As an incentive for the highest-ranked mommy bloggers (based on their follower count or traffic to their blog), Bob Evans gave each a company gift card to use or offer to their blog readers as an online giveaway.

Bob Evans tracked and measured the following statistics from this initiative:

- The extended reach of the selected mommy bloggers provided 1.5 million potential tweet impressions (the number of Twitter followers times the number of tweets about the Bob Evans post/Bob Evans Gift Card giveaway).
- Traffic on Bob Evans saw a 106 percent uptick in page views and a 120 percent increase in site traffic between April and May 2009.
- Bob Evans's search engine referral traffic increased 3,241 percent.

Since running this initial campaign, Bob Evans has seen such positive success it continues to run its social media efforts, expanding into new content and promotions (Figure 11.14).

It's Biscuit & Gravy Week! See how we're celebrating http://tinyurl.com /mokhpr; today's prize = $50 #BEF Gift Card!
10:57 AM Sep 7th from web
BobEvansFarms
Bob Evans Farms, Inc

Figure 11.14 Bob Evans continues to expand its Twitter promotions.

The Main Points

- Always tie your data analysis to your objectives. Try to think of what you want to measure while you're thinking of what you want to accomplish through Twitter.
- Be sure that you take baseline readings for the things you'll want to analyze over time, so that you'll have something against which to gauge your progress.
- Analyze Twitter's impact on your website traffic, particularly because Twitter's 140 characters *is* limiting and you can say a lot more on your site.
- Analyze your actions, choosing the actions from which you can see a direct cause and effect from your Twitter efforts.
- If you're entering Twitter hoping to gain specific value from it, define how you will measure this value, particularly against historical values you already know.

IV

Month 3: Maintain Your Twitter Presence

You now have the fundamentals to market your business through Twitter. Part IV teaches you how to maintain, learn from, and refine your efforts according to how well they help you reach your goals. Some of this will be based on your ability to institutionalize your Twitter marketing efforts. You may even want to take your campaign to the next level, opening up to multiple Twitter accounts to accomplish multiple goals. You might also want to prepare for any backlash that could occur against your company. In Month 3, we'll help you through these various scenarios and build your Twitter confidence before you set out on your own.

Week 9: Institutionalize Maintenance

As we've discussed throughout this book, a lot of Twitter marketing involves doing the same tasks repetitively. After all, there's not much you can do in 140 characters, right? As you've seen in several different user case studies, you can enrich your tweets in many ways. The effort, however, won't be worthwhile if you don't execute, listen, learn, monitor, measure, refine, and repeat what's working and perhaps change what's not. In order to accomplish this, you need to institutionalize the maintenance of your Twitter marketing activity. The person you put in charge of your Twitter marketing initiative really must own *it so that you can progress rather than fall back with your activity. That's what this chapter is all about.*

12

Chapter Contents

Monday: Hold Weekly Meetings

If you're executing Twitter marketing for business, it's a good idea to set up a weekly status update meeting with any parties involved to touch base and review how your efforts are going. During this meeting, you're going to want to review key findings, identify strengths and weaknesses, talk about surprises and successes, both small and large, and flesh out next week's adjusted action plan.

Review Key Findings

When you meet each week to review your Twitter marketing efforts, you really want to focus first on evaluating what you've done to date to help plan future efforts. Using the measurement methods discussed in this book, review how your work over the past week has helped you accomplish your goals. Expect to perform this data analysis on Fridays to be available for this Monday update meeting, and plan to discuss such questions as the following:

- Did we gain or lose followers this week? The answer to this question might lead you to discuss the next question.
- Do our tweets help, hurt, or do nothing for our cause?
    - How many tweets did we make this week that were not `@replies` or DMs?
    - Are our tweets too self-promotional?
    - Do we have enough balance between giving and taking kinds of tweets?
    - Are we having enough conversations?
    - Are our tweets linking to informational content getting the click volume we want? Do we even know what kind of click volume we'd like to see?
    - Which kinds of links generate more clicks than others? Can we come up with more of the type of content that people like, and will it help us achieve our Twitter marketing goals?
- Do we feel connected to the people with whom we are tweeting?
    - Are these people our customers? Our peers? Our competitors? Do we know and do we care?
    - Are people retweeting us and, if so, what about?
    - How many unsolicited positive `@mentions` did we receive (ones that had nothing to do with customer service or complaints)?
    - Did we turn any negative tweets into a positive experience with our brand?
- How is our Twitter initiative helping our brand?
    - Did we receive brand mentions?
    - What is the tone of those mentions?

- Did we connect with the people who were mentioning the brand with an appropriate response?
- What was the outcome of the communication?

Regarding the content of your tweets, over time, if you want to compare what you're doing now with what you did then, remember that you can't rely on Twitter's archive for this. Consider instead using one of the tweet archiving solutions mentioned in Chapter 6, "Week 3: Use Twitter Search and Other Tools to Improve Your Experience." Viewing your past tweets in a historical context might help shed light on trends you might not see otherwise. Also remember, if your goal is to increase awareness for your brand, you are tweeting to millions of people who can see your tweets at any given time through a search.

Turning a Negative into a Positive

Bradley Hospital (`@BradleyHospital`), a pediatric psychiatric hospital in Providence, Rhode Island that helps families of children with autism and Asperger's syndrome, posted this tweet:

> *"What is autism and Asperger's? Our expert Dr Barrett explains these developmental disabilities & how best to treat them.* `http://bit.ly/NptPs`"

As a result, they received a negative tweet back from a user who had Asperger's and who took offense to the tweet, accusing the hospital of calling people like him "ill" and "diseased."

A conversation ensued:

> `BradleyHosp @xxxxxxx` We meant no offense. Our goal is to offer information to families of children who may benefit from the care we provide.
>
> `Xxxxxxx @BradleyHospital` You should check out this article from Harvard Business School `http://hbswk.hbs.edu/item/5869.html`
>
> `BradleyHosp @xxxxxxx` Thank you for sending that great, interesting article. Sounds like a wonderful company to work for!
>
> `Xxxxxxx @BradleyHospital` Indeed it is. However, not many people have heard of it and so, most aspies don't know what to do in their adult life.

The user went on to describe his personal situation and those of fellow "aspies" who have succeeded in life thanks to companies who understood how to take advantage of the common strengths found in people with Asperger's.

The hospital representative went on to laud the user's employer, apologized for any undue offense, and wished the user well. The user then went on to praise the hospital for their efforts in caring for and informing people about autism and Asperger's.

Some of the questions previously posed can be answered by performing data analysis, while others are more qualitative in nature, which is why it's helpful to "gather the troops" involved with your Twitter efforts. You can share insights and interpretations, and have a more complete discussion to prepare you for the week ahead.

Lay Out the Week's Action Plan

During your weekly Twitter update meeting, you'll also want to lay out any steps you want to take in particular for the week. This dialog should also include anything you'll need to prepare this week so that it will be ready in time for future weeks.

1. **Share "the Twitter Luv."** As your Twitter marketing efforts take hold, more and more departments in your organization may want some Twitter attention. Human Resources may want you to tweet job openings, product managers may want you to announce new items, and your media relations team may have industry statistics to share. To manage an ever-increasing demand for Twitter time, you may want to develop a system to handle and process such requests. This system should include a means to reach out to certain company contacts each week to discuss their needs, to evaluate and prioritize each request, and, if deemed possible, to work it into your weekly action plan in such a way that it does not detract from your core Twitter objective(s). Of course, you can also take a proactive position, asking your followers what kind of content they'd find valuable and about which you could be tweeting.
2. **Define the objectives for any new initiatives.** If the demand for other Twitter uses for your brand is great or someone on your core team comes up with a great new idea, just as you did before, you should define your objectives for any new initiatives before undertaking them.
3. **Identify your target metrics and take baseline readings.** If you're defining new objectives, you'll want to go through the same process of identifying the metrics you'll want to relate to your activities, and then you'll need to understand where you are by taking baseline readings before you engage in them.
4. **Develop the weekly "give."** As we've discussed, your Twitter use should be less self-serving and more giving. Unfortunately, giving doesn't just happen; in fact, oftentimes it takes work that, to some extent, you need to plan for in advance. For example, someone should be identifying breaking news and other helpful information about your field that you think people should know about. How about topical retweets? You might want to assign someone to perform Twitter searches to locate useful subject matter to retweet.
5. **Estimate timelines.** For those more self-serving tweets, you should factor in a whole lot more planning and lead time, particularly if a promotion or event is involved. If you are planning to write a topical blog post, you should allocate time for this. Does your contest need its own landing page or microsite (not to mention a review of contest rules by legal)? Remember these kinds of planning and production timelines.

Assign Roles and Responsibilities

Assigning roles and responsibilities doesn't require any thinking when you conduct your Twitter marketing as a team of one, but if you have multiple staff members working on your tweeting, you'll also want to assign certain tasks to specific individuals as you lay out your action plan. For instance, one person could be watching news sites, monitoring breaking news, and posting new tweets accordingly, while another can be working on strategic marketing priorities, while yet another can be doing the evaluation. Working as a team certainly can be beneficial because there are so many aspects to Twitter marketing that need to be managed in order to be truly effective.

It's commonly recommended that someone be assigned the morning Twitter review. This review entails the assigned person setting aside a 15-minute time period every morning to log into Twitter (or your third-party Twitter client) to locate and evaluate brand mentions, product mentions, and retweets even before starting daily `@replies` and executing any planned tweets. This allows your assigned tweeter time to get situated and adjust any original tweeting plans accordingly. It also allows you to understand the impact of any tweeting you may have done the day before.

The morning review person should share any key take-away findings with the person assigned to content production and idea generation of self-guided tweets because this information too might affect the day's tweeting plans. For example, if you had intended to spread your news and information tweets throughout the day, but your morning review reveals you have consistently generated the most retweets of these posts before noon, you probably want to concentrate your deliberate tweeting in the morning to test your theory. This would require swift action on the part of your content producer if he or she were not yet prepared to have content ready before noon.

Throughout the day, your brand might receive `@messages` to which you'll want to respond. Do you want to assign this responsibility to a single person or to several people? If you have complex operations such that a single person might not be able to answer all questions, do you want to have this person act as a filter and direct the questions to the appropriate party for an answer? Alternatively, you could have key members of each department log into Twitter throughout the day to respond to questions within their areas of expertise. Whatever you decide to do, however, roles and responsibilities must be clearly defined, as should be the expectations for response time. Everyone on your Twitter team should understand that Twitter is a real-time medium where people expect responses to their tweets in less than 24 hours.

Finally, how do you want to end your day of tweeting? Do you want to do an end-of-day review to help prepare for the next day? Do you want to conclude the day on an up note with a deliberate tweet to set the tone for the next day? Do you want to impart some final tip or words of wisdom to your followers? Remember, your tweets will always appear on your public timeline, so think about your last tweet of the day as the closing credits on a film—what would you want people to see if they stopped by after hours? Whose responsibility will this be, and what kind of tweets might you want people to see? It's a good idea to give these kinds of questions some thought.

Monday's One-Hour Exercise: Hold a Twitter Status Meeting

Using the preceding guidelines, in an hour or less, conduct a weekly Twitter status update meeting.

Tuesday: Implement Weekly Action Plan

Now that you've conducted your weekly Twitter marketing status meeting, you should have a pretty clear idea of what you want to accomplish during the week to come. In addition to your action plan of brand-directed initiatives, there are a few other actions you should consider institutionalizing.

Your Commitment to Others

After you conduct your first-thing-in-the-morning review, you might want to heed the advice of power user Scott Stratten (`@unmarketing`), who sends out the daily reminder shown in Figure 12.1.

Daily reminder to take 5 mins to reply/retweet others. Nothing about u. Interact, engage, build.

8:50 AM Sep 16th from Endless Tweets

Figure 12.1 Scott Stratten's regular reminder

This is a good routine to incorporate into your daily tweeting, and it will go a long way toward building trust with your followers.

Check on New Followers

Daily if possible, but at least several times a week, it's important to check on new followers. If you hold your status meeting on a Monday, Tuesday might be a great day to check on new followers, since you've already settled into your work week. Even though your strategy as a brand might be to follow every one of your followers back, regularly checking on them helps you understand how well you are accomplishing your objectives.

Are you attracting the kind of followers you ultimately hope will be engaged with your brand? Are you attracting followers who already evangelize your brand? Are you attracting industry peers with whom you can communicate and network? Alternatively, are you attracting people who seem completely contrary to your goals?

By reviewing your followers, you can also stay aware of your bearing in the Twitterverse. Followers you wouldn't want to miss include the following:

- **Competitors.** Are your competitors following you first or vice versa? What are they tweeting? Who are their followers and who else are they following?
- **Brands marketing to a similar audience but who are not competitors.** How are they using Twitter? Who are their followers and should you also be following those users?
- **Potential customers.** Review user bios. Can you identify anyone clearly in your target demographics? Maybe you want to initiate a welcome tweet with them—they'll likely be incredibly impressed and flattered if you do.
- **Important tweeters in your field.** If you attract a power user, you might be doing something right and you'll definitely want to follow them back to learn from their experience. Welcome them and perhaps establish a relationship early on by posing a question to them.
- **Interesting/fun tweeps.** Even as a brand, there's nothing wrong with taking pleasure from folks who just make you smile, who impart bits of wisdom, or who share interesting quotes. They are just great people with whom you can engage in the Twitterverse...and they can also probably help you more than you realize.

Address Brand Mentions

With your daily morning review, you've seen your brand `@mentions`, retweets, and direct messages, but you should also regularly search for your brand and products by name and not by your user handle. It's critical that you know what people are saying about your brand. Obviously, we'd all like to believe that our brands are held in the highest esteem in the world of social media, but that's not always the case. It's important that you have a plan to address negative mentions. Recognize that, in today's world of social media, consumers expect to have their opinion heard at any given moment. One bad mention can easily turn into a huge campaign against your brand, which in turn can become a full-blown public relations crisis. (For more on handling crisis, see Chapter 13, "Week 10: Prepare for Crisis Management.")

If you have positive mentions, be sure to thank the tweeter. (See the dialog in Figure 12.2.) If you have negative mentions, first bring it to the attention of senior management and then refer to your plan on how to address the situation. No response can be much more damaging in today's social media world than a botched one.

@ matthewjared07 At rhode island hospital this morning!!! Traffic was non existant!! 10:33 AM Aug 18th from UberTwitter
RIHospital: @matthewjared07 Hope everything is OK!
@ matthewjared07 Wow. Who knew I'd get a tweet from rhode island hospital after my visit!!! How awesome! @rihospital about 3 hours ago from UberTwitter
@ matthewjared07 @RIHospital it was wonderful. My second trip to rih. Was there for work at the apc building!!! Thanks for the tweet!!! about 3 hours ago from UberTwitter in reply to RIHospital
RIHospital: @matthewjared07 SURPRISE! Yes, we're tweeting! Follow us! :) Glad to hear everything is going well!

Figure 12.2 A tweet thread between Rhode Island Hospital and one of its patients

Trending Topics

Once you've checked on and addressed your brand mentions, you might want to check out breaking news and Twitter Trending Topics. Does anything tie into your brand, your industry, or relate to you in any way? Can you add to the conversation or raise a thought-provoking question to generate conversation? What information that you think will be helpful under the circumstance can you relay to your followers? Maybe you just want to retweet a few noteworthy items and position yourself as a reliable filter and conduit of information.

Launch into Action

Now you've covered all the basics for the day, so you can launch into whatever the rest of your daily Twitter action plan entailed. Get to tweeting, keeping it relevant and helpful, but also supporting your brand.

Tuesday's One-Hour Exercise: Perform Action Plan Prep Work

Before you launch into your action plan, try developing and executing a daily routine such as the work described previously—one that you can stick with and execute every day.

Wednesday: Oversee Production Requirements

As we've discussed in earlier chapters, oftentimes deliberate Twitter marketing initiatives require the production and posting of additional content, creative assets, or other behind-the-scenes support materials. Some of your plans may even require signatures or approvals from upper management.

Considerations for Production

What kinds of tactics might require this kind of additional work?

- Contests or sweepstakes
  - Contest rules and regulations
  - Approval of prize(s)
  - Processing of entries
- Games
- Loyalty or rewards programs
- Job recruitment
- Special offers, discounts, or promotions
- Downloadable white papers
- Blog posts
- Videos, podcasts, or photo montages
- Surveys or polls
- Research results
- Tweetups or Twitter-exclusive events
- Fundraising drives
- Creating whole new Twitter profiles
  - New Twitter backgrounds
  - New landing pages to correspond with your profile URL

As we discussed yesterday, someone (or perhaps several people) needs to be assigned the responsibility for the development of all the content required for your planned initiative. If you have multiple initiatives planned at once, or change initiatives from week to week, be sure to give yourself enough lead time to get them done.

We've discussed estimating timelines during Monday's status meeting so that you can plan ahead, and we've discussed assigning roles and responsibilities on Tuesday. Mid-week (Wednesday) is a good day to check in with your production team to see if they're on time with your production needs. If they are on time, you can go ahead with your initiative as intended; if they're behind or have run into an obstacle, you'll want to regroup and adjust your calendars accordingly. In effect, managing Twitter marketing campaigns is really no different than managing any other marketing project.

Remember to be proactive. Rather than waiting for different members of your company to ask for your help by using Twitter to do this or that for them, plan to check in with them on a weekly basis. As part of your Twitter action plan, be prepared for others to ask you to share the Twitter Luv. Proactivity on your part means that you have more control over requests and whether or not and when they can be implemented. Again, like ordinary project management, much of institutionalized Twitter marketing maintenance is about good communications and setting proper expectations.

Reminder Remember your daily first-thing-in-the-morning routine: spend about 15 minutes on retweets, direct messages, @responses, and brand mentions.

Wednesday's One-Hour Exercise: Coordinate Production

Checking on current production doesn't take all that much time, so take some time today to talk with your production team about long-term production possibilities. The aim is to determine how long it could take to produce the assets for the various Twitter marketing ideas you may be contemplating.

Don't just talk, however; make a chart or some kind of table to document these production timelines so, if and when you're ready to pursue these ideas, you don't have to refer to your memory or scattered notes to know how far in advance you have to plan your lead times.

Thursday: Prepare Documentation

Once you have institutionalized your Twitter marketing maintenance, by Thursday there shouldn't be a whole lot of new activity. Instead, you should be settled into your daily routines, confident about your production schedule (or at least feeling like your fires are under control) and seeing regular engagement with the Twitter community.

Reminder Check on your new followers. Are there any you want to reach out to with a personal @message or retweet?

Considerations for Documentation

On Thursday, you can take some time to start to prepare the documentation you need to review with your team during the weekly status meeting and present to upper management if needed. This kind of document usually involves a quick check of the metrics related to your objectives, perhaps a recap of staff time absorbed by Twitter, and any significant Twitter occurrences. Copy, note, and/or forward any important brand mentions in Twitter to upper management so you can help substantiate the company's efforts and build management's trust in the medium. If you're being asked to provide documentation to upper management, also be prepared to talk about anecdotes and lessons learned from your week in Twitter, especially if your company is measuring its

Twitter activity in terms of return on engagement. Many early Twitter initiatives are set up as proof of concepts: what do you need to document to prove or disprove the concept?

In addition to this preparation, continue with the daily requirements of Twitter activity: read tweets and links, listen to what the community is sharing, respond to `@messages` and DMs, participate in the larger discussion, and learn from everything you're doing.

Reminder Search Twitter for topics your brand cares about. What comes up? Do any of the references directly impact your brand? Are there any topics you want to save as a search for a quick refresh check later?

Thursday's One-Hour Exercise: Prepare Documentation

Use this time to help prepare the documentation you need to provide to upper management. If you don't need to report to upper management, go through the motions and see if you learn anything for yourself, regardless.

Friday: Deliver Results to Management

Today you'll be taking the documentation you assembled yesterday and delivering it to upper management. Public relations and advertising professionals already know the value of providing clip packets to senior leadership. It's been a standard a way of proving the value of your efforts when you show your company's name in print, provide them with a CD of a news segment from the national news broadcast, or present the portfolio of ads that have run. If your upper management hasn't yet completely bought into the value of building brand loyalty through social media, imagine their response when they see a log of all the brand mentions your company received this week. It should be very pleasing to them to see a positive, personal interaction between you and someone in the Twitterverse that clearly builds loyalty for your brand.

To document your Twitter efforts for upper management, devise a format for a weekly recap to be shared with key stakeholders in your company. This recap can include new followers, conversations and the results of those conversations, brand mentions, and anything else that you know appeals to your upper management. It's also interesting to include in the recap where your followers hail from—are they local or are they spread throughout the nation? Even though you might be a local entity, nationwide followers help your brand extend its reach and awareness. You should then tie all of these data points into your strategic marketing goals.

Legal Considerations

It might be worthwhile to have an internal discussion with your management and legal team about the inclusion of entire tweet threads in any corporate recaps. Legal will likely view this as a liability, since all e-documentation can be subpoenaed in lawsuits and, once something is in a memo or emailed, it is subject to the e-documentation laws. If your company has these kinds of concerns, you might want to avoid including actual tweets in recaps.

If possible, don't just email a report or drop a printout on someone's desk. Instead, at least from time to time, try to review your Twitter activity with management in person. This probably means scheduling some once-monthly time with upper management, but the more positive outcomes you can show them, the more likely you'll be to retain and grow their buy-in.

If you need management's approval to move forward on a Twitter initiative, however, try to get that approval before your next weekly status meeting.

Your Friday Routine

Other than delivering your documentation to management and preparing for next week's Twitter status meeting, you'll want to continue your institutionalized Twitter maintenance routine: do your first-thing-in-the-morning review and everything else you do on an ordinary basis. Bear in mind, too, that because today is Friday, it's also Follow Friday (`#FollowFriday`). Yes, as a brand you can also recommend people to follow. In fact, as a brand, your recommendation of someone will be viewed by them as even more flattering. If you receive a `#FollowFriday` recommendation, you'll want to thank that person for their recommendation, but you'll also want to look them up and see what types of conversations you may have engaged in with this person to figure out why you've received a `#FollowFriday` honor.

You might find that, because it's Friday, people are in a more light-hearted mood. As a consequence, Friday is a good day to have fun with Twitter. Try sharing a good, clean joke or being more playful in your tweet engagement.

If your company does not tweet over the weekend, it's probably a good idea to have a "final tweet of the week." This tweet should be a kind of sign-off that lets visitors to your profile know that they shouldn't expect you to return tweets until Monday at the earliest. It could be something simple like,

> *"Signing off until Monday. Have a great weekend, everyone!"*
>
> or,
>
> *"Can't wait to hear how YOU spent your weekend. Please share your activities, and we'll pick our favorite to RT on Monday when we return!"*

Whatever you choose to write, the point is that, to the best of your ability, you're trying to manage people's expectations if they decide to tweet you over the weekend.

Tweeting Nights, Weekends, and Holidays

The real-time nature of Twitter can lead its users to expect 24/7 responses. If you plan on using Twitter for customer service, you might want to assemble a rotating team of weekend tweeters. If you're not using Twitter for customer service, as a brand you don't have to feel obliged to tweet over the weekends or during holidays. Be aware, however, that many brands, particularly those represented by a single dedicated tweeter, *do* tweet during off-hours. It's not a competition. It's just that many tweeters are very passionate about Twitter and find it hard to stay away!

Friday's One-Hour Exercise: Wrap Up Your Week

Summarizing Friday's activities, do the following:

- Deliver your Twitter report to management.
- Get organized for the next week's status meeting.
- Perform your daily Twitter routine.
- Participate in Follow Friday.
- Have a little more fun today.
- Leave a tidy sign-off message if you plan to be off Twitter the entire weekend or on a holiday.

The Main Points

- Twitter maintenance can be institutionalized. Certain activities should be repeated as a routine daily...or even throughout the day.
- When implementing your Twitter marketing action plan, balance new initiatives with the activities that you've institutionalized.
- True Twitter marketing will likely require the production of other content and creative assets that you'll need to plan and oversee. Give yourself enough lead time to plan accordingly.
- Prepare and provide documentation to upper management to retain their support of your Twitter marketing efforts.
- Friday is a day like no other. Have a little more fun with it.
- Repeat all of this institutionalized activity weekly. Make it part of your ongoing regular Twitter routine.

13

Week 10: Prepare for Crisis Management

The inspirations for this week's chapter are two high-profile public relations crises exacerbated by the speed at which bad news spreads on Twitter. Let's start this week a little differently by discussing these cases to give you the appropriate perspective before we describe how to create your own Twitter crisis management plan.

Chapter Contents

The Reality of Twitter Crises

Twitter's real-time platform probably makes its greatest impact when there's news to spread. We've already discussed instances, such as natural catastrophes, government upheaval, and celebrity gossip, where news spread more rapidly on Twitter than through other traditional media. The ability to spread information rapidly becomes a form of power: power to attract readers, power to make someone an overnight sensation, or power to attack a brand. This power, used with different purposes and to different ends, can be either good or bad, depending upon which end of the stick you fall on. The magnitude of this power has taken a few brands by surprise.

Motrin Ad Makes Moms Mad

One might assume that women who tweet are educated, progressive thinking, and early adopters of technology. As it so happens, not all Twitter users advocate all things hi-tech. Some Twitter-using moms (and dads) are fans of what is called *baby wearing,* or carrying children in slings or wraps rather than pushing them in strollers or carrying them in their arms. For some parents, baby wearing is something they do because it keeps their hands free; for others, it's part of a philosophy of being as close to their baby as possible for as much of the time as possible.

It's not hard to imagine, therefore, the kind of ruckus caused by a November 2008 ad campaign associating the practice of baby wearing as a fashion statement to be endured despite pain to the back, neck, and shoulder, and at the risk of looking tired and crazy. (View the television ad on YouTube: `http://www.youtube.com/watch?v=XO6S1TUBA38`.) Motrin, the advertiser responsible for the campaign, thought they could position their pain relief product as a solution for the kind of pain caused by baby wearing, but the presentation of the idea backfired. All of a sudden, Twitter was on fire with moms raging at the makers of Motrin for the ad, even calling for a product boycott. They created a hashtag (`#motrinmoms`) to track their unhappiness and began shouting to the masses that generic ibuprofen is better than Motrin. The volume of tweets containing the `#motrinmoms` hashtag became so great, it appeared as a Trending Topic.

Take a look at how quickly word spread on Twitter from angry moms (Figure 13.1). The ad was posted on the Motrin home page on a Saturday morning and by Sunday afternoon (the "six hours ago" in the graph), word was still spreading as rapidly as it had on Saturday afternoon (note that this all happened on a weekend, when most working professionals are off).

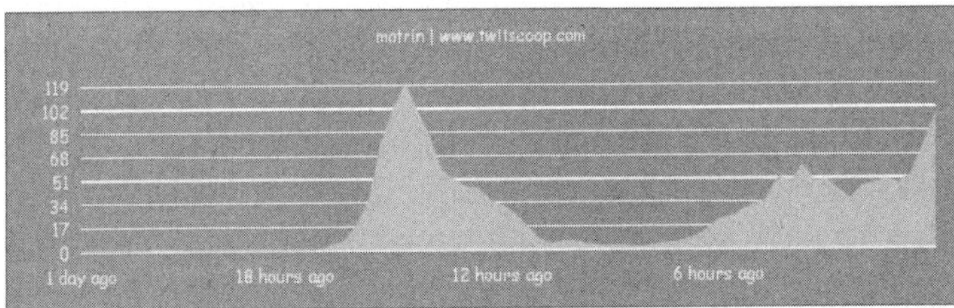

Figure 13.1 A Twitscoop graph demonstrating the Twitter activity on the keyword "motrin" during the time period shown

The Motrin ad was on the company's home page for only 16 hours before they took it down, but it was 16 hours too late. In fact, there was so much backlash that, looking to capitalize on a corporation's pain (no pun intended), One True Media, a do-it-yourself video-mixing and -sharing site (`http://www.onetruemedia.com`) created a nine-minute video (`http://www.youtube.com/watch?v=LhR-y1N6R8Q`) with screen shots of as many tweets as they could find. One True Media then sent the montage to Motrin to highlight the fact that the brand gravely misjudged this audience and that a negative response on Twitter can easily change people's perceptions and hurt a brand's reputation.

To make matters worse, although Motrin took down the ad, they didn't respond to the angry moms on Twitter for days, which on Twitter is an eternity. It took them three full days to respond—and when they did respond, it was by blogging about it and emailing some vocal mommy bloggers. The company was too ignorant about Twitter to know how to respond there.

On the blog, Kathy Widmer, vice president of marketing at McNeil Consumer Healthcare, the company that markets Motrin, said,

> *"One bright spot is that we have learned through this process—in particular, the importance of paying close attention to the conversations that are taking place online. It has also brought home the importance of taking a broader look at what we say and how it may be interpreted."*

To consumer brands, the lesson Motrin learned brings home the fact that you and your advertising and marketing agencies need to understand the ramifications that Twitter and other social media channels can wreak on your brand. You may choose not to engage proactively in this space, but you at least need to *understand* and *monitor* it in order to be able to respond to your audience and protect your brand reputation.

Keep in mind, too, that you should never assume you really know your target audience. Never assume that the sentiment will always be positive just because you created something viral. Consider instead tapping into and getting input from your target audience through social media before you go live. You might not only save yourself from a tarnished image, you might also save yourself from thousands or millions of wasted dollars.

Mother's Day Flower Deliveries = #Fail

On Mother's Day 2009, several moms didn't receive their flowers that had been ordered from FTD, even though the orders were placed several days ahead of time. People began tweeting about it (Figure 13.2), making some of the following comments, which were compiled by TechCrunch (`http://www.techcrunch.com/2009/05/11/ftds-mothers-day-mishap`):

> *"Firing off an angry letter to FTD. They are liars, use 1-800-Flowers or call an actual, real florist on the telephone."*
>
> *"Calling FTD...mothers day flowers that were not delivered...."*
>
> *"FTD had two days to get RA's mom her mothers day flowers and they FAILED. I am SO waiting this 15 minute hold time to rip someone a new one."*
>
> *"FTD resolution was terrible; solution to missed Mother's day flowers; send flowers tomorrow & discount the service charge!"*

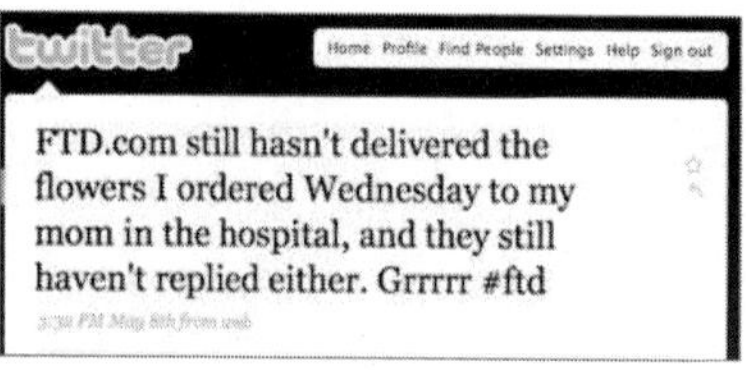

Figure 13.2 A tweet from an unhappy FTD customer

FTD sent the affected customers an email, offering discounts on their orders, but they never addressed the concerns on Twitter, exacerbating the problem. By not communicating directly with upset customers in the social network where they were complaining —Twitter in this case—FTD failed to come to its own defense in the minds of the broader public. Failing to do so left lingering negativity.

TechCrunch did a sentiment analysis of FTD's brand using the reputation management tool Twendz (`http://twendz.waggeneredstrom.com`); the analysis was not pretty. Twendz looks at the sentiments expressed about a brand or topic, as represented by a keyword search, and measures tweets for positivity, neutrality, or negativity (Figure 13.3). According to the Twendz, 63 percent of the tweets about FTD were negative, and that figure climbed to 83 percent for tweets that include "FTD" and "Mom."

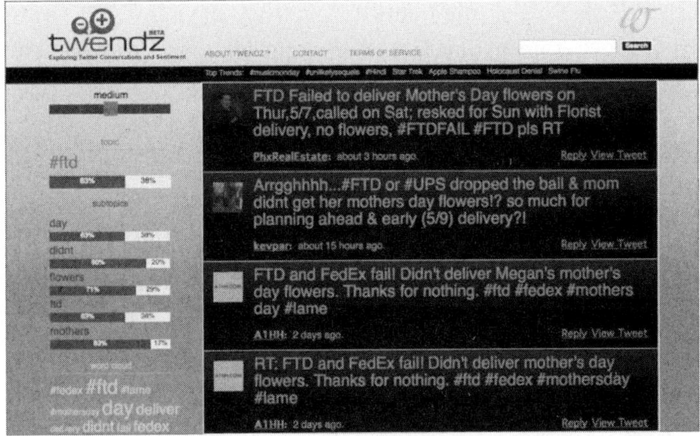

Figure 13.3 Twendz displayed very high negative sentiment for FTD during its Mother's Day debacle.

Although FTD wasn't the only flower delivery company to fail and suffer the wrath of Twitter on that Mother's Day weekend, its competitor, 1-800-Flowers.com, was on hand to do some damage control (Figure 13.4). As a consequence, its Twendz score wasn't nearly as high as FTD's, with only 33 percent of all tweets judged as negative.

Figure 13.4 1-800-Flowers.com tried to placate disgruntled Mother's Day customers through Twitter.

At the time of this writing, FTD (USA) seems to have recovered from its hard-won lesson (Figure 13.5), although the company still appears to be absent from Twitter.

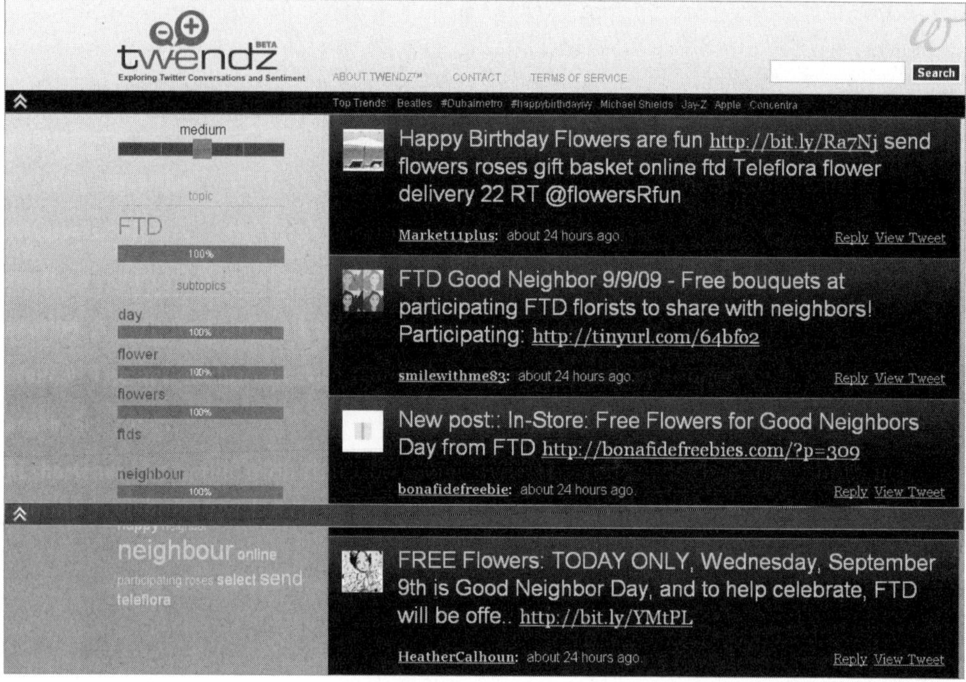

Figure 13.5 Twendz reading for FTD at the time of this writing

Crocs: Crisis Averted

Footwear-company Crocs (`@crocs`) knows one of its main target audiences pretty well: adult females. Many of Crocs' most ardent fans also engage in some form of social networking or blogging, so in July 2009 Crocs took the opportunity to participate in the ever-more-popular targeted blogging conference BlogHer. George G. Smith, Jr., Crocs' social media specialist, led the charge. Crocs hosted a special product preview event for members of its Crocs community attending BlogHer, hosted at one of Crocs' nearby Chicago stores. As is typical for a conference, the company also came armed with lots of giveaways, including free shoes.

Apparently, one female blogger didn't get a free pair of shoes and wasn't going to stand for it. Recognizing Smith as the Crocs man, the blogger approached him in the conference hotel lobby and complained that she didn't get the free shoes. Smith apologized, but the woman went on to threaten Crocs: "Ya know, if you don't give me shoes—I could totally write something bad about you on my blog." Disbelieving, Smith asked her to repeat herself, to which the woman replied, "It's just a pair of shoes. It's a lot easier to give them to me than deal with the negative press I could make."

Knowing Crocs' solid reputation among the blogging community, Smith forced her hand, telling the woman, "I could pick up my phone here and get in contact with so many people and tell them what just happened that you would be afraid to go near your computer, let alone attempt to blog again." The woman left without her shoes, and Crocs avoided a possible PR crisis, but her action left Smith with a bad taste in his mouth. Maybe in an effort to discourage similar future threats from other consumers now wielding media power, Smith wrote a post called "Threatened at BlogHer" on his personal blog (`http://nosenseoftime.org/2009/07/threatened-at-blogher`). He also tweeted about his blog post, which spread through the Twitterverse and then the mainstream news media like wildfire when some power users got a hold of it.

Whether it was by luck that this social media blackmailer didn't really have the guts to go through with her threat or whether it was because of Smith's surprising response, this experience also sends a message to brands. They need to be on the lookout and prepared for ill-intentioned consumers trying to do harm to the brand without due cause. This is another reason businesses need to become immersed in social media: so they know how to defend themselves if victimized this way.

Bloggers Beware

Bloggers and other social media professionals who receive cash or in-kind payment from brands in exchange for their endorsement must now disclose such compensation. A Federal Trade Commission (FTC) ruling in early October 2009 requires bloggers, research firms, and celebrities that help promote a product to disclose these payments or face penalties of up to $11,000 per violation.

…tential Crises

…pare your company to deal with a crisis on Twitter, it's best to imag-
…se scenarios so you can think through how to deal with them *before*
…en. Let's first review some best practices.

…Can't afford a social media strategist? You still need to have a skilled
…place, and this person needs to be empowered to speak for the

Listen. …gle and Twitter alerts for your brand and product names. Use a social media monitoring tool for tracking purposes as well.

Be involved. Try not to just observe from the sidelines. Join in the conversation and be ready to respond to both positive and negative commentary. Learn how to use social media so that, if there is a crisis, you won't be fumbling your way in the dark at the height of danger. Remember that although solving a problem in a phone call creates a happy customer, solving a problem on Twitter can spread good feelings to thousands of users and it can amplify positive sentiment about your brand.

React early. Don't wait for a disaster to get out of hand. Make your audience aware that you know of the problem and that you're working on a solution or how they can get resolution.

Stay involved. Don't hide out. Avoiding a situation is a sure way to get more people to complain about it.

Be transparent. If the problem you're trying to deal with is a difficult one involving more than just a quick fix, don't worry about sounding like a broken record. Keep reassuring people as to exactly when and how the problem will be resolved. Communicate reasonable expectations and update your audience frequently.

Recruit brand advocates. Whether these are your own employees or people who love your brand and let you know it, get them Twittering on your brand's behalf. These tweets will counterbalance negative ones if they come along.

Maintain integrity. Make sure everyone's honest about their tweets on behalf of your brand. Do not pay your brand advocates for their tweets, because if you do face a crisis and it's revealed that your positive tweets are paid ones, you'll have a fiasco on your hands.

The Crisis List

Now that you know what you should be doing, you need to think about crisis scenarios for which you might want to prepare:

- Delivery delays
- Rogue employees
- Product recalls
- Server outage
- Natural disaster
- Terrorist attack
- Negative industry information
- Corporate fraud
- Executive misconduct
- Product contamination
- Product tampering
- Senior executive death
- Litigation
- Labor dispute
- Workplace violence

- Harassment or HR issues
- IT security failure
- Activist attack
- Government unrest (if you do international work)
- Operational failures
- A blogger who consistently writes negative posts about you, the company, or your brands
- Negative comments on blogs or discussion boards
- Negative comments that spread like wildfire before you have time to tend to them
- The potential of not seeing negative comments in another social network
- Online security attacks
- Online brand attacks
- Company or brand hijacking

Although you can't anticipate every possible scenario, there are common themes and incidents. A little bit of planning up front can quickly turn a crisis situation into a manageable story.

Monday's One-Hour Exercise: Create Your Crisis List

Treat the preceding crisis list as a starting point. Based on your organization's history, industry issues from the past, information that could be deemed controversial, or market-specific concerns, write down what you think your crisis list looks like. Think through every possible scenario, ask your colleagues to review the list and add to it, and even ask people in your industry that you trust to review the list and add to it. Start to think about a single crisis you'd like to explore tomorrow as a fire drill. It should be a crisis that's actually likely to happen.

Tuesday: Create a Fire Drill

Did you select a single crisis to pursue from yesterday's exercise? If not, choose one now because you're going to use it to develop a *fire drill*—a plan of action—around. The first thing you have to do when factoring Twitter into your crisis management plan is to determine who in your organization will be responsible for monitoring Twitter for potential crisis situations, how that person (or those people) will communicate for the company, and when it's time to go into full-crisis mode.

The three major phases of any Twitter crisis plan are as follows:

1. **Preparation.** Try to have every possible detail planned out before a crisis hits. You can't plan for every scenario, which is why you'll choose one today to work with, but having a plan can help guide everyone.

2. **Response.** Fast, concise, honest, transparent, and simple is the key to any proper crisis response.
3. **Recovery.** The dialogue created on Twitter can greatly help your recovery. Monitoring what is being written about the response to a crisis helps guide your recovery decisions.

The Public Relations Society of America (PRSA) publishes a newsletter called *The Strategist*. In an article about digital crisis communication, they created a list of items to consider that also applies to Twitter. The list describes the following:

- As soon as a crisis is determined, use Twitter to distribute a brief and crisp message. A company could create a crisis by responding to something that isn't true or isn't serious enough to be considered a crisis. Examine the issue carefully before responding, but be prepared to respond quickly.
- Always provide a direct email address as a way for people to respond.
- Keep in mind that things happen online 24/7, and a digital crisis can occur at any time of the day or week. Rapid response to true crises is the most effective way to address digital situations.

Reminder Be cognizant of the fact that everything you (and others) post digitally is there for posterity. As you develop your crisis management plan, think ahead to the future and pretend you are reflecting on the past. Ask yourself, "Did we respond to this matter as effectively as we could have? What did we issue, do, or not do that we wish people could not see or find later?"

Controlling everything is impossible, but do try to minimize your future consequences by your present actions.

Make It Realistic

As you create your fire drill, think about how to make it as realistic as possible. Only you and one other person within your company should know the exact scenario so the drill is not compromised. Think about these seven elements, which are fundamental to a crisis management plan:

- **Create a listening program.** Be aware of any issues or negative comments in real time—not hours, or even days, later. Refer to the social media monitoring tools discussed in Chapter 7, "Week 4: Track and Monitor What Twitter Generates for You." Even if you're focused on Twitter, listen to all social media channels because you never know where an issue might arise.
- **Get CEO buy-in and involvement.** The CEO must buy into, and be part of, the crisis management strategy from its inception. The CEO sets the tone for the

importance of crisis management throughout the entire organization. Most likely, the CEO also will be the spokesperson in a crisis so he or she *must* be credible. For your Twitter crisis management strategy, make sure your CEO at least understands Twitter and how it works, so preferably he or she can use it to relay the response message directly.

- **Be thorough.** Think through every possible scenario when you create your crisis management plan. What could happen internally? What might employees be hiding? Is there a delivery problem or product tampering that your customer service department knows about, but is hiding in hopes of fixing it before the CEO finds out? What could be happening externally that could damage the brand? Do you have the network and buzz agents on Twitter to help you spread the word when you respond? Are your followers passionate enough to help you through a crisis? How would you respond to negative or potentially negative tweets? Every last detail is what is going to save you. Don't skimp here.
- **Get your legal team on board...now.** If you don't, there could be conflict between legal and the crisis team, which causes delays. The longer you delay, the more the wildfire spreads, allowing your detractors to speak for you.
- **Utilize internal assets.** Always use employees as your brand stewards during crisis. They're typically on the front line with your customers and can communicate what you're doing about the crisis through their own Twitter handles.
- **Be truthful.** Don't dismiss transparency, honesty, and authenticity. If part of your strategy is to videotape your CEO and drive your Twitter followers to your YouTube channel for the message, but he or she is traveling internationally and technology is sketchy, be prepared to say so and let your customers know when to expect a message (just don't make it more than a few hours).
- **Maintenance.** A crisis usually happens because there was no advance planning or the plan was not current. After you develop your fire-drill scenario, deploy it and then evaluate how you performed. Make sure you review your crisis management plan at least monthly to keep it top-of-mind, and update it as changes in the Twitter ecosystem, your company, or your industry demand it.

You might also want to subscribe to the blog Fight Against Destructive Spin (`http://www.spinsucks.com`), which often discusses topics such as these.

Tuesday's One-Hour Exercise: Execute Your Crisis Management Fire Drill

Have you determined what crisis to put to the test in your fire drill? Using the steps described in this chapter, put together a crisis management plan to execute for that crisis, and plan a time to run the fire drill at your company. Execute all the steps except anything that would actually be broadcast publicly—no live tweeting, for example!

Wednesday: Write a Twitter Crisis Management Action Plan

In the event of a crisis, the key to protecting your company's reputation on Twitter successfully is to have a Twitter crisis management plan in place, and to have practiced at least one pre-crisis fire drill. Yesterday, you planned for, and maybe even executed, your fire drill. Today, you're going to write your full-blown Twitter crisis management plan. As you begin to write this plan, think about what to include:

- **Assessment of potential risks.** (You did this when you created Monday's crisis list.)
- **Crisis response team.** Who responds to what, who has the most influence on Twitter, and how do they use their buzz agents to deliver messages?
- **A target audience assessment.** Do you call your customers? Do you send emails? Do you post things to your website? Do you use reporters and bloggers to add third-party credibility? How do you use Twitter to drive your audiences to other mediums?

Flesh Out Your Components

Let's delve deeper into the previous components before you create your Twitter crisis management action plan.

Crisis Response Team

Every crisis response team must include the CEO, your legal counsel, and at least one senior-level communications professional. If you don't have internal counsel or communications, either contract them for this purpose or use your trusted advisors to help you. Educate them on the crisis plan and give them copies. They can even help you communicate your message quickly, should it become necessary.

The crisis response team *must* be empowered to act quickly. Practice a fire drill to keep everyone on the same page.

Identify the Target Audience

Your Twitter crisis management plan must identify the target audience. Who do you want to reach? How will you reach them? What key messages do you want to deliver? Your audiences may include, but are not limited to the following:

- Customers
- Employees
- Suppliers/vendors
- Business partners
- Stakeholders
- The media

- Social media fans, followers, and friends
- Stockholders
- Your board

Now think through how you will use Twitter to advance your message to your audience but also to engage your followers. How will you use Twitter to guide people to your website, blog, YouTube channel, Facebook fan page, or other social networks? Write down the answers to these questions; they will go in your crisis management plan.

Consider Other Possibilites

When developing your Twitter crisis management plan, also take these other considerations into account:

Be prepared at all times. No one knows in advance when a crisis will happen, which is all the more reason you need to treat the management of it like you're an emergency room doctor on call. If a crisis happens, you need to be able to respond immediately. Your detractors don't care if you're on vacation or it's the middle of the night. If they're angry about something, like what happened with Motrin on a weekend, it won't matter when or where it is. They'll rally their online communities and create a firestorm while you're not paying attention.

Respond in the medium. If the crisis breaks on Twitter, like the examples given at the beginning of this chapter, then Twitter should be the first place you respond. If it happens on YouTube, like the unsanitary video made by employees of Domino's Pizza and posted on YouTube, you must respond on YouTube (Figure 13.6). Respond first wherever the crisis first broke.

Figure 13.6 Domino's Pizza's response video to their employees' unwelcome one

Twitter also makes a great support channel though, because you can use your Twitter network to respond to the crisis and push people to your YouTube video as well.

Have materials prepared in advance. Even though it's nearly impossible to predict the kind of detailed content you'll need to respond to a specific crisis, you can prepare background material and a "dark" online media room. Prepare skeleton materials and create an online media room that isn't live until necessary. This media room should contain an RSS feed; video, photo, and audio downloadables; interactive press releases with multimedia; a company fact sheet; the company boilerplate; registration for email news alerts; contact information; and SEC filings if your company is a public company. If a crisis happens, you can quickly move the media room to live and fill in the blanks of the skeleton materials.

Having these components ready enables you to respond within minutes, instead of hours or days. Remember, a crisis usually becomes a crisis because the company isn't properly prepared to handle it. Thinking "I'll get to this later" is what will get you in trouble should something happen. You can't predict a natural disaster, a rogue employee, a tampered product, or a really dissatisfied customer, so be ready!

Wednesday's One-Hour Exercise: Create Your Twitter Crisis Management Plan

You've done your fire drill and gone over the components of a solid Twitter crisis management plan. You should now feel confident about developing your plan, so take the time to do so now.

Thursday: Know How to Really Say "I'm Sorry"

When JetBlue passengers were stranded on the runway for 11 hours without food or water, the founder and CEO of the airline, David Neeleman, described how he felt about the incident as "humiliated and mortified." Throughout this book we've talked about being authentic and transparent on Twitter, and Neeleman proved he could do just that with his apology. He demonstrated the humility to admit mistakes quickly without spin and without making excuses. He reacted by showing he genuinely cared about his customers.

Marketing guru Seth Godin has a great graph he uses to describe the "Local Max," which is when a company begins to have success (Figure 13.7). You'll go from point A to the Local Max fairly quickly, but then you dip to point B and even further to point C. Godin's point is that you have to decline in order to get *really* big results (the "Big Max.") Most companies, however, are so afraid of going to points B and C that they stay at the Local Max.

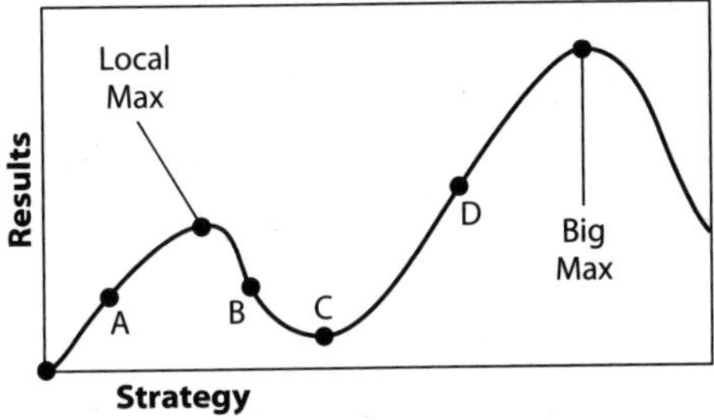

Figure 13.7 Seth Godin's success graph

Let's relate this theory to JetBlue's situation. After humbly apologizing for the incident, Neeleman provided refunds to the stranded customers, which was a huge financial risk to the company. JetBlue hit point B. Neeleman next created a Customer Bill of Rights (Figure 13.8) that penalizes JetBlue financially and rewards customers for every hour they spend stranded on a plane. With this move, JetBlue hit point C. This innovative bill of rights, however, protects JetBlue customers and may force the airline industry to face its miserable customer service record, squarely putting JetBlue at the Big Max.

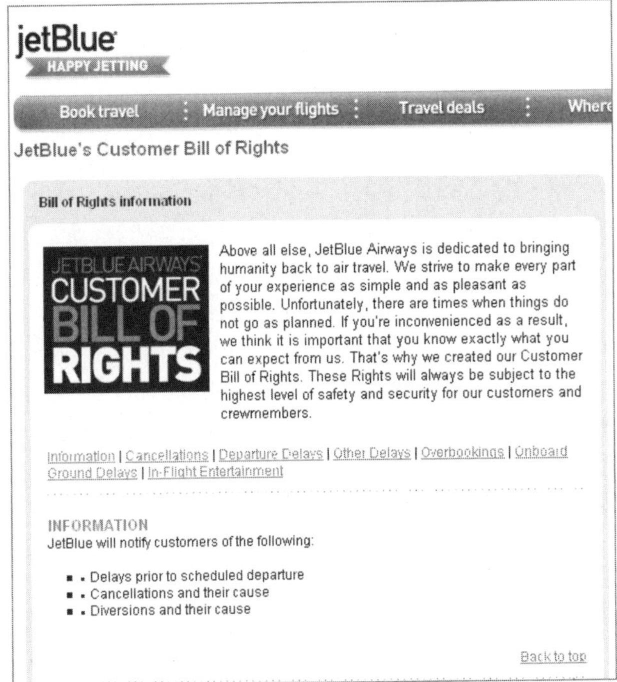

jetBlue
HAPPY JETTING
Book travel
Manage your flights
Travel deals
JetBlue's Customer Bill of Rights
Bill of Rights information
JETBLUE AIRWAYS CUSTOMER BILL OF RIGHTS
Above all else, JetBlue Airways is dedicated to bringing humanity back to air travel. We strive to make every part of your experience as simple and as pleasant as possible. Unfortunately, there are times when things do not go as planned. If you're inconvenienced as a result, we think it is important that you know exactly what you can expect from us. That's why we created our Customer Bill of Rights. These Rights will always be subject to the highest level of safety and security for our customers and crewmembers.
Information | Cancellations | Departure Delays | Other Delays | Overbookings | Onboard Ground Delays | In-Flight Entertainment
INFORMATION
JetBlue will notify customers of the following:
• Delays prior to scheduled departure
• Cancellations and their cause
• Diversions and their cause
Back to top

Figure 13.8 To show its commitment, JetBlue displays its Customer Bill of Rights prominently on its website.

Apologize When Appropriate

In a crisis, don't posture. Don't spin. Don't excuse. Don't blame. You'd be surprised how far "We're sorry" goes, mostly because in today's litigious society, very few companies ever say it for fear of being sued. Do say "We're sorry. We screwed up. We're going to fix this." Then provide as many details as you can about your game plan.

Live It

Is your company doing its best to avoid disasters? Are you doing everything you can to make it possible to do so? This boils down to having everyone in your organization live and breathe the company values. Get serious about them. Don't just provide laminated cards for everyone to keep at their desk and pull out when the CEO walks by and asks them to repeat the values. You company's leadership needs to exemplify these values. Your company needs to communicate about and reinforce these values. Hire only people who believe them. Only then can you be genuinely intent on extending these values to your external audiences. When you do this, not only will it be a lot easier for your company to say "I'm sorry" and really mean it, but many more people will believe it, too.

Thursday's One-Hour Exercise: Remind Yourself of Your Company Values

This exercise, though here in your Twitter marketing book, is a good one to perform at your company sporadically:

1. Clearly define your company's values.
2. Define a plan to communicate these values if you don't have one already.
3. Communicate these values to everyone in the organization. Don't do it through a one-off email. Plan to communicate it in person, even if you can't do that right away.
4. Create daily goals to which you hold yourself accountable to make sure you're living and breathing the values. Plan to practice these goals on a daily basis.
5. Share these goals with at least three members of your organization who can hold you accountable. Make them hold you accountable, even if you're the CEO.

Friday: Distribute Your Crisis Action Plan

As you finalize your Twitter crisis action plan, make certain the following items are included:

- A "dark" online media room with information that can quickly be updated and taken live should a crisis hit.
    - Make sure your website's servers can handle the intense spikes in traffic you might experience. If you're in a crisis and people can't access your site, you'll have an even bigger problem on your hands.

- If you don't already have a blog, consider creating one so that you have readers, fans, and brand ambassadors to help you spread the word in times of crisis.
- Build relationships in advance of any crisis. Get to know bloggers and reporters who cover your space.
- Begin to live and breathe your values, communicate them consistently, and make your internal stakeholders your best brand ambassadors.
- List emergency contacts that include numbers and emails for top executives, your crisis team, and your PR spokespersons. Also consider adding your customers and key partners and suppliers to the list. Give copies of this list to all internal people on the list. All of these people should also have hard and electronic copies of the list off-premises should natural disaster strike.
- Develop a process for being able to record video to put on YouTube quickly. Create a channel, if you don't already have one, and know how to use your video camera. Understand fully how to upload video quickly to the Web and disseminate it to your audiences. Keep your camera's battery charged.
- Create fact sheets, questions and answers, templates for news releases, and other materials on which you can quickly fill in the blanks.
- Designate an appointed spokesperson who will speak to the media, be videotaped, do interviews, and become the face of the crisis. In the JetBlue example, the spokesperson, David Neeleman, is the founder and CEO. That may make sense for your company, or it may make sense to have someone else who is more comfortable in front of a camera, has been with the organization for some time, and has experience handling a crisis.

Then pull together your team, review the plan, make needed changes to it, run another fire drill if you still need to work out some kinks, finalize your plan, and then distribute it to everyone in your organization. Then put it away for three months. Review it every quarter with your crisis team, make changes, update it with new technologies and new company information, and finalize it again. Schedule these reviews in advance so you know that you'll do them. It may feel redundant, but if the time comes when you're faced with a crisis, you'll feel much more confident and you will minimize the damage if you're prepared.

Friday's One-Hour Exercise: Search Twitter for Crisis Management in Action

At any given time, Twitter is a great place to find newsmakers, companies, and individuals handling crises. In today's exercise, we going to have you pay attention to a crisis breaking on Twitter and analyze how it's being handled.

1. Review the week's news. It's bound to have some examples of crisis or disaster.
2. Try to select a few stories on a corporate crisis or misfortune.

3. Go to Twitter Search and see what's being tweeted about this crisis or incident.
    a. Are there many tweets?
    b. Who's tweeting?
    c. Does the affected company have a Twitter account?
    d. Is the affected company addressing the incident head-on through Twitter?
    e. Assess the company's handling of their incident through Twitter, and jot down any items you'd want your company to do differently or better.
4. Perform as many of these searches and reviews as you feel are necessary until you've exhausted all the "We'd handle this differently if it were our problem" situations you can find.

The Main Points

- Small or large, a crisis eventually hits every company. Thinking through a list of most-likely scenarios will help you prepare to deal with, or even avert, a crisis.
- To further prepare for a crisis, conjure up a mock crisis and create and execute a fire drill to respond to it.
- Your company should include Twitter in its overall crisis management action plan.
- A little contrition goes a long way.
- Once you complete the exercise of preparing for a crisis, don't just shelve it to collect dust over time. Bring it out on a regular basis and review it with key stakeholders. In other words, always expect the unexpected.

Week 11: Develop a Direct Response Promotion for Twitter

Throughout this book, we've shown many ways to use Twitter for building awareness and building relationships. We've also talked about brands getting involved on Twitter, not for any specific gain, but to avoid loss *(the ROI we described as a negative "return on influence" or the "risk of ignoring").*

There are, however, businesses using Twitter for direct gain. These companies market or promote through Twitter to generate a direct response. Some might view these companies as mavericks, while others view them as exploiters. The reality is, Twitter is another channel to influence action, and some companies are out there doing so. Let's see what the development of such a campaign would look like if executed over a week's time.

14

Chapter Contents

Monday: Define the Need

Today you're going to spend your hour defining a specific marketing challenge or need that requires attention and determining how Twitter can be used to address it. It's important to take the time to define fully the problem or need you are attempting to resolve and the resolution or outcome you're seeking. Much like branding statements or brand tenets, these definitions will guide how the campaign is executed and the goal is achieved. Without clear objectives, campaigns often try to be all things to all people.

With a team of three or more people, you can best execute the definition process by setting up a brainstorming session. During this session, as with any brainstorming process, you should let the ideas flow without regard for how hard or easy they would be to implement. Generate a list that is as long as needed to highlight the existing challenges and needs of your marketing plan. Build an inclusive list so that you can prioritize the items that are the most critical to the business, as well as the best candidates for Twitter. You can always delete items from consideration later.

Some types of campaigns work well for Twitter and others do not. You need to know how your current customers interact with you to determine if Twitter would be a viable channel to promote your direct response message. If you provide a product or service that people don't feel comfortable discussing in public, for example, you'd have to approach a direct response strategy on Twitter with sensitivity and a lot of smarts.

Consider Direct Response Campaigns

The purpose of a "direct response" campaign is to elicit a response or action. Bearing that in mind, what actions are you trying to drive and what goals are you trying to accomplish? Keep them in mind as you ponder your brainstormed list.

Direct Response Tied to Brand Awareness

Twitter's broad reach might lead a company to believe it's a good channel for driving brand awareness. Used properly by itself, Twitter can help promote your company as tech-savvy, forthright, and engaged with your customers, but expecting increased awareness for an established brand is a lofty goal. For new companies trying to create brands, however, some campaigns have been truly effective.

For example, leveraging Apple products as giveaway incentives, two companies, Squarespace (`http://www.squarespace.com`) and Moonfruit (`http://www.moonfruit.com`), executed awareness-building campaigns in the summer of 2009 (Figure 14.1). Each tweet containing the respective brand name in a hashtag entered the user into a prize drawing. The campaigns performed so well that both companies saw their hashtags appear as Trending Topics on Twitter, which brought even more awareness as people wondered what the names represented. The campaigns, however, also unleashed considerable backlash as users tired of the insignificance of the hashtags and viewed the tweets as spam. Running a similar campaign is inadvisable now that the ground has been spoiled, but these two companies benefited from being pioneers and from weathering the storm brewed by the ensuing controversy.

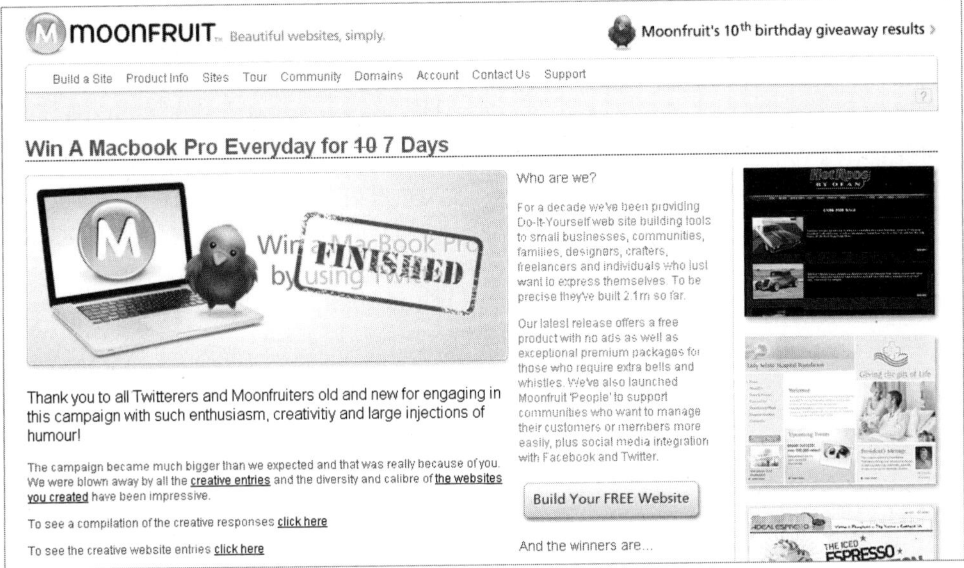

Figure 14.1 Moonfruit's give-away entry page

Get More Twitter Followers or Facebook Fans

Many bloggers and authors have implemented this type of strategy. Oftentimes, these strategies have multiple prongs involving a contest or give-away (perhaps their book for authors; perhaps free attendance to a webinar for bloggers) in exchange for becoming a new Twitter follower and/or Facebook fan. The promotion can also be tied into other actions such as a follow plus a tweet or a follow plus a photo posting. These kinds of promotions can get pretty creative, depending on what the promotional host demands as action versus what they're giving away.

Drive Traffic to Your Website

Twitter can be used not only to drive traffic to your website but also to drive that traffic to specific content on your website, to any specific page, or to another website altogether. For example, a common Twitter marketing word-of-mouth technique is to promote your videos on YouTube. Videos tend to be watched all the way through, whereas website content might be abandoned more readily for the next closest thing. Of course, in order to attract traffic to any site, the content needs to be intriguing enough to attract users and valuable enough to keep them there and encourage retweets. Commonly successful content components include instructional or thought-provoking blog posts, free tools, or some kind of calculator. Setting specific web traffic goal figures, however, is not encouraged because attaining these goals exclusively through Twitter can be difficult.

Events

Promoting events on Twitter works well. The goal, of course, is event registration. The more an event appeals to Twitter users, the more likely they'll be to help promote it. Because Twitter first attracted bloggers, venues like BlogWorld and SXSW have had success direct marketing through Twitter. Other kinds of social media or web-related conferences have had similar success, but now that Twitter has attracted such a diverse audience, the direct marketing of any kind of event is fair game. Charity fundraisers, seminars and webinars, open houses and grand openings, sports leagues, and of course, tweetups—all kinds of events have found their way to Twitter marketing (Figure 14.2). If you visit `http://search.twitter.com` and search for "webinar," you'll see numerous results indicating how powerful this medium is and how easy it is to use.

Figure 14.2 Webinars, open houses, and sports leagues are all promoted through Twitter.

Sales Promotion

Most people would agree that Twitter is a better mechanism for conversing with your existing and/or potential customers than for pursuing sales. Companies that only tweet sales and promotional content will likely find themselves negatively affecting followers and influence. Earlier in the book, we cited such examples as Dell, and KFC's "Free Grilled Chicken" campaign. KFC's attempt, paired with Oprah if you recall, was so successful that they had to stop honoring their coupon by midday. One KFC parking lot overflowed so badly that an attendant had to direct traffic to the drive-through lane. Many people who arrived after midday had their coupons turned down. Was this a sign of a successful campaign or the makings of a PR disaster? Although KFC succeeded in driving awareness of its new product, it also left many customers frustrated in the short run.

Hewlett-Packard (HP)

During the 2008 Christmas holiday season, two of Hewlett-Packard's divisions—the Personal Systems Group and the Imaging and Printing Group—partnered and decided to use Twitter as another channel to support their broader integrated holiday campaign. Recognizing that consumers would be asking their Twitter networks for product recommendations and sharing insights into how to select a new printer or personal computer, HP enthusiastically decided to give Twitter a try (`@HPHolidayCheer`). They intended to use Twitter as an avenue to have conversations with existing and potential new customers and, more importantly, to measure how folks would engage with their brand.

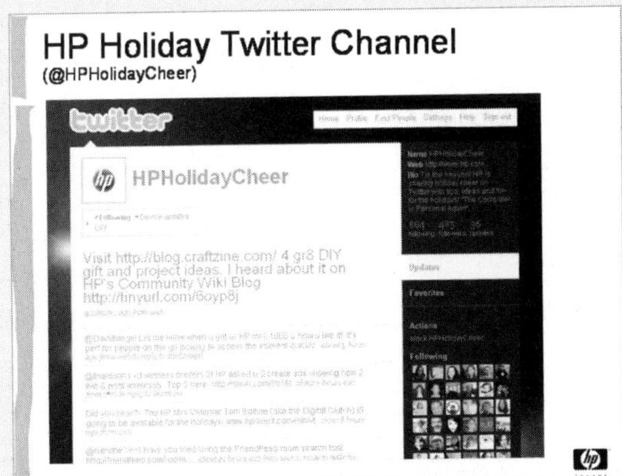

The HP team created content and activity with a 40-day editorial calendar, including a theme for each week. The planned content included weekly promotional awareness about existing coupons and specials. In the spirit of sharing good content, they also posted interesting trivia, gift ideas, and unique activities to do at home during the holidays.

Continues

Hewlett-Packard (HP) *(Continued)*

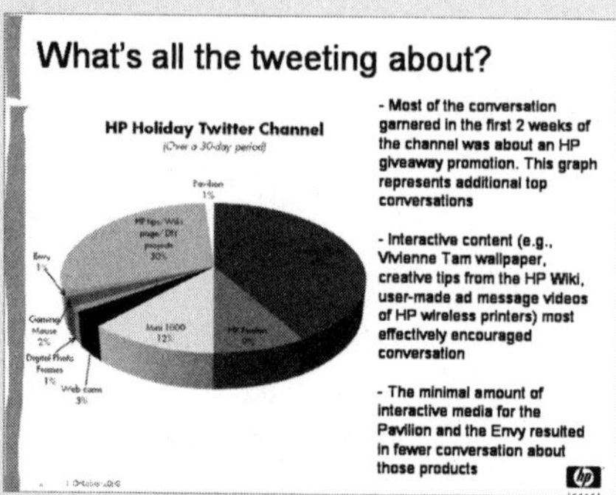

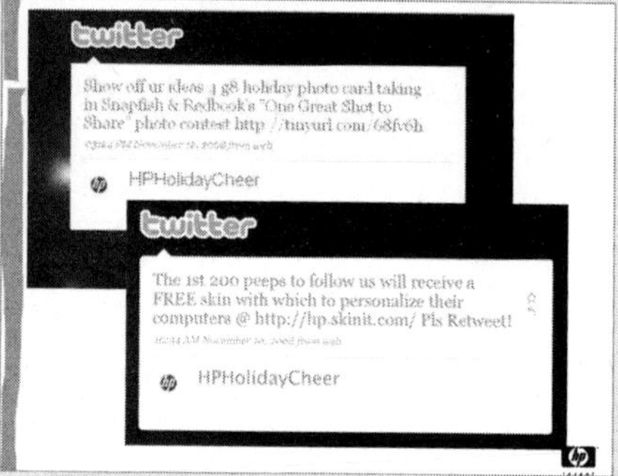

According to Angela LoSasso, U.S. social media manager at HP, "What really surprised us and our executives was the level of engagement we received. The lessons were invaluable in helping us understand not only how customers and fans want to talk with us, but also what's most appealing to them with regards to content and context as evidenced by the replies and retweets. This was a much larger upside than the click-thrus and transactions."

Here are a few examples of HP helping its followers:

- A customer was panicked over not having enough Christmas cards for her dinner party. An HP employee on Twitter pointed the prospective customer to the HP Creative Studio where she could design a card herself and print it at home.
- HP's tweeted idea of creating a custom cookbook to be printed at home and given as a gift received a great response.

Noted LoSasso, "With Twitter, it's incredibly efficient to ask and get answers about what interests [consumers] the most, and in my mind, there's no doubt these positive conversations help solidify our brand loyalty." She noted that during that holiday campaign their follower count went up by over 1,000 followers.

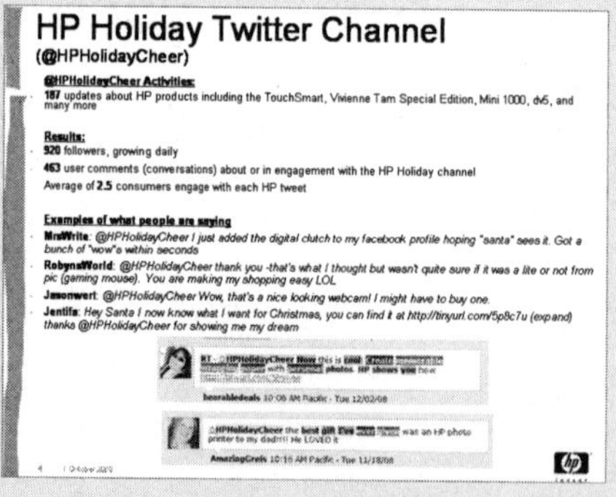

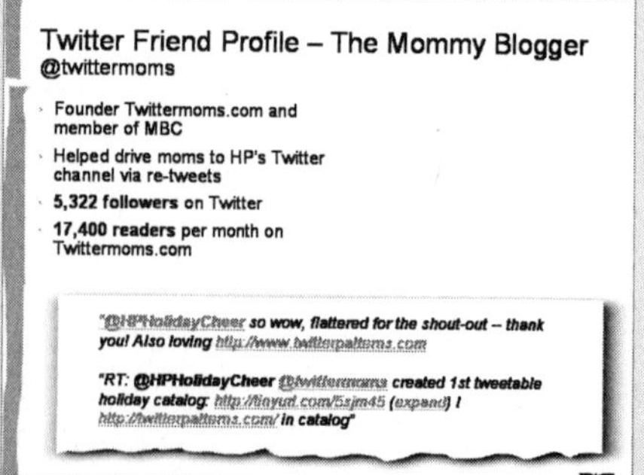

Take Action for a Cause

Devise a campaign specifically to promote a cause. For example, National Breast Cancer Awareness Month takes place every year in October, and various breast cancer organizations launch initiatives to help raise awareness. One of the most visible reminders is the color pink, as retailers, manufacturers, sports apparel, and organizations adopt the color in support of the campaign.

Since Twitter has come along, yet another channel for awareness campaigning has been added. To show your support, you can add a pink ribbon from Twibbon (`http://twibbon.com/join/Breast-Cancer-Research`) to your avatar (Figure 14.3), make $1.00 pledges to Susan G. Komen for the Cure by tweeting the hashtag `#tweetsforboobs` (Figure 14.4), turn your avatar pink to generate donations for the Breast Cancer Network of Strength (`http://www.networkofstrength.org`), or follow any number of nonprofit organizations on Twitter and undertake the activities they ask of you in order to generate donations from corporate sponsors (Figure 14.5).

Breast Cancer Research
Show your support for breast cancer survivors, and the ongoing research to stamp out the disease! And please use this Twibbon if you're a survivor yourself!

Figure 14.3 The Breast Cancer Research Twibbon

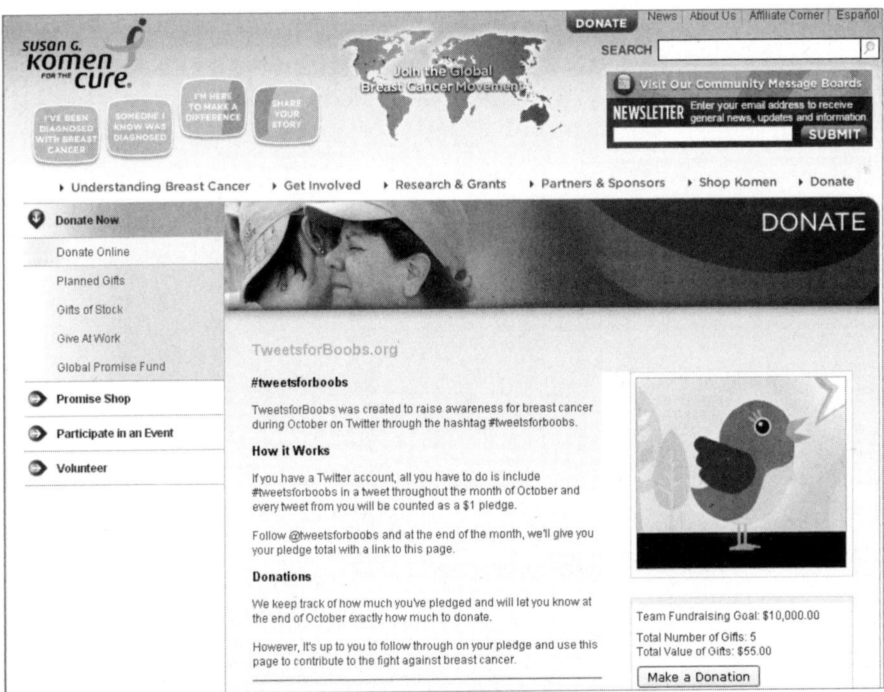

Figure 14.4 Susan G. Komen's `#tweetsforboobs` fundraising idea

We just hit the $30,000 mark! A big thank you to everyone who updated your Yahoo! status for breast cancer! http://ow.ly/sezb

5:53 PM Oct 1st from HootSuite

NBCF

Figure 14.5 The National Breast Cancer Foundation uses Twitter to instruct its followers on how they can help raise donations.

LIVESTRONG

In July of 2009, the Lance Armstrong Foundation (`http://www.livestrong.org`) launched a unique viral campaign encouraging users to update their Twitter avatar with the LIVESTRONG yellow band to build awareness of the campaign and drive support for Lance Armstrong's return to the Tour de France. The LIVESTRONG campaign and Lance Armstrong have a very loyal following. The key to making this campaign successful was how easy they made it to update your avatar. The microsite they created (`http://www.livestrongaction.org/avatar`) wrote a direct interface to the Twitter account settings to update your avatar with only a few clicks.

Monday's One-Hour Exercise: Define Your Need

Let's get started with a Twitter-for-sales strategy with the following exercise:

1. Define the problem or need that requires the most attention and conforms to Twitter's platform.
2. Conduct a brainstorming session on how Twitter could be used to solve the problem or address the need.
3. From your list of ideas, select the winning solution you'll want to implement.
4. Consider the elements of direct response action you want to associate with your solution.

Tuesday: Define Campaign Components

After yesterday's exercise, brainstorming and selecting a winning solution to fulfill via a direct response promotion on Twitter, it's time to transition to more details of planning the specific promotion. When you think about this specific campaign, you'll need to identify the various components needed to make it a success. More importantly, how will you define success? What will your success metrics be? You will want to answer all of these questions upfront.

Content

The critical element in a Twitter marketing campaign is the content. The need you've identified and the solution you've chosen to address it will dictate the specific content you'll need to create. What kind of content do you want Twitter users to share? What action do you want these users to take? How can you best help this campaign go viral? Twitter's ease of use and potency as a word-of-mouth tool makes the sharing of content and, therefore, the viral opportunity as powerful, if not more powerful, than email.

Consider these elements of content production:

- **Articles, blog posts, opinions, and other written material.** Are you going to write content from scratch or compile it from outside sources? Who will compose or compile this material?
- **Graphics and multimedia.** Do you need to create graphics, audio, video, or something similar for the page to which you're sending people?
- **Landing page(s).** Do you need to build custom landing pages for this campaign?
- **Lead time.** What's your lead time to create the content components you've considered?
- **Measurements and metrics.** How will you measure progress throughout the campaign? How often do you need status updates from the people on the team to make sure everything is on track?

- **Pre-launch marketing.** What will your announcement strategy be prior to launch? Do you plan to tease your campaign or keep it completely under wraps?

You may want to develop a Twitter Task Allocation Worksheet to assign specific content deliverables and tasks to team members as well (Table 14.1).

▶ **Table 14.1** Sample Twitter Task Allocation Worksheet

Owner	Key Deliverable	Notes
John	Copywriting	Compose 20 tweets and 200 words for the custom landing page.
Carly	Graphics	Create 10 versions of a branded logo tied into campaign graphic.
Samone	Interactive	Develop or source a blog widget that allows users simultaneously to post and promote the event to their Facebook, Twitter, and LinkedIn accounts.
Nick	Landing page	Conceive, get approval for, and register a dedicated campaign URL. Produce the landing page with the components generated by John, Carly, and Samone. Imbed Google Analytics and any other necessary tracking code into the page.
Angela	Twitter team	Define the team that will monitor Twitter during day of the launch and beyond; define the team's respective roles. Oversee communication with IT, Legal, PR, senior management, and any other departments or people outside of the team who need to be kept in the loop.

Timelines

Once you have defined your various content component needs and allocated tasks, you'll want to create a production timeline that accounts for all your campaign elements. If you truly want to launch your campaign within a week, all your content elements will need to be completed in an expedited fashion, which of course can also open the door for hasty mistakes. Trying to think through every last detail of production and building them into your timeline can help minimize errors. Even if you were to give yourself more than a week to produce and launch your campaign, which is a more realistic case than the exercise we're walking you through, it's a good idea to create a comprehensive production timeline.

Measurement Criteria

Anyone who's ever conducted a direct response marketing campaign knows that it's all about the numbers. Direct response campaigns directly tie into measurements that ultimately determine whether the campaign was a success or failure. Likewise, with a Twitter marketing direct response campaign, you'll want to define how you will measure success. Of course, your measurement criteria need to be tied into your campaign objective, but they should also be as specifically defined as possible. For example, if your objective is to generate event registration, your measurement criteria will likely include the following:

- Number of tweets containing the event link you and your team push out
- Number of retweets generated containing your event link
- Number of clicks on your event link (bearing in mind that people have a propensity to change your link into something they can track on their own)
- Number of visits to your event landing page
- Number of completed registration forms
- Number of actual attendees to your event versus those who registered

Now, for each of these criteria, you should also assign benchmarks or thresholds you'd like to achieve. If you've never done this kind of campaign before, these objectives may be closer to an educated guess than anything else, which is OK so long as you give yourself advanced permission to fail at reaching these benchmarks. For marketers in this kind of predicament, treat this first campaign as a learning experience more than anything else. For other actions to consider during the development of your campaign, you might want to refer back to Table 11.1 in Chapter 11, "Week 8: Monitor, Measure, and Valuate."

You may also want to measure secondary values related to engagement and influence. These would relate to questions such as these:

- What were our follower counts before and after the campaign?
- What was the power of our influence before and after the campaign (as measured by the total reach we have based on our followers' followers)?
- Did our content drive any correlating discussions online?
- Are people sharing the content we posted?

To keep track of whatever measurement criteria you determine appropriate to your campaign, you can develop a *dashboard*. This dashboard, which can be a simple spreadsheet, can then easily be translated into a report card to facilitate a campaign post mortem. You should also sign up for one of the tweet backup solutions recommended on Monday in Chapter 6, "Week 3: Using Twitter Search and Other Tools to Improve Your Experience." Direct response campaigns on Twitter tend to be high volume, and you don't want to rely on Twitter's pitiful 3,000-tweet archive limit to locate a tweet or provide proof of delivery.

Announcement Strategy

The pre-launch marketing of your campaign can be thought of as your announcement strategy. It covers your plans to reveal (or not) your campaign to the public in the days leading up to and including the launch. There's definitely an art to the announcement strategy. Some direct response campaigns benefit extremely well from early momentum and interest built before the campaign actually goes live, while others seek the element of surprise or compressed campaign duration to have the biggest impact.

Once you know which way you want to launch your campaign, you can plan your announcement strategy. Consider using influential bloggers and Twitter elite to help spread your message. Depending on the size of your company or how much you have invested in this particular campaign, you may want to have a formal webinar briefing for bloggers of influence to ensure that your message or campaign details are distributed properly. Recognize that you won't be able to control every detail, but if your intentions are justifiable and you do your best to help others in the Twitter community, you'll improve your chances for success. If you've developed solid Twitter relationships over time, you can also probably call in a favor or two with influential tweeps to help get the word out.

Buying Influence

If you're running a direct response campaign where success really matters, you might consider a controversial tactic: pay-per-tweet. There are about a half-dozen solution providers that provide matchmaking services between Twitter users and advertisers/marketers. The verdict isn't in yet on whether or not these kinds of paid tweets will be accepted or effective. If you're curious to learn more, here's a blog post I wrote about the subject: `http://www.webadvantage.net/webadblog/the-landscape-of-pay-per-tweet-1887`.

Would your campaign benefit from a hashtag? Would it help you track your campaign, generate buzz, and provide an anchor to which the "Twitterati" can latch? If so, consider a hashtag long enough to communicate meaning, but short enough that it won't take up too many characters of the total tweet.

In addition to planning how to recruit help to get the word out after your campaign launches, you may also want to think about teasing your campaign before it launches. Do you want to "leak" the news through outside channels or tease your audience directly? Do you want to do so in a splashy way or a low-key one instead? Be creative or mysterious. You can actually have a lot of fun with the pre-launch, building to a crescendo with the actual launch.

You can also create your tweets in advance and preload them to go live throughout the week leading up to the launch. In previous chapters, we covered a number of individual- and enterprise-level Twitter management tools that allow you to schedule tweets. Play around with the days of the week and times of day. You'll learn from the experiments, and you'll relieve your team of some of the burden of tweeting in real time by knowing what to post and when. The day you launch your live campaign, however, you'll want all hands on deck so you have as many people able to respond, engage, and interact with anyone talking about your promotion.

> **Twitter Direct Response Marketing for Higher Education**
>
> Social media marketer Mike D. Merrill's (`@mikedmerrill`) client at a recently founded southwestern university wanted to test the power of social media to drive traffic to an upcoming one-day sale at their technology store, as well as raise overall awareness of the new store itself. Merrill and his client created a Twitter account for this test, and using Twitter searches, they found and followed the university's students, staff, and alumni. (There is now a new site in beta that can assist those seeking college students and alumni: `http://beta.campustweet.com/Schools`.) The team placed links to the Twitter account and the school's Facebook fan page on the home page of the technology store site.
>
> With only this nominal effort, the team quickly accumulated over 500 relevant Twitter followers. For seven days leading up to the sale, the school started leaking specific promotions; eventually, it posted a full sale price list. A photo of it was posted to TwitPic and then tweeted, as well as linked from Facebook. Thanks to loyalty to the university and the brand, followers on campus and throughout Twitter retweeted the messages about the sale and the link to the price list. From reviewing Google Analytics and TwitPic stats, Merrill could tell that they had doubled web traffic to the store's home page and experienced over 2,500 views of the price list posted on TwitPic. On the day of the sale, the social media marketing campaign worked so well, a line formed two hours prior to the store's opening and the line continued for the next four hours. More importantly, through the power of social media, the university *tripled* their sales from the previous one-day sale record.

Tuesday's One-Hour Exercise: Outline Your Campaign

If you're ready to proceed to creating a campaign, the next step is for you to flesh out the steps you'll need to take.

1. Define the components of your campaign, start to finish.
2. Assign roles and responsibilities.
3. Plan your campaign timeline.
4. Define the campaign criteria you want to benchmark and measure.
5. Develop your announcement strategy.

Wednesday: Move to Production

For Wednesday, we're going to let you off the hook because we covered production previously (see Wednesday in Chapter 12, "Week 9: Institutionalize Maintenance") and because the elements of production from one direct response campaign to another are likely to vary. Just make sure that, as your team members move on to their respective production roles, everyone is clear on such details as the expectations of deliverables, when to provide regular status updates to the rest of the team, and, of course, the final deadlines for their components. Also, if your legal department is going to have to approve anything, get them on board as quickly as possible. We all know how Legal can hold up (or kill) entire projects!

Timing Production

If, for the sake of following along with this chapter, you're truly going to try to execute your direct response campaign in only one week, you'd better have a pretty aggressive production schedule. Of course, under ideal circumstances you'd have far more time. We like to give ourselves at least six weeks, but you might need more and when pressed, almost anyone can do it in less.

Wednesday's One-Hour Exercise: Activate Production

There's no time to waste. For this one-week exercise, you'll want to limit production to no more than a day or two at most. What are you waiting for? Get a move on!

Thursday: Work Your Announcement Strategy

On Tuesday, we discussed the announcement strategy as one of the direct response campaign components to consider. If you determined that you do want to tease your campaign pre-launch, and if you haven't already begun to do so, today's the day! Here's a useful reminder listing ways to help your announcement strategy:

- Encourage people to follow you to get word of your campaign when it breaks.
- Produce a hashtag if appropriate.
- Schedule your tweets in advance.
- Have loyalists retweet your message.
- Recruit (and train) bloggers and Twitterati to help promote your campaign and/or your teasers.
- Develop a pre-launch incentive to encourage retweeting ("The first 50 followers to RT our launch announcement will receive…").
- Tweet clues.
    - You can make a game and offer an incentive for this too ("The first 10 people to figure out the puzzle and tweet it, win…").
- Milk other media.
    - Leverage other social networking platforms:
        - Your own blog
        - Facebook
        - Digg or StumbleUpon

- LinkedIn
- SlideShare
- YouTube
- Send out an email blast.
- Draft and distribute a press release.
- Update your ad campaigns.

- Don't forget the mundane.
    - Talk to your family and friends. Have your team do likewise.
    - Send a company-wide memo. Keep everyone informed.

Final Preparations

Today you'll also be mired in production deadlines. As components become finalized, don't forget the following:

- **Testing.** There's nothing worse than a simple, unobtrusive broken link or image to spoil the user's experience and your campaign success.
- **Staging.** Post any microsites or web pages that will need to go live when it's time.
- **Final authorizations.** Do you need someone's final blessing before the campaign can go live?
- **Check in with IT.** If you've done everything right to promote this launch, you could experience a large surge on your web servers. Make sure the IT department has you covered.
- **Regroup.** At the end of the day, bring the team back together for a status update and ensure that everyone knows their role for the day of launch.
- **Plan B.** You know the saying: "Even the best-laid plans...." Be prepared for a few hiccups by thinking ahead, especially as it pertains to feedback you might get from campaign participants. If a real crisis arises, refer to Chapter 13, "Week 10: Prepare for Crisis Management."

Thursday's One-Hour Exercise: Execute Your Announcement Strategy

We've given you the guidance. Now put your actual announcement strategy in motion. At the end of the day, put in a little extra time to finalize your details before launch.

Friday: Launch Your Campaign

Today's D-day. You're going to press a button, click a few keys, and away you go! Remember, Twitter marketing is instantaneous and real-time, so be prepared to do a lot of care and feeding during the first hours and days of your campaign. You'll want to reply to `@messages`, thank those who retweet, showcase campaign stats worthy of public consumption, and do all that you can to keep the momentum high. The faster you respond to those who engage your brand, the better the experience and the more reach you will see from your campaign.

Something to keep in mind is that people's Twitter streams reload fairly quickly, and the more users that someone follows, the greater the chance that your message will be missed. As a result, you will want to tweet your message at different times throughout the day. Do not, however, just copy, paste, and tweet the same message. In fact, in an effort to cut down on spam, Twitter now restricts and filters for duplicate tweets, so you *have* to avoid repetition. Use your marketing creativity to massage your message into something slightly different each time. In fact, you may want to have a few different places to point (link) people to so that you are actually keeping your tweet content as fresh as possible.

What to Look For

As your campaign gathers momentum, pay attention to the responses you're receiving, both literal and qualitative.

- What are people saying?
- What aren't they saying?
- Is what they're saying what you expected?
- What did they say that's unexpected?
- Are you getting responses or actions the way you wanted to get them?
- What's working or not working?

In other words, play scientist/researcher/sleuth/anthropologist, all at the same time. Remember to learn, even at the hands of failure.

On the measurement side of your campaign, if you've been backing up all your tweets, you've got part of the strategy covered. Make sure to save all retweets and direct messages received by you as part of your monitoring strategy; they are a testament to the number of users who have engaged your brand—and, if you've offered an incentive or contest to certain first tweets, you need to know whose tweet actually won.

Chances are that you've set up your campaign to run more than a single day, so it's not necessarily the time to run all your numbers or conduct your postmortem just yet—but there's no harm in doing a Day 1 dry run for practice. Gather the team and collect their thoughts. Capture all your key metrics and measure them against planned goals. How much further do you have to go to reach your goal? Are you on pace with your expectations? Do you need to adjust your campaign to iron out weak spots? If you're running a transactional campaign, are you able to attribute direct revenues to your efforts? Are you pleased with the results so far?

One last thing: if you really do launch a direct response campaign on a Friday, do not lose all your momentum by letting the whole team take the weekend off. Remember that Twitter users expect 24/7 access and rapid response, so have at least a few people prepared to put in some overtime during these first few critical days.

May you have bountiful success.

Friday's One-Hour Exercise: Launch!

Not much to say here. It's time to pull the trigger and get your campaign started!

The Main Points

- Before you can know what kind of direct response campaign to develop, you need to determine where you need to generate the most response. Usually it's a problem spot or area of new development for your company. Identify your need first, so you can begin planning.
- Content, timelines, measurements, and your pre-launch and launch strategies are the components you'll need to produce in order to execute a Twitter direct response marketing campaign effectively.
- Under ordinary planning and development circumstances, give yourself enough lead time to produce the various components of your campaign.
- Your announcement strategy plays a major role in getting the word out about your campaign and generating early action.
- Once your campaign goes live, you can't expect your work to be done and to manage the campaign on autopilot. You need to feed your campaign, interact with and respond to the Twitter community, and monitor and gauge your performance.
- Never stop learning.

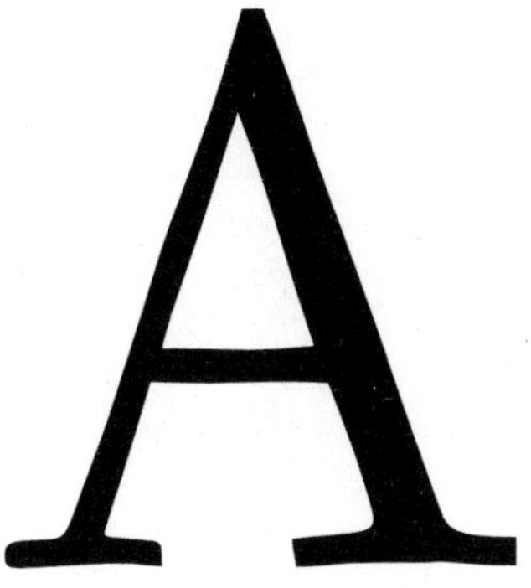

Twitter-Related Glossary

@mention Referring directly to another Twitter user by including their `@username` in a tweet.

@message Sending a tweet to one or more Twitter users by including their `@username(s)` in the tweet.

@reply Responding to another user's tweet by including their `@username` first.

Advanced Search Twitter's in-depth, real-time search tool, available at `http://search.twitter.com/advanced`.

affiliate marketing An Internet-based marketing practice in which a business rewards one or more affiliates for each visitor or customer.

alert Email or text notifications from Twitter about its accounts and services, which can be turned on or off at any time.

application program interface (API) A collection of web programming tools made available to third-party developers, such as those offered by Twitter, for the purpose of creating new applications based on the original.

apps Short for applications; an app is any type of third-party application that enhances Twitter.

auto-DM An automated direct message (see *direct message*); auto-DMs must be set up and managed through a third-party application.

avatar A small image, usually a photo or self-portrait, that represents a Twitter user.

blog A type of website that publishes frequently updated journal-style entries relating news, opinion, entertainment, and other content.

blogging The practice of writing and publishing blog posts, usually on a routine basis.

blogosphere Refers to the large community of blogs and bloggers on the Web.

bookmarklet A small application (also called an applet) stored inside of a URL bookmark or hyperlink that launches when clicked.

bot A software program that performs automated tasks online, often for the purpose of spamming.

brand hijacking Posing as a brand on Twitter by setting up an account and tweeting on their behalf, without the brand's knowledge or approval.

browser See *web browser.*

collector In a social network, a user who aggregates information from multiple sources.

command Any text-based command used to control and manage Twitter functions.

community manager An employee whose job description is to promote and oversee a brand's social media initiatives and marketing efforts.

corporate tweeting Using Twitter for business, such as in a corporate environment.

corporate tweeting (or Twitter) policy A company-wide policy governing employee use of Twitter as it relates to the company's online presence and reputation.

creator In a social network, a user who produces original content.

critic In a social network, a user who reviews, rates, comments on, or reacts to other people's content.

crowdsourcing Outsourcing a specific task or project to a large group of people, often for the purposes of gathering feedback or input.

Digg (`http://www.digg.com`) A popular social bookmarking site where users submit, vote on, and discuss news items and other articles.

direct message (DM) A private message sent or received via Twitter between two users.

direct-to-consumer (DTC) An ideal relationship in which brands are able to market to a consumer directly.

DM See *direct message.*

early adopter One who is eager to embrace new technology and services.

enterprise-wide approach A Twitter-for-business strategy that promotes the use of Twitter at all levels of a large company, from the CEO to the general staff.

evangelist One who finds great value in a product or service, and eagerly promotes it.

Facebook A popular social networking site, available at `http://www.facebook.com`.

Fail Whale A humorous graphic that appears as part of an error message when Twitter is down or experiencing technical difficulties.

favorite A saved tweet in Twitter determined by the individual user and linked to their account, similar to bookmarking favorite websites. Favorites are publicly accessible.

follower A Twitter user who follows someone's, or a company's, Twitter updates.

FollowFriday A popularized Twitter activity that occurs on Fridays whereby users recommend their favorite people to follow. The recommendation is indicated by the hashtag `#FollowFriday` or `#FF`.

follower count The current number of individuals following a Twitter user.

following A Twitter user whom you are following.

following count The current number of people that a Twitter user follows.

friend A Twitter user you follow who also follows you back (reciprocal).

ghost tweeter Someone who tweets on another person's behalf, similar to a ghost writer.

Google The most popular search engine, available at `http://www.google.com`.

handle A Twitter username, preceded by the "at" symbol (@). For example, `@hollisthomases`.

hashtag A keyword or label preceded by the pound symbol (#) included in a tweet to help organize conversations by topic and/or provide further context For example, `#TMHAD` is the hashtag for this book.

inactive In a social network, a user who does not participate.

inbound tweets Tweets other people send to you.

instant messaging A form of real-time, text-based communication over the Internet; often referred to as chatting.

Internet The worldwide network of online computer networks.

Internet Service Provider (ISP) A company that provides connectivity to the Internet.

IRL Abbreviation for "in real life;" commonly used when people want to arrange to meet in person.

joiner In a social network, a user who is eager to sign up for an account, but who does not participate much.

LinkedIn A popular social network for professionals, available at `http://www.linkedin.com`.

live-tweeting Sending tweets about an event in real time, as it unfolds.

lurking Using Twitter in a "look before you leap" manner to read other people's tweets without contributing your own.

mashup A mixture of content or elements; an application that was built from routines obtained from multiple sources; a website that combines content and/or scripts from multiple sources.

meme An idea, part of speech, or other cultural reference that spreads rapidly from one user to another, and influences community behavior.

micro-blogging A casual, low-commitment form of blogging via brief text updates, such as those used by Twitter, Identica, and similar services.

mobile device Any type of handheld computing gadget (such as cell phones, smart phones, or netbooks) with SMS capability and/or Internet connectivity.

mobile Web Refers to any browser-based Internet service accessible from mobile devices.

multiuser approach A Twitter business strategy in which a business maintains multiple active Twitter accounts.

MySpace A popular social networking site, available at `http://www.myspace.com`.

name squatter Someone who creates a Twitter account for the sole purpose of staking a claim to a desirable username.

newbie A user who is new to Twitter and unfamiliar with its conventions.

OAuth An open protocol to allow secure API authorization in a simple and standard method from desktop and web applications.

open-source software Web and computer-based software in which the code is freely available.

power user A Twitter user who is so-deemed by the community. A power user tends to tweet often, contribute original ideas and content, usually has a large follower base, and adds value to the community.

profile A public page that displays a Twitter user's name, location, bio, following/followers count, and latest tweets.

Really Simple Syndication (RSS) Web feeds to which the user subscribes that publish frequently updated content, such as news, blogs, and podcasts in an easy-to-digest format.

real-time search Search results that are generated in "real time" or on an "as it happens" basis.

referral traffic Traffic to a website that has been referred (or generated) by another source, such as search engines, ads, or other websites.

retweet or re-tweet (RT) To repeat another user's tweet in your own tweet stream by preceding the original tweet with "RT" and crediting who said it.

RSS See *Really Simple Syndication*.

RT See *retweet*.

saved search A quick link to the real-time results of a Twitter search that one performs often.

Short Message Service (SMS) A standardized, mobile communications protocol used for text messaging.

shortened URL A URL that has intentionally been shortened using an application, mainly for the purpose of saving character counts. Many URL shortening services also have built-in tracking capabilities (see *trackable URL*).

SMS See *Short Message Service.*

social media policy A company-wide policy governing employee use of social media as it relates to the company's online presence and reputation.

social network A website with an online community of users who use it to socialize, network, and create and share content.

social networking The act of participating in social networks, such as making friends, joining discussions, posting content and status updates, and keeping in touch.

spammer In the context of Twitter, an account that uses Twitter for the sole purpose of self-promotion; often an automated account running a bot (see *bot).*

spectator In a social network, a user who absorbs information but very seldom participates in discussions or contributes original content.

team tweeting A Twitter-for-business strategy whereby multiple people control and contribute to a single Twitter account.

techie A person who is interested in all things technology-related, sometimes called a tech geek or computer geek.

Terms of Service (TOS) Twitter's statement of rules, policies, and legalities, available at `http://twitter.com/tos`.

text message A brief text-based message transmitted between mobile devices, using SMS. See *Short Message Service.*

third-party applications Twitter-related applications created by independent developers unaffiliated with Twitter.

TOS See *Terms of Service.*

trackable URL A URL that has been shortened with a URL-shortening service and provides useful stats, such as how often it is clicked and from which geographical region.

transparency A concept in which brands strive to be open, honest, and humanized on Twitter.

twapp Short for Twitter application; any type of third-party application used to access Twitter or enhance its functionality.

tweep A Twitter user (short for Twitter people or "peeps").

tweep affinity The relationships between Twitter users.

tweet stream A Twitter user's updates, or tweets, in chronological order.

tweet tripping When someone discovers an interesting tweet posted by someone they don't follow and begins following that person.

tweet volume A Twitter user's number of tweets in a given amount of time. For example, many users have a heavier tweet volume on Fridays.

TweetDeck A popular Twitter desktop UI application, available at `http://www.tweetdeck.com`.

tweeting The act of sending a tweet on Twitter.

tweets Brief, 140-character text-based updates sent on Twitter.

tweetup or tweet-up A real-life gathering or "meet-up" of Twitter users.

twetiquette Twitter etiquette; the socially acceptable "dos" and "don'ts" of using Twitter.

twibe A Twitter group focused on a particular goal or topic.

Twitter The most popular microblogging service, available at `http://www.twitter.com`.

twitter addict People who cannot live without Twitter.

Twitter, Inc. Refers to the corporation that owns Twitter, founded in 2007.

Twitter stream See *tweet stream*.

Twitterati The Twitter elite or anyone from whom a user seeks to gain the attention or approval.

Twitterdom Refers to Twitter in general (see also *Twitterverse* and *Twittersphere).*

Twitterese Twitter-speak, or Twitter-related slang used by Twitter users.

twittering The act of using Twitter (*see tweeting*).

Twittersphere *See Twitterverse.*

Twitter-to-conversion A desired action or goal achieved through the use of Twitter.

Twitterverse Refers to the large community of Twitter users.

twoosh A perfect 140-character tweet.

Twooting A verb meaning talking about Twitter.

unfollow The act of choosing not to follow a Twitter user any longer.

update See *tweet*.

URL shortener An application that takes lengthy URLs and turns them into shortened versions (see *shortened URL*).

Verified Account A Twitter account that Twitter has verified as being registered to the person or entity who claims to be the owner.

viral When interesting content becomes popular and spreads rapidly, it is said to have "gone viral."

Web See *World Wide Web.*

Web 2.0 Refers to the social evolution of the Web whereby users create much of the content, and the focus is on interactive exchange between those creating and consuming the content; the advent of social media sites.

web browser A software application used to view web content, such as websites, images, and other information on the Internet.

webinar A seminar conducted online via the Web.

Wikipedia A free, online encyclopedia with content that is written collaboratively by volunteers around the globe, available at `http://www.wikipedia.org`.

wired An adjective describing someone who's constantly online and "in the know" about the latest and greatest.

World Wide Web (WWW) The collective network of interconnected websites published on the Internet.

B

Twitter-Related Tools and Resources

12seconds.tv http://www.12seconds.tv

30+ Funny & Weird Twitter Applications http://techxav.com/2009/07/05/30-funny-weird-twitter-applications

Alerts Grader http://www.alertsgrader.com

The Archivist http://www.flotzam.com/archivist

AudioBoo http://www.audioboo.fm

backtweets http://www.backtweets.com

BackupMyTweets http://www.backupmytweets.com

bit.ly http://bit.ly

Brands That Tweet http://buzzmarketingfortech.blogspot.com/2008/12/brands-that-tweet.html

BubbleTweet http://www.bubbletweet.com

budURL http://www.budurl.com

CEOs Who Use Twitter - BusinessWeek http://images.businessweek.com/ss/09/05/0508_ceos_who_twitter/index.htm

ChatterBox http://chatterboxhq.com

ChessTweets http://www.chesstweets.com

Chirbit http://www.chirbit.com

ChirpCity http://www.chirpcity.com

Cision http://www.cision.com

CoTweet http://www.cotweet.com

Create Your Simpsons Avatar http://www.simpsonsmovie.com/main.html

CTOlist http://ctolist.com

Cymfony http://www.cymfony.com

DestroyTwitter http://www.destroytwitter.com

Die Fail Whale http://www.diefailwhale.com

Digsby http://www.digsby.com

DoesFollow http://www.doesfollow.com

Echofon (formerly Twitterfon) http://www.echofon.com

Echofon for Firefox (formerly TwitterFox) http://www.echofon.com

ENGAGEMENTdb Social Media Report http://www.engagementdb.com/Report

ExecTweets http://www.exectweets.com

Face Your Manga http://www.faceyourmanga.com

Featured Users Publishers Network http://featuredusers.com/publishers

FileTwt http://www.filetwt.com

Filtrbox http://www.filtrbox.com

Flickr http://www.flickr.com

FlipMyTweet http://www.flipmytweet.com

FriendFeed http://www.friendfeed.com

FriendorFollow http://www.friendorfollow.com

GovLoop http://www.govloop.com

HashDictionary http://www.hashdictionary.com

HelloTxt http://www.hellotxt.com

Hootsuite http://www.hootsuite.com

is.gd http://www.is.gd

JournalistTweets http://journalisttweets.com

Klout http://www.klout.com

Localtweeps http://www.localtweeps.com

MadMenYourself http://www.madmenyourself.com

Make a 3-D Avatar http://www.meez.com

Media on Twitter Directory http://www.mediaontwitter.com

monitter http://www.monitter.com

Mr. Tweet http://mrtweet.com

Mrs. Toon http://www.mrstoon.com

My Caricature http://www.mycaricature.com

My First Follow http://dcortesi.com/tools/my-first-follow

MyTweetSpace http://www.mytweetspace.com

Non-Profit Twitter Users Directory http://mashable.com/2009/03/19/twitter-nonprofits

The Oatmeal Twitter Addict Quiz http://theoatmeal.com/quiz/twitter_addict

***ouT*wit.me** http://www.outwit.me

ow.ly http://ow.ly

PeopleBrowsr http://www.peoplebrowsr.com

Ping.fm http://ping.fm

PollDaddy http://www.polldaddy.com

Posterous http://www.posterous.com

Qik http://www.qik.com

Qwitter http://www.useqwitter.com

Radian6 http://www.radian6.com

***Re*Tweetability Index** http://www.retweetability.com

Retweetist http://www.retweetist.com

Retweetrank http://www.retweetrank.com

RichTweets http://www.richtweets.com

Seesmic Desktop http://www.seesmic.com

Sentiment Metrics http://www.sentimentmetrics.com

shortText http://www.shortext.com

SiteVolume http://sitevolume.com

SM2 http://www.techrigy.com

Small Business Twitter Users Directory http://smallbiztrends.com/2009/01/the-ultimate-small-business-twitter-list.html

snipURL http://snipurl.com

Social Mention http://www.socialmention.com

SocialOomph (formerly TweetLater) http://www.socialoomph.com

socialseek http://www.sensidea.com/socialseek

SocialToo http://www.socialtoo.com

Sports Twitter Users Directory http://www.sportsin140.com

Spymaster http://playspymaster.com

SurveyMonkey http://www.surveymonkey.com

Sysomos http://www.sysomos.com

Tagalus http://www.tagalus.com

Tagdef http://www.tagdef.com

Tinker http://www.tinker.com

Tinychat http://www.tinychat.com

Tiny Twitter http://www.tinytwitter.com

Top CMOs on Twitter http://www.systemicmarketing.com/top-cmos-on-twitter

Top Follow Friday http://www.topfollowfriday.com

Topify http://www.topify.com

tr.im http://tr.im

Trackur http://www.trackur.com

Trendistic http://trendistic.com

Trendrr http://www.trendrr.com

trottr http://trottr.com

TruReputation http://www.trureputation.com

Tumblr http://www.tumblr.com

twalala http://www.twalala.com

Twanalyst http://www.twanalyst.com

TwapperKeeper http://twapperkeeper.com

Twazzup http://www.twazzup.com

Twecipe http://www.twecipe.com

TweepSearch http://www.tweepsearch.com

Tweet Congress http://blog.tweetcongress.org

Tweet Scan http://www.tweetscan.com/usersearch.php

TweetBackup http://tweetbackup.com

TweetBeep http://www.tweetbeep.com

Tweetburner http://www.tweetburner.com

TweetChat http://www.tweetchat.com

TweetDeck http://www.tweetdeck.com/beta

TweetDumpr http://bradkellett.com/experiments/tweetdumpr

TweetFind http://www.tweetfind.com

TweetFunnel http://www.tweetfunnel.com

TweetGrid http://www.tweetgrid.com

Tweetie http://www.atebits.com/tweetie-iphone

TweetMeme http://www.tweetmeme.com

TweetMic http://www.tweetmic.com

TweetMondo http://www.tweetmondo.com

TweetPsych http://www.tweetpsych.com

TweetStyle http://www.tweetstyle.com

Tweetake http://tweetake.com

Tweetwhatyouspend http://www.tweetwhatyouspend.com

TweetWorks http://www.tweetworks.com

Twellow http://www.twellow.com

Twemes http://www.twemes.com

Twendz http://www.twendz.com

TwerpScan http://www.twerpscan.com

TwibbleMobile http://www.twibble.de

twibbon http://www.twibbon.com

Twibes http://www.twibes.com

Twibs http://www.twibs.com

Twilert http://twilert.com

TwInbox http://www.techhit.com/TwInbox/twitter_plugin_outlook.html

TwInfluence http://twinfluence.com

Twistory http://twistory.net

TwitTruth http://www.twittruth.com

Twit4 http://www.twit4.com

Twitalyzer http://www.twitalyzer.com

TwitBacks http://www.twitbacks.com

TwitDir http://www.twitdir.com

Twithority http://www.twithority.com

TwitLOL http://www.twitlol.com

TwitLonger http://www.twitlonger.com

TwitPic http://www.twitpic.com

TwitR http://twitr.org

Twitrratr http://www.twitrratr.com

Twittelator http://www.twittelator.com

Twitter 100 http://twitter100.com

Twitter Analyzer http://twitteranalyzer.com

Twitter Best Practices http://govsocmed.pbworks.com/TwitterBestPractices

Twitter Buttons http://www.twitterbuttons.com

Twitter Clients User Statistics http://twitstat.com/twitterclientusers.html

Twitter For Busy People http://www.t4bp.com

Twitter Games Directory http://twitdom.com/tag/games

Twitter Grader http://www.twittergrader.com

Twitter Karma http://dossy.org/twitter/karma/

Twitter Mashups Directory http://www.programmableweb.com/mashups/directory/1?apis=twitter

Twitter Mobile http://m.twitter.com

Twitter Patterns http://www.twitterpatterns.com

Twitter Search http://search.twitter.com

Twitter Terms of Service http://twitter.com/tos

Twitter Tools (WordPress) http://wordpress.org/extend/plugins/twitter-tools

Twitter Widgets http://twitter.com/goodies/widgets

TwitterBackgrounds http://www.twitterbackgrounds.com

Twitterbacks http://www.twitterbacks.com

Twitterberry http://www.orangatame.com/products/twitterberry

TwitterCounter http://www.twittercounter.com

Twitterfall http://www.twitterfall.com

Twitterfeed http://www.twitterfeed.com

TwitterGadget http://www.twittergadget.com

Twitterholic http://www.twitterholic.com

TwitterKeys http://www.twitterkeys.com

Twitterific http://iconfactory.com/software/twitterrific

Twitterless http://www.twitterless.com

TwitterLit http://www.twitterlit.com

TwitterLocal http://www.twitterlocal.net

TwitterMoms http://www.twittermoms.com

Twittersheep http://www.twittersheep.com

TwitterSnooze http://www.twittersnooze.com

twittervision http://www.twittervision.com

TwitTruth http://www.Twittruth.com

TwitVid http://www.twitvid.com

Twollow http://www.twollow.com

Twooting http://www.twooting.com

Twoquick http://www.twoquick.com

Twrivia http://www.twrivia.com

Twtlong http://www.twtlong.com

Twtpoll http://www.twtpoll.com

twtQpon http://www.twtqpon.com

Twtvite http://www.twtvite.com

Twubs http://www.twubs.com

UberTwitter http://www.ubertwitter.com

unTweeps http://www.untweeps.com

US Government Twitter Users Directory http://twitter.pbworks.com/USGovernment

Ustream http://www.ustream.com

Utterli http://www.utterli.com

Verified Twitter Accounts http://twitter.com/help/verified

Viralheat http://www.viralheat.com

Vistage Twibe Directory http://www.twibes.com/group/Vistage

Web Designer Depot http://www.webdesignerdepot.com

WeFollow http://www.wefollow.com

What the Trend http://www.whatthetrend.com

When Did You Join Twitter `http://www.whendidyoujointwitter.com`

WhoShouldiFollow `http://www.whoshouldifollow.com`

Xpenser `http://xpenser.com`

yfrog `http://yfrog.com`

Zoomerang `http://www.zoomerang.com`

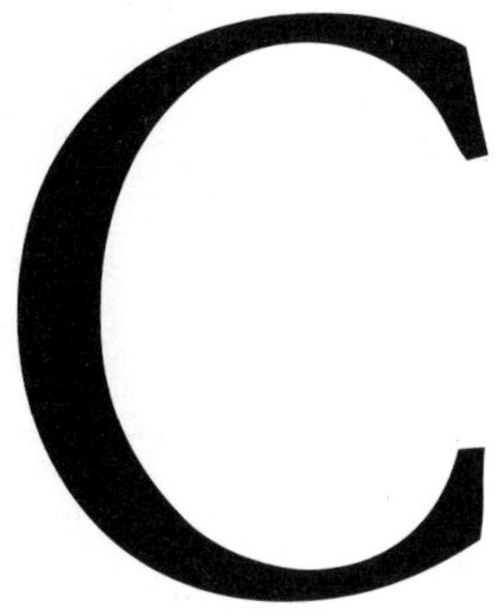

Tips from Tweeps

In the spirit of Twitter's crowdsourced community, we bring you tips from people who live and breathe Twitter business marketing every day…all in 140 characters or less! (If you see a tweet longer than 140, it was culled from another useful compilation: `http://smallbiztrends.com/2009/07/137-small-business-twitter-tips.html`*.)*

We hope you find these "Tips from Tweeps" helpful and thought-provoking. If nothing else, notice some of the commonly repeated themes.

soodonims Stay on theme to be perceived as an expert, don't pander, don't over-Twitter & create a blog and link to it. They will follow.

beebow Don't cram the conversation space with self-promotion. Listen to your target audience! You'll learn so much and earn "street cred."

bill4time Twitter always keeps you in your customers' short-term memory. So make sure your Twitter followers come away engaged, informed, or included.

danieldubya Never approach Twitter as "What's in it for me?" but only as "What do I share that's valuable to the community?"

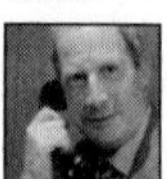

garyhonig A complementary method to our normal marketing to distinguish our firm as experts in the industry.

molsonferg Be an open listener and respectful of opinion—people will likely be open to you and respectful back.

shannonpalmer Set up keyword searches for Twitter & converse w/those talking about your topics. You'll find your audience + it builds prospects' trust.

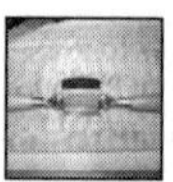

renaissanceww Be yourself—talk about what you know, but don't be a sales pitch. Offer advice and ask for advice, show you're human.

chickdowntown To captivate your followers so they identify with you and your brand, mix up your tweets with business and personal content.

prgully Incorporate Twitter for your business into your everyday life. It doesn't mean hours and hours. Just find the time, it's worth it.

umassdilo 1) Don't over think getting involved. 2) First listen. 3) Then analyze. 4) Engage. 5) Be a human and be authentic.

esthersteinfeld Identify your customers' pain points. Figure out what need that your product fulfills, then connect with people who need you.

mikedriehorst To gain followers, focus most tweets on benefits to audience members wrapped around your product/service. Show value. Self-promote < 25%.

julito77 The person who controls the Twitter experience is you. All the advice means nothing if you are not yourself. Be honest & true. Control it.

mikedriehorst Don't rely just on Twitter. Have another social presence online, even if it's a blog on your site. Twitter's not a be-all, end-all.

abbief Engage, converse, have fun. Best way to build a brand is to participate in the process.

ginidietrich Take five minutes every day and RT someone new. Connect. Engage. Participate. Don't make it all about you.

amywoo Don't be afraid to show some personality! The more people feel like they "know" someone in your organization, the better they'll respond.

matt_mcgowan Reinforce customer relationships, encourage conversation and feedback around your products & services, thank them for their participation.

amywoo It's not about what you say—It's what others say about you and how you respond to it that counts.

vincebuscemi Twitter lets businesses reach & keep a large audience of current & potential clients instantly informed. Valuable connections made daily.

glenngabe Tweet valuable information every day (don't skip days often). You must commit to Twitter before you can see any tangible results or impact.

tomdemers Use Twitter search to follow your own company/name mentions.

bayinghound Use LinkedIn contacts or your business card collection to look up and follow vendors, peers, and competitors in your field. Then browse through who they are tweeting with and add them.

joemanna Commit. Don't just tweet and neglect it, focus and commit yourself to at least a half-hour a day to discovering and tweeting.

thesmallbiznest Identify keywords as well as the "experts" in your industry. Then use Twitter search to search those terms. Once you identify the right people, look at who they're following and who is following them as your potential pool of people you should follow.

auraleigh Listen carefully first before joining the party, then offer information that is valuable and helpful.

mpdotcom Find a valuable blog post referenced on Twitter, leave a comment on the post, then retweet it. This further endears you to the author, while making a more meaningful connection with your followers.

franchiseking Post a link to a recent press release or blog post daily, mixed in with several links to great resource articles and blog posts.

angelaathp Sharing expertise, sharing tips, answering questions to help others is a great use for Twitter.

deniseoberry When the people you are following put out a tweet for help, answer back. Don't let the tweet die in cyberspace.

imnotadoctor Setup an RSS Feed of Twitter Search for your brand name and major keywords. Then interact your heart out in real-time.

craig_burgess How to Tweet: Think. Write. Review. Edit. Review. Edit. Think. Post.

carenmagill Challenging a conversation is great for creating interest, but don't be negative or derogatory.

shergraham49 Make Twitter part of your business protocol in the morning just like reading and answering emails.

daraynor Use Twitter to ask for help in small doses.

michaelhartzell Create a unique landing page for Twitter with a greeting, service, and introduction.

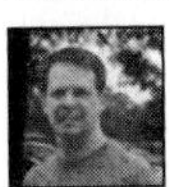

louisvillesoup Post a link to your job postings on Twitter. That's how I found my latest new hire.

webdesignseo Omit Needless Words. Write each word like it matters, because it does.

awsamuel Find people to follow via MrTweet. It suggests people to follow based on who you're already following.

dougdavidoff Tweet from the perspective of your desired reader. Most importantly respect your audience. Always have fun.

thisistrue Even if you can't think of anything to 'Tweet,' you should get on Twitter to monitor what others in your areas of interest have to say.

y2vonne Be approachable, honest, and helpful. Share links and professional info, but be sure to add a personal note now and then.

carloshernandez Just because you think it, doesn't necessarily mean you need to tweet it. "Think" is still a valid principle.

Happytown09 It's not about you; it's about your audience. Be sincere, honest, and provide something meaningful.

nimperiale Tweet your own horn or it might go untweeteth.

abbyharenberg Be yourself, treat others the way you want to be treated. Network with people, be helpful, respectful & caring.

What would a Tips from Tweeps section be without a few tips from your author?

hollisthomases Tweet deliberately. Provide context to readers who might join your conversation mid-stream; always be mindful of your tweet stream's big pix.

hollisthomases Don't be afraid to take your Twitter relationships off-line. Set up tweetups, lunch, or coffee meetings to build relationships further.

hollisthomases Still adhere to the Golden Rule: treat tweeps as you'd want to be treated yourself, which includes thanking people for their help.

hollisthomases Click on RT even before visiting a link if you think you might want to share it. You won't lose your place as your tweet stream advances.

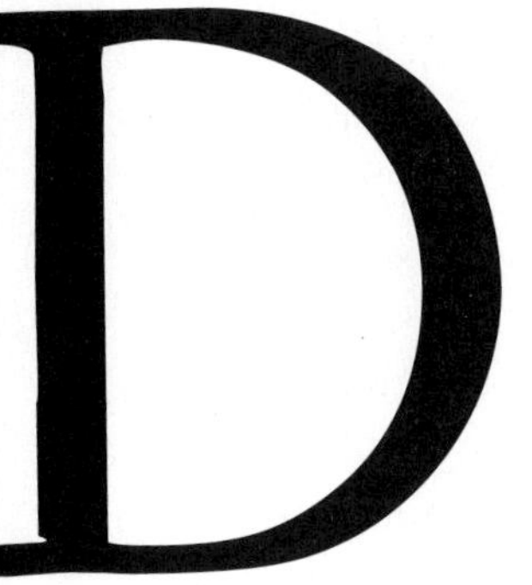

Social Media Guidelines

Organizations large and small are wrestling with creating guidelines for social media—what's appropriate and what's not, how do we seem genuine and personal without getting too personal, how do we stay on message while remaining interesting and relevant, what can we allow employees to say, and what should we try to restrict?

As part of his contribution to my book, Jeffrey Hayzlett (`@jeffreyhayzlett`*), chief marketing officer and vice president of Eastman Kodak Company, was kind enough to provide Eastman Kodak's Social Media Corporate Guidelines. Thinking other organizations might find these guidelines helpful, I asked if we could have permission to reprint them in their entirety. Though social media is ever-changing, I hope you find these guidelines a useful blueprint for using Twitter and other social media.*

Eastman Kodak's Social Media Corporate Guidelines

Getting Involved in Social Media?

Follow these procedures to comply with our one-voice policy, and to protect Kodak and your own privacy and resources.

Kodak has been growing its participation in social media to strengthen our brand and our connection with customers and key influencers.

Networking sites like Facebook, Twitter, and MySpace, news sharing and bookmarking sites like delicious and Digg, and photo- and video-sharing sites like flickr and YouTube can be exciting new avenues for communication in our professional and personal lives. Used responsibly, they provide an effective way to keep abreast of new trends and topics, and to share information and perspectives. Kodak has thousands of followers who have subscribed to keep up with Kodak blogs, podcasts and "tweets" each day. The number continues to grow, as does the number of viewers watching content on KodakTube, our YouTube channel.

Given the reach of the internet, it's important that when you use these various media, you follow some basic procedures that support our "one voice" policy as described in the Business Conduct Guide. That policy applies to Kodak employees when they blog or participate in social media for work, but it should also be considered if personal blog activities may give the appearance of speaking for Kodak. Adhering to the following points in either situation will provide protection for you and Kodak.

Maintaining a good reputation—yours and Kodak's

1. **Live the Kodak values.** Always express ideas and opinions in a respectful manner.
   - Make sure your communications are in good taste
   - Be sensitive about linking to content. Redirecting to another site may imply an endorsement of its content.
   - Do not denigrate or insult others, including competitors

   In a real-life lesson, a worker in one company made disparaging 'tweets' about a client's headquarters city. Needless to say, some of the client's employees followed the individual on Twitter and were offended. Right or wrong, they were upset not just with the individual, but with his company as well.
2. **Be yourself—and be transparent.** The story above illustrates how difficult it is to keep distinct lines between your personal and professional life in the online world. Even when you are talking as an individual, people may perceive you to be talking on behalf of Kodak. If you blog or discuss photography, printing or other topics related to a Kodak business, be upfront and explain that you work for Kodak; however, if you aren't an official company spokesperson, add a disclaimer

to the effect: **"The opinions and positions expressed are my own and don't necessarily reflect those of the Eastman Kodak Company."**

Also, only those authorized by a company may use that company's logos and trade dress in communications, so be sure you do not include Kodak brand symbols or trade dress—or that of other companies—in your personal blogs or postings.

3. **Protect confidential information and relationships.** Online postings and conversations are not private. Realize that what you post will be around for a long time, and could be shared by others. Given that,
   - avoid identifying and discussing others—including customers; suppliers, your friends and co-workers—unless you have their permission;
   - obtain permission before posting pictures of others, or before posting copyrighted information;
   - never discuss proprietary Kodak information, including sales data and plans, company finances, strategies, product launch information, unannounced technology or anything considered "confidential."

   To better understand what is—and is not—acceptable in any type of communication, review the Kodak Business Conduct Guide.

4. **Speak the truth.** If you are in a discussion that relates to Kodak or its products, don't make unsubstantiated claims about features, performance or pricing. If you need to respond or make a comment on something specific, verify details through company-published information (such as product pages on kodak.com). Also, because situations change, make sure references or sources of information are current.

5. **Keep your cool.** One of the aims of social media is to create dialogue, and people won't always agree on an issue. When confronted with a difference of opinion, stay cool. Express your points in a clear, logical way. Don't pick fights, and correct mistakes when needed. Sometimes, it's best to ignore a comment and not give it credibility by acknowledging it with a response.

6. **Stay timely.** Part of the appeal in social media is that the conversation occurs almost in real time. So, if you are going to participate in an active way, make sure you are willing to take the time to refresh content, respond to questions and update information regularly, and correct information when appropriate.

Protecting your, and Kodak's, privacy and resources

7. **Be careful with personal information.** This may seem odd, since many sites are created to help promote sharing of personal information. Still, astute criminals can piece together information you provide on different sites and then use

it to impersonate you or someone you know—or even re-set your passwords. Similarly, "tweeting" real-time about your travels may confirm you aren't at home—letting someone target your house. So, be careful when sharing information about yourself or others.

8. **Don't be fooled.** If you do post personal information on a site like *Facebook* or *Twitter*, criminals can use it to send you emails that appear to come from a friend or other trusted source—even the site itself. This is called "phishing." The lesson is: Don't click links or attachments unless you trust the source. For example, be wary of emails that say there is a problem with your account, then ask you to click on a link and input your username and password. The link may connect to a site that looks exactly like *Facebook*, *Twitter*, your bank's web site, but is really a fake site used to get even more personal information. This ploy can also be used to infect your computer with a virus or keystroke logger.
9. **Disable dangerous privileges.** If a site allows others to embed code—like HTML postings, links, and file attachments—on your page or account, criminals can use them to install malicious software on your computer. If possible, disable the ability of others to post HTML comments on your home page.
10. **Heed security warnings and pop-ups.** There's a reason your security software provides warnings like:

    - "A process is attempting to invoke xyz.exe. Do you wish to allow this?"

    or

    - "The process 'IEXPLORE.EXE' is attempting to modify a document 'X.' Do you wish to allow this?"

    Never allow or say "yes" to such actions, unless you know that they are safe.

Social media is growing at an amazing rate—and Kodak is a leader in this area. The ability to engage online with our customers, prospects and industry influencers is an important part of our marketing and our brand strategy. Following these procedures will help ensure we stay on course as a company, and at the same time safeguard your personal privacy.

Index

Note to the Reader: Throughout this index **boldfaced** page numbers indicate primary discussions of a topic. *Italicized* page numbers indicate illustrations.

B

C

D

E

F

G

H

I

J

K

L

M

P

Q

R

S

T

U

V

W

X

Y

Z